THE BUILDINGS OF SCOTLAND

EDITOR: COLIN MCWILLIAM
CONSULTANT EDITOR: JOHN NEWMAN

GLASGOW

ELIZABETH WILLIAMSON, ANNE RICHES AND
MALCOLM HIGGS

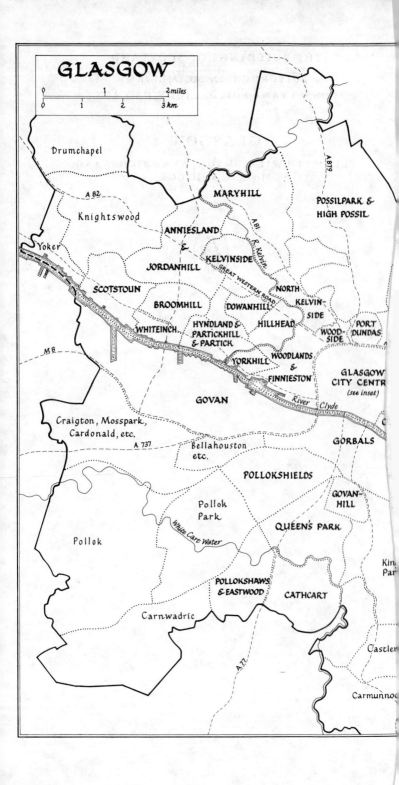

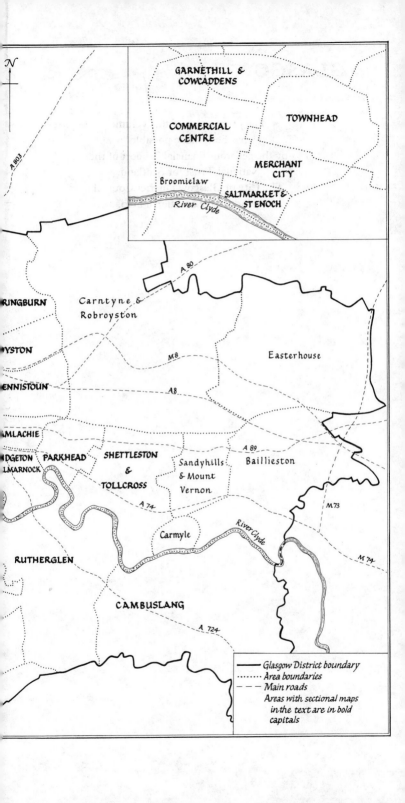

The preparation of this volume
has been made possible
by the generous financial support of the
National Trust for Scotland.
The City of Glasgow District Council
kindly gave additional help.

Glasgow

BY
ELIZABETH WILLIAMSON,
ANNE RICHES
AND
MALCOLM HIGGS

THE BUILDINGS OF SCOTLAND

PENGUIN BOOKS

IN ASSOCIATION WITH
THE NATIONAL TRUST FOR SCOTLAND

PENGUIN BOOKS
Published by the Penguin Group
27 Wrights Lane, London W8 5TZ, England

Viking Penguin Inc., 40 West 23rd Street, New York, New York 10010, USA
Penguin Books Australia Ltd, Ringwood, Victoria, Australia
Penguin Books Canada Ltd, 2801 John Street, Markham, Ontario, Canada L3R 1B4
Penguin Books (NZ) Ltd, 182–190 Wairau Road, Auckland 10, New Zealand

Penguin Books Ltd, Registered Offices: Harmondsworth, Middlesex, England

—

First published 1990
10 9 8 7 6 5 4 3 2 1

—

—

Filmset in Linotron Plantin
Made and printed in Great Britain
by Butler & Tanner Ltd, Frome and London

TO DR DAVID M. WALKER
AND IN MEMORY OF
COLIN McWILLIAM
(1928–89)
EDITOR OF THE BUILDINGS
OF SCOTLAND SERIES 1974–89

CONTENTS

For orientation, see the maps on pp. 2–3 etc. and the Alphabetical
Register of Districts below

SUBURBS NORTH OF THE CLYDE

SUBURBS SOUTH OF THE CLYDE

CROSSINGS OF THE CLYDE AND KELVIN BY TED RUDDOCK

ALPHABETICAL REGISTER
OF DISTRICTS

LIST OF FIGURES IN THE TEXT

FOREWORD AND ACKNOWLEDGEMENTS

Glasgow has long been found remarkable by tourists. Its praises were sung by Defoe and Smollett and by one John Macky who, in 1723, claimed it to be 'the beautifullest little City I have seen in Britain; it stands deliciously on the banks of the Clyde . . .'. By the 1890s, trade and industry had transformed Glasgow from a burgh of little more than four fair streets and a medieval cathedral into 'the Sixth City of Europe'. Then, a million people lived within what are now its boundaries – in the city itself and in the independent burghs and districts that Glasgow devoured after 1900. Now (in 1989) the population is 715,621, reduced by shifts of population to the New Towns and by comprehensive redevelopment that has rearranged the city into a new pattern.

To those just passing through, Glasgow now looks much like any other large industrial city, with spreading C20 housing schemes and roads brutally forced through the older fabric. A visitor with time to spare will find that the city centre is rich with remarkable buildings from the height of its industrial prosperity and that the grandest suburbs are planned on a scale comparable with many European capitals. In the centre, large and showy commercial buildings stand alongside the dignified houses and institutions of the pre-Victorian city on streets planned in the earliest years of Glasgow's expansion. East and north of the centre and along the Clyde lie the once intensely industrial suburbs, their churches, Board schools and burgh halls the chief signs of their former independence as towns and villages. These districts developed as quickly as Glasgow itself during the C19, and have changed as rapidly again since 1945. Their close texture of tenements and factories has mostly given way to a looser, more chaotic one of high-rise, low-rise and industrial estates. To the more salubrious west and south-west are the spacious and leafy C19 suburbs, planned but speculative developments for affluent Glaswegians, remarkably preserved, with numerous inventive variations on the themes of terrace, villa and tenement. Beyond these stretch the C20 schemes that house nearly half of Glasgow's population in cottages, high-rise flats and tenements, punctuated only by churches, schools and the engulfed relics of castles, country houses and villages.

Glasgow's hills, which rise suddenly and steeply some way from the Clyde (Dr Lawson explains their geology in the essay that follows), provide some of the city's most memorable images: the Necropolis bristling with monuments, Woodlands Hill with its Romantic crown of terraces and towers, the High Victorian silhouette of Glasgow University riding on Gilmorehill above Kel-

vingrove Park, and the spire of Townhead and Blochairn Church vying with Royston Hill's tower blocks. The Clyde now flows serenely (though downstream at Govan and Scotstoun there is still some shipbuilding). The city that for more than a century turned its back on what was a working, noisy and grimy riverside is turning towards it again in the last decade of the C20 as industrial buildings throughout the city are converted or demolished to make way for offices, houses and tourism.

Glasgow's physical and architectural development are described in more detail in the following introductory essays, the first (on topography and building materials) by Dr Judith Lawson, the second (on Glasgow's prehistory and Roman past) by J. N. Graham Ritchie and Gordon S. Maxwell, who also wrote the associated gazetteer entries. They received valuable assistance from Miss Helen Adamson and Mr A. Foxon of Glasgow Art Gallery and Museum, Kelvingrove, from Mr R. Mowat of the Royal Commission on the Ancient and Historical Monuments of Scotland (RCAHMS), and Dr L. Keppie and Dr E. W. Mackie of the Hunterian Museum, Glasgow University. Mr Alistair Gordon's contribution to this essay brings the story up to the medieval period. One of Scotland's most important medieval buildings, Glasgow Cathedral, is perceptively interpreted by Dr Richard Fawcett in the gazetteer. Two special aspects of the C19 and C20 called for particular expertise: industrial buildings, which are classified and described in the introduction by John Hume, and the crossings of the Clyde and Kelvin, analysed by Ted Ruddock at the end of the gazetteer.

The experts already mentioned formed part of a small army of contributors mustered to produce this volume, the fourth in the Buildings of Scotland series. John Gifford, head of the Buildings of Scotland Research Unit, had, before we began, mined the major architectural periodicals for references, which his assistant Yvonne Hillyard cleverly identified. These extracts guided us to many of Glasgow's C19 and C20 buildings and to the appropriate documents. Our research assistants, Margaret Stewart and Simon Green, hunted indefatigably through libraries and record offices and often chased their quarry into the field. Their research was facilitated by the remarkable resources and staff of the Glasgow Room in the city's Mitchell Library and of the Strathclyde Regional Archive. In Edinburgh, much was found in the National Library, in the City Library (especially the Fine Art Library and the Scottish Library) and in the National Monuments Record of Scotland, whose staff proved unfailingly helpful.

Chief among our advisers was David Walker, who, with Andor Gomme, opened everyone's eyes to Glasgow's architecture. He unstintingly contributed information from his research as well as judicious comment. Among his staff at the Scottish Development Department's Historic Buildings and Monuments division, Judith Anderson, Ranald MacInnes, Aonghus MacKechnie and Mark Watson have also generously contributed their own information and insights. At the Royal Commission on the Ancient and Historical Monuments of Scotland, Miles Horsey kindly arranged for us to be supplied with photographs for publication from the photographic survey of Glasgow that he organized, as well as providing valuable facts and figures about Glasgow's multi-storey housing. Dr Frank Walker kindly allowed us to consult the dissertations written by his students at the Department of Architecture and Building Science at Strathclyde University, and Professor Andy MacMillan those by his students at the Mackintosh School of Architecture. From the outset, Mr James Rae, the City's Planning Director, showed interest in the project. His staff, particularly the Conservation Officer, Mr David Martin, have fed us with invaluable planning documents and answers to long lists of inquiries. All the departments of the City Council that we have approached for information have been most co-operative. In addition, Dr Derek Dow, Archivist to Greater Glasgow Health Board, has given us historical guidance on the city's hospitals, Mr Donald Farmer helped with information on excavations by the Scottish Urban Archaeological Trust, and John Gerrard of the Scottish Civic Trust kept us abreast of changes to the city. Architectural practices, too numerous to mention individually, have kindly answered questions about their own buildings.

Many people with special local knowledge have been helpful, particularly Mr Peter Aeberli (County Buildings and Courthouse), Mr James Aitchison and Mr Hewitt Graham (Springburn), Ms Elizabeth Arthur (Camphill House and E. A. Taylor), Dr Patricia Cusack (Lion Chambers), Mr Alistair Gordon (Rutherglen), Ms Juliet Kinchin and Mr Jonathan Kinghorn (Pollok House), Mr Michael MacAulay (Broomielaw), Mrs Jean Marshall and Mr Ian Robb (Cathcart), and Mr Peter Trowles (Glasgow School of Art). The staff of the People's Palace made useful criticisms of the description of Glasgow's East End, and Mr Nicholas Morgan offered some stimulating comments. No contributor can, of course, be blamed for our subjective, and sometimes contentious, comments, or for our mistakes. Any corrections or amendments to the text will be gladly received in anticipation of a revised edition. Research was only one strand of our endeavour: fieldwork was equally important, and we are very grateful to all those ministers and priests, officials and owners who allowed us to visit their premises. Especial thanks are due to Hamish Pollock for enthusiastically following miles of our 'perambulations' and intelligently commenting on them, to Sally Rush for casting her informed eye over many stained-glass windows, and to Dr James Macaulay, who entertained us so liberally in Kirklee.

The transformation of our typescript into this book was undertaken by Judith Wardman, who meticulously edited the text and cheerfully sorted out numerous problems, by Margaret Stewart, who prepared the Index of Artists, by Susan Rose-Smith, who organized the illustrations so imaginatively, by Richard Andrews, who drew all the plans, by Reg Piggott, who composed the skilful maps, and by Kathryn Penn-Simkins, who tied up many annoying loose ends. Above all, we are indebted to the late Colin McWilliam, who invited us to write this volume and who sadly died just as it was going to press, and to the National Trust for Scotland, whose support enabled us to pursue our research.

Finally, a practical note. The gazetteer is necessarily only a selection of the city's significant buildings, chosen in general because they are of some architectural interest. Churches, which often give a focus to an otherwise drab or confusing suburb, are the exception: all churches used by Church of Scotland and Roman Catholic congregations are mentioned, though not all the churches of other denominations. Churches now in secular use still appear under their ecclesiastical names. Convents and cemeteries are listed after churches.

Public buildings, like government offices, burgh halls, and libraries, are almost all mentioned but only the best examples of schools and colleges. They are grouped together in what, according to Buildings of England tradition, is rank order: that is, municipal and public offices; museums, libraries and theatres; colleges and schools; hospitals and institutions; and, finally, public utilities and transport buildings. Wherever possible, each building is given the date when its detailed design was approved and the date of completion (e.g. 1900–5).

A word of warning: churches are almost always locked (although ministers, priests and church officers are invariably kind if approached for access), and many of the secular buildings included are private and not freely accessible, even where the interior has been mentioned. As a rule, we have avoided describing in detail interiors to which there is no hope of admission. Church furnishings are described where they are noteworthy, but furniture and paintings in secular buildings are omitted, unless they form part of a decorative scheme.

ACKNOWLEDGEMENTS FOR THE PLATES

We are grateful to the following for permission to reproduce photographs:

Architectural Review: 115

Ralph Burnett: 72, 74

City of Glasgow District Council: 100, 101, 103

Conway Library, Courtauld Institute: 39, 67, 82, 92, 93, 94, 95

Alan Crumlish: 44

Department of the Environment, Edinburgh: 116

Ann Dick: 23

Four Acres Charitable Trust: 49, 50

Glasgow Museums and Art Galleries: 11, 12, 15, 16

Glasgow School of Art: 73, 75

Guthrie Photography: 13, 17, 20, 29, 78, 111, 118, 122

Alastair Hunter: 119

Patricia Macdonald: 1, 34

Douglas MacGregor: 2, 3, 10, 14, 18, 19, 27, 33, 36, 37, 38, 42, 46, 47, 48, 51, 52, 61, 62, 63, 65, 66, 70, 71, 76, 77, 83, 85, 86, 87, 89, 97, 105, 109, 120, 121

Hugh Martin Partnership: 123

Ralston: 4

Royal Commission on the Ancient and Historical Monuments of Scotland: 21, 22, 25, 26, 28, 30, 31, 32, 35, 40, 41, 43, 45, 53, 54, 56, 57, 58, 59, 60, 68, 69, 79, 80, 81, 84, 88, 90, 91, 96, 98, 99, 102, 104, 106, 108, 110, 112, 113, 117

Henk Snoek: 114

Scott, Brownrigg & Turner: 55

Scottish Development Department: 5, 6, 7, 8

Starthclyde Regional Council: 107

Strathclyde University: 64

The plates are indexed in the indexes of artists and buildings, and references to them are given by numbers in the margin of the text.

THE CITY OF GLASGOW:

INFORMATION AND ABBREVIATIONS

City Architects and Engineers

From 1890, the City Engineer acted as the city's architect, and in 1914 the role of City Engineer was combined with that of Master of Works. This post ran in parallel with that of City Architect and Planning Officer, created in 1951, until local government reorganization in 1975, when a Director of Architecture and Related Services was appointed. An independent Planning Department was established in 1967.

James Cleland, Superintendent of Public Works	1814–34
John Strang, Superintendent of Public Works	1834–54(?)
John Carrick, Superintendent of Streets	c. 1844–54
Superintendent of Works	c. 1854–62
and also City Architect	1862–89
Alexander Beith McDonald, City Engineer	1890
and also City Surveyor	1891–1915
Thomas Nisbet, Master of Works and City Engineer	1914–24
Thomas Somers, Master of Works and City Engineer	1925–41
Robert Bruce, Master of Works and City Engineer	1941–8
James Ridder, Master of Works and City Engineer	1950–62
A. G. Jury, City Architect and Planning Officer	1951–60
City Architect and Director of Planning	1961–6
City Architect	1967–71
James Kernohan, City Architect	1972–4
Director of Architecture and Related Services	1975–7
William Worden, Director of Architecture and Related Services	1978–85
Christopher Pursloe, Director of Architecture and Related Services	1985–

Directors of Planning

A. G. Jury, see above	
Robert Mansley	1967–74
James H. Rae	1975–

Directors of Housing

Peter Fyfe	1919–23
John Bryce	1923–8
Robert W. Horn	1928–31
William McNab	1932–41
Ronald Bradbury	1943–7
A. G. Jury	1948–51

After 1951, responsibility for the design of housing was taken by the City Architect and his successors.

Major boundary extensions since 1800

1800 Ramshorn and Meadowflat lands
1830 Necropolis and Blythswood
1843 Port Dundas
1846 Anderston, Calton and most of Gorbals
1872 Broomhill, Kelvingrove and Glasgow University
1891 Crosshill, Govanhill, Hillhead, Maryhill, Pollokshields, Springburn, Possilpark, Langside, Kelvinside, Mount Florida, Shawlands
1896 Bellahouston and Craigton
1905 Kinning Park
1909 Mosspark
1912 Govan, Partick, Pollokshaws, Shettleston and Tollcross, Cathcart, Knightswood, Temple
1931 Carntyne
1938 Easterhouse, Darnley, Penilee, Drumchapel, Summerston
1974 Rutherglen, Cambuslang, Baillieston, Carmyle, Springboig

Population (in thousands)

1450	2	1801	77	1881	511	1981	763
1556	4	1821	147	1891	656	1989	716
1600	10	1841	226	1901	761*		
1707	15	1861	395	1971	898		

*With the outer districts incorporated in 1912, about 1 million, an almost constant figure until the 1960s.

Scottish Special Housing Association

Chief Technical Officers

Walter Fairbairn	1937–9
J. Austen Bent	1945–59
Harold E. Buteux	1959–78
J. H. Fullarton	1978–

Chief Architects

R. H. Mottram (consultant)	1937–9
T. O. W. Gratton	1945–6
A. Waddicar	1951–62
E. W. Smith	1962–80
W. A. Jessop	1980–2

ABBREVIATIONS

C.D.A.	Comprehensive Development Area
G.E.A.R.	Glasgow Eastern Area Renewal
S.S.H.A.	Scottish Special Housing Association

INTRODUCTION

TOPOGRAPHY AND BUILDING MATERIALS

BY JUDITH LAWSON

Glasgow is situated on low ground, rarely rising above 100 m, on 1 either side of the River Clyde. Although of low altitude, the ground away from the Clyde is hilly, with a swarm of 'drumlins', i.e. smooth elongated low hills, often with steep sides, characteristically formed from deposits of till or boulder clay underlying an ice sheet. Their presence is reflected in the suffix 'hill' in many Glasgow names. Near the Clyde, and sometimes surrounding the drumlins, which must formerly have stood out as islands in the sea, are flat areas of raised beaches formed when sea level was higher than at present. There is also alluvium associated with the River Clyde of today.

The Clyde was for most of historical time a shallow river with small tributaries, often with irregular seasonal flow. None of the waterways was navigable until the C18, when improvements to the Clyde, including the engineering work carried out by *John Golborne*, allowed shipping to reach Glasgow itself. In medieval times, therefore, Glasgow, unlike many major cities in England, had no easy means of transport for bulky, low-value materials such as those used in building the Cathedral. Building materials had to be of local origin, and it is this local character, particularly the use of sandstone, begun in medieval times, which has continued to give Glasgow its distinctive appearance.

Rock exposures are rare in Glasgow, but bedrock occurs at only a shallow depth below much of the surface. This bedrock is largely formed of sediments of Carboniferous age. The overall structure is a syncline plunging to the E, so that younger rocks, higher in the succession, outcrop towards the E (see Fig. 1). In detail the whole area is much faulted, and the outcrop pattern is often very complicated. Conditions of sedimentation varied enormously during the Carboniferous, and the sediments themselves vary in both lithology and thickness, rapid alternations of different sediments being very common. The sediments are predominantly shales (fine-grained, black) and sandstones (medium-grained, light-coloured, white, cream or occasionally pink or red) with coals and a few very thin limestones. The proportions of the sediments vary in different parts of the succession, and some of the beds are quite local. Sandstones may

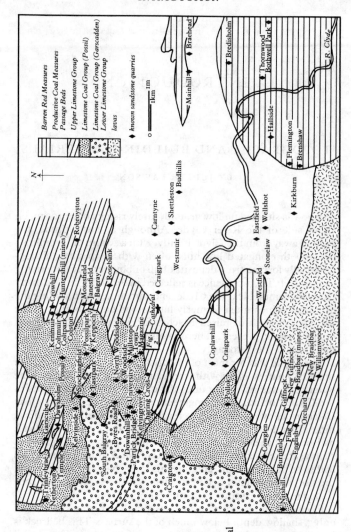

Figure 1. Sketch map showing simplified geology of the Glasgow area and sites of quarries. (Traditional names are used which do not necessarily reflect the true character of the rocks; thus the Limestone Groups and Limestone Coal Group do not in fact contain much limestone)

(Redrawn from an original by Judith Lawson)

occur at any level, even in the so-called 'Limestone Group' or 'Limestone Coal Group', in beds from a few centimetres thick up to, exceptionally, 20 m. Most are 1–5 m thick. The sandstone is relatively soft and easy to cut, even with primitive tools. Some of the thickest horizons of good-quality stone underlie the area immediately w of the original site of Glasgow at no great depth below the surface, and it was these sandstones which were used for medieval Glasgow.

Figure 1 gives the location of some of the largest or longest-working quarries and a key to the main geological horizons and their traditional names. There were undoubtedly many other smaller quarries whose sites can no longer be seen, and large estates would always have had their own quarries to supply stone for the house and outbuildings. Certain horizons contained thicker sandstones, and quarries were subsequently concentrated at these outcrops. In general, the sandstones of the Possil sub-group of the Limestone Coal Group are individually thin, white or cream-coloured, and often streaked with dark carbonaceous material. This darker matter shows up the ripple laminations in the stone. The cement often contains calcium carbonate, and its weathering properties are not good. Such a stone can be seen in the main walls of Glasgow University's main building. Quarries often worked more than one bed; the university's own quarry on Gilmorehill used five separate beds, with a maximum about 4 m thick.

Some of the best-quality sandstone occurs just above the base of the Upper Limestone Group. This is often a white or cream 'liver' freestone, with good weathering properties, which can be up to 20 m thick. At times it becomes pebbly towards the base. Associated with the 'liver' rock is ripple laminated stone. Some-times the two are mixed, as in St Andrew's Church, or they are used in separate buildings, e.g. Nos. 248 and 250 West George Street. The Bishopbriggs stone and Netherton (Garscube) quarries at Anniesland were also on this horizon. A little higher was the often excellent but geographically very limited Giffnock stone, just outside Glasgow but extensively used within the city boundary. Both at Bishopbriggs and Giffnock the best stone was mined. The hill between the Giffnock quarries of Braidbar and New Braidbar, which were some 300 m apart, was almost com-pletely undermined, with galleries 10 m high separated by broad stoops of sandstone left to support the roof. Similar but not quite so extensive mines also occurred at Bishopbriggs. Towards the top of the Carboniferous period, conditions of sedimentation changed. As the climate became drier, red iron oxides coated the grains of sand, and the sandstones are therefore often pink or red, sometimes uniformly coloured, sometimes irregularly stained red, pink and white. The irregularly coloured stone was less popular in buildings but can be seen, outside the Glasgow area, in Formakin House near Bishopton (Renfrew District, Strathclyde). The red sandstone from Bredisholm Quarry can be seen in Yoker Old Church, Dumbarton Road.

Intrusive igneous rocks, generally whin, also occur in the area.

Whin (dolerite), a dark, fine-grained crystalline rock, is common in the E, and there were several quarries, including a large one, still visible, on Necropolis Hill near the Cathedral. Dolerite is hard and generally breaks along joints into rather small pieces. It has been used extensively only for road material. It can still be seen in setts, particularly in side streets, e.g. Dundas Street, or as kerb-stones, but never in buildings. Lavas, extrusive igneous rocks, also occur to the SW, where there are several quarries, but like the intrusive whin the rock was used as road metal.

The drumlins overlying the Carboniferous sediments are of much more recent origin. They are made of till, often referred to as boulder clay. There is a great deal of such clay, and it might be considered surprising that bricks are not more commonly seen in buildings in Glasgow. However, the presence of the pebbles and boulders means that good bricks of uniform quality are not easy to make. Only where the sea winnowed the clay from the pebbles were good, uniform brick clays, generally blue or brown, found. These clays were frequently used for brickmaking, but early firing methods did not always give a uniform quality. Early brickmaking was on a small scale near current building works. Later there were larger brick-fields, e.g. at Polmadie, Belvidere and Drumchapel. Small brick kilns were often situated in quarries where both clay and any suitable underlying rock were excavated. Bricks were commonly used for internal walls, gables (e.g. at the 1771 tenement No. 394 Gallowgate) and stairtowers, where they could more easily be built in a curve, but they were only rarely used in the front or 'visible' parts of buildings. 'Composition' bricks were also made, using Carboniferous shale excavated during coalmining and left in spoil heaps or bings; little was quarried directly for this purpose. There were once large spoil heaps from coalmining in several parts of Glasgow; firms such as P. & M. Hurll in the Knightswood and Anniesland areas used such material for brickmaking. Generally bricks were more commonly used for industrial buildings such as cotton mills, stables etc. A fine example was the famous Templeton Carpet Factory in Calton (1888).

The development of new and existing quarries in Glasgow reflects the growth and history of the city in medieval times. The Cathedral and Bishop's Castle dominated the small town built either side of the High Street, down towards the river. The small domestic houses and shops were built of the easily hewn and transported timber which was common in the surrounding countryside; the roofs were of thatch. Stone was more expensive and used only for larger structures and by the richer townspeople. By far the largest amount of stone was used in the Cathedral (C13–15) and the Bishop's Castle, with their associated ecclesiastical buildings. The ashlar blocks for the Cathedral, which has a very uniform appearance both inside and out, are of white sandstone. The stone in the Bishop's Castle, since recycled in newer buildings which in turn have disappeared, would certainly have come from the same source. The smaller buildings, of which only Provand's Lordship (1471) remains, were of similar sandstone used in more irregular blocks or rubble. Some of the larger houses in the town would also have had at least some stone in their construction, and the first wooden bridge over the Clyde was replaced by a stone one c. 1400. Glasgow continued to use its local sandstone and it is fortunate that most of it was of good quality.

The exact location of the old quarries is not known, but several references indicate that the area N of George Square was quarried over a long period of time. The Cathedral records suggest a quarry a short distance to the W, in what would be Ramshorn lands. City records mention 'the querrel hoill of Ramishorne' in 1574, and a Johnne Bole 'quariour' in 1610. Little new stone would have been needed during the c 15, c 16 and early c 17 after the Cathedral and its associated buildings had been completed.

Two events led to a major change. Disastrous fires in the second half of the c 17 swept through the timber and thatch houses, spreading quickly through these flammable materials. The council decreed that non-flammable materials only should be permitted in the town in the future. Secondly, Glasgow began to expand; trade with both Europe and the colonies increased dramatically, particularly with the tobacco boom in the first half of c 18. The population increased steadily from about 10,000 in 1600 and perhaps 15,000 in 1700 to 25,000 in 1755, then 36,000 in 1785 as Glasgow began to expand westwards.

The quarries N and NW of the westward-expanding city (Fig. 2) prospered with the new building. Uphill, and only a short distance from the new centre of activity, Cowcaddens became virtually one huge quarry. Cracklinghouse Quarry, near the Crackling House, where the tallowmakers rendered down animal carcases, was certainly in operation by 1708, when it was rented by James Montgomerie from the Hutchesons' Hospital Trustees. A little further uphill, Provanside (Bells), Cowcaddens and East (Little) Cowcaddens were also being worked. Provanside, which probably had a very long history from medieval times, continued and expanded; in the 1820s it was worked by Robert Aitken, who had five cranes operating there, and produced 'a large quantity of very fine white rock got here (quite in contrast to the coarse Cowcaddens rock) and many fronts were made out of it.' In 1823 surveyors estimated nearly 13,000 'solid' (? cubic) feet of sandstone left, and the face was some 60 ft (18 m) high in places. The sandstone in Cowcaddens was rather too coarse for good-quality masonry, but East (Little) Cowcaddens produced good stone. St Andrew's Church (1739–56) is known to be built of stone from the area, and so too, probably, was much of the early Merchant City. The St George's Tron Church (1807–9), St Andrew's R.C. Cathedral (1814–17) and St David's (Ramshorn Kirk, 1824–6) all used the ripple laminated sandstone almost certainly from this area.

Other quarries to the NW also supplied stone as demand increased. Hutchesons' Hall (1802–5) was built with Possil sandstone, supplemented by some from Woodside. The Town Quarry, quarrying three separate beds, must also have been used;

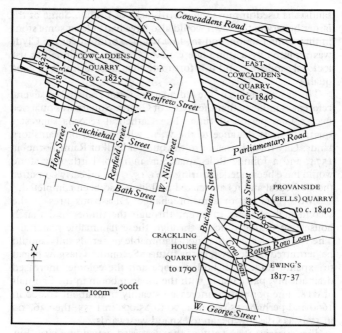

Figure 2. Sketch map of the Cowcaddens area showing outlines
of the quarries and their approximate date of working
(Redrawn from an original by Judith Lawson)

it also contained a coal seam. The eastern extension of Glasgow
along the Gallowgate used stone from the E, generally a cream
and red sandstone such as was visible during refurbishment of
tenements at No. 394 Gallowgate.

Very little stone was brought in from outside the area at this
time. An exception is that used when the Royal Exchange, in the
former Cunninghame mansion, was extended in 1828–9; the
sandstone was brought from Humbie, near Linlithgow (West
Lothian), presumably by canal. The Forth and Clyde Canal was
used by the immensely successful Netherton of Garscube Quarry
for many years. Most of this sandstone was exported via Bowling
and the Clyde. It can still be seen in Greenock Customs House
(Renfrew District, Strathclyde).

Plans of Cowcaddens Quarry show great activity in the early
C 19. However, the sandstone was becoming exhausted and the
land was needed for the ever-expanding city. Cracklinghouse
Quarry was filled in by 1790, when Buchanan Street was laid
out. Cowcaddens Quarry had streets over it by 1828. East
Cowcaddens Quarry became the site of the Caledonian Railway
Buchanan Street Station by the 1840s, while James Ewing, who
had bought the original Crawford Mansion, sold the ground to
the Edinburgh & Glasgow Railway in 1837 for Queen Street

Station. The whole area has been somewhat lowered as a result of the quarrying.

The arrival of the railways in the 1840s changed the whole pattern of quarrying in the area. No longer did stone have to be local or near water transport, as railways could be taken to the quarries and the stone transported relatively cheaply. Stone could now be chosen for appearance and quality more than convenience. Several areas, mainly outside the city boundaries, became important. In the N, quarries near Bishopbriggs expanded. Crowhill was bisected by the new railway, and other quarries developed on either side of it. However, by 1899 nearly all the ground had been quarried. These quarries supplied much stone for the northern suburbs of Glasgow. Huntershill continued until 1908, when a major roof-fall caused abandonment.

In the S, the excellent Giffnock liver rock was quarried in a similar pattern, with rapid expansion in the second half of the C19. This sandstone thins rapidly in all directions and had virtually been quarried away by 1900. Like Bishopbriggs, it was extensively mined. It was used particularly to the S of the river, although an early use was for the column under the statue of Sir Walter Scott in George Square (1837).

In the W, numerous small quarries were opened up in the Hillhead and Partick Bridge area to build those suburbs. They had largely disappeared by the 1870s. A quarry on Gilmorehill, on the site of the present Western Infirmary, was opened specially for the construction of the new university in 1867–71. Its stone was used for the main walls; dressing stones came from Bishopbriggs (Kenmure) and Giffnock, with Craigleith (Edinburgh) flags 'imported' for steps and landings. A glance at the walls shows the difference in weathering between Kenmure and Gilmorehill stone.

To the E, there were large quarries in the upper part of the Carboniferous supplying pink, red or white stone. Space was not in such demand here, and many of these quarries continued until the C20, including Kirkburn (white, closed in 1906), Westfield (red and white, 1902), Eastfield (pink, 1911), Bredisholm (red, 1909) and Bothwell Park (red and white, 1913).

The centre of Glasgow was close to railway termini, and much stone was imported in Victorian times from the area S of Stirling (Central Region), between the Forth and Campsie Fells. A cream or white sandstone from the Upper Limestone Group, it is similar to the local stone. Dunmore (closed in 1906, but recently reopened) is seen in the Merchants' House (George Square) and, with Polmaise (closed in 1909), in the City Chambers; Plean (closed in 1907), used with Hermand from West Lothian, can be seen in former Inland Revenue offices at the NE corner of George Square. Overwood Quarry in the Productive Coal measures near Stonehouse in Lanarkshire also supplied material, which can be seen in the Stock Exchange.

Until about 1890 virtually all Glasgow building stone came from the Carboniferous. Gradually, as the quarries became exhausted, other sources of stone were sought. A new sandstone was imported in immense quantities between 1890 and 1914. This red sandstone lies above the Carboniferous and is of Permian or Triassic age, i.e. the New Red Sandstone. It is even-grained and often shows very large-scale cross-bedding. The sand grains are coated with red iron oxide, which gives it a pink or red colour. This New Red Sandstone may be hundreds of metres thick and is easily quarried. There were a relatively few, but very large, quarries in Ayrshire and Dumfries-shire. A good example of cross-bedding (upside-down!) can be seen in the entrance to *A. N. Paterson*'s Liberal Club in Nelson Mandela Place, West George Street, which has matching blocks on either side. As Bishopbriggs and Giffnock were reduced to one quarry each, those of Ayrshire and Dumfries-shire expanded rapidly, and by 1898 some 1,500 men were employed in the red sandstone quarries. New tenements, e.g. at Hyndland and Broomhill, were built of this stone, as were Glasgow Art Gallery and Museum, Kelvingrove (Locharbriggs and Cove exterior, Giffnock interior), King's Theatre, Charing Cross Mansions (Closeburn), Strathclyde University (Closeburn, with Cove), several schools, including Balshagray, Queen Margaret Bridge (Corncockle) and the former *Evening Citizen* building in St Vincent Place (Mauchline). The main sources of sandstone are summarized in Table 1.

In the c 20 those architects who preferred to continue using cream sandstone imported Northumberland Carboniferous sandstone from Blackpasture (Mitchell Library; also Nos. 17–29 St Vincent Place; the former Parcels Office in Waterloo Street, which also had some from Prudham) and Blaxter (the Scottish Legal Assurance Society building, Nos. 81–107 Bothwell Street). Similar stone is increasingly being used today as facing blocks. The last major stone building, St Margaret's Church, Knightswood (1929–32), used New Red Hollington stone from Staffordshire.

Other stone was seldom used. A small amount of Old Red Sandstone, from below the Carboniferous, was brought from Bonhill (pillars in Glasgow University) and Wemyss Bay (Ardgowan Terrace in Sauchiehall Street; Partick Bridge). Portland Limestone can also be seen in a very few buildings, where it was used as cladding (Nos. 84–94 St Vincent Street of 1908–9). And, although Glasgow was overwhelmingly a sandstone city, granite was sometimes used, particularly in Victorian times, in the lower storeys of major buildings. The City Chambers has unpolished pink Correnie granite from Aberdeenshire; Strathclyde University has the flesh-pink Stirlinghill granite from Peterhead; and the former *Evening Citizen* building in St Vincent Place has the pink Shap granite from Cumbria with its typically large feldspar crystals. Igneous rocks were mainly used for road setts, granite in main thoroughfares, whin in side streets and as kerb-stones. Crarae, Furnace, Ailsa Craig, Bonawe, Aberdeenshire and Peterhead all provided granites, and some were even imported from Scandinavia. The whin was of more local origin. Pavements were of flagstones, from the Arbroath area or from Caithness.

Table 1   *Main sources of sandstone used in Glasgow buildings, with approximate dates of working*

	Pre-1700	1700–1790	1790–1840	1840–1890	1890–1914
Central Glasgow					
Provanside (Bells)	●	●	●		
Cracklinghouse	?	●			
Cowcaddens		●	●		
Town, Magazine etc.	●	●			
North Glasgow					
Possil, Keppoch, Balgray etc.		○	●	○	
Bishopbriggs			○	●	○
West Glasgow					
Woodside			●	○	
Hillhead – Maryhill etc.			○	●	
Netherton of Garscube			●	○	
East Glasgow		○	●	●	○
South Glasgow					
Pollok, Cowglen etc.	○	○	○	○	
Giffnock			○	●	○
Stirlingshire				●	
New Red Sandstone, Ayrshire and Dumfries-shire (Locharbriggs, Closeburn, Corncockle, Mauchline, Cove)					●

● = relatively important
○ = less important

Slates used for roofing were either the intensely black slates, with small cubes of pyrite, coming from Easdale and Ballachulish, or those coloured grey, green or red from Luss.

Later in the C 20 most buildings were of concrete or steel, using stone only occasionally as a thin veneer (up to 100 mm: 4 inches). Such stone can come from anywhere in the world, and one city cannot be distinguished from another by its modern buildings. It is only by looking at the older buildings that a town's distinctive character becomes apparent.

PREHISTORIC, ROMAN AND
EARLY HISTORICAL GLASGOW

BY J. N. GRAHAM RITCHIE, GORDON S. MAXWELL
AND ALISTAIR GORDON

The magnificent sweep of the Kingston Bridge high above the River Clyde symbolizes Glasgow's geographical importance today at the heart of a busy region. In earliest times it was also for its river-crossings that the area played a crucial role, for here was one of the lowest points for fording the river, near its confluence with the Molendinar Burn. It is perhaps not surprising that the expansion of a modern conurbation has revealed traces of the earliest inhabitants of the area; often the building development is itself the reason for the chance discovery of Bronze Age burials or bronze objects. From Glasgow many finds reflect not only the importance of the river, with discoveries of objects from the Clyde, including wooden boats (doubtless used for fishing as well as transportation), but also its position as a place of trade and exchange even from earliest times.

The small groups of people who made their way into the area from about 8,000 years ago were primarily interested in harvesting the natural resources of this part of the river basin; the Clyde must have been an important focus for fishing and its wooded banks for hunting and for gathering the seasonal fruits of the forest. No definite traces of such communities have been found in Glasgow; reports of banks of oyster-shells near Duke Street are tantalizingly vague. But excavations at Woodend Loch, just to the E of the city, have revealed many examples of the chert, mudstone and flint tools associated with such mesolithic communities; flakes, scrapers and tiny flint implements known as microliths show that there was a camp-site or working-place near the water's edge. The fact that not all the raw material for the tools was of local origin shows the importance of trade even at such an early date, perhaps in the sixth or fifth millennium B.C.

More permanent settlement of the area, with an economy based on agriculture and stock-rearing, had probably begun by *c.* 4000 B.C., but all traces of the homes and farms of the earliest agricultural communities have been swept away by urban development. The buildings of these settlements would have been of timber, probably of quite sophisticated construction; but wood rots, and not even traces of post-holes indicating the ground-plan are likely to survive beneath later foundations.

Contemporary burial cairns with their stone-built chambers are more commonly found; such tombs are known from adjacent areas of Dumbarton and Stirling, though not from the immediate vicinity of Glasgow. The presence of Neolithic folk is, however, indicated by many discoveries of their most distinctive tool – the polished axehead of stone. Examples have been found at several locations in the city, in some cases rather incongruously: a Neolithic axe was found at the corner of Sauchiehall Street and Buchanan Street in 1848, another in 1854 in the Clyde at Rutherglen Bridge, and in 1866 one was found at Kingston Dock. More recently axes have been discovered in gardens in Newton Mearns (just s of the city boundary) and in High Burnside, Rutherglen. The stone for these axes may have been the object of exchange and trade over considerable distances: axes of North Welsh and Antrim stone are not uncommon; the tanged flint arrowhead found during the excavation of Queen's Dock in 1875 may also have been an object of trade. Perhaps the most surprising import is the polished stone axehead found inside a logboat in 1780 at Old St Enoch's Church, for it is made of a jadeite known to occur in the Alps.

Logboats, formerly known as 'dugouts' or 'dug-out canoes', are among the best-known archaeological discoveries in the Glasgow area, and feature in many accounts of the history of the city. Twenty-one examples have been recorded within the present District, revealed by engineering and construction works since the c 18 A.D., and several more are known from the Lower Clyde. Logboats found in other parts of Britain have frequently been proved to be of medieval date, but the geological contexts of some of the examples from Glasgow, as well as the jadeite axe from the logboat at Old St Enoch's Church mentioned above, indicate that some are of greater antiquity. Two examples are prominently displayed in the Hunterian Museum, University of Glasgow; one was found during the enlargement of the Springfield Quay c. 1848, and the other, certainly from the Clyde, may also have been found at Springfield at the same time.

The discovery of burials of Bronze Age date either in stone cists (or coffins) or as cremations in large cinerary urns of coarse pottery may indicate the presence of a contemporary settlement nearby; often such burials are discovered in the course of building work or sand and gravel extraction, activities which make the finding of the more fugitive traces of settlement sites unlikely.

In the late 1930s the attention of Glaswegians and Clydebankers was caught by the excavation by L. MacL. Mann of a prehistoric site known as the 'Druid Temple' at Knappers to the w of Great Western Road. Although Mann's interpretation of the multiple rings of timbers and low serpent-shaped banks as an astronomical site was regarded with distrust at the time, it is clear from the character of the associated finds that the location was of some importance; it seems to have been a centre for exchange, ritual and burial in the later Neolithic period and the Early Bronze Age. (An intriguing 'modern' ancient monument is the circle of stones set out with astronomical precision in 1979 at Sighthill Park, a viewpoint with extensive views over the city.)

The working of a sand-pit at Greenoakhill, Mount Vernon, in

1928 led to the discovery of cists containing inhumation burials
accompanied by food vessel pottery; four of the cist-burials have
been reconstructed in the Glasgow Art Gallery and Museum,
Kelvingrove, where they offer an insight into the careful deposition of the dead *c*. 1500 B.C. In 1927 two cists containing food
vessels were discovered in a garden in Newton Avenue, Cambuslang, and similar pottery was found in 1936 on Springfield
Farm, Baillieston. Cists containing food vessels were discovered
in 1930 during the construction of Dalton School, Cambuslang.
Finds made during the clearance of overburden at a quarry in
Victoria Park show that several deposits probably associated with
burials had been made there in the early second millennium B.C.
Other examples of urns and cremations found in the course of
the industrial and mercantile expansion of Glasgow in the later
C 18 and C 19 A.D. came from the Clyde Iron Works (1786),
Springfield Quay (1877), West Sand Quarry, Mount Vernon
(*c*. 1895), and Garngad Quarry (1899). Among the best-preserved
cinerary urns are those found in 1904 on the S side of Earls Park
Avenue, Newlands, the careful recording of which owed much
to the efforts of Mann. The urns (now in the Royal Museum of
Scotland, Queen Street, Edinburgh) contained cremated
remains, and one of them was accompanied by a bronze object,
possibly a razor, which survived as no more than a bright green
stain. Several finds of Bronze Age bronzework have been
recorded, including flat axes from High Crosshill, and from the
River Cart, near Spean Street; a spearhead was discovered at
Gartsheugh, Millerston, in 1952. A socketed axe of Late Bronze
Age date was found in the Clyde in 1864 on the site of the former
York Street Ferry on the Broomielaw. A Late Bronze Age leaf-
shaped sword with its bronze chape (the tip of the sword scab-
bard) and another sword were dredged from the bed of the River
Clyde near Bowling to the W of the city and are now preserved
in the Glasgow Art Gallery and Museum, Kelvingrove.

Another indication of activity in the area in the second millennium B.C. is the boulder decorated with distinctive cup-and-
ring markings formerly situated in the Bluebell Wood, Langside
(now in the Glasgow Art Gallery and Museum, Kelvingrove).
The smooth upper surface is decorated with two examples of
cupmarks surrounded by four rings, one example of a cup and
three rings, and about a dozen plain cupmarks.

Sadly, there are few remaining traces on the ground of Bronze
Age and Iron Age date, but a large mound on Pollok Golf Course
still survives. There were formerly several cairns on the top of
the Cathkin Braes; the largest, traditionally the spot from which
Mary, Queen of Scots, viewed the battle of Langside in 1568,
was originally surrounded by a ditch and bank and stood to a
height of about 5·5 m. In *c*. 1792 about twenty-five 'urns' inverted
on flat slabs and filled with 'earth and human bones' were discovered, and a large (empty) cist was found at the centre of the
cairn; but the stones of the cairn were robbed to build walls, and
nothing now survives. One of the puzzling features about this
cairn is the discovery of a number of bronze objects of Iron Age

date: a button-and-loop fastener was found in one of the urns, part of a comb in another; and a distinctive three-linked bit of the C 1 or C 2 A.D., the most northerly example in Britain, was found with bones close to the central cist. This evidence suggests that the cairn, already an old burial place, was used again in the late Iron Age. A ditched mound of comparable date still survives at Gallowflat, Rutherglen.

The shores of the Clyde below Glasgow and the lochans now to the E of the city were the focus for settlement in the later first millennium B.C. and the earlier first millennium A.D., with, for example, crannogs at Bishop Loch and Lochend Loch (the latter in Monklands District); crannogs are timber or timber-and-stone-built houses, set on small islands of artificial or partly artificial origin at the edge of rivers and lochs. The finds from the crannog in Bishop Loch were meagre, but include coarse pottery, a metalworker's crucible and a socketed iron axehead of later first millennium B.C. date.

An unusual ditched enclosure, probably of Iron Age date, was excavated at Shiels, Govan, in advance of redevelopment in 1973 and 1974. The enclosure was about 42 by 36 m, with a single entrance to the E, and a rectangular timber building 5 by 3 m; air photographs indicate the presence of ring-ditch structures, possibly round timber houses. The earthworks at Camphill in Queen's Park and at Pollok Park are also of Iron Age date, or even later. The former, excavated in 1867 and 1951, produced evidence of paving and perhaps a corn-drying kiln in the interior, and pottery from the bank and ditch suggests that the earthwork is of Iron Age origin, but was re-used as the site of an earth and timber ring-work castle of medieval date. Excavations at a similar earthwork at Pollok Park in 1959 and 1960 revealed traces of a rectangular house, and a medieval date was suggested.

The geographical situation which commended the area of Glasgow to prehistoric man as suitable for settlement drew the attention of the Roman invader also. Apart from the need to control major centres of native population, there were the demands of military and political policy. During the Roman Iron Age, according to the C 2 Alexandrian geographer Ptolemy, the dominant local tribe was that of the Damnonii, whose territories extended through western Scotland from the shores of the Firth of Clyde S of Irvine as far N as western Tayside. Six inhabited sites (whether they were Roman forts or native settlements is uncertain) are assigned to them by Ptolemy, but none is likely to have lain within the present boundaries of the city; the nearest was probably Colania, which may be identified with Castlecary near Cumbernauld.

Of the three major phases of occupation, all but the last necessitated the deployment, for a longer or shorter time, of garrisons on the line of the Forth-Clyde isthmus; the tactics and strategy of the exception, the early C 3 campaigns of the Emperor Septimius Severus, restricted troop movements and fort-building to the E coast. The first occasion was during the fourth season of operations conducted by Gnaeus Julius Agricola, governor of Britain from c. A.D. 77 to 83. According to the historian Tacitus (who happened to be Agricola's son-in-law), this particular year, A.D. 80, was taken up with consolidating the gains made in previous advances; 'for the waters of the Clyde and Forth ... are separated by a narrow neck of land, and this he secured with a chain of garrisons'.

Where these garrisons lay has long been debated by scholars. For many years it was thought that their forts were hidden beneath the structures of the Antonine Wall, built across the isthmus some sixty years later. It now seems that this may be only partially true, for the discovery of a late C I fortlet at Mollins, roughly halfway between the Wall-forts of Cadder and Castlecary, but about 6 km S of the Wall, strongly suggests that the isthmus defence-lines of the two periods are not exactly co-extensive. As it is probable that the garrisons forming the Agricolan frontier were separated from each other by an average interval of from 10 to 13 km, there is a strong likelihood that a member of the chain awaits discovery in the city. Roman material has in fact been recorded from Glasgow Green, overlooking the confluence of the Molendinar and the Clyde, and a coin was found on the opposite bank from the confluence with the Cart; either site could have served as a convenient intermediate station between Cadder and the Agricolan fort at Barochan on the S shore of the Clyde. Wherever the fort was situated, its existence as a member of a linear system is unlikely to have lasted for more than a winter or so. If, however, it occupied a bridgehead position on the bank of the Clyde, there is a good chance that it survived slightly longer, perhaps until c. A.D. 86, when many of Agricola's northern conquests appear to have been abandoned. Doubtless it was in this short period that the Roman artefacts, including two handsome bronze skillets stamped with the Campanian maker's name, CONGALLUS or CONVALLUS, came into the possession of the natives living in the probable homestead at Gallowflat, presumably by way of trade.

Shortly after the death of the Emperor Hadrian in A.D. 138, the decision was taken to reoccupy at least the southern part of Scotland. The precise reason for this sudden change of policy is not known, but, although the sole historical reference indicates that 'barbarians were driven away', the pressure may have been political as much as military. The succeeding emperor, Antoninus Pius, had been an able administrator but lacked any reputation as a soldier. He may have felt that a successful campaign in the remote province of Britannia would provide the correct degree of military lustre, even though it was in fact won by his legate, Q. Lollius Urbicus (governor from 139 to c. 142). Behind these considerations lay the possibility that the existing arrangements, involving vast numbers of troops densely packed in the Hadrian's Wall zone, were fast becoming unworkable and unacceptably expensive.

The main thrust of the new strategy was to push forward the limits of the province to the Tay, but to use the outer fringe of

this reconquest as a buffer zone for a northern mural barrier on
the Forth-Clyde isthmus – the Antonine Wall. The new wall was
eventually to be built of turf and earth, although there are signs
that at an early stage in the planning the intention was to construct
it in stone, like the Hadrianic frontier just abandoned. Less
durable the materials may have been, but the new frontier was
no inferior copy of the old; it represented in many ways a considerable improvement, incorporating several technical inno-
vations. It ran from Bridgeness on the Forth near Bo'ness for
about 40·5 Roman miles (c. 64 km) to Old Kilpatrick on the
Clyde, thus traversing roughly 2·2 km of the city area in the
sector to the w of the Kelvin crossing.

The major element of the frontier was a wall made, wherever
possible, of turf blocks on a boulder foundation 4·3–4·9 m wide;
its height may have exceeded 3·0 m (although we have no way of
demonstrating this), and the wallhead possibly incorporated a
sentry-walk up to 1·8 m wide and a wooden breastwork. To the
N there lay a V-profiled ditch of varying width – 12 m or so in
much of the central sector, but only 6·1–7·6 m between Kir-
kintilloch and the Clyde. The spoil produced by ditch-digging
was piled in a great counterscarp bank on its northern lip, frequently in such a way as to obscure the forward view of watchers
on the Wall, offering cover to possible assailants. The military
surveyors who laid out the earliest stages of the frontier, however,
do not appear to have always given much thought to these
matters, occasionally choosing to sacrifice strength of position to
convenience of construction or other factors. Between the Wall
and the Ditch there was a level platform, or berm, 6–12 m in
width, far broader than was required to prevent any chance of
the Wall's weight causing subsidence of the inner ditch-lip.
Together with the Ditch and Outer Bank, this feature created a
zone 120 Roman feet deep in front of the turf curtain, whose
presence as a formal cordon, rather than a defence, seems frequently to have dictated the siting of the Wall itself. The sector
lying within the city provides a fine example of such a pre-
occupation. The final linear element of the frontier, and one
which Hadrian's Wall was not to possess until much later, was a
communication road, known as the Military Way; it ran roughly
parallel to the Wall about 15–45 m to the s.

The garrison which manned this complex series of works was
housed in an array of forts, fortlets and lesser enclosures, whose
form and significance archaeologists are still attempting to define
by aerial survey and excavation. It was only recently that it was
realized that these too had been subject to a process of evolution,
the earliest plans for the frontier having called for about seven
primary forts, each capable of accommodating a full auxiliary
regiment, and an unspecified number of fortlets set at intervals
of a Roman mile in most cases, but occasionally further apart;
the latter could have held no more than a handful of troops,
probably drawn from the units in adjacent forts. At some stage
in the Wall-building programme it was decided that a greater
density of manning was required, and secondary forts were

added, some replacing or physically supplementing already existing fortlets.

The early concept of the frontier also included a range of minor
installations, possibly intended to provide facilities for signalling
and surveillance: one category, known to early antiquaries as
'expansions', took the form of square platforms, 6 m across,
abutting the s face of the barrier; the other, about which less is
known because it was only recently detected, seems also to have
been square on plan but defined by a low bank and ditch. Both
types may be compared in size with the turrets found on Hadrian's Wall, but their distribution along the frontier is severely
restricted.

An example of both major categories of Wall-installation can
be found within the city area: at Balmuildy there is a splendid
primary fort, one of the two sites on the frontier to be defended
by a stone wall; and about one Roman mile to the N W at Summerston (N S 574723) aerial survey has identified a fortlet.
Although the whole of the perimeter is yet to be established, the
fortlet probably measures about 30 m square over the rampart.
The curtain of the Wall itself served as the northern defence, the
other sides being defined by a turf rampart of slighter scale. Trial
excavation revealed that the site had been severely disturbed by
quarrying, possibly by the 'laird of Dougalstoun' in the 1690s,
when he destroyed the foundation of the Antonine Wall to
provide stone for his park dyke. It was not possible therefore
to identify any traces of the small timber barrack-block which
originally must have stood in the interior, and even the single
enclosing ditch had in places been totally removed. The ditch
was well enough preserved on the s, however, to make it possible
to demonstrate its structural relationship to a small temporary
camp which aerial survey had revealed nearby; the camp measured about 140 by 165 m, and it covered an area of about 2·4 ha
(6 acres). At least twenty such camps are now known in the
vicinity of the Wall, although only three of these are situated to
the w of Kilsyth, which makes the discovery of the Summerston
example particularly important. It is believed that such camps
housed the working-parties of legionary troops that built the
Wall and its installations, and their distribution can therefore
cast light upon the vexed question of how the building work was
allocated and how long it took. At Summerston it was evident
from excavation that the camp was just a little earlier than the
fortlet; the latter was thus a primary element in the building
programme, like the nearly identical fortlet at Wilderness Plantation, 2·8 km, or almost exactly two Roman miles, to the E – a
strong indication that in this sector strictly regular fortlet spacing
was being observed.

The troops, probably of the Second Legion, who built the
adjacent stretch of wall and bivouacked in the labour camp
'signed' the end and beginning of each of their work-lengths with
a pair of carved stone panels known as Distance Slabs, one set
into the front face of the curtain and the other into the rear.
Frequently embellished with decorative elements portraying

scenes of victorious warfare or celebrations of conquest, these slabs were more than utilitarian records; they were also vehicles of propaganda, and handsome advertisements of the skills deployed by legionary craftsmen. At the junction between every pair of lengths there were originally four such stones, two from each legion, and thus at a point roughly midway along the sector which extends W from Balmuildy, on the farmlands of East Millichen and Summerston (c. N S 572725), there once stood two slabs erected by the Sixth Legion and two of the Second Legion. One stone of each pair, recording identical Wall-lengths of 3,666$\frac{1}{2}$ Roman paces, has survived: that of the former unit, found in 1803, is displayed in the Glasgow Art Gallery and Museum, Kelvingrove; the Second Legion's stone may be seen in the Hunterian Museum, University of Glasgow.

Between the completion of the fully developed building programme which these inscriptions recorded in c. A.D. 144 and the final abandonment of the frontier, barely twenty years elapsed. Apart from a brief interval around A.D. 155 the native communities of the lower Clyde had become accustomed to enjoying the fruits of occupation quite as fully as they might have complained about its constraints. There was stability, there was trade, and there was peace. When the troops were eventually withdrawn c. A.D. 163, the economy would have crashed, and the political structures would have been transformed. But the 'barbarians' living to the N had by then learned their lesson. Decades of being treated as the peoples literally beyond the pale had forged them into a redoubtably hostile nation, as the successors of the Damnonii were too soon to learn.

The remains, both structural and material, which have survived in the Glasgow area from the Prehistoric periods and from the period of the Roman occupation until the abandonment of the Antonine Wall give some clue to the nature of settlement in the area. From the centuries following that event, however, no such remains survive which might suggest a settlement pattern. Within the area there have been isolated finds of Roman coins dating to the C3 and C4, but these have been mostly stray and unassociated. While these coins might suggest continued contact between native and Roman, more likely they are stray losses of a later, possibly much later, date, and they are therefore of little value as evidence in this respect.

Some material does survive from the C5 to the C9, but it is from a site outside Glasgow's boundaries, Alt Clut, Dumbarton Castle Rock. From within the city there appears, at present, to be nothing until material of the mid-C10 and the C11 at Govan Parish Church – hogbacked stones, a stone sarcophagus, standing crosses and cross-slabs. There is also, in the Glasgow Art Gallery and Museum, Kelvingrove, a censer from Bearsden of the C11 or possibly C12. This paucity of material, at least for the immediate post-Roman and Early Historical periods, may be because the capital of the kingdom of Strathclyde was Alt Clut, not Glasgow, or perhaps because the rapid expansion of the city from the late C18 onwards has obscured or destroyed evidence.

Glasgow came securely into historical record when Earl David of Strathclyde (later David I, King of Scotland, 1124–53) instituted his inquest into its former possessions during his establishment of the medieval see of Glasgow between 1114 and 1118. The origins of the bishopric and Glasgow date to the late C6 or early C7, when St Kentigern (whose death is recorded in the *Annales Cambriae* as 612) was given land, the 'green hollow' (*glas cau*), by the then king of Strathclyde, Rhydderch Hael, to found a monastery. The land, which later became the site of Glasgow Cathedral, was by tradition the site of a cemetery consecrated perhaps a century earlier by St Ninian. It is thought also that Kentigern was created the first bishop of a diocese, the extent of which would be co-terminous with the boundaries of the kingdom. It would seem strange that Rhydderch Hael chose to give land for the monastery and seat of a bishopric so far, some 23 km (14 miles), upstream from his *oppidum*, Alt Clut, but there is some substance to the tradition that there was a royal seat at Partick, only about 3 km (2 miles) away. Partick is mentioned as royal demesne land in a charter of 1136, when David I granted it to the church at Glasgow. Traces of an earthwork were known to exist on the summit of Yorkhill (now the site of the Children's Hospital), and this site, had it been excavated with modern techniques, might have yielded some needed evidence.

After the death of Kentigern, there is a gap in the episcopal succession until the C11, when three bishops appear on record. It is uncertain whether they occupied the see. It is more likely that they were suffragans attached to the Archbishop of York, who claimed jurisdiction over the see of Glasgow, but it is to David and his first bishop, John, that the re-establishment of the see must be credited.

There are two 'lives' of the saint, both written in the C12, one between 1147 and 1164, the other between 1174 and 1199. Research has shown that these relied on earlier sources – sources, however, not earlier than the C11. Nevertheless, this earlier material may have contained yet older local traditions about St Kentigern, which helped to establish or to continue a cult of the saint. Certainly from the C12 onwards this cult was to benefit both the see of Glasgow and the town itself.

The second important early ecclesiastical site, now within the city, is that of Govan. This site may have been established some time in the mid-C7 under the influence of the then expanding Columban church, but there is no documentary or secure archaeological evidence to substantiate this theory. Only the shape and layout of the enclosure, its wall being relatively modern (although it may follow an older line), the fact that the surviving sculptured stones originally stood in the cemetery, and that the medieval parish church, demolished in 1762, was on the site of the present church, suggest that this may be an early foundation. It is more likely that it was established in the early C9 during the Norse raids on the W coast. Govan Church is dedicated to a St Constantine, and it is possible that the relics of this saint were moved from a site in Kintyre for safety, finding a new home at Govan. Whichever theory is accepted, it is clear, on the evidence of the amount of material surviving in the church enclosure, that by the end of the c 9 or early in the c 10 Govan had become an important ecclesiastical site. It could be argued from the surviving material that by the c 10 Govan was the more important ecclesiastical centre in the area, as no material earlier than the c 12 has so far been found in the neighbourhood of Glasgow Cathedral. The size of the medieval parish of Govan corresponded to the size of parish normally associated with an early English minster. Was Govan therefore established at the time of the Northumbrian domination in the c 8? But the tradition of the cult of St Kentigern maintained the importance of Glasgow through the intervening centuries until its re-emergence in the c 12. Many questions remain until archaeological research can be undertaken on both sites.

One further observation must be made about Govan. The presence of the hogbacked stones suggests either that in the wake of the Norse incursions into Strathclyde in the c 9 some Norsemen did not return but, as happened in the Western Isles, remained to settle and become Christianized, one of these settlements being in the neighbourhood of Govan, or that there was considerable communication, either by trade or intermarriage and settlement, with Cumbria, where there was an existing Scandinavian tradition, since the hogbacked stones at Govan show considerable similarity to those in Cumbria.

Despite the importance of Govan, the cult of St Kentigern seems to have attracted a small community to establish itself around the original site of the 'green hollow'. It is from this site, now that of the present cathedral, that Glasgow is thought to have developed. On this early site Bishop John constructed what is thought to be the first stone-built cathedral, consecrated in 1136, while the community gradually extended down the hill towards the River Clyde. However, there are new indications that, while a small community did exist round the cathedral area, the earliest nucleus of the city developed near the river, in the area of the Bridgegate and Saltmarket, the land between the two communities being open land or farm land. The true development of Glasgow as a commercial centre began with the granting of a charter to the bishop by William the Lion some time between 1175 and 1178, by which the community was created a Burgh of Barony. Some years later Bishop Jocelyn began the enlargement of the earlier cathedral in order to enclose the traditional burial place of St Kentigern. Work on this new church was sufficiently advanced to allow its consecration in 1197. It may be from this church that sculptured fragments of stone, Romanesque in style, and one of them painted, remain. These are not the only sculptured stones of the period to survive in the area; fragments from the Old Parish Church of Rutherglen (a former royal burgh, but now part of Glasgow), which was built c. 1180 and demolished in 1794, are preserved in Rutherglen Museum.

MEDIEVAL TO TWENTIETH-CENTURY
GLASGOW

BY ELIZABETH WILLIAMSON

MEDIEVAL AND RENAISSANCE ARCHITECTURE

Almost all traces of Glasgow's MEDIEVAL ARCHITECTURE have
5 been swept away, leaving the Cathedral as the key to the importance of the upper, Bishop's town, and the much widened and
straightened cross of streets well to its S to represent the trading
settlement near the river. Of the first and probably simple
cathedral, built in the early C 12 by Bishop John in an uncertain
relationship with St Kentigern's tomb, a painted voussoir is the
only likely relic. Bishop Jocelyn's late C 12 enlargements probably
established the arrangement of upper presbytery (then with
salient chapels) and crypt, but only a small spur of masonry, with
a shaft topped by a stiffleaf capital, and part of a wall bench
survive: the rest was probably destroyed by the rearrangement
to an aisled presbytery made in the early C 13. From the evidence
of the basecourses, the transepts and the nave seem also to have
been laid out then. Bishop Bondington began to build again in
the mid-C 13, with a very much longer eastern limb. The nave
and probably one of its western towers (destroyed in 1846 and
1848) seem to have followed almost immediately. It is the remarkable homogeneity of the mid- and late-C 13 design that distinguishes Glasgow Cathedral, Scotland's most important
building of the period. Ideas, such as the suppression of the
middle storey of the interior elevations in the nave, were borrowed from the North of England, but Scottish preferences,
particularly for weighty arcade piers, are obvious, and the sophisticated design of the crypt seems to owe nothing to English
models. That the plate tracery of the choir should have survived
is rare in both England and in Scotland. The plan, a cross
within a rectangle with a rectangular ambulatory (chosen perhaps
because of the need for circulation round a feretory), is made
extraordinary by its numerous accretions: the uniquely two-
storey chapter house, the once two-storeyed treasury and sacristy
and the lateral Blackadder Aisle. The only later contributions –
apart from repairs made after lightning struck c. 1406 – were the
reconstruction of the chapter house, the building by 1454 of the
squat central tower and its (unusual for Scotland) broach spire,
and the vaulting of the transeptal aisle by Bishop Blackadder
(1483–1508).
    Evidence of other medieval chapels and churches (principally

the C15 collegiate church on the site of the Tron Kirk) and of the parishes that ringed Glasgow (Cathcart, Eastwood, Govan and Rutherglen) is extremely scarce, and what there is (at Govan and Rutherglen) has already been discussed by Mr Gordon (*see* Prehistoric, Roman and Early Historical Glasgow, above).

The Bishop's Castle dominated the crown of the hill s w of the 9 Cathedral from the C13 until the C18. Its big stone tower house, built in the first half of the C15, is known only from descriptions and pictures, its early C16 curtain walls from excavations as well. Round it was grouped a precinct of thirty-two prebendal houses, of which Provand's Lordship, the house of the prebendary of 10 Barlanark, is the only survivor, though excavations have revealed the footings of two others, both apparently similar in form. The timber-framed buildings that lined the wynds off High Street are known only from the limited excavation of Old Vennel at the s E end. Nothing remains of the two religious houses, Blackfriars and Greyfriars (founded in 1246 and 1479 respectively), and nothing medieval of the university (established in 1451), neither on its original site off the High Street nor on Gilmorehill, to which some relics were moved in the C19.

The prebendaries of the Cathedral had country seats as well as town houses. Provan Hall, the late C15 courtyard house of the prebendary of Barlanark, was partly rebuilt in the C17 and C18 and still exists at Easterhouse. The relics of three medieval feudal castles come within the city boundary: Crookston Castle (Pollok) with a late C12 ringwork enclosing the ruins of an early C15 tower house of unusual plan; a tiny fragment of the Maxwells' C14 and C16 Laigh Castle in Pollok Park; and the lowest courses of the C15 keep of Cathcart Castle.

The scarce remains of LATE SIXTEENTH AND SEVENTEENTH CENTURY Glasgow have been self-consciously preserved. Earliest are three steeples, venerable relics of the buildings to which they originally belonged: the Tron of *c.* 1592 13 with a spire of 1630–6, the Tolbooth of 1625–7 by *John Boyd*, 14 and the Merchants' Steeple of 1665, all of them Gothic in profile but acknowledging the Renaissance in detail. The same proto-Renaissance spirit is felt in the rich cable decoration of the L- 11–12 plan tower house of 1585, Haggs Castle (Pollokshields). The fragments from the second half of the C17 speak more eloquently of the Northern Renaissance, with its taste for liberal applications of strapwork and rustication, in particular those elements salvaged from the Old College in High Street (fragments of the main façade of 1654–60 by *John Clerk*, and the Lion and the Unicorn staircase of 1690 by *William Riddell*) and incorporated in the Victorian university on Gilmorehill. The Old College, the demolished Hutchesons' Hospital of 1649 and Merchants' Hospital of 1659 shared characteristics of plan as well as elevation, for all of them had low courtyard ranges offset by tall towers. With the gateway of Rutherglen Church, designed by *John Scott* in 1662–3, there is a clear advance (perhaps because of the church's aristocratic connexions) into a more Italian Mannerism, which makes the classical flourish of 1647 on the gateway at Provan Hall (Easterhouse) look old-fashioned and half-hearted.

EXPANSION AND ARCHITECTURE 1700–1840

Glasgow, like Edinburgh, expanded suddenly and rapidly after 1750. In Glasgow the stimulus was a great increase in trade, particularly transatlantic trade in sugar, tobacco and, later, cotton. Its new, initially residential, suburbs E and W of the medieval city were begun not as a civic enterprise but as private speculation and so grew up piecemeal. The first to move out of the overcrowded medieval city were the tobacco merchants, who built themselves mansions beyond the West Port. Most of these houses vanished when those who owned property along Trongate turned developers and laid out, between 1750 and 1800, the long straight parallel streets of the southern part of the New Town (the Merchant City) over their land, along the lines of the medieval riggs.

Planned development, by London standards, came late. The Town Council initiated it when in 1772, perhaps encouraged by the inception of Edinburgh's New Town five years before, they commissioned from *James Barry* a plan for their lands just N of the earlier streets; but it was Barry's published plan of 1781 that inspired the existing layout, begun *c.* 1782. Plans of 1792 by *James Craig* continued to spread Glasgow's characteristic, relentless grid of streets over the Town Council's Meadowflat lands and even further W over the adjoining Blythswood estate from 1800. So successful was the formula of the New Town of Blythswood that, in the 1820s, the grid was extended over the southern part of the estate to a plan by *James Gillespie Graham*, and to the N over Garnethill.

The push westward, away from the industrial suburbs that were mushrooming E of the old city, was irresistible. The smart eastern suburb on the edge of Glasgow Green in Calton, which began in 1771 with an unexecuted plan for a single square, had begun to founder with the influx of industry by the 1820s. Attempts to establish similar suburbs (also on grid-iron layouts) S of the Clyde after 1790 met with the same problems. Laurieston, begun in 1801, failed to meet David Laurie's ambitions for a positively aristocratic suburb after only two very grand terraces (Carlton Place) had been built. As industry and commerce inundated the C18 and early C19 suburbs, the affluent moved even further W, both N and S of the river. The planning here was far more varied and generally on a grander scale, as we shall see later.

The best of Glasgow's ECCLESIASTICAL ARCHITECTURE of this period reflects the growth of her trade and the consequent wealth of her merchants. St Andrew's, begun in 1739, was Glasgow's first completely new church after the Reformation, and remained her most sophisticated ecclesiastical building for over seventy years. This free reinterpretation of James Gibbs' St

Plan of the City of Glasgow and its environs by Smith & Collie, 1838

Martin's-in-the-Fields, London, by *Allan Dreghorn* and *Mungo Naismith* was surely derived from Gibbs' illustrations of his design, published eleven years before, for here, as in the drawings, the building stands freely (though the formal setting of the square came later), and on to it has been grafted one of the versions of the tower of St Mary-le-Strand, London, depicted in the same book. The size of St Andrew's and its Anglican plan, with aisles and chancel, distinguish it from contemporary Scottish churches. Its craftsmanship, especially the plasterwork of the 1750s by *Thomas Clayton*, is as rich as anything in a country house – indeed the only comparable contemporary plasterwork is at Pollok House. More modest and, surprisingly, less Anglican in form is the neighbouring St Andrew-by-the-Green Episcopal Church of 1750–2, just a box by the masons *William Paull* and *Andrew Hunter* clothed in a mixture of Baroque and Palladian styles in the manner of William Adam. The Tron Kirk, rebuilt in 1793–4 by *James Adam*, is equally retiring with a minimum of Neo-classical detail. It was not until 1807 that the inventive *William Stark* gave the classical box 21 some new life at St George's Tron, where his Baroque tower possesses enough vigour to serve as the focal point of an important vista and to punctuate the oblique view along Buchanan Street.

Country churches look very plain: Carmunnock of 1762–7 (with early c19 alterations) is T-plan; Tollcross of 1805–6 by *John Brash* large but plain and square and with a lumpish tower of 1834–5; and Maryhill of 1826 (much altered) and Baillieston of 1833 the plainest pedimented boxes.

GOTHIC first appeared in the late c18 at the ham-fisted Gothick Barony Church built in 1793–1800 by *John Robertson* to designs by *R. & J. Adam* (since demolished), and was soon 26 given more serious treatment by *James Gillespie (Graham)* at St Andrew's Roman Catholic Chapel (now Cathedral) of 1814–17. Indeed his was the most seriously Gothic church in Scotland at that date, with Dec and Perp details, though mixed, from good sources, and an interior in which galleries were originally combined with aisle arcades. There is more mixed and delicately done Gothic in *Rickman*'s T-plan Ramshorn Kirk of 1824–6: its tall tower of Perp outline makes a most effective *point-de-vue*. Later but still Gothick is the country church tower of 1831 by *James Dempster* at Cathcart. Two more Gothick towers should perhaps be mentioned here, although they are not ecclesiastical: the Adamish clock tower at Pollokshaws of 1803 (all that remains of the old Burgh Buildings) and the more Tudor Balgray Tower at Springburn, a belvedere built *c.* 1820. Late Gothick occurs again domestically further up Balgray Hill at Mosesfield (designed in 1838 by *David Hamilton*), and in the splendid ribbed and pendant plaster vault of *David Cousin*'s Cambuslang Church (1839–41). For the exterior, Cousin used the Norman (or, more accurately, Transitional) style, perhaps consciously harking back to his church's medieval predecessor. Otherwise, despite the popularity of *Rundbogenstil* throughout Europe at this time, in

Glasgow only *David Hamilton* and *Charles Wilson* used it (for the cemetery gates described further on).

The city's major PUBLIC BUILDINGS of the C18 have gone. The Town Hall, begun in 1737–40 by *Allan Dreghorn* adjoining the C17 Tolbooth, continued only slightly more grandly the stone houses with piazzas round Glasgow Cross, but in 1792 *Robert Adam*, who managed to secure a number of commissions in the city, designed two much more imposing buildings. His domed Infirmary was swept away for the present hospital, but the triumphal arch centrepiece of his Assembly Rooms is preserved on Glasgow Green as the McLennan Arch. Adam's elegant Neo-classicism was succeeded early in the C19 by the weightier Greek style. *William Stark*'s Justiciary Courthouse of 1809–14 (rebuilt 23 with some alterations in 1910–13) was a very early descendant of Smirke's Covent Garden Theatre in London and imported the idea of the grand and pure Greek Doric portico into Glasgow. The County Buildings and Courthouse, for which *Clarke & Bell* won the competition in 1844, is larger, more complicated and infected by Romanticism. It stands raised self-importantly on a podium above its island site in the manner of Liverpool's St George's Hall, but its Greek detail, though well done, is still conventional. Also Greek but far more cautious, is *John Stephen*'s Custom House of 1840.

Whilst Glasgow's New Town (the Merchant City) was being completed in the late C18 and early C19, INSTITUTIONS moved in. Though their buildings were exclusive, a great deal of attention was paid to their public faces. *Robert Adam*'s new hall of 18 1791–4 for the Trades' House, composed with a bold columned centrepiece and a dome, gained additional prominence at the end of a vista when Garth Street opposite opened in 1793, and seems to have set the fashion for the opportunistic siting of major buildings that gives the very flat, long straight streets of the Merchant City their visual surprises. For Hutchesons' Hall in 17 1802–5, *David Hamilton* exploited a position facing down Hutcheson Street to even greater effect, distinguishing, like Adam, the hall itself by the use of columns on the *piano nobile* but using a very dignified French Neo-classical style and adding a steeple, perhaps as an echo of the charity's demolished C17 hospital. The steeple is distinctly Baroque, a style revived both by Hamilton and, as we have seen at St George's Tron, by William Stark. 21 Hamilton used a bolder tower still, though this time Graeco-Roman, in his conversion of the C18 Cunninghame mansion to the Royal Exchange in 1827–32, and advertised the Exchange's presence at the end of Ingram Street with the most grandiose temple front of its date in Glasgow. The former newsroom, a columned Roman hall, is equally grand. Older, but with a similar quasi-public function, is the unusually secretive little former Tobacco Exchange of *c.* 1819 in Virginia Street, with its classical tiers of booths.

Glasgow's reputation in the late C17 and C18 as one of the most beautiful cities in Europe rested on its four wide medieval streets lined with handsome HOUSES, all built, after fires swept through Glasgow Cross in 1652 and 1677, with stone fronts and on specified building lines. Illustrations show that, round the Cross itself, they had 'piazzas' or arcaded walks in the manner of Inigo Jones's Covent Garden, but none survived the work of the City Improvement Trust in the late C19. W of these, beyond the West Port, successful merchants built themselves mansions in large gardens. Of these, all long since gone, *Colen Campbell*'s Shawfield Mansion of 1711–12 (demolished in 1792) must be mentioned as an extremely early reassertion of C18 Palladian principles.

Some of the first houses of the new C18 suburbs were detached but more modest, although, like the Shawfield Mansion, they often had symmetrical façades and a central pediment. One of 1775 by *John Craig* still stands in Miller Street, another of *c.*1780 in Charlotte Street (the sole survivor of a street of such houses), and another of 1792 in Blackfriars Street, the last two with Adamish detail. Merchants continued to build mansions just beyond the city, but the only one left, enveloped in the Royal
25 Exchange, is that put up by the Cunninghames of Lainshaw in 1778–80. Most houses were terraced or tenemented. Tenements of 1771 and *c.*1780 on the fringes of the medieval city in Gallowgate are still rather rustic, with minimal classical allusions. The palace-fronted tenement block seems to have made its first, and simple, appearance in St Andrew's Square soon after 1786, and the formula was repeated at about the same date in George Square, where the surviving block has a Neo-classical cast. *Peter Nicholson*'s planned and grandly uniform Carlton Place, the showpiece of the southern suburb of Laurieston, continued the theme far more ambitiously in 1802–18 with terraces of large houses masquerading as two palaces looking out over the River Clyde. In the New Town (the Merchant City) and along the road to Dumbarton, tenements sprang up alongside business chambers and warehouses, most of them with stark classical façades indistinguishable from those of their commercial neighbours, such as Virginia Court and the fashionable Soanian Virginia Buildings of *c.* 1817 in Virginia Street. Because they were more economical to build, tenements took over in many of the neighbourhoods, such as Garnethill, Calton and Laurieston, which had been begun with villas and terraced houses.

The few early tenements that do survive display a variety of PLANS, all of them, at this date, incorporating a turnpike stair. The earliest, the free-standing No. 394 Gallowgate of 1771, is entered at the back through the circular stairtower that led to three floors of houses. More urban examples, tightly fitted between neighbours in the street, usually have a close leading through to a rear courtyard and to a separate external entrance in the stairtower (as at Nos. 106–14 Argyle Street): this was perhaps the most common solution until well into the first half of the C19. More sophisticated than this (and popular for the smartest residential tenements up to the 1870s, and thereafter for more humble ones) are separate entrances to the ground-floor house or houses and to the close, which leads to a partly extruded or an internal turnpike stair at the back (found in a commercial example at Nos. 47–55 Virginia Street of *c*. 1817). Alternatively, the staircase (sometimes cantilevered) filled the centre of the block and was reached from a central close, as was the case at Spreull's Land, Trongate, of 1784 (demolished in 1979). Years of alterations have obscured the original internal arrangements of each house, but most seem to have been of several apartments plus kitchen and watercloset and, in the early C 19, sometimes a bathroom.

The houses that gradually filled the streets of Blythswood New Town were almost all designed as variations on a single theme, that of the terrace composed of individual houses, three storeys high plus a basement. Some, like those in West Regent Street, are composed of houses all slightly different in size and detail; but a few are united into a single composition. There are three main versions: the terrace with slightly taller and slightly projecting ends, seen in Bath Street (Montague Place of *c*. 1830) and, at its most Neo-classical, in Blythswood Square, where the terraces, built in 1823–9 by *John Brash*, may have been designed by *William Burn*; the terrace with taller ends and a taller centre (also in Bath Street, at Athol Place of 1833–60, probably by *John Baird I*; and in St Vincent Street); and, rarest, most elaborate and perhaps slightly old-fashioned, the palace-fronted terrace (Adelaide Place, Bath Street, of 1839–62, by *Robert Black*). Within such a terrace, the houses vary slightly in size, the broader centre pavilions sometimes being taken up by whole houses (e.g. No. 218 St Vincent Street), the end ones sometimes by flats. What little remains of their interiors (many blocks have been altered or completely gutted) seems simple and remarkably consistent, especially the entrance halls, with their columned screens and flying, top-lit staircases with cast-iron balustrades.

The houses and tenements already discussed were built within the confines of the city or in its immediate vicinity. The ring of COUNTRY MANSIONS now engulfed in Glasgow's suburbs was then well beyond it. J. Guthrie Smith in his *Old Country Houses of the Old Glasgow Gentry* (1870) illustrated dozens, of which some were ancestral seats and some were country villas built by successful Glasgow merchants. In 1870 the suburbs were fast encroaching, and several had just gone or were derelict; now only four with any pretensions are left. Pollok House is the oldest and 15 most important of them. Though originally of little more than villa size, it was the ancestral seat of the Maxwells and superseded their medieval castle in 1747–52. Its tall, spare, blockish form and (probably somewhat altered) double-pile plan, with asymmetrically placed oval stair, is of the type invented by Sir William Bruce and developed by William Adam. *William Adam* produced a plan for Pollok in 1737 but there is no evidence that what stands is his. The interior, as in many William Adam houses, is rich 16 with plasterwork (some of it Edwardian pastiche) in the manner of *Thomas Clayton*. The only other plasterwork of any note is later and Neo-classical, and decorates the remarkably grand house that 20 the entrepreneur David Laurie fitted out for himself in 1804 in

Carlton Place. There are no other interiors as opulent as these.
Camphill House of 1800–18 and Aikenhead House of 1806 and
1823, both merchants' villas, are severely Neo-classical, even
Soanian, inside and out, and closely resemble each other. *David
Hamilton* perhaps designed both houses. Otherwise, almost on
the city boundary, there is only Cathkin House of 1799 by *James
Ramsay*, an Edinburgh architect.

URBAN AND SUBURBAN DEVELOPMENT 1830–1914

In the 1830s, Glasgow began to creep westward beyond Blythswood with more spaciously planned developments of crescents
and circuses. Terraces, screened by pleasure gardens laid out by
the Edinburgh architect *George Smith*, along Sauchiehall Street
and on the lowest slopes on Woodlands Hill in the 1830s and
1840s set the pattern for later development. The West End (or
Kelvingrove) Park, designed by *Joseph Paxton*, formed part of a
grand design conceived by *Charles Wilson* in 1854. His layout of
terraces encircling the upper slopes of Woodlands Hill, accented
by the towers of *J. T. Rochead*'s Park Church (1856–8) and his
own Free Church College (1856–7), and linked by majestic flights
of steps, combines the classical and the picturesque in a way
only half-heartedly tried before in Glasgow. After the high-level
bridging of the Kelvin and the opening of the Botanic Gardens
c. 1840, Glasgow made another spurt westward along the Great
Western Road beyond Kelvin Bridge and into Kelvinside (for
which *Decimus Burton* provided a plan of terraces and villas in
1840, revised in 1859 by *James Salmon*), Hillhead (a grid laid out
in the 1850s), Dowanhill (planned by *James Thomson c.* 1850)
and, towards the end of the century, Dowanside and Hyndland.

South of the Clyde as well, superior suburbs were planned in
the w away from industry. The first of them, Pollokshields, shows
a very different taste from the classical circuses and crescents N
of the river, albeit transformed by the topography. At Pollokshields the layout of 1849 by *David Rhind* is more loosely
picturesque, with roads lined with villas following the contours
of the hills. *Alexander Thomson*'s layout of 1853 for Langside is
in the same spirit, but the speculative venture, Regent's Park,
which he began on a flat site at Strathbungo in 1859 is disciplined
into straight terraces. Other suburbs were planned but failed, as
Laurieston had done earlier, to attract the wealthiest because of
the encroachment of industry. Kinning Park (planned in 1834)
and Dennistoun (begun in 1854 on a layout by *James Salmon I*)
soon had to be content with plain grids of middle-class tenements,
though Stobcross (started by *Alexander Kirkland* in 1849) was
partly built as intended with the remarkable curving tenements
of St Vincent Crescent, Minerva Street and Corunna Street. Not
all of the more desirable suburbs were planned: several, like
Mount Vernon, Crosshill, Partickhill, Bellahouston, Burnside
(Rutherglen) and Cambuslang, grew from small clusters of
country villas built in salubrious spots by city businessmen. All

of these suburbs increased greatly after the arrival late in the C 19 of the trams and the suburban railways.

The INDUSTRIAL SUBURBS that discouraged the affluent from moving E, both N and S of the river, grew apace throughout the C 19, promoted by exploitation of coal and iron ore. Thousands of utterly plain four- and five-storey tenements (the majority of which have gone) were added to the existing rural stock of single-storey cottages and two-storey tenements. Two attempts were made by proprietors to create model industrial settlements, but they have been demolished. One was a group of cottages designed for railway workers at Cowlairs by *Andrew Heiton* in 1863, the other the model town of Possilpark (which survives in name) established by Walter Macfarlane for workers at his Saracen Ironworks in the 1870s. A similar but more rural settlement, Gordon Park, survives at Scotstoun, where a few streets of substantial cottages, designed by *Alexander Petrie*, were laid out by Gordon Oswald for his estate workers in 1885. The scheme expanded on a commercial basis after 1895 with a large grid of similar cottages put up by the *Scotstoun Estate Building Co.*, which began a similar development, Thistle Park, at Cardonald in 1906. Summerfield Cottages, Whiteinch, of *c.* 1877, was another philanthropic exercise, this time in low rental, by Lord Rowallan's son. Some model housing was also provided during the 1870s by co-operative ventures, at Farme Cross, Jordanhill and Springburn, though not on the scale that had been initiated in Edinburgh a decade earlier. Like the Edinburgh housing, this takes the form of flatted cottages, the upper ones entered from outside staircases on one side of the terrace, the lower ones from the other side.

But by far the greatest amount of non-speculative housing for the artisan class (it was too expensive for the poorest) was built by the City Improvement Trust, established in 1866, as part of its huge programme of URBAN RENEWAL. In the overcrowded medieval city and in the industrial areas immediately to the N and E, the Trust cut wide new roads, such as Bain Street and Abercromby Street, and widened and realigned old ones, including Trongate (which involved cutting a carriageway through the 13 base of the Tron Steeple), Saltmarket, High Street, Bridgegate, Bell Street and the lower part of Albion (then Nelson) Street. This of course involved extensive amounts of rebuilding. Although the Trust had orginally intended only to clear sites and sell them for development, lack of interest from developers forced it to build housing and warehousing itself, sometimes to the designs of the city's *Office of Public Works*, sometimes to designs submitted in competition by commercial architects. The Trust's first buildings, in Saltmarket (1880–7), were designed by the City Architect *John Carrick* and made some attempt to echo the C 17 houses they replaced. More followed, especially in Trongate (1891–1900), Bell Street (warehouses and tenements of the 1890s) and in High Street (1899–1902) to an ingenious Baronial design 70 by *Burnet, Boston & Carruthers*, well tailored to the curve of the street as it rises up the hill to the Cathedral. A group of very

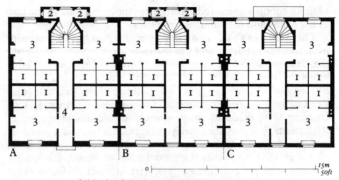

A block of single-ends off Saltmarket for
the City Improvement Trust, 1890
A ground floor, B first floor, C second floor
1 bed, 2 w.c., 3 room, 4 close
(Redrawn from an original plan)

large warehouses went up at the corner of Trongate and King Street (1899, by *John McKissack*) and between High Street and Trongate (by *McKissack & Son*, 1899 and by *Thomson & Sandilands*, 1904–12). One of the Trust's last projects was the remodelling of Glasgow Cross to improve the flow of traffic, designed in 1914 by *Keppie & Henderson* but not carried out until 1922. Beyond the old city centre, the Trust's housing survives in individual blocks, the most ambitious externally and internally being at the top of Hope Street (then part of Cowcaddens) by *Honeyman, Keppie & Mackintosh* (1906–7) and at St George's Cross by *Burnet, Boston & Carruthers* (1900–1).

The TENEMENTS put up by the City Improvement Trust for the respectable working classes may have been slightly larger, better-ventilated and better-plumbed than most of their speculatively built counterparts, but their internal PLANNING was very similar and changed little throughout the C19 and C20. Many tenements are of four storeys with a central close leading to common stairs, either at the back or front of the block. Individual houses were often designed with two apartments (a room and kitchen, each with a box bed), but could be slightly larger, or even as small as the notorious 'single end' (room and kitchen combined). W.C.s, which at first were in the communal courtyard, later (especially after new regulations of 1892) opened off the landing, either integral or as makeshift projections. Also, after 1892, access by means of open balconies at the back of the blocks was favoured (e.g. in the City Improvement Trust's Morrin Square, Townhead, of 1894–7 (now Strathclyde University flats), and its Hope Street block of 1906–7). Communal yards or drying greens at the back were sometimes replaced by flat rooftop drying areas, recognizable from the street by their railed parapets, as at Camphill Gate, Pollokshaws Road. The tenements associated with branches of the Glasgow Savings Bank (e.g. at Parkhead and Anderston) had washhouses fitted

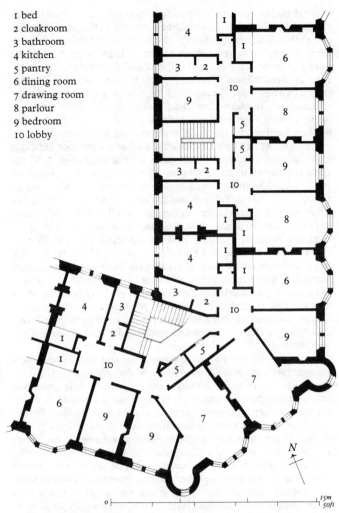

1 bed
2 cloakroom
3 bathroom
4 kitchen
5 pantry
6 dining room
7 drawing room
8 parlour
9 bedroom
10 lobby

City Improvement Trust tenements for the middle classes:
St George's Mansions (Woodlands), 1900–1. First-floor plan
(Redrawn from an original plan)

into the tops of the corner towers. The best of such tenements,
designed for the artisan or the clerk, have larger houses of up to
four simple apartments, often, after 1900, with bathrooms, as
can be seen in unaltered fashion at No. 145 Buccleuch Street of
1911 (the National Trust for Scotland's Tenement House). The
middle classes lived in tenement houses more varied in plan,
with rooms of different sizes and for specific uses, often cleverly
adapted to corner sites. W.C.s were consistently incorporated
into such houses as early as the 1830s and bathrooms by the
middle of the century. More of them are organized into houses

entered by street doors ('main-door houses') and upper houses
reached from a common stair, but a common close and stair was
acceptable. The arrangement with two houses of two storeys one
above the other is less common than in Edinburgh but can be
found in large numbers in Hillhead and sometimes elsewhere,
e.g., at Breadalbane Terrace (1845–56) and Niddrie Square
(1895, by *Alexander Petrie*). Such tenements are as sophisticated
as London's mansion flats, and indeed by the early C20 had
begun to style themselves 'mansions' in order to live down what
by then had become the socially inferior tag of 'tenement'.

The ARCHITECTURAL TREATMENT of the exterior indicates
quite accurately the original status of the tenement. Middle-
class tenements of the 1830s to 1870s look, at their simplest,
remarkably like the terraced houses of that date, as is shown by
the cream sandstone flat-fronted blocks with mildly Italianate
(or sometimes Greek) cornices over the windows, and doors and
ground floors of channelled rustication, along much of Pollokshaws Road at Queen's Park, along Paisley Road West at
Ibrox and in Hillhead and East Pollokshields. There are slightly
larger and coarser versions along Argyle Street and Sauchiehall
Street and much more showy ones on Garnethill (Peel Terrace,
1841–2, and Breadalbane Terrace, 1845–56). Very rarely does
this kind of tenement take on the challenge of a corner, the
35 notable exception being the pilastered curve from Argyle Street
into Minerva Street designed so confidently by *Alexander Kirkland* in 1856.

Variations in the flat front appear in the late 1850s, most
idiosyncratically in *Alexander Thomson*'s Walmer Crescent
(1857–62), where big square bays interrupt the façade and channelled rustication and a continuous band of windows tie it
together. Other tenements, e.g., of *c.* 1878 in Nithsdale Street,
have Thomsonish features but none the relentless logic of this
design. Bay windows started to appear more generally on houses
and tenements in the late 1850s (e.g. in the Bath Street block by
J. Burnet) and eventually became ubiquitous in bow or bay
form in all but the meanest tenements. Rows and rows of them
characterize the streets of spacious suburban districts like
71 Queen's Park, Tollcross or Hyndland, where they are usually set
behind areas or strips of garden. Oriel windows, probably first
52 employed on the houses of *Rochead*'s Buckingham Terrace in
1852, appear early on the tenements of Walworth Terrace, Kent
Road, *c.* 1858–60. They were most popular in more densely
packed streets, where they allowed a neater, more economical
line at ground-floor level, but they became a decorative cliché in
the modelling of hundreds of façades.

Fashions in the design of tenement façades, and the change
c. 1890 from cream to red sandstone, followed the same pattern
as the rest of Glasgow's buildings. From the 1870s, French
Second Empire became popular and is seen early at Broomhill
(from 1871), in *W. M. Whyte*'s fanciful Balmoral Crescent (1884–
6), in Trongate (1891–1900), and, most ebulliently, at *J. J. Burnet*'s Charing Cross Mansions (1889–91). Diluted Baroque

appears everywhere, particularly in the work of *Burnet, Boston & Carruthers*, Glasgow's most prolific tenement designers; but the Glasgow Style is rarer. The best examples are in Terregles Avenue (1895–6, by *H. E. Clifford*); in Helenvale Street (1902, by *John Hamilton*); in Pollokshaws Road (Springhill Gardens, 1904, and Camphill Gate, 1905–6, by *John Nisbet*); and in Balgrayhill Road (1903, by *Beattie & Morton*). *John Gordon*'s tenements and terraced houses in Maryhill Park (1901–3) have a peculiar interest. Along the main roads and at important junctions, like Parkhead Cross or Charing Cross, corners received especial attention, with extra decoration, elaborate oriels and fancy rooflines, or domes. The public domain extends to the close, which is, therefore, decorated in all but the poorest tenements with hygienic ceramic (or 'wally') tiles. The smartest ones, like those in Camphill Avenue (1903, by *John C. McKellar*), have handsome exterior doors as well.

With the development of the new suburbs beyond the medieval and c 18 city, TERRACED HOUSING became firmly accepted in Glasgow. It enabled speculators to provide individual houses for the affluent middle classes economically, just as it had done in London since the c 17. Designers in the second half of the c 19 elaborated on the cohesive compositions of the earlier c 19 terraces and in doing so achieved some results of exceptional grandeur, grander than anything in Scotland or provincial England. The earliest terraces of the West End by *George Smith* (especially Woodside Terrace, 1835–42) have some of the unremitting severity of his native city, Edinburgh. *Charles Wilson*'s designs of the 3, 34 1850s for Woodlands Hill are richer and more inventive than the simple classical elevations of *John Bryce*'s Queen's Crescent (1840): Wilson's outer circuit of the hill looks French, his inner one, Park Circus, Italianate.

The grandest show is along Great Western Road, where the terraces show remarkable variety in design, mainly playing on Italian themes. The solidity of the robustly detailed palazzo-style Kirklee Terrace of 1845–64 by *Charles Wilson* contrasts with the 51 lighter Venetian framework, as repetitive as a prefabricated cast-iron façade, of *J. T. Rochead*'s Grosvenor Terrace of 1855. 53 Rochead's Buckingham Terrace (1852 and 1858) introduces 52 delicate first-floor oriels linked by a cast-iron balcony into an otherwise plain and monotonous Italianate façade, and Belhaven Terrace of 1868–74 by *James Thomson* develops this more ponderously. These terraces, very long (Grosvenor Terrace is of eighty-three bays) and seen in sharp perspective, needed careful orchestration. End, and often centre, pavilions provide the simplest punctuation, as can be seen at Kew Terrace (1849, by *Brown* and *Rochead*) and Belgrave Terrace (1856, by *Gildard & MacFarlane*). Wilson at Kirklee Terrace added weight to each end with counterbalancing end bays set back, and *Alexander Thomson* at Great Western Terrace (1869) developed the idea 54 with Greek grandeur, seeming to thread a lower block through taller pavilions set in somewhat from the ends.

Variations appear elsewhere in the West End – end pavilions

in many examples (see, e.g., *James Thomson*'s Kirklee Gardens
of 1877–8), bays at *Burnet*'s Cleveden Crescent of 1876 and,
within a strong Greek framework, at *Alexander Thomson*'s
Westbourne Terrace (Hyndland Road) of 1871. It was Alexander
Thomson who in, for example, Oakfield Avenue (1865) and
Northpark Terrace, Hamilton Drive (1866), showed the surest
touch in relating individual elements and decoration to the mass
of a terrace. At this period, only Nos. 28–41 Westbourne Gardens
of *c*. 1876 breaks away from the classical into Gothic; but around
the turn of the century, the Free Style offered an escape from
the symmetrically composed terrace into ones that are full of
movement, such as *J.J. Burnet*'s in University Gardens (1882–
4), or that develop asymmetrically from one end to another, such
as *Campbell*'s in Kirklee Road (1900–9). Lowther Terrace on
Great Western Road takes this to extremes in a composition,
reminiscent of London's Cadogan Square, of three distinct
houses (by *James Miller* and *A. Sydney Mitchell*, 1894–1909).
Much more modest and generally plain Italianate terraces, flat-
fronted at first but after 1860 sometimes with bays, are scattered
thinly throughout Glasgow's suburbs and indicate where there
was once a middle-class enclave, e.g. in Govan, Dennistoun,
Ibrox, Mount Vernon, Maryhill Park, Broomhill, East Pollokshields and Jordanhill. Only a few have architectural pretensions, for example the exquisite Moray Place of 1859–61 by
Alexander Thomson and Millbrae Crescent, Langside, of the late
1870s, possibly by *Thomson & Turnbull*.

Such isolated terraces are usually the less affluent neighbours
of VILLAS. The earliest (of the 1850s, 1860s and 1870s), whether
built in haphazard groups out in the countryside or as part of
planned suburbs, were generally modest in size and picturesque
in outline. Most famous are those by *Alexander Thomson*: the
33 Italianate The Knowe, begun in 1852 and one of the first villas
of the new suburb Pollokshields, and Nos. 25–25a Mansionhouse
Road, Langside, of 1856–7, where picturesque effect and
imposing size were so important that a semi-detached house was
disguised as a single asymmetrical villa. There are *cottages ornés*
at Crosshill, Mount Vernon, Tollcross and in Merryland Street,
Govan, and rather ordinary bigger villas in the north-eastern
streets of Pollokshields (though *Alexander Thomson*'s mysterious
Ellisland of 1871 and its neighbour, No. 202 Nithsdale Road, are
remarkable exceptions), in Dennistoun (the beginning of the
failed suburb), on Partickhill and Dowanhill and at Burnside
(Rutherglen). As usual at this date, the West End has the best
collection, and none in Glasgow can vie with *James Boucher*'s
opulent ironfounder's palazzo of 1877 that is now St Mungo's
Academy Centenary Club.

The most rewarding of the later villas are S of the river in
West Pollokshields, Newlands, Dumbreck and Bellahouston, and
Langside. Pollokshields has the largest and most varied houses by
well-established local architects, but there are some prosperous
houses N of the river in Kelvinside, especially around Cleveden
Road. The Baronial style was predictably popular (*McGibbon*'s

own house of *c.* 1880 in Nithsdale Road, two more of 1886 in Dalziel Drive, a fearsome display of 1896 by *Thomson & Sandilands* in Sherbrooke Avenue, and, with a French flavour, *W. Hunter McNab*'s Beneffry of 1910 in Springkell Avenue), but English Domestic Revival styles made themselves felt in conjunction with Baronial features (at Kelmscott, Springkell Avenue, by *John Nisbet*, 1903), in free-planning and half-timbering (Stoneleigh, Cleveden Drive, almost stockbroker Tudor of 1900–6 by *H. E. Clifford*, and Oaklands, Sherbrooke Avenue, by *J. C. McKellar*, 1902), and with the Queen Anne style (by *John Gordon* in Hamilton Avenue, 1895). The English taste for a large two-storeyed living hall with rooms opening from it also affected internal planning (e.g. of Clifford's Stoneleigh, and of Matheran and Woodmailing in Sherbrooke Avenue, both of 1902–3 by *Burnet, Boston & Carruthers*). The most idiosyncratic house, with a suspicion of the developing Glasgow Style, is *W. J. Anderson*'s black and red Balmory of *c.* 1893 in Sherbrooke Avenue. These tailor-made houses are accompanied by streets and streets of mass-produced single and double villas (many of them of 1895–1905 by *Fryers & Penman*), and the same pattern was followed in Bellahouston and in Newlands in the 1890s and 1900s.

Only a fragmentary idea can be gathered from the surviving (and accessible) evidence about Glasgow's DOMESTIC INTERIORS. The contemporary detail that survives in the mid-C19 terraces of the West End (e.g. in Park Circus) suggests that most terraces followed the conventions of those in Blythswood, with columned screens in entrance halls and reception rooms. *Alexander Thomson*'s Great Western Terrace has majestic staircase halls with handsome ironwork at Nos. 4 and 11, and No. 4 also has painted decoration in the manner of *Cottier*. Among Thomson's other houses, his own in Moray Place, the double villa at Mansionhouse Road, and No. 202 Nithsdale Road still have his characteristic lithic style of joinery and big disks and daisies in the plasterwork. More conventional but more sumptuous are the interiors by *Boucher* in No. 22 Park Circus and in the mansion he designed at No. 998 Great Western Road. *Honeyman*'s original decoration of Craigie Hall, Bellahouston (1872), is in similar vein. Later interiors are generally more individual; several display remnants of the Glasgow Style. Purest and most complete is the interior of *Charles Rennie Mackintosh*'s own house (reconstructed within the Hunterian Art Gallery), but there is also notable interior decoration at No. 12 University Gardens by *J. Gaff Gillespie*, 1900; at Hugh McCulloch's house, Hughenden, in Langside Drive, done *c.* 1902–4 by *E. A. Taylor*; at No. 26 Huntly Gardens (1907) and No. 11 Whittingehame Drive (1908) by *John Ednie*; at No. 22 Park Circus by *Salmon & Gillespie* (1897–9); and an organ by *Mackintosh* in the music room at Craigie Hall, part of some handsome refitting done in the 1890s by *Honeyman & Keppie* with Art Nouveau touches which bridge the gap between undiluted classicism and the Glasgow Style. Examples of committed medievalizing (like that by *Lorimer*, *c.* 1900, at Burrell's house in Great Western Terrace) or of c 18 revival (most charmingly done at No. 10 Lowther Terrace, *c.* 1909) seem to be rarer.

It is often STAINED GLASS that gives these rooms, whatever their style, their vitality and charm. Sometimes, as at Hughenden, where the glass was designed by *David Gauld* and *Harrington Mann*, it was part of an overall scheme for a discerning patron, in this case the stained-glass manufacturer Hugh McCulloch. Elsewhere, it is in a variety of styles ranging from non-figurative glass in domes and decorative panels in doors (often supplied by *Oscar Paterson*) to figurative staircase windows (e.g. at Ross Hall, Crookston, No. 56 Cleveden Road, or Stoneleigh, Cleveden Drive). The quantity and quality of the glass in Dowanhill are exceptional. Stained glass brightened up clubs, pubs and offices 83 as well. Some of the very best (of 1901–3 by *W. G. Morton* for *John C. Hall*) is in an art publishers' in Darnley Street, Pollokshields, where sea monsters, mermaids and seasonal figures probably advertised the proprietor's greeting cards.

The creation of PARKS was an important catalyst in the growth of many of Glasgow's suburbs. The improvements made to Glasgow Green in 1813 under the aegis of *Cleland* proved a stimulus, though a short-lived one, to the building of smart houses on its fringes, and the resiting of the Botanic Gardens in 1839–42 encouraged development beyond it. Kelvingrove Park was, of course, intrinsic to a great suburban development; and, following this model, the Corporation, in annexing and drawing up plans for its parks, feued the lands round them for suburban development. At Queen's Park, the feus were accompanied by strict conditions to maintain salubrity and to provide several church spires as picturesque features. *Paxton* provided the plans for both Kelvingrove Park (1854) and Queen's Park (1860), though neither was laid out quite as planned. Most parks were opened for the recreation of neighbouring workers as the industrial suburbs gobbled up the countryside. First was Alexandra Park, laid out by the City Improvement Trust in 1866–70; next, but much later, in 1883–4, Elder Park, Govan, given by the local shipyard owner. The Corporation followed suit in the next decade with parks at Maryhill, Ruchill and Springburn in 1892 and with Tollcross and Richmond Parks in 1897. One or two parks served affluent and industrial suburb alike (Victoria Park, provided by the burgh of Partick in 1886–7, and Bellahouston, 1896), but only Maxwell Park (1878) was exclusively an ornamental pleasure ground for surrounding villadom. Three of the parks incorporate WINTER GARDENS or conservatories. They 44 range in ambition from the circular Kibble Palace of 1863–6, transported to the Botanic Gardens from John Kibble's Dumbartonshire house, to that of 1893–8 enclosing the back of the People's Palace and the elegantly simple one of 1899–1900 in Springburn Park.

In the city centre, OPEN SPACES are few and far between. c 18 speculative development rarely allowed for garden squares of the London or Edinburgh type. George Square, St Enoch

Square (the latter invaded first by St Enoch Station and then by the St Enoch Centre), and Blythswood Square were the exceptions, the first two initially just railed plots grazed by sheep. The others (St Andrew's Square, St George's (now Nelson Mandela) Place, and Royal Exchange Square) were filled by buildings which look outward and are significant as landmarks in a wider setting. In the West End, pleasure gardens were incorporated 34 into the suburban layout. The broad bands of garden introduced in the 1830s in streets such as Woodside Place to separate the terraces of houses and their carriageways from the thoroughfare were repeated to great effect along the Great Western Road. And it was not only the grand layouts of the West End that admitted gardens: they were even set, in European fashion, between the tenements off Great Western Road (e.g. Lansdowne Crescent) and in middle-class Hyndland. The City Improvement Trust opened up one or two green lungs in overcrowded districts; Overnewton Square at Yorkhill (1866) and, on a larger scale, Cathedral Square Gardens (1879) still have their walks and shrubs.

The parks and squares are studded with free-standing SCULPTURE; indeed George Square and Cathedral Square are showcases for bronzes of famous Scotsmen and their monarchs, assembled there in the C19. Earliest is the stiffly classical equestrian bronze of William III (1735) moved from Glasgow Cross to Cathedral Square Gardens. In George Square, Victoria (1854) and Albert (1866) by *Baron Marochetti* are also mounted, and so is the Duke of Wellington (1844, by the same sculptor) in front 93 of the Royal Exchange. The finest equestrian monument by far is that by *Harry Bates* to Lord Roberts (1916) in Kelvingrove 92, 9: Park. Most other figures are standing or seated. Their sculptors were not always Glasgow men, though *John Mossman* was responsible for a lot of them. *Flaxman* did the first public statue in George Square (1819) – Sir John Moore gazing s towards his home in Miller Street. *Chantrey* added the pensive James Watt (1832) and *Hamo Thornycroft* the vigorous Gladstone (1899– 94 1902). Further afield, there are statues of philanthropic industrialists: of Mr and Mrs John Elder in Elder Park, Govan, the husband by *Boehm* (1887), his wife by *Macfarlane Shannon* (1905–6), who also did the busts of the couple (1901–3) inside the Elder Library; of another Govan shipbuilder, Sir William Pearce, by *Onslow Ford* (1894), opposite the institute his wife founded; and of James Reid of the Hydepark Works by *Goscombe John* (1903) in Springburn Park.

Statues were not the only means of commemoration. The most dramatic PUBLIC MONUMENTS were obelisks and columns. First (and the first public monument in Britain in honour of Lord Nelson) was the plain but exceedingly tall obelisk of 1806 by *David Hamilton* and *A. Brockett* on Glasgow Green. Glasgow's columns are to two Scottish heroes of very different kinds: John Knox (by *William Warren*) gazes censoriously from *Thomas Hamilton*'s Greek column of 1825 on the brow of the Necropolis; and, in George Square, Sir Walter Scott, a joint effort of *John*

Greenshields and *A. Handyside Ritchie* ponders atop *David Rhind*'s splendid Graeco-Roman one of 1837. Of equal serious-ness is *Sir J. J. Burnet*'s Cenotaph (1921–4) in front of the City Chambers.

FOUNTAINS also served as reminders of public-spirited citi-zens. *James Sellars*' Stewart Memorial Fountain of 1872 in Kel-vingrove Park is a grand object celebrating an important man, but scattered throughout the parks and streets are humble cast-iron drinking fountains, mostly made by *Walter Macfarlane & Co.*'s Saracen Foundry, like the Aitken Memorial Fountain of 1884 at Govan Cross and the Jubilee Fountain of 1897, now in Overtoun Park, Rutherglen (which can also boast a fine iron bandstand of 1914 by *J. & A. McFarlane*). Two of Glasgow's fountains are positively spectacular, designed as showpieces for
86 Glasgow's two International Exhibitions, one a confection of imperial themes in Carrara Stoneware by *Doulton & Co.* (1888, now on Glasgow Green), the other Graeco-Roman in cast-iron
87 by the *Saracen Foundry* (1901, now in Alexandra Park). *Doulton & Co.* also made the simpler fountain of 1907 in Maxwell Park, Pollokshields, designed by *Burnet, Boston & Carruthers*.

BURIAL MONUMENTS were banished from inside Scottish churches in 1581, so most of those found there now are purely commemorative. Glasgow Cathedral has only three medieval monuments and four of the C17 – three wall monuments and a tomb-chest, none of them at all exceptional. It also has the very few later monuments of any artistic value. The best are bronze reliefs, one by *Sir Alfred Gilbert* (*c.* 1900) and two others by *Pittendrigh MacGillivray* (1891 and 1901), one of them a plaque to Dr Peter Lowe † 1612, whose damaged monument stands in the graveyard, alongside an array of imposing though not particularly sophisticated wall monuments of the C17 to the early C19. Neither are there any monuments of great significance in the rural church GRAVEYARDS, though their watchhouses (Tollcross, Cathcart) and stone wardens' boxes (Carmunnock, Rutherglen) have historical value and some charm.

CEMETERIES at their finest doubled as parks and displays of memorial sculpture. There is no better example of this than
28 Glasgow's Necropolis, important as only the third 'hygienic' cemetery in Britain (it opened in 1833 after St James's, Liverpool, 1829, and Kensal Green, London, 1832) and wonderfully pic-turesque, with monuments and evergreens bristling from its craggy sides. Its arrangement into regular plots is conventional, but its topography makes it special, and so do its fine architectural set-pieces in Mannerist style by *John Bryce* (1835–6) and the
29 proud monuments and mausolea of its uppermost (in every sense) levels. Other cemeteries soon followed, though none had such prestige and therefore such sculptural and architectural richness. The Necropolis and the Southern Necropolis of 1848 have gloomy Romanesque lodges by *David Hamilton* and *Charles Wilson* respectively. Other lodges were small and classical (Sight-hill, by *John Stephen*, 1839; Eastern Necropolis, probably of the 1860s; Lambhill, by *James Sellars*, 1881). CREMATORIA came

late (*James Chalmers'* for the Scottish Burial Reform and Cremation Society at the Western Necropolis was the first, in 1893–
5) and did not reach any impressive size until the C20 (*Thomas
Cordiner*'s Linn Crematorium of 1962).

ECCLESIASTICAL ARCHITECTURE 1850–1918

The major ECCLESIASTICAL EVENTS of the C19 – the Dis-
ruption of 1843, when about a third of the members of the Church
of Scotland left to form the Free Church, and the formation in
1847 of the United Presbyterians by those who had previously
seceded from the Established Church – ushered in an era of
feverish building as each of the three churches provided for itself
and vied with its rivals. The effects on church design are perhaps
too subtle to occupy us here, except to say that the United
Presbyterians often advertised themselves by unusual, sometimes
almost secular designs, and that the Free Church was, with
notable exceptions, the most restrained.

It is perhaps surprising that the Presbyterians took any notice
of the Tractarian movement, but the fashion for a more correct
GOTHIC eventually proved irresistible. *J. T. Emmett*'s Independent Chapel in Bath Street of 1849–52 (now Renfield St
Stephen), like a Decorated parish church complete with aisles
and chancel, and with a spire that paid undisguised homage to
Pugin's St Giles, Cheadle, was a false dawn. Its nearest Gothic
contemporaries, Maryhill High of 1846–8 and Rutherglen West
of 1848–50, both designed by *Charles Wilson* for the Free Church,
are still preaching boxes, though the latter is a charming one with
pinnacled tower and well-nigh complete furnishings. It took
nearly a decade for the archaeological accuracy of Emmett's
chapel to become a general standard, and until the last decades
of the century, when Ecclesiology formally took root in Scotland
(the Glasgow branch of the Ecclesiological Society was founded
in 1893), almost all of Glasgow's Presbyterian churches demonstrate an uneasy compromise between liturgical needs and the
demands of Gothic authenticity.

The first churches are variously English and French Gothic
and make good use of the opportunity for SPIRES and TOWERS
as landmarks in their suburban settings; indeed, spires were a
prerequisite for all the churches built along the north edge of
Queen's Park. The first notable tower after Emmett's steeple is
still Perp and is all that is left of *Rochead*'s Park Church of 1856– 3
8. Lansdowne U.P. Church of 1862–3 by the scholarly *John
Honeyman* was the most convincing E.E. church to date, with an
elegantly slender spire. The greatest heights were reached by the
broach spire of *J.J. Stevenson*'s Townhead Church (1865–6),
which, like the rest of the church, has an idiosyncratic boldness,
and by that of the contemporary Dowanhill Church by *William* 49
Leiper. Leiper, strongly influenced by J. L. Pearson, for whom

he had worked in London, chose French Gothic ten years later
59 for the spire of Camphill Church (now Camphill Queen's Park),
a United Presbyterian rival to *Campbell Douglas*'s Established
58 Queen's Park High Church (now Crosshill Queen's Park) of
1872–3, with its more inventive spire, probably by J. J. Stevenson.

French Gothic became generally popular in Glasgow *c.* 1875
and is used in a robust manner by *John Burnet Snr* to control a
picturesque composition of church and halls at Woodlands (now
St Jude's Free Presbyterian) U. P. Church in 1874–5. It was
James Sellars who kept most literally to a French model, the
57 Sainte Chapelle, in his Belmont Hillhead Parish Church of 1875–
6. Glaswegian Gothicists of the 1870s absorbed ideas from their
influential English counterparts: Sellars had evidently looked at
William Burges when composing the W front of Belmont
Hillhead, but Pearson's influence was perhaps most pervasive,
starting in the mid-1870s with a taste for Normandy Gothic
exteriors, such as Leiper's Camphill Queen's Park and Sellars'
former Belhaven U. P. Church of 1876–7 (now St Luke's Greek
Orthodox Cathedral) and continuing into the 1880s with the
lofty, aisled and Ecclesiologically correct interiors discussed
below.

The unobstructed PLAN of Sellars' Belmont Hillhead Church
was particularly well adapted to Presbyterian requirements, but
most architects of Gothic churches in the middle of the century
had to struggle to combine a longitudinal form with galleries and
platforms. Honeyman at Lansdowne Church sidestepped the
problem with enclosed passage aisles and broad shallow
transepts. The more usual formula was to use archaeologically
unacceptable tiers of arcades carrying galleries just as in the
earlier preaching boxes; but the inconvenience of this is clearly
felt at Stevenson's exceptionally long, tall and narrow Townhead
Church, so the nave was often widened into the boxy shape used
at Crosshill Queen's Park. No such problem arose, of course,
with Episcopal churches, such as *David Thomson*'s St Ninian
(Pollokshields) of 1872–7, where medieval precedents had reformed liturgy and buildings alike. *Sir George Gilbert Scott*'s St
Mary's Episcopal Cathedral of 1871–4 is an entirely conventional
English Gothic cruciform church.

Although many of these CHURCH INTERIORS of the 1860s
and 1870s are architecturally disappointing (particular exceptions being Stevenson's Townhead Church, with its boldly
repeated pierced foiled figures and portrait headstops, and Sellars' lantern-like Belmont Hillhead Church), some at least have
to be imagined with the PAINTED DECORATION which completed decorative schemes that are now mostly only reflected in
the stained glass. Most dramatic was the blue, red and black
scheme by *Cottier* at Townhead, which accompanied the window
by *Morris & Co.* (the only window by Morris of this early date
in Glasgow). Only tiny fragments of this painting survive but
some of that at Dowanhill Church, for which Cottier also
designed the glass, is being uncovered (in 1989).

After 1880, Gothic designs became more varied, more confident and much more interesting as the influence of the Ecclesiological movement led to an abandoning of the strictures of auditorium plans and consequently to opportunities for a wider choice of sources. The Scoto-Catholic minister John Macleod, in his pursuit of the 'beauty of worship' for the working classes of Govan, made a significant move in this direction, modelling the brief for his new Govan Parish Church on Italian preaching churches and commissioning *Robert Rowand Anderson* to carry it out (1883-8). Here for the first time in Glasgow is a large church with passage aisles, deep chancel and side chapels in a plan inspired by Pearson's St Peter, Vauxhall, and, almost uniquely, a complete scheme of stained glass designed by *Kempe* as part of the grand design. Here Scottish sources are used too (the chancel elevation is modelled on Pluscardine Abbey), as they are by *J. J. Burnet & J. A. Campbell* at the Barony Church of 64 1886-9 and by Campbell alone at Shawlands Old of 1885-9, who followed the bluntly Gothic east end of Dunblane in their heavily modelled compositions, and by *J. J. Stevenson*, who took as his pattern for the crown spire of the Kelvin Stevenson Memorial (formerly Free) Church (1898-1902) that of King's College, Aberdeen.

Inside, the Barony has much in common with Govan Parish Church, with a similar plan also adopted from Pearson. Passage aisles, as in English churches of the date, proved a useful way of giving an uninterrupted view of the communion table and preacher. A number of architects used them, e.g. *H. E. Clifford* who set the pattern at Pollokshields Titwood in 1893-5 (now St James Pollok). Communion tables were now frequently pushed into the apse like an altar, though often with elders' stalls behind. Many platforms and organ recesses were remodelled for the purpose, either with enclosing organ cases, as *H. E. Clifford* did in 1913 at Pollokshields, or with the organ displaced, as designed by *P. Macgregor Chalmers* for Cambuslang Parish Church in 1913.

Galleries on three sides were not banished from all designs, however, and Free churches certainly favoured them. At this late date, they were usually set within tall stone arcades, and for this purpose the Perp style was particularly useful. One of its most elaborate manifestations is at Shawlands Cross, a Free church of 1900-3 by *Miller & Black*, but it was adapted most inventively by *W. G. Rowan* at Eastbank Parish Church (1901-4), where Art Nouveau creeps into the tracery and the Glasgow Style into the charming furnishings, and, above all, by *C. R. Mackintosh* at Queen's Cross in 1896-9. 66

Silhouettes at the turn of the c20 were usually sturdy and spireless. Just a few are unusual – e.g. the English village church outline of *Rowan*'s St Margaret Tollcross of 1900-1 (again with Glasgow Style furnishing); the Baronial-cum-Arts and Crafts Broomhill Trinity Congregational by *J. J. Burnet* of 1900-8; and the castle gate *Westwerk* of St Andrew's East by *James Miller* of 1903-4. An orthodox strain of Gothic lingered on, expressed for the Episcopalians by *G. F. Bodley*, who began St Bride's,

Hyndland Road, in 1903 (a rare employment of an Englishman), and by *W. F. McGibbon*, who did a serious French Gothic Free church at Shettleston (now Shettleston Old Parish Church) in 1895–1903. The ROMAN CATHOLICS commissioned one of the first examples of French Gothic (*George Goldie*'s St Mungo, Townhead, built for the Passionists in 1866–9), but under the patronage of Archbishop Eyre (1878–1902) they mainly employed *Pugin & Pugin*, who did numbers of their large but pedestrianly Dec churches with ugly rock-faced finishes and pinnacled marble altars (St Francis, Gorbals, 1878–95; St Bridget, Baillieston, 1891–3; St Agnes, Lambhill, 1893–4; St Patrick, North Street, 1898; St Alphonsus, London Road, 1905).

ROMANESQUE came late into the repertoire (although it had made two earlier appearances – at Cambuslang and at Blackfriars Church (Dennistoun) by *Campbell Douglas & Sellars*, 1876–7). Its chief promoter was *Dr Macgregor Chalmers*, whose churches, like Whiteinch-Jordanvale (1912–13), usually look so unpromising outside and are surprisingly interesting, even though rather drily correct, within. His first church at Cardonald (1888–9), in the simplest lancet style, promised little, but the imposing St 65 Margaret Episcopal at Newlands (Cathcart), designed in 1895, and the very similar Merrylea Church of 1912–15 boast a high degree of finish in building and in the Norman-style furnishings. *James Chalmers*' Romanesque at All Saints' Episcopal (Jordanhill) of 1904 and Scotstoun West of 1905–6, both laden with symbolism, verges on the eccentric. A hybrid of Romanesque and Byzantine was favoured for SYNAGOGUES in the later C19, and Glasgow's example of 1878–9 in Garnethill is of good pedigree, designed by *John McLeod* with the advice of *Nathan Solomon Joseph*, architect of the Bayswater synagogue in London. Others follow the same style in simpler form.

More easily adapted to Presbyterian needs, the CLASSICAL box stayed popular in Glasgow throughout the C19. GREEK or, as frequently, GRAECO-ROMAN lingered on, used by most denominations, into the 1880s. St Jude's Episcopal of 1838–9 by *John Stephen* was the earliest assemblage of Greek detail, but *Burnet* gave the style new sophistication and a grand scale with his pure Elgin Place Congregational Church of 1855–6. *Peddie & Kinnear* put the columns of the portico *in antis* at Trinity Duke Street U.P. Church (now Kirkhaven Day Centre) two years later; but the formula of a hexastyle Greek portico survived into the 1880s, with a chaste French Neo-classicism at *T.L. Watson*'s Wellington United Presbyterian Church (1882–4) and, more grandiloquently, with very Victorian figurative sculpture, at the *Barclays*' St George's-in-the-Fields (1885–6). It was *Alex-* 40 *ander Thomson*, at Caledonia Road Church of 1856–7 and St Vincent Street Church of 1857–9 (both built for the United Presbyterians), who injected real originality into the Greek style with massing (exceptionally responsive to the sites) and forms taken from Schinkel, and bizarre ornament of Eastern origin probably from the illustrations in James Fergusson's *Handbook of Architecture* (1855). Thomson's Queen's Park Church of 1862, with its huge pointed dome, was most original of all but, sadly, has gone. In St Vincent Street Church (his only surviving church 42 interior), his architectural imagination embraced the furnishings and fittings, transforming an average galleried plan. Thomson's influence was pervasive and can be seen in the rather old-fashioned but charming former Finnieston Parish Church of 1879–80 and in the former Cowcaddens Parish Church of 1872–3, both by *Sellars*; in *T. L. Watson's* Baptist churches, Adelaide Place of 1875–7 (mixed with Roman arches) and Hillhead of 1883; and in the massive Graeco-Roman Langside Hill Church, a Free Church of 1894–6 by Thomson's former assistant, *Alexander Skirving*.

Glasgow's ITALIANATE churches have as much distinction and originality as her Greek ones. Most remarkable of all is *Rochead's* former John Street U. P. Church of 1858–60, which followed no ecclesiastical precedent but used Mannerist forms (unusual at that date) to clothe a galleried box. *Honeyman* produced two original façades, one of 1878–80 for the United Presbyterians at the Barony North Church, which resembles a Palladian palazzo lavished with statuary, the other in 1880–1 for the Free Church (now Belhaven-Westbourne), where twin towers give a distinctly Italian air to a clever synthesis of Neo-classical rustication with a two-tiered portico in the manner of Wren's St Paul's Cathedral. The Roman Catholics were particularly keen on the style, seen at its crudest in *Goldie & Child's* St Mary (1841–2) in Abercromby Street (Calton) and in its most sophisticated High Renaissance form at St Aloysius (Garnethill) by the Belgian *Charles Menart* (1908–10). Menart's basilican Sacred Heart (Bridgeton) of 1900–1910 is Roman, *Honeyman's* St Anthony (Govan), unusually for its date in Glasgow (1877–9), is North Italian Romanesque without, Renaissance within. *Pugin & Pugin* made an exception to their usual Dec with Early Christian at Holy Cross (Govanhill) in 1909–11.

CHURCH FURNISHINGS were restricted to the unrewarding essentials in most churches. They are best when they were conceived as part of the architectural whole, as at *Thomson's* St Vincent Street Church, *Burnet* and *Campbell's* Barony Church, *Mackintosh's* Queen's Cross, *W. G. Rowan's* St Margaret Tollcross and Eastbank, and at *Macgregor Chalmers'* St Margaret Episcopal and Merrylea. Otherwise there is nothing worth singling out, except from Episcopal churches: *Scott's* pulpit and font in St Mary's Cathedral; a reredos in St Ninian's painted in 1901 by *William Hole*; and, as a curiosity, the angel font at St Margaret's by *Galbraith & Winton* after *Thorwaldsen*.

STAINED GLASS was considered appropriate from about 1860, and most churches have some. The *Morris & Co.* window in Townhead Church (1866) and *Cottier's* Morris-influenced ones in Dowanhill Church, are among the earliest glass and have already been discussed. Now that the Munich glass installed in the Cathedral in 1856 has been removed to store, there seems to be nothing from before the 1860s, except the complete scheme of non-figurative glass by *Ballantine & Allan* in Sandyford-

Henderson Church, 1857. There are sparkling examples of the 1860s, by *Ballantine & Allan*, in Ibrox (originally Bellahouston) Parish Church of 1863, but most glass is much later. In the Ramshorn Kirk, a selection of the best-known makers' work, nearly all from 1887–8, instructively juxtaposes windows by *William Meikle & Sons*, the *Kiers, Ward & Hughes*, *Ballantine* and *Clayton & Bell*. There is a good display of glass by several C19 firms in St Mary's Episcopal Cathedral and by *Heaton, Butler & Bayne* in St Ninian's Episcopal Church. Pollokshields Church has a magnificent display of *Stephen Adam*'s work, ranging from his clearly drawn and coloured windows of 1878 to his late (and often decayed) experiments. Govan Parish Church, as has been said before, has the only planned scheme of windows (by *Kempe*), as well as one or two by *Clayton & Bell* and *Heaton, Butler & Bayne*. There are late windows by *Morris & Co.* (1893) and by *Cottier & Co.* (1893–1903) at Belmont Hillhead. Much of the best glass is secular, but that has been dealt with elsewhere.

PUBLIC BUILDINGS AND INSTITUTIONS
1830–1914

60 Glasgow's City Chambers takes pride of place in a list not only of Glasgow's, but Scotland's, PUBLIC BUILDINGS, for, although its design, by *William Young*, a moderately successful Scottish-born architect who worked in London, is a little plod-
61, 62 ding, its size and the splendour of its interiors are unsurpassed. Its Italianate style was considered conservative by 1882, when Young won the competition, and came near the end of a long tradition in Glasgow for classical and especially Italianate public buildings, institutions and clubs. Both Rutherglen and Govan have fully-fledged Town Halls befitting their once independent
43 status, Rutherglen a naively Baronial one of 1861–2 by *Charles Wilson*, Govan an eclectic monster of 1897–1901 by *Thomson & Sandilands*. Other former burghs have their own halls too. The French Renaissance halls of Partick (designed by *Leiper* in 1865) and Maryhill (1876–8, by *Duncan McNaughtan*) are the earliest. Two of the later ones (Pollokshields, 1888–90, by *H. E. Clifford* and Pollokshaws, 1895–8, by *R. Rowand Anderson*) reveal the same growing interest in Scottish styles that is expressed in the philanthropic institutes designed for the Coupers in Cathcart by *James Sellars* (1887–8) and for the Pearces in Govan by *Sir R. R. Anderson* (1902–6).

Glasgow's public offices are not especially rewarding. The best were put up by the Post Office, whose architects *Matheson, Robertson* and *Oldrieve* designed the handsome Italianate General Post Office in George Square (1875–1916) and the huge Parcels Office in Waterloo Street (1903–5). Other public offices were the responsibility of the City Architect and Engineer and his *Office of Public Works*. Of the fine series of police stations by *John Carrick* there is now only the Eastern District's neat palazzo of 1868-9 in Tobago Street; Partick has a similar one of 1853 by *Charles Wilson*. Early fire stations are almost as scarce and have been converted to other uses, like those in High Street (1898-1900) and Wallace Street (1914-16). Many districts still have the baths and washhouses built after 1880 in substantial numbers and in a variety of styles, ranging from the plain Italianate Woodside of 1880-2 to the gabled Franco-Flemish Whitevale of 1899-1903, and the Wrenaissance Govanhill (1912-16). The earlier façades screen cast-iron trusses and columns, the later ones ferro-concrete arches over swimming ponds and washhouses. Private bathing clubs pre-date these municipal ventures, and two of them (the Arlington of 1869-71 by *J. Burnet* and the Western of 1876-81 by *Clarke & Bell*) still have well-preserved interiors.

There are three C19 markets, all cast-iron structures with a fair amount of swagger about the façades, French Empire by *Clarke & Bell* at the former Fish Market (1872-3) and Roman by *John Carrick* at the Meat Market (*c.* 1875). The City Markets in Candleriggs, first of the series and still with its hall of 1852-3 by *Bell & Miller* and *John Baird*, incorporates the City Halls, begun in 1841 by *George Murray* as Glasgow's main assembly and concert hall and now with an Italianate main front of 1882-6 by *Carrick*.

This brings us to Glasgow's CULTURAL BUILDINGS, with which, in the broadest sense, the centre and the suburbs were well endowed. The majestic Graeco-Roman St Andrew's Halls by *James Sellars* (its shell is now the Mitchell Theatre) took over the cultural functions of the City Halls in 1877; as for commercial theatres and music halls, there were many, but few survive. The Theatre Royal (burnt out and reconstructed several times), the King's (1901-4, by *Frank Matcham*) and the Pavilion (1902-4, by *Bertie Crewe*) are conventionally glamorous inside.

After 1899, almost every district gained a library, mostly small buildings skilfully managed to look grand. *J. R. Rhind*, who did Bridgeton, Dennistoun, Govanhill, Maryhill, Parkhead, and Woodside in Baroque style between 1902 and 1906, was especially adept. His Hutchesontown Library of 1904-6 is bigger and charmingly Loire-style, and *J. J. Burnet*'s Elder Library (Govan) of 1901-3 is like an elegant park pavilion. Some are plainer (*W. B. Whitie*'s Springburn, 1902-6; *John Fairweather*'s Townhead, 1907; and *George Simpson*'s Possilpark, 1911-13, and Langside, 1912-13); and some retain much of their characteristic woodwork, like Possilpark, which also has lugubrious contemporary murals by students from Glasgow School of Art. Of this series, the *pièce de résistance* is the Mitchell Library, rather flabby Baroque by *William B. Whitie* (1906-11), but with a splendid interior.

The city provided two museums. The Glasgow Art Gallery and Museum in Kelvingrove Park by *J. W. Simpson & E. J. Milner Allen* (1891-1901), opened during the International Exhibition of 1901, its romantic towered roofline the stone counterpart to *James Miller*'s temporary exhibition buildings. At the East End is the self-explanatory People's Palace of 1893-8 by the

City Engineer, plainer but still substantial and with a wonderful winter garden.

EDUCATIONAL BUILDINGS are equally prominent and, in the suburbs, vie with the churches, with towers among their eye-catching devices. *David Hamilton*'s former Free Normal Seminary of 1836–7 (now just in Garnethill) has a dignified classical tower, but *Charles Wilson* made his Free Church Trinity College of 1856–7 a landmark, with three soaring towers. The new building designed in 1864 for Glasgow University on Gilmorehill (after it had been exiled by the railway from High Street) has both tower and spire and is a rarity in Glasgow – a major public building in Gothic style by an eminent English architect, *Sir George Gilbert Scott*, who blended Franco-Flemish Gothic with Baronial bartizans. The real *tour-de-force* is not the tower but 47, 48 the Randolph and Bute Halls, with their sombre undercroft and vibrantly decorated interior. The two other colleges at all comparable in scale – the Royal Technical College of 1901–5 (now part of Strathclyde University) and Jordanhill College for teacher training (1913–22) – are just variations on the mixed Renaissance themes the *Barclays* used for schools in the 1900s, Jordanhill College stripped down to quite a powerful silhouette. *Honeyman & Keppie*, with *Mackintosh* as their principal assistant, won the competition for the School of Art in 1897 with a design as practical as it was idiosyncratic in detail. The fluid Art 72, 73 Nouveau of Mackintosh's detailing became in the second phase 74, 75 (of 1907–9) more geometric and Secessionist, with some of the starkness of C17 Scottish architecture.

SCHOOL ARCHITECTURE was not dominated by any one architect. Although the Glasgow School Board, established in 1874, preferred a number of fairly standard plans, exterior treatment was very varied. School Boards in the encircling burghs – Eastwood, Govan, Maryhill, Cathcart, Rutherglen, Shettleston – adopted a similar line, though Govan employed *H. & D. Barclay* almost exclusively. The earliest schools were the most modest in size and the most varied in plan, though of the sixty-two built by the Glasgow Board in the first ten years very few survive. From the outset, the separation of boys and girls was a significant factor, achieved ingeniously by *Honeyman* at Rockvilla (Possilpark) and Tureen Street (Calton) between 1874 and 1877 by entwining two staircases in a single tower. Alternatively, the towers were placed at each end of the block, as *Burnet* did at Overnewton (Yorkhill) in 1876–7. However planned, the staircases led to large classrooms over a ground-floor hall. By 1881 the central hall for exercise and assembly, used first by *H. & D. Barclay* for the private Glasgow Academy in 1878 and then at Abbotsford School in 1879, was made a standard design. Dennistoun by *Salmon & Son* (1883) is a transitional type, with stairs filling the central space, but most central halls were galleried with classrooms leading off them and with staircases quite separate.

The most ingenious plans are by *C. R. Mackintosh*: the Martyrs' School with its central hall for the Glasgow Board (1895– 85 8) and Scotland Street School, with classrooms one above the other over a ground-floor hall, for the Govan Board (1904–6). Mackintosh's two completely different designs show, not only how his work evolved from Art Nouveau to a style prefiguring Art Deco, but what a range of invention was permitted. Even the earliest schools vary from the Tudorbethan made popular for schools in England (*Salmon & Son*'s Lambhill, 1875–6, and Dennistoun, 1883), to a picturesque version of that style (*Honeyman*'s Rockvilla), to the Northern Renaissance (*Burnet*'s Overnewton), the Italianate (the best of them by *H. & D. Barclay*, e.g. Lorne Street, Annette Street and Abbotsford), the Gothic 84 (the anonymous Queen's Park), and the positively cottagey (*James Thomson*'s Crossmyloof, 1877–8). The most popular style for later schools (mostly larger, in red sandstone and surviving in greater numbers) was, *à la* Robson, mixed Renaissance (*John McKissack*'s Eastbank, 1894), sometimes with English Baroque elements (*Andrew Balfour*'s Langside, 1904), though compositions could be looser and more domestic, with Glasgow Style touches, such as those by *Duncan McNaughtan* (Royston, 1906, and Gallowflat, 1907) or more obviously Glasgow Style, such as *H. E. Clifford*'s handsome Elmvale School (Springburn) of 1901. Halls sometimes reached the huge proportions of the *Barclays*' 1904 Balshagray School.

Private schools, or, more genteelly, 'academies', served the former Elmbank or Glasgow Academy of 1846–7, an Italian palazzo by *Charles Wilson*, taken over by the Glasgow School Board in 1878 (and by Strathclyde Regional Council nearly a century later). The West End has two: the second Glasgow Academy by the *Barclays* (1878) and Kelvinside by *Sellars* (1877–9), the latter one of the city's most dignified classical compositions with long wings of classrooms of Thomsonesque severity and a raised temple front marking the first-floor hall. On a similar plan but Gothic is *Robert Baldie*'s Bellahouston Academy of 1874–6. The Roman Catholic St Aloysius College of 1882–3 by *Archibald Macpherson* is appropriately Italianate (a Venetian palazzo), and *Thomson & Sandilands*' endowed Hutchesons' Girls Grammar School of 1910–12 is a richer mixture of the High Renaissance and Vanbrughian styles familiar from Board schools.

The spate of school building was paralleled by three decades of HOSPITAL BUILDING, ended by the construction in 1901–14 of *James Miller*'s vast and, from the outset, much criticized Royal Infirmary, to replace *Robert Adam*'s Neo-classical hospital of 1791–4. Its mixed style, in this case, Scottish Baronial and Edwardian Baroque, is typical of its contemporaries, though its plan, with wards and service towers strung out along a long corridor, was unusual and partly dictated by the restricted site. Plans vary. There are separate ward blocks at the infectious diseases hospitals, such as Belvidere of 1874–7 and Ruchill of 1895–1900 (the latter apparently modelled on the Johns Hopkins Hospital of the 1870s in Baltimore), but also at the Combination Poor Law Hospital at Stobhill of 1900–4. The Govan Poorhouse and Hospital of 1867–72 (now the Southern General), the Western Infirmary of 1871–4, and the Victoria Infirmary of 1882–

1906 all have finger plans, the Eastern District (now Duke Street) Hospital, a radial one (1901–4). Stylistically, brick-built Belvidere is the simplest, Ruchill and Stobhill the most elaborate, grouped round magnificent water towers. Lunatic asylums were on an even bigger scale, and started with the innovative one of 1809 by *William Stark* (long since demolished). *Charles Wilson*'s model Gartnavel Hospital of 1841–3, which masquerades as a Tudor palace, was followed much later by the Elizabethan Leverndale (begun in 1890 by *Stark & Rowntree*) and the Baronial Gartloch (1890–7, by *Thomson & Sandilands*), both as big as villages. On a smaller scale, the Glasgow Institute for the Deaf and Dumb of 1876–8 by *Salmon, Son & Ritchie* (now part of Langside College) is, unusually for a secular building in Glasgow, Ruskinian in colour and detail. Smaller still and more domestic is *J. J. Burnet*'s Elder Cottage Hospital of 1910–12.

Many of Glasgow's professional and commercial INSTITUTIONS continued to present proud architectural faces to their fellow citizens throughout the C19, though some made do, as we shall see, with remodelling existing houses. Gothic, rejected in
38 1854 for the Royal Faculty of Procurators' Hall and Library in favour of *Charles Wilson*'s rich essay in the Italianate style of London's clubs, never became popular and made a rare secular appearance in the city centre twenty years later when *Burnet*
56 cribbed Burges's Law Courts competition entry for the Stock Exchange (1875–7). He had used the Italianate for the Merchants' House in 1874, completing a range along the west side of George Square begun by *Rochead*'s Bank of Scotland but adding a tower that smacked of self-importance and of nostalgia for the Merchants' old building. It was made even more swagger in 1907–11 by the younger *Burnet*, whose first Glasgow building on his return from Paris, the Athenaeum of 1886, was in chilly Beaux-Arts classicism, quite new to the city and not repeated so purely until the C20. The extension he made in 1891–3 was equally radical and supplied a popular formula for the narrow façade common in Glasgow as buildings were reconstructed taller on existing single plots. (*Campbell* used the formula nearly opposite in Buchanan Street at the former British Workman's and General Assurance office of 1898–9, *Robert Thomson & Andrew Wilson* in Buchanan Street for North British Rubber, 1898, and in Hope Street for the *Daily Record* a year later, and the *City Engineer*'s assistant for the Kingston Halls of 1904–5.) *Burnet* was also responsible for the most elaborate of all these institutional buildings, that of the Clyde Navigation Trust (in the Broomielaw),
63 begun with rich but beautifully controlled detail in 1882–6 and finished with the Baroque bravura of the Trust Hall in 1905–8. The English Baroque of *J. B. Wilson*'s contemporary Institute of Engineers and Shipbuilders, though very grand, can hardly compete.

The CLUBS informally patronized by the professional and merchant classes, like their London and Edinburgh counterparts, initially took the form of Italian palazzi (e.g. *D. & J. Hamilton*'s

Mannerist Western Club, 1839–42, and *David Bryce*'s subtle Junior Conservative Club, 1868–71), but *James Sellars* broke the mould at the New Club (1877–9) with his mix of French Empire and Thomsonish motifs. *A. N. Paterson*'s Liberal Club of 1907–9 is still a palazzo but much freer in composition. Clubs and professional institutes sought a combination of style and comfort for their members. The grandest of the C19 clubs, the Western Club and the New Club, have tragically been gutted, but the Liberal Club still has its huge dining room. Several clubs occupied existing houses. In 1892–3 *John Keppie* remodelled the hall and added a gallery (with similar Renaissance-cum-Art Nouveau details to those at Craigie Hall) at the pair of Bath Street houses occupied by the Glasgow Art Club. *Mackintosh* and *George Walton* did the same for the Lady Artists at No. 5 Blythswood Square in 1908. *James Miller*'s remodelling of the Royal Scottish Automobile Club in 1923–6 made their terrace in Blythswood Square exactly like a grand hotel. *J. J. Burnet* gave Blythswood houses libraries and meeting halls for the Institute of Accountants and Actuaries (1899) and for the Royal Faculty of Physicians and Surgeons (1892–3).

RESTAURANTS, more informal meeting places, often sought to entice and detain customers by artistic or novel decoration. All but one of them have been stripped bare. Miss Cranston, the doyenne of the Glasgow temperance restaurant, was one of the most enthusiastic patrons of *avant-garde* young architects, employing *Walton* and *Mackintosh* in 1896 at her charming little striped Buchanan Street restaurant by *George Washington Browne* (gutted for the Clydesdale Bank) and at the tenement in Argyle Street (remodelled for her in 1897–8 by *H. & D. Barclay*), of which a Walton door and other fragments are preserved in the People's Palace. Mackintosh also worked for her at Nos. 205–17 Ingram Street in 1902 and 1911 (his Chinese Room of 1911 has been reconstructed in the Glasgow Art Gallery and Museum, Kelvingrove Park) and, most memorably, in 1903–4 in Sauchiehall Street, where his remodelling of the street façade was as revolutionary as the decoration and furniture in what became known as the Willow Tearooms.

COMMERCIAL BUILDINGS 1830–1914

The invasion of BANKS into the Merchant City and Blythswood set the seal on their transformation from residential into commercial districts. Two banks merit particular attention. *Archibald Elliot II*'s chaste Greek temple for the Royal Bank of Scotland, built in 1827 as the nexus of that fine piece of urban design, Royal Exchange Square, was perhaps Scotland's first really remarkable bank. *John Gibson*'s National Bank of 1847 (moved from Queen Street and converted to Langside Halls in 1902–3) was among the first of the string of palazzo-style banks for which he became famous. The Italianate style was the one that caught Glasgow's imagination. Gibson's lead was followed in 1853–7 by *Rhind* at

36, 37 the former Commercial Bank in Gordon Street (with as much loving attention to detail as Gibson had applied); by *Burnet* in 1866 at the Glasgow Savings Bank in Glassford Street (much altered by his son); by *Rochead* at the grand Bank of Scotland of 1867–70 in George Square; and, as a close neighbour to that, by *Burnet* in Venetian style for the Clydesdale in 1871–4. Burnet struck a different note in the former Union Bank (1876–9) in Ingram Street with a complex North Italian Mannerist façade derived from Cockerell. The same taste continued until late, with *J. M. Dick Peddie*'s unwieldy National (now Co-Operative) Bank in St Vincent Street of 1898–1906 and *A. N. Paterson*'s Edwardian Mannerist National (now Royal) Bank in St Enoch Square (1906–7), but it was not quite exclusive. *Rochead*'s City of Glasgow Bank in Trongate of 1855 was an early and rare essay in the Baronial, *T. P. Marwick*'s former National Bank in the same street a late Baroque one (1902–3). The banking hall that *J. J. Burnet* added to his father's Glasgow Savings Bank in 1894–1900 is fully-fledged Edwardian Baroque.

In the late 1880s the British Linen Bank and the Glasgow Savings Bank began to open branches in the suburbs, moving into working-class tenement areas and actually combining banking hall and tenements in their branches. About 1900, following, it seems, the initiative taken in 1897–1900 by *Salmon,* 82 *Son & Gillespie* at the British Linen Bank at Govan Cross (the first of a series by these architects), the Glasgow Savings Bank also began to advertise its presence by eye-catching corner build- 81 ings – at Anderston Cross (by Salmon, Son & Gillespie, 1899–1900); at Shawlands Cross and on New City Road (both by *Neil C. Duff*, 1905–6); on Govan Road (by *E. A. Sutherland*, 1906); and at Parkhead (by *Honeyman, Keppie & Mackintosh*, 1908).

INSURANCE COMPANIES followed the banks into Blythswood. Many of them occupied buildings just like speculatively built office blocks, and indeed most of them were designed to be partly let. Just a few have a more distinct image: *Leiper*'s Francophile Sun Life Assurance of 1889–94, with sculptural allusions to the firm's name; and the Prudential with its familiar hard red face in a late example of 1888–90 by *Paul Waterhouse*.

The earliest remaining COMMERCIAL BUILDINGS in the Merchant City are, as we have seen, indistinguishable from their late C18 and C19 domestic counterparts. Most are very plain, though the block of *c.* 1790 on Wilson Street, attributed by Bolton to the *Adam Brothers*, has some embellishments. Greater sophistication came in the 1830s with the ranges of offices round Royal Exchange Square, all part of a single composition, and in the courts either side of it. This courtyard pattern, once much more common, survives in part again at *John Baird*'s Prince of Wales buildings (now much altered to form Princes Square) of 1854 in Buchanan Street, but it was not ubiquitous. Many offices were, even in the mid-C19, just blocks following the line of the street with shops below, and in the case of the Paris-inspired Bothwell Chambers of 1849–52 by *Alexander Kirkland* and *John Bryce*, with saloons extending the shops behind. The style of all

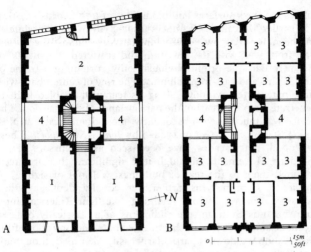

Atlantic Chambers, Hope Street, by J. J. Burnet, 1899–1900.
A ground floor, B first floor
1 shop, 2 warehouse, 3 office, 4 light-well
(Redrawn from *Academy Architecture*, 1899)

these chambers was classical and generally subdued, ranging from *Boucher*'s Italianate stockbrokers' chambers of 1875 in Nelson Mandela (St George's) Place to the French Renaissance block of *c.* 1875–8 by *J. J. Stevenson* at Nos. 67–79 St Vincent Street.

Relatively few mid-century offices remain, for most of them, and many of the houses in the Merchant City and especially in Blythswood, were replaced later in the century by bigger office blocks – not always wider, for many of the old plots were retained, but taller and deeper. After *c.* 1880, new building regulations, together with the introduction of lifts, permitted heights of up to 100 ft (30 m). The greater depth was managed by the introduction of light-wells, often either side of a central service core, forming a 'dumb-bell' plan like that used in 1899–1900 by *J. J. Burnet* at Atlantic Chambers and Waterloo Chambers. Iron framing (and, after 1895, occasionally steel framing) with load-bearing outer walls allowed tailor-made arrangements of partition walls. Insignificant entrances and long passages between ground-floor shops invariably make for dull interiors.

BUSINESS CHAMBERS built speculatively are less common before 1880 than those built for rent as part of banks or insurance companies, though *Alexander Thomson*'s Grosvenor Building of 1859–61 is an early exception. Like the Grosvenor Building, speculatively built chambers, untrammelled by 'house style', were often more extravagant or experimental. Most novel among later office buildings were the exceptionally tall and narrow blocks by *Salmon, Son & Gillespie*: the Hatrack building of 1899–1902, 79 where the large amount of glass is held by a stone framework of Art Nouveau sinuosity, and Lion Chambers of 1904–7, in which 90 pre-cast concrete, used to achieve maximum floor space, distantly

echoes the stark surfaces and mouldings of C17 Scottish castles.
76 The earlier Mercantile Chambers (1897–8) by the same architects
had been, for Glasgow, equally innovative, its almost sheer stone
wall front wall with its 'few, thin and scattered ornaments' of
distantly Baroque origin obviously only curtaining a frame of
steel beams and cast-iron columns. The row of canted bays with
large patent steel windows along its rear wall enabled light to
penetrate deep inside from the narrow lanes of Blythswood. The
device was much used subsequently, most dramatically at Nos.
84–94 St Vincent Street of 1908–9 by *John A. Campbell*. These
functional rear façades have been seen as precursors of the
'Modern Movement', although it is significant that architects
confined them to the rear of buildings, well out of sight. *J. J.
Burnet* and Campbell, his partner, were equally adept at avoiding
excessive ornament, whilst retaining, like their American forerunner Louis Sullivan, the rudiments of a classically ordered
façade. Campbell's love of sheer canted bays hanging above fully
glazed shop windows is particularly easily identified, though his
78 style ranges from the romance of Nos. 157–67 Hope Street (1902–
3) to the more conventional Nos. 122–8 St Vincent Street (1904–
6). The more usual way of coping with large and tall buildings
was to pile up what J. J. Stevenson called 'Free Classic' details
and turn the corner with a handy tower in Baronial, French
château, Flemish or even Scandinavian style (as at *Duncan
McNaughtan*'s Baltic Chambers of 1899–1900). Two of the best
of this conventional type are the Castle Chambers of 1898–1902
by *Frank Burnet & Boston*, put up by the Castle Brewery, and
the Liverpool and London and Globe Assurance building of 1899
by *J. B. and W. A. Thomson*. In their typically more orthodox
fashion, *Peddie & Kinnear* made their huge Central Chambers
(1890) French Second Empire, recalling the design they had
made for a hotel on the site in 1877.

The city centre's Victorian and Edwardian WAREHOUSES
look just like their other commercial neighbours, except for some
of those by the Broomielaw, purpose-built for storing particular
goods shipped into the quayside (as described by John Hume,
below). Warehouses for storage and for retail (what we would
call shops or department stores), which were concentrated in
Argyle Street, Buchanan Street and Sauchiehall Street, shared
the same characteristics. Like banks and offices, the earliest ones
are usually Italianate, e.g. *Alexander Kirkland*'s Venetian Eagle
Buildings of 1854 in Bothwell Street (now reduced to a façade)
and *Black & Salmon*'s refined Miller Street palazzo of 1849–50
for Archibald McLellan. The style went on into the 1870s and
1880s with the ebullient Teachers' building in St Enoch Square
by *Boucher*, 1875, and three similar façades in the Merchant
City (in Montrose Street, 1878, Brunswick Street, 1883, and
Candleriggs, 1912). Much rarer was Baronial, seen in *Billings*'
bizarre façade in Ingram Street (1854–6). *Alexander Thomson*
brought his usual ingenuity to bear on warehouse façades. The
solidity of Grecian Buildings (1865) gives way at the Egyptian
Halls (1871–3) to a screen-wall of superimposed orders and exotic

ornament, but it was the simpler façade of his partly demolished Dunlop Street warehouse (1864) that was imitated throughout the 1880s (e.g. in Drury Street and Bell Street). In the more familiar mixed Renaissance styles, most elaborate is *James Thomson*'s Teutonic façade of 1898–1900 in West George Street for Connal & Co. *H. & D. Barclay*'s Cumming & Smith warehouse of 1891–5 in Sauchiehall Street is big with bold arches, canted bays and lovely sculpture. Biggest of all are those designed for the Scottish Co-Operative Wholesale Society by *Bruce & Hay* (1886–95) and by the Society's own architect *James Ferrigan* in 1919. Smaller but more original are two warehouses in Howard Street, one brick and Arts and Crafts style by *H. E. Clifford* (1902–5), the other Glasgow Style of 1903 by *G. M. Beattie & Morton*.

Warehouses, like some office blocks, were usually constructed with cast-iron stanchions and with timber, cast-iron or, later, steel beams. Such construction survives from the early C19, for instance in a warehouse of *c.* 1800–15 in Robertson Lane. Central light-wells, often of substantial proportions, were common (as in Nos. 65–81 Miller Street or Hunter Barr's warehouse in Queen Street by *David Barclay*, 1903). The same plans were used for retail warehouses, and indeed the most famous galleried light-well was in Wylie & Lochead's original warehouse of 1855 in Buchanan Street, burnt down and reconstructed more heavily in 1883–5 by *James Sellars* with a magnificent fireproof terracotta casing (now Frasers'). Occasionally, not only the structure was of cast-iron but the façade as well: Jamaica Street has a particularly fine run. Gardners' (now Martin and Frost), a pure 39 and subtle design of 1855–6 by *John Baird* carried on a system patented by *R. McConnel*, is among the best of its type in Britain; and *Honeyman*'s Ca' d'Oro of 1872, like Gardners', turns a corner beautifully but with more obvious bravura. Other cast-iron fronts, slotted between conventional buildings, imitate stone: the Colosseum building of 1856–7 by *Barclay & Watt*; *Honeyman*'s Nos. 24–30 Jamaica Street of 1864, and, round the corner in Argyle Street, *James Thomson*'s Nos. 217–21 of 1863. Just a few façades combine cast-iron with timber or stone, including those of *c.* 1854 and 1879 by *William Spence* in Jamaica Street and Buchanan Street, and another in Buchanan Street by *Boucher & Cousland*, 1853–4. Concrete framing was introduced in Glasgow early in its British history: first in 1903 at the Sentinel Works, Jessie Street, and in 1904 at Lion Chambers, both on the *Mou-* 90 *chel-Hennebique* system. The alternative system, supplied by Kahn's *Trussed Concrete Steel Co.*, was used at Weir's (1912) and the Wallace-Scott Institute (1913–22) in Cathcart, and at the Albion Motor Works in Scotstoun (1913).

Victorian and Edwardian ARCHITECTURAL SCULPTURE is abundant. From the 1840s until the 1890s, *John Mossman*'s work appears on almost all public buildings, most effectively integrated at the former St Andrew's Halls of 1873–7. High Victorian figurative tableaux appear in the pediments of the *Barclays*' St

George's-in-the-Fields (by *Birnie Rhind*, 1885–6) and of the City
Chambers (by *George Lawson*); statues of artists and musicians
on *Burnet*'s Athenaeum (by *John Mossman*, 1886); men of learn-
ing, also by Mossman, on *Charles Wilson*'s former Glasgow High
School (1846–7) in Elmbank Street; and, unusually for a
Presbyterian church, of the Evangelists on *Honeyman*'s Barony
North Church (1878–80).

These buildings promoted their historical or cultural connexions by sculptural means; commercial buildings advertised
their names, their branches, their wares and their virtues. The
National Bank (now Langside Halls) has a magnificent display
37 of arms by *John Thomas*; the former Commercial Bank in Gordon
Street, charming reliefs of minting and printing money by *A.
Handyside Ritchie*; the Clydesdale in St Vincent Place, badges of
its branches by *Mossman* and *Charles Grassby*; and *Paterson*'s
former National Bank offices in St Enoch Square (1906–7), Prudence and Fortitude by *Phyllis Archibald*. Michelangelo was
frequently an inspiration, e.g. to *William Birnie Rhind* on *Leiper*'s Sun Life building (1889–94), to *Richard Ferris* on *Salmon,
Son & Gillespie*'s Scottish Temperance League (1893–4), and to
Albert Hodge at *James Miller*'s Caledonian Chambers (1901–3).

Carved detail can be equally rewarding, ranging from the
Greek frieze of *Wilson*'s Queen's Rooms (1857) to the ency-
clopaedic diversity of classical and pre-classical motifs in *Thomson*'s work, the medieval diapering and niches of the Stock
Exchange and the scholarly Renaissance vocabulary devised by
W. J. Anderson in 1885–9 for *T. L. Watson*'s *Evening Citizen*
building. Masonry was often treated with precision and even
subtlety, particularly in the Italianate work of *Wilson* and *Rhind*.
The Free Style gave sculpture a more active and, sometimes,
literally a supporting role. Oriels and balconies were carried by
82 men, carved by *Derwent Wood* (Bank of Scotland, Govan, 1899–
1900), or maidens, by *Kellock Brown* (Castle Chambers, 1898–
1902) and *Derwent Wood* (Mercantile Chambers, 1897–8).
Figures loll against the arches of the *Barclays*' Cumming & Smith
warehouse (1891–5) in Sauchiehall Street. Styles encompass the
77 spirited New Sculpture of *Frampton* and Derwent Wood and
81 the more hieratic medievalizing figures at the former Glasgow
Savings Bank, Anderston Cross (1899–1900) by *Albert Hodge*,
whose serene groups of Europe and America flank the Clyde
Navigation Trust's dome of 1905–8. Hodge was a superb local
sculptor, *Kellock Brown* less distinguished, although he could
manage the formal figures on the People's Palace (1893–8) as well
as the Pre-Raphaelite girls on Castle Chambers (*see* above). St
Mungo and the attributes of the arms of Glasgow (tree, book,
fish and bell) appear in numerous guises, most powerfully at
67 Glasgow Art Gallery and Museum (1897–1900) by *Frampton*
(who also did the St Mungo on the Glasgow Savings Bank in
Ingram Street, 1894–1900), most delicately on Hutchesontown
Library of 1904–6.

PLANNING AND PUBLIC HOUSING 1914–90

Glasgow doubled its area in 1912 when it annexed several large independent burghs (Govan, Partick, Pollokshaws, Cathcart). In addition, the Corporation bought tracts of agricultural land for the building of public housing on a scale never attempted by the City Improvement Trust. The model, as in most British cities, was the garden suburb. The first to be started was Riddrie, well beyond the city centre, in 1919, followed by Mosspark and Knightswood in the early 1920s. Acres of cottages and cottage flats, with almost no concessions to the garden-suburb ideal, were built in every outer suburb during the 1920s and 1930s, but these houses were out of the reach of all but the best-paid artisans. The cheaper alternative was tenements. Hundreds replaced decayed C19 housing in blighted districts like Calton and Royston, and slumdwellers were decanted into thousands more in outer areas like Blackhill.

The Second World War prompted a reassessment of future, and, it was hoped, planned, growth. The regional Clyde Valley Plan of 1946 by *Matthew* and *Abercrombie*, which envisaged several New Towns to relieve Glasgow's housing problems (it was estimated that 100,000 new houses were needed), had little effect on the city's development. The city opposed a loss of population, and *Robert Bruce*, the City Engineer, proposed instead a number of satellite townships within the city boundary, proposals upheld in the City of Glasgow Development Plan of 1951. So the pre-war practice of moving citydwellers to the fringes of the city reached new heights in the 1950s and 1960s, particularly at Pollok, Castlemilk, Easterhouse and Drumchapel. All of these townships, ranging in population from twenty-five to forty-seven thousand, degenerated for lack of funds into housing schemes without amenities or transport. Bruce's utopian plans for completely rebuilding the city centre were rejected, but the idea of totally redeveloping the industrial suburbs with zoned industry and housing, initiated in 1953 by the first Director of Architecture and Planning, *A. G. Jury*, was acted upon. Twenty-nine Comprehensive Development Areas were designated in the next few years, but fewer than half that number were completed, starting in 1957 with Hutchesontown-Gorbals and continuing with Anderston, Woodside, Royston, Springburn, Townhead, Laurieston-Gorbals, Cowcaddens, parts of Govan, and Sighthill.

It was the ring road, put forward by Bruce in 1946 but revised in the Glasgow Central Area report and Highways Plan of 1965, that had the greatest impact upon the city centre, by cutting it off from its immediate surroundings (though only at the SW corner, which fell within the Anderston C.D.A., and along the fringes of the new road was there complete rebuilding). It is still not complete in 1989. By the time the road was abandoned in the mid-1970s, the tide against comprehensive redevelopment had turned (the creation of C.D.A.s was suspended in 1974), and so most of the centre's historic buildings were reprieved, supported by Lord Esher's report of 1971 in favour of conservation.

The initiative in conservation had been taken in housing. A team of students from Strathclyde University, under their banner of *Assist*, had realized in 1970 that replumbing with kitchens and bathrooms could give tenements new life. (It had often been observed that most tenements were structurally sound.) The Corporation acted upon this principle for the first time at Old Swan Corner, Pollokshaws, in 1971, and by 1973 Housing Action Areas, selectively cleared or improved, had become established policy. The new approach was followed during the eight-year Glasgow Eastern Area Renewal Project (G.E.A.R.), established by the Corporation, the Scottish Development Agency and other interested agencies in 1976 in Calton, Bridgeton, Dalmarnock, Parkhead and Shettleston. Housing associations and private contractors have played a major role in G.E.A.R. and in the other former C.D.A.s. Throughout the 1980s, under the guidance of Local Plans (instituted in 1978) which identify local character, social needs and development potential, the city has been swiftly rebuilt with the minimum of aesthetic control.

As a result of the explosion of PUBLIC HOUSING since 1918, Glasgow is three-quarters C20. In Cardonald or Drumoyne, Haghill or Blackhill, Easterhouse or Castlemilk, houses and tenements appear with minor variations on standard themes, most of them beyond our scope here. The first Corporation housing was provided by the City Improvement Trust in the C19 and has been dealt with already. The next, post-World War I phase began in the same spirit of slum clearance, but in a cosier style at the notorious Garngad (now Royston) in 1918–20, where the City Engineer, *Thomas Nisbet*, built tenements in individual brick-and-render blocks together with cottage flats. This formula was developed in 1919–27 at Riddrie for the Corporation's Director of Housing by *Robert Horn*. Here, as well as tenements, there are Arts and Crafts-style cottages on the Government-approved model that was followed throughout England. The layout, though fairly formal, has greens and verges in garden-suburb fashion. Tenement blocks are repeated at Craigton (1921–3), but at Mosspark Horne abandoned tenements and introduced a wider variety of semi-detached and terraced cottages and cottage flats (designed in 1920) laid out along the contours of the hill. Knights-100 wood was begun in 1921 on exactly the same lines, but, as it grew large (the W side was not finished until the 1940s, long after government subsidy had been withdrawn), the numbers of house types and the variety of their picturesque details were severely reduced. Some of the later houses have the suntrap windows and tubular balconies of the 1930s; the last are of the type experimented with, as we shall see, at Penilee in the 1940s. The cottages and cottage flats built in huge numbers throughout the 1920s and 1930s in the outer suburbs, at Shettleston, Drumoyne, Cardonald, Carntyne, and so on, are mostly of the simple blockish type with minimal brick decoration on the roughcast, though the original picturesque form occasionally occurs (e.g. at Hawthorn, Possilpark, 1925–7).

The tenements designed for poorer families are blocks of three or four storeys, sliced off at street corners to admit light and air; the first of this new type appeared in 1923. Usually built of reconstituted stone blocks, they are devoid of frills, except where a prominent site on a main road, at a major junction or in an established area demanded something smarter. In Dennistoun and at Anniesland Cross, they have red sandstone facing; on Shettleston Road and at Anniesland, cantilevered balconies. In Barrowfield (Parkhead) and in Larchgrove Road, Springboig (1938–46), a degree of streamlining was also tried. Those at 101 Blackhill, Calton, Haghill, Possilpark, Govan and in many smaller pockets look depressingly plain. Though the cottages at Rutherglen and Cambuslang by Lanarkshire County Council are less appealing than Glasgow Corporation's best, their tenements have more panache, with rounded corners, Art Deco brick trim and metal windows.

Flat roofs had been flirted with in the 1920s by the contractor *John McDonald*, who built a number of his Sunlit Homes for the Corporation at Carntyne (now disguised by pitched roofs), but shortages during the Second World War stimulated more interesting experiments. At Penilee, between 1939 and 1947, the first houses were built of foamed slag, partly in blocks, partly cast *in situ*, and then fitted with details, such as the gridded balconies, made at the Corporation's own factory in Amulree Street, Shettleston. The houses are in conventional tenement blocks and flatted cottages, but their style is International Modern, horribly spoilt in the 1980s by hipped roofs and cosy details. Several other experimental types were tried, and appear in the greatest concentration at Barmulloch, where in 1948 the Scottish Housing Corporation contracted to build two thousand non-traditional houses, including Glasgow Corporation's Penilee model, the Scottish Special Housing Association's Swedish timber houses, and several kinds of part-prefabricated steel-framed and concrete houses. Then there were the more familiar single-storey prefabs: a group of Aluminium Permanent Houses is still in well-maintained existence in the shadow of Hampden Park football ground.

Huge Corporation schemes, many of them postponed because of the war, were begun after 1945 at Cranhill, Ruchazie, Milton, Barmulloch etc. Four peripheral schemes – Pollok (begun as a 103 garden suburb of the Knightswood type in 1937, but not completed until 1951), Easterhouse, Castlemilk and Drumchapel – were envisaged as independent satellite townships with a mixture of housing and amenities gathered into neighbourhoods round a town centre on the pattern of contemporary New Towns, to which these townships were intended to be an alternative. Their very idealism proved their downfall in the face of financial stringency. Rural sites and exceedingly low density meant isolation for former citydwellers, especially as amenities proved too expensive to build, and the housing degenerated into monotonous tenement blocks unsoftened by landscaping. The design most prevalent in the earliest neighbourhoods was tried out in 1949 on a small number of houses at Fyvie Avenue, Eastwood, by *A. G. Jury*, then Housing Director. To the International Modern traits of the 1940s tenements (flat roofs, long shared balconies and porthole windows, all done in brick and colour-washed render), he added shallow pitched roofs. This style, softer and potentially more cheerful, can be seen at Calfhill Court, a women's hostel of 1952 at Pollok. Its details, however, became meaner throughout the 1950s and early 1960s, and plans were reorganized to give a small individual, and aesthetically insignificant, balcony to each house. The few cottages built were equally simple, though at Castlemilk and Drumchapel they have evocative small-paned windows. The S.S.H.A.'s contemporary schemes (e.g. Cadder, begun in 1947, and Arden, of the 1950s) are remarkably similar in type, though much smaller and with a larger proportion of cottages. The layouts (by *T. O. W. Gratton*) are more imaginative and so are the details (e.g. the coloured tubular porches at Cadder). These schemes are still distinguished (in 1989) by better maintenance and landscaping.

The Corporation's first experiments with multi-storey flats were made in the late 1940s and early 1950s at Crathie Drive, Partick (of 1946–54 and still with the geometrical severity of the 1940s tenements); at Moss Heights, Cardonald (1950–4), which had, until crudely reclad, the jolly curves and colours of the 1950s; and by the S.S.H.A. at Toryglen (1954–6). But it was not until comprehensive redevelopment and Government subsidy began in the late 1950s that the experiments really took root. Over one hundred high-rise blocks were envisaged – and built. Most interesting are the high-rise blocks designed as part of mixed developments by individually commissioned architects. Most original is *Sir Basil Spence*'s great wall of slabs in Hutchesontown-Gorbals (1960–6), with sweeping concrete pylons and hanging garden decks. Its neighbours are smaller and more friendly slabs by *Sir Robert Matthew, Johnson-Marshall & Partners* (1958–65).

Some sites called for special treatment, like the slopes below the Cathedral, where mannered slabs by *Honeyman Jack & Robertson* (1961–4) are effectively grouped with partly stone-clad flats scaled down to surrounding streets, or at Ibroxholm (1962–6), where towers and maisonettes by the *City Architect* are integrated with suburban streets, or at Pollokshaws, where slickly detailed slabs by *Boswell, Mitchell & Johnston* (1961–74) are ranked along the village street and White Cart Water. Pollokshaws has the most interesting low-rise as well, in the curtain-walled tenements of Well Green by *Dorward, Matheson, Gleave & Partners* (1960–71). At Cowcaddens, housing has been made an island in the midst of city traffic by *Walter Underwood and Partners* (1968–75). The S.S.H.A. under *Harold Buteux* was particularly sensitive to siting and layout. The Wyndford scheme (1960–9), a classic of mixed development, is within the walls of a former barracks; the Broomhill slabs (1963–9) crown a hill; and at Hutchesontown (1961–5) formal squares seek to capture the essence of the original Georgian layout. Deck-access blocks, the later, unsuccessful alternative to high-rise, were designed by the *City Architect* at Hillpark (1966–73), at St Andrews Drive,

Pollokshjelds (1966–72), and at Springburn (1964–8) to reflect the scale of the villas they replaced. At Woodside (1970–4) *Boswell, Mitchell & Johnston* even tried to reflect the character of local tenements, a significant step towards designing in context.

Right from the beginning of its comprehensive redevelopment programme, the Corporation had hoped to keep up with its huge housing problem with the package deals in industrialized building offered by contractors. Towers and slabs built by such methods were particularly useful for filling small or awkward sites. The first went up at Royston in 1959–61, followed by dozens more of these no-fines blocks by *George Wimpey* (distinctively L-shaped, with glazed attic storeys); by others (of panel construction) by *Reema* at Springburn, Maryhill, Scotstoun and Ibrox; and by *Crudens'* Brutalist slabs on the Truscon system at Sighthill (1964–9). The epitome of this approach was the sub-sublimely arrogant slabs and towers of 1962–70 at Red Road, 113 Springburn, designed by *Sam Bunton & Associates*. Almost none of the high-rise blocks can be seen in the original livery. Cladding with coloured metal panels and the addition of pitched or curved roofs (partly for insulation but mainly for style) became a mania in the 1980s. Dull system-built blocks like those at Woodside, Springburn and Red Road now sing out across the city, but unique designs like Moss Heights and *Spence*'s slabs have been irrevocably spoilt.

With the introduction of Housing Action Areas in 1973, housing associations began to play a big part in the rehabilitation of tenements and the building of small pockets of new houses. The taste throughout has been for brick two-storey terraced houses round pedestrian courts, sometimes punctuated with taller blocks of flats. Their origins lie in the English New Towns, and they have transformed Glasgow's inner suburbs like Calton, Bridgeton and Woodside, once densely walled with tenements and factories, as completely as high-rise did in the previous two decades. The S.S.H.A., at, for example, Calton (1984–7) and North Kelvinside (1981–5), have, as usual, the best layouts and landscaping. *Simister, Monaghan, McKinney, MacDonald* have designed the most imaginative small schemes at Govanhill (1979–83), at Govan (1984–6), Whiteinch (1986–7), and Bridgeton 122 (1986–8), and *Ken MacRae with McGurn, Logan, Duncan &* 121 *Opfer* have skilfully reinterpreted the tenement in North Kelvinside (1987–8). In a more monumental manner, redolent of the surrounding villas, are the handsome 1970s flats in Langside Avenue by *Derek Stephenson & Partners*. Styles have nothing particularly Scottish about them (there are pantiled roofs, stained timber, polychrome brickwork and Post-Modern details in abundance, especially *à la* Frank Lloyd Wright), though the allegiance to Mackintosh, manifested in grid patterns and in lettering, is even more noticeable than it is in England.

The C20 has contributed almost no speculative housing of interest. While great tracts were being gobbled up for public housing, the more affluent exiled themselves to the bungalows of Bearsden, Milngavie and Bishopbriggs beyond the city bound-

dary. There are indifferent houses and flats slotted into the
established Victorian suburbs and patches of bungalows on their
fringes. The speculative houses of Kelvindale and King's Park
by *Mactaggart & Mickel* are not much different from those they
were building for the Corporation during the 1920s and 1930s,
and Garrowhill, conceived in 1923 by J. M. Scott Maxwell as an
enlightened garden suburb, was built as an ordinary speculative
scheme by *George Arthur & Son* from 1934. Best from the 1930s
108 is the block of flats at Anniesland by *J. N. Fatkin*, Kelvin Court
(1937–8), a late manifestation of the English arterial road manner.

The boom in private development during the 1980s has not
produced anything of architectural note either. Glasgow has been
scattered with small houses of the sort seen in every town and
village in Britain, and with graceless blocks of flats like those
built by *Laing* (1986–8) close to the Kingston Bridge. None
has any feeling for siting or for Glasgow's particular character,
though the tenements at the w end of St Vincent Street (1985–
7) show a perverse imagination. At the time of writing, contractors are busy in the blighted peripheral estates putting a neo-
vernacular or Post-Modern finish on flats they have bought from
the Corporation. The private developers' architectural success
has been in the city centre, where they have turned dozens of
redundant warehouses into flats, beginning in 1978 with Albion
Buildings in Ingram Street. Most handsome of the buildings
thus saved are the great railway warehouse in Bell Street and
Wylie & Lochead's cabinet works in Kent Road. A whole block
119 of the Merchant City has been revived by *Elder & Cannon*'s
well-integrated mixture of conversion and new build (1984–9).

CHURCHES AND PUBLIC BUILDINGS 1914–90

The suburban developments of the C20 called for a greater
number of new churches. Each new neighbourhood was provided
with at least one Roman Catholic church and one Church of
Scotland. Other denominations' churches were spread more
thinly. Although many were cheaply built and not especially
inventive, these churches are often the only buildings besides
schools to identify individual neighbourhoods in the most
amorphous housing schemes.

Two of the earliest, St John Renfield, Kelvindale (Kelvinside),
by *J. T. Thomson* (1929–30) and St Margaret's, Knightswood
(1929–32), by *Lorimer & Matthew*, are among the best, traditionally planned and stone-built, but with powerful silhouettes.
Drumchapel Old Church of 1936–9 by *Launcelot Ross* is in a
traditional but more rustic manner. Few of the others aspire to
this standard. Most inter-war churches have mean historicist
details, lack towers and are often in brick, though this formula
can be successful, as at *Hutton & Taylor*'s King's Park Parish
Church, designed in 1931 as a prototype for the 1930s Church

Extension scheme. Some new churches were, of course, also built in established suburbs between the wars, especially by the Roman Catholics, who patronized particularly the practice of *Gillespie, Kidd & Coia*, in which *Jack Coia* was by then the principal. His 1930s churches are some of the most interesting of any date in Glasgow, large, inventive and well-crafted, with a beautiful combination of bricklaying and stone-carving. St Anne's White-104 vale Street (Dennistoun) of 1931–3 is an amalgam of Early Christian and Roman Renaissance, St Columbkille, Rutherglen (1934–40), and St Columba, Hopehill Road (1937), Italian Romanesque as it might have been interpreted by Dudok. St Columba's is constructed round a concrete portal frame, the most common means of cheap construction throughout the 1950s, used extensively by *Thomas Cordiner*, whose churches generally reveal their construction frankly, e.g. the barn-like St Margaret Mary, Castlemilk (1956–7), the harmonious Our Lady and St George, Cardonald (1957–9), and, most dramatic of all, the A-framed Immaculate Conception, Maryhill (1955–6). The portal 110 frame is often disguised, even as a Spanish mission church (e.g. St Laurence, Drumchapel, and St Augustine Milton of 1954–7) by *R. Fairlie & Partners. Alexander McAnally*, almost as prolific as Cordiner, designed distinctively in brick. His sub-Romanesque style with domestic overtones is most fully expressed at St Teresa of Lisieux, Possilpark (1956–60).

Gillespie, Kidd & Coia's churches of the late 1950s and 1960s stand quite apart from these economical solutions. The last of their traditional basilican churches were St Paul, Shettleston Road (1957–9), and the Perret-influenced St Charles, North Kelvinside (1959–60). Younger partners (*Andy MacMillan* and *Isi Metzstein*) and the dictums of the Second Vatican Council led to experiments in the footsteps of Le Corbusier, some of which have led to severe building failure and to unsympathetic remedies, as at St Martin's Castlemilk (1959–61). Their large centrally planned churches – all of them (except Our Lady of Good Counsel, Dennistoun, 1964–6) within the peripheral housing schemes – are dominated by dramatic roofs (timber inside, copper-clad without), indirect lighting, exposed brick interior walls with the subtle patterning that Coia enjoyed, and chunky furnishings. Simplest is the countrified St Benedict's, Easterhouse (1962–5), most sophisticated St Benedict's, Drumchapel, with its sail-like roof (1964–70). Only *Rogerson &* 111 *Spence*'s Victoria Park Parish Church of 1968–70 shows anything of the same spirit, this time for the Church of Scotland.

Gillespie, Kidd & Coia's churches have by far the most interesting CHURCH FURNISHINGS, many of them independent works of art. The carving on Coia's earliest churches was by *Archibald Dawson* and *Jack Mortimer*; *Walter Pritchard* and *William Crosbie* painted the chapel vaults in St Columbkille; and *Benno Schotz* modelled the curious Stations of the Cross and designed the sanctuary lamp in St Charles. *Lorimer* designed, with *Phoebe Traquair*, the triptych in All Saints, Jordanhill (1920–1), and, with *Matthew*, the furnishings in his own St

Margaret, Knightswood, to which *Alexander Russell* added in
1950–1 some appropriate Arts and Crafts-style stained glass. The
best ensemble of 1950s furnishings is not in a C20 building but
in Cambuslang Parish Church, where *Sadie McLellan* designed
in 1957–8 a complete decorative scheme, including stained glass
and tapestry. *Gordon Webster*'s glass is ubiquitous, but for a more
comprehensive display of late C20 glass the Cathedral is the
showcase.

SCHOOLS, like churches, were mostly built to serve the new
suburbs. School Boards were abolished in 1919, but under the
local authority their plans remained fairly standardized. The
'butterfly' or 'aeroplane' plan was ubiquitous, developed,
perhaps, from Glasgow's C19 independent academies in Kelvinside and Bellahouston, as well as from the Board schools with
'marching corridors' found in England after 1900. (A prototype,
Jordanhill College's Demonstration School, designed in 1913 by
Honeyman, Keppie & Mackintosh, was built in 1920.) It consists
of a central administration block with assembly hall projecting
at the back and long symmetrical and often splayed wings of
classrooms entered from continuous corridors. Secondary
schools were more elaborate than elementary schools, usually
with additional accommodation (gymnasium, laboratories, etc.)
opening off either side of a longer central spine. From the late
1920s (e.g. at Hillhead, by *E. G. Wylie*, of 1928–31; the former
105 Possil School, 1930–4, by *J. T. Thomson*; and Cloberhill, 1929–
32, by *Keppie & Henderson*, now St Ninian's Primary), the 'open-
air' movement in education meant open corridors and sometimes
also sliding screens to classrooms, which could be opened in
favourable weather. These standard plans were variously, but
almost invariably well, dressed by a number of different architects – classically as at Knightswood Secondary (1930–4, by *Ross
& Buchanan*, now Knightswood Primary); in Wrenaissance style,
as at the former Balmore School (1929–32, by *J. A. Laird*, now
Parkhouse School for the Partially Hearing); or with Art Deco
details (Albert Higher Grade School by *Wright & Wylie*, 1926–
7). Cloberhill, with cleverly articulated plan and clean details, and
109 *Thomas Cordiner*'s mannered Notre Dame School on Dowanhill
(designed in 1939 but not completed until 1953) are the most
successful. Lanarkshire schools, such as St Bridget's Primary,
Baillieston, 1931–7, and Garrowhill Primary, 1935–8 (by the
County Architect, *John Stewart*), followed the same principle,
but the wings were intended to completely enclose a polygonal
courtyard, though few were completed like that. They are usually
rendered and have stripped classical details.

After the Second World War, planning changed to the loose
assemblages of linked blocks of different heights familiar
throughout Britain, with the flat slab roofs and porthole windows
used also for contemporary tenements. This model was followed
throughout the 1950s and 1960s, when large numbers of schools
were built in peripheral housing schemes, constructed partly of
brick, partly of coloured cladding panels. Many were designed
by the *City Architect's Department*, but some of the best in

this idiom are by independent practices, e.g. a neat pair in Hutchesontown by *J. L. Gleave & Partners* (1961–4), and one (Hutchesons' Boys Grammar School, by *Boswell, Mitchell & Johnston*, 1957–60) for an independent foundation. *Gillespie, Kidd & Coia* brought a new style to schools in the late 1950s, as they had to churches, with the exposed concrete construction of their extension to Our Lady and St Francis in Calton (1958–64) and King's Park Secondary (1956–63). Since then, few schools have been built and almost nothing of interest.

The expansion of HIGHER EDUCATION, particularly after 1960, involved an extensive building programme. Between the wars, Glasgow University put up a handful of exceptional buildings: the Zoology Building and the Chapel by *Sir J. J. Burnet & Dick*, 1923–7, and the Reading Room (1939–40), Institute of Chemistry (designed in 1936) and a Sports Pavilion (1936), all by *T. Harold Hughes*. Post-war buildings for the Universities of Glasgow and Strathclyde (the latter created in 1964) are mostly uninspired. Glasgow University's only real extravagance was the soaring Brutalist towers of *William Whitfield*'s Library and 115 Hunterian Museum and Art Gallery Extension (*c.* 1968–81), though some of the outlying buildings are more interesting, particularly *Building Design Partnership*'s Wolfson Hall (1961–5) and *Keppie & Henderson*'s Hydrodynamics Laboratory and Astronomy Building (1964–7) at Garscube. Strathclyde University employed a wide range of architects but has little to boast of except the unassuming Department of Architecture of 1964–7 by *Frank Fielden & Associates* (who did an equally discreet Refectory at Glasgow University), and, because they are an interesting instance of Glasgow contemplating her own architectural navel, the halls of residence by *G. R. M. Kennedy & Partners* 120 (1983–4). Their near neighbours, the crisply Corbusian Central College of Commerce and College of Building and Printing (both of the early 1960s, by *Wylie Shanks & Partners*) show far more confidence; so does *Sir Robert Matthew, Johnson-Marshall & Partners*' shipshape College of Nautical Studies (1962–70), which seems to enjoy its riverside site. In contrast, the Royal Scottish Academy of Music and Drama (1982–7) is insulated from its noisy surroundings in a monumental skin typical of *Sir Leslie Martin*. The local authority's further education colleges of the 1960s (Anniesland by *Ross Doak & Whitelaw*, 1962–4; Barmulloch by *D. Harvey, A. Scott & Associates*, 1960–4; and Langside by *Boissevain & Osmond*, 1958–65) are close in style to contemporary schools but crisper and more serious. *Keppie, Henderson & Partners*' Crawfurd Building at Jordanhill College (1962–3) takes a softer line.

Glasgow was so well furnished with PUBLIC BUILDINGS in the C 19 that few additional ones have proved necessary since 1914. There have been only three major ones: the expensive and monumental Sheriff Court by *Keppie, Henderson & Partners* 116 (completed in 1986), the long-awaited home in Pollok Park for the Burrell Collection by *Barry Gasson & John Meunier* (1972– 118 83), informally composed (to a confusing degree) to unite art, landscape and architectural relics, and the Concert Hall (1987–90) designed by *Sir Leslie Martin* to close Buchanan Street.

Useful public buildings serve the outer suburbs, but few of those rise above the strictly functional. Interwar public HALLS and LIBRARIES at Shettleston (1922–5), Whiteinch (1923–6) and Riddrie (1935–8) by Glasgow's *Office of Public Works* in an abstracted version of Wren's Hampton Court style have a certain dignity; post-war libraries (several, like Ibrox and Cardonald, by *Rogerson & Spence*) are more informal. The City Engineer, *Thomas Somers*, designed the cleanly modern Community Centre at Knightswood (1937–8), and the Denmark Street Health Centre at Possilpark (1936–7). On an equally practical level, HOSPITALS have been enlarged or rebuilt, mostly with little grace. The slab block Gartnavel Hospital by *Keppie, Henderson & Partners* (1968–73) represents the linear ward plan, the great squat blocks at the Western Infirmary (completed by the same architects in 1974) and at the Royal Infirmary by *Sir Basil Spence, Glover & Ferguson* (1971–82), the net plan. At Yorkhill, the busy mannerisms of the Queen Mother's Hospital (1964, by *J. L. Gleave & Partners*) contrast with the crudely detailed Royal Children's Hospital by *Baxter, Clark & Paul*, 1968–71. In comparison, the Sewage Works at Shieldhall by *Rogerson & Spence* (*c.* 1980) are surprisingly stylish.

CINEMAS were the supreme and abundant source of popular entertainment between the wars. Glasgow still has a large number, though many others have gone and some are in a sorry state at the time of writing. The earliest opened were solidly stone-built in a pared-down classical, often French, style, e.g. the Vitograph of 1914–15 by *John Fairweather* and La Scala of 1908–12 by *Neil C. Duff* in Sauchiehall Street; the Waverley, Shawlands (1923), by *Watson Salmond & Gray*; and the Parade, Dennistoun (1921–2), by *McKay Stoddart*. Some, such as the former Grand Central created in a Jamaica Street warehouse of 1915 by *W. B. Whitie*, were converted from other uses, particularly from theatres and music halls. Slightly later, the styles became more fanciful – Egyptian, like the former Govanhill Picture House (1925–6, by *E. A. Sutherland*); Hispanic, like the Kingsway, Cathcart (1929, by *James McKissack*), and the Toledo, Muirend (1933, by *W. Beresford Inglis*); and Art Deco, like the New Bedford, Gorbals (1932, by *Lennox & Macmath*). Largest of all was Green's Playhouse (1925–7, by *John Fairweather & Son*) in Renfield Street, now demolished.

The late 1930s saw the super cinema spread from the centre, which still has the Paramount (now the Odeon), Renfield Street (1933–5, by *Verity & Beverly*), to the suburbs. Most streamlined are those by *C. J. McNair & Elder* (the Lyceum, Govan; the Ascot, Anniesland; and the State, King's Park) but, although most of Glasgow's cinemas were designed by a few architects for a few proprietors, no house style can really be discerned. The flagship of Singleton's Vogue chain (at Rutherglen, Possilpark and Riddrie) was his 'art cinema', the Cosmo (now Glasgow Film Theatre) in Rose Street, designed in 1938–9 by *W. J. Anderson*

11 of *John McKissack & Son* in homage to Thomas Tait's famous Curzon in Mayfair.

FOOTBALL, of course, vied in popularity with the cinema, and *Archibald Leitch*, the Scot responsible for the s stands for both Rangers and Celtic and for the layout of Hampden Park, was, nationwide, the doyen of football stadium design. At Parkhead, his stand of 1929 has been remodelled by *Lang, Willis & Galloway* (1988), but its contemporary at Ibrox Park still shines forth in its harsh red brick glory. Two equally populist but temporary entertainments, the Empire Exhibition of 1938 masterminded by *Thomas Tait* and the Glasgow Garden Festival of 1988, have left little behind them. The neglected Palace of Art by *Launcelot* 106 *Ross* in Bellahouston Park hardly conjures the spirit of Tait's magnificent tower, though the former Beresford Hotel, built for exhibition visitors in Sauchiehall Street by *Weddell & Inglis*, still has something of its verve.

COMMERCIAL BUILDINGS 1914–90

While the suburbs were growing apace in the 1920s and 1930s, the city centre was also being changed by a new generation of monumental buildings modelled on American Neo-classical examples. The first of this type, the former Phoenix Assurance offices (now the Bank of Credit and Commerce), was built just before the First World War in 1912–13 by *A. D. Hislop*. It was followed by others on a much bigger scale, e.g. *James Miller*'s former Union Bank (now Bank of Scotland) in St Vincent Street 99 (1924–7), its design directly derived from an American example, and by the largest of all, *E. G. Wylie*'s Scottish Legal Assurance Society in Bothwell Street (1927–31). On a smaller scale but in the same vein are *J. T. Thomson*'s Metro-Vick (now Fortune) House in Waterloo Street (1925–7), *Miller*'s former Commercial (now Royal) Bank in West George Street (1930–7) and *Graham Henderson*'s Bank of Scotland in Sauchiehall Street (1929–31). *Sir J. J. Burnet*'s No. 200 St Vincent Street (1926–9) has all the 98 monumentality of these designs but none of the literal Neo-classicism.

Most of these buildings are discreetly ornamented (Thomson's building by *Phyllis Bone*, Miller's Commercial Bank with a frieze by *Gilbert Bayes*, Henderson's bank with figures by *Benno Schotz*, Burnet's building by *Archibald Dawson* and *Mortimer*), but Wylie's design is more elaborately finished with carved reliefs by *Dawson* and decorative metalwork. Of the equally decorative shopfronts of the period, best are the classical Ciro in Buchanan Street (1926–7, by *George Boswell*) and the slick Rogano's (1935–6, by *Weddell & Inglis*) just round the corner in Exchange Place.

Another spate of OFFICE BUILDING started in the late 1950s, when new blocks were fitted into the centre's older fabric, with varying degrees of success, and the whole south-western sector was developed as part of the Anderston C.D.A. In the first category, the most conscientious efforts were made by *Wright &*

Kirkwood in 1958 at No. 249 West George Street, with acknowledgements to the classical vocabulary of Blythswood
Square, and by *Gillespie, Kidd & Coia*, whose dark-faced B O A C
building (now Halifax Building Society) of 1968–70 took up the
colour, texture and rhythm of its neighbours in Buchanan Street.
In the second category, *Derek Stephenson & Partners* did some
big and brutal piles that fill whole blocks of the centre's grid
plan. Heron House (*c.* 1967–71) is the most ambitious, cleverly
stepped up the hill, a powerful and, some would say, insensitive
foil for St Vincent Street Church. Slabs and towers like these are
confined to the fringes: the first was *Arthur Swift & Partners'*
St Andrew's House of 1961–4 in Sauchiehall Street. It was also
in the 1960s that the bad habit of gutting historic buildings and
rebuilding behind their façades began with the annexation of the
Western Club as part of *Leslie C. Norton*'s Scottish Life building
of 1968–72. The 1970s brought an epidemic of 'gutting and
stuffing' (the New Club, John Street Church, and many of
Blythswood's terraces are just examples), and of designs which
show greater deference to the existing streetscape. Two slick
formulas are endlessly repeated: the first has horizontal or vertical
bands of cream sandstone and tinted glass (e.g. Hume House,
West George Street, by *R. Seifert Co-Partnership*, 1974–7), the
second, big bays of tinted glass within a framework of polished
red sandstone, done first and well by *King Main & Ellison* at
Amicable House, St Vincent Street (1973–6), and pushed to
extremes of size and opulence by *Holmes Partnership* at No. 100
Bothwell Street (completed in 1988), by *Scott, Brownrigg &
Turner* for Coats Viyella (completed in 1986), and above all by
Hugh Martin & Partners for Britoil (1982–6). On a mammoth
scale, there is the Anderston Centre (1967–73), a megastructure
of flats, shops and amenities which never functioned as it was
planned, the Charing Cross complex (1971–5), already out of
date when it was started and never finished to the original designs
(both by *Seifert*), and the St Enoch Centre (1981–9) enveloped
in a vast glass tent by *Gollins Melvin Ward Partnership* and
Reiach & Hall. In the mid-1980s, shopping flourished with the
low-key conversion of the Fish Market into the Briggait Centre
by *Assist Architects* (1983–6) and the overwhelmingly opulent
one of Princes Square by *Hugh Martin & Partners* and *The
Design Solution* (1985–7).

BANKS have, as usual, been given strong personalities, the
most flamboyant the extension to Burnet's Clydesdale Bank by
G. D. Lodge & Partners of *c.* 1980, the most reticent outside the
National Bank of Pakistan in Sauchiehall Street by *Elder &
Cannon* of 1981–2. The latter's interior is intriguing and so is the
Brutalist-in-miniature one of the Clydesdale Bank in Buchanan
Street, converted by *Wylie, Shanks & Partners* from Miss Cran-
ston's Tearooms in 1968–71.

Interesting COMMERCIAL BUILDINGS of a heavier duty are
few. *George Boswell*'s extensions to Templeton's factory (1934
and 1936), Weir's amenity building at Cathcart by *Wylie, Wright
& Wylie* (1937), (*Sir*) *Owen Williams*'s Daily Express building in

Albion Street (1936), the Luma Lightbulb Factory at Shieldhall (1936–8, by *Cornelius Armour* of the Scottish Co-Operative Wholesale Society), the offices at Temple Saw Mills (Anniesland) by *Laird & Napier*, and the warehouses by *Thomson, Sandilands & McLeod* in the Merchant City are the best of that decade. Still with a 1930s look but of 1945–53 is the Wills tobacco factory at Dennistoun and what remains of Queenslie Industrial Estate, planned in 1945 by *George Boswell* for Scottish Industrial Estates Ltd. The only memorable later building is the Scottish Co-Operative Wholesale Society's headquarters of 1962–9 by the SCWS's architect *Kenneth F. Masson*, as brash as the earlier warehouses.

Fine ART is not much seen in public places. Glasgow University has a sculpture by *George Rickey* of 1972, Strathclyde University one by *Gerald Laing* of 1971, and Buchanan Street another of 1977 by *Neil Livingstone*. There are huge doors of 1977 by *Paolozzi* at the Hunterian Art Gallery, and tapestries of the 1980s by *R. A. Stewart* at Strathclyde University and in the City Chambers. Perhaps, though, the mélange of mosaics, glass, murals and ironwork at Princes Square and the liberal use of sculpture at *Page & Park*'s Italian Centre in John Street (1987–9) are signs that Glasgow's decorative tradition is reawakening.

INDUSTRIAL BUILDINGS

BY JOHN R. HUME

Glasgow was for more than a century one of the world's great industrial cities. Within the boundaries of the city as they were redrawn in 1912 lay shipyards, engineering works, whisky blending stores and textile mills of international scale and repute, and myriad industrial premises engaged in almost every known trade, from iron smelting to fancy box making. The city served international markets for metal products, textiles, pottery, drink and some foodstuffs, and, locally, it was the manufacturing centre for the W of Scotland. Its satellites complemented and reinforced its position, although they made a great virtue of their administrative independence. An appreciation of the range and scale of Glasgow's industries is necessary to understand the city's industrial buildings. There is an underlying quality about many of them found more consistently here than anywhere else in Britain, a quality that is not necessarily ostentatious (though it can sometimes be aggressively so) but is more the result of a certain dignity and lack of pomposity on the part of both owners and designers. The design of industrial buildings was to some extent governed by the constraints of materials, of construction, of the machinery used, and the product made; but within that framework room was found for a sense of proportion, for careful detailing, and for an economical elegance.

The forces which have radically changed the Scottish economy since the late 1950s have made a sharp reduction in the number of Glasgow's industrial buildings, and many of those that
survive have been converted to domestic or commercial use.
Enough, however, remains to evoke some of the grandeur
of industrial Glasgow, and the growing interest in the city's industrial heritage should ensure a future for many of these fine
buildings.

The GRAIN-USING INDUSTRIES, the earliest industries of
any size in Glasgow, were mostly sited on the Molendinar, partly
because of its suitability as a mill-stream; but the only two
surviving water-powered grain mills, neither with a wheel, are
on other water-courses. Cathcart Mill lies on the River Cart; it
was almost certainly worked as a grain mill in the C18, although
it was converted to a papermill early in the C19, and also ground
snuff for a short period. Bishop Mills of 1837 in Partick stands
on an ancient site by the River Kelvin.

The most impressive of all grain mills can be found at Port
45 Dundas, where the City of Glasgow Mills at North Spiers Wharf
(built from c. 1850) and its associated warehouses form part of the
grey wall of industrial buildings dominating the city's northern
skyline. Of the three grain mills in Washington Street, the Anderston Grain Mill is the oldest, part-converted from a cotton store
in 1845, which later became a rice mill. Its particularly good
brick addition was purpose-built as a grain mill in 1865. On the
other side of the street are the Crown Flour Mills of 1862 and
the Washington Mills, with C19 buildings of several different
dates and a C20 concrete silo. Scotstoun Mills is the only working
survivor of the great Kelvin mills, its one old block with its water
tower (of 1909) swamped by buildings of the 1960s and 1970s.
W. F. McGibbon's castellated riverside part of the complex (1898)
has gone, and so have the massive Regent Mills of 1887–90 on
the other side of the river. In Tradeston, one former mill remains,
the Victoria Grain Mills in West Street, a dignified group of
1886–96, also by W. F. McGibbon.

Almost all the grain ground in Glasgow after the 1840s came
in by sea to the many warehouses which lay to the N of the
Broomielaw quay. The oldest of these, at 34 Robertson Lane,
dates from c. 1800–15. Those in James Watt Street make a magnificent group of four classical buildings of outstanding elegance,
built between 1847 and 1861 (one was largely rebuilt as a bonded
46 warehouse in 1910–11). In 1912, the function of these warehouses
passed to the Clyde Navigation Trust's vast granary at Meadowside, Partick, and in 1989, they are, alas, threatened by sweeping
redevelopment proposals.

Few of the other grain-using industries are still active. Mech-
anized bread and biscuit bakeries, pioneered in Glasgow in the
late 1870s by J. & B. Stevenson, have been, so far as still-
functioning historic structures are concerned, reduced to a single
example of each, and the older buildings (1875, 1893–7) of the
Gray Dunns biscuit factory in Stanley Street are heavily disguised by render and refenestration. Otherwise, only the former

bakery in Clarendon Street (City Bakeries, 1924–8) has some style and quality of materials.

Glasgow's breweries were once numerous. Only Greenhead (now a bottling plant) retains any original features, though its two late C 19 kilns are almost hidden from public view. Late C 20 plant sometimes has vitality, as at the much modernized Wellpark Brewery or at the Port Dundas distillery, where the rather bland distillery buildings of c. 1900 are complemented by a gutsy dark grains plant of the early 1970s. Part at least of Port Dundas retains a traditional flavour, especially along North Canal Bank Street, where monumental warehouses exude a pervading odour of maturing whisky. Just to the W of them, the Scottish Grain Distillers' cooperage occupies the mid-C 19 remains of Dundas-hill Distillery.

The great monuments to the whisky trade are not the distilleries but the bonded warehouses and offices round the city centre. As well as buildings adapted for the purpose, there are still about a dozen bonded warehouses intact. The fine example in Oswald Street of c. 1844, with its later classical front, seems to be the oldest; the most spectacular (and one of the finest industrial buildings in Glasgow) is the Glasgow & South-Western Railway's massive Bell Street bond of 1882–3, well proportioned and with excellent detail. Lowrie's bond in Washington Street (1897–1906), with its Roman detail, is almost as monumental. The other large bonded brick-built warehouses in Borron Street (1897–1911, by *Burnet & Boston*) are conspicuous chiefly because of their size. On a smaller scale there is a pleasing little pink sandstone bond in York Street, rebuilt in 1895–1901, and Waterloo Street has a quite extraordinary warehouse and offices designed by *James Chalmers* in 1898–1900 for the distillers Wright and Greig.

Only a few other buildings connected with food and drink merit attention, in particular a grand tea warehouse in York Street (1843), with chunky Victorian detail. Most of the late Victorian and Edwardian cold stores have now gone, but there is a simple terracotta example, with a brick ice factory, in Osborne Street by *Alexander Adam* (1901–2). Once there were some very large and grand confectionery works, notably in Kinning Park, Bridgeton and Port Dundas, but all have been demolished.

We turn now to the TEXTILE INDUSTRY. Glasgow's reputation as a major industrial city was founded on the cotton industry, which was drawn to the city by its trading connexions and by local expertise in the linen trade. Before steam power was introduced on any scale in the late C 18, Glasgow merchants David Dale and James Finlay dominated the rurally based, water-powered cotton-spinning trade. Only one water-powered spinning mill was built in Glasgow – on the Kelvin in South Woodside. After the introduction of steam power in 1782 at Springfield on the S bank of the Clyde, cotton spinning rapidly became the staple trade, concentrated in Anderston, Bridgeton, Dalmarnock, Mile-End and Calton in the East End. Much of the yarn produced was 'put out' for weaving into cloth throughout the W of Scotland, and then often bleached, printed, dyed or embroidered in factories throughout the region. Finally, it was packed and dispatched, commonly to export markets. From the mid-1820s power looms were introduced and weaving factories were built either independently or integrated with spinning mills. Some of the yarn was twisted into sewing thread; although Paisley came to dominate this trade, Glasgow also had some thread mills. Glasgow's cotton spinning trade was relatively short-lived, ceasing to grow after 1840 and generally declining from the 1860s, although two large spinning mills were built in the 1870s and 1880s. Weaving, however, boomed and new factories were built until c. 1900, most of them specializing in fancy muslins, shirtings and other high-quality products.

This great industry generated a very large number of buildings, many of considerable size and some of high architectural quality. A significant proportion survived the steady run-down of cotton manufacturing during the C 20, finding new uses as warehouses, workshops and lodging houses; but most of them have been demolished since the 1950s. Of the remaining spinning mills, the oldest are the much altered Mile End Mills at Nos. 91–7 Fordneuk Street, built c. 1835 and rebuilt in 1914; the Old Rutherglen Road Mill of 1816–21, embedded in later extensions but notable for its early cast-iron columns and beams; and the Falfield Cotton Mill in Falfield Street (c. 1840). All of these mills are or were brick buildings, multi-storey, with multi-paned cast-iron window frames. The Barrowfield Spinning Factory in Reid Street (c. 1846) is similar. The first iron-framed 'fireproof' building in Glasgow, Houldsworth's Anderston Cotton Works, had been built in 1803–4 (demolished in 1968), but most later mills had timber beams and floors. In Carstairs Street, part of the Glasgow Cotton Spinners Company's giant terracotta brick factory (1884–91), with hollow-tile floors on cast-iron beams and columns, is a piece of Lancashire transplanted to Glasgow by an Oldham millwright, *Joseph Stott*. Only one thread mill still exists, but that is a particularly splendid Italianate one (now the Great Eastern Hotel, Duke Street), designed for R. F. and J. Alexander by *Charles Wilson* in 1849. Most of the weaving factories have been demolished too, although examples can be seen in French Street, Dalmarnock (the Barrowfield Weaving Factory, 1889–99, by *M. S. Gibson*), and in David Street (the Fordneuk Factory of c. 1862). The Boden Street Factory of 1881–1907, demolished in 1989, was the last to close (in 1987). The characteristic weaving factory was a block of single-storey brick sheds, often with two-storey preparation rooms; Fordneuk, even in its decayed state, is a classic example of the type.

The last stages of finishing and packing were generally city-centre operations, and many of the buildings in the district now called the Merchant City were at some stage occupied by textile firms. The block bounded by Cochrane Street, John Street, Ingram Street and South Frederick Street is perhaps the best-surviving section, although the conversion work in progress in 1989 will probably obscure the little courtyards with their wall cranes for handling bales of cloth. Of the calender works used for imparting surface gloss to cloth, there is nothing left at all.

The linen industry was introduced into Glasgow in the early c 18, and the city then became an administrative centre for the hand spinning and weaving of linen. There were few linen mills in the city, and only three small short-lived jute mills, all founded in the boom years of the mid-1860s. None of them survives. Woollen manufacturing also failed to take root in Glasgow, with the exception of carpet weaving and, more recently, hosiery manufacture. Carpet weaving became one of the city's greatest industries from the last decades of the c 19, Templetons' manufactory in particular becoming world-famous for carpets of high-quality. Of the empires built by Templetons and their principal rivals, Lyles, there is relatively little architectural evidence, but some of what does still exist is outstanding. The complex of buildings adjacent to Glasgow Green is dominated by one of the most theatrical industrial buildings anywhere in the world; the so-called Doges' Palace, its brick Venetian Gothic show front 68 (1888) designed by *William Leiper*, is as vigorously polychromatic as any carpet. The accompanying buildings, ranging in date from the 1890s to the 1960s, are at worst workmanlike and at best distinguished, the streamlined showroom of 1934 by *George Boswell* at the corner of Templeton Street being particularly good. The rather heavy concrete-framed, brick-clad style favoured by the carpet makers in the interwar years is also to be found in four-storey blocks in Abercromby Street (1927) Crownpoint Road (1929) and St Marnock Street (1923). Templetons moved out of Templeton Street in the 1970s to a purpose-built factory on the site of the Govan Ironworks in Cathcart Road, a building distinguished only by sheer bulk and now abandoned to the modern gods of Cash and Carry.

The dyeworks, printworks and bleachworks which served the city's textile trade have left only obscure fragments: so too have the silk industry and hemp ropemaking, although British Ropes' office block in Farmeloan Road, Rutherglen, is a nice Glasgow Style essay of 1912 by *E. A. Sutherland*. Laundries, near-relations of the finishing trades and ubiquitous between *c.* 1900 and the 1950s, are almost extinct, apart from the Cathkin Laundry in Rutherglen, which still operates in architecturally nondescript buildings. The finest surviving laundry building is a much neater little one at the corner of Darnley Street and Albert Drive, Pollokshields, designed *c.* 1895 as the Glasgow Laundry and Carpet Beating Works.

The only other interesting buildings belonging to the textile industry are the clothing workshops. Glasgow was one of the great British centres for ready-made clothing production in the late c 19. Much of this industry was conducted in small workshops, often in re-used buildings, but occasionally a larger firm emerged and built on a grander scale. There are three particularly notable workshops, two of them in Ingram Street. The oldest of them, at the E corner of Albion Street, was built for Fraser Ross in the 1870s and is now flats. The other, much larger and now offices, is the great seven-storey red sandstone block by *James Thomson* built in 1897–8 for Stewart & Macdonald at the corner of Montrose Street. Fraser Brothers also built, to the designs of *H.E. Clifford*, the six-storey red sandstone clothing warehouse (1906) on the w corner of Albion Street. The most remarkable of all Glasgow's former clothing works was the Wallace-Scott Tailoring Institute at Spean Street, Cathcart, designed by *Sir J.J. Burnet* in 1913–22, with great attention to the employees' welfare. This fine building has been disfigured for the South of Scotland Electricity Board. Just enough remains, however, to recall Burnet's handsome design, with its polychrome brick patterns and extensive formal gardens.

SHIPBUILDING was one of the most characteristic industries of the Glasgow area. The first yard was at Stobcross, where the Finnieston crane now stands, and was established in 1818. From the late 1830s, iron ships were built in increasing numbers on both banks of the Clyde. As land values rose close to the city centre, firms moved down-river. By the 1880s the Clyde was the most technically advanced shipbuilding area in the world. After the First World War contraction began, but it was not until the late 1950s that foreign competition and changing demand resulted in a rapid rundown.

The dramatic contraction of the Clyde shipbuilding since 1960 has had a serious effect on the buildings associated with it. The sole surviving merchant yard, Kvaerner Govan, still boasts the elegant Italianate offices in Govan Road designed for the Fairfield Shipbuilding & Engineering Co. by *John Keppie* (1889–91). There are some other old buildings within the yard, including the engine works (described later) and the mould loft, but the great steel sheds in which most of the work is done date from after 1960. Yarrow's in South Street, Scotstoun, is also active. The oldest parts of this yard were constructed before the First World War, but thoroughgoing modernization has enabled both the building and the fitting out of frigates to be done under cover. Little else remains; just the office block of D. and W. Henderson, in Castlebank Street, a pleasant Italianate building of 1885, and undistinguished fragments of other yards in South Street.

Glasgow's ENGINEERING industries were the most varied in Britain, and probably in the world, by the beginning of the C20. Born out of the requirements of the textile and grain-milling industries, engineering developed its own momentum. After the application of a mill engine to propel a ship (Henry Bell's *Comet* of 1812), marine engineering became a Glasgow speciality, and from it iron shipbuilding grew in the 1830s. The techniques of marine engineering could be applied to locomotive building, and from that developed one of Glasgow's most important industries. The private builders, with works in Springburn and Polmadie, amalgamated in 1903 to form the North British Locomotive Company Ltd, the largest firm of locomotive builders outside the United States of America. Sugar-machinery manufacture, like marine engineering, was an offshoot of the textile machinery industry and became a speciality.

Round the core of these industries grew other firms supplying components. Iron and brass founders, forgemasters, tube makers, rivet, bolt and nutmakers produced basic parts; machine-tool builders provided the means for finishing them. Boiler-makers, pump manufacturers, crane builders, air-conditioning engineers and a host of others were tied into a network of enter-prise. The availability of engineering skill and capacity acted as a magnet for new ideas. Sewing machine manufacture, motor vehicle and steam lorry building, hydraulic machinery manu-facture, structural steel production, all came to Glasgow for that reason, and were drawn into the net. For a variety of complex causes, predominantly foreign competition and technical change, the engineering and shipbuilding industries suffered severely in the interwar years and since about 1960 have contracted markedly. This contraction has been followed fairly quickly in most instances by demolitions, as the larger engineering build-ings usually have little potential for re-use.

To begin with the creation of basic materials, there is only one historic ironfoundry building left in Glasgow, the Cranstonhill Foundry in Elliot Street (c. 1854). With its tall round-headed windows and large semicircular fanlight in the doorway, it is an outstanding example of its type externally, despite being much modified inside. Brass foundries have also survived by being given other uses, like the one of 1869 in Minerva Street (now a timber store) and that built in 1897 by Steven and Struthers of the Anderston Brass Foundry in Eastvale Place (now a galvanizing works). The original Anderston Brass Foundry in Elliot Street of 1870–83 with its fanlighted door is particularly fine. The largest brass foundry to survive (in Bulldale Street, Yoker) is a tall single-storey building of c. 1901, with side aisles and a large fanlighted doorway. Apart from some nondescript sheds in Woodville Street, the only remaining coppersmith's shed (of 1876) is in Tradeston Street. In Admiral Street there is a two-storey red and white brick former rivet works dating from c. 1888.

The oldest engineering works is now the Eglinton Engine Works at the corner of Cook Street and West Street. Although the two-storey stone block dates from c. 1855, the main shops, with their four-storey pattern store, were built in the 1860s and 70s. Close by in Scotland Street are two other early works: on the corner of West Street, the former Scotland Street Engine Works (dating from 1850 onwards), and opposite it a well-detailed little works dating from 1871–2, both of which were at different times used by the marine engineer, James Howden & Co., the last heavy engineering concern active in central Glasgow. This firm occupies (in 1988) the former Glasgow Subway Power Station (see below) as well as a purpose-built works, the oldest parts of which date back to the 1890s. Another early engineering works is that of Glen & Ross, specialists in steam-hammer making, whose Greenhead Engine Works in Arcadia Street date from 1859–63.

Two major marine engineering works still survive, both no longer in production but both exceptionally fine. The Fairfield

Engine Works, used as the central stores for Govan Shipbuilders, was built in 1874 and represents an advance in design on the Randolph, Elder engine works which stood in Tradeston until 1968. The former's simple brick exterior is poor preparation for the splendid, boldly constructed interior. (The simpler and more elegant earliest part of Alexander Stephen & Sons' engine works built at Linthouse in 1873 was dismantled in 1988 and has been re-erected at the Scottish Maritime Museum at Irvine.) The North British Diesel Engine Works, Whiteinch (but *see* Scotstoun) built to a German design in 1912–13, has all the sophisticated, complicated steelwork of German design at that period. The Scotstoun Works of Harland & Wolff in South Street, which had their origin in a gun-mounting shop built for the Coventry Syndicate in 1907, became one of the largest groups of steel-framed engineering shops in Glasgow; they survive as part of the Albion Motor Works. Other marine engineering works were on a smaller scale, the most important and impressive being the now disused works built between 1884 and 1905 for British Polar Engines in Helen Street, Govan.

Most interesting of the other heavy engineering works was Penman's Caledonian Boiler Works in Strathclyde Street, Dalmarnock, built as the Heavy Machinery Hall for the Glasgow International Exhibition of 1888, but this has been moved again (in 1989) to the Scottish Railway Preservation Society at Bo'ness. The huge Dalmarnock Ironworks, home of the celebrated bridge-builders Sir William Arrol & Co., has been much reduced, but part of the complex, built between 1889 and 1911, is still in use for other purposes. Alley & McLellan's Sentinel Works in Jessie Street, Polmadie (1903–5), Glasgow's first reinforced concrete building, dominates some undistinguished steel-framed shops. On the other side of Polmadie Road are some steel-framed workshops built in 1904–14 as part of the North British Locomotive Company's Queen's Park Works, but that important company is more fittingly remembered by the imposing offices (now Springburn College) that *James Miller* designed for it in 1909.

Lighter engineering is represented by the Holm Foundry of G. & J. Weir, in Newlands Road, with its two early reinforced concrete buildings of 1912 and 1913 and a splendid Modern Movement amenity block of 1937 by *Wylie, Shanks & Wylie*. The oldest part of Anderson Strathclyde's factory in Broad Street built for Mavor & Coulson in 1896–7 has nothing particular to distinguish it as one of the first purpose-built electrical engineering works. The first mass-production engineering works in the city were sewing machine factories. That built by Singers' has gone, but part of one built in 1872–3 by their rivals, the Howe Company, still stands in Fielden Street and Avenue Street, Mile-End. Of premises associated with motor vehicle building, most interesting are William Park's reinforced concrete coach-building works of 1913–14 in Kilbirnie Street and the nearby Leyland Motor Co. depot in Salkeld Street, a stylish design by *James Miller*, probably of 1937.

Glasgow was a major centre for the CHEMICAL INDUSTRY

and activities related to it from *c.* 1800. These industries were at first primarily suppliers of materials for the bleaching and dyeing of textiles. The St Rollox Chemical Works of Townhead, founded in 1799, was perhaps the largest in the world for much of the C19, but its only relics, the once noisome waste-heaps, have been landscaped and built over with the slab blocks of Sighthill. At the height of their success in the third quarter of the C19, St Rollox and the neighbouring Townsend's chemical works boasted the largest chimneys in the world, about 150 m (500 ft) high; but these have disappeared, as have all the heavy chemical plants save that of R. & J. Garroway at Parkhead. Worth mentioning, though, are the buildings that survive from the chemical-related industries. The paint industry, which grew up largely to supply specialist paints for ships, shows the most impressive remains. The oldest is the dignified three-storey ashlar Tradeston Paint Mills (1866) at the corner of West Street and Cook Street. In the same complex are Blacklock & McArthur's massive paint warehouse of 1888 by *H. & D. Barclay*, and their elaborate Venetian Gothic block designed by *W. F. McGibbon* in 1900. Other paintworks are built of brick: for instance, the mildly Gothic Milton Colour Works (1873) in Dobbies Loan and the Kinning Park Colour Works (*c.* 1895) in Milnpark Street and Middlesex Street, a good example of *Bruce & Hay*'s idiosyncratic polychrome style.

Adjacent to the Glasgow Lead & Colour Works in Ruchill is the Glasgow Rubber Works of *c.* 1876–1911, the last of a small group of rubber factories in the city. Its most striking buildings, of *c.* 1876 and *c.* 1900, face the Forth and Clyde Canal. The firm of R. & J. Dick, which specialized in working in gutta-percha and balata, natural products related to rubber, had works in Greenhead Street (1872–89) with a façade designed to resemble its handsome tenement neighbours facing Glasgow Green.

Tanning has been important in Glasgow since the Middle Ages; boots and shoes, horse harness, upholstery leather and industrial driving belts were made in large quantities. Almost all the traditional tanneries have gone now, together with their distinctive louvred drying sheds, but several sizeable buildings connected with the leather trade remain, including the stone-fronted Tannery Buildings of 1876–7 in St Andrew's Square, Schrader Mitchell's red sandstone block of 1903 in Howard Street, and the innocuous St Catherine's leather works of 1910 in Ingram Street, which were all leather warehouses.

From the C18 to the First World War, Glasgow was celebrated for its potteries, which turned out a wide range of wares until competition from Staffordshire and changing taste forced them out of business. The only substantial pottery buildings to survive are the handsome former White's clay pipe factory in Bain Street, Calton, only part of a once much larger polychrome brick composition of 1876–7 by *M. Forsyth*, and the Eagle Pottery in Boden Street (of 1869). Below the Belmont Street Bridge, beside the Kelvin Walkway, can be seen the much reduced but preserved remains of the North Woodside Flint Mill, which operated from

1846 until the 1960s, latterly producing ground flint for a Paisley sanitary ware factory.

PRINTING is an industry more often associated with Edinburgh, but, though book printing was indeed an Edinburgh speciality, two major printers and publishers, Blackie & Sons and William Collins & Sons, once operated in Glasgow. Except for part of the Collins' works which has been adapted by Strathclyde University, both companies' buildings have gone, including the offices that Alexander Thomson designed for Blackie's in 1869. Glasgow's great strength was, and still is, in printing newspapers. The former offices and printing works of four daily and two evening papers are slotted into the city centre, with, generally, multi-storeyed offices at the front and basement print rooms at the rear. Architecturally they are just as pretentious as their commercial neighbours. Two are by *Honeyman Keppie & Mackintosh*: the Mitchell Street block of the *Glasgow Herald* (1893–5), with its dramatic water tower, and the *Daily Record* Printing Works of 1900, almost hidden off Hope Street between Renfield and St Vincent Lanes. Both, in their different ways, are tailored to restricted sites. The first is only part of a group of buildings whose classical face (by *Sellars*, 1879–80) is turned to Buchanan Street. The *Evening Citizen* building in St Vincent Place (by *T. L. Watson*, 1885–9) was one of the first offices in Glasgow to be constructed of red sandstone, and is distinguished by scholarly detail and excellent craftsmanship. The Glasgow *Daily Record* offices of 1899–1900 in Hope Street is an equally inventive design (by *Robert Thomson & Andrew Wilson*), this time for a narrow plot and with some good sculpture. Least skilful is the *North British Daily Mail* block of 1898 in Union Street, designed with a heavy-handed classicism by *Clarke & Bell*. (*Sir*) *Owen Williams' Daily Express* (now *Glasgow Herald*) building of 1936 in Albion Street is, with its sheer curtain-walling, one of the city's most distinguished interwar buildings, a close relative of the paper's works in Fleet Street and Manchester. By comparison, the colour printing extension of 1986–8 by *Frank Burnet Bell & Partners* is neat but bland, though not as anonymous as the *Daily Record*'s slab of *c*. 1970 on Anderston Quay.

Among general printing works, one or two look far from non-detailed Glasgow-Style exercise of 1901–3 by *D. B. Dobson*, with, inside, wonderful stained glass by *W. G. Morton*. The Kelvinbridge Artistic Stationery Works in Herbert Street (1898, by *Thomson, Turnbull & Peacock*) nicely shows the influence of the Arts and Crafts movement; and McCorquodales' extensive premises in Howard Street and Maxwell Street incorporate some workmanlike Thomsonesque frontages of 1868.

ROAD TRANSPORT gave rise to a number of significant and specifically designed buildings (as well as bridges and tunnels, which are dealt with below; *see* Crossings of the Clyde and Kelvin). Earliest are the two remaining tollhouses; an unusual circular one of *c*. 1820 in Pollokshaws Road and a bow-fronted example in Dalmarnock Road. Of the great stable establishments which were built between 1850 and 1914, four notable ones are left. Architecturally the best is Wylie & Lochead's vast block of livery stables of 1870–3 in Kent Road. Carting stables are represented by the former Wordie & Co.'s in West Street (1895); by the Clyde Shipping Co.'s former stables in Carlton Court (c. 1895); and by the striking red brick Glasgow & South-Western Railway building of c. 1900 in Bell Street. Until converted to offices and flats, the last two still had the open ramps and galleries which took horses to the upper levels.

From the early 1900s, motor vehicles were provided with covered garages in which they could be both maintained and housed. As this habit died out, most of these garages went or were adapted for other purposes. Two remarkable survivors are the early and fine Botanic Gardens Garage of c. 1906–11 in Vinicombe Street, Hillhead, with its faience frontage and refined iron-framed interior, and the huge reinforced concrete garage designed in 1938 by *Thomson, Sandilands & McLeod* for Road Transports Co. (Glasgow) Ltd on the Broomielaw, to accommodate both lorries and their drivers.

Two of the three CANALS which were constructed to serve Glasgow have left no significant monuments. The Glasgow, Paisley and Ardrossan Canal, opened in 1811, was converted to a railway in the mid-1880s, and the Monkland Canal, opened in stages from 1773 to 1790, became a motorway in the 1970s, although fragments of its Cuilhill Coal Basin (c. 1843) survive just inside Glasgow's eastern boundary near Baillieston. Most of the 'Cut of Junction' between the Monkland and the Forth and Clyde Canal has also been obliterated by road construction, but much of the Forth and Clyde Canal survives. As well as the canalside structures, built for industries attracted by ease of bulk transport, there are five significant aqueducts, locks, and an intriguing range of bridges over this canal. The biggest of the aqueducts, a superb four-span structure designed by *Robert Whitworth* over the Kelvin at Maryhill, was said to be the largest of its kind in Europe when it was completed in 1790. The earliest are two small single-span viaducts, one of 1777 over the E of Lochburn Road, Maryhill, the other of c. 1790 (now bypassed) at Possil Road. The other three major aqueducts, over Maryhill Road (1881), Bilsland Drive (1879), and Possil Road (c. 1880), are all similar in design, with semicircular arches on either side of massive segmental arches carrying the canal channel; all were part of road improvement schemes. The principal flight of locks on the canal at Maryhill (1787–90), stepping down from the summit level to that of the Kelvin Aqueduct, is still, with its intermediate basins and dry-dock, spectacular canal engineering, although the lock chambers have been somewhat altered by repairs. There is a flight of three locks just beyond the city boundary near Knightswood (1790), and another group at Temple (1790), none of which has operated since the mid-1960s. Happily, at the time of writing the canal is being improved and partly reopened after decades of neglect.

The oldest type of canal bridge in Glasgow is the cast-iron and wooden bascule bridge, necessary to accommodate masted vessels on the Forth and Clyde, a ship canal. The original design was conceived c. 1780, but the three bridges left at Netherton, Port Dundas and Hamiltonhill have all been altered to some extent. The bascule bridge of 1931–2 at Bearsden Road, Anniesland (once electrically operated, but now fixed), dates from a major road improvement in the 1930s. The hand-operated railway swing bridge at Port Dundas was built by the Caledonian Railway during the 1880s when trade was shifting from canal to rail.

Passenger services operated on the canal from its inception, but competition from improving road transport forced the introduction of a better service in 1830. This required the construction of a series of stables at intervals between Glasgow and Falkirk to provide changes of barge horses. The first stage from Port Dundas was at Lambhill, where the stable block still exists, somewhat altered. At North Spiers Wharf, Port Dundas, the little canal office of 1812 has a surprisingly elegant façade.

RAILWAY BUILDINGS AND STRUCTURES are now much less numerous than they were, depredated by the triple assaults of decline, modernization and rationalization. Almost all of the earliest structures have disappeared: the oldest complete examples are now the unusual station at Pollokshaws West, with the adjacent viaduct over the Cart, and an accommodation bridge nearby, all dating from 1847. Earlier, but now much altered and obscured by later extensions, is the long sequence of brick arches which formed the approach to, and the undercroft of, the first Bridge Street Station, opened in 1840 by the Glasgow Paisley Joint Railway. The Queen Street tunnel of 1842 is substantially intact, but with a southern portal dating from the 1870s; the Buchanan Street Tunnel, opened by the Caledonian Railway in 1849, has been blocked at its northern end and largely obscured at its southern.

Of the 1850s, there is the Maryhill viaduct built c. 1858 for the Glasgow Dumbarton and Helensburgh Railway, but almost nothing is left from the 1860s or earlier 1870s. It was in the later 1870s that Glasgow's first modern terminals were built. The grandest of them, St Enoch, built by the Glasgow and South-Western Railway as the terminus of the joint Anglo-Scottish services with the Midland Railway, has gone; but enough remains of the original Central Station of the Caledonian Railway and of Queen Street, the North British Railway's Glasgow terminus, to give some idea of the prosperity and technical achievement of the mid-Victorian years.

Survivals from the 1880s and 1890s are more numerous. Suburban railways were first built during that period; Cathcart, Maxwell Park and Pollokshields West (c. 1894) have charming wooden stations with the then novel island platform layout. More sophisticated stone-built stations are Bridgeton Central of 1897–8, with flanking red sandstone tenements, and the infinitely more sophisticated Kelvinside of 1896, disguised as a villa by *J. J. Burnet*. This, and a wall of Glasgow Green Station (1896), are the only remains of the original buildings of the underground

Glasgow Central Railway, most of which were designed by *Burnet* and by *James Miller*. The circular Glasgow Subway, opened in 1896, had only one station with any style, the diminutively Baronial St Enoch of 1896 by *James Miller*. Also of 69 this period are the giant Bell Street bonded warehouses of the Glasgow & South-Western Railway (already described), the second Bridge Street Station of 1889–90 by *James Miller*, and the first part of the Central Hotel in Gordon Street begun in 1882–4 by *Robert Rowand Anderson* as railway offices. The former St Rollox Works of the Caledonian Railway were also rebuilt in the 1880s.

The last decade of grand-scale British railway building was 1901–10. In Glasgow this was dominated by the completion of the extensive rebuilding (by *Donald A. Matheson* and *James Miller*) of Central Station in 1899–1908, which included a new bridge over the Clyde, an extension to the Central Hotel and new offices in Union Street (1901–3), and transformed Central Station 97 into one of Britain's great railway termini. The Glasgow & South-Western's St Enoch Station was also enlarged between 1897 and 1902, but of this work only the massive steel-arched Union Bridge over the Clyde (*see* Crossings of the Clyde, below) outlived the destruction of the station in 1977.

Another phase of station building began in the 1960s after a long pause. The solidity, and even grandeur, of the pre-1914 stations has gone, but the stations of the rebuilt Argyle Line (Rutherglen–Partick) and of the Underground stations are refreshingly bright and cheerful. But although additions of 1987 to Central Station respect the ingenious designing of the concourse, many fine older railway buildings have been cavalierly demolished.

Glasgow's TRAM SYSTEM (established in 1872) was one of the first in Britain; the part that ran through to Govan (from 1878) was the first urban steam tramway in the world; and the electrified system (operating throughout by 1902) was probably the best in the world long before the First World War. It produced some of the finest tramcars in Britain. The system was run down from 1955 until its final closure in 1962. Of the network of depots, workshops and substations which served the tramways, only a handful survive. There is one depot of the Glasgow Tramway and Omnibus Company in Tobago Street, Calton, built in 1883, in the polychrome brickwork popular at that time; and the ground floor of a similar depot of *c.* 1883 is incorporated in a more modern building in Thurso Street, Partick. When Glasgow Corporation took over the operation of the tramways from the Tramway and Omnibus Company in 1894, a complete set of new depots was built, two of which rather precariously survive: the Springburn Depot in Keppochhill Road (1893–4) and the Coplawhill Depot in Pollokshaws Road and Albert Drive (begun in 1894). All these depots housed the cars on the ground floor, with ramps to the stables above. The Springburn Depot was extended in 1898 by an electricity generating station for the experimental electrification of the Mitchell Street to Springburn route, a pioneering but otherwise insignificant building still standing behind the main depot. The whole network was electrified by 1902, and grew to be one of the largest systems in the United Kingdom, served by a vast network of facilities of which only a handful survive, including the red brick depots for electric cars in Brand Street, Govan (1913–14), and Hawthorn Street, Possilpark (1900). The extensive Coplawhill workshops built in Albert Drive in 1894–1912 are partly demolished, partly used (in 1989) as a public auditorium.

The first of Glasgow's DOCKS was built in the second half of the C19. Until the late C18, the city's first and only harbour was at the Broomielaw on a site now largely overshadowed by the Central Station and King George V Bridges. This sufficed to handle the trade carried in small barges which navigated the shallow River Clyde until the late C18, when commercial pressure forced the deepening of the river. The expansion of the harbour followed, first by forming quays along the river banks and then, as these moved down-river to the point where road transport to the centre became uneconomic, by building docks.

The first of many projected dock schemes actually to be built was the Kingston Dock in 1867, followed by the much larger Stobcross or Queen's Dock in 1878–80, and by the even bigger Prince's Dock in 1894. Further down-river, Rothesay Dock was opened in 1907 for mineral traffic, and in 1931 the King George V Dock was completed, the first of five projected large basins. With the exception of the entrance or canting basin of 1893–7 at Prince's Dock, and the little Yorkhill Basin of c. 1907 at the mouth of the River Kelvin, all the commercial docks within the city have been filled in. Most of the quays, too, have been altered to provide walkways and leisure facilities. Nevertheless, there are surviving features of interest, most pleasing as architecture the two hydraulic pumping stations which served Queen's Dock and Prince's Dock, the former of 1877–8, the latter of 1894. *John Carrick*'s 1877–8 building is elegantly Italianate, dominated by the campanile which housed the hydraulic accumulator. The brick Prince's Dock station has a much more exuberant accumulator tower by *Sir J.J. Burnet*. The Finnieston Crane of 1931 (technically an aptly named titan crane which dominates views of the river) is now almost the last and certainly the largest harbour crane left, though there are privately owned cranes of similar type and larger lifting capacity at Govan Shipyard and at the North British Diesel Engine Works. Undoubtedly the largest dockside buildings are the series of granary buildings at Meadowside (*see* above). At Windmillcroft Quay, Tradeston, is the last early example (dating from the 1860s) of the single-storey brick warehouses, known as transit sheds, which once characterized Glasgow's quaysides and, adjacent to it at Bridge Wharf (Clyde Place), stands one of the most recently built (in 1929), partly as a passenger steamer terminal. The long range of transit sheds at Yorkhill Quay was built *c.* 1907. Less obvious reminders of the city's riverborne trade are the many miles of quay wall with granite copes and cast-iron bollards.

In contrast, one of the largest dockland relics is the group of dry docks (graving docks) at Govan, built between 1869 and 1898 to provide ship repair facilities for vessels using the river, but also, and predominantly, to allow vessels built on the Clyde to be dry-docked before delivery. Each of the three docks was capable of taking the largest ship afloat at that time, and the development of constructional techniques is well illustrated in a series of changes in design ranging from the massive granite walls of No. 1 dock (1869–75) to the mass concrete of No. 3 (1898).

Glasgow's PUBLIC UTILITIES were provided on a scale and with a sense of style equalled in few major cities. Outside the boundaries, the great Loch Katrine Water Supply Scheme (1856–60) was bold in conception, and executed with a real sense of fitness: the intake of Loch Katrine (not on public view); the sluice house at Loch Vennachar, and the gauge basins, reservoirs and filters at Mugdock are all beautifully designed and executed. The duplication of provision between 1882 and 1896 was of the same high standard. The only visible sign in the city of this splendid enterprise is the ornamental Stewart Memorial Fountain of 1871–2 in Kelvingrove Park, which lacks the simplicity and grandeur of the waterworks themselves.

Glasgow as a municipality took over its own water supply in the 1850s to remedy the deficiencies of the privately owned systems. For the same reasons it began making gas in 1869. The larger works of the old companies were retained and modernized, and at Dalmarnock an elegant gas-holder of 1872 survives. All the coal-gas plants have now gone, but some office and store buildings still exist, notably at Provan, the last new works to be commissioned (in 1900). The dominant remains of the coal-gas industry are the gigantic holders at Provan (1900–4) and Temple (1893, 1900), whose monumental quality can redeem earlier impressions of ugliness: indeed the sight of the Provan gas-holders from the Monkland motorway is always dramatic, and in some lights is compelling. At the corner of Blackfriars Street and Walls Street are the former workshops of the Corporation Gas Department (built 1881–1903), and in Virginia Street the remarkably ornate office of the Glasgow Gas Light Company (1867–70, by *Melvin & Leiper*), the last surviving link with the old private companies.

Electricity supply was municipalized in 1890–3. There were at that time two primitive stations, both now gone. The original form of the purpose-built Kelvinside Electricity Generating Station (1892) has been obscured by demolition and addition; and the only other existing generating station – the St Andrew's Works at Eglinton Toll (1899–1900), designed to serve the South Side – was condemned to early closure by the inadequacy of its water supply. Its massive terracotta brick walls and steel-framed roof now enclose the Strathclyde Regional Printing Works. To distribute electricity from the central station, high-tension cables were laid to substations, where the voltage was reduced to a level suitable for individual consumers. The earliest of these were large buildings designed to house the heavy rotary machines

needed to reduce direct current voltage, like those in Osborne
Street (1912) and in Flemington Street, Springburn (1906), both
tall single-storey terracotta brick buildings with round-headed
windows. An unusual example in Haggs Road (1908) was
designed in stone to harmonize with residential development,
and in the city centre, 'architectural' examples exist in Buchanan
Street (1922) and in Virginia Street (1925). Once the National
Grid had been introduced in the 1920s, more compact static
transformers supplanted rotary converters, and substations
became smaller, like that of 1937 in Lauderdale Gardens, Hyndland.

Telephone services were in the hands of private companies
from the 1880s. Glasgow Corporation introduced a service in
competition with them in 1900, but it was short-lived, because
the telephone system was nationalized in 1907. Early Post Office
telephone exchanges survive in Highburgh Road (a fine banded-
stone building, designed by *Leonard Stokes* in 1907 to complement neighbouring tenements) and in Cubie Street (a suave
Edwardian affair of 1910 by *H. M. Office of Works*). Best from
between the wars is the well-proportioned former Bell exchange
of the 1920s in College Street; the Pitt Street exchange of 1937
and 1939 is much duller.

A city of Glasgow's size requires extensive sewage disposal
systems. Until the 1890s, sewage ran into natural watercourses
and thence into the Clyde. Exploiting new techniques of sewage
purification, a system of intercepting sewers was then built on
both sides of the river, with purification works at Dalmarnock,
Dalmuir and Shieldhall. All have been rebuilt since 1945 (Shieldhall is a quite dramatic structure of *c.* 1980 by *Rogerson &
Spence*); but the sewage pumping stations at Partick (1904) and
Kinning Park (1909–10) remain to show comparable architectural
pretensions. The Partick station in Dumbarton Road is fairly
ornate, although it was recently shorn of its fine chimney; but
the Kinning Park station, in Admiral Street, is monumental and
well proportioned.

Glasgow Corporation had a well-developed cleansing system
from the mid-c 19, with horse-drawn vehicles collecting domestic
and industrial refuse. Until the 1880s dry closets were in general
use, and the night soil was collected, mixed with street sweepings
(largely horse manure) and sold to farmers. One of the central
stables of 1896–8 stands in Bell Street. After the watercloset
became general at the end of the c 19, refuse destructors were
built, with exceptionally tall chimneys to carry off the smoke. All
of these early examples have gone, but the Ibrox Destructor, built
in the 1930s, is still in operation. This and the later destructors of
the 1950s and 1960s at Polmadie and Dawsholm (though not
described in the Gazetteer) have a strong and not unattractive
industrial character.

Thirty years ago the dense matrix of buildings in Glasgow
incorporated perhaps fifteen hundred industrial buildings and
complexes. Of those, more than two-thirds have gone. There has
been some new building, mainly of small non-specific factory

units, although until the 1980s this was sadly uninspired. The best of such developments are to be found in the Scottish Development Agency's estates in the East End. The remaining pre-1939 industrial buildings are, in 1989, still declining in number, but the fine quality of many of them is at last being generally recognized. Glasgow's place in history is firmly that of a great industrial city, so it behoves all those planning its future to ensure that the best surviving industrial buildings have a place in it, and that new buildings have a quality that helps to engender a proper pride in Glasgow's continuing industrial enterprises.

FURTHER READING

Until the growth of interest in Victorian and Edwardian architecture in the 1950s and 1960s, only the Cathedral had received much scholarly attention. Then, in the mid-1960s, two influential books appeared. The first was very modest but has remained, through all its editions (the first dated 1965, the most recent 1983), one of the most useful: *Glasgow at a Glance*, edited by A. M. Doak and Andrew McLaren Young, which showed in intelligently captioned photographs the vast array of architecture from medieval to C20 that Glasgow possessed. The second, *Architecture of Glasgow* by Andor Gomme and David Walker, published in 1968, excited enthusiasm with its absorbing descriptions and analyses, backed up by painstaking research, and its dramatic black-and-white photographs of the Victorian and Edwardian buildings on which it concentrated. This book (revised in 1987, showing a cleaner Glasgow in less seductive pictures) is still the most authoritative text.

Unfortunately, since 1968 too many books have recycled the information Gomme and Walker gave, and little new light has been shed on a city that has as many buildings from after 1914 as before it. The most interesting research has dealt with the evolution of the city rather than its architecture and can be found in Andrew Gibbs's *Glasgow: The making of a city* (1983); J. M. Kellett's essay in *Historic Towns* (ed. M. D. Lobel, 1969); M. A. Simpson's on 'The West End of Glasgow' in *Middle Class Housing* (ed. M. A. Simpson and H. Lloyd, 1977); and F. A. Walker's on 'The Glasgow grid' in *Order and Space in Society* (ed. T. A. Markus, 1982). F. A. Worsdall has described the evolution of Glasgow's housing up to the 1960s in *The Tenement: A way of life* (1977). John Hume's *The Industrial Archaeology of Glasgow* (1974) is particularly valuable as an exhaustive record of what stood until swept away by comprehensive development: his essay in this book brings the story up to date. For other, especially C19 books, articles and local periodicals, the extensive bibliography in the 1987 edition of *Architecture of Glasgow* is the most convenient source.

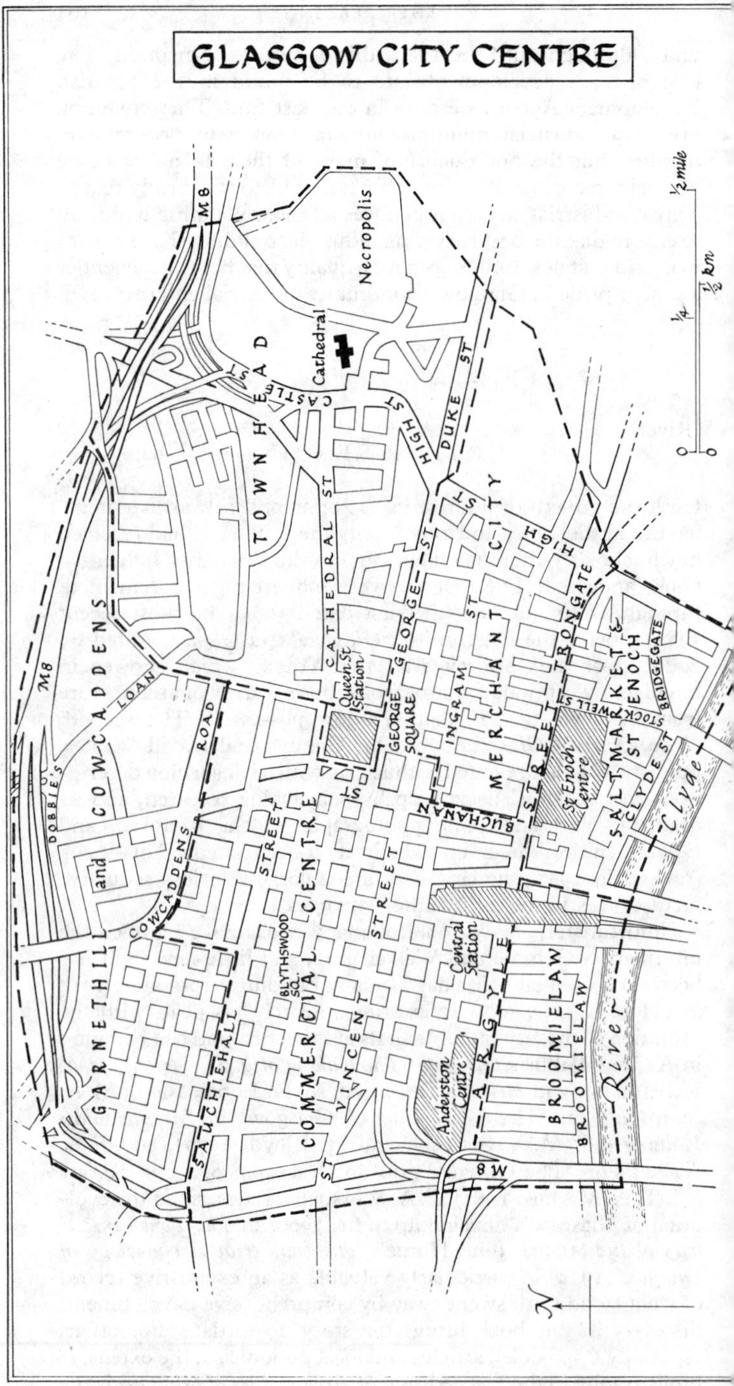

GLASGOW CITY CENTRE

Necropolis

Cathedral

CASTLE HEAD

TOWNHEAD

M8

HIGH ST

DUKE ST

CATHEDRAL ST

Queen St. Station

GEORGE ST

GEORGE SQUARE

INGRAM ST

CITY

MERCHANT

TRONGATE

High

St

St Enoch Centre

S·A·L·T·M·A·R·K·E·T

STOCKWELL ST

CLYDE ST

BRIDGEGATE

ST ENOCH

River Clyde

BUCHANAN STREET

COWCADDENS and

GARNETHILL and

DOBBIE'S LOAN

COWCADDENS ROAD

COWCADDENS

BLYTHSWOOD

STREET

COMMERCIAL CENTRE

ST VINCENT STREET

STREET

SAUCHIEHALL ST

Central Station

Anderston Centre

ARGYLE

BROOMIELAW

BROOMIELAW

M8

½ mile

¼

½ km

0

N

THE CITY CENTRE

INTRODUCTION

The City Centre is clearly defined by the motorway (which on
the N and W forms a barrier as strong as any city wall), by the
River Clyde, and, on the E side, by the less physical boundary
of the essentially medieval route between Cathedral and river.
Within these confines, there are dramatic changes in the topography. On the E side, the steep northern ridge drops abruptly
to the flat river plain; on the W, the land falls from the equally
steep Garnethill to the valley of Sauchiehall Street before rising
into the gentler drumlin of Blythswood Hill above the flat riverside. The buildings and their disposition are just as dramatically
varied. On the NE ridge stand the Cathedral and one prebendal
house (all that remains of the bishop's precinct) amid the 1960s
flats and educational buildings of the thinly redeveloped Townhead. Below lies the cross of medieval streets and their much
expanded wynds with the C19 stamp of the railway and the City
Improvement Trust firmly upon them. Just W of Glasgow Cross
are the long straight streets of the city's first suburb, laid out
along the medieval riggs in the late C17 and the C18 and now
tightly packed with C19 and C20 warehouses. The strict grid of
streets and squares that was begun in the late C18 marches
regardless of the contours over the flat land N and W of this and
over the steep drumlins further W still. Blythswood Hill still has
the terraces of houses that once lined the whole grid – except on
Garnethill, which had villas and tenements. Everywhere else are
taller and grander commercial buildings, mostly Victorian and
Edwardian in the broad commercial spine around the railway
stations, late C20 in the comprehensively redeveloped S W corner.
S of Blythswood, by the Clyde, there is, though this is threatened,
a different pattern with long straight streets of warehouses (probably echoing the old ropewalks) at r. angles to the Broomielaw,
once Glasgow's bustling quayside.

The straggling shape of Glasgow's medieval core, established
by the mid-C16, seems to have resulted from the fusion of two
separate settlements, one by the Clyde, and one around the shrine
of St Kentigern, popularly St Mungo († 612), on the hill N of
it, where the Bishop's Castle was established after the first of
Glasgow's three successive cathedrals was built between 1110
and 1136. A long street joined the upper town with the riverside
settlement, where it met two E–W streets (Gallowgate and Trongate) at Glasgow Cross. The southern settlement grew vigorously

after burghal rights for Glasgow were granted to Bishop Jocelyn by William the Lion between 1175 and 1178 and again after the river was bridged. (The first timber bridge was mentioned in 1285 and rebuilt in stone *c.* 1400.) Just N of Glasgow Cross were the monasteries of Blackfriars (founded 1246) and Greyfriars (1479), and the university, founded in 1451 and built between 1460 and 1475. Fire swept through the area around the Cross in 1652 and 1677, and thereafter the tall tenements with uniform stone fronts that impressed so many travellers rose along the main streets. Defoe, in 1726, found these streets 'the fairest for breadth, and the finest built that I have ever seen in one city together...'.

A few new straight streets had been laid out in the C16 and C17, but development was accelerated during the C18 by great increases in the tobacco, sugar and cotton trades, particularly after the Clyde was made navigable up to Broomielaw in 1770–1 and the Forth and Clyde and the Monklands canals were completed in the 1780s. The mansions and gardens, then only recently built beyond the West Port, were swept away by speculators who developed what by the 1790s was known as Glasgow's 'New Town' (now dubbed 'the Merchant City'). Between 1750 and 1790 all the streets W of High Street and Saltmarket, as far W as Jamaica Street and Buchanan Street and as far N as Ingram Street, were laid out piecemeal following the lines of the long medieval plots or riggs, but they were not built up until the early C19, by which time industry had infiltrated. Only a scattering of contemporary houses or warehouses survives, but churches and public buildings still close the vistas down the long straight streets magnificently. (For the C18 development E of Saltmarket, *see* Calton.)

The almost relentless grid of streets that covers the rest of the City Centre seems to have been initiated by *James Barry*, who in 1772 drew up a layout of the Town Council's Ramshorn lands (just N of Ingram Street). This was Glasgow's first attempt at planned growth, late by London standards but only some five years after James Craig's plans for Edinburgh's New Town. The Council did not proceed until 1782 with the grid of streets focused on a large square, inspired no doubt by Barry's plan of 1781. From 1800 the grid spread across the Corporation's adjacent Meadowflat lands and the Campbells' Blythswood estate further W, probably according to two separate but harmonious plans of 1792, by *James Craig*. Each had a grid of streets lined east-to-west with individually designed terraces of houses. By 1840 there were terraces as far W as Blythswood Square on the top of Blythswood Hill (where they survive in reasonable concentration), but building continued until the 1860s. In the 1820s the grid was extended S of St Vincent Street to a plan by *James Gillespie Graham* and N over Garnethill, where villas and, later, superior tenements were built instead of terraces. S of Blythswood, by the river, the long streets were built up as far W as the village of Anderston, first with houses *c.* 1820 and then with warehouses to store the goods unloaded at the Broomielaw.

NE of Garnethill, round the canals, industry and the associated artisan housing took a strong foothold.

As a result of this industrial success and the opening of the railways, the City Centre E of Blythswood Hill was mostly rebuilt between 1845 and 1914. Many buildings of the first three decades were warehouses, surprisingly opulent and built in particular concentration in the streets between the railway stations. The smartest retail ones were in Argyle Street, Buchanan Street and Sauchiehall Street, which today are still the principal shopping streets. Just W and S of George Square, banks and offices replaced houses, and in George Square itself the residential terraces gave way to commercial buildings in the 1870s, and then in the 1880s to the civic grandeur of *William Young*'s City Chambers.

In the second half of the C19 attention was again focused on what had been the medieval town, by then decayed into teeming slums. Glasgow University moved to Gilmorehill in the 1860s, and railway yards were created on its site in High Street. What remained of the old town after that (mostly C16 and C17 buildings), from the Cathedral to the river, was replaced by tenements and warehouses under the auspices of the City Improvement Trust, founded in 1866, and the roads and wynds (some already improved in the C18) were widened and realigned.

It was the ring road, begun in the early 1960s, which gave the City Centre its unnatural isolation from the industrial area to the N and SW and from the smart West End, disconnecting the roads, like Bath Street, Sauchiehall Street and Argyle Street, that linked them. The ring road (envisaged by the City Engineer in 1946, together with the entire rebuilding of the City Centre with high-rise slabs) brought in its wake a fortunately limited amount of comprehensive redevelopment: in the SW quarter, which was given over to the Anderston Cross megastructure of offices and flats and to office blocks and hotels; and in Townhead and Cowcaddens, where simple tenements were replaced by an enclave of educational buildings and high-rise housing. The Broomielaw is the latest subject for redevelopment, subject in 1989 to plans for the currently fashionable 'mixed use'.

The centre falls into seven manageable segments, which bear some relationship to historical development but more to the conceptions of post-World War II planners:

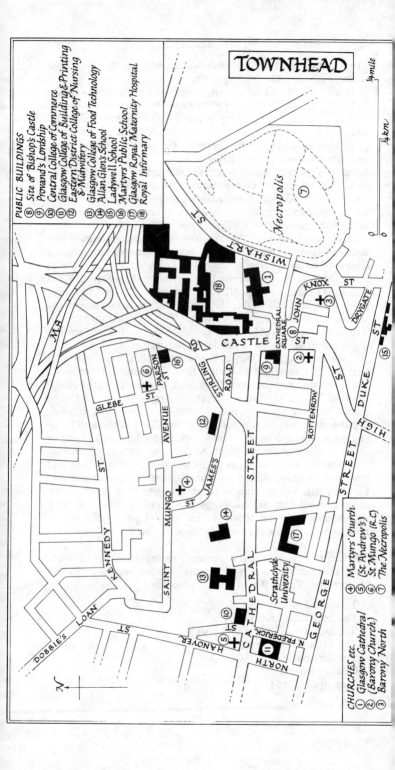

TOWNHEAD

PUBLIC BUILDINGS
⑧ Site of Bishop's Castle
⑨ Provand's Lordship
⑩ Central College of Commerce
⑪ Glasgow College of Building & Printing
⑫ Eastern District College of Nursing
   & Midwifery
⑬ Glasgow College of Food Technology
⑭ Allan Glen's School
⑮ Ladywell School
⑯ Martyrs' Public School
⑰ Glasgow Royal Maternity Hospital
⑱ Royal Infirmary

CHURCHES etc.
① Glasgow Cathedral
② (Barony Church)
③ Barony North
④ Martyrs' Church
   (St Andrew's)
⑤ St Mungo (R.C.)
⑥ St Mungo
⑦ The Necropolis

¼ mile
¼ km

TOWNHEAD

Glasgow Cathedral boasts as fine a hillside site as many other
European cathedrals, a naturally defended position above the
Molendinar Burn chosen, as tradition has it, by St Kentigern in
the late C6 for his monastery. It has, however (and this comes as
a shock to most visitors), no venerable medieval surroundings at
all; they were razed by the 'improvements' of the C18, C19 and
C20. Though placed high, the Cathedral stands as if accidentally
pushed aside. It was the Bishop's Castle that dominated the 9
crown of the hill, that temporal and ecclesiastical seat of the
bishops of Glasgow (archbishops after 1488), who not only ruled
the burgh of Glasgow by right of a charter issued in 1176 or 1178
by William the Lion, but dominated Scotland from Skye to
Carlisle and were rivalled only by the bishops of St Andrews.
Around it, by the time the Cathedral was completed in the C15,
stood St Nicholas's Hospital and thirty-two prebendal houses
(increased by Bishop Cameron (1426–66) from the original six).
It takes a feat of imagination now to conjure all this when nothing
remains other than the Cathedral and a single prebendal house,
Provand's Lordship.   10

Three streets fanned out S of this precinct; Drygate (now
obliterated) led E, High Street very steeply SW, and Rottenrow
(mostly gone) W along the top of the ridge. In 1789–92 *Robert
Adam*'s Infirmary (itself replaced a century later) took the place
of the Bishop's Castle, in 1792 the Bridewell was built at the foot
of Drygate, and in 1833 Scotland's first 'hygienic' cemetery, the
magnificent Necropolis, opened on the hill on the far side of the
Molendinar Burn. High Street (this part was known as Bell o'
the Brae) still had low thatched cottages until the late C19, when
the City Improvement Trust replaced them with a picturesque
curve of tenements, but the rest of the district, especially to the
N and W, had been built up with ordinary tenements for workers
in the many local industries encouraged by the canal and the two
big railway depots.

Nearly all of this went in the 1960s as a comprehensive development scheme replaced tenements and industry with housing and
an educational campus including Strathclyde University. The
density is low, the traffic routes tyrannical and the majority of the
buildings uninspiring. *Mackintosh*'s Martyrs' School, stranded
above the main road with only St Mungo's Church as a
companion, once belonged to the densely tenemented area that
stretched north to Royston (*q.v.*), where Townhead Parish
Church and Public Library stand.

Various attempts have been made to show the Cathedral to
better advantage. The development proposed in 1987 by *Page &
Park, Ian White Associates* and *Ian Begg* (to be completed in
1990) seems on paper to be a sadly misjudged mixture of the
formal (with bold approaches to the W front of the Cathedral,
not its best aspect) and a picturesque re-creation of an earlier
street pattern, with a stolid Scottish Baronial visitors' centre
along what little remains of Castle Street to recall the Bishop's

Castle and tenement blocks along John Knox Street. Surely more could be made of that powerful trio of silhouettes – the Infirmary, the Cathedral and the Necropolis.

GLASGOW CATHEDRAL

BY RICHARD FAWCETT

CHRONOLOGY

Glasgow's early diocesan history is bound up with the figure of St Kentigern (or Mungo); but, apart from a reference in the *Annales Cambriae* to his death in 612, all that is recorded of him comes from accounts written in the C 12. The lives composed for Bishops Herbert (1147–64) and Jocelyn (1174–99) apparently relied on sources no earlier than the previous century, and there is a disconcerting lack of the early artefacts which might reason-ably be expected from such a venerable site. Nevertheless the tradition of Kentigern as the first bishop of an area corresponding to the British kingdom of Strathclyde and based on Glasgow appears inherently acceptable, although the attempt to establish continuity with earlier Christian history in the area by placing his church within a graveyard consecrated by Ninian is less so.

Bishops begin to appear on record again in the mid-C 11, although the first three are likely to have been suffragans of York, having no active connexion with Glasgow. Re-establishment of the diocese must be attributed to Earl David (the future David I), who made his erstwhile tutor, John, bishop. Despite much of John's energy being spent in furthering David's policy for a Scottish church autonomous of York, the *Melrose Chronicle* records the consecration of a cathedral in 1136.

This first cathedral, on analogy with what little we know of other Scottish cathedrals of the early C 12, and on the basis of a single painted voussoir which may have belonged to it, is unlikely to have been of any great architectural complexity – however richly painted it may have been. But by 1181 the *Melrose Chron-icle* says that Bishop Jocelyn was gloriously enlarging the build-ing. This was probably in the form of a cruciform extension around the high altar at the main level and Kentigern's tomb in the crypt below it. Work was interrupted by a fire, but enough was completed by 1197 for a consecration to be performed.

Jocelyn's death in 1199 was followed by a series of elections of bishops who can have had little opportunity for building. When work was eventually recommenced – in the earlier decades of the C 13, on the architectural evidence – a modified plan was adopted which must have necessitated the destruction of some of the masonry by then existing. In this modified plan there appear to have been aisles rather than salient chapels flanking the pres-bytery, and non-projecting transepts were planned in the position in which they were eventually built about a half-century later.

At the same time a nave to the existing plan was laid out. But this was a period of rapidly changing architectural and liturgical ideas, and the new work cannot have risen to any great height before Bishop William Bondington (1233–58) in turn abandoned the work then in hand in order to build a very much longer eastern limb.

In the three forms to which the eastern limb appears to have been successively set out between the 1130s and the early C 13, it is doubtful if more than the presbytery at the upper level and the tomb site below, along with flanking chapels, were accommodated; in each case the choir of the clergy was probably intended to be largely within the E part of the nave. It was perhaps the progressive expansion of the complement of secular canons serving the Cathedral, and the prospect of the eventual adoption of a constitution based on that of Sarum in 1258, which made an architecturally distinct choir on the newer English pattern a more attractive proposition to Bondington.

Building of the extended E limb was underway by Lent of 1242, when the faithful were exhorted to contribute to the work. Incorporating an extended crypt of outstanding architectural quality, it was also provided with a two-storeyed chapter house at the NE corner. As something of an afterthought a treasury and sacristy block was added on the N side of the choir, and a southward-projecting lateral aisle was appended against the lower parts of the S transept wall which had already been built in the early C 13. Work on the transepts themselves followed the choir, and was probably nearing completion by 1277, when the Lord of Luss provided timber for the bell tower and treasury, according to the Glasgow *Registrum*. There seems no reason to doubt that construction of the nave followed immediately, although its completion may have been delayed by the outbreak of war with England at the end of the century. Certainly Bishop Robert Wishart (1271–1316) was accused of making siege engines from timber provided for the building, suggesting the work was not complete before the start of hostilities.

The place of the asymmetrical western towers in this chronology is uncertain, since they were destroyed in 1846 and 1848, before sufficiently detailed records of them were made. Archbishop Eyre, in his essay on the towers in *The Book of Glasgow Cathedral* (1898), states that, during the demolition, evidence was observed that the N aisle had had a window pre-dating the tower on that side. Nevertheless, the N tower appears to have been started within the C 13, from what we know of its details, although its superstructure may well be later. The squat S tower, however, appears to have been a late addition, and excavations made in 1988 suggested that it might be of the C 15.

By the end of the C13 the building was substantially complete, although extensive repairs and rebuilding were to be needed after damage by lightning *c*. 1406, according to a letter of Benedict XIII to Bishop Matthew de Glendenning (1387–1408). The progress of the repairs is well mapped by heraldry. Bishop William de Lauder (1408–25/6) started reconstruction of the

chapter house and rebuilt the central tower; Bishop John
Cameron (1426–46) completed its stone spire and continued
reconstruction of the chapter house; and this latter operation was
completed by Bishop William Turnbull (1447–54). There was
presumably a reordering of the choir when the internal structural
work was largely complete, and in 1420 papal permission was
sought to move Kentigern's relics into a shrine of gold or silver.

Once rebuilding was finished works were largely confined to
the effort of containing structural defects, such as settlement in
the choir aisles, and adding new fixtures and furnishings. Robert
Blackadder (1483–1508), who in 1492 became Glasgow's first
archbishop, was an especially active prelate, and amongst his
benefactions was the vaulting of the transeptal aisle, which has
been generally attributed solely to him. He also is known to
have provided canopies for the canons' choir stalls, and to have
endowed additional altars.

Post-Reformation works

After the Reformation of 1560 the Cathedral was progressively
adapted for reformed worship, a process which, whilst not
invariably accomplished with the highest delicacy, at least meant
that Glasgow, alone among the mainland cathedrals, survived
virtually intact. By 1635 at the latest the choir had been walled
off for the Inner Kirk congregation which had worshipped in it
since the Reformation; in 1647 the five western bays of the nave
were also walled off, for the Outer Kirk congregation, in existence
since 1587. Galleries were placed in the aisles of these parts in
1657 and 1647 respectively. Since 1595 a third congregation, that
of the Barony, had been housed in the crypt, possibly per-
petuating a medieval parochial usage.

A view that the Cathedral should be treated with greater
respect emerged in the early c 19. In 1805 *William Stark* was
refitting and remodelling the choir, and in 1812 *David Hamilton*
made improvements to the nave, whilst *John Herbertson* provided
new seats. From the early 1830s growing alarm about structural
defects, coupled with increased appreciation of the Cathedral's
architectural merits, led to a movement for wholesale restoration.
In 1833 Archibald McLellan published a plea for action, and in
the following year *George Meikle Kemp* prepared drawings for
ambitious and rather extraordinary augmentations, including
new w towers and enlarged transepts. Some jockeying for position followed, in which *James Gillespie Graham* made an attempt
to secure the job with further designs, whose more scholarly
nature may have owed something to the influence of A. W. N.
Pugin. Both designs were published in a report by J. Cleland in
1836, which led to acrimonious exchanges.

One regrettable area of general agreement which did emerge
was over the unacceptability of the irregular western towers, and
in 1846 and 1848, in the expectation that they would be rebuilt
to Gillespie Graham's designs, they were demolished in cavalier
fashion. Soon afterwards it became apparent that funds would

not be found, and the present inadequate W front was cobbled together by *Edward Blore* as part of the general programme of repairs. Blore was working on behalf of the government, since it had come to be recognized that the Act of Annexation of 1587 and the final abolition of episcopacy in 1689 had left the Crown in technical ownership of the building. Reinstatement of the interior as an extension of the same operation had been rendered more feasible with the construction of a new building for the Outer Kirk in 1835, leaving a single congregation within the cathedral (a new church for the Barony congregation had already been provided *c.* 1798). In 1852 the galleries within the choir were removed – albeit leaving the piers dreadfully damaged. Much of the process of restoration was directed by the government's Clerks of Works, *William Nixon* and *Robert Matheson*, but both Edward Blore and *William Burn* were extensively consulted.

Brief reference must be made here to the glazing of the Cathedral as part of the mid-C19 restoration process. After many of the crypt windows had been filled by various artists, a committee (in which *Charles Heath Wilson* played a prominent part) was formed to discuss a more unified scheme for the rest of the building. Against considerable opposition, the Royal Establishment of Glasspainting at Munich, under the leadership of *Maximilian Ainmüller*, was commissioned to undertake the work, which was executed largely between 1859 and 1864. Decay of the painted detail and changing taste – together with a degree of xenophobia – soon left the glass with few admirers, although a longer perspective allows the modern eye to appreciate its qualities. In the 1930s it was decided that the glass should be removed and replaced by modern work, but it was not until after the Second World War that large-scale replacement became possible. The only figurative panels of the Munich glass still in place are in the E clearstoreys of the transepts, but the heraldic achievements from many of the nave windows have been reset in modern clear glass.

The last major operation of structural significance was the replacement of the greater part of the roofing between 1909 and 1912 by *W. T. Oldrieve*. The consequent extensive destruction of original timber was a cause of concern, but in the process evidence seems to have been found for earlier states of the choir roof (see Peter MacGregor Chalmers' volume in Bell's Cathedral series, 1914), although little record was made of these findings. The green colour of the copper roofing provided at that time is not a happy element in the Cathedral's external appearance.

ASSESSMENT

Glasgow Cathedral has a complicated architectural history, in which building campaigns were instigated and superseded in startlingly quick succession. But it is as a strikingly complete and homogeneous building of the mid- and later C13 that it must now be seen. (Only a later C12 fragment in the crypt, the early

C 13 lower walling at the W end of the crypt and along the transepts and nave, together with the C 15 central tower and its spire, impinge significantly on this unity.) As such it is now the most important building of its period surviving in Scotland, which in general has suffered such a disproportionate loss of its medieval ecclesiastical architecture.

The details and planning of the Cathedral vividly illustrate that when it was built there was still a free exchange of architectural ideas between Lowland Scotland and Northern England. Nevertheless, Glasgow is in no sense a derivative building dependent purely on English prototypes. The sophistication of the spatial modelling in the crypt, in particular, is of outstandingly high quality and without obvious contemporary parallels in Northern England. A degree of Scotticism that is of significance for the future is seen in the preference for arcade piers of comfortingly solid profile, as earlier at Holyrood. This is despite the fact that the choir carries no high vault, and that one of the ultimate models for the choir design – Lincoln – had been particularly adventurous in the slimness of its piers. One other fascination of the choir is the range of plate tracery to be found in the aisle windows, since so little of such tracery now survives in either Scotland or England.

The nave design has received less critical acclaim than the choir, and some puzzlement has been shown over its date – for which there is no documentation. However, regarded as a late C 13 attempt to reconcile, on the one hand, the tight pier rhythm dictated by existing wall-shafts in the outer wall and, on the other, changed ideas for church interiors, it must be seen as a more successful piece of design than is generally allowed. Despite the early model of St David's Cathedral in Wales for linkage of triforium and clearstorey, the revived C 13 northern interest in reducing the impact of the middle storey, as at Southwell and York, makes it fully acceptable to place it within the later decades of that century. Such a date receives corroboration from the tracery types employed.

THE PLAN

The most striking feature of the plan is the contrast between the strict rectangular containment of the main mass and the almost randomly accretive relationship of the ancillary structures around that mass. Within the main body the simplest elements are the transepts and nave. The former, whilst rising to the same height as the nave, do not project beyond its aisles, and the consequent compression of space concentrates attention, to great advantage, on the dramatic flights of steps leading up into the choir at the centre, and down into the crypt on either side. The nave is an aisled space of eight bays. To the W of the nave the asymmetrical towers were joined to the main body only by their E walls, and thus projected fully to the W. Prominently salient towers – either singly or in pairs – were to be relatively common in Scotland, as at Holyrood and Dunkeld, although the canyon-like space between Glasgow's towers has no precise parallels. The N tower was used as a consistory house in the Middle Ages, and the S was a library.

Even more unusual was the so-called Blackadder Aisle, stretching out four bays from the S transept, for which the only known Scottish counterpart was an abortive C13 scheme for a lateral arm at Iona. No more than the crypt of this feature at Glasgow was completed, but it seems improbable that its main storey was intended to rise higher than the aisles of choir and nave. It is possible that the aisle was intended to cover the burial place of Fergus, whose hearse Kentigern is said to have followed to Glasgow.

Within the eastern limb the rectangular space was more elaborately articulated than in the nave. To the E of an aisled five-bay space, which served as canons' choir, presbytery and feretory, a rectangular ambulatory was returned, with four chapels off its E side. Such a plan type had been evolved by the Cistercians as a simple means of housing a large number of altars (possibly used previously in Scotland at Newbattle, see Buildings of Scotland, Lothian), but it is best explained in a secular cathedral as a relatively economical means of providing circulation for pilgrims to a feretory behind the high altar. Certainly, references to offerings by Edward I in 1301 indicate the presence by then of both a tomb in the crypt and a separate feretory near the high altar. The choice of choir plan in turn dictated the main dispositions of the crypt. But within this matrix the lower space was magnificently manipulated to provide twin points of focus on the tomb site towards the W end and on the Lady Chapel to its E; the positioning of the latter in the crypt shows the importance accorded to this level.

Two ancillary structures were placed off the N of the choir. Projecting fully to the N and partly to the E of the NE ambulatory chapel was the two-storeyed chapter house. Whilst its double height appears never to have been imitated, its square centralized plan may have been the prototype of many others, e.g. at Crossraguel, Jedburgh and Glenluce. The second of these ancillary structures housed the sacristy and treasury, and abutted the W bay of the N aisle. The sacristy on the upper storey, which had been destroyed by the 1830s, was entered directly from the choir aisle, whilst the treasury below, for reasons of security, could only be reached by a mural stair. (The existing external and internal doors into it are modern.) A two-storeyed block to house these functions was to become a relatively common appendage of major Scottish churches, as at Arbroath and Dunkeld, or in more elongated form at Dunblane and Fortrose. But the necessity for a crypt at Glasgow fostered an exceptional arrangement in which it was the treasury which was at the lower level.

EXTERIOR

At Glasgow it is particularly illuminating to start a tour of the Cathedral by examining the basecourses, although the

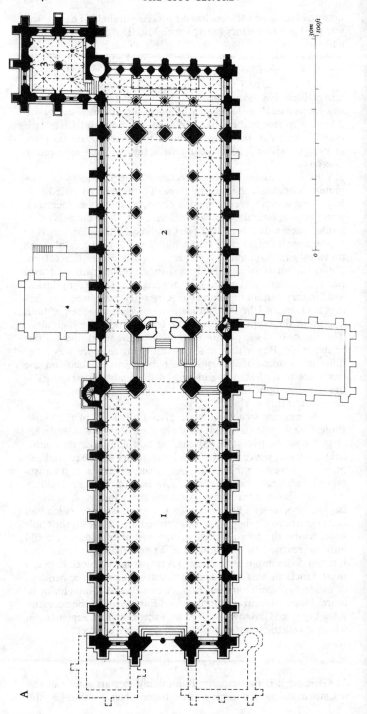

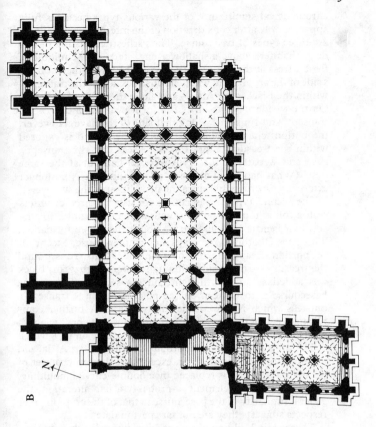

B

N

A upper church
B lower church

1 nave
2 choir
3 sacristy
4 crypt
5 chapter house
6 Blackadder Aisle

(Redrawn from measured drawings
by Geo. S. Hill)

chronological significance of the various types becomes fully apparent only after consideration of the internal details. There are three types of basecourse. The earliest, consisting of two deep chamfers above a shallower one, starts in the middle of the buttress at the centre of the second bay from the W on the S side of the crypt, from where it runs back across the transept – within the Blackadder Aisle – and along the S side of the nave. On the N side it starts in its full form near the E end of the transept, and runs back along that side of the nave. However, the bottom chamfer alone extends further E and is exposed within the treasury. From this it is clear that the transepts, nave and W parts of the crypt were all laid out at the same time. (What happened at the W end of the nave is no longer externally ascertainable since the demolition of the W towers.)

The second type of basecourse consists of three chamfers with a roll at top and bottom, with a smaller chamfer for the sub-base, and a beak-like string above the whole formation. This runs all around the crypt and chapter house, except for the portion already referred to on the S side. It also runs around the treasury on the N side, although it appears that this block was added as an afterthought, since a section of the same basecourse is to be seen on the portion of the N transept E buttress which is now inside the treasury. (A further complication is that this same buttress also appears to have a length of the bottom chamfer of the earlier basecourse on its E face.)

The third basecourse runs around the Blackadder Aisle, and is similar to that of the crypt, except that the top chamfer of the main formation is replaced by a double-curved moulding. Although this last element is probably a late alteration, the general similarity of the basecourse to that of the crypt in other respects suggests they are not far apart in date.

Three main building phases are thus immediately apparent, and all are of the C 13, as will become clear internally. (It may be added that a double-curved moulding for a plinth, as on the Blackadder Aisle, is not inconceivable in the mid-C 13, since a similar detail is found on the C 13 basement of the tower at Brechin Cathedral; but, on balance, at Glasgow it appears more likely to be a later modification.) The late C 12 operations of Bishop Jocelyn are not represented externally, although it is presumably the survival of the one internal relic of them behind the third buttress from the W on the S which results in the curious mid-buttress basecourse change at that point.

CHOIR. The stepped massing of the eastern limb of Glasgow Cathedral is one of its most memorable aspects, and the extra height afforded by the crypt adds so greatly to the effect that it may be doubted if any of the other variants on the square ambulatory type can have offered such drama. This, at least, is more than adequate compensation for the undeniable disappointment of the first sight of *Blore*'s W front at the other end of the building.

The finest view of the choir is from the E. At the lower levels are two ranks of paired lancets per bay, lighting the two levels of chapels at crypt and main choir levels. In the crypt the two central pairs of lancets are linked by containing arches, reflecting the fact that it is only in these bays that the vaults do not have an intermediate mid-bay intersection. The bays are strongly marked by buttresses, which have broadly chamfered angles at the upper level.

Rising to the same height as the choir aisle is the two-storeyed chapter house, although the difference of floor levels within this block is marked by the squatter windows of the lower level. The major C 15 reconstruction of the chapter house is indicated at crypt level by no more than the recutting of the bases of the window reveals, but at the upper level the windows are entirely rebuilt, with simpler mouldings, flatter arch heads and rectangular daylight openings. Responsibility for this reconstruction is denoted heraldically on the w face, where the arms of Bishop Lauder (1408–25/6) are at the lower level and those of Bishop Turnbull (1447–54) at the upper. A curious feature of the remodelled upper level is the stepping of the buttress-head weathering; this may have reflected some feature of the rebuilt roof, but, if so, further reconstruction of the roof within crowstepped gables by Archbishop Law (1615–31) has left no trace of this. (Law's initials are said to have been on the roof ridge.)

The roof above the chapels and ambulatory has also been altered on at least two occasions, the present flattened form being probably attributable to *William Stark* in 1805. The roof he replaced may have been of the same vintage as that now over the chapter house, since it is shown in Slezer's *Theatrum Scotiae* (1693) as having crowstepped single-pitch gables. The medieval form of the roof is now unascertainable, although it seems likely that the lowest portion of the lancets in the eastern gable must have been externally built up to a higher level than is now the case, to allow the abuttal of a roof. The gable of the main body of the choir has also been modified, since Slezer depicts higher flat-topped lateral sections which may have been intended to carry more substantial pinnacles than the C 19 ones now there. Nevertheless, all these changes cannot detract from the magnificence of the quadruplet of lancets which pierces this gable.

There is greater variety of treatment along the flanks of the choir than at its E end. At crypt level the aisles have intermediate buttresses, corresponding to the additional arcade piers inside, and most of the half-bays are lit by single lancets embellished by finely moulded reveals with engaged shafts. The exceptions are the wider bays at the ends of the ambulatory, which have paired lancets, and the w one-and-a-half bays on each side. On the s side, the reason for the differences at the w end is that the masonry at this point, as indicated by the basecourse, is of the early C 13 campaign, although the two windows within it are evidently considerably restored. On the N side the bays are blank because of the abuttal of the truncated treasury, a structure which is now largely modern externally.

In the fourth bay from the W on each side a small doorway was provided to give access to the Lady Chapel. With blind arches on the flanking buttresses, and well-detailed stiffleaf caps to the door shafts, these entrances further emphasize the importance of the crypt. That on the S is covered by a porch between the buttresses.

At the level of the choir aisles the windows are treated yet more ambitiously. Lighting the ambulatory ends and the SE chapel are plate-traceried two-light windows. Lighting the aisles proper are some of the most extraordinary and inventive examples of three-light plate tracery to survive anywhere in Britain. There are no precise parallels for them, although the triforium openings in the nave of Lincoln are perhaps as close as anything now to be seen. The windows of the N flank are especially intriguing for the sloping engaged shafts to either side of some of the tracery lights. In the W bay on the N, the window is largely rebuilt, since it was here that the sacristy was adjoined; the area of modern masonry under the sill shows the position of its doorway, which is also recorded in some detail in one of Blore's measured drawings. On the S, the second window from the W is a four-light bar-traceried opening of the standard Westminster chapter-house type; it was presumably placed here at the time of the transept construction, perhaps suggesting this bay had been left open for access until then.

At clearstorey height there are groups of three lancets in each bay except the W, where there are only two. The flatter arches of these lights, along with the simpler chamfered reveals, are clearly some decades later than the lancets of the crypt.

BLACKADDER AISLE. This projection from the S transept is of four by two bays. Its chronological relationship with the rest of the building is not immediately apparent because it is not coursed with the early C 13 masonry of the lower part of the transept, which it abuts. The arms of Archbishop Blackadder (1483–1508) on a tabernacle corbel on the upper part of the W face and on the central buttress of the S face have led to general acceptance of his responsibility for its entire construction. However, the masonry of which the heraldic corbel forms a part seems to be secondary, since it is irregularly bonded with the adjacent masonry; and the arms on the S face appear to be cut into existing masonry. Beyond this, most of the moulded detail of the aisle is more consistent with a mid-C 13 rather than a late C 15 date. The similarity of the basecourse to that of the eastern limb has already been mentioned, and it will be seen that the window reveals, of the E face in particular, are closely similar to those of the choir crypt, although the windows themselves have probably been modified at a later stage.

Thus it is likely that the aisle was started, but left unfinished, by the same master mason who built the choir; and the one fragmentary window reveal of the aborted upper storey, on the W side, would also seem to be his. Blackadder's contribution was therefore largely confined to the vaulting of the aisle, and the minimal remodelling of the plinth and windows externally. Rather more enigmatic are the carvings above the windows, whose date and significance are open to question. Those still identifiable are: on the E face from N to S, Adam and Eve, a leopard, a camel and a dragon; on the S face, a centaur; on the W face from N to S, a unicorn and a wyvern.

TRANSEPTS. The position of the non-projecting transepts was defined in the early C13 campaign on the evidence of the basecourse, with provision for strengthened buttresses which was laid out at this point. But the main body of each of the transepts, which are distinguished by fine bar-traceried windows, is unlikely to be much before the 1270s. The earliest documented Scottish examples of such tracery, at Sweetheart Abbey and Elgin Cathedral, are of that decade, and such a date accords well with the agreement over timber for the bell tower and treasury of 1277.

Collie's engraved elevations of 1835 and *Blore*'s own surviving drawings show that the latter must have considerably embellished the transept windows, although the basic forms are authentic. On the S side, two two-light windows at aisle level indicate that all idea of building the upper storey of the Blackadder Aisle had been abandoned by that stage. Above these a splendid five-light window rises through triforium and clearstorey levels and up into the roof space, with a transom at the level of the clearstorey base string. With paired lancets and an oculus in the flanking sub-arches, and a larger oculus above the single central light, this window is essentially similar to the E window of Sweetheart, although now enriched by a plethora of modern trefoils.

Rather less effort was taken over the corresponding great window of the N transept, which is related to windows on the N side of the nave. Here there are six lights grouped in two triplets reaching up to the sub-arch heads, with an oculus below the apex.

TOWER AND SPIRE. These were rebuilt by Bishops Lauder and Cameron, whose episcopates extended from 1408 to 1446. The former's arms are on the tower parapet. The tower rises only a single storey above the crossing and is pierced by four lights of equal height on each face. This formula, redolent of, e.g., the Romanesque tower of Winchester, was to be adapted for use elsewhere in late medieval Scotland, as in the three-light variant in the tower at Haddington. The spire, which rises to about 67 m (220 ft) above the floor level of the crossing, is relatively unusual in Scotland for being of broached rather than splay-foot form. Pinnacles rise from the broaches, and crested bands divide the spire into three stages, although there are four levels of lucarne windows. The present termination of the spire is probably due to mid-C18 repairs by *Mungo Naismith* after lightning damage.

NAVE. As in the transepts, the early C13 basecourse dictated the basic plan and buttress rhythm of the nave, although the main brunt of construction was postponed to the last decades of that century. Simpler buttresses along the N side, and in the W bay on the S, may suggest that these parts had been built up to a greater height than the rest in the first campaign; but this is by no means certain, since the N side is generally treated more simply than the S in other respects too. The N aisle, for example, has simple three-light windows with all lights reaching up to the main arch, whereas the S aisle has groups of three uncontained trefoils in the tracery field. A curiosity of these latter is the different sections employed for form-pieces and mullions. In the window above the main lay entrance, in the third bay from the W in the S aisle, is an even more elaborate design, with a circlet containing six trefoils. This S aisle tracery is the external feature which most obviously proclaims the late C13 date of the greater part of the nave. At clearstorey level the treatment is simpler, with pairs of Y-traceried windows in each bay, separated by narrow strip-like buttresses with chamfered angles.

The W front was the area of the Cathedral most radically altered in the C19, because of the refacing necessitated by the removal of the towers in 1846 and 1848. The W door, however, appears to have been left unaltered, although *Blore* could not resist enriching the window above it, which, like the inserted window in the S choir aisle, was of the paired two-light and circlet pattern. The W doorway and window, together with the S doorway, could have been amongst the first parts of the resumed nave campaign to be tackled, and may be contemporary with the transepts. The S doorway is of four orders of engaged shafts, whilst the W doorway is of six. The latter has an attractively treated lintelled tympanum: within two sub-arches concentric with the main arch are triplets of blind arches, between which is a central niche flanked by quatrefoils.

INTERIOR

The architectural complexity of the Cathedral is more apparent internally than externally. Ideally it should be visited in a chronological succession of its parts, but this would require an over-complicated itinerary. Nevertheless the first part to be visited should certainly be the S W corner of the crypt, where the earliest *in situ* masonry is to be seen.

SW COMPARTMENT OF CRYPT. On the E side of the third crypt bay S aisle, and at a point corresponding with the break in the external plinth course previously discussed (p. 116), is a small northward spur of masonry with a squat keeled shaft surmounted by a disproportionately large early stiffleaf cap. It rises from a wall bench of an earlier form than any other in the Cathedral. This is the only fragment still in place of Bishop Jocelyn's church, which is known to have been underway in 1181 and ready for a consecration in 1197. Its position strongly suggests that it formed part of a cross wall originally intended

Glasgow Cathedral: western elevation
(Reproduced from James Collie's *Plans, Elevations . . .
and Views of the Cathedral of Glasgow*, 1835)

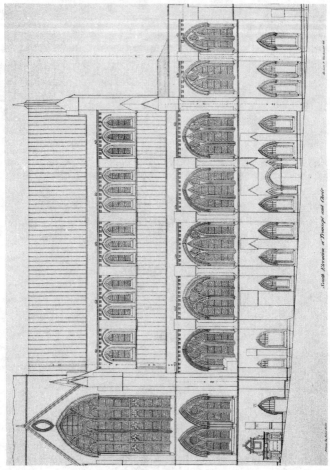

Glasgow Cathedral
Right south elevation of
transept and choir
Below longitudinal sections through
the nave and through the choir,
Lady Chapel, crypt, etc.
(Reproduced from James Collie's
*Plans, Elevations ... and Views
of the Cathedral of Glasgow,* 1835)

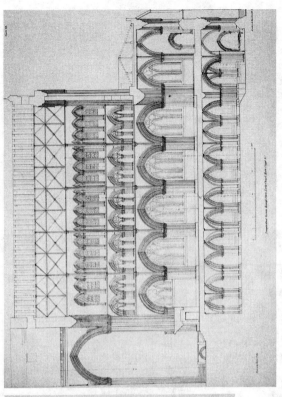

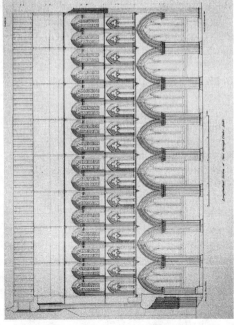

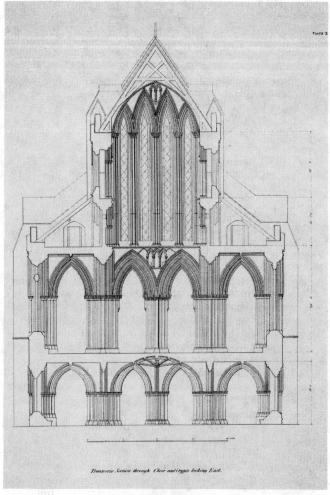

Glasgow Cathedral
transverse section though the
choir and crypts looking east
(Reproduced from James Collie's
*Plans, Elevations ... and Views
of the Cathedral of Glasgow*, 1835)

to extend further to the s, and, taking account of the position of Kentigern's tomb, the most likely explanation is that it was part of the E wall of a laterally projecting chapel. Assuming a corresponding projection on the N, together with a reconstructed presbytery and supporting crypt, this indicates some form of cruciform plan to the eastern limb, with the tomb below the presbytery.

The large size of the cap suggests that it was not designed for such a short shaft, and that it was placed here either in the repairs following the fire which interrupted Jocelyn's campaign, or when that campaign was finally abandoned in the early C13. The wall running W from Jocelyn's fragment is the earliest part of the C13 operation, and it evidently truncated the projection of which Jocelyn's work formed a part. Since the keeled vault rib profiles in this compartment show it was covered over at an early stage of the new operation, it may be that the cap on the wall-shaft was a discarded piece placed here to make superficial sense of the fragment and to receive the structurally redundant rib extended to it. The whole has a make-do-and-mend air not seen elsewhere in the Cathedral.

CRYPT. Apart from the sw compartment, the crypt is entirely the result of Bishop Bondington's E limb extension of the mid-C13. Its plan with ambulatory and E chapels was dictated by what was intended for the choir above, but the disposition of the central space is a work of genius. Thomas Watson, in his fascinating *Double Choir of Glasgow Cathedral* (1901), suggested a complex sequence of developments leading to what was eventually built, based largely on changes of rib profiles. His interpretation is probably over-complicated, although it does indeed seem likely that the arrangement was developed only progressively as building advanced.

In order to give the impression of Kentigern's tomb being at the heart of the crypt, unequal sections were cut off to each end, that at the E being set apart for the two-bay Lady Chapel, that at the W being simply a form of vestibule. Particular attention was concentrated on the tomb by constructing a 7 close canopy of vaulting carried on four piers around it. By comparison, the Lady Chapel was allowed to fill the full width available, and was covered by a slightly domical lierne vault of considerable complexity and with lavish foliate bosses at the intersections. To E and W of the tomb, the square areas of three by three bays were each supported on a single central pier, so that there is a most effective counterpoint between the more open and the more concentrated spaces. As well as the variety of rib types already mentioned, there is a surprising range of pier types: of those surrounding the tomb, for example, the two to the W differ from those to the E.

There is also a considerable range in the quality of carving. Only the caps associated with the more important areas have stiffleaf foliage, and those on the W of the tomb and in the E ambulatory chapels are distinctly superior to the rest. The foliage of the vault bosses also varies greatly, but none approaches the luxuriance of the best caps, and many have a rather mechanical quality.

The steps which now lead down the full width of the crypt from both the Lady Chapel and the aisles do not reflect the original arrangement, and post-date the mid-C 19 use of the crypt as a burial chamber. Of the four E chapels, those at either end are differentiated by having intermediate vaulting ribs towards the E, and by having attractive arched screens between them and the central chapels. The central chapels, however, have dogtooth to the window jambs.

LOWER CHAPTER HOUSE. This projection is entered through a delightful, but surprisingly weathered, door of three orders. The outer and inner orders are carried on engaged shafts with stiffleaf to the caps, but the middle order is continuous and carved with a rich foliage trail. On the S side, figures at the base and within the trail have something of the appearance of a Jesse Tree, although the charming dragon on the N seems unlikely to be intended as a descendant of Jesse.

To gain extra height the room is several steps below the floor of the rest of the crypt. It is still largely of the mid-C 13, although there has evidently been much remodelling after the lightning damage of c. 1406. The reconstruction was started by Bishop Lauder (1408–25/6), who on the new president's seat he installed at the centre of the E wall inscribed: wilms : fuda^t : istut : capilm̄ : dei. Several of the wall-shaft caps have been replaced in the operation, some having foliage carving, as has the moulded cap of the central pier. The vault also appears to have been partly reconstructed, albeit with the original ribs, since it has the arms of Bishop Cameron (1426–46), Queen Joan Beaufort († 1445) and the fifth Earl of Douglas († 1439). The vault is carried on a central pier, with additional intersections around the walls.

BLACKADDER AISLE. The internal architectural similarities between the choir crypt and that of the Blackadder Aisle are very marked. The wall-shafts in the two parts are virtually identical, and the aisle piers are very similar to the lesser piers in the crypt, although without being extended on one axis because of the need to carry the arches beneath the choir arcades. The similarities also extend to the bases and to the wall ribs. By contrast, the vault ribs are of much heavier and less undercut profile than in the crypt, and there would be no need to doubt that these were indeed work for a late medieval bishop, even if Blackadder's arms were not liberally applied to the bosses; his also are the foliage caps.

Nevertheless, although the shell seems clearly to be Bondington's and the vault Blackadder's, the precise chronological relationship of the aisle to the rest of the church is undeniably complex. The door of three orders leading into it, which cuts into the early C 13 basecourse, has its decorated side facing into the crypt, which suggests that it was originally designed as an external entrance before there was any thought of the aisle. But, in a building where mercurial changes of intention are the norm, there is no reason to doubt that the aisle's addition was made as a slight afterthought in the Bondington campaign.

In adding his vault Blackadder took over the outer shafts of the door to support the ribs of an intermediate cell, which was necessitated by the position of this opening on the principal N–S axis. Immediately facing the door, on the web of the vault, is a rather crude depiction of the Fergus whose hearse Kentigern is said to have followed to Glasgow as a prelude to his missionary activity here. With it is the inscription THIS.IS.YE.ILE.OF.CAR[?].FERGUS, perhaps suggesting that Fergus was believed to have been buried in the area covered by the aisle.

The choir is reached from the crypt by way of flights of steps which rise from tierceron-vaulted vestibules below the transepts, and which still afford a memorable spatial progression, despite their partial blocking by the altar bases which Blackadder built in front of the pulpitum. A central flight then passes through the pulpitum.

CHOIR. This part of the Cathedral has suffered from a covering of brown paint to the arcade to hide the extensive cement patching which presumably followed the removal of the galleries. Despite this, the first impression on entering through the pulpitum is sublime. It is not a large building in European terms, but the sense of scale far outstrips its real dimensions. The greatest initial impact is made by the four enormously long lancets, which rise above the twin arcade arches opening into the ambulatory, and which extend through triforium and clearstorey levels up to meet the soffit of the wagon ceiling. It is possible that the daylight opening of these lancets was originally less than now, in order to accommodate the ambulatory roof in its earlier form, although the rear arches must always have been as we now see them, so that the effect is unlikely to have differed greatly.

The proportions of the choir are helped by the extra height provided by the wagon ceiling, the apex of which is about 22·5 m (74 ft) above floor level, adding about 4·4 m (14 ft 6 inches) to the total internal height. In its present form this ceiling is of 1912, although its delicately cusped profile was dictated by the wall rib in the E gable, and Brown's view of 1822 shows that the diagonal lattice of ribs reflects what was presumably the C15 design as modified after the fire of c. 1406.

The flanks of the choir have two pairs of triforium openings in each bay, and at clearstorey level there are triplets of equal openings flanked by narrower blind arches, except in the more compressed end bays. For the design of this vaultless clearstorey an inspiration may have been the recently finished nave of Jedburgh, in which Glasgow's bishops, as the successors of one of its founders, took a close interest. The design of the two lower levels is within the tradition established by the choir of Lincoln, although the immediate source of inspiration is likely to have been one of the more recent variants on this idea, e.g. at Rievaulx. The similarity with Rievaulx is especially marked in the end bays, where the sub-arches of the triforium openings are concentric with the containing arches, and the tympana are pierced by foiled openings. In the central bays the sub-arches are cusped and flatter. Some similarities with Rievaulx are also to be seen in the solidity of the piers, although Rievaulx's are developments on the bundled shaft form, whereas Glasgow has combinations of shafts and rectangular sections which offer an almost Romanesque sense of mass.

However, Lincoln may also have had a more direct influence at Glasgow. The analogies between the Glasgow choir aisle windows and the triforium openings in Lincoln nave have been suggested above, and it may also have been Lincoln nave
6 which prompted the use of stiffleaf on the arcade caps of Glasgow, except at the corners below the high E gable. This stiffleaf is difficult to study in detail because of its modern covering of paint, but it is certainly of very high standard, although the rather gritty carboniferous sandstone from which it is carved did not encourage the same degree of undercutting as at Lincoln, and there is perhaps a slightly repetitive quality. Within Scotland the same carver may also have been responsible for the N door at Paisley.

The calibre of Glasgow choir's master mason continues in evidence in the ambulatory and eastern chapels. Although the equal vault heights give this area something of the appearance of a hall church he has subtly introduced a directional axis to the chapels by giving their vaults an intermediate intersection towards the E, as in the corresponding outer chapels of the crypt. He has also introduced differentiation by concentrations of stiffleaf to the caps of the window wall, in contrast to the moulded caps of the ambulatory piers, and has further enriched the two outer chapels with bands of dogtooth to the window jambs.

The vaults of the eastern limb, which have ridge ribs in both directions throughout, in general show ample evidence of the settlement which was a perennial problem both before and after the lightning damage. Amongst the arms on the bosses which point to necessary repairs are those of Cardinal Walter de Wardlaw (1367–87) and Archbishop James Betoun (1508–23).

UPPER CHAPTER HOUSE. Paradoxically, although the upper is the loftier and presumably the more important of the two chapter houses, it is entered by a simpler door than its lower counterpart. Apart from carvings to the hoodmould corbels, this door is devoid of foliage carving. The room itself has been extensively rebuilt in the C15, the only original parts being in the lower outer walls, where the shaft bases survive, and the wall adjoining the choir, where the shafts survive to full height together with one vault springing adjacent to the small entrance vestibule. Otherwise it is the work of Bishops Cameron and Turnbull, the former of whom had the good sense to insert a fireplace. An intriguing feature of the new work is the rebuilt central pier, which is not strictly biaxially symmetrical, and which consequently does not sit altogether happily on its more orthodox base.

TRANSEPTS. It is in the transepts that the unbroken continuity of operations throughout the C 13 is most clearly apparent. The early C 13 campaign is represented in the wall responds to the W tower piers, which have canted faces with attached half-shafts. The tower piers themselves are particularly interesting for the way in which they so precisely reflect the surrounding piers and responds, and thus demonstrate that the changes of design to either side of the crossing are not separated by any gap of time. This is also borne out by the way in which the caps towards both transepts and nave are already of the multiple moulded type which was to be employed in the nave.

The principal features of the transept end walls are the great windows, which have already been discussed, and which are rather overwhelming within such tight spaces. The other elevations show significant changes of design between E and W at triforium level. On the E, the rather flattened containing arches simply embrace a triplet of lancets, whereas on the W they contain a pattern of intersecting arcs within which are trefoiled circlets. At clearstorey height on both sides, the windows foreshadow typologically those of the N nave aisle and, like several other features already referred to, suggest that later work on the transepts and earlier work on the nave overlapped.

The crossing is covered by the only high vault in the Cathedral. But, although it must be of the originally intended form, with tierceron ribs and a central ring, what is now seen is a C 19 reconstruction. A more jarring C 19 intrusion is represented by the over-massive parapets around the crypt descents, which copy the pulpitum parapet and were constructed to *Blore*'s design in 1855.

NAVE. The early C 13 campaign played a more formative role in the design of the nave than of any other part. The lower walls in both aisles have keeled vaulting shafts which are clearly part of that campaign, and internally it is evident that the W wall was also laid out then, since its arcade responds are of essentially the same form as the W responds to the tower piers in the transepts. The nave plan, with its tighter arcade rhythm, was thus governed by the early work, whilst the elevations are almost entirely of the later decades of the C 13.

Nevertheless, the break with Bondington's choir campaign is not so complete as first appears, and the arcade bases, for example, are closely similar in their pronouncedly waterholding form above concave flared sub-bases. The arcades are carried on octofoil piers in which the cardinal shafts are filleted and the diagonal shafts are angled in a way which may be an updated attempt to reflect the earlier keeling of the aisle wallshafts. The caps carried by these piers, which were anticipated in the transept piers, are profusely moulded in the manner which had become more common in the later decades of the century.

Within the aisles there are slight differences of vaulting between the two sides. That on the S has ridge ribs throughout, as in the choir, whilst that on the N has ridge ribs only in the third and fourth bays from the crossing. These variations are possibly due to various repairs which are indicated by the arms of several of the later occupants of the see. At the E end of the N aisle may be seen an ogee-headed opening off the stair which leads up to the wallloft. This opening was evidently to give access to the rood loft, which must have crossed the nave in front of the W crossing piers; however, it is of secondary construction, and from what we can gather of the positions of altars it may not have remained in use for long.

Above the arcades the two upper storeys are linked by a pair of embracing arches in each bay, within which the trefoil-headed triforium openings are set back on a recessed plane. Such a general disposition places the elevations in the initially western tradition of design established at St David's and developed at Dublin, Pershore and further N at Southwell. But, whereas at the last two of these the triforium was almost suppressed, at Glasgow it was simply reduced in importance. In this it provides a parallel strand to other late C13 experiments in the integration of the upper storeys, as in the nave of York, started some years later.

The nave is now covered by an open timber roof with tie-beams, of early C20 construction, which replaced a plaster ceiling of polygonal section. Brown's view of the nave, published in 1822, before the great campaign of C19 restorations, appears to show that the medieval ceiling was of arched wagon form, with ribs corresponding to the bays, but without the additional lattice of ribs as in the choir.

FURNISHINGS

Crypt

ST KENTIGERN'S WELL. Well-head in S wall of SE chapel. SHRINE BASE. Fragments of a finely detailed mid-C13 miniature arcade have been reconstructed in the SE chapel. Mac-Gregor Chalmers suggested they formed part of a benefactor's tomb; George Hay more plausibly identified them as Kentigern's shrine base. ARCHITECTURAL FRAGMENTS displayed in SE chapel. – PAINTED VOUSSOIR, probably found beneath choir floor in 1916. Painted palmette on one face. Presumably from first cathedral, though on stylistic grounds likely to post-date consecration of 1136. Probably from rear arch of window, suggesting that the first building relied on flat painted decoration rather than architectural sophistication for

effect. – Various fragments probably from the cathedral consecrated in 1197, including base of keeled shaft with spurs,
volute caps and keeled vault ribs. Carved figurative corbels of
C15 said to have come from W towers, reminiscent of early
C15 corbels at Melrose; could they be further examples of the
work of *John Morow*, who included Glasgow amongst his list
of works? Other C15 foliate bosses and corbels. ARMORIAL
DISPLAY FROM GATEHOUSE OF BISHOP'S CASTLE in N
aisle.* Arms of Archbishop Dunbar (1523–47) and Subdean
James Houston (1526–50), within balusters, and arms of James
V in chief. Removed to Mochrum Park, Wigtonshire, then
returned here in 1965. TAPESTRY, W wall, on theme of St
Kentigern. Designed by *Robert Stewart* and made by *Edinburgh Tapestry Company*, 1979.

STAINED GLASS. Some of the windows retain heraldry
from C19 glass in modern settings. N aisle, St John Baptist
(memorial to Edward Irving, founder of the Catholic Apostolic
Church); S S Kentigern and Columba, and post-Reformation
archbishops, by *Ballantine & Allan*, mid-C19.

E chapels, second from N, Te Deum by *Gordon Webster*,
1979; S chapel, one panel of a St Kentigern window by *Clayton
& Bell*, 1869.

S aisle, C16 Low Countries roundels on various themes.

MONUMENTS. W bay, grave-slab decorated with foliate
cross; badly worn stiffleaf decoration indicates mid C13 date.
SW compartment, grave-slab with eroded figure of cleric on
top and interlace decoration on edges; possibly the work of a
mason from W Highland area and of C15 date. Robert Burn
Anderson † 1860, brass plate and bronze sculpture of sword,
belt and wreath by *R. Jackson*. S end of ambulatory, tomb of
Margaret Colquhoun, Lady Boyd, † 1601; large chest-like
tomb with panelled front and inscribed stone on top. On dwarf
wall between central E chapels, effigy of (headless) bishop in
Mass vestments flanked by miniature figures at head and foot.
The effigy is known to have been moved to the area of Kentigern's tomb in 1843, but was returned to its present site in
1866. Although it is too long for its position, excavations in
1965 showed it to be above a burial chamber. Traditionally it
is associated with Bishop Robert Wishart † 1316, and the
carefully modelled broad drapery of the chasuble would be
consistent with such a date. N aisle, but originally on E external
wall of treasury, Covenanters' Memorial; incised slab commemorating execution of covenanters at Glasgow Cross 1660–
88; repaired and relettered 1827. N descent to crypt, Dr George
Stewart Burns † 1896; marble relief plaque with angel extending laurel branch towards portrait medallion, by *Kellock
Brown*.

Choir

The choir was seated with pews between 1851 and 1856, before
the vogue was established in the later C19 for refitting the

choirs of major Scottish churches with stalls and screens which
reflected their likely medieval furnishing. Despite some
rearrangement and remodelling of the pews in 1957 they are
thus set out on an essentially parochial pattern. COMMUNION
TABLE, c. 1890. Gothic with relief of Last Supper on W face.
CHOIR PULPIT. Early C17 panelled oak pulpit with semicircular front to square body; originally used by Barony congregation in crypt and returned to the Cathedral in 1905, when
it was heavily restored and remodelled. CHOIR LECTERN. C17
French, timber eagle on column. ORGAN SCREEN. Massive
timber arcade and gallery backing on to pulpitum. LECTERN
in E chapels. Brass eagle on Gothic base, given to Cathedral in
1890 and presumably made shortly before then.

STAINED GLASS. Main E window, Four Evangelists by
Francis Spear, 1951. N aisle, from W to E, Christ and the
World's Work by *Herbert Hendrie*, 1939; grisaille by *Robert
Armitage*, 1951; Christ and the World's Happiness by *Herbert
Hendrie*, 1946; grisaille by *Robert Armitage*, 1953; Christ and
the World's Beauty by *Sadie McLellan*, 1955; S S Andrew and
James by *Herbert Hendrie*, 1940.

E chapels from N to S. SS Ninian and Columba by *Marion
Grant*, 1954; Nativity, Crucifixion, Resurrection and Ascen-
sion by *Francis Spear*, 1953; S S Stephen and Lawrence by
Gordon Webster, 1975; St Margaret and David I by *Christopher
Webb*, 1958.

S aisle from E to W. Masonic window by *Robert Armitage*,
1957; three St Mungo windows by *Sadie McLellan*, 1951, and
William Wilson, 1954 and 1956; Trades House window by
William Wilson, 1951; St Nicholas by *Marion Grant*, 1955.

MEMORIAL, SE chapel. Tall two-stage monument to Archbishop James Law † 1632; lower stage with inscription in
cartouche, flanked by terms capped by obelisks and strapwork
volutes; upper stage a Corinthian aedicule containing a prayer
desk. Now unfortunately painted.

Upper Chapter House

DOOR, the only surviving medieval door in the Cathedral; vertically boarded. ROYAL ARMS, early C19, probably from W
gallery of Inner Kirk.

STAINED GLASS. Windows illustrating works of mercy and
Christian mission by *Henry Hughes*, 1862–5.

Blackadder Aisle

STAINED GLASS. E side from N to S, all by *Harry Stammers*.
Archbishop Blackadder, 1960; Annunciation to Virgin and to
Shepherds, 1956; Nativity and Epiphany, 1956; Presentation
and Flight into Egypt, 1956. W side, all by *Harry Stammers*,
aspects of ministry of Christ, 1960. S side, C16 Swiss panels
of Last Supper, Resurrection, Crucifixion and Passion, some
evidently based on wood-block illustrations.

Crossing and transepts

PULPITUM. Below E crossing arch; probably constructed as part of early C15 reordering of choir. Three-centred arched doorway with continuous mouldings, flanked by walls articulated by thin decorative arcading, the whole capped by a heavily reticulated parapet punctuated by elaborated miniature buttresses. Supporting the buttresses are figurative corbels of uncertain iconography. Traces of cut-back corbels at midheight within arcading indicate earlier presence of images, which were presumably removed when altars were built to either side of the doorway.

ALTAR PLATFORMS. A very rare survival. Added in front 8 of the pulpitum in 1503 by Archbishop Blackadder: to N dedicated to Name of Jesus; to S dedicated to Our Lady of Pity. Originally connected to transept floors by bridges, but now with modern cap stones. Arms and initials of Blackadder on flanks; crudely carved saints holding scrolls in front. On N base are five saints under triangular canopies; on S are six saints under ogee canopies.

STAINED GLASS. E clearstoreys of transepts. The only major relics *in situ* of the scheme for reglazing the main spaces of the Cathedral with windows by *Ainmüller*'s Munich Königliche Glasmalereianstalt, 1859–64 (*see* above). N transept N wall. Scottish Regiments, Navy and Air Force windows by *William Wilson*, 1960. S transept S wall. The Scottish Divisions window by *Gordon Webster*, 1951–4.

Nave

PULPIT. Grainger Memorial, late Gothic, designed by *Peter Macgregor Chalmers*, 1903.

BELL displayed in N aisle. Inscription dating from recasting of 1790 says it was first donated by Marcus Knox, 1594, but it is now believed to have originally been one of the bells given by Archbishop Gavin Dunbar (1523–47). OFFERTORY CHEST. C16 Dutch, iron-bound.

STAINED GLASS. Some windows retain heraldry from Munich windows within modern clear glass. W window. Creation, by *Francis Spear*, 1958. W end S aisle. Three Cameronian windows by *Harry Stammers*, 1954, and *William Wilson*, 1958. N aisle. W end, Scots Guards window by *Harry Stammers*, 1956; fifth bay from E, Moses by *Douglas Strachan*, 1936.

MONUMENTS. S aisle. Minto Memorial, in third bay from crossing. Rectangular stone frame, with a higher section capped by a broken pediment with the date 1605, flanked by volutes (only one surviving) and containing an arch with emblems of mortality. Brass plate in main panel depicting knight kneeling towards divine glory, with inscription commemorating members of the Stewart of Minto family. 74th Highlanders killed at Tel-el-Kebir 1882, relief of battle scene within Egyptian frame surmounted by Sphinx, by *Alexander Macdonald & Co*.

w end s aisle. Andrew Cochrane † 1777, canted marble frame flanked by consoles and surmounted by high-relief angel placing laurels on urn. w end N aisle. Lt John Stirling † 1828, Grecian detail with flanking inverted torches and surmounted by draped urn, by *Clelands & Co*.

N aisle from w to E. Lt Col. Henry Cadogan † 1813, sarcophagus of 1816 on plinth surmounted by arms by *David Hamilton & Sons*. William Graham † 1855, bronze relief of c. 1900 with serpents and doves around spray of poppies, emblematic of future awakening, by *Sir Alfred Gilbert*. Lt Donald Campbell † 1835, austere marble *stele* with 'Illyrian' helmet, shield and sword at base, by *William Behnes*. Dr Peter Lowe † 1612, founder of the Royal Faculty of Physicians and Surgeons, by *James Pittendrigh MacGillivray*, 1891. Bronze memorial relief symbolizing health, with angel holding caduceus, flanked by old man with boy and woman with baby treading on serpent. (Lowe is buried in the graveyard.) 93rd Sutherland Highlanders killed in Crimea 1854–6, white marble with goddess Fame above dying standard-bearer, by *Sir John Steell*, 1859. Lt Robert Burn Anderson † 1860, knightly arms in bronze by *Robert Jackson* above marble sarcophagus with brass plate. Major William Middleton † 1859, white marble, two soldiers flanking tomb and portrait medallion above draped flags, by *Mossman*. Dr James Hedderwick † 1897, alabaster Gothic niche by *T. L. Watson* with bronze portrait medallion by *J. Pittendrigh MacGillivray* of 1901. 71st Highland Light Infantry killed on N W frontier 1863; one soldier places wreath on cenotaph and another shows it to kilted boy. By *William Brodie*, 1867.

FURTHER READING

Glasgow Cathedral is fortunate in having had considerable interest shown both in its architecture and in the documentation associated with it. James Collie's *Plans, Elevations ... and Views of the Cathedral of Glasgow*, published in 1835, was a rare attempt to provide accurate measured drawings of a Scottish church. The Scottish historical clubs cast much light on the Cathedral's history with the publication of the *Chronica de Mailros* (Bannatyne Club) in 1835 and the *Registrum Episcopatus Glasguensis* (Bannatyne and Maitland Clubs) in 1843.

Another landmark in the appreciation of the Cathedral was the publication in 1898 of *The Book of Glasgow Cathedral*, edited by George Eyre Todd; inevitably, many of the ideas included have been superseded, but several of the essays, especially John Honeyman's sensitive analysis of the building, are still well worth reading. Interest in the Cathedral was furthered by Thomas Watson's *Double Choir of Glasgow Cathedral* (1901) and Peter Macgregor Chalmers' *Glasgow Cathedral* (1914). The former is a fascinating, if outmoded, study; the latter, although inclined to be dogmatic, is one of the best volumes in the Bell's cathedral series.

In recent years there has been more research on the documentary than the architectural side. Invaluable summaries of what is known of the Cathedral establishment and its clergy are to be found in Ian B. Cowan and David Easson's *Medieval Religious Houses, Scotland* (1976) and Donald Watt's *Fasti Ecclesiae Scoticanae Medii Aevi* (Scottish Record Society, 1969). The results of work by John Durkan, George Hay, David MacRoberts, Lionel Stones and others have been published in a wide range of articles and notes in the *Innes Review*; and the Friends of Glasgow Cathedral have instituted a promising series of occasional publications.

GRAVEYARD

Flanking the s door of the Cathedral, two handsome tombs. On the E, a two-storeyed wall tomb with lots of strapwork, originally erected, according to the inscription, before 1670 to the memory of Thomas and George Hutcheson, renovated in 1857 and 'new restored' in 1903 by the preceptors and patrons of Hutchesons' Hospital. On the w, a High Victorian Gothic canopied tomb to George Baillie, philanthropist, † 1873, with his portrait head. Signed by *J. Burnet* and *J. Mossman*.

Lining the graveyard walls, a number of C17, C18 and C19 tombs. To judge from the inscriptions and the later finials, several of the wall tombs seem to be C17 ones reused in the C19, and not, as might seem more likely, early revivals of the Jacobean style. – s of the gate, first on the w wall, an undated but apparently C17 wall tomb, inscribed 'Property of Mis ... Hamilton'; the usual type of tiered architectural wall monument with an attached colonnade on the lowest tier, armorial tablets above and a Mannerist pediment. – Next, an C18 version of the same type of tomb but canted out to give the impression of a free-standing monument and with Batty Langley Gothic details. Property of Andrew Scott and his wife Marion Stark, who married in 1740. – On the s wall, the much-restored tomb of Peter Lowe, founder of the Royal Faculty of Physicians and Surgeons, † 1612. – Next to the E, within a burial enclosure, what seems to be a three-tier C17 tomb, reused by George Brown † 1831. – A little further on, a lower tomb, also apparently C17 and reused, this time by George Lyon † 1830. – Provost James Bell's heirs have a more interesting tomb of 1734, with a Piranesian arched base below a Jacobean-style tester. – Next to the E, a badly weathered wall tomb with attached columns to McKin ... and dated 1770. – Close to this but free-standing, a fine Victorian column to James Young, merchant in Glasgow, † 1855. Greek base *à la* Thomson, well-carved Corinthian column and, on top, a classical lantern. – On the E wall, a bas-relief sarcophagus delicately carved with gryphons and eternal flames; to George Roger, Jr, † 1821. – Then a very late example of the Jacobean type of wall tomb with columns and strapwork; inscribed to John Anderson, Douhill, Provest (*sic*) of Glasgow. – Nothing else of interest until the middle of the N wall and a panel of Victorian patterned encaustic tiles to Alexander Smith, slater of Glasgow. – On the W wall N of the gate, the wall tomb of William Leckie † 1822, with Salomonic columns and female grotesques. – Lastly, just N of the gate, the single-storey wall tomb of John Marshall † 1708, with a winged head.

CHURCHES

BARONY CHURCH, Castle Street (now the ceremonial hall of Strathclyde University). 1886–9, by *J. J. Burnet* and *J. A. Campbell*, winners of a competition adjudicated by J. L. Pearson, and with a strong flavour of Pearson inside. It succeeded a Gothick church built in 1793–1800 by John Robertson to designs by *R. & J. Adam*, which stood SE of the C18 Infirmary. Low, powerful and Scottish outside, lofty and loosely modelled on Gerona Cathedral via Pearson within. The exterior in snecked red sandstone, with its S front modelled on Dunblane, simple lancets and a squat SE porch, has the spare bold modelling especially characteristic of Campbell. The delicate little *flèche* makes an almost frivolous contrast. Inside, a tall severe clearstorey and rustic timber roof above aisle arcades in which complex arch mouldings die into plain round piers. Fully developed chancel with aisles opening to the nave in tightly squeezed arches. The details here are more conventionally E.E., with finely moulded arches, capitals and wall-shafts.

FURNISHINGS. REREDOS. 1900, by *J. J. Burnet*, with three generous arches. The lettering and symbols of the Agnus Dei and Evangelists carved by *William Vickers*. – CHANCEL STALLS, handsomely carved with angels. – LECTERN. 1889 and typically Arts and Crafts in its sturdy form and angel reliefs. It rests on the memorial stone from the previous church. – ORGAN. 1949, by *Harrison & Harrison*. – WAR MEMORIAL in the Cunliffe Chapel. 1921 by *P. Macgregor Chalmers*. – STAINED GLASS. All installed between 1935 and 1955. By *Herbert Hendrie*, that in the chancel, transept, E and W aisles. – By *Douglas Hamilton*, the S window, one light (Ruth) in the W aisle, two windows in the Cunliffe Chapel. – By *William Wilson*, the windows in the John White Memorial Chapel, including a representation of Dr White (Minister of the Barony 1911–51), badges of the institutions and buildings with which he was associated.

The HALLS to the N are part of the same spreading composition effectively filling the site. Inside like a rustic barn, with an ingenious timber roof and one aisle of timber posts.

BARONY NORTH (Glasgow Evangelical) CHURCH, 14–20 Cathedral Square. 1878–80, by *John Honeyman*. Built for the United Presbyterians but taken over by the Evangelical Assembly in 1978. Its original setting has gone, making this highly individual design seem extremely unbalanced. All the elaborate detail is on the W side facing the gardens (the S and E sides, formerly hidden by close-packed tenements, are completely unadorned), yet the internal arrangement is a conventional longitudinal one with a gallery. What appears to be the apse at the N end houses the gallery stair.

Remarkably Italianate and lavish main elevation, the centre like a Palladian palazzo, with its deep rusticated base pierced by tiny windows (the larger ones to the basement halls are screened by a rich rinceau-pattern railing), and strongly modelled upper walls with the architrave projecting over three-quarter Corinthian columns, each set against a pair of pilasters between big arched windows. Both the plainer end bays were intended to rise into towers: only the N one was completed, with a handsome top, more English C18 than Italian. Its bell-stage, a squared-off oval, carries a cupola with a ribbed stone dome and a tall cross. In niches over the doorways, statues of St Paul (N) and St Peter (S), and along the cornice figures of the Evangelists – a display of free-standing statuary (by *M'Culloch* of London) unusual for a Glasgow church at this or any date.

Well-preserved interior with a curved gallery on thin cast-iron columns and pews beneath them following the same line. Gallery fronts and organ pipes painted green, gold and terracotta. Central mahogany PULPIT. The vestibule is equally handsome. Classical timber screen and doors with etched glass, encaustic tile floor and, most impressive, a staircase in the apse starting in one flight and dividing into two, framed by pairs of black marble columns and with a boldly patterned cast-iron balustrade. – STAINED GLASS. S windows, obscured by the organ. The Transfiguration over all three lights with figures in C17-style architectural frames. By Messrs *Kier* and contemporary with the church.

MARTYRS' CHURCH, St Mungo Avenue. Of the 1970s. One long monopitch rises to the E with a clearstorey just below it. Otherwise the orange brick walls are blank.

ST ANDREW'S FREE CHURCH, 72 North Hanover Street (subdivided as a showroom). 1844, one of *J. T. Rochead*'s cheap stone churches, with its large Perp W window blocked.

ST MUNGO (R.C.), 56–8 Parson Street. A Passionist church of 1866–9 by *George Goldie*. Early French Gothic in yellow snecked rubble. The SW tower still lacks its spire. Lancets except for the big plate-traceried S window. Beneath it, an arcade of three pointed arches on stubby polished granite piers with crocket capitals. Over the arches, triangular hoodmoulds, their fleur-de-lis finials enfolding portrait heads, one of them a bishop (St Mungo?). At the end of the E aisle, a small polygonal angle tower and a window with a foliate plaque in its head. The nave arcades have polished pink granite piers, the roof exposed timbers. Polygonal apsed sanctuary and monastic choir with side chapels. Charming Gothic timber confessionals in recesses in the aisles. Goldie gave final touches to the interior, such as the angel corbels and foliage capitals towards the E end, and the bosses, in 1877.

ST MUNGO'S RETREAT (the monastery) has a red rock-faced and terracotta-trimmed façade of 1892, still French Gothic but more domestic, by *Father Osmund Cooke* from Paris. It conceals older and plainer buildings. Facing N, the church hall was built as part of St Mungo's Academy (*see* Calton) by *Joseph Cowan & Sons*, 1902.

28 THE NECROPOLIS, Cathedral Square. The craggy silhouette of this drumlin, bristling with monuments, is one of Glasgow's most memorable images. The Necropolis, opened in 1833, was the third 'hygienic cemetery' in Britain (after St James's, Liverpool, 1829, and Kensal Green, London, 1832). The idea of a garden cemetery, following the model of Père Lachaise in Paris, had been proposed by a number of leading citizens in 1828. They suggested to the Merchants' House that their plantation of Fir Park (established on Craig Park when the rest of Wester Craigs was feued in 1750: *see* Dennistoun, below) could be put to commercial use in this way. The E side of Fir Park was already being quarried, but otherwise only the summit of this private pleasure ground was occupied – with the monument to John Knox, erected at public expense in 1825. The Jews led the way by buying a burial ground on the NW slope in 1830. The next year, a competition was held for the layout of the new cemetery, with 'economy, security and picturesque effect' as the guidelines. Five designs were pre-miated, and *John Baird* and *David Hamilton* were appointed to combine them into a single design, soon abandoned. Instead, *David Mylne*, a landscape gardener, was made first super-intendent of the Necropolis, and he designed the final layout, a simple one with equal compartments divided by the principal walks on the level ground and planting with evergreen shrubs.

The architectural features were professionally designed, and so were many of the monuments, all of which were vetted after 1835 'to prevent the construction of monuments in very bad taste'. Most carefully adjudicated were the designs of the pro-posed neighbours to the Knox Monument: proximity to this was considered most prestigious and was sought by leading families even after the cemetery had been extended E into the former quarry in 1857, and E again after 1894. The major mausolea and tombs are in the old part and date mostly from between 1833 (when the first Christian burial was made) and 1860. The material in this part is mainly sandstone. Loudon praised the variety of designs. The later monuments are more modest and predominantly of granite, except for a few tombs of Carrara marble or cast-iron. A great many monuments of all dates and stones were carved by the *Mossmans*, either to the designs of others or to their own.

The entrance is from Cathedral Square through a GATEWAY of 1833, designed by *James Hamilton* (the partner of his father David), with cast-iron gates by *Thos. Edington & Sons*. Just beyond them is the neo-Norman and originally castellated GATEKEEPER'S LODGE by *David Hamilton*, 1839–40, and a later Tudorish LODGE dated 1890. Until the old Barony Church was demolished, gates and lodge stood further E at the W end of *James Hamilton*'s BRIDGE, 1833–4, which crossed the Molendinar Burn (now culverted under Wishart Road) in one dramatic 60-foot (18-metre) span to reach the actual burial ground. Facing the E end of the bridge is THE FAÇADE, designed by *John Bryce* in 1835–6 like an Italian Mannerist garden feature, semicircular to allow hearses to turn. In the centre, the entrance to a tunnel leading through to the quarry on the far side of the hill, which had already been earmarked as a cemetery extension. The tunnel was to have been a catacomb for secure 'aristocratic' burial, but, because of the success of the Anatomy Act of 1832, it was never used; neither were the two mausolea in the wings. Over the tunnel entrance, an inscription referring to the 'adjoining bridge', transcribed from an obelisk demolished before 1857.

The main carriageway crosses in front of The Façade. The N part turns back S on itself as it climbs the hill. At the bend a path runs N to the JEWS' BURYING GROUND, tucked in at the foot of the hill. The GATEWAY with its scrolled arch is by *John Park* of Anderston. Now blocked and without its iron gate by *Thos. Edington & Sons*. The tall, Assyrian-looking COLUMN, intended to recall Absalom's column in the King's Dale in Jerusalem, was designed by *John Bryce* before 1836.

Back on the main carriageway and just below the hairpin bend, the crocketed Gothic monument of Mrs Lockhart † 1842, designed by her brother-in-law, *Wallace* of London, with sculpture by the *Mossmans*. – Further along the carriageway, an anthemion-inscribed pylon (with urn) and tomb-chest to the Revd A. O. Beattie, Minister of St Vincent Street U.P. Church, designed by *Alexander Thomson*, 1858, and carved by the *Mossmans*; the small mausoleum of Robert Black, c. 1837, with Doric columns *in antis*, built into the slope; and the tomb of William Motherwell † 1835, by *James Fillans*, 1851, with a copy of the original Parian marble bust beneath a Tudorish canopy. – The first really noteworthy mausoleum is that of the Misses Buchanan of Bellfield, mid-C19 and chastely Greek, with draped urns flanking the entrance. Probably by *John Stephen*, with gates (since removed) by *Hutcheson*. – Next, immediately under the Knox Monument, is the Greek gateway to the EGYPTIAN VAULTS, designed by *David Hamilton* (the gates with reversed torches by *Thos. Edington & Sons*) to provide a number of tombs for temporary burial.

The tall pink granite cenotaph of 1855 to Henry Monteith of Carstairs by *C. H. Wilson* (sculptor *Mossman*) marks the point at which the carriageway divides. The E branch leads up

to 'the most richly embellished division of the whole Necropolis' (Blair). – Opposite the obelisk, the earliest of many
versions in the Necropolis of the Choragic monument of Lysicrates. This one, a cenotaph to John Dick D.D. † 1833, by
Robert Black, 1838. The dome with curious scrolled ribs originally sheltered a vase. – Behind it, the tapering High Gothic
cross by *J. A. Bell* (1861) of the Revd Duncan MacFarlane
† 1857. – Further E, the actor-manager John Henry Alexander
of the Theatre Royal is commemorated by a Baroque design
by *James Hamilton*, with an appropriately theatrical scene by
A. Handyside Ritchie, representing the stage and proscenium
of a theatre flanked by 'Tragedy' and 'Comedy', 1851.

An obelisk marks the division of the carriageways. – Near it
on the W branch, another monument by *James Hamilton*, to
David Robertson, bookseller, 1854. – Further W, the Elizabethan-style tomb of Robert Stewart of Omoa † 1854,
designed by *James Brown* of *Brown & Carrick*, executed by
one *M'Lean*.

At the end of this avenue, a broad plateau covers the top of
the hill, with panoramic views over Glasgow and the
Cathedral. – John Knox's monument (1825) stands on the W
edge of this arena. On top of a tall and massive Greek Doric
column, designed by *Thomas Hamilton*, a 12-foot-high (3.6 m)
statue of Knox designed by *William Warren* and carved by
Robert Forrest. – In this superior neighbourhood, a number
of interesting monuments. To the NE, the Saracenic sepulchre
of the traveller William Rae Wilson † 1849 (author of *Travels
in the Holy Land*), designed by *J. A. Bell* of Edinburgh to
resemble 'one of the numerous sepulchral monuments in Pale-
stine' (Blair). – Next to this, the Houldsworth Mausoleum
by *John Thomas*, 1854, Graeco-Egyptian and topped by a
clearstorey (originally with stained glass) which lights a figure
of Faith, flanked by angels, inside. Hope and Charity stand
outside against the chamfered corners of the chamber. – To
the E, a late version (1891) of the Choragic monument type
by *James Thomson* of *Baird & Thomson*, to Charles Clark
MacKirdy. – Close by to the E, the handsome Edwardian
Baroque tomb of Walter Macfarlane of the Saracen Foundry
† 1885. The bronze portrait panel with Art Nouveau details
by *Bertram MacKennal* of London is dated 1896. – Beyond,
in the most recent part of the cemetery, the only distinctive
C20 slab, designed by *Talwin Morris* for the Blackie family,
carved by *J. & G. Mossman Ltd*, 1910.

Back S towards the Knox Monument, a seated Carrara
marble figure of Charles Tennant of St Rollox † 1838 by *Patric
Park*, just like the one in Leeds Parish Church. – SE of that
monument, the plain granite tomb-chest of James Ewing of
Strathleven † 1853, one of the principal promoters of the
Necropolis, designed by *John Baird I*. The bronze relief panels
by *Mossman*, sadly, have been removed. – Further SE still,
off the main carriageway, the stubby Greek Doric tester and
sarcophagus of Robert Muter † 1842 by *John Stephen* of *Scott*,

Stephen & Gale, 1844. – Back on the carriageway, *John Bryce*'s big Flemish Mannerist monument to William McGavin (1834, one of the first to be erected on the Necropolis). Executed by *Ritchie* of Edinburgh, and with a statue of McGavin by *Forrest*. – On the l. side of the avenue s of McGavin's tomb, a tall-domed severely Roman Doric memorial to William Dunn of Duntocher; 1848, by *J. T. Rochead*. – Also in this zone, a modest Celtic cross to Andrew McCall by *C. R. Mackintosh*, 1888.

Further w, on the edge of the hill, the cemetery's most prominent and showy mausoleum, housing the remains of 29 Archibald Douglas Monteath. It is a substantial circular building of 1842 with polygonal clearstorey stage, the exterior richly detailed by *David Cousin* in his favourite Romanesque style. – Its neighbour is to James Buchanan of Dowanhill † 1844, by *James Brown* of *Brown & Carrick*, the hexagonal base derived from the Tower of the Winds, the top (rebuilt with a central cylinder after 1856) from the Choragic monument of Lysicrates.

Opposite McGavin's monument, a path descends to the main carriageway, passing a poor statue of Life with a dashed torch by *Mossman*, 1840, commemorating Peter Lawrence. – Just behind it, flanking a side path, is the monument to Mrs Matthew Montgomerie, designed before 1856 by *Charles Wilson* in the manner of a Decorated Gothic wall tomb, and executed by *Hamilton & Miller*. Figures of Hope and Resignation by *Mossman*. From the bottom of the carriageway paths reascend the hill.

To the s, on a spur of the hill, the largest, latest and most lavish mausoleum, reminiscent of a High Renaissance *casino*, designed for the Aikens of Dalmoak by *James Hamilton II*, c. 1875. The arcaded centre bays have splendid cast-iron gates crowned by a coffered stone dome, the pedimented wings pairs of polished pink granite columns. – Along the left-hand path, a flight of steps leads up to the Davidson of Ruchill mausoleum by *J. T. Rochead*, 1851, a sombre Greek pseudo-peripteral temple with screens of channelled masonry between rectangular-section piers. – Further s along the same terrace, the family burial ground of Laurence Hill, Collector to the Merchants' House, a semicircle cut out of the rock, with several tablets of early date (one of 1833) set into the artificially rugged background, enclosed by a balustrade.

PUBLIC BUILDINGS

BISHOP'S CASTLE. Of the curtain-walled castle that crowned the hill and extended over an area corresponding to the whole square in front of the Cathedral and the Jubilee Wing of the Infirmary, there is nothing to be seen above ground, apart from a section of excavated walling to be preserved within the Cathedral Visitors' Centre and the line of part of the curtain wall to be outlined on the paving outside. Its pillaged remains

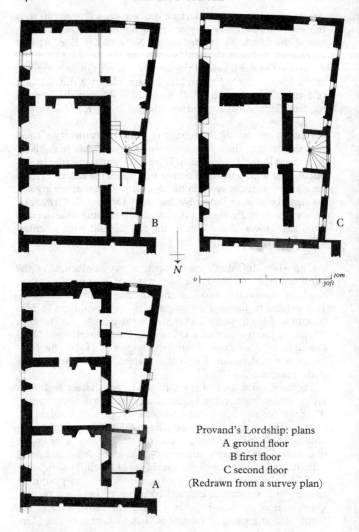

N

Provand's Lordship: plans
A ground floor
B first floor
C second floor
(Redrawn from a survey plan)

stood, as many views show, until 1789, when they were swept away for the Infirmary, all except some of the curtain wall and a last tower (Beaton's Tower) which remained until 1792.

First mention of the castle was made in 1258, but its early form, whether of timber or of stone, is not known. It was substantial enough to be garrisoned by Edward I in 1301. (A ditch that may mark an early timber structure was unearthed on the s edge of the Infirmary car park in 1969.) Major building work was done by Bishop Cameron (1426–66), who built a large tower house of three or four storeys (the section of fine ashlar foundation walling to be incorporated in the Visitors'

Centre may relate to this); but whether there was an earlier residence on this site is unknown. Archbishop Beaton (1508–22) surrounded this with a curtain wall which enclosed an irregular hexagon extending into a S arm parallel with Castle Street. Obtruding from the SE angle was a five-storey per-imeter tower with bastions and crowstepped gables. (This section of curtain wall and tower was excavated in 1986–8 at a point just N of John Knox Street and just E of Castle Street.) Just N of it, Dunbar (1524–47) built the square gatehouse with two big circular embattled towers. These fortifications were indeed necessary; the castle was stormed six times between 1515 and the final attack by Moray in 1568. It was restored by Spottiswood in 1611, but by 1689 was ruinous again except for Beaton's Tower.

PROVAND'S LORDSHIP (Museum), 3 Castle Street. The only medieval prebendal house ('Provand' is a corruption of 'pre-bend') to have survived the C19 City Improvements was saved and restored in 1906 by the Provand's Lordship Society, founded for that purpose. In 1927 Sir William Burrell helped to provide C16 and C17 furnishings.

It was built in 1471 by Bishop Andrew Muirhead (whose arms, almost illegible, are carved on a skew on the SE gable) as part of St Nicholas's Hospital, which he had founded and which adjoined to the S. At some time later, it was acquired by the prebendary of Barlanark, whose country seat was Provan Hall (*see* Easterhouse, below: Public Buildings). The masonry is substantially medieval and so are the oak floor beams, but the window openings are C17 or C18, and the N end was curtailed in the C19. At the back, a wedge-shaped extension with crowstepped gables, built in 1670 by William Bryson, a tailor (*see* the datestone).

Inside, the original arrangement is preserved: three rooms of equal size on each of the three floors. The upper rooms were probably originally reached by an external timber stair and galleries on the W side. The broad stone winder stair between two small rooms per floor in the C17 extension replaced this. All the rooms have fireplaces on their S walls. The downstairs ones are crude, with breasts corbelled out on huge rough imposts. The first-floor rooms are altogether more elaborate: the fireplaces have proper jambs and lintels and relieving arches in the big square breasts, the windows little seats in the reveals.

N of Provand's Lordship stood Govan Manse (the ruins of which were not cleared until after 1843) and, N of that, Renfrew Manse (replaced in the C17). Both, according to the footings found in 1979, apparently corresponded in form and alignment to Provand's Lordship.

CENTRAL COLLEGE OF COMMERCE, 300 Cathedral Street, and GLASGOW COLLEGE OF BUILDING AND PRINTING, North Hanover Street. Two striking buildings completed in 1964 and designed by *Peter Williams* of *Wylie Shanks & Partners* in a Corbusian manner, with expressionist rooftop plant and penthouses, and a crisp cladding of black Vitrolite and smooth travertine. The Central College of Commerce is a rectangular seven-storey block with glazing wrapped right round between the floor slabs and slender *pilotis* along the street front; Glasgow College of Building and Printing is a tall, curtain-walled, coffin-shaped slab on sculptural raw-concrete *pilotis*.

EASTERN DISTRICT COLLEGE OF NURSING AND MID-WIFERY, St James's Road. By *Sir Basil Spence, Glover & Ferguson*, 1985–7. Horizontal layers of red-brown brick and glass interrupted by a square tower.

GLASGOW COLLEGE OF BUILDING AND PRINTING. *See* CENTRAL COLLEGE OF COMMERCE, above.

GLASGOW COLLEGE OF FOOD TECHNOLOGY, 230 Cathedral Street. By *Keppie, Henderson & Partners*, 1970–8. Depressing brown and beige brick.

ALLAN GLEN'S SCHOOL, Cathedral Street. Founded in 1853 as Glasgow's first school for training in science and practical subjects. The present school buildings date from 1961–3 (by the *City Architect's Education Department*): a curtain-walled slab of labs and classrooms, screened from the road by a glass-walled hall and dining room, and, to the NW, a block of workshops and a gym.

LADYWELL SCHOOL, 94 Duke Street. 1858, by *John Burnet Senior*. Built as Alexander's School for the proprietor of the adjacent mill (*see* Perambulation 1, below). Italianate, with a tall slim tower asymmetrically placed by the entrance. Blind Ionic loggia between the pedimented end bays. In the spandrels, heads of Homer, Aristotle, Shakespeare, Michelangelo and Milton, carved by *John Crawford*. Inside altered in 1924.

MARTYRS' PUBLIC SCHOOL (since 1983 the Forum Arts Trust), Parson Street. 1895–8, by *Honeyman & Keppie*. *Charles Rennie Mackintosh* was the senior assistant in the practice, and his hand is evident in many aspects of the design. When viewed from Parson Street, it appears a rather jumbled composition, but from the pedestrian bridge to the E the ordered arrangement that derives from its symmetrical plan is more obvious: the elegant roof ventilators, masquerading as cupolas, indicate the straightforward plan beneath. Access was from a large playground (now much reduced in size) to E and W entrances with their own staircases. Classroom blocks of three storeys each side of a central open galleried well and a further classroom block on the axis to the N. The elevations are made restless by the number of different window shapes and a mixture of sashes and leaded glazing. The overall appearance is not enhanced by the clumsy junction between the main block and the N classroom block, nor by the single asymmetrical chimney on the S elevation. There are light touches, however, where Mackintosh's flair for details is apparent; in the short run of projecting eaves with swept timber corbels over the staircase windows and in the swirling Art Nouveau motifs around the entrance doorways.

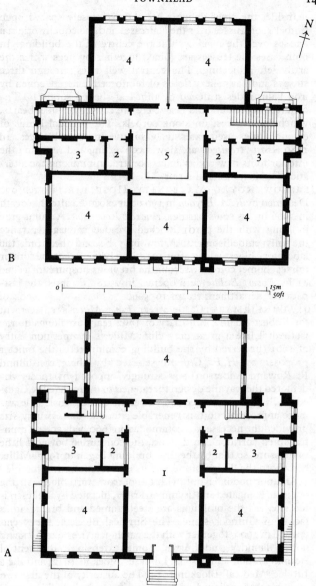

Martyrs' Public School: plans
A ground floor, B first floor
(second-floor plan is identical to first)
1 hall, 2 cloaks, 3 staff, 4 classroom
5 light well (hall below)
(Redrawn from a survey plan of 1984)

Inside, the chief delights are the six closely spaced open timber roof trusses over the staircases and the equally original trusses over the main well at the centre of the building. In both cases the trusses are joined together by pegs which are artily left projecting. The central well rises through three storeys and has gallery floors of reinforced concrete edged by iron balustrades stiffened by thin leaf-shaped supports. The concrete floors here and elsewhere are carried on steel beams, which in turn rest on stone corbels. The original bands of coloured tiles used extensively survive in several places. In 1989 *Assist Architects* are slowly converting and restoring the interior to its new use as an arts centre, minimizing the alterations to the original interior.

GLASGOW ROYAL MATERNITY HOSPITAL, Rottenrow. Designed by *R. A. Bryden* in 1903 but executed after his death in 1906 by his son's partner, *Andrew Robertson*. A gaunt grey building with the partly blocked arcaded carriage entrance the only embellishment. A few bays beyond the pend, the laboratory block, added after 1914, and beyond that the former nurses' home, converted from the previous hospital (of 1879–81 by *Robert Baldie*) and opened in 1928. To its S, the outpatients' department etc. of 1955–60.

ROYAL INFIRMARY, Castle Street. *James Miller*'s replacement for Robert Adam's Infirmary of 1792 rears up alongside the Cathedral like a great grey cliff. Miller's competition entry of 1901 (preferred by the building committee to the quieter proposal by *H. E. Clifford* selected by their consultant, R. Rowand Anderson) was strongly opposed by those who deplored the way the design threatened to intimidate the Cathedral. But the committee considered that its Scottish style was more appropriate to this venerable site, and that its very size provided the necessary accommodation (660 beds and an uninterrupted corridor). In the end, the committee bowed a little to pressure, so that by the time building began in 1907, Miller had shorn the design of most of its excrescences.

An unorthodox layout, with tall narrow ward blocks strung out in an elongated and asymmetrical H, dictated by the restricted site. All the buildings are steel-framed and brick with a facing of Giffnock stone. The Surgical Block at the N end opened in 1909 (together with the gatehouse (*see* below), power house, laundry and nurses' home extension); the central Administration and Special Diseases Block in 1912; and the S Jubilee (Medical) Block in 1914. The austerity of the first two ward blocks is relieved on their main fronts only by big square central towers with simple bartizans, by some open arcading and much balustrading, and by almost free-standing 'sanitary towers' with Baroque, not Baronial, cupolas. The back is bleak enough for a prison, the centre unmodelled and connected to the end towers only by an attic-level corridor – a convalescents' promenade. The JUBILEE BLOCK (with which the idea for rebuilding began in 1897) is completely Beaux Arts classical, with a tall mansard roof, lots of emphatic horizontal rustication, and a centrepiece with giant columns *in antis* and an insignificant dome instead of the big square Scottish-style towers of the other blocks.

The long, low GATEHOUSE (Accidents and Emergencies) forms a screen along Castle Street. At its N end, on the wall of the LISTER LECTURE THEATRE (1926–7), a plaque records the site of the surgical wards where Lister worked (added to Adam's Infirmary in 1861 by *Clarke & Bell*).

In the Surgical Block's entrance hall, a bronze MEDALLION of Lord Lister by *Johan Keller*, 1909. – In the CHAPEL, on the ground floor, eight STAINED-GLASS windows of 1912, four of them by *R. Anning Bell*.

EAST CHAPEL AVENUE, N of the N wing, gives access to an additional ward block and mortuary, and to the curtain-walled PATHOLOGY DEPARTMENT of 1957 and 1963. N of the Avenue, the former BLIND ASYLUM, incorporated in the hospital in 1940 and mostly derelict in 1989. The original building by *William Landless* (1879) is excruciatingly Franco-Flemish, with a spire bristling gargoyles. Figure of Christ restoring sight to a blind child, carved by *Charles Grassby*, 1881. Then, following the curve of Castle Street, a long range of plain stone warehouses with timber shopfronts below, apparently part of Landless's remarkable design. The asylum buildings which they concealed have gone, replaced by the Infirmary's Outpatients' Department of the late 1940s (also derelict in 1989).

Beyond lies the W gateway to the huge QUEEN ELIZABETH BUILDING, designed by *Sir Basil Spence, Glover & Ferguson* as the first phase (1971–82) of a complete rebuilding programme, with five- to seven-storey blocks rising above a continuous four-storey podium. The two blocks that have been built are massive and monotonous, with narrow horizontal layers of white concrete and glass. The blue brick podium projects on the NE. Under the deck, the entrance to the out-patients' waiting room, as unfriendly as an airport lounge. Within each block, a regular grid of wards etc. Standing to the NE, the brick-clad STAFF RESIDENCES; to the NW the BIOCHEMISTRY DEPARTMENT, both in a similar vein. (For the associated Eastern District College of Nursing, *see* above.)

UNIVERSITY OF STRATHCLYDE

Glasgow's second university received its charter in 1964. It is a lineal descendant of Anderson's Institution, begun in 1796 for education in the sciences and mechanics along the lines envisaged by John Anderson, Professor of Philosophy at Glasgow University, in his will of 1795. Anderson's library and scientific instruments formed the basis of the college, which in 1886 was incorporated with the College of Science and Arts (developed from the Mechanics' Institution) and with the Atkinson Institution (for the instruction of artisans) into the Glasgow and

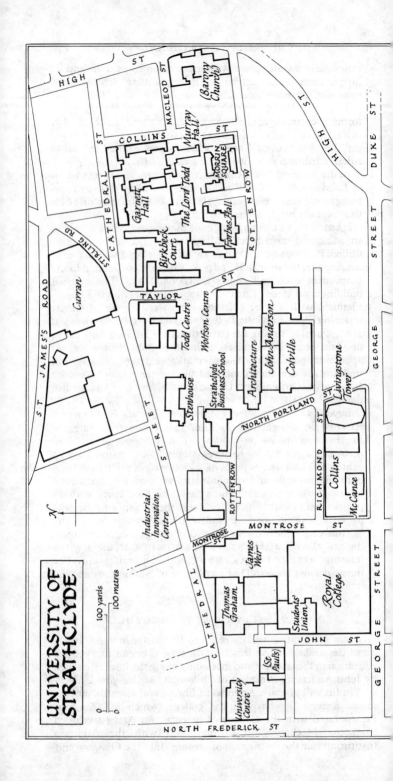

West of Scotland Technical College (after 1912 with the prefix Royal). In 1964, just before it acquired university status, the Technical College was merged with the Scottish College of Commerce.

Several of the university's buildings, grouped behind the original Royal College on the slope up to Cathedral Street, pre-date 1964. There is no real campus, though pedestrian routes and landscaped courts link the buildings. Neither was there any aesthetic master-plan, though *Sir Robert Matthew* was the consultant; various architects were employed, and the result is a motley collection of designs. The scale of the buildings is generally modest (rarely more than six storeys), the materials predominantly dreary brown brick and exposed concrete, especially along Cathedral Street, where large expanses of blank brown walls and an irregular and gappy building line make a depressing streetscape.

Important to all the designs is the very steep fall of the land, especially from Rottenrow to Richmond Street, where artificial terracing has been used to house servicing and laboratories in tall podia. Styles range from the solid conservative brick of the earliest addition to the Royal College, through the quiet and thoughtful Department of Architecture and the sharp geometry of the Wolfson Centre, to the monumental silhouette of the Stenhouse Building. The late 1970s and 1980s have brought a conspicuous historicism and, as in the rest of the city, the re-use of old buildings, the Barony Church as a hall for ceremonial, the former Collins factory as a library and classrooms, and tenements as student flats.

The obvious place to start a tour is the ROYAL COLLEGE on George Street, built for the Glasgow and West of Scotland Technical College. *David Barclay* won the competition of 1901 with a design that shows none of the refinement of the earlier *H. & D. Barclay* practice. Four wings round two open light-wells were finished in 1905: the Dumfries-shire stone façade came last. There is little to distinguish it from a contemporary warehouse. It is extremely flat, with a scarcely modulated skyline and the device, familiar from commercial buildings, of uniting each bay of windows within a single tall arch. Attic storeys make the end bays into towers, a freely interpreted temple-front marks the centre. The entrance is especially self-effacing and leads into a cramped hall, dominated by the dark marble WAR MEMORIAL designed by *T. L. Watson* and *Colin Sinclair*, 1920–1. On the staircase off the s spine corridor, a statue of James Watt by *John Greenshields*, once part of the façade of the Mechanics' Institution, built on this site in 1833. The unexciting Assembly Hall, its flat ceiling spanned by open trusses, is best reached from the big NE extension, the JAMES WEIR BUILDING (Engineering) by *Wylie, Shanks & Underwood*. Brown brick, with a tall stairtower at the junction of old and new (1957–8), and an additional six-storey slab (1960–4) facing Cathedral Street.

The THOMAS GRAHAM BUILDING (Chemical and

Process Engineering), next along Cathedral Street to the w, is a tough five-storey concrete slab of 1960–4 by *Walter Underwood & Partners*, with horizontal bands of windows and a lower, partly open corner entrance block where the ground drops steeply to the sw.

Beyond John Street, the blank brown walls of the UNIVERSITY CENTRE by *Covell Matthews Partnership*, 1975; and, adjacent to it, facing John Street, St Paul's Parish Church of 1905–7 (now CHAPLAINCY CENTRE) by *John McIntyre* of Edinburgh, cavalierly subdivided and extended by *Wylie, Shanks & Underwood* in 1957–8. William Adamish exterior, with a tall thin se tower with arcaded and domed bell-stage. *Wylie, Shanks & Underwood* did better in 1954–7 with the STUDENTS' UNION opposite, a nice mix of punctured stone and glass curtain walling. N extension by *Walter Underwood & Partners*, 1976.

Now back down to George Street, E of Royal College, where a brutal car-parking deck overhangs a row of shops. Sitting on top of it, an ill-assortment of buildings all designed by *Covell Matthews & Partners*, in a collaboration of university and commercial interests. The McCANCE BUILDING (1962–3), with its mannered concrete frame, coloured mosaic and projecting wedges of lecture theatres, was designed for the university. In the library, two murals by *William Mitchell*. The lozenge-shaped LIVINGSTONE TOWER (1965–8), with its vivid orange framing and dark-green curtain walling, was originally speculative offices (now Social Sciences). The retiring blue-brick COLLINS BUILDING, containing library and art gallery, was sandwiched between them in 1973. All are entered from Richmond Street.

Behind them lies Glasgow Royal Maternity Hospital (*see* Public Buildings, above). E of this, the COLVILLE BUILDING (Civil Engineering and Metallurgy) fills the steep NE corner of North Portland Street and Richmond Street with a wedge-shaped blue-brick podium containing laboratories and an upper lecture-room block, strongly banded in white, in a clean-cut design typical of *Sir Robert Matthew, Johnson-Marshall & Partners* at that date (1964–7).

Rottenrow, along the top of the hill, now leads w only; its ancient line has been interrupted by a landscaped court best approached from Cathedral Street via Montrose Street at the w end of Rottenrow. At the NE corner of Montrose Street, *Walter Underwood & Partners'* CENTRE FOR INDUSTRIAL INNOVATION (1968–9), with a dreary blank wall to Cathedral Street. Beyond it to the E, the STENHOUSE BUILDING (Business Administration) is a more ambitious design of 1972 by the same architects. Bold silhouette with the topmost storeys cantilevered one above the other on the N side and two massive staircase towers on the s. Open framing shelters a staircase up to the level of the landscaped courtyard behind.

This steeply mounded grassy court, crossed by a thickly planted rivulet and a winding flight of steps, is the university's most congenial spot. At the centre, a rhythmic alignment of curved Cor-Ten steel posts (CALLANISH by *Gerald Laing*, 1971), inspired by prehistoric sites on Lewis. To the W, the showy STRATHCLYDE BUSINESS SCHOOL by *G. R. M. Kennedy & Partners*, 1974–5, with vertical panels of yellowish brick and bronze glazing answering the vertical accents of the Wolfson Centre (*see* below).

Forming a low continuous backdrop to the court, the DEPARTMENT OF ARCHITECTURE AND BUILDING SCIENCE (1964–7), designed by *Frank Fielden* (then Professor of Architecture) *& Associates*. This wall of blue engineering brick is gently articulated by the rows of monopitch rooflights and by the projecting square bays, glazed at first-floor level and faced with copper sheets along the second floor. On the ground floor, partly screened by the mound in front, shallower canted bays beneath the strongly modelled cantilever. Open-plan interior with a spine of lecture rooms and library and a row of offices along the S face. Beneath, in the podium, the boilerhouse served by the slender silver chimneys to the W.

The WOLFSON CENTRE FOR BIO-ENGINEERING (1970–1, by *Morris & Steedman*) is the monumental serrated block at the E end of the court, with slits of bronze glazing between the triangular vertical members of ribbed concrete which conceal the ducting. In the galleried entrance hall, a TAPESTRY by *Robert A. Stewart*, an excellent design of Léger-like entwined tubes.

A raised deck across the line of Rottenrow links the Wolfson Centre and the JOHN ANDERSON BUILDING (Natural Philosophy), a panel-clad L-shaped slab by *Building Design Partnership* (1968–71), on a wide and very tall podium that contains much of the accommodation and overlooks Richmond Street below. In the foyer, the plain Kilsyth stone MEMORIAL SLAB to Professor John Anderson † 1796, moved from the Ramshorn Kirk in 1973.

Steps from the deck lead down to the remaining E part of Rottenrow (*see* below) at its junction with Taylor Street. At the N end of Taylor Street, the uncommunicative TODD CENTRE FOR BIOCHEMISTRY (1973–7), also by *Building Design Partnership*. Opposite, two remaining parts of William Collins's Herriot Hill Stationery and Printing Works, founded in 1861, sweep round at the end of Cathedral Street, heavily disguised as the CURRAN BUILDING, a remodelling for the Engineering Applications Centre and Scottish Hotel School by *Walter Underwood & Partners*, completed in 1983, and as the ANDERSONIAN LIBRARY by *Faulkner-Brown Hendy Watkinson Stonor*. The form and, at the back, the fabric of the earlier building can be discerned despite the skin of brown and red brick that reduces the windows to slits. Towards St James's Road, gates from the Royal College building.

STUDENT VILLAGE. Student accommodation is concentrated on the S side of Cathedral Street. The staggered brown brick and white weatherboarded flats of BIRKBECK

COURT (1972–4, by *George Wimpey & Co. Ltd*) flank a pedestrian street down to Rottenrow. w of Birkbeck Court, the
hard red brick of *G. R. M. Kennedy & Partners*' group of
residences, with their Post-Modern variations on various
Glasgow themes, such as (for GARNETT HALL and FORBES
HALL, 1985–6) canted bays and oriels (here mirror-clad),
grids of glazing bars and repeated squares of headers *à la*
Mackintosh, channelled brickwork reminiscent of Thomson,
and, most obviously (at MURRAY HALL, 1983–4), big round
corner towers derived from Scotland Street School. Other
details, such as silly metal eyebrows and pediments like
coathangers, are more trivial. The elevations are quite subtly
adjusted – within the court to answer the square blocks of
Birkbeck Court, and along Rottenrow to continue the flat
fronts of the City Improvement Trust's tenements of 1894–7
(formerly Morrin Square) that have been converted into
student flats. In the centre of the courtyard, the LORD TODD
(1983–4), combining student centre and local pub in three low
pavilions linked by a glass-roofed corridor. Dark roof trusses
dominate inside.

There are a few university buildings further afield; *see* especially:
ALEXANDER TURNBULL BUILDING: *see* Nos. 161–9
  George Street (under Merchant City, below: Streets).
Former BARONY CHURCH: *see* Churches, above.
CLYDE HALL: *see* Jamaica Street (under Saltmarket and St
  Enoch's, below: Streets).
JAMES TODD BUILDING: *see* Merchant City, Streets:
  Ingram Street.
MARLAND HOUSE: *see* George Street (under Merchant City:
  Streets).
Former RAMSHORN KIRK: *see* Merchant City: Churches.

PERAMBULATIONS

1. *Cathedral Square and its surroundings*

CATHEDRAL SQUARE. The Cathedral, Infirmary and craggy
silhouette of the Necropolis are the dramatic backcloth to this
broad plateau, formalized in 1917 by the City Engineer, *A. B.
McDonald*, and to be reordered, by 1990, with orchestrated
approaches to the Cathedral and buildings reinforcing the
street pattern (*see* above). The Infirmary tends to dominate by
its very size, leaving the Cathedral to stand almost accidentally
between it and the gates of the Necropolis. Provand's Lordship
on the w side (*see* Public Buildings, above) is the only visible
medieval relic. Most of its neighbours of all dates have been
demolished in the ruthless path of a feeder road to the M8.

On the s side the Square opens directly into CATHEDRAL
SQUARE GARDENS, created by the City Architect, *John
Carrick*, in 1879. Turning its NE corner, the nicely judged
informality of the former DISCHARGED PRISONERS' AID
SOCIETY, designed in 1894–6 for the inmates of the Bridewell

(*see* below) by *Campbell Douglas & Morrison*. Facing the gardens, the elegant Italian façade of Barony North Church answers the red Gothic bulk of Barony Church on the w side (*see* Churches, above).

CIVIC STATUES. All but one are bronze figures of a straight-forward commemorative kind: none is outstanding. All to be reordered by 1990. – David Livingstone, 1875–9, by *John Mossman*, moved here from George Square in 1959. Very naturalistic. Pictorial reliefs round the base. – Within the Infirmary garden, James Lumsden, stationer and local benefactor, † 1856, by *John Mossman*, 1862. – Flanking the Necropolis gate: on the l., James White of Overtoun † 1884, begun by *John Mossman*, completed by *Frank Leslie*, 1890; on the r., James Arthur † 1885, a truculent figure by *G. A. Lawson*, 1893. – At the NW corner of Cathedral Square Gardens, Revd Dr Norman Macleod, Queen Victoria's chaplain † 1872, modelled in his robes by *John Mossman*, and cast by *Cox & Son* of Thames Ditton, 1881–2. – Facing Castle Street from Cathedral Square Gardens, a stiff but handsome equestrian statue of William III in the classical mould. It was presented to the city in 1735 by James Macrae and stood at Glasgow Cross until 1923. The tail, on a ball-and-socket joint, is supposed to move in the wind!

HIGH STREET runs down the hill from the SW corner of Cathedral Square to Duke Street (and thence S to Glasgow Cross; *see* Merchant City, below: Streets). Its broad curve, and the red sandstone ashlar tenements with shops below that line it, are the City Improvement Trust's work of 1899–1902. [70] The composition of big chimneystacks, attic-level oriels, cast-iron-edged shallow canted bays, crowstepped and coped gables, and panels carved with the city arms unfolds with subtle variety and no two bays the same, in a happy Arts and Crafts reinterpretation of the C17 Scottish tenement by *Burnet, Boston & Carruthers*, who won the limited competition in 1899.

Just round the corner into DUKE STREET, the LADYWELL HOUSING SCHEME (1961–4, by *Honeyman, Jack & Robertson*). It was built on the site of Glasgow's Bridewell, which was first erected in 1792 and demolished *c*. 1950, except for the cut-down remains of the boundary wall. Along Duke Street, three fifteen-storey slab blocks with mannered, angled W elevations and part-open access corridors along the E sides. Across the slope that climbs steeply up to Cathedral Square, rows of two- to four-storey tenements, detailed with harling and stone cladding in deference to the site, enclose a grassy court with a few spindly trees. To the E, the shining silver pipework of WELLPARK BREWERY (*c*. 1967–74, by *Thomas Cordiner, Cunningham & Partners*), the successor to a series of buildings on a site reputedly established as a brewery by the Tennents as early as the 1550s.

On the other side of Duke Street, Ladywell School (*see* Public Buildings). This was built for James Alexander, the proprietor of the adjacent fireproof cotton-thread mill designed by *Charles Wilson* (1849). It was given wrought-iron roof trusses and mass-concrete on corrugated-iron shuttering for the top two floors when converted to the GREAT EASTERN HOTEL for homeless working men by *Neil C. Duff* in 1907–9. Duff's only alteration to the mill's impressive tooled ashlar façade, with its projecting end bays and rusticated quoins, was the addition of the top storey and the Baroque centrepiece with its flowing lettering.

2. *Townhead N of Cathedral Street*

A perambulation round the N part of Townhead lacks interest. The only rewarding buildings, St Mungo's R.C. Church and the former Martyrs' Public School (*see* Churches and Public Buildings, above), are on the E edge, perched high above the motorway link that cuts them off from the Cathedral. Otherwise, the dense mixture of industrial buildings and the plainest C19 tenements (which in 1962 housed most of the area's 19,000 people) was replaced between 1967 and 1970 with sufficient homes for 7,000, spread out in high- and dreary flat-roofed low-rise blocks (to which pitched roofs were added in 1987) round the perimeter of a series of featureless open spaces. *George Wimpey & Co.*, in association with the City Architect, produced the design, which has none of the imaginative strokes of the earliest C.D.A.s.

Below in Cathedral Street, almost nothing but the schools and colleges of this educational zone of the C.D.A. (*see* Public Buildings). At the E end, the CLYDESDALE BANK COMPUTER CENTRE, Cathedral Street, a pavilion of purplish engineering brick and silvered glass by *McKay & Forrester* (1981) forming an effective *point-de-vue*. The illusion of a transparent box overlaid with wafer-thin sheets of brick gives way at the back to more solid geometry.

Due N, in the N industrial fringe that was once the hinterland of Port Dundas (*see* below), but is now divorced from it by the M8, very few old buildings now. Most interesting and eye-catching across the corner of DOBBIE'S LOAN (Nos. 58–70) and Kennedy Street, the TOWNHEAD WRIGHT WORKS (former Milton Colour Works), a weakly French Gothic former oil and colour works in red and white brick, dated 1873. Beyond to the W lies Cowcaddens (*see* below).

THE MERCHANT CITY

The eastern edge of the Merchant City is that part of the High Street between Townhead and Glasgow Cross, historically a section of the long medieval street between the Cathedral and

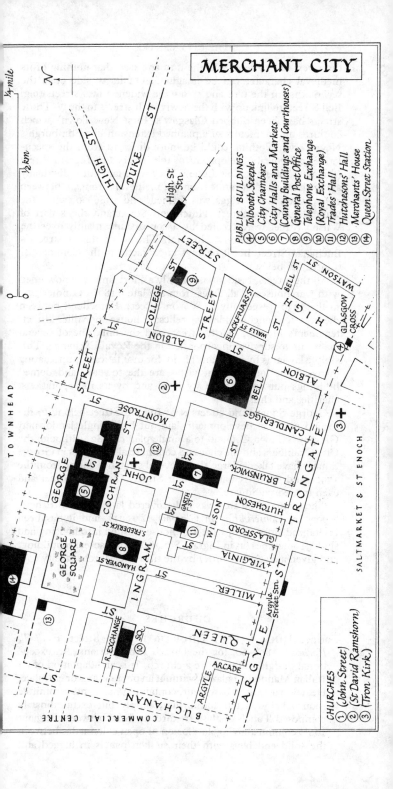

MERCHANT CITY

PUBLIC BUILDINGS
④ Tolbooth Steeple
⑤ City Chambers
⑥ City Halls and Markets
⑦ (County Buildings and Courthouses)
⑧ General Post Office
⑨ Telephone Exchange
⑩ (Royal Exchange)
⑪ Trades' Hall
⑫ Hutchesons' Hall
⑬ Merchants' House
⑭ Queen Street Station

CHURCHES
① (John Street)
② (St David Ramshorn)
③ (Tron Kirk)

the river, but so rebuilt in the C19 and C20 that nothing of its medieval character can be imagined. Off its w side open the wynds that in the C18 and C19 were widened into streets (e.g. Bell Street) to link up with the newly built streets to the w. Those streets have been dubbed Glasgow's 'First New Town', which conjures up the picture of a planned extension like Edinburgh's New Town. Nothing could be more different from the speculative, piecemeal development of the streets s of Ingram Street (the medieval Back Cow Lone). They were laid out individually along the riggs that ran N from the medieval Trongate between 1660, when Candleriggs was formed, and 1786–90, when the wider Brunswick Street, Hutcheson Street and the E part of Wilson Street were created by a consortium, mainly over the grounds of Hutchesons' Hospital. The westernmost street is Buchanan Street, but it belongs in character to the Commercial Centre (*see* below).

All the streets, residential for only a short time, are now lined with warehouses of all dates from the late C18 (in Candleriggs) to the 1930s (especially in Wilson Street). Embedded between them, a few once-residential relics: a house in Miller Street, tenements in, e.g., Garth Street, and the only one of several mansions to survive, incorporated in the Royal Exchange. This simple layout is by no means bland, for dramatically punctuating many of the long straight vistas are the towered and domed buildings put up by the City itself and by its incorporations, charities and churches.

George Square and streets N of Ingram Street belong to the second phase of development, laid out by a single landowner, Glasgow's Town Council, to a single plan *c.* 1782. Although the City Chambers and the civic and commercial buildings in George Square have taken a large slice, several stretches dating from the 1790s and 1800s remain in John Street, Cochrane Street and even in George Square.

The virtue of all this was rediscovered late (in Lord Esher's report on *Conservation in Glasgow* of 1971), and it has been revitalized since then, with warehouses turned into housing and shops, sometimes (as in Ingram Square) with discreet rebuilding, and given a distinct identity by the title 'the Merchant City'.

CHURCHES

Former JOHN STREET CHURCH, 18 John Street. By *J. T. Rochead*, 1858–60, for the United Presbyterians. An exceptional design, quite unlike a church. It is an adaptation of an Italian Mannerist palazzo, without an obvious axis or entrance. Heavily rusticated basement, containing halls and committee rooms, below a tall auditorium, simply but extraordinarily composed. Panels of glass are directly fitted between the giant Ionic columns, giving an illusion of open colonnades between the solid end bays with their sunken panels in lugged and scalloped surrounds. Alas, the crisply cut detail has been scoured away, and the fine galleried interior butchered in the conversion to a bar and offices in 1987–8, though there is still notable plasterwork by *James Steel*.

ST DAVID (RAMSHORN KIRK; owned by Strathclyde University), 98 Ingram Street. 1824–6, by *Thomas Rickman*, who provided 'Working Drawings with some alterations' on the basis of plans drawn up by *James Cleland* after a meeting with Rickman on the site. (It replaced a church of 1719–24 destroyed when Ingram Street was extended w.) Thinly Gothic but with a tall tower, the first of such boldness among Scottish Gothic Revival buildings, impressively sited on axis with Candleriggs. The body of the church is T-plan and exceptionally tall because of the crypt stipulated by Cleland. The details are much simplified, indeed rather delicate, late C13, with early use of Geometrical tracery in the larger two- and three-light windows along the front and at the ends. Inside, a flat ceiling, ribbed in plaster to imitate quadripartite vaulting, but meeting in flat classical plaster roses rather than bosses. W gallery with Gothic tracery, on thin cast-iron columns. Side galleries removed 1886–7 and session house extended. Stripped of pews but with the organ case still *in situ* on the S wall.

STAINED GLASS. An astonishingly complete display, mostly of 1887–8. No individual window is of outstanding quality. – W arm: S wall, Hezekiah and Josiah in bright clear colours with lots of plain glass by *Ward & Hughes*; Peter, James and John by *Kier*; Armour of God hanging in a trellis of foliage by *Clayton & Bell*; W wall, all three (Baptism, Resurrection and Presentation of Christ) in muddy colours by *William Meikle & Sons*; N wall, John the Baptist and David I, both by *Ballantine*. – Under the gallery (from W wall to E wall): Work, 1911, by *Alf. Webster*; Christ Blessing the Children by *J. & W. Guthrie*; the Preaching and the Conversion of Paul, and Moses, all by *Kier*; Dorcas and Phoebe, *c.* 1930, by *C. E. Stewart*. – E arm: N wall, Good Samaritan by *Meikle & Son*, 1911; Aaron by *Kier*; E wall, all three (Old Testament prophets) by *Kier*; S wall, Ruth and Naomi, and Faith, Hope and Charity, both by *Meikle*; David and Solomon by *Ward & Hughes* to match that W of the organ. – Gallery (from W side): St Andrew by *Kier*; Solomon and Queen of Sheba designed by *Stewart* of Glasgow, made by *Hooper & Edwards*; heraldry by *Meikle*; The Faithful Servant, 1903, by *Stephen Adam*; 'I am the Way' by *W. & J. Kier*; Ecce Homo, 1911, by *Stewart*; heraldry by *Kier*. – Front stair: Mary Magdalene, and Christ and St Peter, both by *Kier*.

The CRYPT (with a groin vault carried on cast-iron columns) houses the bones of many celebrated Glaswegians (David Dale, John Glassford, John Campbell etc.) disturbed when the graveyard was curtailed for the new street and church. – MONUMENT to *James Cleland*, designed by himself and erected in 1825.

Handsome railings to a long GRAVEYARD of 1719, extended 1767 and c. 1800.

TRON KIRK, 71 Trongate. Now the Tron Theatre, converted from the former Tron or Laigh Kirk. Straddling the pavement, the TRON STEEPLE, which at some time housed the tron or public weighing beam which gave it its name. The steeple is all that remained, after a fire in 1793, of the original church on this site, founded in 1484 as the collegiate church of St Mary and St Anne, and reconstructed as a city kirk in 1592. Set back behind the steeple and independent of it, the replacement church of 1793–4.

The harled tower (begun c. 1592) and stone spire of 1630–6 are late Gothic. The spire takes its cue from Glasgow Cathedral, but Renaissance influence creeps in with the simplified balustrades round the parapet and the spire. The Tudorish pedestrian arches were cut through by *John Carrick* in 1855. Pretty vault with winged shields of the city arms and figures of St Mungo. In similar vein, and also decorated with the city arms, the adjoining No. 73 Trongate: also by *Carrick,* 1857–8. The Baroque courtyard wall and gateway are by *J. J. Burnet,* 1899–1900, a virtuoso display to screen a Caledonian railway tunnel air-shaft. The church is disappointing – just a simple bow-fronted harled box with stairtowers projecting at the NE and NW corners, two storeys of sash windows and a hipped roof – a fragment of an elaborate proposal by *R. & J. Adam,* including tenements along the street. The interior was converted c. 1981 by *McGurn, Logan & Duncan.* Above the theatre's gallery-level auditorium, a saucer dome with oculus and simple plasterwork.

PUBLIC BUILDINGS

TOLBOOTH STEEPLE, Glasgow Cross. 1625–7, by *John Boyd.* A tall slender square tower, unrelieved (except for the stringcourses which mark the seven storeys, the small windows, each with a little strapwork, and the buckle quoins) right up to the top with its clock and modest crown. As might be expected at this date, the crown is Gothic only in concept: it is pared down to the simplest forms and given a Renaissance cast with obelisk finials and naively classical balustrade. It originally had twenty-eight bells, replaced in 1881 by sixteen small bells and one large one by *John Wilson & Co.,* Gorbals.

The steeple still stands in its original position, although the rest of the Tolbooth, to which it was attached on the W side (*see* the rebuilt W side, without stringcourses), was demolished in 1921, when *Graham Henderson* of *Keppie & Henderson* reorganized Glasgow Cross (*see* Streets, below). The Tolbooth of c. 1626, in a similar mixture of late Gothic and Renaissance styles, had been rebuilt and Gothicized in 1814 by *David Hamilton.*

CITY CHAMBERS, George Square. 1882–90, by *William Young*. The lavishness of Glasgow's municipal buildings admitted no doubt of the city's wealth and importance. William Young, a native of Paisley with a London practice, won the second competition (1882) with a design that admirably fitted the brief. The foundation stone was laid in 1883, and Queen Victoria formally opened the building in 1888, although the interior, started in 1887, was not finished until 1890.

The EXTERIOR is chiefly memorable for its huge physical 60 presence, its main façade a gleaming white backdrop to the wide expanse of George Square. The style is conservative, a 'free and dignified treatment of the Italian Renaissance' (according to the architect), with Venetian influence predominant on the main façade, a more Roman *gravitas* elsewhere. Each elevation is different, reflecting the disposition of rooms within. The articulation of the MAIN FAÇADE is rather half-hearted: shallowly projecting central bays under a pediment, more pronounced angle pavilions (at all four corners) with proto-Baroque domes and, set well back behind the façade, the tall tower demanded in the brief, eclectically composed but with a heavy debt to the tower of Thomson's St Vincent Street Church. The rusticated *basimento* conceals two storeys of offices. The *piano nobile*, with suites of public rooms, is on the second floor, distinguished by an unbroken band of much-ornamented Serlian windows between coupled Ionic columns in the manner of Sansovino's St Mark's Library in Venice. More Serlian windows on the third floor, both in the centre, where they light the double-height Council Chamber, and in the domed end pavilions. The elaborate SCULPTURE is judiciously reserved for emphasis: for the Jubilee Pediment (by *George Lawson*), with Queen Victoria and the countries of Great Britain receiving homage from all over the world; the spandrels (by *John Mossman*), with the trades and industries of Glasgow; the figures of Peace, Plenty, Prosperity etc. at attic level; and the panels over the entrance, showing the peaceful victories of Art, Science and Commerce.

The N FRONT, almost as rich, has coupled, fluted Corinthian columns projecting between the three Serlian openings that light the Banqueting Hall, and more sculpture (groups representing Peace and Justice above the columns, *putti* in the spandrels, and bold rinceau along the parapet). The S and E FRONTS are plainer and more Roman, with pedimented windows, the S ones slightly more elaborate. On the S side a projecting bay with a pair of giant unfluted Corinthian columns and twin domes at the main entrance to the courtyard, disappointingly cramped, with a triumphal arch entrance to the W range and the Rates Hall projecting along the E side.

The large E BLOCK of 1914–23 by *Watson, Salmond, & Gray,* linked by arches over John Street, takes up the theme of Young's Cochrane Street elevation with Beaux Arts severity and refinement. It was intended to stretch to Montrose Street.

White Polmaise (N and W fronts) and Dunmore stone (S and

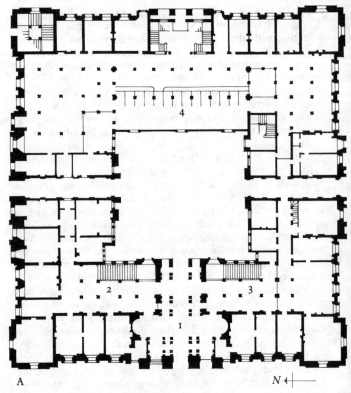

City Chambers: plans
A ground floor, B second floor
1 loggia, 2 banqueting hall staircase, 3 council
chamber staircase, 4 rates hall, 5 banqueting hall,

E fronts) and a granite plinth form a thin skin over Young's fireproof structure of brick, iron, steel and concrete, with timber confined to the roofing pegs, and to internal joinery and floors. There was electric lighting from the outset. The building contractors were *Morrison & Mason*, the sub-contractors and craftsmen *D. & J. Mackenzie* (plasterers); *Charles Carlton & Son* (painters); *Galbraith & Winton* (marble work and mosaic); *Stephen Adam* (stained glass); *Starkey, Gardner & Co.* (wrought-iron gates); and *George Adam* (wrought-iron lamps). The sculptors, apart from Lawson and Mossman, were *Farmer & Brindley*, *Charles Grassby* and *Edward Good*. Furnishings and furniture (except where stated) were provided by *Wylie & Lochead*. Young's assistant throughout was *H. D. Walton* of Glasgow.

INTERIOR. The entrance hall or LOGGIA, as Young called it, is immediately overwhelming in its opulence, reminiscent

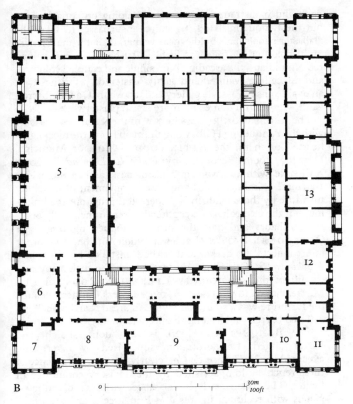

6 mahogany reception room, 7 octagonal salon, 8 satinwood
salon, 9 council chamber, 10 Lord Provost's dining room,
11 Lord Provost's room, 12 library, 13 council rooms
(Redrawn from *The Builder*, 1882)

of a luxury hotel, with gleaming mahogany, bevelled glass, and
coloured polished granite lit by pendant bronze lanterns. The
sources are mixed Italian, the columned and saucer-domed
'nave' and apsidal-ended transepts resembling (according to
Young) 'a Roman church of the Renaissance period', the tessellated vaults with *grotteschi* having 'Pompeian character'.
Massive stone doorcases, with figures of the Arts and Virtues
and mottoes transcribed from the old Tolbooth and, flanking
those to the staircases, caryatids (by *Mossman*). The expensive
but commonplace furnishings of 1983 are best ignored,
especially the reception desk, given an altar-like significance
by its backdrop, a TAPESTRY of the grey Glasgow hills by
R. A. Stewart.

  The STAIRCASES, simple in plan but with Baroque grandeur of scale and decoration, can be seen in one *coup d'œil* on 61
the first floor. The Council Chamber staircase (s) is magnificent enough, with alabaster-panelled walls, breccia marble

dado and balustrade, and tiers of arcading on square piers; but the Banqueting Hall (N) staircase surpasses it. Here the alabaster panels have bold evocative markings, the marbles are multi-coloured (purple breccia, black Irish and strongly veined red Numidian), the arcading is on single and coupled columns, and the ceilings vaulted and richly plastered. It finishes with an oval Louis XVI-style gallery and, above that, a long barrel-vault with central dome and more lavish plasterwork.

The RECEPTION ROOMS lie NW of the N staircase, *en suite* with the Banqueting Hall. Along the main front, the most light-hearted of them, the SATINWOOD SALON or Municipal Drawing Room, decorated by *Wylie & Lochead* in Louis XVI style, with satinwood and silk damask, and an anomalous Italianate chimneypiece. Sadly, the complement of matching furniture by the same firm is dispersed throughout the building, but the electroliers (exceptionally) retain their frilly opalescent shades and give the proper subdued lighting. The OCTAGONAL SALON (Ladies' Boudoir) in the NW corner interconnects. Its darker amberwood, installed by *Alexander Mackenzie & Co.*, forms the prelude to the mahogany and walnut of the MAHOGANY RECEPTION ROOM, also by Mackenzie's, and with heavier, more-or-less Carolean details; the furniture was also in that style. An arcade carries shallow, coffered barrel-vaults along the fireplace wall.

62　　　The BANQUETING HALL is vast, double-height and barrel-vaulted. Its decoration, supervised by *Leiper* and executed by *McCulloch & Co.*, clearly shows the influence of the French buildings visited by the advisory committee of bailies. The style is early Renaissance, with leaded windows, panels with reclining figures *à la* Primaticcio, and acanthus-decorated pilasters, arranged on the S wall to echo the Serlian windows opposite. Somewhat at odds with this revivalist scheme are the MURAL PAINTINGS, in 1899–1902 the most modern work Glasgow could offer. The main panels, describing the history and progress of the city of Glasgow, were painted by the so-called 'Glasgow Boys'. The scenes on the S wall of 'Legendary Glasgow' by *Alexander Roche* (The Legend of the City Arms) and 'Medieval Glasgow' by *E. A. Walton* (Glasgow Fair *c.* 1500) are in those artists' atmospheric and rather lugubrious style. *Lavery*'s 'Modern Glasgow', a bravura collage of scenes from local industry, breaks with their conventional composition and brownish palette. *George Henry*'s 'Granting of Glasgow's charter by William the Lion' (over the dais) has even brighter colours and a medievalizing manner. The smaller panels (Virtues) by *Alexander Walker*, showing the progress of culture, are later (1915). On the W wall, personifications of the Forth, Clyde, Tweed and Tay by *William Findlay* (1911) and 'Glasgow unfolding her plans for the future' by *D. Forrester Wilson* in the lunette. The *Templetons'* carpet duplicates the pattern of gilt-and-turquoise coffering in the ceiling.

The COUNCIL CHAMBER, its decoration designed to be

'of sombre and solid aspect, befitting the deliberations of a Town Council', fills the centre of the main front. Mahogany panelling, twin fireplaces at each end (glimpsed through Serlian openings) and a small public gallery. Above them, a deep frieze of greenish-gold Tynecastle Tapestry, a richly coloured and gilded ceiling with a central dome filled, like the windows, with greenish patterned glass. The horseshoe of seating, fitted in 1912 when the burgh was extended, faces the Lord Provost's chair, Queen Victoria's gift at the formal opening (1888).

The LORD PROVOST'S SUITE is in the SW pavilion. The decoration of the LORD PROVOST'S ROOM has been altered and given a Louis XVI air, with silk wallcoverings instead of the original 'distressed' Tynecastle Tapestry, satinwood furniture with blue leather tops instead of heavy Jacobean pieces, and a Neo-classical-style electrolier. The fireplace tiles painted with Pre-Raphaelite maidens have also gone. The octagonal upper part of the room, with its thickly enriched plaster ceiling, reflects the dome above: it rests on squinches. In the LORD PROVOST'S DINING ROOM, to the N, discordant eclecticism: rococo plasterwork, a William Adamish timber chimneypiece and Tynecastle Tapestry wallcovering.

The decoration of the suite of three COMMITTEE ROOMS and library along the S range, chosen by a committee of bailies, happily survives intact and displays an equally curious mixture of tastes. In the LIBRARY, at the W end, Chinese Chippendale-style bookcases continued above the Persian-tiled fireplace with the suggestion of a C17 oriel. Red and cream Tynecastle Tapestry wallcovering has been replaced with something more sombre, but the gold-green frieze embossed with *grotteschi* (repeated in the carpet) and the rococo decoration of the coved ceiling, originally more brilliantly coloured, survive. The middle committee room has imitation Tynecastle Tapestry wallpaper of 1986; the other two have mellow original versions below deep embossed friezes. The carved woodwork, where *in situ*, is mahogany and walnut.

The FAIENCE CORRIDOR links these rooms round the inside of the S, E and N ranges. With its glazed and embossed ochre and green tiles (by *Burmantofts*), it has the flavour of a monstrous Victorian vase.

CITY HALLS AND MARKETS, Candleriggs. These have their origin in the Bazaar (founded on this site by James Cleland in 1817), which housed the green and cheese markets long established in this neighbourhood. By 1914 Scotland's chief wholesale fruit market was held here: it was moved to Blochairn in 1969, and one of the two market halls became a general retail market.

The City Hall (the 'Great Hall') was added to the Bazaar in 1841 by *George Murray*. It stands, very plain and with sash windows on each side, almost concealed at the centre of the market, raised on iron columns and a perimeter of flat stone arches originally open to the walled but otherwise open area

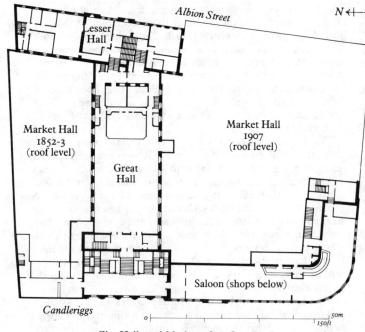

City Halls and Markets: first-floor level
(Redrawn from a survey plan of 1972)

of the Bazaar. (This open ground floor was built up as a store in 1967–9, when the Halls were remodelled as Glasgow's main concert hall.) The E block, with a flat Greek façade, faces Albion Street, and was designed to house a staircase and smaller halls. After Murray's death, the N end was added by *John Baird* in 1843–5, with an entrance into the part of the Bazaar he had roofed in 1842. This pend now gives access to the market hall of steel, cast-iron and glass constructed by *Bell & Miller* under *John Carrick* in 1852–3 to replace Baird's structure. In the galleried interior, the individual stalls and name-boards stand abandoned. The stone arches beneath the Great Hall can also be seen from here. At the Candleriggs end, the short section of façade with cast-iron pilasters and plate glass (now painted) originally fronted two storeys of shops, finished in 1855.

The bold Italianate entrance façade to the halls on Candle-riggs was added by *Carrick* in 1882–6 when he enlarged and recast the hall and markets, adding the vestibule, a new stair-case, and a short S range of shops (with saloon above), extended round into Bell Street in 1898. Except for the ware-house and Cheese Market adjacent in Bell Street (*see* Streets be-low), the classical red sandstone SE section, designed in 1907 by *A. B. McDonald* for the Office of Public Works, was the last ex-tension to the Bazaar: it replaced Carrick's Central Police Office.

Carrick's wide STAIRCASE rises from the Candleriggs entrance through three storeys and is lit from an iron-trussed glass roof. The rest of his work was remodelled in 1967–9. The GREAT HALL is large but dull. Gallery, platform, long Renaissance-style organ case (the organ of 1904 was sold in 1956) and window surrounds date from 1851–4, when Baird remodelled the hall. In the windows (now shuttered externally), PAINTED GLASS badges of the main city organizations, such as the Clyde Trust and Trades' House. The Albion Street block has also been modernized, all except the LESSER HALL, with its deep-coffered ceiling and linked-chain motif running round the cornice, possibly by Mr *Caird*, 1844.

Former COUNTY BUILDINGS AND COURTHOUSES, 40–50 Wilson Street. A vast Greek Revival building that fills a whole block of the Merchant City, *Clarke & Bell* won the competition in 1841 with a design incorporating the county offices, sheriff court, and the Merchants' House. Later, they enlarged and remodelled it to provide new county offices and more space for the courts (1868–71) and, after the City Chambers been built, reorganized the whole building for the courts (1892).

Each phase can be identified. The first building was L-plan, with the wing facing Wilson Street housing the county offices and sheriff court, and that along Hutcheson Street a new Merchants' House (moved from Bridgegate; *see* Saltmarket and St Enoch's, below: Public Buildings: former Fish Market). Each wing has a distinct façade. To Wilson Street, a hexastyle portico of fluted Ionic columns is raised above the rusticated ground floor, which reads as a tall stylobate. No steps to the portico: instead, along the stylobate, there is a frieze of classical figures by *Walter Buchan*. Insignificant entrances, formerly to the county offices (w) and the quite separate sheriff court (E), in the bases of the heavy, characteristically Greek Revival end pavilions. To Hutcheson Street, the Merchants' House is given equal importance by a colonnade of six giant fluted Corinthian columns *in antis* between two pairs of corresponding piers, and a classical frieze by Buchan. It faces down Garth Street to the Trades' House.

The block added in 1868–71 to rehouse the council offices, and rebuilt again in 1892 as part of the courts, faces Ingram Street. The Corinthian portico, which answers that at the s end, was cannibalized from the original Corinthian colonnade, which had been similar to that on Hutcheson Street but completely disengaged. The long range along Brunswick Street, plain except for a central pavilion echoing those at the corners, was also built in 1868–71 for court use. At the same time, the original building (including the Merchants' House, which moved again to George Square; *see* Streets, below) was entirely refitted for the same purpose.

The interior has been butchered in the poor-quality remodellings of 1892 and the 1960s. Nothing of the superior early and mid-Victorian character survives. In 1989 the building awaits yet another remodelling and repair by *Building Design Partnership* for a new use as a fashion centre.

GENERAL POST OFFICE, 1–7 George Square. The Italianate façade in, say, the manner of Scott's Foreign Office, is of 1875–8 by *Robert Matheson* of H.M. Office of Works for Scotland. The original building was T-shaped; the great side blocks were added in 1914–16 by *W.T. Oldrieve* and his successor as the Board of Works' principal architect for Scotland, *C.J.W. Simpson,* using the *Mouchel-Hennebique* method of concrete-framing. Between these blocks and facing Ingram Street, the stem of the T, remodelled in 1892–4, with an elaborately decorated façade, as a sorting office by *W.W. Robertson,* also of the Board of Works. (This construction entailed the demolition of Robert Adam's Assembly Rooms of 1792; *see* Calton, Public Buildings, Glasgow Green: McLennan Arch.)

Former CENTRAL FIRE STATION. *See* Streets, below: High Street.

TELEPHONE EXCHANGE, 29 College Street. A Bell exchange of *c.* 1922. Handsome stripped classicism in grey sandstone, with large semicircular windows. 1938 wing to Ingram Street.

Former ROYAL EXCHANGE, Royal Exchange Square. Converted for the Royal Exchange by *David Hamilton* in 1827–32 from the mansion built in 1778–80 by William Cunninghame of Lainshaw on farmland W of the city. Hamilton remodelled the old mansion, adding the portico and a newsroom at the back. Stirling's Library, founded in 1791 and originally housed in Miller Street (*see* Nos. 48–56, under Streets, below), moved here in 1954.

25   A noble Graeco-Roman design, especially as a termination of Ingram Street, but evidently a sum of its parts rather than a comfortable whole. In front of the former mansion, a grand octostyle, double-depth portico of fluted Corinthian columns (capitals by *James Fillans*), and a circular *tempietto* with flattened ogee cap, raised above it on a squat drum. The sides of the house have been completely encased. Two storeys and an attic articulated by giant pilasters, with the smaller order of the ground-floor windows threaded behind them. First-floor windows with pediments on long consoles. The high mansard is later and underlines the intentional disparity between the former mansion and Hamilton's W addition. The addition was always much lower, and, although the pilasters continue, the ground floor is taller with arched windows, the first floor only half a storey with square ones. On each side, a free-standing colonnade of six fluted columns carrying an elaborate parapet. Bold iron railings with lamp standards.

27   Hamilton's great NEWSROOM is Glasgow's most magnificent early C19 interior. Broad nave and aisles, divided by fluted Corinthian columns of sandstone which run across the almost fully glazed W wall, and as a screen in front of the E apse, with its glazed vault. Richly coffered ceiling, segmental over the nave, flat over the aisles. Ugly C20 library fittings do their best to destroy the grandeur. Nothing of interest is left

in the original mansion except the layout of rooms and the central saloon with its domed oval light-well and double tier of galleries with cast-iron balustrades. Simple cornices in the flanking rooms, but upstairs nothing at all is left. The entrance hall and basement library were marble-panelled *c*. 1954, the crude sheets of glass put in the windows in 1989.

STATUE in front of the portico. Duke of Wellington, eques- 93 trian bronze by *Baron Marochetti*, 1844. On the tall granite base, bronze reliefs of the battles of Assaye and Waterloo, the Return of the Soldier, and Peace and Agriculture.

TRON THEATRE. *See* Churches, above: Tron Kirk.

MERCHANTS' HOUSE. *See* Streets, below: George Square.

TRADES' HALL, 85–91 Glassford Street. 1791–4. *Robert Adam* designed it for the Trades' House, which had developed from the federation of the Fourteen Incorporated Trades founded in 1605. The façade is Adam's only surviving work in Glasgow, 18 and even this was completely refaced by *John Keppie*, 1927. The design, however, is full of characteristic motifs. The formula is Palladian with a *piano nobile* and attic storey over a rusticated ground floor, but the silhouette is Neo-classical, with emphasis on the outer bays rather than the centre. The dome is not dominating but small and set well back. Lots of Adam's favoured 'movement' in the lines of the parapet, the deeply set Venetian windows (now lacking their lunettes), and the projecting raised portico, not a conventional temple front but with unfluted Ionic columns drawn back into two pairs either side of the central window. The broad ground-floor openings originally gave access to shops, but the building has been altered and extended several times. The outer bays are more Italianate: the S one dates from 1837–8, when *David Hamilton* added a kitchen and a saloon at the back; the N one (undated) screens a wing rebuilt in 1888 by *James Sellars* to provide a new hall and smoking room, which has a characteristic façade to Virginia Passage.

S of the central passage (vaulted in Adam's design), the RECEPTION ROOM, created by Keppie out of one of the shops in 1929, with Adamish roundels between the deep ceiling beams. (Everything N of the passage is divided off for use by the neighbouring bank.) The STAIRCASE is by Sellars, François I in style, lit from a barrel-vault and overlooked by a stained-glass window of Sellars' own design with the badges of the Trades. The HALL is dominated by the timber ceiling of 1955 by *Walter Underwood & Partners* which replaced Hamilton's rich Italianate 1840 ceiling of similar form. (Adam's ceiling may have been flat and quite simple.) Round the walls, panelling and name-boards by Sellars, and a Belgian silk frieze of 1902–3, depicting the Trades in well-drawn figures. The delectable chandeliers came from the Grosvenor Restaurant (*see* Nos. 72–80 Gordon Street, under Commercial Centre, below: Streets). All that is left of Adam's design is the simple white marble fireplace: a matching one has been moved from here to the SALOON, which was refurbished with new

panelling and doors by *John Keppie* in 1916, and with a coffered
ceiling by Underwood in 1955. In the window, by *Guthrie &
Wells,* medallions of James VI, Mary, Queen of Scots, and the
Deacon of the Trades' House who held office in 1605. The
DEACON CONVENOR'S SUITE is contemporary with the
Reception Room and was converted by Keppie from the small
hall in Sellars' extension.

HUTCHESONS' HALL (Glasgow and West of Scotland headquarters of the National Trust for Scotland), 158 Ingram
Street. 1802–5, by *David Hamilton* (builder *Kenneth Mathieson*), to replace the hall lost when the C17 Hutchesons' Hospital, which stood due S in Trongate, was demolished for
Hutcheson Street to be laid out on the hospital's lands. George
(† 1639) and Thomas († 1641) Hutcheson of Lambhill, leading
benefactors of C17 Glasgow, founded the hospital for aged
men (*see* the frieze inscription). The hall was a meeting place
for the patrons of the charity, which was dispensed in pensions
after the destruction of the C17 building. Hutchesons'
Grammar School, founded by Thomas (now in Pollokshields;
see below), moved to an adjacent building from Crown Street,
Gorbals, in 1840. It used a room above the hall as a classroom
until the interior was completely remodelled by *John Baird II*
in 1876.

17   Hamilton's façade and steeple (the crisp polished ashlar
long-since painted) terminate Hutcheson Street. The style is
extremely idiosyncratic, a mixture of French Neo-classicism
and the English Baroque of Wren and Gibbs, executed with
some of the delicacy of Robert Adam. The façade, with the
centre of the tall *piano nobile* recessed behind two attached
Corinthian columns, and a low rusticated 'basement', strongly
resembles the garden front of J.-A. Gabriel's Petit Trianon at
Versailles. Even the unusual hoods of the recessed windows
(though not the long consoles) can be traced to this source.
The oval Roman altars over the pilastered end bays are redolent
of Robert Adam. The statues of George and Thomas Hutcheson by *James Colquhoun* (1649), in niches created for them
in 1824, come from the C17 hospital. Much more conventional
is the side elevation, with two pedimented tripartite first-floor
windows. The steeple, with a sharp reeded needle spire, harks
back to the tall tower of the first hospital. Its models (like
Stark's at St George's Tron) must have been Baroque, but the
treatment is extremely chaste, without any Baroque sinuosity.

Baird in 1876 raised the height of the ground floor, replaced
the staircase in a different position, and removed the second-
floor schoolrooms over the hall to make it double-height. The
style of the HALL, with its pedimented doorcases and windows
and compartmented ceiling, imitates Hamilton's manner, but
the present scheme of pastel neo-Adam decoration bears no
relation to the rich Victorianism of Baird's hall. Between the
timber panelling of the walls and ceiling (originally stained
dark and varnished), the walls were diapered on a reddish-
gold ground and the cornice painted blue with bright stars and

coloured ornaments. This, Baird felt, was in keeping with the original building. The STAINED GLASS, with portraits of the founders and view of the C17 hospital, and the bold stripy tiling in the fireplaces have survived redecoration. The staircase and panelling in the BOARDROOM (now shop) are late C17 in style, perhaps also harking back to the C17 hospital.

QUEEN STREET STATION, West George Street. The High Level station opened as the W terminus of the Edinburgh & Glasgow Railway in 1842. Nothing remains of the original station. The grim offices of 1968–9 on West George Street screen a fine iron arched roof, 1878–80, by *James Carsewell*. The car park has replaced the former goods station. The approach by train via the Cowlairs Incline and a half-mile of tunnel (on a 1-in-46 gradient) is perhaps as dramatic as the terminus. The engineer in 1842 was *James Miller*. Only the N end of the tunnel (*see* Springburn, below: Public Buildings) is still as built in 1842: the S end was cut back in 1878–80.

The Low Level station serves the N bank suburban lines of the former Glasgow & District Railway (electrified in 1959–60).

STREETS

ALBION STREET

Along its W side just N of Ingram Street, the glittering wall of (*Sir*) *Owen Williams'* former DAILY EXPRESS BUILDING, built for Beaverbrook in 1936 and now occupied by the *Glasgow Herald*. Its reinforced concrete portal-frame structure (a type invented by Williams for Boots' factory at Beeston, Notts, in the 1920s) is, like the famous *Daily Express* predecessor in Fleet Street, wrapped in a slick curved skin of glass and black Vitrolite, covering both the low front block containing the presses and the taller office block behind. But this building is not a showpiece, more a functional factory, and it lacks super-ficial styling. The extension by *Frank Burnet, Bell & Partners,* 1986–8, follows the same principles nicely, but with a curved skin of cream GRP and a structure of coloured steel.

S of Ingram Street, the City Halls and Markets (*see* Public Buildings, above). This part of the street (opened between George Street and Ingram Street in 1806) was widened and straightened by the City Improvement Trust, and so was the stretch (formerly Nelson Street) S of Bell Street, where the warehouses belong to the rebuilding of Trongate (*q.v.*).

ARGYLE STREET

Argyle Street joins Trongate just beyond the point where the West Port stood until 1749 and is split into two contrasting halves by that magnificent Central Station viaduct, the 'Highlandman's Umbrella'. The part E of the viaduct is one of Glasgow's three main shopping streets, the equivalent of, say, London's Oxford Street, with a generally depressing mixture of commercial architecture and a few barely recognizable tenements from the beginning of its development c. 1750 from just a rural route w to Dumbarton Castle. One or two c 19 warehouses and a few bold 1930s stores stand out amongst a larger number of mass-produced late c 20 shopfronts.

For Argyle Street w of the viaduct, *see* Commercial Centre, below: Streets.

Trongate to Central Station

No need to linger over many of the commercial productions. First on the N SIDE, the long low MARKS & SPENCER of 1966–8 by *Monro & Partners,* with its wide cantilevered canopy. Then comes the previous MARKS & SPENCER by *James M. Munro,* 1929–31, with a chamfered, tower-like corner; a c 19 warehouse (Nos. 26–34, DOLCIS) of familiar type by *James Thomson,* 1873; and the cheap and nasty Nos. 36–8, designed for WOOLWORTH'S in 1960–2, before we get to *J. A. Campbell*'s No. 50 on the w corner of Miller Street, its sheer red sandstone walls apparently suspended above plate-glass shopfronts.

Back to the junction with Trongate and, on the S SIDE at the corner of Stockwell Street, Nos. 1–11, a thin, angular parody of Glasgow's Victorian buildings in light pink Corsehill sandstone by *Scott, Brownrigg & Turner,* 1986–7, replacing one of the last substantial c 18 tenements in the street. Nothing after that, except a row of low shopfronts incorporating the entrance to Argyle Street Underground Station, until the quadrant block of *Alexander Thomson*'s BUCK'S HEAD warehouse (1862–3) at the corner of Dunlop Street (No. 63). There is almost nothing of Thomson's usual monumentality about the insubstantial curtain of iron-framing (with windows fitted directly into it), though the pilasters are stone on the first floor and timber in the attic, with the usual incised and other Greek details. Overlaying this, a delicate skeleton of cast-iron colonnettes with Schinkelesque winged brackets and an insubstantial balcony of filigree acanthus. The portion facing Dunlop Street, which seems to have been added in 1864 and lacks the exposed outer columns, was truncated, along with the street itself, in 1974.

From Dunlop Street for a whole block on this (s) side, LEWIS'S department store (or, more evocatively, Polytechnic) by *G. de Courcy Fraser* of Liverpool and *Clarke, Bell & Craigie,* 1932: seven storeys of Portland stone with minimal classical detailing and some Art Deco touches along the attic. Just beyond, the canopied entrance to the St Enoch Centre (*see* Saltmarket and St Enoch, Streets, below: St Enoch Square) pushes in alongside two more modest buildings, one the towered CROUCH'S WONDERLAND THEATRE, designed by *George Boswell* in 1912 and gutted by him for a cinema in

1939; the other a CLYDESDALE BANK (Nos. 163–165) by *Baird & Thomson*, 1934. Then another big store, ARNOTT'S, a 1938 building by *W. J. B. Wright* recast in 1960–2 by *Gordon Jeeves* with a handsome black polished granite SW tower, curved canopy and row of flagpoles (recapturing a 1930s flavour), white mosaic cladding on the five storeys that step back from the street, and a bold curtain wall with red spandrels curving round to meet a wing in Jamaica Street.

On the N SIDE again, back at the entrance to Queen Street, an early C19 classical building (No. 78), with timber cornices and consoles of the mid-C19 (poorly reconstructed in 1987); and another retail development by *Scott, Brownrigg & Turner* (1984–7) of pinkish sandstone with peculiar details in black polished granite plus a Thomsonish attic. More low shops before the entrance to the ARGYLE ARCADE, cut through an old tenement (Nos. 98–102) disguised by pebbledash. Don't be misled by the 1962 entrance; the arcade itself is a long narrow passage in the Parisian fashion, glass-roofed for John Reid Robertson in 1828 by *John Baird*, with timber trusses held in a delicate 'hammerbeam' framework of cast-iron. Above the shops, divided by the piers that carry every second truss, a deep glazed clearstorey.

A painted Italianate façade (No. 104, TRUEFORM) intervenes between the arcade and Nos. 106–14, a ten-bay C18 tenement roughcast and given an 'olde English' bargeboarded gable and oriel, plus fancy dormers and a tower with a spire at the back in Morrison's Court, by *H. & D. Barclay* in 1897–8. The remodelling was for Miss Cranston's Crown Lunch and Tea Rooms; next to nothing, alas, is left of the interior decoration by *George Walton*, nor of *Mackintosh*'s alterations of 1906 (except the fragments now kept in the People's Palace). At Nos. 116–20 another Italianate façade, in buff sandstone with tiers of arcading, fronted Arthurs' and Frasers' warehouse of 1873 by *William Spence*, which originally extended through to Buchanan Street. At the corner of Buchanan Street, BURTON'S (Nos. 122–32), its white 'Empire' artificial stone and blue-painted cast-iron busily moulded with zigzags and Egyptian motifs: 1938, by Burton's architects, *R. I. Pierce & N. Martin*.

Infinitely more serious, the massive warehouse (Nos. 134–56) of 1900–3 by *Horatio Bromhead* for Campbell, Stewart & Macdonald, with ponderous French details and sculpture (e.g. the Atlantes flanking the main door) by *W. Vickers*. Next, at the tunnel-like entrance to Mitchell Street, a slighter warehouse of *c.* 1876 (Nos. 158–60), with arcading at each of its four storeys; and a three-bay Italianate façade (Nos. 162–66), slightly overlapping the curved and chequerboard curtain wall of BOOTS, a dazzling display of 1959–62 by *Colin St John Oakes*.

There are two more things of interest just before the Central Station viaduct, the poetically named Highlandman's Umbrella (*see* Commercial Centre, Public Buildings, below: Central Station), bars the view W and divides Argyle Street into two: on the S SIDE at No. 188, Art Nouveau-flavoured timberwork applied to an early C19 tenement by *J. H. Craigie* of *Clarke & Bell* in 1908; and, opposite, the classical cast-iron front of Nos. 217–21, by *James Thomson,* in association with ironfounder *R. McConnel,* 1863. A three-bay façade, each bay subdivided into three: fine moulded semicircular arches over second-floor windows and a heavy console cornice at roof level.

BELL STREET

The W part of a C17 wynd, made into a street in the C18 and widened and rebuilt for the City Improvement Trust.

Facing up Walls Street, cream ashlar City Improvement Trust tenements (Nos. 55–66) with shallow oriels and shaped gables carved with the city arms: 1895–6, by *A. B. McDonald* of the Office of Public Works, extended W in red sandstone. More for the City Improvement Trust flanking the S entrance to Albion Street. One of these two big but unenterprising office blocks by *Thomson & Sandilands* stretches to Trongate (*q.v.*) and links with the rest of this extensive rebuilding scheme approved in 1904. On the opposite side, another huge building of the same sort, this one a warehouse extension to the City Markets made in 1902–5 by Glasgow's *Office of Public Works,* with a big Vanbrughian aedicule marking the centre, and the single-storey-and-basement former CHEESE MARKET at the back.

W of Albion Street, the City Halls and Markets fill a whole block (*see* Public Buildings, above). Facing them, at Nos. 6–20, a tall steel-framed warehouse of 1914–21 by *Campbell, Reid & Wingate,* with some outsize Greek details, notably the giant metal antefixae along the parapet.

E of High Street, a great cliff of warehouse (Nos. 105–69), built in 1882–3 for the Glasgow & South-Western Railway, with massive, roughly rusticated walls concealing a structure of huge cast-iron columns carrying concrete arches, an early example of the use of mass-concrete in Glasgow. Converted to flats in 1984–8 by *James Cunning, Cunningham & Partners,* as part of a housing scheme that will eventually embrace much of the adjacent goods yard.

Opposite, and round the corner in Watson Street, a pair of large warehouses of *c.* 1880, in the style of the Dunlop Street range of Thomson's Buck's Head warehouse, with giant pilasters and incised decoration. Facing them, large but less powerful, the red rock-faced former CLEANSING DEPARTMENT DEPOT, built for the Corporation by the Department's engineer, *A. W. Wheatley,* 1896–8, and, beyond that, THE STABLES (No. 174), also for the Glasgow and South-Western Railway, *c.* 1900. Terracotta brick front with simple arches on corbels at eaves level and flats fitted in where the ramps and stalls once were.

BLACKFRIARS STREET

Blackfriars Street takes its name from the Dominicans, whose convent (founded *c.* 1246) lay on the E side of High Street. The street (and an unsuccessful associated square) was laid out to a plan by *R. & J. Adam* as Stirling Street between 1794 and 1804. Evidence remains of succeeding waves of C18 houses and C19 warehouses and industrial buildings.

N SIDE. The street's most distinguished building, BABBITY BOWSTER'S at Nos. 16–18, is a reconstruction by *Nicholas Groves-Raines* with *Tom Laurie Associates,* 1984–5, of a detached classical five-bay house of *c.* 1794, the last relic of the Adams' street and with an elevation in their manner. The tripartite Roman Doric doorway is original, but the top storey and pediment are new, though apparently a faithful reconstruction. The bar has painted ceiling beams, imitating an earlier tradition, and a ceramic panel by *Mary Wilson* showing a kilted Scot dancing the Babbity Bowster. Nearly next door, a former fruit-broker's warehouse (Nos. 26–8) of 1899, tall and red, with an arcade cut in low relief along the upper storeys.

S SIDE. The same broker's brick warehouse of 1904 by *Brand & Lithgow* faces his other premises. Turning the corner of Walls Street, BLACKFRIARS COURT, the former workshops of the Corporation Gas Works, now converted into flats. The S block in Walls Street, with an attic of lunette windows, dates from 1881, although the simple classicism of this and all the rest (corner block, 1888; Blackfriars Street block, 1903, by *G. Sinclair*) looks much earlier.

BRUNSWICK STREET

Brunswick Street, Hutcheson Street, and Wilson Street were the last three streets S of Ingram Street to be developed. They were laid out by a consortium in 1786–90. The former County Buildings (*see* Public Buildings) fills the hollow square between them.

E SIDE. *Billings'* Baronial warehouse turns the N corner from Ingram Street (*see* below) with a gabled tower. This and all the buildings along the E side form the W side of Ingram Square (for which *see* Candleriggs, below). The warehouse at Nos. 108–10, of a later kind than Billings', with more window than stonework, was built in 1883 for Simon Jacobs & Co., fruit merchants, with a top floor added *c.* 1913 by *Thomson & Sandilands* who built the same proprietors' warehouse at Nos. 87–99 Candleriggs (*q.v.*). The flats behind in Ingram Square re-establish the original link between them. Next, another change of scale down to No. 106, a three-bay three-storey house which may pre-date the street by about two decades, and then another defiantly unorthodox façade (Nos. 102–4, built in 1859) that might also be by *R. W. Billings*. The conglomeration of crazily angled hoodmoulds, diagonally set chimneys, and the doorway topped by an octagonal light beggars description. All this is repeated on another wing behind. After this, *Elder & Cannon*'s Post-Modern vocabulary breaks out of Ingram Square in a block of flats turning the corner into Wilson Street with an enjoyable glazed circular tower. Below Wilson Street, the street narrows and finishes in a narrow passage (a wynd earlier than the street) leading to Trongate. Just two stretches of much-altered buildings of *c*. 1800.

119

CANDLERIGGS

Opened up in 1668 from Trongate to the industrial premises exiled to the NW of the old town centre after fires in the mid-C17. There are two substantial stretches of pre-Victorian buildings but nothing earlier than the late C18. At the N end, the C19 City Halls and Markets (*see* Public Buildings, above), the successor to markets established in this area as early as the C17. Candleriggs, both straight and narrow, still conveys the severity that much of the Merchant City must once have had. Sadly, its canyon-like symmetry from Bell Street to Trongate was lost when the whole of the E side was demolished in the 1970s, but the long perspective is still dramatically closed by the Gothic tower of the Ramshorn Kirk (*see* Churches, above).

W SIDE. From the S end up to Bell Street, an all but complete stretch of sheer four- and five-storey warehouses and shops, begun in 1790 by *James & William Carswell*, builders from Kilmarnock, which were originally mirrored by an almost identical range on the E side.* The surviving façades, once utterly plain apart from moulded eaves, are marred by cement frames applied in 1963, by the coat of paint, and by the taller GOLDBERGS', 1936–7, by *G. A. Boswell*, which breaks in towards the S end. Behind, a (contemporary?) pedimented range.

Along the same side, N of Bell Street, a mixed range of buildings incorporated into an extensive piece of urban renewal, called INGRAM SQUARE, which occupies a whole block between Candleriggs (E), Ingram Street (N), Brunswick Street (W) and Wilson Street (S). Several of the C19 and early C20 buildings along the street have been retained and converted to flats and offices, but others now have only façades masking new flats that turn Post-Modern faces towards internal courts. A handful of others have been replaced in the same eclectic manner. All this by *Elder & Cannon*, 1984–9.

The buildings that face Candleriggs start at the SW corner with Nos. 81–5, an orange-red stone-clad steel-framed building of 1932 by *Hamilton & Forbes*, its tower of Rationalist outline complete with a stylized eagle. Next, an infill block; and, then, a handsome fruit-broker's warehouse (Nos. 87–99),

119

* Being replaced (1989) by a heavily disguised multistorey car park (by *Carl, Sibbald, Fisher*) stretching E to Albion Street.

its slender stone framework modelled with François I details. It formed the E side of large premises, established in 1883, that stretched through to Nos. 108–10 Brunswick Street (*q.v.*); this side was rebuilt in 1912 by *Thomson & Sandilands,* almost to the original pattern but in red sandstone. Beyond, a terrace of *c.* 1800 (Nos. 109–23, MERCHANT COURT) with plain, regularly spaced sash windows and shopfronts reconstructed in appropriate style. An office block of 1937 by *James McCallum & Gordon* turns the corner of Ingram Square into Ingram Street. (For the buildings that form the other sides of Ingram Square, *see* Ingram Street, Brunswick Street, Wilson Street.)

Inside the courts, disappointingly thin and cheap façades, little more than graphic renditions in sugary colours of the distinctive motifs of Alexander Thomson and Secessionist architects. The fruit-broker's premises have been replaced by student flats round a hollow court raised above the car park. In this court, the utilitarian white tiles of industrial buildings.

COCHRANE STREET

Part of the planned development of the Ramshorn lands, Cochrane Street was opened from W to E by *c.* 1800. At the W end on the S SIDE, a terrace built as offices and warehouses for handling cotton about this date (Nos. 45–57), the remains of a stark unbroken line that once stretched all the way to Montrose Street. Plain classical façades, with rusticated ground floors, pilastered doorcases, and cornices over the first-floor windows: behind them were square and octagonal courts with wall-mounted cranes, but everything has been reconstructed in 1989 by *Page & Park* as the Italian Centre, which also involves similar warehouses round the corner in John Street (*q.v.*).

DUNLOP STREET *see* ARGYLE STREET

GARTH STREET

Opened in 1793 and still partly lined with the plain tenements that were advertised to let in 1799.

GEORGE SQUARE

Glasgow's civic square, of impressive size, presided over by the City Chambers. It is laid out in the usual Victorian manner, with islands of lawn and flowerbeds, and has a splendid array of public monuments around the tall Doric column of the Scott Monument. The square was laid out *c.* 1782, and the houses appeared between 1787 and the early 1820s (three-storey on the N, S and (tenemented) W sides, two-storey on the E), but only one of these Georgian terraces survives. The Bank of Scotland on the corner of St Vincent Place was first to step out of the domestic scale in 1869, closely followed by the General Post Office, the Merchants' House and the City Chambers, but in fact the bolder presence of these buildings and their c 19 and c 20 neighbours fits the size of the square better than their predecessors.

N SIDE. This has the only vestige of the Georgian square, but also the worst buildings as neighbours. The COPTHORNE HOTEL embodies one of the two terraces of *c.* 1807–18 that filled this side, although it was converted with an extra storey and attic into the North British Hotel in 1903–5 by *Baird & Thomson*, and further marred by the ungainly conservatory added *c.* 1986. Rather thin detail of fluted Corinthian pilasters marking the end bays survives. The bolder and better-preserved of the two terraces was replaced in 1978–9 by the unrewarding bulk of *Cockburn Associates*' GEORGE HOUSE. The NW corner falls away with the bathetic office block of *c.* 1969 fronting Queen Street Station's fine shed (*see* Public Buildings, above).

W SIDE. An underlying unity of composition is still evident, despite the overbalancing Edwardian storeys added to the N block. At the S end, the BANK OF SCOTLAND by *J.T. Rochead,* 1867–70, a solemn palazzo with its entrance in St Vincent Place. Heavy details, from the vermiculated basement to the shell-enriched segmental pediments over the first-floor windows and the bracketed cornice, overburdened with a balustrade and vases. Over the entrance, a weighty shield of arms supported by two Atlantes carved by *Mossman*. Equally serious is the double-height banking hall, where caryatids, ranged above the main architrave, carry the deep-beamed ceiling with its glazed dome. *Campbell Douglas & Sellars*' BANK BUILD-INGS, designed in 1874, continue Rochead's elevation along the W side, with the addition of an attic storey, aedicules round the first-floor windows and vermiculated quoins to make a more emphatic centrepiece, but symmetry was upset from the outset in 1874 by the Merchants' House at the N corner.

J. Burnet made the MERCHANTS' HOUSE self-important, with a corner tower and dome, an effect increased by the columned upper storeys of offices, incorporating the existing tower, added by *J.J. Burnet* in 1907–9. The main façade is on West George Street, and here Rochead's format is abandoned, with more florid detail and figurative sculpture by *Young*, and an emphasis on the end bays, where a pair of oriels repeats the one on the E front. The simple marble-lined staircase entered from No. 7 West George Street leads to the suite of Merchants' Hall, Directors' Room and Dean of Guild's Room, remodelled by J. J. Burnet. It fills the W range of this courtyard building. In the entrance door, a stained-glass roundel depicting a galleon, its sails faceted to catch the light, and, over the door inside, a stone relief salvaged from the c 17 Merchants' House; it depicts pilgrims. Screened from the anteroom, the DEAN OF GUILD'S ROOM, with black and gold Tynecastle Tapestry

wallcovering of 1912 and a big STAINED-GLASS window by
W. & J.J. Kier, 1877–8, the partner to one on the staircase
(donation by James VI of the Letter of Guildry in 1605, which
established the Merchants' House and the Trades' House, and
the First Court of Guildry). In the DIRECTORS' ROOM, lit
from the oriel and with the same handsome wallcovering, a
Neo-classical marble relief built into the overmantel, commemorating Archibald Ingram, Dean of Guild and Lord
Provost in the mid-C18. Supposed to have come from the
original House and to be signed *C.R.* The HALL, altered in
1907–9, is in J.J. Burnet's most opulent Baroque style. Over
the directors' platform, a giant aedicule embracing the arms
of the Merchants' House; at the S end an apse lined with
Corinthian columns. Below the windows, with their simple
trails of fruit and flowers, Jacobean-style panelling incorporates the painted panels recording bequests that were
brought from the C17 House.

S SIDE. W of Hanover Street, two seven-storey office blocks
tower over a thinly detailed palazzo of *c.* 1870 at No. 11. The
W office block, with arched top storey, faces Queen Street
(*q.v.*), the E one (LOMOND HOUSE, 1922–4, by *James Miller*)
is clearly a framed building with cast-iron panels handsomely
moulded with classical motifs, and a bracketed cornice. The
General Post Office (*see* Public Buildings) fills the whole block
E of Hanover Street, and the square ends quietly at the SE
corner with a block of *c.* 1800 just in Cochrane Street (*q.v.*).

PUBLIC MONUMENTS. A notable selection of C19 monuments
by local and nationally known sculptors. – SCOTT MONU-
MENT, 1837. The first monument to Walter Scott ever erected,
only five years after his death. *David Rhind*'s fluted Doric
column with Greek ornament, a handsome Greek base and an
anthemion-decorated pedestal for the statue is superior to the
rather flaccid figure of Scott wearing a plaid, designed by
John Greenshields and carved by *A. Handyside Ritchie.* – The
CENOTAPH. By *Sir J.J. Burnet,* 1921–4. A slab that was
intended to be softened by its reflection in a sunken pool; the
lions and an intricate figure of St Mungo by *Ernest Gillick.*

From the Cenotaph clockwise. – Thomas Graham, chemist,
† 1869. Seated and gowned figure by *William Brodie,* 1872,
cast by *R. Masefield & Son* of Chelsea. – Thomas Campbell
† 1844, editor of the *New Monthly Magazine,* in Regency
dress, by *Mossman,* 1877. – Lord Clyde † 1863, bristling
Indian Army commander leaning on a palm, by *J. H. Foley,*
1868. – Sir John Moore † 1809, slightly bowed and shrouded
in a cloak. By *Flaxman,* 1819, the first statue to be erected in
the Square. – Robert Burns, 1876–7, by the local *George Edwin
Ewing,* cast by *Cox & Son* of Thames Ditton. On the base,
reliefs by Ewing's brother *J. A. Ewing,* depicting 'The Cottar's
Saturday Night', 'Tam O'Shanter', 'The Twa Dogs', and 'The
Vision' (1885–7). – James Watt † 1819, serious seated figure
by *Chantrey,* 1832. – Queen Victoria and Prince Albert, equestrian bronzes by *Baron Marochetti.* That of Victoria, a spirited

young empress on an equally spirited mount, was placed in St Vincent Place in 1854, to commemorate her visit to Glasgow in 1849, and was moved to accompany the more stolid Prince Albert when that statue was erected here in 1866. – Robert Peel † 1850, simple standing figure by *John Mossman*, 1859. – Sir William Gladstone † 1898, in the robes of the Rector of Glasgow University; by *W. Hamo Thornycroft*, 1899–1902. On the tall base, two bronze reliefs, one of Gladstone felling a tree at his Welsh family home, Hawarden, the other of him in the House of Commons. Originally sited in front of the City Chambers. – James Oswald, local M.P., † 1853, in contemporary dress by *Baron Marochetti*, 1856. Moved from Sauchiehall Street.

94

GEORGE STREET

George Street (opened in 1792 as part of the planned development of the Ramshorn lands) leads from the NE corner of George Square.

The N SIDE begins at the corner of George Square with the Italianate former INLAND REVENUE OFFICES of 1885, by *W. W. Robertson*, of H.M. Office of Works, unexceptional but neatly turning the corner. Next, at No. 266, the former PARISH COUNCIL OFFICES by *Thomson & Sandilands*, 1900–2, compositionally a near relation of J. J. Burnet's Waterloo Chambers (*see* Commercial Centre, Streets, below: Waterloo Street), but in a dense and confused mixture of styles. Two-storey oriels along the first and second floors, coupled fluted Ionic columns and a Doric entablature, of Beaux-Arts inspiration, above them between the windows of the ornate top-floor Council Chamber, which is also lit from an insignificant dome. From here E to North Portland Street, all the buildings belong to Strathclyde University (*see* Townhead, above).

Opposite them, on the S SIDE, EXCHANGE HOUSE (1983–6, by *Ian Burke Associates*) successfully mediates, without loss of character, between the City Chambers' earlier classical lines and the red sandstone of the Royal College building, mirrored in its bronze glass walling. Unresolved roofline. Rounding the E corner of Montrose Street, MONTROSE HOUSE (No. 187 Montrose Street), designed before the Second World War but built in 1951–3 by the *Ministry of Building and Public Works*. The big circular corner with fins still looks 1930s, but the detailing, especially the abstract-pattern railings, entrance foyer and staircase, is distinctly 1950s. Its late C19 warehouse neighbour (Nos. 151–9, by *Frank Burnet & Boston*, 1897) is now the ALEXANDER TURNBULL BUILDING of Strathclyde University.

Beyond here, the only noticeable building is on the N side: MARLAND HOUSE by *Arthur Swift & Partners*, 1960–1 (now part of Strathclyde University). Not an obvious choice for its Civic Trust Award. George Street ends with tenements that turn N into High Street (for which *see* Townhead, above: Perambulation 1).

GLASGOW CROSS

A chaotic traffic junction with nothing except the isolated Tol- 14 booth Steeple (*see* Public Buildings, above) to recall the Cross's historic role as the hub of the city from the Middle Ages until the C18. Round the steeple, an ill-coordinated mixture of buildings. The present arrangement is a partial realization of the scheme by *Honeyman & Keppie* that won the competition for improving this congested crossroads in 1914. They intended to rebuild the Tolbooth Steeple as the focal point of the perspectives down Trongate and High Street, and to set it off, in Beaux Arts fashion, with two quadrants of offices flanking High Street and a warehouse on the gushet between Gallowgate and London Road. However, they were not allowed to move the steeple from its historic site and were left without the central pivot that made sense of their plan. Work did not begin until 1922.

Only one of the quadrants proposed in the 1914 plan was built and then not to the original convex design. The present concave one, by *A. Graham Henderson* of *Keppie & Henderson*, links the two big City Improvement Trust warehouses on the corner of High Street and Trongate (*qq.v.*) with a giant Ionic order. The answering quadrant is sorely missed, for, on its own on the E side, A. Graham Henderson's handsome MERCAT BUILDING of 1925–8 lacks impact on the bleak acres of tarmac and on the view from Trongate. Its façade is deeply modelled, with an apsidal recess screened by a pair of giant Ionic columns. Crouching figures on each façade by *Proudfoot, Archibald Dawson* and *Benno Schotz*, who carved 'Painting' and 'Sculpture' on the main front. Dwarfed by this warehouse is the MERCAT CROSS, a weak reinterpretation by *Edith Burnet Hughes* (1930) of the C17 style of mercat cross with a proclamation platform and unicorn-topped column. It represents one removed from Glasgow Cross in 1659.

Nothing enclosing about the buildings on the S side of the Cross either. The City Improvement Trust tenements on the S side belong to Trongate (*see* below).

GLASSFORD STREET

A very wide street being laid out from 1786 across the gardens of *Colen Campbell*'s Shawfield Mansion, built in 1711–12. It faced Trongate and was demolished in 1792 to complete the S end of the street, then known as Great Glassford Street.

The street has nothing to offer until nearly halfway up from the S end. Then, on the W SIDE, a block of red-brick flats (GLASSFORD COURT by *McGurn, Logan, Duncan & Opfer,*

1987–8) faintly echoing its close warehouse neighbours – the two big steel-framed red sandstone corner blocks, which belong to *Thomson, Sandilands & McLeod*'s series of 1930s warehouses along Wilson Street, and the handsome Glasgow Style warehouse by *Robertson & Dobbie* of 1908–9 (Nos. 61–5), its details (particularly the torpedo-shaped bartizan and the complicated window surrounds) reminiscent of Salmon & Gillespie's work. Remodelled inside, eliminating the courtyard and various Art Nouveau details, by *T. M. Miller*, 1965.

18 Beyond is the TRADES' HALL (*see* Public Buildings, above) with *Robert Adam*'s façade of 1791–4 facing the later and abandoned hall of its rival, the Merchants' House, down the length of the mostly late C18 Garth Street. Ending the street, the former Glasgow Savings Bank (*see* Ingram Street, below). On the opposite E SIDE, past the Adamish block that faces Wilson Street (*see* below), ranges of the street's original and very plain buildings, with one or two nice pub and shop fronts.

HIGH STREET

Glasgow Cross to George Street and Duke Street

The appearance of High Street amazes the unsuspecting visitor who expects to find the High Street of medieval Glasgow leading from Glasgow Cross to the Cathedral (for the N part, *see* Townhead, above: Perambulation 1). But, although the line of the street is the same, only a single building survives from before the late C19. The railways are mainly to blame, especially the North British and Glasgow & South-Western Railways, which swept away the buildings of Glasgow University in the 1870s for the College (later High Street) Station and the huge College Goods Yard that covered the whole university site and the medieval Old Vennel on the E SIDE of the street. (Old Vennel's timber-framed houses with stone-lined cellars and pits, probably used for tanning, have been excavated.) At the N end of this side, the North British Railway established its goods station in 1904. Both stations have been abandoned, and every building along here bar one demolished. At the S end, a magnificent railway warehouse of 1882–3 (*see* Bell Street), converted to flats.

The City Improvement Trust was responsible for much of the other, W SIDE. At Glasgow Cross, a big red warehouse that forms part of the City Improvement Trust scheme round the corner in Trongate (*q.v.*). After Bell Street, BOWS EMPORIUM, by *John Carrick* and *A. B. McDonald* (1889), extended W and made more French by *Burnet, Boston & Carruthers* in 1905–6. Beyond it, the curiously flat classical façades of City Improvement Trust tenements at Nos. 73–99 (1891–3, by *A. B. McDonald* of the Office of Public Works); the more Baroque Nos. 101–3 of 1892–4 by *Bruce & Hay*; one small plain house of *c.* 1800 at the corner of Blackfriars Street

(No. 111); and, beyond that, what was the city's principal FIRE STATION, 1898–1900, also by *A. B. McDonald* (City Engineer). The broad High Street front of Locharbriggs stone, with shallow oriels, nicely carved strapwork panels beneath the windows, and a freely treated achievement of the city arms in the gable, looks like a slighty superior tenement block with shops below: it did, indeed, contain sixteen houses for the firemen. On the similar Ingram Street front are the arches of the engine room and, above it, were officers' houses and duty rooms.

N of the Fire Station, the street (in 1989) is being filled with lacklustre brick housing. The most serious loss (in 1973) was the pair of Neo-classical tenement blocks of 1793–5 designed by *R. & J. Adam* to house some of the staff of the university. They flanked the entrance to College Street and were meant to frame a vista, terminated by a domed corn market, from the main gate of the College. Just one interesting survival, at No. 215, a narrow red sandstone tenement above a former British Linen Bank by *Salmon, Son & Gillespie* dated 1905 (cf. Govan, Gorbals, below). Mostly conventional Renaissance detail and only hints of the small-scale Art Nouveau decoration found on their St Vincent Chambers (*see* Commercial Centre, Streets, below: St Vincent Street). Topping the crowstepped gable is a classical figure, over the oriel a classical *tempietto*.

HUTCHESON STREET

Mostly laid out, together with Brunswick Street and Wilson Street, between 1787 and 1790 on the backlands of the old Hutchesons' Hospital, which stood set back a little from Trongate and was demolished in 1795 to allow the street to be completed.

The s half of the street, below Wilson Street, had the same tunnel-like quality as Candleriggs, until the early c19 buildings on the e side were demolished. Like Candleriggs, it frames a focal point much grander than the street itself (Hutchesons' Hall, rebuilt on Ingram Street; *see* Public Buildings). The w SIDE still has a row of plain early c19 tenements (Nos. 25–37), much altered but with palmettes decorating a few of the doorways.

N of Wilson Street, facing the former City and County Buildings (*see* Public Buildings, above), severe tenements of *c.* 1790.

INGRAM SQUARE *see* BRUNSWICK STREET, CANDLERIGGS, INGRAM STREET, WILSON STREET

INGRAM STREET

Development of Ingram Street began in 1772 along the line of the medieval Back Cow Lone, between Candleriggs and Virginia Street. It opened in 1781, but its line was later continued E of

Candleriggs as Canon Street, which ended at Shuttle Street. In
the 1860s the City Improvement Trust straightened Canon
Street and continued it to High Street, renaming the whole street
Ingram Street; so of the little that is left at the E end, all is mid-
Victorian or later.

High Street to Montrose Street

There is in fact nothing much at the far E end, which has suffered
the same creeping dereliction, demolition, and uninspired
infilling as High Street, except *J. W. & J. Laird*'s gaunt ST
CATHERINE'S LEATHER WORKS of 1910 at Nos. 12–20,
on the N SIDE. Further on, an earlier warehouse, ALBION
BUILDINGS (Nos. 54–64), *c.* 1875, the first warehouse in
the Merchant City to be converted to flats (1980). Debased
Italianate, with rows of windows within arcades or under
basket arches. Further W, two red-sandstone-fronted clothing
workshops on a larger scale: on the corner of Albion Street, a
sturdy one of 1900–6 by *H. E. Clifford* (used as the JAMES
TODD BUILDING of Strathclyde University), and, past St
David's Ramshorn Kirk (*see* Churches, above), another (Nos.
110–12) for Stewart & Macdonald by *James Thomson*, 1897–
8, with just a few decorative touches culled from J. W. L.
Campbell's earlier warehouse opposite, to which it was linked
underground.

   The façade of the earlier warehouse (S SIDE, Nos. 115–37)
by *Robert Billings,* 1854–6, is a catalogue of uncouth and
mostly unorthodox Baronial and C17 motifs, topped by a row
of shaped gables, which wraps round the corner and continues
down Brunswick Street, punctuated effectively by the diagonally perched corner tower. The façade was always a
separately designed screen but now conceals, not the
original structure, with its cast-iron columns, designed by *John
Baird I*, but late C20 flats belonging to Ingram Square (*see*
Candleriggs).

Montrose Street to Frederick Street

Along the next stretch of Ingram Street, the commercial buildings are earlier (of grey ashlar) and more classical. On the N
SIDE after Montrose Street, a long mid-Victorian front (Nos.
126–36), its upper two storeys embraced by giant Ionic pilasters with incised Greek decoration and a more Italianate
attic above that. Then, before Hutchesons' Hall (*see* Public
Buildings, above), another of *c.* 1840, with a classical ten-bay
façade (Nos. 144–54), a balustraded parapet and a central pend;
and, beyond John Street, yet another, earlier (*c.* 1820) plain
classical range (Nos. 162–6), and the more elaborate, symmetrical former Bank of Scotland (Nos. 174–6), by *William
Burn,* 1828, that forms the *point-de-vue* at the end of Glassford
Street opposite. On the S SIDE, Nos. 159–61 of *c.* 1860 bears
the same relationship to John Street.

Glassford Street to Queen Street

From here, buildings on a larger scale frame the Royal Exchange in the Merchant City's grandest formal vista. The S SIDE has the important buildings; the N side has only the back of the General Post Office (*see* Public Buildings) and the blank side of the Bank of Scotland (*see* Queen Street). *J. J. Burnet*'s Baroque banking hall (1894–1900) of the former Glasgow (now TRUSTEE) SAVINGS BANK forms a low but powerful corner to Glassford Street. Strongly sculptural in itself, it is embellished by sculpture full of imagination but strictly subservient to the architectural forms. Designed by *Frampton* and carved, except for Frampton's own St Mungo, by *William Shirreffs*. At the same time, J. J. Burnet reconstructed the rest of the bank (designed by his father, *John Burnet*, in 1866 as the headquarters of the Glasgow Savings Bank) and made it more Baroque. He added the colonnaded attic and rusticated hollow chamfered angles to the simple square palazzo facing Glassford Street. Nothing quite so lavish about the interior of the banking hall (the boardroom is in similar style): the minor modifications are by *Honeyman, Jack & Robertson,* 1973–5.

The former UNION BANK (now Lanarkshire House), further W at No. 191, has undergone a similar evolution. It was built, on the site of the C18 Virginia Mansion, to designs by *David Hamilton* in 1841. The plain sides of this building are clearly seen behind the unrelated façade applied in 1876–9 by *J. Burnet,* who achieved great splendour with a North Italian Mannerist style like that of Sanmichele, and the use of colour and carving. It grows increasingly elaborate from the ground floor to the top storey, with free-standing classical figures and a rich and heavy attic, cornice and parapet. (Hamilton's façade was moved to the Princess (later Citizens') Theatre (*see* Gorbals, below) and later destroyed.) The interior has a high well-staircase with a glazed barrel-vault, and a domed former telling room at the back (reconstructed by *James Salmon I* in 1853 and again in 1988 by *David Le Sueur Partnership* as justiciary courts).

Flanking the entrance to Miller Street, two big French blocks. The first (Nos. 205–17), *c.* 1875, contained a branch of Miss Cranston's Tea Rooms, famous for their decoration of 1902 and 1911 by *Mackintosh* (dismantled and moved to the Kelvingrove Art Gallery in 1971). The second (Nos. 223–9), 1875, by *James Boucher*, is crested and trimmed with cast-iron. This side ends with a 1950s building turning the corner into Queen Street (*q.v.*).

JOHN STREET

Along the W SIDE, a symmetrical terrace of warehouses (Nos. 7–17) of *c.* 1840, its centre pedimented and with long pedimented first-floor windows, the wider end bays with tripartite windows over arched pends, originally to small courts. All reconstructed behind the façade round a large single court by *Page & Park* (1987–9) for the ITALIAN CENTRE, and given a less dignified public face with the superfluous 'piazza' built out over the pedestrianized street and a liberal application of sculpture (Neo-classical figures on the theme of Mercury by *Alexander Stoddart* on the façades, more abstracted figures by *Jack Sloan* on the courtyard canopy). At the NE corner, the former John Street Church (*see* Churches, above).

MILLER STREET

A narrow street of close-packed and mostly mid-C19 warehouses and factories. It was surveyed and laid out in 1762 by *James Barry*, according to James Muir, for the speculator John Miller (it involved demolishing half of his new mansion), but the first plot was not taken until 1771, and the street was not opened until 1773. By 1778, it was still only half-developed with detached houses along the S end. Only one C18 house remains.

Argyle Street to Ingram Street

E SIDE. At No. 42, the earliest house to have survived in the Merchant City, and the only one left of the detached houses that lined this end of Miller Street until the mid-C19. It is a compact house of 1775 (by *John Craig*, wright), seven bays and two-and-a-half storeys with a scarcely projecting pedimented centre, rusticated quoins – a composition that harks back to Campbell's Shawfield Mansion of over sixty years before. But its broad proportions (not helped by the ugly C20 mansard) look decidedly naive, particularly the wide doorway with its fluted Corinthian pilasters.

Then, past the E entrance to Virginia Court (*see* Virginia Street), the former STIRLING'S LIBRARY (Nos. 48–56), built in 1863–5 on the site of Stirling's house, where the collection of books he bequeathed in 1791 for public use was originally housed. (For the present Stirling's Library, *see* the former Royal Exchange, Public Buildings, above.) This yellow ashlar palazzo was designed by *James Moyr Smith* under the direction of *James Smith*, and finished, after J. M. Smith left Glasgow in 1864, by *Melvin & Leiper*. Obvious Mannerist inspiration in the enormous attic, with lugged surrounds to blind windows and the central stack flanked by volutes, yet the doorway to the library itself has almost Gothic decoration.

Further N, a clothing factory of *c.* 1870 (Nos. 60–70), its upper floors embraced in narrow blind arches. Next door at Nos. 74–80, a tall Edwardian intruder by *G. S. Kenneth*, 1900–2, sandwiched between the factory and a Thomsonish warehouse of *c.* 1877 (Nos. 84–90).

The W SIDE (also from halfway up the s side) has three remarkable warehouses. The first (Nos. 53–9) of 1874 rather more curious than beautiful, with crude mixed detail, ranging from the ogee hoodmoulds of the top windows to the broad capitals carved with *grotteschi* on the first floor. Nos. 61–3 of 1854 by

J. Burnet is far less strident, with a row of round arches along the top floor of the Italianate façade. Nice carved detail, coarsened by paint. Inside, the huge galleried light-well was partly retained to form access to flats fitted into this and the next warehouse (Nos. 65–81) by *John Drummond & Partners, c.* 1986. Both warehouses have been christened CANADA COURT, although historically that name belongs to neither. Nos. 65–81 was a complete rebuilding in 1849–50, as an independent warehouse, of the rear block of premises that originally extended through to Queen Street and enclosed the open Canada Court. (The Queen Street block, rebuilt after a fire in 1848 by *James Wylson,* was demolished in 1967.) This front by *Robert Black & James Salmon I* is exceptionally fine, possibly because it was designed for the connoisseur Archibald McLellan. The Italian palazzo façade has an unusual neo-c18 flavour. Its rhythm is subtle, with three sections differentiated by the arrangement of segmental pediments over the windows, those on the first floor shell-enriched. The tripartite entrance bay is equally cunningly arranged.

MONTROSE STREET

The street (the E edge of the Ramshorn development) was opened in 1787 but has nothing as early as that now.

On the E SIDE, nothing of interest except the former leather merchant's warehouse (Nos. 14–22) of 1878, erected by a fruit-broker of Candleriggs and very like his later warehouses in that street and Brunswick Street (*qq.v.*), though this one is more Venetian than French Renaissance in style. Central bays left unglazed as access balconies, revealing ugly dropped floors, the result of the conversion to flats by *Miller Urban Renewal* in 1986–7. The façade makes a bold termination to the view down Cochrane Street.

On the W SIDE, at the corner of Cochrane Street, the Corporation's SANITARY CHAMBERS, a Flemish Mannerist compilation of 1895–7 by the City Engineer, *A. B. McDonald,* displays a positive *horror vacui*. It is smothered with Gibbs rustication, blocked columns, vermiculation, swags and roundels. 'Hygeia' stands over the central bay.

For Montrose House, *see* George Street.

QUEEN STREET

Laid out in 1766 by *James Barry* and the speculator Walter Neilson along the line of the old Cow Lone. The most substantial of the street's individual mansions survives embedded in the former Royal Exchange, set in an early c19 square, but along most of the street the c20 has made its presence strongly felt.

Argyle Street to George Square

Well into Queen Street, first on the W SIDE, plain but four-storey early C19 warehouses (Nos. 25–41), unified by later cornices and dwarfed by their red sandstone Edwardian neighbours. On the E side, the office block at Nos. 32–44 (1912–14, by *Thomson & Sandilands*) has shallow bays squeezed between Ionic columns along its upper storeys. Opposite, GUILD HALL (Nos. 45–67), salmon-pink and with overscaled and unmoulded Franco-Flemish details of exceptional crudity, was Hunter Barr and Co.'s warehouse by *David Barclay*, 1903. Converted to offices by *Covell Matthews Partnership*, 1983–7; light-well roofed over and furnished with wall-climber lifts and bold stained glass (by *Glashaus Ltd*). Much fussier carving on the next warehouse (Nos. 67–71) by *George S. Kenneth* for Charles Buchanan, 1899–1907.

Plainer, lower buildings then resume on both sides. On the E side, QUEEN'S COURT (Nos. 54–72), warehouses of *c.* 1833 with segmental-headed windows before the podium of the tall CHARLOTTE HOUSE by *John Drummond* (1968) breaks in at Nos. 78–82. On the W side, at Nos. 73–87, business chambers by *Robert Black* for John Leadbetter, *c.* 1830: they incorporate the stylish 1930s front of the former LANG'S BAR, and continue behind in two lower wings flanking SOUTH EXCHANGE COURT and in one four-storey, slightly more elaborate range down ROYAL EXCHANGE COURT.

25 ROYAL EXCHANGE SQUARE forms an elegant backwater. The former Royal Exchange (*see* Public Buildings) almost fills it. Behind, at the head of the square, the ROYAL BANK OF SCOTLAND by *Archibald Elliot II*, 1827, solemnly Greek Revival with a hexastyle Ionic portico, and two flanking archways, which frame the entrances to Royal Bank Place and Exchange Place, pedestrian passages to Buchanan Street. (For the bank's later extension, *see* Commercial Centre, Streets, below: Buchanan Street.) The bank is the nexus of the square, planned by Elliot (with some assistance from *Robert Black*) but completed between 1830 and 1839, probably by *David Hamilton* and his son-in-law, *James Smith*. Which of them was responsible for the design of the flanking three-storey business chambers and shops is not clear. The N and S terraces are plain between pavilions made taller by panelled attics instead of balustraded parapets and emphasized with Ionic pilasters and, on the return façades to Queen Street, with attached Ionic columns. The perspective narrows towards the W end with two stretches of plain terrace brought forward from the line of the rest, and pairs of giant pilasters on the short return blocks flanking the bank. This is Glasgow's most self-conscious piece of early C19 town planning, far more ambitious than anything on Blythswood Hill. It was initiated by the proprietors of the Royal Bank, who in 1827 sold off the former Cunninghame mansion, which they had occupied for ten years, for conversion to the Royal Exchange, built their new premises behind it and feued the rest of the grounds for the new square.

Nos. 151–7 Queen Street (*c.* 1834, probably also by *David Hamilton*) continues the composition of the neighbouring pavilions. The finish, however, is far superior, perhaps because the client was the connoisseur Archibald McLellan. Crisply carved Corinthian capitals, and acanthus repeated above them in the fluted frieze.

The crucial buildings flanking the entrance to Ingram Street show no regard for the square opposite. Curving round the s corner, offices and shops by *Frank Burnet & Boston* of 1954–7, though the fins, cantilevered canopy and detailing look 1930s. The BANK OF SCOTLAND and its tower of offices (1967–72, by *T.P. Bennett & Son*) fill the N corner with dilute Brutalism. At the corner of George Square, OLYMPIC HOUSE, a speculative office block of 1904–6 by *James Miller,* with the popular Edwardian formula of tower-like outer bays flanking colonnaded upper storeys.

ROYAL EXCHANGE SQUARE *see* QUEEN STREET

TRONGATE

One of the four main streets, meeting at Glasgow Cross, of the medieval riverside settlement. It originally stretched only as far as the West Port which stood by the early C14 about on a line with Old Wynd. It was known as St Thenew's Gait until a charter for a weigh-beam or tron was granted in 1490. It was also the site of the Tolbooth, first mentioned in 1508 but rebuilt in 1626 (the Tolbooth Steeple being its only relic). The magnificent street shown in so many views dated from after the fires of 1652 and 1677. The tall narrow stone-fronted houses with ground-floor arcades or 'piazzas' were interrupted only by the Tolbooth, by its neighbour the C18 Tontine Hotel (designed as the Town Hall), and by the Tron Church's steeple. The C17 Hutchesons' Hospital and the C18 merchants' mansions, including Colen Campbell's Shawfield Mansion, stood beyond the West Port (demolished in 1749). The E end suffered the same widening and rebuilding by the City Improvement Trust as the rest of the medieval town; at the W end, a more motley commercial assortment.

s side (*Glasgow Cross W to Stockwell Street*)

The first stretch of cream sandstone tenements flanking Glasgow Cross (Nos. 3–39), 1891–1900, by *A.B. McDonald* of Glasgow's Office of Public Works, are part of the City Improvement Trust's alterations to the street. Their style is French Renaissance, plain and rusticated up to the second floor, then with some thinly carved detail, pedimented dormers linked by a balustrade, and circular pavilion roofs like sliced-off cones at each end. Quite generous houses inside, of three and four apartments with bathrooms.

Next, punctuating the street's rigid line, the Tron Steeple

13

(*see* Churches, above). Beyond it, more of the Improvement Trust's work (1895–1900, by *A. B. McDonald*) at the corner of King Street (Nos. 79–89). A mixture of Flemish and Baronial, with big crowstepped and shaped gables and plenty of carving concentrated towards the top. The block continues in King Street with some plainer bay-windowed tenements.

On the w corner of King Street, a simple pilastered warehouse (Nos. 97–101) of 1849, designed by *J. T. Rochead* for the Buchanan Society, is clasped by *McKissack & Son*'s big red sandstone warehouse built for the City Improvement Trust in 1901–2. Most of it lies behind, along King Street (*see* St Enoch, Streets, below), but it emerges at No. 103 as a tall and narrow Dutch-style façade topped by a wide shaped gable. The next remarkable building (Nos. 109–115), although built as a warehouse in 1857, housed on the second and third floors the BRITANNIA MUSIC HALL. The shell of the music hall and its proscenium and gallery (designed by *Thomas Gildard & R. H. M. MacFarlane,* according to the *Building Trades Directory* of 1868) still survive, with a rear staircase of 1869 by *Hugh Barclay* and other alterations for cinema use by *Boswell & McIntyre,* 1904–10. The façade is exceedingly rich, clad in an assortment of debased borrowings from Italian palazzi. Each storey is different: the first and second are arcaded and enriched with rustication and vermiculation (first floor) or long festoons (second floor). Along the top floor, an open-arcaded loggia, and interlaced over it, a narrow fluted band.

Beyond the curtain-walled C & A of *c.* 1964, with its rooftop canopy, the narrow cream sandstone front of Nos. 137–9 by *James Sellars* for *Campbell Douglas & Sellars,* 1886–7, completed by a deep Art Nouveau cast-iron parapet. Nos. 151–5, plain and mid-C19, bridges Old Wynd. Its neighbour, the seven-bay Nos. 157–63, may be a late C18 or early C19 house, lightly disguised. Next to it, another debased palazzo front of *c.* 1850, and last but certainly not least on this side, turning the corner of Stockwell Street and running right down to Osborne Street to the s, the angular and coarse REARDONS' (No. 179), a warehouse with a big copper dome over the sharply chamfered corner. Built by the Corporation in 1923–30 to *Burnet & Boston*'s designs, as part of the widening of Stockwell Street. Flanking the entrance, atrocious figures of Neptune and Ceres.

N *side* (*Glassford Street* E *to Glasgow Cross*)

This side starts boldly with *T. P. Marwick*'s NATIONAL (now Royal) BANK OF SCOTLAND, 1902–3, turning the corner of Glassford Street (Nos. 2–4), its Baroque-Baronial style in the same vein as Edinburgh's almost contemporary Scotsman Building. Even the angle bartizans have a classical cast. The white stone is from Plean, and the carving is by *W. Birnie Rhind.* Adjoining it, the worthless replacement of Spreull's

Land, 'a large and elegant tenement' (J. Guthrie and Smith) of *c.* 1784, which was, alas, demolished except for the back wall in 1978.

On the E corner of Hutcheson Street, the early Victorian warehouse (Nos. 166–74) looks, from its slivers of pilaster and timber architrave, as if it could be of cast-iron and timber. After that, nothing worth noting until Nos. 138–44, superficially similar but more decorative and of stone, with slim shafts as mullions and a cast-iron cresting. The range of simple four-storey, sash-windowed buildings between No. 130 and No. 106 on Candleriggs corner may be late C18 or early C19 in origin. Nos. 130–6 has a little Greek decoration, and Vitruvian window surrounds.

The next two modest buildings (a BANK OF SCOTLAND at Nos. 100–4 by *George Bell*, 1894–7, with the classical orders hierarchically applied, and the plain Nos. 96–8 of the 1840s with an Edwardian Baroque ground-floor refacing) are put in the shade by *J. T. Rochead*'s overwhelmingly vulgar Baronial display of 1855 for the CITY OF GLASGOW BANK at Nos. 74–92. Rochead, even more than Billings in Ingram Street (*q.v.*), delighted in stringcourses and hoodmoulds in a plethora of complicated mouldings and patterns, in crowsteps, machicolations, broaches and bartizans. The elevation to Albion Street is a little more restful.

With the huge orange-red warehouses which extend not only along the rest of Trongate (Nos. 20–40) but all the way up Albion Street, we get back to work of the City Improvement Trust. The W part (by *Thomson & Sandilands*) of this large but conventional mixed-classical design was approved in 1904, that facing Trongate in 1912. The third block, round the corner in High Street, was not completed until 1916 (*see* the datestone).

VIRGINIA STREET

Laid out by Andrew Buchanan in 1753 and developed from the S end halfway up by 1778. The N end was opened in 1796, as far as the C18 Virginia Mansion, which closed the street and which now has the domed banking hall of the former Union Bank on Ingram Street (*q.v.*) in its place. The oldest buildings are early C19.

Argyle Street to Ingram Street

W SIDE. No hint from the front of Nos. 31–5, with its later pilastered shopfront of *c.* 1850, of the enchanting CROWN ARCADE behind, designed as the Tobacco Exchange *c.* 1819, and afterwards used as the Sugar Exchange. A passage through the fore-building leads into the glass-roofed three-tiered arcade. Arched shopfronts with Doric details carry the first gallery (which has similar arched shops set back behind the walkway), fluted Ionic columns the second, rather mutilated one. At the W end the well-staircase, at the E (over a nice moulded stone, and possibly once exterior, doorcase) an oriel, said to have been the auctioneer's box.

Next door (Nos. 37–45), more or less contemporary business chambers that look mid-C18 but for the windows within blind arches and the anthemion incorporated in the sturdy Ionic doorcases. The pend leads to VIRGINIA COURT, flanked by almost identical wings. Another pend on the far side opens into Miller Street. VIRGINIA BUILDINGS (Nos. 49–55), *c.* 1817, looks down Wilson Street (with a slightly earlier C19 tenement on the corner, *q.v.*). The façade has paper-thin, Soanian details, though the tripartite doorcase is slightly more robust – and old-fashioned. The close at No. 49 give access to a winder stair at the back. Further up, a neat classical ELECTRICITY SUBSTATION of 1925.

E SIDE. Tucked into Virginia Passage, the rear façade of the Trades' Hall (*see* Public Buildings). S of Wilson Street, a small palazzo (No. 42) designed in 1867–70 for the Glasgow Gas Company by *Melvin & Leiper*, with big and bold Roman Doric aedicules framing the first-floor windows and gigantic consoles carrying the doorhood. It has been incorporated in the Marks & Spencer store that stretches back from Argyle Street (*q.v.*).

WILSON STREET

Laid out generously in the same phase as Hutcheson Street and Brunswick Street: it opened in 1793 but was much rebuilt in the 1930s with warehouses, e.g., the two by *James Taylor Thomson* of 1931–2 between Glassford Street and Brunswick Street.

Candleriggs to Virginia Street

At the E end, beyond the impassive S façade of the former City and County Buildings (*see* Public Buildings, above), the Post-Modernism of Ingram Square (*see* Candleriggs) breaks through in a long stretch of angular flats. In the central section between Hutcheson Street and Glassford Street, the last, mal-treated classical block designed as offices *c.* 1790 and attributed by Bolton to *R. & J. Adam*. Its façades are indeed more distinguished than many of its Glasgow contemporaries, with giant Ionic pilasters doubled in the end bays below Diocletian windows and a rusticated ground floor with broad arches that were originally open. Its lumpish quality dates from 1925–7, when *Thomson, Sandilands & McLeod* reinforced it with steel and gave it an attic.

W of Glassford Street, on the S side at No. 89, a simple six-bay tenement of *c.* 1800: its rear turnpike stairtower is visible from round the corner in Virginia Street (*q.v.*), where there are commercial buildings of just a little later. All of these sober façades are cowed by the orange-red swagger of the former SCOTTISH LEGAL LIFE ASSURANCE OFFICES (N side,

Nos. 76–84), designed in 1884 by *Alexander Skirving* with his
usual fondness for combining Greek and Roman detail. His
original dome was more French, pointed and ornate.

SALTMARKET AND ST ENOCH

The bones of this quarter, between Trongate and the Clyde, are
medieval, C16, C17 and C18 but much disturbed in the C19 and
C20 and with none of the close-knit character of the Merchant
City. Saltmarket (originally Waulkergait) is part of the same long
street from Cathedral to river as High Street. It was originally
stopped short of the river by the Molendinar Burn, and was
extended s to a new bridge only in the 1790s. The curving
Bridgegate took the traffic SE to Glasgow Bridge (first mentioned
in 1285, rebuilt in stone *c.* 1400). Stockwellgate (originally Fish-
ergate), connecting Bridgegate with Trongate, was certainly in
existence by the late C13. Straight new streets were cut through
to link these main streets (Old and New Wynd in 1573, then
Gibson's Wynd and Armour's Wynd in 1689, the last continued
in 1722 into the long straight King Street on axis with Candleriggs). All or part of these streets survive but in the guise of the
City Improvement Trust, for which the present tenements and
warehouses were built.

Westward (and eastward; but *see* Calton) expansion took hold
here, as it did N of Trongate, in the second half of the C18, with
the laying out of Jamaica Street and of Clyde Street along the
river. The intervening streets, St Enoch Square, and the second
Clyde bridge followed. Throughout the C19, C18 buildings,
many of them residential, gave way to the present warehouses,
including the remarkable ones of cast-iron along Jamaica Street.
There was an even more dramatic invasion in the form of St
Enoch Station, which arrived in the 1870s with its broad swathe
of railway lines and viaducts; its bulk is now represented by a
monster of the 1980s, the St Enoch Centre.

St Enoch Square turns its back on the riverside, where warehouses replaced most of the C18 merchants' mansions built just
w of Bridgegate, the Town Hospital and most of the early C19
terraced houses, a context in which the Roman Catholic Chapel 26
(now the Cathedral) made sense. The Customs House and the
former Fishmarket obviously belong to the riverside, the Merchants' Steeple, enclosed in the Fishmarket, to the medieval
Bridgegate. The Justiciary Courthouse, built close to the river 23
on the later bit of Saltmarket, still stands there lonely and grand.

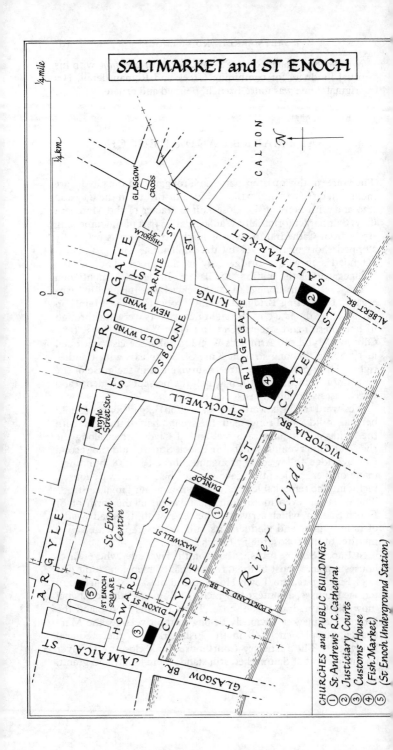

SALTMARKET and ST ENOCH

CALTON

GLASGOW CROSS

TRONGATE

CHISHOLM ST

PARNIE ST

NEW WYND

OLD WYND

OSBORNE ST

KING ST

BRIDGEGATE

SALTMARKET

ALBERT BR.

② ST

CLYDE

④

STOCKWELL ST

VICTORIA BR.

Argyle Street Stn.

ST

St Enoch Centre

DUNLOP ST

①

MAXWELL ST

River Clyde

SPORTLAND ST BR.

ARGYLE

⑤

ST ENOCH SQUARE

HOWARD ST

DIXON ST

CLYDE ST

JAMAICA ST

③

GLASGOW BR.

¼ mile

¼ km

N

CHURCHES and PUBLIC BUILDINGS
① St Andrew's R.C. Cathedral
② Justiciary Courts
③ Customs House
④ (Fish Market)
⑤ (St Enoch Underground Station)

CHURCHES

St Andrew's Cathedral (R.C.), 170–88 Clyde Street.
This Roman Catholic chapel of 1814–17, which became the
cathedral in 1889, is by *James Gillespie* (later *James Gillespie
Graham*), as the inscription on the entrance arch soffit makes
quite clear. Here, and at his R.C. chapel in Edinburgh of 1813,
Gillespie Graham introduced a new standard of archaeological
correctness into Scottish church architecture, in both plan (a
tall nave and lower aisles, like those of a medieval church)
and detail. The silhouette is latest Perp with tall octagonal   26
buttresses, panelled with tracery and rising into turrets either
side of the high nave gable, which is topped by a tabernacle
housing St Andrew and outlined with an open quatrefoil
parapet. Battlemented parapets and tall pinnacles over the
aisles and along the now revealed length of the nave. The
details are Dec. The façade windows have curvilinear tracery,
the doorway a multitude of thin shafts and mouldings (with
foliage trails and dogtooth) and naturalistic oakleaf and acorn
capitals in the style of Southwell chapter house. Aisle windows
and those in the shallow three-sided chancel Dec, but Perp
tracery in the clearstorey. At the NE corner, Cathedral
House, lumpily domestic in yellow concrete block *c.* 1986,
by *Wagner Associates*.

Gothic rib-vaults of plaster, originally painted to represent
stone, throughout the interior. The narthex (with w gallery
over) has a lierne-vault with a central tracery roundel and big
foliage boss. From the nave (lowish and broad, but high
enough to have had galleries until 1904) a simpler lierne-vault
with foliage bosses continues into the sanctuary, which is
marked only by a broad segmental arch with painted mouldings. Simple quadripartite vaults with ridge ribs over the aisles.
The nave vaults rise on shafts from clustered arcade piers with
curious capitals: a fringe of hanging leaves shelters randomly
distributed flowers.

FURNISHINGS. Much of it by *Pugin & Pugin*, who renovated the chapel for use as a cathedral in 1889, 1892 and 1904. –
ALTAR. By Pugin & Pugin, 1893. Alabaster frontal, traceried
marble reredos with figures of S S Andrew and Paul, brass and
jewel-encrusted tabernacle. Later classical canopy instead of
the original elaborate superstructure. – SIDE ALTARS. By
Pugin & Pugin, 1892. Pinnacled and traceried. – SANCTUARY
SCREENS. By Pugin & Pugin, 1904. – FONT. Dec bowl on
porphyry shafts. – STAINED GLASS. In the sanctuary, medievalizing and brightly coloured, with much white glass. – In
the other windows, quatrefoils with saints' heads set in white
glass.

St Andrew-by-the-Green, Turnbull Street. *See* Calton,
below.

St Andrew's Parish Church, St Andrew's Square. *See*
Calton.

PUBLIC BUILDINGS

JUSTICIARY COURTS, Saltmarket. 1809–14, by *William Stark*, who won a limited competition for the courthouse, municipal offices and gaol against David Hamilton (who also produced a Greek scheme) and Robert Reid (who submitted a Roman one). His Greek Revival building was remodelled by *Clarke & Bell* in 1845, and completely reconstructed as courts alone by *J. H. Craigie* for Clarke & Bell in 1910–13.

23   The solemn Greek Doric portico (which preserves the fluted drums of Stark's original columns) is the purest piece of Greek Revival in Glasgow, and among the first of this monumental size and purity in Britain. Smirke's Covent Garden Theatre, conceived in 1807 and complete by 1809, set the fashion. The portico and the long low silhouette of Stark's building, with its end pavilions marked by coupled pilasters, are certainly related (though perhaps fortuitously) to Smirke's design. Craigie's reproduction played down Stark's very French banded rustication and bold linking stringcourse, and spoilt the carefully calculated balance of the pavilions by making the upper windows tripartite and omitting the open pediments from the lower ones.

Inside, Craigie made two courtrooms in place of Stark's single courtroom with colonnaded apse (inspired, it seems, by Thomas Harrison's at Chester Castle, 1791–1801). Craigie's scheme does not lack grandeur. A colonnaded vestibule leads into a top-lit atrium. The Ionic capitals were probably salvaged from the earlier building. On either side, galleried courtrooms with bowed ends incorporating the columns from Stark's apse.

CUSTOMS HOUSE (now the Procurator Fiscal's Office), 298–306 Clyde Street. 1840, by *John Taylor*, the Irish-born customs official also responsible for Dundee Customs House. Unassuming Greek Revival façade of uncomfortable proportions in well-cut yellow sandstone ashlar. Lower wings with Venetian windows later.

Former FISH MARKET, Bridgegate and Clyde Street. *Clarke & Bell*'s Fish Market was built here in 1872–3 and extended
E, enveloping the Merchants' Steeple, in 1886 and again in 1903. The Merchants' Steeple was once the centrepiece of the Merchants' House, which with its associated hospital was built on this site in 1659; the steeple was retained when the rest was replaced by tenements in 1817. After the traders moved to Blochairn in 1977, the building was converted to a shopping centre in the fashion of London's Covent Garden Market, by *Assist Architects*, 1983–6; it is awaiting a new use in 1989.

Painted stone façades screen a galleried market hall of cast-iron and glass. The river front, a grand essay in Second Empire French classicism, is dominated by two tall columned gateways, suggestive of water gates. Arched shops on the ground floor; above, circular openings filled, like the gate arches, with intricate cast-ironwork. To the r., the later extension. The Bridgegate front is less pretentious, and more Italianate. The E extension has segmentally arched shops on this side.

The Merchants' Steeple emerges through the roof of the extension. Although dated 1665, it is still Gothic, with nothing post-medieval about it except for the two upper balustrades. Lancet bell-openings, intersecting tracery on the next stage, and canopied lucarnes on the short spire, which bulges like an onion at the top. For the finial, the badge of the Merchants' House, a ship on a globe. The attribution to Sir William Bruce, first mentioned in Cleland's *Annals of Glasgow* in 1816, seems to have no basis. The lower half, completely enclosed, consists of 'a naked square tower' (Reid).

The conversion of the market's interior, with shop-booths reconstructed beneath and along the galleries, and a broad nautical staircase added to reach the upper level, was admirably simple.

ST ENOCH UNDERGROUND STATION (now Travel Centre), 69 St Enoch Square. *James Miller*'s most charming building (1896), a miniature Baronial essay in red sandstone with curly carving on the gables, balconies and oriels, and Arts and Crafts capped bartizans. It ends the view down Buchanan Street delightfully – or did until the dreadful entrances to the remodelled underground got in the way.

ALBERT BRIDGE, VICTORIA BRIDGE, SOUTH PORTLAND STREET SUSPENSION BRIDGE, GLASGOW BRIDGE. *See* Crossings of the Clyde and Kelvin, below.

STREETS

BRIDGEGATE

Bridgegate probably dates from the late C 13, when the town spread SW of Glasgow Cross towards the earliest known river bridge, first mentioned in 1285. The Merchants' House built their hospital here in the C 17: its steeple is still incorporated in the former Fish Market (*see* Public Buildings, above). Nothing else survived the C 19 city improvements and the building of the railways. On the W corner, some Corporation tenements (Nos. 128–36) of 1905 by *A. B. McDonald* of Glasgow's Office of Public Works, going round into Stockwell Street with a saucer dome between tall chimneystacks.

CLYDE STREET

As late as 1830, Clyde Street was only patchily developed, with the town slaughterhouses at the ancient E end, industry and depositories of shipped wood at the newer W end (opened in 1773), and, between them, houses (the offshoot of the residential St Enoch Square), the Roman Catholic Chapel, the Town Hospital, and three villas, including the famous mansion built by the

merchant Dreghorn in 1752 just w of the medieval Bridgegate.
In the C 19, most of this made way for the Custom House,
Fish Market and warehouses, one of which (demolished *c.* 1980)
engulfed the Dreghorn mansion. Now the warehouses have
become offices and flats, and along the river is a landscaped
walkway (completed in 1975 by the *Director of Planning*, with
Crouch & Hogg as engineers) of CUSTOMS HOUSE QUAY,
30 with the stately classical South Portland Street Footbridge (*see*
Crossing of the Clyde and Kelvin, below).

Saltmarket to Jamaica Street

Near the E end, the Salvation Army's HOPE HOUSE (Nos. 14–
26), the former police barracks of 1891–3 by *A. B. McDonald*
(City Engineer), extended in 1913 and converted to a hostel
c. 1936 by *J. Thomson King*. After the railway bridge (*see*
Crossings of the Clyde and Kelvin, below), the former Fish
Market (*see* Public Buildings, above). w of Stockwell Street,
St Andrew's R.C. Cathedral (*see* Churches, above) enjoys a
little breathing-space between bulky neighbours: (E) jaunty
flats by *Davis Duncan Partnership*, 1989, and a large plain
red sandstone warehouse (Nos. 144–58), built speculatively in
1896–9 (and unhappily refenestrated in its 1984–8 conversion
to flats by *Nicholson & Jacobsen*); (w) *H. E. Clifford*'s cork
warehouse of 1914, transformed by the same architects in
1987–8 with dark glazing. SOGAT HOUSE by *R. W. K. C.
Rogerson*, 1961–5, on the corner of Maxwell Street, blithely
continues many jazzy mannerisms of the 1950s. It adjoins the
street's only surviving terrace of houses (Nos. 228–46), built
as Claremont Place before 1828, with a positively Regency
flavour. Ground floor and basement with very flat rustication
with wide channelled joints, and a few surviving cast-iron
balconies. All in painted ashlar, except the single, taller granite-faced No. 238. Past two more tall early C 20 warehouses (the
striking almost Perp one at Nos. 242–62 by *Eric A. Sutherland*,
1906–7), the remains of a handsome yellow ashlar classical
tenement of *c.* 1855 (No. 286) on the corner of Dixon Street.
Similar façades continue N up Dixon Street. Clyde Street ends
with the dignified but modest Customs House (*see* Public
Buildings), and the towering Clyde Hall of Strathclyde University (*see* Jamaica Street, below).

DIXON STREET *see* CLYDE STREET

HOWARD STREET

The w end from Jamaica Street to the E side of St Enoch Square
was laid out in 1768. It was extended E from St Enoch Square
along the line of the old Rope Walk in 1798. Nothing looks older
than the early C 19, and most is much later. Most of the N side

was consumed by St Enoch Station in the 1870s, and now the St
Enoch Centre (*see* St Enoch Square, below) has cruelly reduced
the street to little more than a service road.

Jamaica Street to Stockwell Street

The street starts very narrow but has nothing of interest until,
past the supermarket's curtain wall, a row of buildings on a
domestic scale, and possibly early c 19 in origin, forming part
of the s side of St Enoch Square. Quite a nice classical, pilastered pub front at No. 40 on the corner of Dixon Street.
Further E the buildings are more interesting. Rounding the
corner of Maxwell Street, the pilastered façade of what was
McCorquodales' printing works of 1868: it continues s w into
Fox Street with a section rebuilt in 1870 by *D. Thomson*.
Beyond Maxwell Street, the conventional design of 1903 by
A. Balfour for the leather warehouse at No. 114 shows up the
idiosyncrasy of its contemporary neighbour (No. 118), the
former glass warehouse of William Cotterill by *J. Gibb Morton*
of *G. M. Beattie & Morton*, 1903. The smooth central bow is
flanked by panelled buttresses, ending in what *The Architect*
condemned as 'gratuitous and uncouth gargoyles', but which,
like all the other interlinked flowing forms on this façade, are
just indescribably organic.

The range of commercial buildings along here is interrupted
by the halls of St Andrew's R.C. Cathedral (*see* Churches). It
continues with a warehouse of 1901–2 by *Burnet & Boston*,
remarkable for the size and monotony of its red rock-faced
walls. The street regains two sides here. On the s, the former
CHRISTIAN UNION CHURCH of 1864 by *Robert McAlister*,
a painted ashlar box with a pilastered façade to Ropework
Lane.

Along the N SIDE, past the St Enoch Centre (*see* St Enoch
Square), an intriguing relic of St Enoch Station, commercial
premises fronting an extension to it. Built of red pressed brick
and yellow stone (Nos. 145–95), it curves gently all the way to
Stockwell Street: 1902–5, by *H. E. Clifford*. The proportions
and composition, especially the prominent slated roof, with
big stacks and multi-pane box dormers, are Arts and Crafts.
So are the long windows (some with little Ionic shafts as
mullions) and the numerals on the circular grilles over the
close doors between the shopfronts. The ten bays on the bend
of the street are more elaborate and Flemish, with sharp and
fancy gables, windows in aedicules, strapwork balconies, and
a main gable with a roguish central buttress and little octagonal
turrets. At each end, a taller block with little octagonal turrets
and cupolas.

JAMAICA STREET

Famous for the cast-iron-fronted warehouses that line its w
side. When the street was laid out in 1761–3, only residential
development was intended, but commercial premises soon crept

in and prospered after Glasgow's second bridge was built in 1768–72.

Argyle Street to Clyde Street

W SIDE. The first two warehouses are cast-iron-framed but ashlar-fronted. The first, of *c*. 1860 (Nos. 18–22, now CANNON CINEMA), is lightly clad. The big arch was made by *William Whitie*, who inserted the Grand Central Picture House into the centre of the warehouse in 1915. The second (Nos. 24–30) by *John Honeyman* (1864) for the founders of the Cunard Line, G. & J. Burns, has a more Roman gravity.

39   A. GARDNER & SON's warehouse (No. 36, now Martin & Frost) is one of the most remarkable cast-iron warehouses of its date anywhere in Britain: 1855–6, by *John Baird I*, and built using a structural system patented by *R. McConnel*, ironfounder. The two façades are full of subtleties: the storey heights diminish and the window head profiles vary from four-centred arches at first-floor level to semicircular arches at the top. Also, the main bays are divided into four lights on the Midland Street façade and into five on Jamaica Street. Some refined classical mouldings and fine lettering between the first and second storeys.

Then a break in this row of warehouses. First, a red sand-stone commercial building and pub (Nos. 42–4) by *George Bell* (of *Clarke & Bell*) for a publican, Philip MacSorley, 1894–7. Nice Free-Style details above a pub front with cut and etched glass and glazing bars in Art Nouveau tear shapes. Next, a long brick curtain wall and undulating canopy of 1965 by *D. R. Hickman*.

The cast-iron fronts resume with Nos. 60–6, the N half of the otherwise conventional COLOSSEUM building, 1856–7, by *Barclay & Watt*, an original composition with arched bays and giant pilasters rising through three storeys, and an almost Indian cornice of hanging leaves. No. 72, *c*. 1854, probably by *William Spence*, has superimposed cast-iron columns and a dentil cornice.

E SIDE. Nothing left of interest on this side. The S end is filled with the mosaic-clad podium and eight-storey slab of the former Royal Stuart Hotel (now CLYDE HALL, University of Strathclyde) by *Walter Underwood & Partners*, 1963–5. For Arnott's, at the NE corner, *see* Merchant City, Streets, above: Argyle Street.

KING STREET

Created by the Town Council in 1722, on axis with Candleriggs, to link Trongate and Bridgegate. It was carefully planned to have broad pavements and houses with uniform ashlar fronts of two storeys plus garrets. None of these early houses remains, although the line of the street is still straight and narrow like Candleriggs and the vista from the S ends in the tower of the Ramshorn Kirk.

What still stands (N of Osborne Street) is the late C19 work of the City Improvement Trust.

The W SIDE's two big warehouses were both designed by *John McKissack & Son*, who won the competition for them held by the City Improvement Trust in 1893. The N one, which has one bay facing Trongate (*see* Merchant City, Streets, above) and a lower section along Parnie Street, is of 1901–2; the s one, returning to Osborne Street, dates from 1899.

On the E SIDE, cream sandstone tenements continue from Nos. 79–89 Trongate (*q.v.*). s of these, the wedge between King Street, Parnie Steet and Osborne Street is filled with plainer orange-red Corporation tenements of 1894–1900 by *A. B. McDonald & D. McBean* of Glasgow's Office of Public Works.

OSBORNE STREET

A late C19 creation by the City Improvement Trust cutting across the path of Old Wynd and New Wynd, which were laid out in 1573 to link Trongate and Bridgegate. Nothing much left from before 1914, and nothing of note except the former Corporation ELECTRICITY SUBSTATION of 1912 (electrical engineer *W. W. Lackie*), adjacent to the Wynds, and its neighbour, the more angular former ICE FACTORY AND COLD STORE of 1901–2 by *Alexander Adam*.

Along the s SIDE the railway, itself dismantled, obliterated the s part of the Wynds.

ST ENOCH SQUARE

St Enoch Square was for a hundred years familiar as the open space in front of St Enoch Station and Hotel, but in 1977 station and hotel and railway lines were destroyed. Here the ST ENOCH CENTRE, a huge steel and glass L-shaped tent, wrapped round a multi-storey car park and enveloping a shopping centre and an ice rink, has arisen to designs by *Reiach & Hall* with *Gollins Melvin Ward Partnership*, 1981–9. Only its vastness, its novelty as the largest such structure in Europe at the time of its conception, and its train-shed aesthetic, perhaps appropriate for this site, seem worth remarking on. The design displays none of the structural ingenuity or pleasing refinements of the best High-Tech steel-and-glass architecture.

The station (of the City of Glasgow Union Railway) was itself an invasion in 1870–6 into what had been a select residential square, planned in 1768 by the Corporation on Town property. Development was slow to start; by 1775 there were houses only adjacent to Argyle Street. In 1780 the Corporation provided a new St Enoch's Church at the s end of the square, on axis with Buchanan Street (it was demolished in 1925). The only buildings that truly belong to St Enoch Square are those on the w side. For the buildings on the N and s sides, *see* Howard Street, above, and Argyle Street (under Merchant City, Streets, above).

The square's focal point is the endearing former underground railway ticket office (*see* Public Buildings, above). Close to it, the w side begins with TEACHERS' offices at No. 20, designed for the whisky distillers in 1875 by *James Boucher*, in an Italianate style, with rich carving in the spandrels of the arcades that frame the windows, and some intricate cast-iron balconies. The offices of the ROYAL (formerly National) BANK OF SCOTLAND next door (Nos. 22–4), by *A. N. Paterson*, 1906–7, is taller and of buff Plean stone, smoothly cut except for the Mannerist details concentrated at the top (the strapwork really does look like thick curled leather) and the animated classical maidens (Exchange, Security, Prudence and Adventure) by *Phyllis Archibald*, which appear to support the outer bays. Marble-lined banking hall, with some original fittings, by *Watson, Salmond & Gray*, 1936–7. Nos. 28–32 is equally tall with only the curious Romanesque-gabled aedicules along the top storey to relieve the baldness which succeeded tiers of cast-iron columns, *c*. 1932. Nos. 34–6 (altered in 1888–90 by *Sydney Mitchell* for the Commercial Bank) is similarly plain but has a more conventional and elaborate arcaded top storey. Its ground-floor facing of granite and incised stone dates from 1931 (by *James McCallum*). The next narrow front of the 1870s (Nos. 38–44) is High Renaissance in inspiration, with later top storeys. After it, a very big but uneventful red sandstone office block (Nos. 46–60) of 1895–9 by *Alexander Petrie* completes this handsome run of buildings at Howard Street.

SALTMARKET

In medieval Glasgow, Saltmarket was known as Waulkergait and stretched from the Cross only as far s as Bridgegate, where it ended in South Port. From that point traffic was deflected down Bridgegate to what was then the only bridge across the Clyde. The medieval buildings of Waulkergait were all destroyed in the fires of 1652 and 1677. Saltmarket was extended s across Glasgow Green to a short-lived new bridge built across the river in 1794–5. The thoroughfare's present wide and straight form is a creation of the City Improvement Trust who widened it in the early 1870s and, perforce, because of a lack of private developers willing to build tenements on the empty E side, provided Glasgow's first municipal housing for the artisan classes with one- to three-apartment houses above a row of shops.

On the E SIDE are the first City Improvement Trust tenements (Nos. 109–29), designed by the City Architect, *John Carrick*, in 1880 and completed in 1887. Their gables, with chimneys and crowsteps, and the strapwork over the topmost windows are slight acknowledgements of the C17 houses that at that time still stood on the w side. Otherwise the four-storey tenements look no different from contemporary private developments. They return to the then newly created Steel Street and end in the Tent Hall (*see* Calton, below: Churches).

The almost matching row on the W SIDE are a little later, with one poorly detailed infill block which dates from the rehabilitation of all of Saltmarket's tenements by *John B. Wingate & Partners*, *c*. 1980. Those N of the railway bridge, slightly more obviously Scottish in style (Nos. 15–27), are by *J. J. Burnet*, 1899–1900. S of Carrick's housing, at the corner of Bridgegate, the OLD SHIP BANK BUILDING, C19 but remodelled in 1904 by *R. Horn* for the City Engineer's Department. To the OLD SHIP BANK pub on the ground floor, a nice pilastered front, its glass etched with a depiction of the C18 Ship Bank that used to stand at this junction.

S of this the vista opens up to the river with the solemn Greek portico of the Justiciary Courthouse (*see* Public Buildings, above) facing the expanse of Glasgow Green (*see* Calton, below: Public Buildings).

STOCKWELL STREET

Established as Stockwellgate by the early C14, when the Knights of St John had a tenement there. It was widened by the Corporation in the late 1920s, and it is a warehouse built as part of this plan that lines the E side (No. 179 Trongate; *see* Merchant City, Streets, above).

Almost everything else has been cleared for redevelopment, but at the S end a few Edwardian buildings remain, including Nos. 133–9 by *A. B. McDonald*, the City Engineer, with two square mansard roofs with hefty panelled parapets, and a tenement of 1905, also by *A. B. McDonald*, going round into Bridgegate (*q.v.*).

THE COMMERCIAL CENTRE

The commercial heart of Glasgow coincides with its second major phase of westward expansion, the laying out from 1792 on a strict grid of the Campbells' Blythswood estate as 'the Town of Blythswood' and of the Corporation's Meadowflat lands E of West Nile Street. The first two completely co-ordinated plans for an area bounded by the existing Buchanan Street and Sauchiehall Street, and by St Vincent Street and Pitt Street may have been made by *James Craig*,* but the layout was far simpler than that of Edinburgh's First New Town (its only subtlety being slightly more generous spacing on the easterly slopes) and so was well suited to the speculative development for which it was designed. Its only square, Blythswood Square, crowning Blythswood Hill, was an afterthought, and no strategic positions were reserved for churches and public buildings, which, like the houses, were built

---

* All feuing plans of Blythswood were made by the Campbells' surveyor *William Kyle* and date from after 1800.

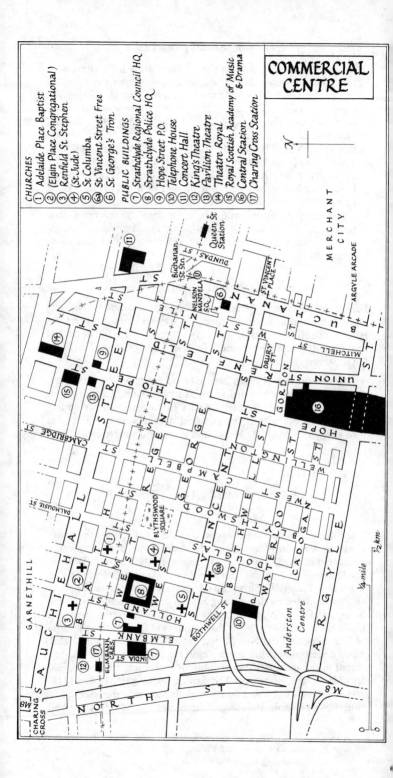

piecemeal. The same grid marched on S to Argyle Street after 1820, according to a plan of *James Gillespie Graham*.

The E-to-W streets, the main streets of the original layout, provided with back lanes between each pair, predominate, with two or three more densely developed N-to-S streets – e.g. West Nile Street, Renfield Street, and Hope Street, which led N to the pre-existing Cowcaddens (*see* below) – threaded through along the eastern edge. The grid is interrupted only by the curiously-angled Union Street and Mitchell Street, remnants of the street pattern of Grahamston village, almost obliterated by Central Station in the 1870s. The grid stops short of Anderston, where village streets gave way in the 1960s to the Anderston Centre. The eastern and northern edges are defined by streets that belong historically to neighbouring districts – Buchanan Street to the Merchant City, Sauchiehall Street to Garnethill – but in character to the commercial heart.

The disciplined grid of streets represented on maps is transformed in three dimensions into vistas of long streets switch-backing over Blythswood Hill. On the top of the hill remain the 24 sedate low grey terraces of houses (not tenements) prescribed in the original Blythswood feuing conditions. These had been built up as far W as Blythswood Square by the 1830s but were not complete until the 1860s. Lower down the slopes and at the foot of the hill on the E side, the richest architectural mixture in the 2, 21 city, where warehouses, banks and offices, ever taller and grander, replaced houses. In the SW corner, totally redeveloped in the 1960s, a larger scale still where many buildings have consumed not just the original plots or groups of them but whole blocks.

The atmosphere of Blythswood Hill is made spacious and relaxed by broad streets lined with low, simply designed terraces of houses. Bath Street has the best of these. From the top of the hill, sweeping views, especially down St Vincent Street and West George Street, take in the tall red and gleaming white stone banks and offices that shoot up alongside the more sedate grey commercial palaces of the mid-C 19 and the early C 19 houses that remain. Buchanan Street, Gordon Street, and St Vincent Street are the most stately, but nearly every street provides a walk full of variety, incident, and surprise.

CHURCHES

ADELAIDE PLACE BAPTIST CHURCH, 209 Bath Street. 1875–7, by *T. L. Watson*. An amalgam of Italianate arches and Greek trabeation in yellowish sandstone. The simple base of channelled rustication ties together the W front (facing Pitt Street) with its raised temple front of slim, coupled, unfluted Corinthian columns, the side elevations with their row of big arched windows, and the pedimented gallery-stair projections, which give greater importance to the Bath Street elevation. Alexander Thomson's influence is quite clear. Grave interior, with a gently curved gallery on thin cast-iron columns. Beneath it, the pews curve towards the platform and the baptistery, which is raised behind it. Behind that, the organ case framed in a giant aedicule with coupled Corinthian columns and a segmental pediment. – STAINED GLASS. Contemporary w windows (Christ and the Wise Virgins; Paul and Isaiah; Timothy and his mother) by *W. & J. J. Kier*.

Former ELGIN PLACE CONGREGATIONAL CHURCH (now Follies discothèque), 24 Bath Street and 193–5 Pitt Street. By *John Burnet*, 1855–6. A handsome, blackened Greek Revival temple of impressive simplicity, with a rectangular auditorium fronted by a hexastyle Greek Ionic portico, raised above the street, with bold rinceau in the tympanum, acroteria and ante-fixae its only decoration. Burnet's strict archaeological approach was rather outdated: his models were, loosely, the Erechtheion (for windows and doorways) and the peripteral temple of Athene Polias, Priene (for the portico). The halls were in the basement, and ancillary rooms in the lower s w wing with its Thomsonish triplet of windows divided by square mullions. Interior (originally galleried and with elaborate plasterwork in the central dome) completely remodelled by *Holmes & Partners*, 1979–83.

JOHN ROSS MEMORIAL CHURCH FOR THE DEAF, 158–64 West Regent Street. *See* Streets, below: West Regent Street.

RENFIELD ST STEPHEN (formerly St Matthew Blythswood), 256½ Bath Street. Designed as an Independent Chapel by *J. T. Emmett* of London in 1849–52, soon after Pugin's St Giles, Cheadle, on which the tall slender s w corner tower and spire (sadly stripped of its lucarnes in 1968–71, when the jarring w addition was built by *Munro & Partners*) seem to have been closely modelled. In fact, the whole boldly Dec design, with aisled nave and a chancel, is, as Hitchcock realized, 'the nearest approach to Camdenian standards Scotland saw at this period'. Reticulated tracery in the liturgically E window (N), intersecting and cusped tracery in all the others. Crisply carved foliage round the doorway. One of the most elegant interiors in Glasgow: a tall clearstoried nave, nave arcades with clustered columns, finely moulded capitals and arches with headstops, and a timber roof with arched braces, cusped windbraces and wall posts on angel musician corbels. No chancel arch, but the end of the w aisle is enclosed by two arches and the corbels here are foliate. – Gothic furnishings all post-1918, except the pulpit of 1915 from Maxwell Church. – STAINED GLASS. Apostles flanking Christ in Glory, above the Virtues: stolid figures by *Norman Macdougall*, 1905. – Two aisle windows of the 1980s, horribly naive.

ST COLUMBA (Gaelic Church), 300 St Vincent Street. 1902–4, by *William Tennant & Frederick V. Burke* of Glasgow, lavish because it was paid for out of the compensation provided by the Caledonian Railway Company when it acquired the site of the former church in Hope Street for the Central Station. This big red rock-faced church is cleverly composed of several well differentiated parts, all with steep slate roofs, to step up the hill from the W and to punctuate the view E with a tall tower and broach spire. Large windows with elaborate Art Nouveau-influenced tracery. Over the door a Gaelic motto (House of my Heart, House of my Love). Cruciform in plan, with halls and meeting rooms linked by the polygonal porch. The size of the interior (justifying its soubriquet, 'the Gaelic Cathedral') is immediately impressive: so, in a different way, are some of the idiosyncratic details. The tall passage aisles, with grey sandstone arches and diapered spandrels on quatre-foil columns with bushy capitals, are quite conventional, and so is the triplet of tall arches to the polygonal-apsed chancel and its flanking organ. But the wall-shafts, with equally bushy corbels and capitals, become partly detached from the piers screening the transepts; and the roof is a curious hybrid, with timber fans of ribs carrying a part-panelled crownpost roof with turned principles. All the woodwork, including the Gothic chancel furnishings, is heavily modelled, the fronts of the W and canted transept galleries particularly so.

ST GEORGE'S TRON, 165 Buchanan Street, by *William Stark*, 1807–9, forms an island in Nelson Mandela (St George's) Place, and an arresting *point-de-vue* at the W end of George Street. With the latter in mind, Stark concentrated on the E front and especially the tower, which shows the Baroque 21 influence occasionally seen in early C19 Glasgow (cf. Hut-chesons' Hall, Merchant City, Public Buildings, above). Wren seems to have been the principal inspiration (particularly the Borrominesque tower of St Vedast Foster Lane and the *tempietto* of St Mary-le-Bow), but Stark's interest in the Baroque may have been kindled by his visit to St Petersburg. Obelisk finials instead of the statues that were shown in the original design, but which proved too expensive. The façade to the E vestibule, with giant Roman Doric three-quarter columns dividing it into three, forms a sturdy plinth for the tower. The rest of the church is a disappointingly plain box, inside and out. Simple W pediment and round-headed windows. Three-sided gallery on thin cast-iron columns and shallow vaults, and a flat ceiling. Circular marble pulpit of 1851, pews of 1884, and organ of 1888.

ST JUDE (now St Jude's House), 278–82 West George Street. A former Scottish Episcopal church of 1838–9 by *John Stephen*, its Greek façade of a powerful pylon form savagely stripped of its detail, except on the side porches. The main porch originally carried a Choragic monument. Behind, a simple rubble box with two storeys of windows; interior sub-divided as offices by *Wylie Shanks & Partners*, 1975.

ST VINCENT STREET FREE CHURCH, 265 St Vincent Street. *Alexander Thomson*'s masterpiece of 1857–9 for the United Presbyterians. Tweed, in his *Guide to Glasgow and the Clyde* of 1872, described it accurately: 'Its lofty situation gives to its 40 raised porticoes a commanding look which in less elevated quarters the Grecian buildings miss. It stands north and south, having a portico at each end ... The tower is disconnected from the church, and it is difficult to bring it into harmony with the temple architecture. It stands at one side, as if there had been more money to spare at the building of the church than people knew what to do with. It is probably a purely Thomsonian structure, and is covered all over with the peculiar ornamentation which that artist lavishes on the humblest as well as the richest of his designs.' The picturesque qualities of the design are indeed striking, even though C 20 office blocks have destroyed the illusion of an Acropolis standing high above St Vincent Street. The tall thin tower and the temple that encloses the upper part of the church sit side by side, as they do at his Caledonia Road Church (see Gorbals, below), on a tall stylobate. This stylobate, which contains the lower part of the church and the upper part of the basement halls, is pierced only by a band of windows punched through the wall between the two main doorways into the vestibule, by a similar band incorporating a doorway towards Pitt Street, and by another, continuous band (lighting the area under the gallery) held in a Greek fret of stone. Above the stylobate, the temple and its two flanking wings (really the upper parts of the aisles) and the tower have an almost independent existence: even the side elevations of the 'wings' end in aedicules, with battered sides and disk ornament, resembling doorways. The ornament is more exotic here than on any other of Thomson's buildings and culminates in the tower, with its banded masonry, T-shaped windows with Egyptianizing caryatid busts as mullions, scrolling (which introduces a completely different style) round the clock faces (of 1884), and the Egyptian, Assyrian or perhaps even Indian elements of the bell-stage and tower top, with its fluted egg-shaped dome.

42   The same wonderful invention continues inside. The vestibule is like an atrium, top-lit and with broad stone staircases to the galleries. Instead of balustrades, solid timber plinths and columns with exotic capitals. The church is extremely tall. Light floods in at each of the three tiers, muted below the galleries, stronger at gallery level (where the neat way in which sheets of obscure glass are fitted into the stone framework is most clearly seen), and more muted again to light the timber roof of Antique type. Cast-iron columns rise daringly from the basement hall to support the gallery and the clearstorey. The capitals are extraordinary. All of them have prickly acanthus, but the lower ones have a hanging bell of leaves, the upper ones gilt claws embracing a padded ring. The capitals, the deep frieze of anthemion and fret, and the roof are richly coloured in terracotta and cerulean blue. Everything gives pleasure, from the gasoliers, like upturned brass dishes, to the curved and tapered pews of solid timber.

The platform is particularly satisfying, every necessary item totally integrated into an architectural whole. The long pulpit is reached from twin stairs that also lead to doorways into the passage behind. Framing the doorways, aedicules which overlay the main architrave just like those on the exterior of the galleries, and, flanking pulpit and doorways, plinths carrying tripod-like lights. The front of the pulpit incorporates a long seat. Above the pulpit, the ORGAN (1904, by *Norman & Beard*) in a case designed for it by *Watson & Salmond* in a remarkably sympathetic manner. The organ console stood where a reading desk now interpenetrates the pews. All this is, like the gallery fronts, in light oak, inlaid with dark patterns of daisies, anthemion and fret. Only the modern plain brass railings jar.

PUBLIC BUILDINGS

STRATHCLYDE REGIONAL COUNCIL OFFICES, Elmbank Street. The council occupies what was, until 1976, Glasgow High School. The central building, by *Charles Wilson*, 1846–7, was built for the private Elmbank or Glasgow Academy, and was bought for the High School by the Glasgow School Board after the Academy moved to Hillhead in 1878.

Only the façade survives of Wilson's grand palazzo, raised high above the street. All the effect is concentrated on the entrance, marked by four projecting rusticated piers carrying figures of Cicero, Homer, Galileo and Watt by *John Mossman*. The doorways between them are heavily enriched: otherwise the classical detail is restrained. The ungainly dormers were added when the rest was reconstructed in 1938–57 by *William McCaig* and *Watson, Salmond & Gray* and given a grim grey E front. The WINGS, quite well matched on the W front and linked to Wilson's façade by arches, are by *J. L. Cowan*, 1886 (N) and 1897 (S). Another archway links the 1931–2 (N) science block (also by *Watson, Salmond & Gray*, and red brick at the back).

On Holland Street, a handsome GATEWAY, part of the 1938–57 reorganization, with the gatepiers merged into the pavilion-roofed lodges in an entertaining manner. To the N the former assembly hall of 1906–7 by Cowan, now used as the COUNCIL CHAMBER.

See also India Street, below, for Strathclyde House.

STRATHCLYDE POLICE HEADQUARTERS, 173 Pitt Street. The former Glasgow and West of Scotland Commercial College by *James Miller*, 1931–4. Two long low wings (E and N) of orange brick (grey brick to the courtyard), with horizontal bands of windows and Portland stone dressings. 1960s S wing. Large W extension for the police along Holland Street, a cascading curtain of silver Astrowall: by *J. C. McDougall*, Director of Strathclyde Regional Council Department of Architecture and Related Services, completed 1984.

Former G.P.O. PARCELS OFFICE. *See* Streets, below: Waterloo Street.

HOPE STREET POST OFFICE, 228 Hope Street. 1910, by *Colin Menzies*. 'Queen Anne' in red ashlar with grey stone dressings. Three S bays of 1937–8 by *H.M. Office of Works* (Edinburgh).

TELEPHONE HOUSE, Pitt Street. By *H.M. Office of Works*, dated 1937 (main building) and 1939 (N block). Stripped classicism in red sandstone.

CONCERT HALL, Buchanan Street. Designed by *Sir Leslie Martin*, 1987, and due for completion by the executive architects, *Robert Matthew, Johnson-Marshall & Partners*, in 1990. Simple monumental brick-clad forms like those of Martin's Royal Scottish Academy of Music and Drama (*q.v.*), but the hinge of the design, between shopping centre to the E (designed in detail by *Seymour Harris*) and concert hall to the W, is crafted into an asymmetrical composition with a curved entrance block to close in a classical manner the end of Buchanan Street. The main elevation of the concert hall, closing in Sauchiehall Street, still carries overtones of the Royal Festival Hall in London.

KING'S THEATRE, 335 Bath Street. 1901–4, by *Frank Matcham*. A long and lowish red Locharbriggs sandstone façade screens the 2,000-seat theatre (Howard & Wyndham's premier touring-company house) from Bath Street. The only theatrical touches are the great ball finials over the arched entrance and matching dummy entrance. A marble-lined foyer with coffered barrel-vault on caryatids precedes the huge auditorium, with its three horseshoe galleries, columned stage boxes and opulent Baroque decoration in fibrous plaster by *McGilvray & Ferris*. The Adam-style ceilings on the Grand Circle staircase and in its crush bar are of 1914, by *William Beattie Brown*, Howard & Wyndham's architect.

Next door, the tall brick office block with a rather industrial vocabulary, by *Thorburn, Twigg, Brown & Partners*, 1984–6, combines backstage accommodation with commercial use.

PAVILION THEATRE, 121 Renfield Street. Originally the Palace of Varieties. 1902–4, by *Bertie Crewe*. A French Renaissance exterior in yellow terracotta with touches of blue and gold mosaic, and big Art Nouveau lettering (N). Segmental pediments *à la* Lescot on the ornamental E front and pavilions at either end of the severe N one. Rich but extremely coarse Rococo decoration in the small oval foyer and in the auditorium, which has serpentine galleries and stage boxes.

THEATRE ROYAL, 254–90 Hope Street. The first theatre on this site (of 1867) burnt down in 1879. The next, by *C.J. Phipps* (1880), burnt out in 1895 but was reconstructed by Phipps inside the remaining walls to substantially the same design. The interior was partly burnt out again in 1970, while in use as television studios. *Derek Sugden* of *Arup Associates* restored it, with some replanning, in 1974–5 as an opera house.

Dull outside, especially now the tower over the entrance in Hope Street has gone. The auditorium had its main entrance on Cowcaddens Road until 1903. The Italianate centrepiece by *George Bell* (to be given a pediment in 1989) and the long cast-iron canopy may have been moved here then. Surprisingly cramped foyers, staircase and corridors in Phipps's manner by Derek Sugden. The splendour of the auditorium (originally decorated in cherry, yellow, terracotta, and peacock blue) somewhat dimmed by Sugden's brown-and-gold colour scheme. The two circles and gallery, columned stage boxes and proscenium have, however, lavish plasterwork with *putti* and strapwork by *Jackson & Co.* Slip boxes remodelled like those at Phipps's Royal Lyceum, Edinburgh (1883).

Former GLASGOW HIGH SCHOOL. *See* Strathclyde Regional Council Offices, above.

INSTITUTE FOR THE ADULT DEAF AND DUMB, 158–64 West Regent Street. *See* Streets, below: West Regent Street.

ROYAL FACULTY OF PROCURATORS' HALL. *See* Streets, below: West George Street (Nos. 62–8).

ROYAL SCOTTISH ACADEMY OF MUSIC AND DRAMA, Renfrew Street. 1982–7, by *Sir Leslie Martin* with *Ivor Richards* and executive architects *William Nimmo & Partners.* Conceived by Leslie Martin along with the Concert Hall (*see* above) in the 1960s and still with the stamp of his work of that period, i.e. a quiet and classically based design done in brick, quite remote from Glasgow's atmosphere. To Renfrew Street and Hope Street, a tall colonnade of square brick piers linking the administration pavilion and the main block, and penetrated by an inviting flight of steps only occasionally used by the public visiting concert hall or theatre on the *piano nobile*. The everyday entrance to the classrooms and circulation spaces in which the theatre and concert hall are bedded is below in the podium. This public face is grand: the rest is solid, protective and dull.

Inside, the brick-lined foyer leads diagonally to the conventional day-lit concert hall, box-like and with raked seating, and to the rather self-conscious theatre, with three tiers of galleries round an apron stage and columns headed with circular lights. Expensive timber finishes in both.

CENTRAL STATION, Gordon Street. Built for the Caledonian Railway and opened in 1879. Extended to thirteen platforms in 1899–1906 by *Donald A. Matheson*, the railway company's chief engineer, who was much impressed by American railroad stations. Part of the steelwork was erected by the *Motherwell Bridge & Engineering Co.* The earlier part of the roof (E of Platforms 9 and 10) has flat trusses, the later part elliptical-arched girders carried on riveted steel columns, and a masonry wall with big biforated windows along Hope Street designed by *James Miller*, who was responsible for the overall architectural treatment. The shed looks entirely functional. Until modernization in the 1980s, the concourse was one of the most 97 atmospheric in Britain, with a massive timber indicator board and matching ticket offices, waiting rooms and restaurant, all laid out in generous curves by Mathieson in 1899–1905 to accommodate 'the tendency of a stream of people to spread out like flowing water and travel along the line of least resistance.' The waiting rooms etc. have been reasonably modified (the indicator board houses a restaurant!), and additional shops in similar style have Post-Modern detailing.

Vehicle access within the vast substructure (the station was high-level to cope with bridging the Clyde). Outside, on Gordon Street, an elegant iron *porte cochère* by *Skidmore* of Coventry, *c.* 1879. The VIADUCT over Argyle Street (nicknamed the Highlandman's Umbrella) was reconstructed in 1899–1906, and screened with classically detailed cast-iron and glass by *McDowell, Steven and Co. Ltd* of Glasgow.

The station is fronted by the CENTRAL HOTEL of 1882–4 by *Robert Rowand Anderson*, designed initially as offices but opened as a hotel. Its massive Swedish-c 17-style tower makes a handsome contribution to the junction of Gordon Street and Hope Street. It is set between two monotonous elevations, generally c 17 in style but threaded with a storey of Italianate biforated windows. *James Miller*'s s extension of 1900–8 substitutes a loggia at first- and second-floor levels. The interior (much redecorated since 1884), with heavy woodwork and plaster-panelled ceilings, is plain, and was fitted out by *W. Scott Morton* and the *Bromsgrove Guild*. Overlooking the concourse, a grand circular columned room by Miller, the dome glazed by *Oscar Paterson & Co.*

Also by Miller, the office block facing Union Street (*see* Streets, below).

The Low Level Station, opened in 1896 for the Glasgow Central Railway, is now part of the Argyle Line.

CHARING CROSS STATION. *See* Streets, below; Bath Street.

KINGSTON BRIDGE, CALEDONIAN RAILWAY BRIDGES, GEORGE V BRIDGE. *See* Crossings of the Clyde and Kelvin, below.

STREETS

ARGYLE STREET

For the first section, from Trongate to Central Station, *see* Merchant City, above: Streets.

Central Station to Kingston Bridge

N SIDE. Most prominent in the view w is the huge and crushingly dull office block by *Greenock & Will*, 1980–8, which rounds the corner of Hope Street with a smooth wall of polished beige granite, monotonously studded with brown window units. Oblivious to its surroundings, it is perhaps the most deadly building in the City Centre. Nothing else of interest until the BLYTHSWOOD HOTEL (Nos. 316–36), *c.* 1899, with Quattrocento details spread thinly over the flat façade. Next, the CLYDESDALE BANK (Nos. 340–4) of red Locharbriggs and pink Corsehill stone on the corner of West Campbell Street. Italian Renaissance, with lots of rich carving, by *James Thomson* for *Baird & Thomson*, 1892.

S SIDE. From Oswald Street to James Watt Street, mostly painted four-storey tenements, similar in style but different in dates (Nos. 279–87 of c. 1870; Nos. 321–33 of c. 1840; Nos. 351–9 of c. 1820), with a bigger Second Empire-style block of c. 1870 (Nos. 335–45) on the corner of York Street. Last, at the corner of James Watt Street, a grain store of 1864, with cast-iron-columned interior.

Argyle Street then undergoes a violent transformation from a shopping street to a shrub-lined dual carriageway, flanked by buildings scaled not to the pedestrian but to the motor car, the result of the comprehensive redevelopment of what was once the village of Anderston split in two unequal parts by the M8. For the w part, *see* Woodlands and Finnieston, below: Perambulations 3 and 4.

On this side of the M8, the ANDERSTON CENTRE by *R. Seifert Co-Partnership* (1967–73), intended to house many of Anderston's inhabitants and their needs within a single mega-structure, with car parking, services and a bus station under a deck carrying shops and three tower blocks of flats and, in the original plan, a department store and vast polygonal entertainments centre. (The smaller polygon at the e end was a restaurant.) Nothing at all attractive on the badly treated lower level, where a messy mixture of part-painted, board-marked and textured concrete and facing brick screens two floors of parking and services from Argyle Street and the banal office block of pre-cast units at the e end. The upper decks are gloomy, neglected and deserted by shoppers in favour of business concerns (in 1989), but the blocks of flats are of a coherent, neatly sculptural design, each raised on a podium of shops. Alongside, the HOLIDAY INN by *Cobban & Lironi*, 1979–82, an example of the soulless ring-road hotel.

Opposite (S SIDE), KENTIGERN HOUSE (Ministry of Defence offices) by the *Property Services Agency*, 1981–6, stepped back from the street like a half-open chest of drawers, each concrete-block layer linked by a slope of bronze glass, the whole topped by a big lead mansard. On the e side, more complicated projections and a lead relief of the legend of St Kentigern (Mungo) and his ring by *William Scott*.

BATH STREET

A broad and, in parts, still elegant street with an interesting variety of terraces. It was the first street to be opened in Blythswood (1800), and became fashionable because of the bath establishment begun in 1804 by the New Town's principal speculator, William Harvey. It had only just reached Pitt Street by 1860.

Buchanan Street to West Campbell Street

At the start, some of the street's original tenements of c. 1830 and two- and three-storey terraced houses. Behind No. 25, with its broad Roman Doric portico, a hall (used by St

George's Tron Church) added by *James Thomson* in 1894 and remodelled on two floors, together with the vestibule and staircase in the original house, by *Andrew Balfour* in 1914–15. The only really noticeable building on the S SIDE is the ugly red sandstone ALBERT CHAMBERS at No. 19, *c.* 1902.

On the N SIDE, No. 38 shoots up beside lower neighbours, its Baroque upper storeys sitting uneasily above the façade of *James Salmon I*'s Palladian former MECHANICS' INSTITUTE of 1860–1, gutted and enlarged as offices by *Arthur Hamilton* for *J. Hamilton & Son* in 1907–9. Beyond it, the spare-framed former GLASGOW TRAMWAYS CORPORATION offices, the corner block of *c.* 1860 by *John Baird II* with a 1904 top floor and an E extension by *Frank Burnet*, 1914.

Beyond Renfield Street, where a few remaining early tenements (e.g. Nos. 63–9, 92–106) are dominated by offices and by the backs of Sauchiehall Street shops, still nothing much of interest. Worth a glance, perhaps, the Beaux Arts REFUGE ASSURANCE BUILDING (No. 49, S SIDE) by *Stanley Birkett* of Manchester, 1932–4.

On the N W corner of Hope Street, the 1930s Watt Brothers (*see* Sauchiehall Street, below) and, opposite, on the S W corner, a nice, though apparently reconstructed and painted, detached house of *c.* 1820, with two storeys above a vermiculated basement, and a hipped roof. There is another early C19 house at the other end of this block, beyond the ribbed-concrete HELLENIC HOUSE of 1970–1 (by the *Lyon Group*'s architect), and two more beyond Wellington Street at Nos. 119 and 121. The two-storey-and-basement No. 121 of *c.* 1840 is the superior, with channelled rustication tailored to fit round–arched door and windows and, inside, Ionic columns screening a top-lit staircase. Next door, at Nos. 127–9, *H. E. Clifford* elaborated on the theme of No. 121 for his (former) Education Offices of 1910–11, adding extra bays and storeys, giant Ionic columns with festoons, and a big rusticated hood round the doorway, which opens into an elaborately tiled vestibule. This is now combined as insurance offices with No. 135, a square-bayed block clad in reconstituted stone (by *King, Main & Ellison*, 1971). Opposite (N SIDE), the Sauchiehall Centre (*see* Sauchiehall Street, below) fills the whole block between Wellington Street and West Campbell Street.

West Campbell Street to Pitt Street

From here the hill begins to rise more steeply, and commercial redevelopment is less obvious, leaving a good impression of the appearance of Blythswood in the 1830s. The stretch between West Campbell Street and Blythswood Street was originally called MONTAGUE PLACE. On each side, a terrace of three-storey-plus-basement houses terminated by taller, five-bay end pavilions. On the N SIDE, the flatted pavilions have been reconstructed, Nos. 152–4 quite convincingly, except for the ugly basement windows and the dormers, by *Boys, Jarvis Partnership*, 1986: their successful N extension is obviously new. Nos. 156–66 were reconstructed as business chambers in 1878: *see* the paired doorcases with tiny consoles. The S SIDE looks less altered, although the E pavilion (Nos. 147–9) was heightened as offices in 1902 and the W was reconstructed in 1988–9. All have wide doorcases with bold cornices on small consoles. Nos. 151, 153, 159 and 163 have Greek Ionic columns in their halls, those at Nos. 153 and 159 (the latter particularly fine) screening top-lit staircases.

Two more symmetrically composed terraces between Blythswood Street and Douglas Street (originally called ATHOL PLACE), both begun in 1833 and completed by 1860 for Hamilton William Garden's Trustees, and probably designed by *John Baird I*. Here the centre and the ends are taller and slightly advanced, and marked by cornices and pediments over the windows, and by very shallow porches of just-detached Greek Ionic columns.

On the N SIDE, Nos. 182, 190, and 196 still have their vestibule screens of Greek Doric columns. Horrible later alterations to the front of Nos. 198–200, almost completely rebuilt in 1920–1 by *Keppie & Henderson* for the CITY OF GLASGOW FRIENDLY SOCIETY, who made the bold Wren-style domed addition behind in Douglas Street to contain boardroom and manager's office. Facing Douglas Street, a statue (by *Kellock Brown*) of the Society's founder, John Stewart, seated in a niche.

The terrace on the S SIDE (Nos. 181–99) is more altered. At No. 183, a pretty and apparently quite early new doorcase and bow window with lotus capitals; and at Nos. 187–91 an internal recasting of two houses by *John Keppie* of *Honeyman & Keppie* for the GLASGOW ART CLUB (1892–3), in François I style with a strong flavour of the Aesthetic movement (Mackintosh, the senior assistant, signed the drawings). In the entrance hall, still with its original Greek Ionic columns, the traceried timber entrance doors, two stained-glass panels, the fireplace, the beginning of the staircase balustrade and (now suspended from the second landing) the flower-like electrolier of beaten metal, are all in that style. In the dining room, opened up with a columned screen, the only Aesthetic touch is the copper firehood. Across the back, a top-lit exhibition gallery, with natural forms carved into the decorative ventilation grilles, and on to the twin fireplaces, one with a languishing female head in bronze relief (entitled 'For Auld Lang Syne') by *Charles Van Stappen*, the other with a bronze clock and winged figures. (The original drawings show fireplaces of channelled masonry.) The two short passages linking the gallery to the main house are glazed with painted scenes of Old Glasgow.

The next stretch, between Douglas Street and Blythswood Street, was called ADELAIDE PLACE: two matching palace-fronted terraces, more ambitious than any of Bath Street's other unified designs, were intended by *Robert Black*. Both were begun in 1839, but only the N one was completed (by 1862), with giant Corinthian pilasters marking the taller end and pedimented central pavilions, and shallow but sturdy Greek Doric porches. Channelled rustication along the ground floors ties the composition together. Many later alterations, most obvious the dormers cut into the main entablature. Only No. 212 still has vestiges of its original interior: Greek Ionic columns with heavy volutes and scagliola shafts in the entrance hall. The S terrace (Nos. 201–5) stops at the former premises (No. 207) of the GLASGOW PHILOSOPHICAL SOCIETY, designed in a similar (but freer) style to its neighbours by *T. L. Watson & W. J. Millar* in 1880. Watson also designed Adelaide Place Baptist Church (*see* Churches, above), which turns its side to Bath Street. It answers the former Elgin Place Congregational Church (*see* Churches) on the opposite (NW) corner of Pitt Street.

Pitt Street to Charing Cross

At Pitt Street we leave the hill and the ambience of Blythswood. This part of the street has been truncated by the ring road and heavily redeveloped. The sharp spire of Renfield St Stephen (*see* Churches) punctuates the view W. There are otherwise only one or two interesting buildings.

On the N SIDE, *John Burnet's* terrace of tenements (Nos. 246–56) of *c.* 1850 breaks away from orthodox classicism above the ground floor with bay windows, strange sub-Romanesque shafts and drooping hoodmoulds. Beyond St Stephen's Church, in the plain classical tenement (Nos. 264–6) of *c.* 1852 that rounds the corner of Elmbank Street, is the GRIFFIN (originally King's Arms), given its Art Nouveau front and fittings (of which some remain) in 1903–4 by *William Reid* to entice the audience from the King's Theatre (*see* Public Buildings, above) on the opposite (SW) corner. Such debased classical tenements, up by 1854, once swept in a long curve all the way to North Street from St Stephen's Church. The longest stretch remains from Nos. 268 to 276.

The CHARING CROSS complex (1971–5) finishes the S SIDE, past the King's Theatre. It is a fragment of the redevelopment planned by the *Richard Seifert Co-Partnership*. These multistorey and low office blocks of chunky white pre-cast concrete units, grouped together with Charing Cross Station on a deck round a sunken garden, were intended to be linked via a bridge, with further offices W of the ring road, an idea astonishingly revived (in 1989) by *Holford Associates'* design for the office block to line the M8 from Bath Street to Sauchiehall Street.

BLYTHSWOOD SQUARE

Blythswood Square, on the crown of Blythswood Hill, is the hub of Blythswood New Town. Initiated in 1821 by William

Hamilton Garden, who went bankrupt promoting it, it was laid out between 1823 and 1829 after William Harley took over from Garden. We know that *William Burn* produced a design for Harley's square, but not whether his design was the one used. *John Brash* certainly executed the façades, whoever designed them. Visually, the square is not entirely successful. The hilltop site, with streets sloping away from the four corners, works against the expected sense of enclosure. The terraces themselves are slightly undersized and too spread out around the central garden. Each terrace of three-storey, three-bay houses is emphasized not in the centre but at the ends, according to the Neoclassical taste which expresses itself even more mildly in the details. Flat, channelled rusticated ground floors and basements, windows and doorways in blank-arched panels, first-floor windows with slight cornices (on consoles in the end bays), and Ionic porticoes each end. One subtlety is the distinction of one house from another by the rhythm of the bays. All the terraces have been extensively altered for offices and clubs.

N SIDE (Nos. 1–7). 1829; much rebuilt behind the façades. At No. 5 *C.R. Mackintosh* made a remarkable play on a classical doorcase, part of his alterations for the Lady Artists' Club, 1908. The house is still mostly early C19, with columned screens in the hall and upstairs room. Mackintosh and *George Walton* made their mark downstairs, Mackintosh in the panelled entrance hall, with its gridded doors, and in the big barrel-vaulted entrance to the partly top-lit L-shaped gallery created out of all the downstairs rooms by Walton in 1896. At the far end, a stone chimneypiece of medieval cast, more in Walton's style than Mackintosh's (cf. a fireplace at Ledcameroch, Dunblane). More of Walton's work of 1896–8 in the basement room at the back: fitted bookshelves, an overmantel with Della Robbia-style musical *putti*, and a window, with Edwardian glazing bars, barred by a grille wrought into flame shapes either by Mackintosh or by Walton.

E SIDE (Nos. 8–13). The whole terrace was completely remodelled by *James Miller* for the ROYAL SCOTTISH AUTOMOBILE CLUB in 1923–6. He gave the façade mansards, the central portico and all the heavier detail; and he opened up the interior with an outmoded Edwardian magnificence, creating a columned hall and first-floor lounge almost the length of the building, linked by an impressive well staircase. At the N end of the ground floor and the S end of the first, pillared dining and reception rooms with Greekish capitals. Panelling by *Wylie & Lochead*, lavish plasterwork and metalwork by the *Bromsgrove Guild*, marblework by *T. Youden & Son* of Glasgow. At the back, the original clubroom of c. 1897 in a totally different style; here panelling and plasterwork are Jacobethan.

W SIDE (Nos. 14–20). This terrace has five-bay, not three-bay, end pavilions, each possibly originally divided horizontally into two houses. At the N end, No. 26, with a full-height bow at the back, was probably the first house in the square to be finished. Interior refurbished imitating the original manner by *G. D. Lodge & Partners*, 1986.

Terraces similar in style meet at the s w and n e corners of the square. At the other corners, mid-c 20 office blocks. For all these, *see* West George Street and West Regent Street, below.

BLYTHSWOOD STREET

A street lined with the side elevations and extensions to the buildings in the streets running E to W. For the best of these, *see* Bath Street. Near the N end, on the E side, the charming *ex-situ* Edwardian shopfront of the FINE ART SOCIETY at No. 134, and at No. 123 (W side) the angular façade designed for the West of Scotland Agricultural College in 1930–2 by *Andrew Robertson*. At the S end, the entrance to the Anderston Centre (*see* Argyle Street, above).

BOTHWELL STREET

Laid out in the 1820s as a residential street, part of the extension of Blythswood New Town. It was widened and commercialized between 1849 and *c.* 1854 by the entrepreneur James Scott of Kelly, beginning at the E end. Under the West End Improvement Act of 1854, Scott linked Bothwell Street in a curve (named Bothwell Circus) to St Vincent Street and the rest of the West End with a bridge over the since obliterated Bishop Street. These improvements were planned by *Alexander Kirkland*: only two of the buildings he designed to line E and W ends of the street were built. The W end was redeveloped in the 1960s as part of the Anderston Comprehensive Development Area.

Hope Street to Wellington Street

BOTHWELL CHAMBERS (Nos. 4–28, N SIDE), a handsome classical range of business chambers and shops designed by *Alexander Kirkland & John Bryce* in 1849–52, formed part of Scott's plan, which was modelled on Parisian examples. The elegantly arcaded shopfronts and interiors of the three E sections have been totally reconstructed: Nos. 4–16 by *T. M. Miller & Partners*, 1976–8; Nos. 14–18 (with slightly different and probably later details) by *Frank Burnet, Bell & Partners*, 1981–3. Behind the shops were top-lit showrooms: at No. 20, a surviving and accessible example. *James Miller* destroyed the symmetry of Kirkland's composition in 1934–5 with the white ashlar pylon of his Commercial Bank (now ROYAL BANK OF SCOTLAND, No. 30). Classical frieze by *Gilbert Bayes* illustrating Commerce, Industry, Contentment, Wisdom, Prudence and Justice. Effective entrance, with Greek Corinthian columns *in antis* against a screen of cast-iron and glass, to a banking hall fitted out by *Scott Morton & Co.*

On the S SIDE, where Scott intended a matching block of chambers with a Parisian-style arcade, we now have the overpowering CENTRAL CHAMBERS (Nos. 91–115 Hope Street, *q.v.*), a grandiose remodelling of a hotel which, though nearly thirty years later (the site had been earmarked for Central Station), was originally sympathetic to Bothwell Chambers. Its more ordinary red sandstone neighbour, the former ALLAN LINE offices (Nos. 21–9), rounding the corner of Wellington Street, is by *Robert Ewan*, 1888–90.

Wellington Street to West Campbell Street

N SIDE. The tall Franco-Flemish former CENTRAL THREAD AGENCY by *H. & D. Barclay* unrolls in three progressively Baroque and richly modelled sections (Nos. 36–44, 1891; Nos. 48–52, 1892–1900; Nos. 58–62, 1901), all thick along the skyline with gables, turrets and chimneys. Differences in date are clearly revealed at the back, with conventional fenestration contrasted with later full-height canted bays of glass between brick piers (cf. the rear of Mercantile Chambers opposite).

S SIDE. The Barclays' display makes *Salmon, Son & Gillespie*'s 76 MERCANTILE CHAMBERS (Nos. 35–69) of 1897–8 look, as the *Builder*'s correspondent noted, 'excessively plain ... its few thin and scattered ornaments seem merely to accentuate its severe simplicity.' The critic could not deny, though, the design's 'daring originality'. The façade is indeed severe, dominated by two sharp gables tied by a completely novel eaves gallery, with arches framing small lantern-like bay windows, but breaks at the very topmost level into a busy skyline of dormers and chimneystalks. The Baroque ornament has an Art Nouveau fluidity and is disposed without classical rationale, above what was originally an open arcade with shop-fronts behind. The sculpture (by *Derwent Wood*) fulfils a strong architectural purpose, especially the four damsels (Industry, Prudence, Prosperity, Fortune) embowered in the consoles that support the balconies. Over the door, a puckish 77 Mercury, seated in a baldacchino carried by a foliage corbel hiding tiny *putti*, 'seems to have collapsed after the fatigues of some long journey' (*Builder*). The façade does not pretend to be more than a curtain concealing a frame of steel beams, cast-iron columns and load-bearing piers; the back wall, to let more light into the deep-plan, is rippled into eight flattened oriels cantilevered on a steel beam, the first of its kind in Glasgow.

West Campbell Street to Blythswood Street

Just two huge blocks facing each other. On the N SIDE at No. 100, the popular 1980s formula of projecting glass bays and polished red granite, here on a grandiose scale and stepped up to a central tower: designed by the *Holmes Partnership* and executed by *Newman, Levinson & Partners*, 1980–8. On the S SIDE, the SCOTTISH LEGAL ASSURANCE SOCIETY (Nos. 81–107) by *E. G. Wylie* of *Wright & Wylie*, 1927–31, the largest American Classical-style building in Glasgow, and the most elaborately finished, with none of the contrasts of plain wall surface and muted decoration used by Miller and Burnet. Wylie seems to have been impressed by Maurice Beresford's then recently completed Cairo Telephone Exchange. Banded rustication to quoins and basement; bronze shopfronts with anthemion cresting by *Charles Henshaw*; bronze entrance doors by the *Birmingham Guild*; reliefs of Industry, Prudence, Thrift, Courage by *Archibald Dawson* between the windows; cartouches; zigzag and lion emblems on the cast-iron window panels and so on are all held within a strong framework. Inside (all originally let by the insurance company, except for the top floor) joinery in exotic woods by *Wylie and Lochead*.

Blythswood Street to St Vincent Street

All at this end of the street dates from the redevelopment of Anderston (*see* Woodlands and Finnieston, below: Perambulation 4). The first two blocks – SCOTTISH DEVELOPMENT AGENCY, No. 120, on the N SIDE, and FRANBOROUGH HOUSE (S SIDE, by *Wylie, Shanks & Partners*, 1979) – are in their different ways equally dull, the first somewhat relieved by planting. The next, between Douglas Street and Pitt Street, is the large and complicated HERON HOUSE by *Derek Stephenson & Partners*, c. 1967–71, which stretches through to St Vincent Street and makes much of the dramatic changes of level, especially where the podium continues as a piazza in front of St Vincent Street Church (*see* Churches, above). At the E end of the podium, two twelve-storey slabs set at r. angles, each modelled with three horizontal blocks projecting from the core and with purposeful hipped roofs. All above the podium is of grey concrete panels set in polished metal. Beneath the podium, shops with a continuous band of glass along the street. Opposite, the dismal brick ALBANY HOTEL of 1970–3 by *James Roberts*, with expensive interior finishes by *Dennis Lennon & Partners* in parts almost obscured by subsequent fussy decoration. Etched zinc RELIEF (Multiple Landscape Image) by *Norman Ackroyd* in the banqueting suite foyer on Douglas Street.

Beyond Pitt Street, the BRITOIL monster (*see* St Vincent Street). The street itself turns at this point into a narrow route between the bulk of Britoil and the back of Dial House (1969–70) below in Waterloo Street. At its entrance, the long façade (the building behind it was demolished in 1984, and the façade is, in 1989, to be relocated within a new building) of *Alexander Kirkland*'s Venetian EAGLE BUILDINGS (Nos. 205–9), a warehouse of 1854. Its continuity and curve are illusory: the twenty bays are divided into four straight sections, repetitive except for the delicately carved and varied keystones. It is the only existing part of Kirkland's never completed plan for this end of Bothwell Street.

BUCHANAN STREET

Glasgow's smartest shopping street. It began as a residential street in the late c 18. In 1763 Andrew Buchanan, tobacco merchant, acquired land on the N side of Argyle Street reaching to Meadowflat Dyke (just N of Gordon Street) and built himself a house at the s end. This he partly took down in 1777 in order to open up Buchanan Street on what was then the very w edge of the city. Work began in 1778 under a trust, after Buchanan's business failed. It was opened as far as Gordon Street in 1780 (though by 1786 there were only four houses) and was extended N by the city fathers in 1804. The earliest houses were substantial mansions, soon succeeded by plain three- and four-storey houses in which shops were early established. By the late 1820s, blocks of shops and houses were being built, encouragd by the links made with Argyle Street (Argyle Arcade) and Queen Street (Exchange Place and Royal Bank Place). Large and showy retail warehouses and offices replaced houses during the c 19, vying with each other to establish the present imposing character. Traffic was banished in 1975 and the street laid out with paving and planters. Near the s end, a weighty bronze bird (the legendary bird brought to life by St Kentigern, which is incorporated in the city arms) unfurls its wings: 1977, by *Neil Livingstone*.

Argyle Street to St Vincent Street

The W SIDE starts with a grand warehouse (formerly Stewart & Macdonald's: *see* Merchant City, Streets, above: Argyle Street), and continues with FRASERS' department store, which occupies a variety of recast and painted buildings along the w side, the result of Frasers' absorption in the 1950s of rivals, Stewart & Macdonald and Wylie & Lochead. The first (Nos. 21–31) was Stewart & Macdonald's original warehouse by *William Spence*, c. 1879, with a classical four-storey front divided by Corinthian pilasters, and an almost unaltered shopfront with thin cast-iron shafts. Next, the former Wylie & Lochead store, itself of three different sections. The Quattrocento-style centrepiece replaced Wylie & Lochead's original warehouse, a famous cast-iron structure of 1855 by *William Lochead* (one of the proprietors?), which burnt down in 1883. For the present building (No. 45), of 1883–5, *James Sellars* followed the original galleried arrangement, but wisely made it fireproof. The *British Architect* claimed it was the first time terracotta had been used on such a scale in Scotland. The façade has a slender frame clad in red terracotta (now painted), and much glass. Magnificent interior, with four tiers of galleries, clad in moulded and embossed cream and pale green glazed terracotta, round an enormously tall glass-barrel-vaulted saloon. The topmost tier, like a clearstorey, is a continuous arcade. A timber staircase bridges across the end of the saloon. To the l. of it, a narrow cast-iron and masonry front by *Boucher & Cousland*, 1853–4 (originally Kemp's warehouse). Its two top storeys were added *c.* 1860 by the same architects to increase Wylie & Lochead's premises. So was the Italianate No. 53 (also by Boucher & Cousland) r. of the original store. The last part of Frasers' (Nos. 55–61) has a simple palazzo front of *c.* 1860 and a few cast-iron columns still exposed inside. All the other cast-iron columns inside these three warehouses were encased and their light-wells filled in when they were amalgamated in 1968.

Next comes (at No. 65) *Sellars'* remodelling of the back of *John Baird*'s 1870 GLASGOW HERALD OFFICE done in 1879–80, its façade (originally with a ground floor of polished granite) more massive than Wylie & Lochead's but clearly setting the pattern for it, with suppressed first floor and attic and bow windows flanking a narrow, recessed central bay. On the first floor, plaques of *putti* with newspapers (by *Charles Grassby*); at attic level, Caxton and Gutenberg by *John Mossman*. (*See* also the more famous refronting by *Honeyman & Keppie* and *Mackintosh* to the w in Mitchell Street, below.) Nos. 71–9 (a former china and glass warehouse by *James Thomson*, 1880, rebuilt with attic in 1887) is described as Romanesque by the *Builder*; the correspondent must have meant Roman.

After this, the former BOAC office (now HALIFAX BUILDING SOCIETY, No. 85), 1968–70, by *Gillespie, Kidd & Coia*, unusual for its date in that its regular arched windows punched in the copper-clad frame respond to the rhythm, the lines and the sculptural depth of its neighbours. Its blackened face once merged happily in the street: now it is (almost) the odd one out. The interior too has its own character. A little classical front of *c.* 1830 (Nos. 87–9) intervenes between this and the exquisitely scaled Northern Renaissance façade of the CLYDESDALE BANK (No. 91), striped delicately in red Locharbriggs and cream Prudhoe stone, and topped by a shaped gable. It was designed as Cranston's Tearooms (with offices above) in 1896 by *George Washington Browne*, and had rather rustic decoration by *George Walton* and *Mackintosh*, of which no trace survives. Now the interior is an independent concrete structure by *Wylie, Shanks & Partners*, 1968–71, well worth seeing but completely at odds with Washington Browne's façade. Plainer classical fronts, among the earliest now remaining in the street, take us up to Gordon Street: Nos. 95–7 (CIRO) of *c.* 1828, with an attic of 1884 by *Boucher*, and a pretty cast-iron shopfront and Rococo shop by *George Boswell* of 1926–7; and Nos. 101–11 of *c.* 1826, one of the first blocks of houses with shops to have been built.

The important-looking towered block is, surprisingly, only an extension to the former Commercial Bank round the corner at No. 8 Gordon Street (*q.v.*). Beyond it, the CARRON BUILDING (Nos. 123–9), a nine-bay Italianate block of shops and offices by *Boucher & Higgins*, 1884, and the return of National Bank Buildings, No. 47 St Vincent Street (*q.v.*).

So, to examine the E SIDE, back nearly to Argyle Street and N of Morrison's Court is the great orange sandstone former Wylie Hill's department store (No. 20) of 1888–9, nominally by *John Hutchison* but probably by his assistant *Andrew Black*. *C. R. Mackintosh* drew the crisp details, unexceptional except for the glazing fitted directly into the stonework. The interior, like Wylie & Lochead's, was originally galleried. The Argyle Arcade (*see* Merchant City, Streets, above: Argyle Street) emerges through the florid Franco-Flemish ARGYLE CHAMBERS (Nos. 28–32) by *Colin Menzies* of *Thomson & Menzies*, 1902–4. Nice (original?) shopfront at No. 32.

Next, the extremely long (twenty bays), plainly classical PRINCE OF WALES BUILDINGS of 1854 by *John Baird I*, the front range of a slightly earlier development of chambers round PRINCES SQUARE, covered over and made into a showy shopping mall by *Hugh Martin & Partners* and *The Design Solution*, 1985–7. The steel-and-glass structure, with free-standing lift cages inserted in the court, copies the C19 Bradbury Building in Los Angeles. Grafted on to it, a ragbag of voguish quotes from Mackintosh and Continental Art Nouveau, with nothing at all vigorous except the Gaudiesque ironwork designed by *Alan Dawson* and made by *Charles Henshaw*, who also did the external canopies. Etched glass on the lifts by *Maria Lafferty*, stained glass by *John B. Clark*, floor mosaic by *Jane Muir*, trompe-l'œil portraits on the entrance escalator by *Dai Vaughan*. E wall topped with an inscribed parapet, basement excavated.

Red sandstone again at No. 62, designed in 1898 for North British Rubber by *Robert Thomson*'s assistant *Andrew Wilson*, with a tall narrow façade, modelled on that of Burnet's then recent Athenaeum extension but with crude medieval Scottish details (cf. also Thomson's Daily Record building, No. 67 Hope Street, *q.v.*). The little Nos. 64–6 (BURBERRY) of 1851 is richly Graeco-Roman, an unusual style for *John Baird*. Beyond Rowan House, an earlier classical range (Nos. 82–90, *c.*1835, by *Robert Foote*) in pale golden sandstone, the attic and Vitruvian window surrounds later. It turns the corner into EXCHANGE PLACE, one of two pedestrian walks that lead into Royal Exchange Square (*see* Merchant City, Streets, above: Queen Street) either side of the Royal Bank of Scotland. In Exchange Place, ROGANO'S OYSTER BAR of 1935–6 by *Weddell & Inglis*, adapted to a restaurant fifty years later by *Weddell & Thomson*. Stylish black and cream Vitrolite front with a giant lobster; inside, 1930s veneer and chromium.

The ROYAL BANK OF SCOTLAND is an extension (on the site of Alexander Gordon's mansion) to the bank that faces Royal Exchange Square (*see* Merchant City, Streets: Queen Street). It was added in 1850–1 by *Charles Wilson*, who gave it its own distinct palazzo front. The ground floor (originally with three classical shopfronts) and the interior of both parts were destroyed *c.*1968 by *Gratton & McLean* (*see* the GRP relief in the foyer by *Charles Anderson*). The upper storeys retain their very large windows with deeply undercut and complex surrounds, and with delicately carved naturalistic foliage and male and female heads.

The last two buildings before St Vincent Street, though perfectly decent, are not exciting. First, on the corner of Royal Bank Place, *Thomson & Sandiland*'s angular ROYAL INSURANCE BUILDING (Nos. 106–10) of 1895–7, in characterless buff Dunmore stone; then, continuing round into St Vincent Street, ST VINCENT CHAMBERS (Nos. 120–6) by *John Baird & James Thomson*, 1902, six storeys of red sandstone with canted bays and French dormers.

St Vincent Street to Sauchiehall Street

St Vincent Street marks (in 1989) a change to a less commercial character, though, at the time of writing, a new shopping centre is planned (by *Seymour Harris*) to dominate this end of the street, and the Concert Hall (*see* Public Buildings, above) is rising to form a *point-de-vue* at the N end.

21   It is the W SIDE that contributes one of the most interesting, varied and well-composed stretches of buildings in the city centre. It is best seen from N of West George Street, the tower of St George's Tron making a strong accent amongst the rich texture of the façades. First, on the corner of St Vincent Street, the former WESTERN CLUB (No. 147), 1839–42, by *D. & J. Hamilton*, an early example of the Italianate in Glasgow, has a preponderance of tripartite openings, still detailed in a frankly Graeco-Roman manner, a bold attic derived from the Genovese Palazzo Doria Pamphilii, with the consoles that carry the cornice between square windows, and other Mannerist detail. The equally rich interior, originally decorated by *George Hay*, was gutted, and the fine ashlar was thickly coated, in 1968–72, when the 1871 extension by *Honeyman* was replaced by the big office block on St Vincent Street (*q.v.*).

56   The former STOCK EXCHANGE (No. 159) by *John Burnet*, 1875–7, follows nicely the lines of the club, though in a well-mixed Gothic dress rare among Glasgow's secular buildings. The elevations are a very close crib of Burges's design of 1866 for the Strand front of the Law Courts (London), with Burges's big biforated first-floor windows omitted and his open second-floor arcade being rendered as triplets of windows on the first floor instead. The gables, machicolations, hefty arcade and roundels (here of Science, Art, Building, Mining and Engineering) against diapered spandrels were certainly borrowed ideas. In the tabernacles, figures of Trade and Commerce. The interior, originally with the clearing house above the first-floor exchange, was gutted in 1969–71 by *Baron Bercott & Associates* and rebuilt with six floors instead of four: the current shopfronts and maltreated stonework are glaring disfigurements. The tamer W extension with an extra storey, which faces Nelson Mandela (St George's) Place, was added by *J. J. Burnet* in 1906.

Next comes St George's Tron (*see* Churches, above), the former Liberal Club, and the former Athenaeum (*see* West

George Street, below: Nelson Mandela Place); then a stretch of plain classical tenements of the 1820s; and lastly, the GEORGE HOTEL (Nos. 235–45), 1907, by *Neil C. Duff*, a thorough remodelling of part of the CLELAND TESTIMONIAL BUILDING (No. 249), a superior tenement by *D. & J. Hamilton*, erected in 1835–6 as a tribute to James Cleland, Superintendent of Public Works † 1834, which bows round into Sauchiehall Street.

On the E SIDE, only three buildings of interest (in 1989), all N of West George Street. TOWER BUILDINGS (Nos. 152–60) by *James Sellars*, *c.* 1877, with Greek details, should have a truncated conical cap on the bowed corner. Beyond it, DUNDAS HOUSE (Nos. 166–8, originally the British Workman's and General Assurance Co.), 1898–9, one of *J. A. Campbell*'s first works after leaving J. J. Burnet's office, and clearly a version of the latter's Athenaeum extension opposite (*see* West George Street, below), but with the gable and a canted corner tower overtopped by the slim chimneystack. Then, in polite camouflage, the ELECTRICITY SUBSTATION of 1922.

CADOGAN STREET

One of the streets of the southward extension of the Blythswood development. Almost entirely rebuilt with post-1960 office blocks as part of the redevelopment of Anderston.

Cadogan Street starts E of Wellington Street in a cul-de-sac, closed by the back of Atlantic Chambers (*see* Nos. 43–7 Hope Street, below) and flanked by Baltic Chambers and Pacific House (*see* Wellington Street, below).

N SIDE (W of Wellington Street). After the dull corner block, APSLEY HOUSE by *Keppie Henderson & Partners*, 1980, the refreshingly bright turquoise spandrels of the curtain-walled FITZPATRICK HOUSE of 1965–8 (Nos. 14–18), followed by the later silvery float-glass of EPIC HOUSE (No. 32), W of West Campbell Street. Both by *King Main & Ellison* and one (Fitzpatrick House) about to be replaced in 1989. The dramatic spiral ramps of a multi-storey car park turn the W corner of Blythswood Street; then there are more bronze mirror-glass bays and brick at HANOVER HOUSE (by *Fewster, Valentine & Partners*, 1984–6) before the street closes in again with the Anderston Centre (*see* Argyle Street, above).

The S SIDE has only the mid-C19 Italianate Nos. 5–7 (on the corner of Wellington Street), with superimposed pilasters and arched central windows, all smothered in chocolate brown; the L-shaped MELROSE HOUSE, built *c.* 1978 of pre-cast concrete units; and, W of West Campbell Street, CORUNNA HOUSE (No. 29), 1982–8, by *King, Main & Ellison*, a close relation of their Scottish Amicable Life Assurance building in St Vincent Street.

CAMBRIDGE STREET

Only Nos. 18–20 on the E SIDE, close to Sauchiehall Street, is worth singling out, and of that only the façade is left: by *Duncan McNaughtan*, built 1890–3 for an optical-instrument maker. Four clearly differentiated storeys, the top one certainly classical, the first one faintly ecclesiastical with narrow shafts between windows with moulded segmental heads.

On the W SIDE, the stylish Fleming House belongs to Garnethill (*see* Garnethill, below: Description).

DOUGLAS STREET

Nothing here but the sides of buildings in the main E–W streets. Most interesting are the Soanian Nos. 95–9 (*see* Nos. 260–80 St Vincent Street, below).

DRURY STREET

HORSE SHOE BAR (Nos. 17–21, S side), incorporated in an earlier warehouse and remodelled in 1885–7 by its horse-mad proprietor John Scouller. The front and the interior with its oval bar (altered in 1901) are largely intact. Horseshoes everywhere. The initials J W Y on the front refer to an owner of the 1920s, John Whyte, as do the Union Jack panes, transferred from Whyte's Union Café.

ELMBANK STREET AND ELMBANK CRESCENT

The former Glasgow High School (*see* Public Buildings, above: Strathclyde Regional Council Offices) looks down on a terrace (Nos. 11–27) of plain three-bay and two-storey-plus-basement houses on the W side, built between 1828 and 1838.

At the corner of ELMBANK CRESCENT (No. 39), the Vanbrughian bulk of the former INSTITUTE OF ENGINEERS AND SHIPBUILDERS (now Scottish Opera rehearsal rooms), 1906–8, by *J. B. Wilson*, in Blackpasture stone. A masculine interior, reflecting shipbuilding and engineering's contemporary prosperity. Broad ground-floor former reading room and library divided by square piers with fine plaster capitals incorporating female masks and galleons; upstairs, former committee, smoking and coffee rooms, plus, on the top floor, a barrel-vaulted meeting hall with some vivid pictorial stained glass in the lunettes by *Stephen Adam & Son* (N: The Lion, a C16 Scottish galleon, full of surging movement; S: a four-funnelled liner). Also by Adam, late and rather decayed heraldic work on the marble staircase, with some figurative panels that repay scrutiny.

Next door at No. 38, one house like those in Elmbank Street. Opposite, Charing Cross Station within a complex of offices (*see* Bath Street, above).

EXCHANGE PLACE *see* BUCHANAN STREET

GORDON STREET

Gordon Street (which extended originally only to Mitchell Street) was opened in 1802 by Alexander Gordon on axis with the site of his Buchanan Street mansion, built in 1804. The Victorian commercial buildings down the whole length of the present street are particularly handsome.

Buchanan Street to West Nile Street

N SIDE. The ROYAL BANK OF SCOTLAND starts the street majestically. The corner block makes the initial impact but is merely an addition to the original bank (No. 8) of 1853–7, one of Glasgow's finest palazzi, by *David Rhind* of Edinburgh for 36 the Commercial Bank. Tweed said in 1872 that it was 'modelled after the Farnese Palace', but the source is remote: only the linked window motif seems to have much in common. The composition, divided by bands of rustication and given a central emphasis by the colonnaded attic, is unusual, but remarkable is the quality of the masonry (by *David Rae*) and the carving (by *A. Handyside Ritchie*). Flat, stylized vermiculation contrasts with an uneven finish on the ground floor and the smoothest ashlar above. In the square panels and pediments, scenes (conceived by *John Thomas*, according to the *Building Chronicle*) of minting and printing money; of 37 Commerce supported by Navigation and Locomotion (centre); Glasgow with Trade and Manufacture (l.); and Edinburgh with Science and Art (r.), all delightfully enacted by children. Rhind's façade is faintly echoed in the 1886–8 extension, but *A. Sydney Mitchell* (another Edinburgh man) designed it to cut a dash in Buchanan Street and used a great domed tower. Both interiors were linked and remodelled in 1938 by the bank's Master of Works, *James McCallum*. In the banking hall, a glass-brick barrel-vault, and plaques of Glasgow's industries by *James H. Clark*, 1941. This part of the street finishes with the sharply chamfered corner (to West Nile Street) of an office block (No. 18) by *T. Aikman Swan*, 1939–40.

S SIDE. Nothing much to catch the eye along this stretch. The five-storey No. 19 (tiled with 'James Craig Luncheon Rooms' on the side) is a very average 1930s production (though with fancy lift doorpieces inside) by *James Carruthers*, 1931–3, sandwiched between two plain corner blocks of *c.* 1815.

West Nile Street to Renfield Street and Mitchell Street

N SIDE. More Edinburgh architects' work on the w corner of West Nile Street, this time a block of shops and houses (Nos. 20–40) by *Peddie & Kinnear*, 1873–4. Their conventional employment of continuous entablatures and pilasters seems unaffected by Thomson's innovative use of them further down the street in his Grosvenor Building. Next (Nos. 42–50) a coarser version, by *Clarke & Bell*, 1886, of Sellars' Glasgow Herald Building in Buchanan Street, with heavy piers carrying urns and antefixae, and an ungainly Britannia over the entrance. The mutilated curve of (originally floodlit) marble set into the corner of the palazzo at Nos. 52–8 was a revamping for Austin Reed by *Westwood & Emberton* (though the drawings are signed by *James W. Reid*) in 1926–7, an early example in Glasgow of what the *Architects' Journal* called the 'modern tendency'.

55 The S SIDE is dominated by the CA' D'ORO, a magnificent palazzo of cast-iron by *John Honeyman*, 1872, originally a furniture warehouse. Its name comes from the restaurant inserted in 1926–7 by *J. Gaff Gillespie*, not from the design, which follows other Venetian models. Above the giant arcade of shopfronts with stone piers, a regular rhythm of huge traceried bays, charmingly enriched with sprays of flowers and other decorative mouldings. The interior (remodelled in the 1920s with ferro-concrete floors to strengthen the original grid of cast-iron columns and *McConnel* patent beams) was burnt out in 1987 and has been replaced by shops round an atrium by *Scott, Brownrigg & Turner*, 1987–9. The two end bays on Union Street are replicas, replacing the 1920s Art Deco extension by *Jack Coia*.

Renfield Street to Hope Street

N SIDE. Another corner remodelling, this time part of a Baroque reworking of *Boucher & Cousland*'s 1858 warehouse (Nos. 66–70) by *J. J. Burnet* for Forsyth's (1896–8; 1900–2). It precedes the GROSVENOR BUILDING (Nos. 72–80), *Alexander Thomson*'s unmistakably disciplined façade weighed down by the swagger Graeco-Roman top hamper added in 1907 by *J. H. Craigie* of *Clarke, Bell & Craigie*. Thomson's building was a warehouse, built speculatively by A. & G. Thomson in 1859–61. It burnt down in 1864 but had been rebuilt, apparently to the same design, by 1866. Perhaps because it was for Thomson himself, the modelling of this façade is heavy and experimentally ambiguous, with conventionally dominant giant pilasters contested by the projecting aedicules, and bold consoles rather than more usual pilasters along the deep attic storey. Craigie's magnificent staircase and restaurant were burnt out in 1967 and rebuilt with dull offices by *R. Seifert Co-Partnership*, 1971–4. The chandeliers have been moved to the Trades' Hall in Glassford Street (*see* Merchant City, above: Public Buildings). This side of the street ends with Standard Buildings (*see* Nos. 94–104 Hope Street, below).

S SIDE. Almost completely filled, except for the debased Italianate building on the corner of Union Street (1850–1, by *Brown & Carrick*), by Central Station (*see* Public Buildings, above).

HOLLAND STREET

Occupied by the backs of Strathclyde Regional Council Offices and Strathclyde Police Headquarters (*see* Public Buildings, above) and by Pegasus House (*see* West George Street, below).

HOPE STREET

Hope Street has none of the grandeur of Buchanan Street or St Vincent Street; but set along its rather unpromising length, the s end overshadowed by Central Station, are some of Glasgow's most interesting buildings.

Argyle Street to St Vincent Street

W SIDE. First, diagonally set as the street funnels out to Argyle Street, a severe narrow warehouse front (Nos. 15–17) by *J. J. Burnet*, *c.* 1900, less cleanly unified than his red sandstone ATLANTIC CHAMBERS of 1899–1900, a little further on past the mid-Victorian façade of Nos. 19–23. Atlantic Chambers (Nos. 43–7) has a strict Beaux Arts axiality, underlined on both tall narrow façades (the main E one to Hope Street and the W one set at a slight angle to Cadogan Street) by the chimneystack breaking through the strong horizontal of the eaves gallery. On the E façade, restrained detail and expressive sculpture; on the W one, plain canted bays to catch the light, and floor heights adjusted to accommodate a floor above the gallery. Dumb-bell plan, with an octagonal staircase and lift hall at its 'waist'. Its neighbour (No. 67) is the DAILY RECORD premises: first the printing shed of 1933–7 screened by a curtain wall; then the offices of 1899–1900 by *Robert Thomson & Andrew Wilson*, one big arched bay in rather lumpen Scots Renaissance.

Between Waterloo Street and Bothwell Street, CENTRAL CHAMBERS (Nos. 91–115), a great French Second Empire-style block that smacks of Haussmann's Paris. First built in 1877 to *Peddie & Kinnear*'s design as the Blythswoodholme Hotel, but reconstructed in 1890 as offices by *J. Dick Peddie*. Nothing between here and St Vincent Street but the flanks of those buildings that face St Vincent Street (*see* below).

E SIDE. This is filled from Argyle Street to Gordon Street by Central Station (*see* Public Buildings, above). On the corner of Gordon Street, STANDARD BUILDINGS (Nos. 94–104 and 82–92 Gordon Street) by *James Thomson* (of *Baird & Thomson*), 1890, with all the interest concentrated in the top storeys added in 1909 by *J. B. & W. A. Thomson*. Next, the little orange-red Franco-Flemish former SCOTTISH TEMPERANCE LEAGUE (Nos. 106–8), 1893–4, officially by *Salmon & Son* but ascribed in his obituary to *J. Gaff Gillespie*, then their draughtsman. Its light-hearted details and profusion of semi-naked figures carved by *Richard Ferris* of *McGilvray & Ferris* (particularly the two females in roundels) showed that pleasure was not confined to imbibers of strong drink! This building was converted for the *Daily Record* in 1919 by *Keppie & Henderson*, and was linked to the DAILY RECORD PRINT-ING WORKS, just behind, between RENFIELD LANE (Nos. 20–28) and St Vincent Lane, designed in 1900 by *C. R. Mackintosh* for *Honeyman & Keppie*. Its apparently 'modern', spare form of white-glazed brick, with canted bays along the top storey, is determined, like the backs of several contemporary Glasgow buildings, by its ill-lit situation. Art Nouveau forms along the ground floor arcade and Secessionist patterns of coloured tile. Interior altered to a clothing warehouse by *Burnet, Son & Dick*, 1937.

St Vincent Street to Cowcaddens Road

W SIDE. Between St Vincent Street and West George Street, two great red sandstone buildings: for the first, *see* St Vincent Street, below. The second is *John A. Campbell*'s great 1902–3 cliff of speculatively built offices (Nos. 157–67), almost sheer up to the two-storey arcaded eaves gallery. The minimal decoration is, surprisingly, conventional strapwork, and the great height relies not on a steel frame but (like Atlantic Chambers) on a load-bearing masonry shell, with cast-iron columns carrying steel beams spanning between brick piers inside. The two façades are quite distinct, with no domed oriel to effect a transition: instead, it is pushed round the side as just one of two canted bays.

There is nothing that actually faces Hope Street on the E side, and nothing of interest between West George Street and West Regent Street, except perhaps, on the E SIDE, a noticeably tall narrow classical elevation with scrolls supporting the wall head chimney, one of a pair of tenements of *c.* 1835 at Nos. 154–66.

On the W SIDE of the next stretch (West Regent Street to Bath Street), just a mutilated terrace of three- and four-bay three-storey houses (Nos. 205–33), much like those round the corner in Bath Street.

90 LION CHAMBERS, 1904–7, the second reinforced-concrete building in Glasgow and among the first few in Britain, rises above the rest of the E SIDE at No. 172. The material was used here to construct a tall building on a very small site, only 10·09 by 14 m (33 ft 1 in by 46 ft); wafer-thin walls (100 mm; 4 ins), carried on a frame of twenty-one continuous columns of 330 to 200 mm (13 to 8 inches) square, saved space. The architects were *James Salmon II & John Gaff Gillespie* (the dominant partner in this design); the system used was *Hennebique*'s, through the British agent *L. G. Mouchel & Partners* (engineer probably *T. J. Gueritte*, working from Newcastle), and the contractors were *The Yorkshire Hennebique Contracting Company Ltd., Leeds*. The client, William G. Black, lawyer and lay member of the Glasgow Art Club, intended the offices for lawyers and the top floor for artists' studios. There is

almost no literal quotation of the 'old rough-cast castle style'
that Salmon thought a suitable basis for stylistic development
in the new material: it was the simplicity of detail and sheerness
of wall-surface that provided the inspiration. The wall's thin-
ness is revealed where it meets the windows in sharp,
unmoulded surrounds, the existence of the frame by the almost
fully glazed side wall and by the way the tower (with its peculiar
parabolic arches) and the square bay overhang the ground
floor. The only ornament is the moulded heraldic shield and 91
the pre-cast judges' head corbels.

Nothing then until Renfrew Street (for Watt Brothers, see
Sauchiehall Street, below), but a glance back s from Sauchiehall Street catches a view with the dome and glazed bays
of Lion Chambers towering over the neighbouring buildings.

On the junction with Renfrew Street, the bunker of the
Savoy Centre (see Sauchiehall Street), the Hope Street Post
Office and the Royal Scottish Academy of Music and Drama;
further N, last on the E side, the Theatre Royal (see Public
Buildings above, for all three). This N end of the street was
widened by the City Improvement Trust in 1903 and ends on
the W SIDE at Cowcaddens Road with one of the Trust's
most lavish tenements (Nos. 307–33), by *Honeyman, Keppie &
Mackintosh*, with *Keppie* probably the architect, 1906–7. Not
only is the round corner tower, with its shallow ogee dome, a
showpiece, but each red sandstone façade has huge curvy
pediments hooding equally sinuous canted bays between giant
chimneystacks carved with Glasgow's arms and the date 1907.
At each end, stairtowers with deeply recessed openings
(making them look more massive) and pavilion roofs behind
pedimented gables. All along, plate-glass shopfronts with
gridded upper lights. Brick back with access balconies: railed
rooftop drying area. All restored in 1975–7 by *William Nimmo
& Partners*.

INDIA STREET

A bureaucratic backwater. All along the E SIDE, STRATH-
CLYDE HOUSE (Regional Council Offices: see also Public
Buildings, above), a twelve-storey wall of engineering brick,
partly set back from the street, by *F. S. Boyer & Partners*,
1974–7. Opposite, between India Street and the M8, PORT-
CULLIS HOUSE (H.M. Customs and Excise and the Inland
Revenue). Horizontal bands of tan brick with recessed sections
of aggregate panel; by the same architects, 1970–3. At its s
end, CLIVE HOUSE, a curtain-walled outpost of the Regional
Council, with speckled mosaic cladding and obliquely set
blocks (1971, by *John Drummond & Partners*).

MITCHELL STREET

On an irregular line reflecting its origin as the beginning of a
country lane from Argyle Street to Cowcaddens.

Best approached from Gordon Street to receive the full of impact of the 150-ft (46-m) water tower on the former GLASGOW HERALD BUILDING (Nos. 60–76), where *Mackintosh*, in 1893–5, was given his head within his firm of *Honeyman & Keppie* in refronting and remodelling *John Baird*'s Glasgow Herald building of 1870 (*see* also Sellars' remodelling of the rear part at No. 65 Buchanan Street, above). This severe façade is made remarkable not only by the tower (inspired perhaps by the same bulging profile of James McLaren's tower at Stirling High School), placed where the street opens out, but by its mutation of quite conventional ornament into something organic. The only remaining simple fittings are in the former editor's room. In the lane to the N, an addition of 1897 and one of 1909, by *J. Beaumont & Sons*.

Some of Mackintosh's thunder is stolen by the almost equally large and red GORDON CHAMBERS (Nos. 87–94) to the N, despite its rather flat and unemphatic façade. This block of offices, motor-car showroom (now shops) and warehouse of 1903–6 was designed for the publican David Ross by *Burnet, Boston & Carruthers*. Original front to Ross's pub (*see* his initials) and to the basement billiard saloon.

At the S end the street becomes a narrow and fume-filled passage lined on the E with the backs of Buchanan Street shops. On the W side, a Thomsonish warehouse of 1876 (Nos. 55–63), with glazing set directly between square stone mullions.

NELSON MANDELA (ST GEORGE'S) PLACE *see* WEST GEORGE STREET

PITT STREET

Lined with the sides of the mostly late C20 buildings that face adjoining streets, and with (from N to S) Elgin Place Church and Adelaide Place Baptist Church, both officially in Bath Street (*see* Churches, above), Strathclyde Police Headquarters and Telephone House (*see* Public Buildings).

RENFIELD LANE *see* HOPE STREET

RENFIELD STREET

A long street without many buildings to call its own. Most of them have their main entrances in the streets that cross Renfield Street and should be looked for under those streets. Despite this, the view down the large ranked blocks S from St Vincent Street to where Union Street curves away out of sight is among the most atmospherically urban in the centre, with nothing to recall its origin as a residential street of Blythswood.

Gordon Street to Cowcaddens Road

First of interest, Nos. 13–17 (W SIDE), the former CRANSTON'S PICTURE HOUSE AND TEA ROOMS of 1914–16, just a tall white faience-clad façade by *James Miller*, all behind it reconstructed by *John McKissack*, *c*. 1935, and again as offices in 1990. No trace now of the lavish ground-floor tearoom (seating 857) decorated by *John Ednie* in Louis XVI style. Nothing interesting on the E side.

N of St Vincent Street, most striking is the PRUDENTIAL ASSURANCE (Nos. 28–36, E SIDE), designed as a furniture warehouse by *James Miller* in 1929–31 and, although related compositionally to his almost contemporary St Vincent Street Bank of Scotland, much more showy in decoration.

Beyond West George Street, again on the E side, the ODEON CINEMA (Nos. 52–6), 1933–5, by *Verity & Beverly*. Built as a 2800-seater cinema for the Paramount chain but subdivided in 1969–70. All its exterior glamour has been lost as well; the curved entrance, its fins, and the blank brick walls should be outlined in neon as they used to be.

On the opposite, NW corner, the red sandstone Baronial-Baroque CASTLE CHAMBERS (Nos. 59–69), the former headquarters of the distillers and brewers McLachan & Co., of Castle Brewery, 1898–1902, by *James Carruthers*, *Frank Burnet & Boston*'s most capable assistant. The big plate-glass windows on Renfield Street lit their showpiece Palace Restaurant. The corner projects as a domed oriel, sheltering two medieval maidens by *Kellock Brown*.

The original PRUDENTIAL BUILDING, opposite, of 1888–90, by *Paul Waterhouse* for *Alfred Waterhouse & Son*, also belongs to Renfield Street (Nos. 73–9). Its harsh Jacobean style in glazed Ruabon brick follows Waterhouse's usual Prudential house-style and makes no concessions to Glaswegian exuberance. On the corner, DE QUINCEY'S BAR occupies the former telling room, lined in *Burmantofts*' buff and pale green faience, with slightly Moorish arches and frieze. De Quincey lived in a house on this site; *see* the plaque on the side elevation.

Nothing of particular interest beyond here now that the huge hulk of the former 4500-seater auditorium of GREEN'S PLAYHOUSE cinema and ballroom of 1925–7 by *John Fairweather & Son* has been demolished (1989). Only the Italianate Nos. 94–8, N of Bath Street, until the Pavilion Theatre (No. 121) on the SW corner of Renfrew Street (*see* Public Buildings, above).

ST GEORGE'S PLACE *see* WEST GEORGE STREET: Nelson Mandela Place

ST VINCENT LANE *see* HOPE STREET

ST VINCENT PLACE *see* ST VINCENT STREET

ST VINCENT STREET

2. Commercial architecture in St Vincent Street is on a monumental scale. E of West Campbell Street, Victorian palazzi are ranked alongside later and even grander Free Style and Neo-classical buildings in a concentration of the highest quality. Further W, beyond the remaining terraces of Blythswood, 'Greek' Thomson's St Vincent Street Church, hemmed in by late C20 office blocks, still governs the hill.

The E end was opened off George Square in 1804, the W end
24 (beyond St Vincent Place) in 1809 as a smart residential street; commercial buildings had begun to take the place of the terraced houses by the middle of the C19.

St Vincent Place

An august start to the street, with a broad enclave of the banks and offices that began seriously to colonize it in the 1850s.

N SIDE. This begins with Rochead's Bank of Scotland (see Merchant City, Streets, above: George Square), followed by James Miller's former ANCHOR LINE offices (Nos. 12–16) of 1905–7, steel-framed at the back and sides, but with a masonry face clad in white Doulton Carrara ware, symmetrical about a portico in antis, jacked up to the third floor, and the gallery above it. Echoes of the sea in the doorcase carving by H. H. Martyn of Cheltenham; and, inside, several rooms with the opulence of an ocean liner (Miller had designed interiors for S. S. Lusitania) have survived alterations of 1975. In complete contrast, the former EVENING CITIZEN offices and printing works (No. 24), by T. L. Watson, assisted by W. J. Anderson, 1885–9. Its red Mauchline sandstone and its style (mixed Renaissance) here made early appearances in Glasgow. Subdued asymmetry (the clock tower had more importance before the tall Anchor Line was built), and rich carving by James Hendry. The portico was originally open.

The Citizen newspaper robbed the CLYDESDALE BANK (Nos. 30–40) of the E end of its intended site, hence the unhappy asymmetry of this Venetian palazzo by J. Burnet, 1871–4. The bank's headquarters (until 1902) occupied only the E part: the towered W section was originally a warehouse. A highly ornamented façade with rustication, superimposed orders, an elaborate parapet, and lots of sculpture (Roman matrons with crouching men (Industry and Commerce) by J. Mossman, reliefs of almost Pre-Raphaelite Spring and Autumn, roundels with the emblems of the towns where the bank was represented and, over the doorway, Father Clyde, by Grassby). Inside, a telling room like a roofed courtyard, with two storeys of arched openings (originally glazed), lit from the glazed coffers of a segmental ceiling and glazed oval dome. One desk composed from the remains of the original counters, by John Notman, architect of the 1978–80 modernization. (For the large N extension, *see* West George Street, below.)

The S SIDE starts with a range (Nos. 7–21) of plain classical offices of *c*. 1830. After this the street widens (and always did). Set back is the SCOTTISH PROVIDENT BUILDING (Nos. 17–29), a very Beaux Arts and rather straight-faced composition with a big mansard by *J. M. Dick Peddie*, 1904–8. The former SCOTTISH AMICABLE BUILDING (Nos. 31–9) is in two parts: the lower Quattrocento-style one in pearl-grey stone and pink granite of 1870–3 is by *Campbell Douglas & Stevenson* (finished by *Campbell Douglas & Sellars*); the Edwardian Baroque top was added by *Burnet, Boston & Carruthers*, 1903–6. A single bay of St Vincent Chambers (*see* Buchanan Street, above) ends St Vincent Place. Outside it, the handsome street-level cast-iron excrescence of the subterranean PUBLIC CONVENIENCES.

Buchanan Street to West Nile Street

N SIDE. On the NE corner, the former Western Club (*see* Buchanan Street, above). The rest of this side is filled with the crisp but relentless SCOTTISH LIFE HOUSE (No. 48) by *Leslie C. Norton*, 1968–72.

S SIDE. On the corner of Buchanan Street, an Italian Mannerist palazzo (formerly National Bank Chambers, now CO-OPERATIVE BANK, No. 47) blown up to giant size, by *J. M. Dick Peddie*, 1898–1906. A huge pedimented doorway, with big shield of arms, leads to a banking hall, lined with pairs of freckled green marble columns, at the bottom of the central light-well. Nos. 57–61 (JOHN SMITH & SON), though by *Rochead*, *c*. 1850, is a far more modest palazzo, its well-detailed five-bay ashlar façade, with aedicules round the first-floor windows, transformed by Edwardian shopfronts. Nos. 63–5, CLYDESDALE (formerly North of Scotland) BANK, a little earlier and a little more elaborate, has an attic and mansard of 1926–8 by *Launcelot Ross*.

West Nile Street to Renfield Street

N SIDE. On the corner (No. 78), Glasgow's first American Classical-style building (1912–13), designed for Phoenix Assurance (now the BANK OF CREDIT AND COMMERCE) by *Alexander D. Hislop* of *Campbell & Hislop*. Narrow-fronted but deep, with an attractive contrast between the grey granite of the ground floor and mezzanine, with their fluted Doric columns on tall pedestals (marking the company's offices), and the buff Blackpasture stone of the severe, slightly French upper storeys. Very sparing decoration: only the bronze gates and the carved trophies (with phoenixes), both by the *Bromsgrove Guild*. Next door, at Nos. 84–94, *J. A. Campbell*'s last work (1908–9), an office block for NORTHERN INSURANCE CO. (he died during its construction). The sheer Portland stone front (the first in Glasgow), with Campbell's characteristic canted bays soaring into towers, is evidently hung on a full steel frame (also Glasgow's first), and the decoration is pared down to the angularity that gives a foretaste of Art Deco. Undulating bays, with *Henry Hope* steel casements all along the back. Interior completely reconstructed by *Covell Matthews Partnership* in 1975.

Two palazzi of the 1850s complete the side, the second (Nos. 102–4) just two-thirds of *Clarke & Bell*'s handsome North British Assurance Company offices of 1853, its *piano nobile* emphasized by windows linked by a continuous cornice carried on Corinthian columns, its Ionic-colonnaded shopfronts sadly lost. Later attic; and all reconstructed behind the façade in 1989.

s SIDE. The buildings on this side are of an altogether smaller scale, beginning with Nos. 67–79 on the corner of West Nile Street, business chambers and shops done by *J. J. Stevenson* from London, *c.* 1875–8, with elegant details and Lescot-like pediments. The next diminutive palazzo, of *c.* 1860 (Nos. 81–91), has crisply carved, ingenious Renaissance details comparable to Salmon's Nos. 65–81 Miller Street or Rhind's No. 8 Gordon Street: note especially the aedicule doorway, the *putti* over the central tripartite window, the swan-necked pediments holding little masks, and the two rusticated arched chimneystacks. A particularly ugly rendering of the American Classical style (BANK OF SCOTLAND CHAMBERS, No. 93) by *Balfour & Stewart*, 1924–6, ends this stretch.

Renfield Street to Hope Street

99 N SIDE. With *Miller*'s BANK OF SCOTLAND (Nos. 110–20, formerly Union Bank) of 1924–7, the American Classical style introduced by Hislop acquired a scale worthy of New York or Chicago. Indeed, Miller's assistant *Richard Gunn* derived his design from York & Sawyer's Guaranty Trust Building in New York. These huge fluted Ionic columns and their massive stylobate dwarf the passer-by. Inside, more monumental marble columns round a noble top-lit atrium. In the foyer, plaques from the Ship Bank in Ingram Street. Nos. 122–8 (for EDINBURGH LIFE ASSURANCE) shows *J. A. Campbell* in 1904–6 being more conventionally classical than usual. Rebuilt behind the façade by *Scott, Brownrigg & Turner* in 1980–1.

At Nos. 130–6, a former china merchants' of 1876 by *James Thomson*, identical to Nos. 101–3 for the same proprietors at the E end of the S SIDE, on the corner of Renfield Street. Both have more window than wall and giant pilasters rusticated above the shopfronts. The shopfront of Nos. 101–3 is a slick design of 1927 by *Watson, Salmond & Gray*, which its later canopy compliments. From the second floor of Nos 105–13 (by *Frank Southorn* for SCOTTISH TEMPERANCE ASSURANCE, 1911–12), with its peculiar green pantiled mansard, two giant seated female figures look down into the street. The lower Nos. 115–17, the former UNION BANK of 1870, is by *John Burnet*, a fairly close relation of his Clydesdale Bank in St Vincent Place (*see* above). Lastly, the tall narow red Locharbriggs sandstone front of the LIVERPOOL AND LONDON AND GLOBE ASSURANCE BUILDINGS (Nos. 121–3) by *J. B. & W. A. Thomson*, 1899–1901 (relieved 'at points' with Peterhead granite) develops in Franco-Flemish elaboration towards an oriel with green onion dome and cupola on the corner, and continues s equally elaborately to another oriel-cum-bartizan some way down Hope Street.

Hope Street to Wellington Street

From Hope Street to West Campbell Street, there is very little that is earlier than the 1890s, and much that dates from the late c 20.

N SIDE. No. 142, by *Burnet, Boston & Carruthers*, 1899-1900, turns the corner with some refinement. Its tall slender canted bays are much more daringly interpreted in its even narrower contemporary neighbour, the HATRACK building (Nos. 142a– 144), by *James Salmon II* of *Salmon, Son & Gillespie*, 1899– 1902. Here the walls have been almost whittled away, to leave a façade mostly of glass held in a stone skeleton full of Art Nouveau curves. What stonework remains has fantastic details on a minute scale: filigree capitals with strands of tiny beads round the doorway; a goat (or is it a dragon or a satyr?) supporting the oriel; and, above the shop window and entrance, little flying lanterns and figures mixed up with bending trees. The rooftop cupola is most curious of all, with projecting finials that give the building its soubriquet, the Hatrack. In the oriel, a galleon in stained glass, and, domi-nating the entrance hall, a decorative iron lift-cage. Its western neighbour is big and bold but thoughtfully designed: SCOT-TISH AMICABLE LIFE ASSURANCE (No. 150) by *King, Main & Ellison*, 1973–6. Strongly modelled, with rectangular projecting bays of tinted glass held in a slender frame of polished granite and neatly stepped back and forward along its length to diminish its bulkiness.

s SIDE. NORWICH UNION CHAMBERS (Nos. 125–7), by *John Hutchison*, 1897–8, answers in similar but more ordinary Northern Renaissance fashion the Thomsons' building on the opposite (E) corner of Hope Street. A narrow classical front in cream sandstone follows (No. 129, former LEGAL & GENERAL ASSURANCE OFFICES, 1927–9, by *James Napier* of *Laird & Napier*). Nothing much of interest then until the very large, plain classical No. 145 on the corner of Wellington Street, which was built for Commercial Union in 1931–2: architects *Burnet & Boston*.

Wellington Street to West Campbell Street

From here, the street runs along the side of a steep N–S slope. Some buildings are better adapted to it than others.

On the N SIDE, a sudden break in the line of the street, where SCOTTISH UNION HOUSE (No. 174), a thoughtfully detailed six-storey block with chamfered brickwork and reeded bronze piers, by *Wylie, Shanks & Partners*, 1965–7, is set back on a deep terrace. Next (Nos. 178–82), a painfully ill-digested medley of canted bays, arches and mansards, built of pink granite and mirror glass in 1988–9; and an average production, dated 1897, by *Frank Burnet & Boston* (Nos. 188–92). At the w corner, the former NORTH BRITISH & MERCANTILE BUILDING (No. 200) of 1926–9, *Sir J. J. Burnet*'s last work in Glasgow. It is of seemingly effortless simplicity. The figure of St Andrew (1927) is by *Archibald Dawson*, the later menacing figures crouching on pedestals by the door by *Mortimer, Willison & Graham*. The same regular fenestration and simple arches continue round the back in yellow brick.

On the S SIDE, the overbearing COATS VIYELLA building (by *Scott, Brownrigg & Turner*, 1983–7), eating unnecessarily into the hillside. Its huge mirror-glass bays strain to compromise between its two narrow classical neighbours to the E (No. 147 of *c.* 1904–5 by *W. Hunter McNab* (also for J. & P. Coats); and No. 149 of 1931 by *James Miller*) and the line of the Blythswood terraces beyond.

West Campbell Street to Douglas Street

On St Vincent Street, only a fragment (four terraces between these streets) remains of the New Town of Blythswood.

Between West Campbell Street and Blythswood Street, two terraces different in design. The truncated and much altered one of individual houses on the S SIDE (Nos. 187–209) is the earlier (*c.* 1825) and simpler; the two centre ones (Nos. 193–201) were completely replaced in 1981–3 by *Hugh Martin & Partners*. That on the N SIDE (Nos. 202–28), with projecting end and centre pavilions and Greek Ionic doorcases, is of *c.* 1830–5 and has been gutted and stuffed by *Keppie Henderson & Partners*, 1987, except for the w and the distinctive centre pavilion (No. 218). *Sir J. J. Burnet* added the solid balcony and small-paned windows in 1898–9, and reconstructed the interior for the INSTITUTE OF CHARTERED ACCOUNTANTS (then Accountants and Actuaries). The entrance hall of No. 218 is still the original Greek Revival one, with shallow dome, Ionic-columned screen and broad staircase through three storeys up to a dome on a windowed drum. On the first floor, another columned screen into Burnet's library, which runs the length of the first floor from front to back. Late-C17-style panelling, with a Baroque overdoor and chimneypieces: it was linked originally with the adjoining front room by means of sliding doors, similar to the more elaborate ones at Burnet's Clyde

Navigation Trust building (*see* Broomielaw, Streets, below: Robertson Street). At the back, a smaller library in similar style, and on the ground floor, beneath the main library, a plainer room with bolection-moulded fireplaces.

Of the next pair of terraces, between Blythswood Street and Douglas Street, only that on the S SIDE (Nos. 217–45), begun *c.* 1825, is complete – and rather grand – with a distinct *piano nobile* on the taller end and centre pavilions, and Roman Doric porches and doorcases. Nos. 233 and 241 have nice original entrance halls. No. 233 (gutted in 1988) had a back extension by *Charles Rennie Mackintosh*, 1898–1900; its open timber roof, very like those in the School of Art, is to be placed elsewhere in the building.

Opposite (N SIDE) the remains of another, different symmetrical terrace of the late 1830s. In the centre, the five-bay No. 242, with fluted coupled columns and a balustrade to the central portico, was a superior house altered by *Sir J.J. Burnet* for the ROYAL FACULTY (now Royal College) OF PHYSICIANS AND SURGEONS in 1892–3. He panelled the staircase hall (which still has its screen of Tuscan columns, though the sequence of saucer domes looks typical of Burnet) and rebuilt the staircase to form a grand axial approach to the College Hall, which he added behind the house above ground-floor classrooms (now altered). A subtle change of rhythm on the top-lit mezzanine landing before the Hall itself, a rather bleak double-height room, its coved plaster ceiling with a large guilloche pattern and its big timber fireplace and doorcase in late C17 style. Across the front of the building at first-floor level, the drawing room of the 1830s house, the plasterwork on walls and ceiling apparently original. Burnet was responsible for the careful modelling of this landing, which until altered by *W. N. W. Ramsay* in 1962–3 was lit from a fine dome above the octagonal gallery that served the second floor. The dome can still be seen from the second-floor library, which was extended across the light-well. All the post-1914 alterations have been quite without Burnet's imagination. On the ground floor, the original dining room, with Corinthian-columned screens and a galleried library, handsomely fitted up by Burnet, was spoilt in 1956 by the mania for stripping varnish. It is now entered from No. 236, a narrower house taken over in 1901 and slightly altered by Burnet. He may have put the gallery in the first-floor drawing room, still with part of a fine 1830s ceiling. This house, No. 234 (taken over by the Royal College in 1980) and No. 232 all have original staircases and columned halls. The terrace ends on the same classical lines, but on a greatly expanded scale, with *James Thomson*'s now gutted Maclean's Hotel (No. 250) of *c.* 1875. The two-storey porch owes much to Thomas Hamilton's Royal College of Physicians in Edinburgh.

Douglas Street to Pitt Street

One more plain painted terrace (Nos. 260–80) on the N SIDE, with a very Soanian E return (Nos. 95–9 Douglas Street). Segmental heads to the windows and to the doorcases with unfluted Greek Doric columns *in antis*. On the S SIDE, the relatively subdued main entrance to Heron House, No. 255 (*see* Bothwell Street, above), next to *Alexander Thomson*'s *magnum opus*, St Vincent Street Church (*see* Churches, above).

Pitt Street to India Street

Beyond Pitt Street, the gilt-glazed BRITOIL monster (by *Hugh Martin & Partners*, 1982–8) squats in ungainly fashion on polished granite legs between Bothwell Street and St Vincent Street. There is no focal point (not even the entrance in St Vincent Street) and no relief other than slightly higher glazed stairtowers at regular intervals along the sides, and functional excrescences on the roof: no advantage has been taken of the steep site.

On the N SIDE, St Columba's (*see* Churches) makes the only strong statement until GUARDIAN ROYAL EXCHANGE ASSURANCE by *Derek Stephenson* of *Royce, Stephenson & Tasker*, 1962–4, a massive T-shaped block banded in crunchy aggregate and smooth grey brick. It stands on *pilotis* above a big podium (originally a petrol station, but converted into offices with Post-Modern embellishments *c.* 1988), just before St Vincent Street takes off over the ring road.

SAUCHIEHALL STREET

Perhaps Glasgow's most famous street, the mecca for shopping and entertainment since the C19, but certainly not its most beautiful. The undisciplined mixture of hidden villas, tenements, warehouses, theatres and, predominantly, late C20 commercial buildings represents the unplanned growth of this E end of it. Until it became the main route to the smart western suburbs in the mid-C19, this part of Sauchiehall Street had three disparate parts; its E end (then Cathcart Street), lined with tenements and shops, belonged to the development just W of George Square; the central stretch was built up with terraced houses like those on Blythswood Hill; and the W end (then a country lane in the valley) was edged with the villas of Garnethill. From the 1860s, villas were joined or replaced by respectable tenements, the terraced houses by grand retail warehouses for the carriage trade of the West End, and numerous places of entertainment – theatres, music halls, restaurants and an art gallery. Many of these went in the 1960s and in the 1970s, when the M8 split the street pattern open and cut this end off from the still suburban W end of the street (*see* Woodlands and Finnieston). The street is very long, and the best buildings are scattered down its whole exhausting length.

Buchanan Street to West Nile Street

Sauchiehall Street starts narrowly with the Concert Hall (*see* Public Buildings) on the N side walling in its E end and a row of early C19 tenements on the S (Nos. 1–21), including the Cleland Testimonial Building which rounds the SE corner (*see* No. 249 Buchanan Street, above).

West Nile Street to Renfield Street

The next stretch was redeveloped in the 1960s. On the N SIDE, ST ANDREW'S HOUSE, by *Arthur Swift & Partners*, 1961–4, the first multi-storey commercial block in the city centre and still the tallest in this part of it. An unmodulated slab towers over a long podium, its upper floor cantilevered over shopfronts.

On the S SIDE, another long podium, carrying a stocky three-storey block, more chunkily detailed in brick and concrete by *Covell Matthews & Partners*, 1962–5. The only old building left along here is the plain former Linen Bank chambers (No. 112) of the 1890s on the W corner.

Renfield Street to Hope Street

All of the N SIDE looks mid-Victorian and Italianate, except for *Boyer & Partners'* block at the W corner, a crude and dreary yellow brick pastiche of its Italianate neighbours, 1987–8. First, the seven-bay Nos. 76–82, with chunky pediments to the first-floor windows; then (after the altered infill of 1927) the former CROWN HALLS (auction rooms) at Nos. 94–102, by *H. K. Bromhead*, 1871, the doorway with its naive timber crown the only incident in the long yellow sandstone façade.

Nothing of interest on the S SIDE with its mixture of late C20 shops (e.g. BRITISH HOME STORES by *G. W. Clarke*, 1966–9, curving round the E corner) and mutilated mid-C19 buildings.

Hope Street to Cambridge Street (N side)

Nos. 116–20 (DUNNS), on the corner of Hope Street, is another, slightly more elaborate palazzo, with enriched triangular pediments alternating with segmental ones on the first floor and with cornices on the second. After the horribly defaced Nos. 122–6 comes the most handsome and lavish warehouse in the whole street (Nos. 128–52), or rather the front of it, for behind its façade it has been rebuilt (by *Gavin Paterson & Sons*, 1971–c. 1979) as part of the SAVOY CENTRE, a shopping mall on the site of *James Miller*'s Savoy Cinema of 1913, once entered either through this warehouse or from Hope Street. The part seen from Hope Street is crude (just a raw concrete box); but *H. & D. Barclay*'s façade of 1891–5 for Cumming & Smith, furnishers, is a feast for the eyes. Dominant are the deeply

recessed arches embracing canted bays, which have only a
slender framework of stone, repeated with a syncopated
rhythm across the whole front. The stubby Ionic columns and
end pediments of the eaves gallery echo the rhythm in a stricter
mood. Below it, delicately-carved classical figures lean non-
chalantly against the heads of the giant arches, carrying palms,
horns, galleons, swords, torches and cornucopia.

Now for an unattractive stretch of low buildings. First
MARKS & SPENCER (Nos. 164–84), whose main building of
c. 1935, executed to *Robert Lutyens*'s standard house design by
James M. Munro, was truncated for an equally unimaginative
extension by *Munro & Partners c.* 1985. Then the showy
BOOTS (Nos. 186–200), with two ugly oriels, by *Cunningham
Glass Partnership*, 1971–3. In welcome contrast, the tall deep-
red sandstone corner building of 1899–1902 (Nos. 202–12), by
James Thomson of *Baird & Thomson*, is remarkable for its
multiplicity of mouldings, especially concentrated on the tall
two-storey dormers with their shaped leaded roofs which grow
out of the tall corner mansard.

Hope Street to Blythswood Street (s side)

WATT BROTHERS, on the corner and all down Hope Street to
Bath Street, is in two parts, both loosely classical. The 'early
Roman' style N one (No. 119), by *Alec S. Heathcote* of Manchester, with two pyramid-capped towers facing Sauchiehall
Street, came first in 1914. The bigger, bolder s block followed
in 1929–30, designed by *Keppie & Henderson*; between its
fluted columns and stone piers with their geometrical ornament, big triangular bays cast by *Walter Macfarlane & Co.*
Nos. 123–33, by *James Carruthers*, 1923–4, is a much less
spectacular job in the same materials. Next to it, the best
building so far on this side (Nos. 137–43), a design of c. 1903–
6 by *John Keppie* of *Honeyman, Keppie, & Mackintosh* for Dr
Walker. Conventional Franco-Flemish Baroque detail well
under control and crisply done in orange-red sandstone. The
former LA SCALA cinema (Nos. 147–63, now shops) runs up
to the corner of Wellington Street, its three tall storeys in the
French Beaux Arts classical style designed for Caledonian
Cinemas by *Neil C. Duff* with *John McKissack*, 1908–12. 1930s
entrance by *Alister McDonald* (1936).

The SAUCHIEHALL CENTRE (1970–4, by *Ian Burke & Partners*) fills the block between Wellington Street and West
Campbell Street. Pettigrew & Stephen's famous Manchester
warehouse of the 1890s (designed by *Honeyman & Keppie*)
was demolished for it; its cupola, apparently detailed by *Mackintosh*, is in the Hunterian Art Gallery (*q.v.*). The original
blank brown brick envelope round a two-storey shopping mall
and top-floor parking (reached by brutal ramps each end) was
given cosmetic treatment by *Bradshaw, Rowse & Harker* in
1987. Outside, along the N and s fronts, big flat projecting
glass bays with a post-Mackintosh blue-painted grid and, along

Sauchiehall Street, a veranda. Inside, more Mackintosh-derived details, together with mirrored surfaces, pools, planting, and wall-climber lifts, shopping-centre favourites of the 1980s.

Then an unexciting range of mid-C19 buildings (those at the E end, Nos. 199–215, reconstructed by *James Munro* in 1901), and, amongst them, at No. 217, the startling stucco façade of the former WILLOW TEA ROOMS, one of Miss Cranston's celebrated restaurants. *Charles Rennie Mackintosh* of *Keppie, Henderson & Mackintosh* converted part of the former warehouse and fitted it out in 1903–4. Miss Cranston's restaurant lasted until 1919, when it was taken over by another restaurateur. In the 1920s, it was absorbed by the then adjacent department store, who owned it until the major reconstruction in 1979–80 by *Geoffrey Wimpenny* of *Keppie, Henderson & Partners*. The façade, which stands out even amongst the showy façades of Sauchiehall Street, is oddly asymmetrical. Although it is of three bays, that to the l. is wider and bowed at second- and third-floor level for no apparent reason. The eye-catching first-floor bow window, with its closely spaced mullions and decorative leaded windows, indicates the position inside of the Room de Luxe. The reconstructed ground-floor window follows the lines of the original, although the roundels are a free interpretation of the lost original, using a design based on the finials at the School of Art.

When the interior was completed in 1904, the entrance doors gave on to a dining room in two parts, which stretched from front to back of the building. The vista remains, with the fireplace on axis at the far end. On the walls to l. and r., a frieze of plaster panels of abstracted willow trees, eight in all. They are all casts from a well-preserved original, removed during the reconstruction. The rear part of the ground floor has an open well offering glimpses of the gallery level above. This was originally reached only by the stair on the l.; the one on the r. is a later insertion. The gallery is all typically Mackintosh, with tapered columns, a lattice ceiling, and balustrades all in timber painted white with, here and there, tiny areas of mauve. Again, a fireplace on axis on the rear wall and leaded windows in a strip to l. and r. Opposite, a metal balcony screen of novel design allows glimpses of the ground floor. Upstairs, the Room de Luxe, now again in use as a tea room. The reconstruction has been done with good intentions to re-create the original room; indeed the famous leaded double doors, the abstract frieze in coloured glass and mirrors, the eccentric 'hanging rail' fireplace surrounds, are all original.

Cambridge Street to Dalhousie Street (N side)

From Nos. 218–38 the dark blue, sheer curtain walls of C & A (*North & Partners*, 1964–7), concealing a bold faience front of 1930 by *North, Robin & Wilson*, and LITTLEWOODS (1964–8 by Littlewoods' own architects). Along the rest of this block, the much altered, painted, four-storey late C19 No. 250, its remaining classical details on a coarse scale. It was extended to the N up Rose Street (No. 6) in 1925 with several stone and cast-iron bays by *E. G. Wylie*.

Beyond Rose Street, TRERONS (Nos. 254–90) has a long and restrained classical front. Designed by *James Smith*, it was originally an art gallery, built in 1855–6 by the merchant and bailie Archibald McLellan to display his large collection of paintings. Paintings and gallery were bought by the Corporation in 1856. After the collection was transferred to Kelvingrove, the building was partly reconstructed by *Burnet & Boston* (the corner dome and shopfronts were created then) and opened in 1904 as Trerons' Magasin des Tuileries. In 1912–13 the City Engineer, *A. B. McDonald*, built new exhibition galleries and public halls (with ferro-concrete roofs and grand staircase) enclosed by the three ranges of the shop; their windowless Neo-classical façade can be seen in Renfrew Street, behind in Garnethill. Nothing remarkable inside the shop, which was gutted by fire in 1986 and rebuilt to designs by *Scott, Brownrigg & Turner*.

Blythswood Street to Douglas Street (s side)

The BANK OF SCOTLAND (No. 235), by *Graham Henderson* for *Keppie & Henderson*, 1929–31, is the only memorable building along here. It follows a well-established formula, giving a nice solid base to the narrow façade, with figures by *Benno Schotz*. Some Greek decoration outside and in the Hoptonwood stone-lined banking hall. Beyond, a mixture of inconsequential C19 buildings (the corner one with a 1930s shopfront); and the unpleasant pink brick WARING & GILLOW (Nos. 249–61) of *c.* 1979–81 by *Scott, Brownrigg & Turner*, with slitty dormers.

Dalhousie Street to Charing Cross (N side)

This side really belongs to Garnethill behind it. One or two of Garnethill's early villas are hidden behind later commercial property; even later buildings, like the Dental Hospital and Albany Chambers, run through N to Renfrew Street (*q.v.*).

The unprepossessing CANNON CINEMA (between Dalhousie Street and Scott Street) has seen many changes. At the E end, the brown brick extension added in 1965–7 by *Leslie C. Norton & C. J. Foster* to what started life *c.* 1900 housing a panorama (Nos. 304–34), was converted *c.* 1910 into Hengler's Circus, and was then partly demolished and redesigned as a dance hall by *Neil C. Duff* in 1927. The centrepiece dates from its conversion to the Regal Cinema by *C. J. McNair* in 1929.

From the E corner of Scott Street, *Alexander Thomson*'s GRECIAN BUILDINGS (Nos. 336–56) of 1865 with, ironically, Egyptian detail dominant over Greek. Almost uniquely among Thomson's commercial work, this occupies a corner site and had to reveal its depth rather than hide behind a screen façade slotted between others. It has solid-looking end pavilions, with windows set in broad expanses of masonry and almost none of the teasing spatial complexity of the centre, where the stumpy tapering columns of the deeply shadowed top floor (they are attached to almost concealed piers, into which the timber windows are set) seem to grow out of the masonry piers between the slightly raised aedicules below. The ground floor represents yet another layer, with large sheets of plate glass set in a narrow timber framework, restored in 1988–9 by *Boswell, Mitchell & Johnston*. No clue, except the central stair, is left to the original plan.

Its neighbour is the Dental Hospital (*see* Garnethill, below: Public Buildings). Then comes a long stretch of Edwardian Baroque red sandstone tenements and shops (ASHFIELD HOUSE, Nos. 396–450, by *T. L. Watson & Henry Mitchell*: W end 1900–3, E end, with a slightly bowed centrepiece and giant Ionic columns, 1907–8), before the impact of the former BERESFORD HOTEL (now BAIRD HALL of Strathclyde 107 University), built in 1937–8 for visitors to the Empire Exhibition and designed in the same mood as the Exhibition buildings by *Weddell & Inglis*. Its dazzling livery of mustard and black faience with red fins has been sadly obliterated with paint. On the ground floor, curved windows repeat the theme of the towers: inside, not much left except some timber veneer.

The much smaller and heterogeneous buildings come as something of an anticlimax after that. There are, however, one or two of interest, especially those relics of the street's original early C19 buildings. First, almost completely hidden behind the entrance to the Mayfair discothèque (No. 478), an early villa: a square, two-storey house with Greek Doric portico and a Greek Ionic screen of columns in the hall. After the ZANZIBAR CLUB (Nos. 500–16, by *Robert Duncan*, 1898), with a big central pediment carried above a very slight framework of red sandstone and fluted cast-iron colonnettes, at No. 518 there is a narrow, approximately-Dutch façade by *Honeyman, Keppie & Mackintosh*, 1903–4, with sinuous details like those on the Glasgow Herald building. It hides a three-storey three-bay house, probably the remains of Albany Terrace, still with a columned screen and original fireplace in its former drawing room. This was the premises of the photographers T. and R. Annan. Next door, Victory still reigns over the mutilated entrance of the former VITOGRAPH CINEMA, converted from a shop by *John Fairweather*, 1914–15; Beethoven presides on the Renfrew Street façade. The NATIONAL BANK OF PAKISTAN (No. 522, by *Elder & Cannon*, 1981–2) is equally narrow. Subdued elevation, with a cladding of blond sandstone (sadly streaked by Glasgow damp by 1989) set in a fine diagonal grid of polished green marble; the interior is more exotic, with brass rings round the cone-capitals and an Islamic pattern frieze.

The landmark of CHARING CROSS MANSIONS, an extrovert design full of incident by *J.J. Burnet* for *Burnet, Son & Campbell*, 1889–91, has a quieter prelude: ALBANY CHAMBERS (Nos. 528–34) of 1896–9, designed by the same architects for the same proprietors, the warehousemen Robert Simpson & Sons. It forms the commercial front of Albany Mansions, entered from the other (N) side in Renfrew Street (*see* Garnethill, below: Description). For Charing Cross Mansions, a block of tenements (or rather mansion flats), Burnet forged a French Second Empire façade in the manner of the Hôtel de Ville into an expansive curve following the corner into St George's Road and, with a dramatic tower, a clock rich with sculpture (by *William Birnie Rhind*), and a band of plate-glass shop windows, closed the view down Sauchiehall Street from the W while entertaining the passer-by. Its effect on the once close-knit road junction can now, alas, only be judged from old photographs.

Douglas Street to Charing Cross (s side)

Tenements with shops of the 1840s to 1870s stretch almost unbroken from Douglas Street to Charing Cross. They are all of four storeys and cream sandstone, and all are of debased classical design; their details vary slightly but not significantly.

Nos. 269–305 (Douglas Street to Pitt Street) are the plainest and earliest, that is, *c.* 1845, with cornices over first- and second-floor windows and blind windows over the close entrances. No. 293 has a Deco shopfront by *Archibald Hamilton & Sons* for MORAY GLASSER, 1929.

Between Pitt Street and Holland Street, Nos. 309–13 (MUIR SIMPSONS of 1904, by *Honeyman, Keppie & Mackintosh*) breaks in with red sandstone and Franco-Flemish gables, but Nos. 315–23 are plain classical tenements of *c.* 1850, and Nos. 325–49 are a more ambitious composition with projecting ends emphasized by quoins, and little shaped hoods over the first-floor windows. An elegant C19 shopfront at No. 335, and a pub and billiard hall by *Clarke & Bell* of 1906 at the corner of Holland Street (No. 349).

Nos. 351–87 (Holland Street to Elmbank Street), also of *c.* 1850, have a greater display of alternating pediments, some tripartite windows, and original shopfronts at the E corner. The 1930s infill at No. 373 still has (just) its contemporary shopfront, designed for Art Fabrics in 1931 by *E. Pollard & Co.* of London. On the W corner, *Holmes Partnership*'s flats and shops of 1984–8 are happily as robustly detailed in buff brick as their neighbours, though they revert, alas, to Post-Modern clichés on Elmbank Street.

Nos. 401–35 (Elmbank Street to Charing Cross) are decidedly coarse: Nos. 401–27 are later (*c.* 1870, by *Horatio Bromhead*), with heavy cornices and daisy-decorated hoods to the windows (blind windows over the closes); and Nos. 431–51, of the 1850s, have flowery consoles to cornices over single and tripartite windows. At No. 417, a Chinese restaurant still with its 1911 cinema guise.

These pleasingly uniform classical terraces stop abruptly against the podium of a nine-storey brick slab of 1968–9 before the extraordinary office block (*see* Bath Street, above) planned to bridge the gulf of the M8. Sauchiehall Street continues in its original residential manner on the far side of the M8 (*see* Woodlands and Finnieston, below: Perambulation 3).

UNION STREET

Being laid out as a new street from the head of Jamaica Street in 1802. The W side still has some of the plain classical earlier C 19 commercial character, but the most interesting buildings are the later ones on the E side.

Argyle Street to Gordon Street

E SIDE. This side starts boldly with Boots (*see* Merchant City, Streets, above: Argyle Street), followed by the narrow Nos. 28–40 (a former restaurant of 1929–31 by *Whyte & Galloway*), but most of it is taken up by a magnificent, unbroken stretch of mid-C 19 warehouses. Nos. 50–76 (1855, by *William (?) Lochead*) is remarkable for the length and consistency of its mostly cast-iron and glass front, held within the slightest masonry framework of superimposed orders and corresponding entablatures. Then, briefly, a more substantial façade at Nos. 78–82, almost identical to James Thomson's Nos. 71–9 Buchanan Street of the 1880s (*see* Streets, above), the grey granite facing of the ground-floor bank with its Doric doorways by *Balfour & Stewart*, 1924.

The theme of the screen-wall of superimposed orders is resumed in more sophisticated manner by *Alexander Thomson*'s EGYPTIAN HALLS (Nos. 84–100), a warehouse of 1871–3 built by James Robertson. Here, the uninterrupted entablatures and repetitive bays seem capable of infinite extension, with slivers of pilaster at each end the only, characteristically subtle, terminations. The four storeys vary in depth of relief and complexity of ornament, from the plate-glass shopfronts flush with their stone surrounds, incised only with bands (all altered to some degree), to the first floor with windows set well back between slender piers with Assyrian scroll capitals, to the shallower second floor, a positive base for the 'eaves gallery' with its continuous band of glazing behind an Egyptian colonnade designed on the same scale as the deep coved cornice, which conceals sloping attic rooflights. The continuous entablatures indeed represented undivided floors behind, supported on cast-iron columns. Breaking the mood, a stodgy design by *George Bell II* of *Clarke & Bell* for the North British Daily Mail (1898) but the Ca' d'Oro (*see* Gordon Street, above) ends Union Street in the highest style.

W SIDE. Starting again at the S end, two neat curtain-walled slabs built for BURTON'S in 1961, framed in black granite and set at right angles (Nos. 1–15) to form the corner with Argyle Street. Plain four-storey commercial buildings of *c.* 1840 follow: first Nos. 19–53, with the centre one of eleven bays slightly recessed and the N half refenestrated in the 1930s; then DUNCAN'S HOTEL (Nos. 57–71), equally long and with wallhead chimneys. Next a dramatic jump in scale to *James Miller*'s CALEDONIAN CHAMBERS (Nos. 75–95), a vast office block of dead buff stone built for the Caledonian Railway in 1901–3 and incorporating a pedestrian entrance to Central Station (*see* Public Buildings, above), which Miller was then remodelling. Mannerist detail remarkably subdued in the middle eleven bays but breaking out with huge aedicules on the tower-like end ones carried on Michelangelesque figures by *Albert Hodge*. In the huge pediments of these, the royal arms of Scotland. This brings us to the building on the corner of Gordon Street (*see* above).

WATERLOO STREET

Much redeveloped.

Hope Street to Pitt Street

N SIDE. This side starts with the big French-style Central Chambers (*see* Hope Street, above). After that, the Inland Revenue's HAMILTON HOUSE (by *R. Seifert Co-Partnership*, 1972), a stocky slab on a brown tile-clad podium. Filling half the block between Wellington Street and West Campbell Street, the former G.P.O. PARCELS OFFICE of 1903–5 by *W. T. Oldrieve*, rather dry classicism on a giant scale.

Several modestly scaled buildings between West Campbell Street and Blythswood Street. First, a slick cube of greenish glass by *Cunningham Glass Partnership*, 1988, set back to display the idiosyncrasies of No. 64, its red sandstone neighbour of 1898–1900 by *James Chalmers*. A fairly conventional front contrasts with the E side's Free Style and a positively peculiar tower, with scalloped top, projecting baldacchini and droopy hoodmoulds. Over the entrance two Highlanders, advertisement for the original proprietors' wares (one of these figures is 'Rhoderick Dhu', after whom Wright & Greig's most famous whisky was named). Over the oriel, a Highland lass with her malting shovel; the baldacchini were meant to have figures of the Seasons. Next door, plain cream sandstone tenements, probably mid-C19 and the earliest buildings in the street; and on the corner, No. 74, FORTUNE HOUSE (originally Metro-Vick House) by *J. Taylor Thomson*, 1925–7, for Metropolitan Vickers Electrical Co. Ltd, American Classical, with two distinct oddities – the blocks of rough stone (intended to be sculpted?), and the animal masks carved after models by *Phyllis M. Bone*.

S SIDE. Back to the E end and, after an unpromising start with the overhanging canopy of a concrete-framed block of 1963–5 by *Leslie C. Norton*, WATERLOO CHAMBERS (Nos. 15–23) of 1898–1900 by *J. J. Burnet*. Although much larger and weightier and with more conventional symmetry, the organization of this façade strongly resembles that of his contemporary Atlantic Chambers round the corner in Hope Street. But for fire regulations, Burnet would have made it two storeys higher still; its red sandstone already dwarfs the plain yellow sandstone corner block of *c.* 1870 at Nos. 27–31.

Next, two boring office blocks take up a long stretch: ALHAMBRA HOUSE by *Newman, Levinson & Partners*, which took the place of J. J. Burnet's exotic Alhambra Theatre in 1971–2 (and was itself transformed in 1989); and MAGNET HOUSE of 1963–7 by *Leach, Rhodes & Walker*. The yellow sandstone palazzo of ELECTRICITY HOUSE, 1930–7, just beyond at Nos. 75–7, is not much more exciting. It was designed in 1927 by *A. McInnes Gardner* for the Corporation's electricity department.

Beyond Blythswood Street, nothing much of interest on either side.

WELLINGTON STREET

Argyle Street to Sauchiehall Street

On the W SIDE, a five-storey cream sandstone warehouse of *c.* 1880 (Nos. 7–11) with a slim framework of superimposed pilasters and a lot of incised Greek decoration. At the entrance, bizarre columns made top-heavy with angle volutes and incised bands. Odd open parapet with antefixae. For Nos. 23–5 *see* Nos. 5–7 Cadogan Street, above.

On the E SIDE, *Duncan McNaughtan*'s pink Dumfries-shire stone BALTIC CHAMBERS (Nos. 40–60), 1899–1900, its Baltic character expressed in the big octagonal slated roofs, with lanterns and handsome weathervanes, over the end bays. Nice strapwork and cartouches, carved by *William Vickers*, on the upper part. A liberal amount of Gibbs rustication gives weight to the ground floor. On the other (N) side of Cadogan Street, PACIFIC HOUSE (*Comprehensive Design Group (Scotland)*, 1981–4) lacks subtlety: canted mirror-glass bays step up to a tall one that turns the corner.

Nothing beyond that except the side elevations of buildings in the streets running E to W (*q.v.*) all the way to Sauchiehall Street.

WEST CAMPBELL STREET

Along the whole length of the street, nothing but the side elevations of buildings in the streets running E to W (*q.v.*).

There are interesting buildings along the whole length. At the E end, many of Glasgow's clubs and institutions set amongst a wide variety of commercial architecture. Beyond Wellington Street, terraces of houses, focussed on Blythswood Square.

George Square to Buchanan Street

A very mixed bag, starting, on the N SIDE, with the dreadful front block of Queen Street Station (*see* Merchant City, above: Public Buildings) and the adjacent office block of 1974 by *Miller & Black* for which the Independent Chapel of 1819 by James Gillespie Graham was demolished in 1975.

On the W corner of Dundas Street (No. 34), a remarkable display of ornament in crimson Locharbriggs sandstone, designed by *James Thomson* of *Baird & Thomson* for Connal & Co., warehousekeepers, 1898–1900. The square bay windows with herms as mullions are copied from the Ritterhaus in Heidelberg, and the heaped-up gables, masses of rustication, blocked columns and so on are all in the same German Renaissance spirit. The heads, carved by *James Young*, represent famous C19 Glaswegians (Watt, Dixon, Baird, J. B. Neilson *et al.*) involved, like Connal & Co., in the iron trade. No. 34 represents James Thomson's late work, its neighbour, Nos. 44–6, of 1871, his earlier Italianate style. Tower Buildings then turns the corner (*see* Nos. 152–60 Buchanan Street, above).

On the S SIDE, after the Merchants' House (*see* Merchant City, Streets, above: George Square), all was rebuilt *c.* 1980. The CLYDESDALE BANK (by *G. D. Lodge & Partners*) on the corner is really an extension to Burnet's building in St Vincent Place (*see* St Vincent Street, above), but takes its cue from the red stone of No. 34, and is thoughtfully swept back at the top to frame the view of St George's Tron (*see* Churches, above). The contemporary DALE HOUSE (No. 21) next door, by *Walter Underwood & Partners*, mediates between its neighbours with heavier modelling in cream sandstone. Its fortified air is functional: it is the Bank of England's cash distribution centre.

Buchanan Street to West Nile Street (including Nelson Mandela (St George's) Place)

This narrow, rather mean square, laid out in 1810, surrounds St
21 George's Tron (*see* Churches). It opens on the S corner with the former Stock Exchange (*see* No. 159 Buchanan Street, above), and this continues all along the S side to where the square closes in again to the width of West George Street with a simple Italianate block of 1872 by *Peddie & Kinnear*. In the SW angle of the square, the tall Italianate back of No. 79 (NILE BAR), identical to its W front in West Nile Street (*q.v.*) but

with a columned entrance to what were stockbrokers' offices on the upper floors: by *Boucher*, 1875.

Back to the E entrance to the square and, at its NE corner, the former LIBERAL CLUB of 1907–9 by *A. N. Paterson*. Rudiments of a conventional classical club design, interpreted on a large scale with Free-Style unorthodoxy in pink ashlar. Shallow bays break out of the flat façade, big chimneystacks and dormers out of the attic; cast-iron windows rise through two storeys. The interior was only very slightly altered in 1928 when the club, together with the neighbouring Athenaeum, became the Royal Scottish Academy of Music and Drama (this moved in 1987: *see* Public Buildings, above). To the original entrance hall and modest stair were added the musical references. Along the S front, a huge apsed club dining room, with masses of rococo plasterwork by *Bankart*, including paired naked figures carrying the main arches. The former ATHENAEUM (No. 60) to the W is an early, Beaux Arts-influenced work by *J. J. Burnet*, 1886, of a severe, disciplined classicism then unparalleled in Glasgow. Above the deep-channelled rustication of the ground floor (with twin entrances leading to the club and classrooms, and pedestals carrying groups by *John Mossman* of teachers and their pupils), four unfluted Ionic columns carry figures of Flaxman, Wren, Purcell and Reynolds, also by Mossman. The back portion of this deep block was refitted in 1890 and linked, via a bridge behind the previous corner building, to an equally novel extension of 1891–3 which faces Buchanan Street (No. 179). Its tall narrow buff sandstone façade, just the width of a single Georgian house, fronts a simple theatre, billiard room, dining room and gymnasium stacked on the narrow plot. Its verticality is emphasized rather than disguised by a division into a single gabled bay with full-height arch embracing shallow canted bays and a more prominent oriel, and a narrow stair-tower with strong vertical mullions and none of the Mannerist embellishments that enliven the rest. The formula proved useful for similar narrow sites.

At the w end, Nelson Mandela (St George's) Place closes in on this N side with *Charles Wilson*'s ROYAL FACULTY OF PROCURATORS' HALL (Nos. 62–8), in the Italianate club style of London's West End, 1854–6. The model is Venetian, e.g. Sansovino's St Mark's Library or Palazzo Corner Ca' Grande. Above the rusticated ground floor, an exceedingly rich *piano nobile* with coupled fluted Corinthian columns between arched and Venetian (E and W) windows (these have deep splayed and enriched reveals), a deep enriched frieze, and a balustraded balcony and parapet. Frieze and parapet have an oddly complicated (though strictly correct) corner detail. Fine masonry, especially the delicately ribbed voussoirs and keystone portrait heads by *Handyside Ritchie*.

Plain single lower hall. The doorway to the upper floor is in the angle of the square and opens into a short wing filled by a dog-leg and top-lit stair. Pendentive vaulting over entrance

passages and stairwell, with enriched plaster mouldings. The
38 READING ROOM is the most handsome room of its date in
the City Centre, lit from each end by Venetian windows and
divided into 'nave' and 'aisles' by square scagliola piers with
gilt plaster capitals and bases. The 'nave' ceiling is beamed
in plaster, the 'aisles' are groin-vaulted. All the ornament,
including the busts of law lords and lawyers on pedestals,
carved by *Mr Shanks*, was designed by *James Steel*. At the N
end, the distinctly C20 classical doorway to the barrel-vaulted
ORR LIBRARY created in 1938–9 by *T. Harold Hughes* in the
adjacent building to the N. Chastely done, with a pair of free-
standing Neo-classical columns and a barrel vault.

West Nile Street to Renfield Street

Once beyond Nelson Mandela Place, there is a dramatic but
fairly short-lived change of scale introduced on the N SIDE by
James Miller's seven-storey gleaming white Commercial Bank
of 1930–7 (now ROYAL BANK OF SCOTLAND, No. 92), one
of his simpler American Classical designs, with only shallow
Egyptianizing decoration on flat pilasters. Its even larger
neighbour, MONCRIEFF HOUSE (Nos. 100–6) by *Baron
Bercott*, 1987–8, has undulating bays that take their cue from
Fyfe Chambers opposite (*see* below). The scale then drops
suddenly back to mid-C19 standards with the three-bay No.
110, with its attenuated Ionic porch; and, on the W corner,
the former SCOTTISH WIDOWS' FUND OFFICES AND
JUNIOR CONSERVATIVE CLUB (Nos. 112–14), a palazzo of
1868–71 by *David Bryce*, rich and with certain subtleties, such
as the ground-floor window surrounds slightly recessed on
the projecting outer bays, slightly proud on the inner ones.
Aedicules with shell tympana round the upper windows,
narrow and closely set. Three balconies along the main front
removed, attic added and interior reconstructed in 1958–60 by
Wylie, Shanks & Underwood.

The S SIDE is all red and pink sandstone of the 1890s and
1900s. First, the seven-storey former ROYAL EXCHANGE
ASSURANCE BUILDING by *Frank Burnet & Boston*, 1911–
13, with a severity reminiscent of J. A. Campbell; then the
restrained FYFE CHAMBERS (Nos. 103–11) by *George Bell
II*, 1894–7, its top floor by *Alfred G. Lochead*, 1937. On the
corner of Renfield Street, the fairly subdued silhouette of
William Leiper's red sandstone Sun Life Building of 1889–
94, now the NATIONAL AND PROVINCIAL BUILDING
SOCIETY, Nos. 117–21 (its big corbelled-out corner tower is
an early, if not the first, example of this popular device). Its
façades, too, are quietly composed despite their remarkable
conglomeration of French Renaissance detail (mostly from the
hôtels of Ecoville and Assézat, according to Donald Bassett).
It was perhaps the design's Francophilia that gained it a silver
medal from the Paris Exhibition of 1900. Much sculpture in

Mannerist vein by *William Birnie Rhind*: over the door, winged figures with the arms of England, Scotland and Wales; on the ground floor, capitals with signs of the Zodiac; at the base of the dome, Aurora; facing Renfield Street, Night, Day and Apollo, literal borrowings from Michelangelo; and, in the panelled corner office, more winged figures on the overmantel.

Renfield Street to Hope Street

From here until Wellington Street the buildings are mostly mid-C19 or mid-C20. As the hill climbs, the basements of the older properties get deeper, the steps to their front doors steeper. *James Thomson* was responsible for rather a lot of sober buildings along here.

The N SIDE begins with two palazzi, the CLYDESDALE BANK (Nos. 134–6) by *J. Burnet Snr*, 1867, transformed by *James Thomson*'s 1898 ground floor and columned banking hall, and Nos. 138–40, a former warehouse of 1859–60, also by *Thomson* and disproportionately tall and flat. The top and ground floors both look later. Nos. 144–6, the former New Club of 1877–9 by *James Sellars* (now JAMES SELLARS HOUSE), makes an astonishing break with the modest symmetry of its neighbours. Traits of the French Second Empire (oval windows and dormers, tall mansard, curved acanthus mullions and cast-iron balconies, delicate, and eroded, François Premier-style sculpture by *William Mossman*) co-exist with Thomsonish bands of windows in an unprecedented, asymmetrical composition of smooth cream sandstone. Sadly, all is of 1979–81 behind the façade. Less inventive François Premier features in the attic of Nos. 150–4 next door (SCOTTISH UNION AND NATIONAL INSURANCE CO.), by *James Thomson*, 1878. Last on this side, a plain house of *c.* 1830, reconstructed with an open plan by *Boyer & Partners*, 1987.

The S SIDE has little left to recommend it. Two more buildings by *James Thomson* of *Baird & Thomson* – Nos. 133–7, the red sandstone PEARL ASSURANCE offices, 1896–7 (at six storeys, one of the first of the larger taller blocks in the City Centre), with ground floor remodelled by *T. S. Tait* in 1935; and Nos. 159–65, a sedate palazzo of 1859–60 for the British Linen Bank – flank the long and dreary BOWRING BUILDING by *R. Seifert Co-Partnership*, 1972–4.

Hope Street to Wellington Street

N SIDE. At the beginning, an effective corner building, the classical Nos. 166–8 (Ballantine House) by *Baird & Thomson*, 1859–60, in the style of 1830, followed by HUME HOUSE (No. 180), again by *R. Seifert Co-Partnership*, 1974–7, but this time well modulated, with the familiar format of shallow square bays. After this, the bizarre ugliness of Nos. 188–94, OCEAN CHAMBERS by *Robert Bryden*, 1899–1900, is welcome, with its lighthouse-and-galleon relief over the door, badly carved Neptune and Amphitrite near the top, and a slightly oriental gable and faceted dome carrying globes. It makes a vulgar neighbour for the refined No. 198, a five-by-five-bay house of the 1820s, possibly originally a flatted pair. Nice central chimneystalk with panelled sides, fluted pots and supporting scrolls.

On the S SIDE, FESTIVAL HOUSE, an angular pastiche of a familiar turn-of-the-century type by *Covell Matthews Partnership*, 1987–8, squeezed between Campbell's powerful office block (*see* Hope Street, above) and the mean ASHLEY HOUSE (Nos. 181–95) by *Newman, Levinson & Partners*, 1969–72, which fills the rest of this side.

Wellington Street to West Campbell Street

At Wellington Street we come to concentrated remains of Blythswood New Town, with inconsistent and maltreated terraces of simple houses leading up to the summit of Blythswood Hill and its square.

The N SIDE (all pre-1828) begins and ends with houses similar to No. 198 on the opposite (E) corner (*see* above). Both are plainer, No. 204 with Greek detail over the first-floor windows, an additional storey, and columns in the entrance hall, No. 226 with fluted Roman Doric columns. Between them, Nos. 208–24, a terrace of five plain two-storey-plus-basement, three-bay houses, with Ionic pilasters to wide doorways. All altered, though Nos. 208 and 224, at least, have their original staircases.

S SIDE. Similar but, alas, even more mutilated houses here. The first one (Nos. 201–3), on the corner of Wellington Street, was replaced in 1880 by *John McLeod* with a very deep block in white Overwood stone, with some crisp François Premier detail. This and its neighbour, Nos. 205–13, were reconstructed as office blocks in 1982–5, the former by *G. D. Lodge & Partners*, the latter completely rebuilt by *McPherson & Bell*.

West Campbell Street to Blythswood Street (Blythswood Square)

The N SIDE has a complete, though very badly treated, terrace of *c*. 1830 (Nos. 232–56). No. 242 looks most intact: cornice on tiny consoles over the door, a screen of Greek Ionic columns in the entrance hall (the same in No. 238).

On the S SIDE, three houses of the original terrace with wide Greek porches (Nos. 237–41), brutally reconstructed with some neo-Georgian frills by *Scott, Brownrigg & Turner*, 1987, flanked by two modern blocks that try to be polite to their neighbours. The W one (No. 227) is plain dull; the other (No. 249), at the corner of Blythswood Square (*see* above), very successfully transmutes classical features, with channelled rustication between chains of windows, and a framed cornice reminiscent of a modillion one: by *Wright & Kirkwood*, 1958. From here, the sweeping view back along the street is decisively closed by the silhouette of St George's Tron.

Douglas Street (Blythswood Square) to Pitt Street

Terraced houses (Nos. 299–309) and Nos. 103–9 Douglas Street (formerly Oakfield Place, *c.* 1825–30) meet at the corner of Blythswood Square. Opposite, the Greek ST JUDE'S HOUSE (Nos. 278–82), a former Scottish Episcopal church (*see* Churches, above).

Beyond Pitt Street, the character changes to that of the redeveloped SW area; *see* the side elevations of the Strathclyde Police Headquarters (Public Buildings, above) and PEGASUS HOUSE of *c.* 1970 by *Derek Stephenson & Partners*, an office tower above a brutal podium.

WEST NILE STREET

Another N–S street, laid out *c.* 1808 and built up with plain tenements (stretches of which survive), but now lined mostly with the ends of buildings that face the E–W streets and with post-war office blocks.

Gordon Street to Sauchiehall Street

First on the W side, past the classical block on the corner of Gordon Street (*see* above), a flashy office block by *Baxter, Clark & Paul*, 1984–8, with a popular Art Deco inverted ziggurat motif introduced in the mirror-glass bays. The next building (Nos. 19–23), by *Burnet & Boston*, 1900, is a close cousin of the adjacent corner building designed by J. J. Stevenson twenty-five years earlier (*see* Nos. 67–79 St Vincent Street, above). The E side is almost completely consumed by the dull FINLAY HOUSE by *Scott, Brownrigg & Turner*, 1977.

N of St Vincent Street, the cream sandstone GRESHAM CHAMBERS of 1904–6 by *John McKellar Ltd* (W side, Nos. 41–9), with battered end bays and almost continuously glazed attic, demonstrates a pared-down version of the Glasgow Style and is perhaps a remodelling of an earlier building. On the E side, the straightforward ROYAL LONDON HOUSE (1958–9, by *H. Bramhill*), its concrete frame (clad in red granite and sandstone) clearly expressed. Next to it, the NILE BAR (Nos. 58–60) goes right through to No. 79 St George's (Nelson Mandela) Place to the E (*see* West George Street, above). Its W and E façades (1875, by *James Boucher*) are almost identical, with tiers of arcading, pilasters and colonnettes of grey and pink granite, and much diapering and odd rusticated patterns on the white stonework. Entrance to the former fish shop on this side, columned entrance to the offices above on the other.

Between West George Street and Bath Street, the W SIDE seems to be dominated by the blank back of the Odeon Cinema (*see* Renfield Street, above): the routine office block at Nos. 67–9 (by *Scott, Brownrigg & Turner*, 1981–6) and the 1987 recladding of the SUN LIFE BUILDING (a tower designed *c.* 1976 by *R. Seifert Co-Partnership*) acknowledge its shiny redness with polished red granite. Last of interest on this side is Nos. 99–107, a warehouse of 1874 by *Alexander Thomson*, its incised detail fudged by the synthetic Linostone. On the E side, past plain classical tenements (Nos. 80–4) and a very average red sandstone office block (Nos. 90–4) by *Brand & Lithgow*, 1914, the restless façade of GENERAL ACCIDENT's offices, 1968–9, by *Baron Bercott & Associates*, forms the *point-de-vue* down West Regent Street. It dwarfs the neat little Graeco-Roman front by *James Smith*, 1837, of the former VICTORIA BATHS next door at Nos. 106–8. Uneasy asymmetry, with double central pilaster and off-centre doorway.

Nothing to venture N of Bath Street for.

WEST REGENT STREET

Though it has a fair proportion of early C19 houses, as a whole the street is only erratically interesting.

West Nile Street to Renfield Street

The red brick side of the Odeon takes up the whole of the S SIDE (*see* Renfield Street, above). Opposite (N SIDE), the surviving half of VICTORIA BUILDINGS (Nos. 2–4) by *Jonathan Anderson Bell* of Edinburgh, 1858–60, in a style reminiscent of Billings's. English Tudor meets Scottish castellated in cream stugged ashlar.

Renfield Street to Hope Street

The N SIDE starts with the former Prudential offices (*see* Renfield Street). Next to it, at No. 58, a Post-Modern variation (by *Comprehensive Design Group*, 1986) of a familiar C19 type of façade, with surprising blue mullions in the bay window. Classical façades and handsome railings at Nos. 64–82; a plainer, much altered house (Nos. 86–8) on the corner of Hope Street; and a matching house (No. 69) facing it from the S SIDE. All of these date from the early 1820s. Thrusting in on this side between the quiet No. 69 and the rich Baroque curves of Castle Chambers (*see* Renfield Street), the crude bays and elephantine cornice of ELPHINSTONE HOUSE, completed in 1989 by *Scott, Brownrigg & Turner*.

Hope Street to Wellington Street

N SIDE. Another disfigured classical house (No. 94) on the first corner is followed by the red sandstone Nos. 98–100, with some crisp Renaissance detail and two figures (Good Shepherd?; St

Margaret?) flanking the main oriel: 1895–7, by *J. L. Cowan* for Glasgow Masonic Halls Co., incorporating a masonic hall amongst business chambers. The rest of this side is late C20 and undistinguished.

S SIDE. The mid-C19 E corner house (No. 79) was made 'Queen Anne' (and unusually English for Glasgow) by *James Salmon Jun.* in 1903–4 by the addition of lead-clad bay windows and a steep hipped roof with dormers. Nos. 83–101 are simple three-bay, two-storey-and-basement houses of *c.* 1820, i.e., among the first in the street. The terrace ends with a harsh five-bay block, Nos. 105–7, where *Alexander Thomson* had his office. He was responsible for remodelling the original early C19 house and extending it northward with offices to No. 122 Wellington Street (into which he moved his own office) in 1872. Nothing obviously from Thomson's hand except, perhaps, the N and W doorcases.

Wellington Street to West Campbell Street

On both sides, terraces composed of individual houses, inconsistent in size and detail. Those on the N side are mostly of *c.* 1835, those on the S slightly earlier.

N SIDE. No. 126 (the former Ophthalmic Institute) has a Greek Ionic portico with pink granite shafts; No. 144, a pilastered and pedimented doorcase; Nos. 154–6, paired doorcases and heavy guilloche-pattern railings.

S SIDE. Nos. 111–13 is similar to No. 126 opposite, though it was reconstructed in the 1870s and altered again in the 1880s; its portico has thin part-fluted Ionic columns, its railings are of interlinked circles. No. 121 has a doorcase with Corinthian columns on pedestals. The next pair, Nos. 125 and 139, was completely rebuilt by *G. D. Lodge & Partners*, 1986–8. The last house (Nos. 141–3) is rather different and of pale grey not cream ashlar. Its side elevation has a flat-topped gable.

West Campbell Street to Blythswood Street (Blythswood Square)

On the N SIDE, a bold red intruder, the former INSTITUTE FOR THE ADULT DEAF AND DUMB, and the linked JOHN ROSS MEMORIAL CHURCH FOR THE DEAF (Nos. 158–64) are combined in a single red sandstone composition. The domestic front of the Institute (1893–5, by *Robert Duncan*) with pyramid-topped bay windows and 'Christ Healing the Dumb Man' carved over the door, continues W with only a central gable, with some mixed Gothic detail, drawn in relief to indicate the church (by *Norman Dick*, 1925). Inside, the church is now offices. Alongside it, two pairs of altered classical houses by *Robert Scott* at Nos. 172–8 and 180–4. Grafted on to their ground floors, with windows in blind-arched recesses (cf. Blythswood Square, above), lumpish Victorian Ionic porches of almost neo-medieval proportions. The taller No. 188, also by *Scott*, 1831–2, is more or less in its original state;

on the side of it (Nos. 116–18), the doorcase has Ionic pilasters with anthemion necking. This block goes with Blythswood Square (*q.v.*), and so do the buildings on the W corner of the S SIDE. The AMALGAMATED ENGINEERING UNION headquarters, a tactless design by *W. H. Dickie* of Motherwell, 1968–70, fills the rest of it (Nos. 145–65).

Douglas Street (Blythswood Square) to Holland Street

More dreary late C20 office blocks heave into view, alas, at the NW corner of Blythswood Square. Beyond Pitt Street, on the N SIDE, three-storey terraced houses with bay windows, late C19 variations of the flat-fronted houses just to the E in Blythswood Square.

THE BROOMIELAW

The Broomielaw lives in popular memory as the departure point for pleasure trips 'doon the watter', and, further back, as the noisy and grimy principal terminus for Glasgow's riverborne trade. The quayside was lined with long low storage sheds, like the one that survives at Clyde Place Quay on the opposite bank (*see* Gorbals, below: Public Buildings), the Broomielaw and streets to its N with warehouses. Many magnificent warehouses survived the closure of the quay in 1947, but they stand idle in gap-toothed surroundings. Redevelopment has begun in 1989 with offices by *Building Design Partnership*. This will, it is hoped, bring a new kind of prosperity, but although some of the most handsome and characteristic buildings will be preserved, many more (and the distinctive street pattern) are making way for offices, housing, and tourist facilities on a more massive scale.

Broomielaw Croft was, as late as 1777, an almost undeveloped heathy tongue of Glasgow that stretched along the Clyde to the Royalty boundary just E of the present Washington Street. Boats were able to reach this far up the river after the removal of a ford in the mid-C16. Broomielaw Quay itself, first established in a modest way in the C17 and rebuilt in 1722, was at first confined to a short section between Jamaica Street and what is now Robertson Street. Behind it (where Central Station now stands) was the village of Grahamston with warehouses and woodyards for imported timber. Further W lay the Delftfield pottery. Improvements in navigation meant that larger vessels could reach the Broomielaw by 1771. Broomielaw Quay was extended W in 1792 to York Street (beyond which lay the village of Finnieston (*see* below), laid out by John Orr of Barrowfield in 1777) and to the Royalty boundary by 1821. By then all the streets leading off it, except James Watt Street, had been laid out, at first mainly with residential property. Houses were replaced by warehouses, mostly for grain and tea. Later in the century, many were converted to tobacco and whisky bonds, and new ones for this purpose were built. Almost all the C19 warehouses are constructed with cast-iron columns, carrying brick jack-arches in the basement and timber beams and floors above. In those originally for grain, the columns have pairs of ribs into which partitions were slotted to subdivide the floor area.

STREETS

BROOMIELAW

Very few buildings of interest have survived along the BROOM-IELAW itself. It starts at Jamaica Street, and first of note is the warehouse (Nos. 6–12) just by the railway bridge (see Crossings of the Clyde and Kelvin, below); it is of 1883 and probably by *Alexander Skirving,* in the style of Alexander Thomson. After the bridge, on the w corner of Oswald Street (see below), a larger shipowners' warehouse (Nos. 54–64) of 1878 with prominent dormers. Next, a former ships' chandler's (Nos. 72–4) with the date 1840 and a plaque of a galleon in full sail on the wallhead chimneystack. On the next corner, the masterly drum and dome of the Clyde Port Authority (see Robertson Street, below).

BDP's huge offices stretch to MARITIME HOUSE (General Council of British Shipping) on the corner of James Watt Street, polite and domestic neo-Georgian of 1958–61 by *A. Gardiner & Gardiner-McLean* in red-brown brick and granite, with copper roofs. Then, on the corners of Brown Street, a Corporation CLINIC of 1942–3 by *Robert Bruce* on modern lines; and the former GLASGOW SEAMEN'S INSTITUTE, 1926, by *R. A. Bryden & Robertson,* with its ugly copper dome and relief of a steamship. Behind it, in Brown Street, the simple former SEAMEN'S CHAPEL (No. 39) of *c.* 1860. Nothing else of note until the big ROTRANSCO BUILDING, a garage and hostel for lorry drivers by *Thomson, Sandilands & McLeod,* 1938, not architecturally distinguished but an interesting period piece.

Broomielaw ends at Anderston Quay, just before the giant pylons of the Kingston Bridge (see Crossings of the Clyde and Kelvin, below), stride across the road. Just by it, on the corner of Washington Street, the huge WASHINGTON FLOUR MILLS, founded *c.* 1849. Tall silos of yellow brick, flanking lower offices and laboratory, by *R. Ewan,* 1937. To Washington Street the yard is screened by the remains of a stone office building built for J. & R. Snodgrass in 1874. In the yard a tall red-brick store and water tower of 1897–8, also by *Ewan,* who altered the engine house for the use of electricity rather than steam in 1926. At the back a rubble building, the oldest part of the mill.

BROWN STREET *see* BROOMIELAW

JAMES WATT STREET

James Watt Street, narrow and enclosed by sheer walls of handsome classical warehouses (the best surviving in Glasgow), recalls the scale of maritime trade along the Broomielaw from the mid-C19. The street was the last in the area to be laid out (the Delftfield Pottery had occupied the site since 1748). *John Stephen* provided the plan in 1847. The earliest (speculative) warehouse, probably designed by Stephen for Wm. Connal & Co., and completed in 1848, is on the E SIDE (Nos. 68–72). Nine bays of grey ashlar with a rusticated basement and four central pilasters carrying a very deep entablature (the original attic) below the pediment. Later attic of 1881. To its S, the former grain and general stores (Nos. 44–54) built for Thomas Mann *c*.1861, is the grandest in the street, with bolder pilasters, pediments at each end, Mannerist window surrounds, and a pseudo-metope frieze with attic windows. Rounding the corner into Argyle Street (No. 82), a plain ashlar former grain store of 1864.

46 A vast T-plan tobacco warehouse (Nos. 27–59) occupies most of the W SIDE. Its earlier core, initially a grain store, is clearly evident. This, originally one-storey-plus-basement, was designed in 1854 by *John Baird*. The second storey was added *c*.1870, when it was converted into a tobacco bond for Connal & Co. The 1854 pediment, 'Tobacco Warehouse' inscription, and royal arms by *John Mossman* were raised then. *Robert Thomson* added the pink sandstone and brick upper storeys and reconstructed the whole interior in 1910–12, with a much discussed new system of reinforced-concrete floors anchored to reinforced-concrete columns. This was reconstructed again in 1932 by *Clarke, Bell & Craigie*. To the N, the façade of a grain and general stores for Harvie and McGavin (Nos. 65–73), *c*.1848, possibly also by *Stephen*. Six storeys and with single end bays marked by pilasters. U-plan.

OSWALD STREET

No. 11, first on the W side from the S end, is the gable end of an early but otherwise utilitarian bonded warehouse of *c*.1844, made more decorative by the addition of a pilastered fifth storey and pediment in 1902. Most of the rest of this side is taken up by pinkish ashlar offices built for the tube makers Stewarts and Lloyds by *J.J. Craig,* the S half (1909) much more Baroque than the N (1901).

ROBERTSON LANE *see* ROBERTSON STREET

ROBERTSON STREET

Once a residential street; the last of the late C18 and early C19 tenements sadly went in 1988.

The street begins with the splendour of the CLYDE NAVI-
GATION TRUST's headquarters (now the CLYDE PORT
AUTHORITY, No. 16) by *J. J. Burnet*, one of Glasgow's most
important and impressive buildings. The bravura corner-
piece, an extension of 1905–8 to the five-bay building of 1882–
6, which faces Robertson Street, continues the earlier composition with heavier, more Baroque modelling. The style is
Roman. A muted entrance (just an open arcade in the lowest,
rusticated one-and-a-half storeys), but, raised above it to the
tall second floor, is a splendid portico of slim fluted Composite
columns *in antis*, lavished with sculpture by *Mossman*. On the
pediment, Neptune and seahorses, within it Neptune receiving
homage. Lower down, two Antique prows emerge from the
wall; and along the recessed attic stand figures (1907) of
Telford, James Watt and William Murdoch. A row of order-
less aedicules projects all along the first floor. They form an
insecure base for the huge corner drum, with its pairs of
Composite columns carrying a Baroque drum and concrete
dome. Flanking the dome, two magnificent groups by *Albert
Hodge* (1908): Ceres leading a bull, and Amphitrite with a pair
of seahorses.

   The design of the interior, complete with original
furnishings, light fittings and mostly heraldic stained glass,
though splendidly rich, is beautifully controlled, with none of
the showy eclecticism of the contemporary City Chambers.
All this splendour was not for the benefit of the public but was
intended solely for the Trustees and their guests.

   The main rooms lie along the TRUSTEES' CORRIDOR on
the second floor, reached by a staircase with sturdy cast-iron
balustrade and a newel-post-cum-lamp-standard spiky with
more Antique prows. The corridor, with its row of gilded
domes, black and gold pilasters and columns, patterned mosaic
floor, and heraldic glass with the Trades' badges, is magnificent
in itself. At the N end, the RECEPTION ROOM, its three- 63
quarter panelling of walnut (a step up from the teak of the
corridor) banded in ebonized wood. Huge sliding doors (their
mechanisms implied by the Viking-style straps at the top)
open into matching committee rooms at each end. Above the
panelling, blue and gold Tynecastle Tapestry, and over the
fireplace, a great display of arms – the royal arms stamped in
gold leaf on the wallcovering, the Trust's carved in timber. The
boarded ceiling, with its coloured ribs, looks like shipwright's
work. In the windows, the arms of the Clydeside burghs and
Glasgow's major institutions. Similar banded wall panelling
but in a later C17 style continues in the later rooms to the S,
i.e. the CHAIRMAN'S ROOM and COMMITTEE ROOM, and
the TRUST HALL, more opulent than all the other rooms but
perhaps less original. The style here is definitely Baroque,
with fleshy plasterwork including female figures, and walnut
panelling with a carved frieze pierced to admit heated air.
Under the dome sat the Lord Provost, Chairman, Deputy
Chairman, General Manager and Secretary, and the forty-two

trustees, originally at individual desks (*see* the few remaining). The two alcoves, flanked by festooned Ionic columns, were for professional officials such as the Engineer. In the upper lights of the windows, handsome STAINED-GLASS panels of the trades, very similar to the much earlier ones by Stephen Adam from Maryhill Burgh Hall (*q.v.*).

On the first floor the Managing Director's corridor is lined with teak screens, the upper halves open between slim balusters. On the ground floor, part of the earliest phase and on axis with the main entrance, a tall BUSINESS HALL with engaged and banded Doric columns at the angles and a boldly coffered ceiling. Near the staircase, the WAR MEMORIAL in bronze, with winged Victory in a *fin-de-siècle* manner: 1920–22 by Burnet.

Further up Robertson Street, now only Nos. 49–63 (W SIDE), built in 1869–70 for the engineer and ironmonger James Gilchrist, probably by *Spence*. Long and low with a range of biforated windows. Behind, a high workshop with cast-iron roof trusses and a decorative cast-iron front to the gallery which serves as the rails for the mobile crane. At the corner of Robertson Lane, a tea merchant's offices (Nos. 71–5) with domed corner tower, eaves gallery and Art Nouveau detailing inside and out: by *J. A. Campbell*, 1899–1901.

In ROBERTSON LANE, the earliest warehouse to survive in this area (No. 34), built *c.*1800, for multiple occupancy. Four storeys and eleven bays of squared rubble. Loading bays alternate with very small windows. Pedimented stairtower of *c.*1815. Inside, cast-iron columns, each with ribs, into which boards could be slotted to subdivide the floor, and timber beams.

WASHINGTON STREET

Laid out in 1815 and with the character of the industrial Anderston (*see* below) to which it then belonged. It meets the Broomielaw (*see* above) at the huge Washington Flour Mills. The Italianate Nos. 66–8 was built as part of the CROWN FLOUR MILLS in 1862 (*see* the wheatsheaf on the pediment); at the back, the original building of *c.* 1848. Flour mills and foundries dominated the street in the 1860s. At the N end of the W SIDE, Nos. 30–46 (claimed by the *Architectural Review* in 1907 to be the largest bonded warehouse in the world) was built in 1896–1907 over the sites of the famous Saracen (*see* Possilpark) and Globe foundries. (The Vulcan foundry was at the SE end of the street.) This bond is of two very similar parts, both of rock-faced Locharbriggs sandstone and red brick, the former (N) by *A. V. Gardner*, 1897, the latter (S) by *H. E. Clifford*, 1906–7. Set back beyond it, the former Washington Street Public School (now ARTS CENTRE) of the plainest four-square type, by *H. E. Clifford*, dated 1890.

On the E SIDE, a confused assembly of buildings used as the ANDERSTON RICE MILLS (No. 27): threatened with demolition in 1989. The earliest, stone building (four storeys, with a brick top floor) was built as a cotton store *c.* 1825, and converted to a steam flour mill in 1845. The second one, a grain mill of red-and-white brick, is of 1865, with a two-storey office block. Inside, wooden floors on cast-iron columns, cast-iron fittings and spiral chutes.

YORK STREET

Initially a residential street, with mansions built on the W side *c.* 1802, and tenements on the E. Near the S end of the W SIDE (Nos. 13–15), offices and stores designed by *W. F. McGibbon* in 1892–3 with a toy-fort air worthy of a barracks. Pretty spider-web heads to the gateways. At the back, a brick warehouse of 1901. Next (No. 23), a big fireproof warehouse of 1843 by *Scott, Stephen & Gale* for William Connal, storekeeper at the Queen's Tea Stores, one of the first warehouses in the street. Coarsely classical with a palatial entrance.

On the E SIDE, which as late as 1989 had a terrace of the original early C19 tenements, a prison-like bonded warehouse (No. 64), originally a grain store of 1877, enlarged in 1895–1901 by *Miles S. Gibson*; and No. 74, designed to a familiar Edwardian formula, with lots of fleshy carving, by *Neil C. Duff*, 1907–10.

COWCADDENS

In the early C18, Cowcaddens was a hamlet set amid grazing land W of the city just S of the road to Strathblane, that is, on what is now Cowcaddens Road between Hope Street and Stow Street. Development began with the opening of Port Dundas (*q.v.*) in 1790. Some of the industrial character has survived comprehensive redevelopment, approved in 1963, but the small amount of tenement housing has been replaced in a single monumental scheme, the huge Caledonian Railway goods yard has been given over to Glasgow College, and the main roads were widened and realigned as major traffic routes that dominate the neighbourhood.

CHURCHES AND PUBLIC BUILDINGS

Former COWCADDENS PARISH CHURCH, 30–4 McPhater Street. Just the shell of this Free church of 1872–3 by *Campbell Douglas & Sellars*, which closed in 1968. Mixed Greek and Italian, with a simple pedimented façade and S W corner tower. Clearstorey, originally lighting the gallery, with almost continuous glazing *à la* Alexander Thomson.

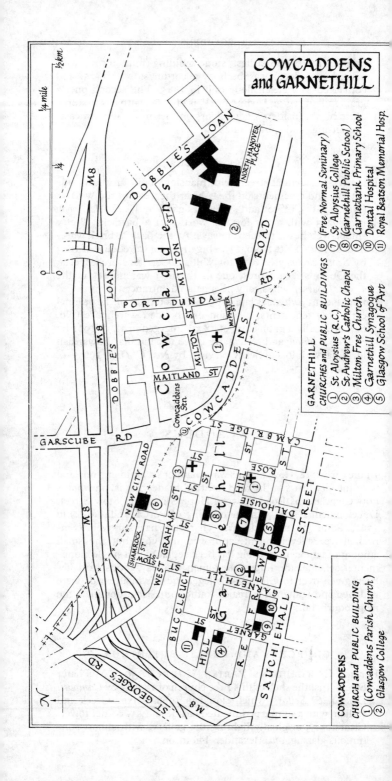

COWCADDENS and GARNETHILL

½ km
½ mile
¼
¼
0
0

M8

DOBBIE'S LOAN

NORTH HANOVER PLACE

②

MILTON ST

Cowcaddens

PORT DUNDAS

DOBBIE'S LOAN

McPHATER ST

MILTON ST

①

MAITLAND ST

COWCADDENS ROAD

RD

GARSCUBE RD

Cowcaddens Stn

COWCADDENS ST

CAMBRIDGE ST

M8

NEW CITY ROAD

③

Garnethill

ROSE ST

①

SHAMROCK ST

ST GRAHAM ST

⑥

DALHOUSIE STREET

WEST GRAHAM ST

⑧

⑦

⑤

ST

SCOTT

ST

②

RENFREW

BUCCLEUCH ST

GARNETHILL ST

GARNET ST

⑪

⑨

⑩

HILL ST

RENFREW ST

④

SAUCHIEHALL

M8

ST GEORGES RD

N

GARNETHILL

CHURCHES and PUBLIC BUILDINGS

① St Aloysius (R.C.)
② St Andrew's Catholic Chapel
③ Milton Free Church
④ Garnethill Synagogue
⑤ Glasgow School of Art
⑥ (Free Normal Seminary)
⑦ St Aloysius College
⑧ (Garnethill Public School)
⑨ Garnetbank Primary School
⑩ Dental Hospital
⑪ Royal Beatson Memorial Hosp.

COWCADDENS

CHURCH and PUBLIC BUILDING

① (Cowcaddens Parish Church)
② Glasgow College

GLASGOW COLLEGE, Cowcaddens Road. By *Borth-wick & Watson,* 1967–72, although, stylistically, 1957 might seem a more likely date. Two eight-storey wings with fussy concrete cladding on a butterfly plan, and a short curtain-walled entrance block across the w end. To the s, a zigzag-roofed gym; to the w the library of *c.* 1980, with vertical slits giving light to all three floors; and, to the N, a slab block with heavily moulded pre-cast window units.

DESCRIPTION

COWCADDENS ROAD is the brutal main artery. At its junction with PORT DUNDAS ROAD, the eye-catching cream pavilion of the BRITISH TRANSPORT POLICE (by the *British Railways Board*'s own architects, completed 1984), holding its own in the shadow of the depressing SCOTRAIL HOUSE (by *Ian Burke, Martin & Partners,* 1965–7), built on the carriage sidings of Buchanan Street Station (closed in 1966). In front of it, a personification of LOCOMOTION, a bronze figure running between two hoops by *Frank Cossell,* 1967. Behind Scotrail House, all along the s side of MILTON STREET, a continuous wall of bronze glass, with a touch of Art Deco revival in the stepped triangles of brick, fronts NORTHGATE, an office development by *Greenock & Will* (1987), completed in 1990 by a twenty-two-storey tower on Port Dundas Road.

w of Scotrail House, looking s on to Cowcaddens Road, the remarkable battlemented warehouse at No. 16 McPHATER STREET is a landmark for many travellers from the city centre. Designed in 1892 by *W. J. Anderson* as warehouses and work-shops, it opened in 1895 as a model lodging house, the Orient Boarding House. The medieval Italian styling conceals exper-imental partial steel framing and concrete floors (cf. Napier House, Govan). The four E bays are slightly later.

Cowcaddens' HOUSING is packed on to a raised deck in the small area between Maitland Street, the sharp curve of Cowcaddens Road and the M8. It is a surprisingly tranquil and well-tended spot, complete with a bowling green. Five-storey brick-built walls of flats enclose the two courts laid out on the deck. On one face they have individual balconies, on the other continuous concrete decks. Marking the three sharp angles (NW, NE and SE), simple twenty-three-storey tower blocks. All by *Walter Underwood & Partners,* 1968–75.

GARNETHILL

Most of those who climb the treacherous slope from Sauchiehall Street almost to the summit of Garnethill are making a pilgrimage to *Charles Rennie Mackintosh*'s School of Art; but it is only one of several interesting public buildings that invaded this once prosperous suburb in the later C19. Just as rewarding as some of the buildings are the curious vistas afforded by the conflict of the steepness of the hill with the rigidity of the grid of streets, and the panoramic views across the city, especially those opened up by the creation of the motorway along the northern and western flanks of the hill.

CHURCHES

GARNETHILL SYNAGOGUE, Hill Street. Opened in 1879, the first purpose-built synagogue in Scotland. It was designed (1878–9) by Glasgow's *John McLeod,* with advice from *Nathan Solomon Joseph,* and follows the same Romanesque-cum-Byzantine style with Moorish touches as Joseph's contemporary Bayswater synagogue in London. Facing Hill Street, a gabled façade to the vestibule and committee room above. Round-arched portal with many highly decorated orders. In the tympanum a round window with star tracery. The body of the synagogue lies at r. angles to this. Ladies' gallery carried on octagonal piers with ornate Byzantine capitals, the ceiling on another arcaded tier. Stained glass in the dome and in all the double-light windows by *J. B. Bennett & Sons.* Underneath, committee rooms etc. with an entrance from Garnet Street.

MILTON FREE CHURCH, 69 Rose Street. By *John Burnet, c.* 1850. Pre-archaeological Gothic, with cast-iron Perp tracery combined with, on the façade, an ogee hoodmould and traceried roundel. Spired bellcote on the gable linked by an openwork parapet to the angle pinnacles.

ST ALOYSIUS (R.C.), Rose Street. 1908–10, by the Belgian *Charles Menart.* Distinctly Italian, like the associated school in Buccleuch Street (*see* Public Buildings, below), but this time Roman High Renaissance and of red sandstone ashlar. Handsome but not imaginative. Pilastered and pedimented main (E) and N transept façades. (Presbytery attached to the concealed S transept.) Excessively tall, sheer NE tower with small domed bell-stage. Bulgy copper-clad central dome of curious and unattractive shape, constructed, like the nave barrel-vault and other roofs, by the *Expanded Metal Co.* using reinforced concrete on concrete ribs.

Sumptuous interior of coloured marbles and (for reredoses, Stations of the Cross etc.) glittering Venetian mosaic, with subdued and mostly top-lighting. This decoration, started in 1927 by *Ernest Schaufelberg,* proved too expensive and was never carried into the bare-looking vault or into the apse. Piers and round arches to the nave and crossing, double Ionic columns of polished marble to the outer aisles, which step up to side chapels and, at the E end, baptistery and mortuary. – ALTARS. Most interesting are the High Altar, an adaptation

of the shrine of St Aloysius in S. Ignazio, Rome, and the s
transept Quattrocento-style altar. The sculptor throughout
was *W. Vickers* of Glasgow. – IRONWORK by *Charles Henshaw*
of Edinburgh. – STAINED GLASS. Mostly dates from 1927–
39. – Dome: bold portraits of Jesuit saints, with *putti* trailing
ribbons, by the studio of *J. T. & C. E. Stewart*. – Outer aisles:
crudely coloured pictorial scenes, several of them probably by
the *Stewarts'* studio, three of them, in debased Arts and Crafts
style, definitely so (Martyrdom of John de Britto, after 1934;
Mother of Good Counsel, both N aisle; and Death of Francis
Xavier, S aisle) and two of these signed. – Apse: two windows
(one of them walled up behind) delicately painted by *Horace
Wilkinson*, *c.* 1930 (St Stanislaus Kostka and the Infant Christ,
Apotheosis of St Aloysius). – In the N transept, a serene Arts
and Crafts rendering of the Assumption, perhaps by *Louis
Davis*, *c.* 1915.

ST ANDREW'S CATHOLIC CHAPEL, Renfrew Street. Mid-
C 19. Small, of ashlar, and with Perp windows.

PUBLIC BUILDINGS

MCLELLAN GALLERIES. *See* Nos. 254–90 Sauchiehall Street,
under Commercial Centre, Streets, above.

GLASGOW SCHOOL OF ART, 167 Renfrew Street. *Charles
Rennie Mackintosh*'s most celebrated building, for many years
revered as a pioneering work of the Modern Movement, but
now correctly appreciated as a brilliant eclectic design, blending, principally, Arts and Crafts and Art Nouveau ideals. The
commission was secured as a result of a competition announced
in February 1896. The winners were named in January 1897
as *Honeyman & Keppie,* although the building has always been
accepted as wholly the work of Mackintosh. A memorial stone
was laid in May 1898; the first section of the School, E from
Dalhousie Street up to and including the entrance block,
opened in December 1899. The project then lay dormant until
1906, when revised plans were requested. These drawings,
dated May 1907, were used for the completion of the building
W to Scott Street.

The plan, which is the clue to understanding the building,
is straightforward and rational. Two blocks of studios with
large N-facing windows have an entrance block inserted
between them. Flanking this sequence of rooms to the S is a
corridor connecting the museum at the centre and, at either
end, more utilitarian stairs (both of them part of the 1907–9
phase) serving a variety of rooms, including, at the W end, the
famous library. In spite of this, everywhere you look about the
building there is subtlety, invention and surprise expressed
through an astonishing diversity of details in timber, stone,
iron, tilework and glass.

It is instructive to look at the façades in an anti-clockwise
sequence, starting with the E front: this not only follows the

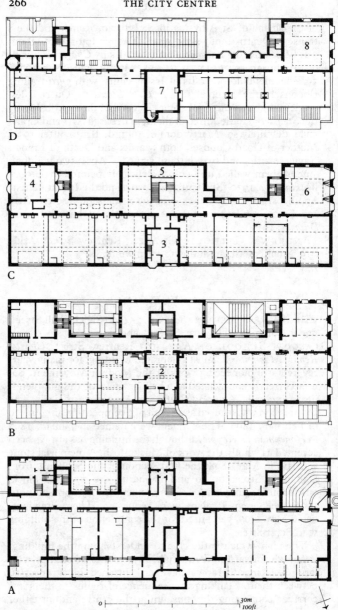

Glasgow School of Art: plans
A basement, B ground floor, C first floor, D second floor
1 board room, 2 entrance hall, 3 director's room,
4 Mackintosh Room, 5 museum, 6 library,
7 director's studio, 8 furniture gallery
(Redrawn from the architects' plans of 1910)

chronology of the building but also shows most clearly Mackintosh's differing approach to the design of details in the two phases of the building. The r. half of the E FRONT is of uninterrupted snecked rubble (the flank wall of the studios), broken into by two windows inserted in 1915 at basement level. The l. half is a Scottish domestic composition typical of Mackintosh, with, from top to bottom, a blank portion masking classrooms; two slender bow windows to the former board room; a double window, with a curved pediment above, serving two staff rooms; and two levels of plain windows to the janitor's house. The two halves are stitched together by a string of windows in the centre, topped by an octagonal turret and with a basement door below, reached by a platform off the steeply sloping street.

The N FAÇADE of smooth ashlar is set back from the pave- 72 ment, and the main entrance, at ground-floor level, is reached by a flight of steps bridging the gap, which reduces in width as the stair rises. The central portion is exceptionally domestic in character, perhaps rightly so, as much of it was designed as a private office and studio, with balconies at first- and second-floor level, for Francis Newbery, who was then the director. Either side of this are the giant studio windows, three to the l., four to the r., all capped by a large oversailing cornice. Above this, a partly hidden attic storey. The whole façade is plain, apart from the elaborate ironwork of the railings, finials and brackets and a single carved stone panel of two female figures in distinctly Art Nouveau style over the entrance.

The W ELEVATION to Scott Street, originally intended to 74 be an almost exact mirror of the E façade, was redesigned in 1907 in the experimental Secessionist style Mackintosh then favoured. The blank snecked-rubble portion flanks the studio, as before; the rest in smooth ashlar is a highly original arrangement of small-paned bay windows, with subtly varied surrounds, including three majestic triple-height versions serving the library and the room above it. The basement door has a zigzag surround of similar design to those at Scotland Street School (*see* Gorbals, below). The S façade can only be glimpsed from here: it was never intended to be seen as a whole. It is almost all harled and is a fine example of Victorian *architecture parlante*.

The main doorway on Renfrew Street leads into the ENTRANCE HALL, a wide space bisected by a sequence of fat, square piers, with a low barrel-vaulted ceiling on either side. Recessed panels at the top of these piers remained empty until 1962–3, when they were filled with inferior mosaic portraits of artists and architects (including Mackintosh). Down the corridor to the l. is the BOARD ROOM, formerly the Secretary's Room. This interior, although within the earlier phase of the building, was created in 1906, and its decoration clearly reflects this. Square grids are everywhere, on the ceiling, on the walls and in the windows. It is this room that has the eight famous Ionic pilasters around its walls. The designs vary, but all of them have tiny volutes and fifteen flutes filled with a pattern reminiscent of an abacus. At the end of the corridor the staircase leads up to the MACKINTOSH ROOM on the first floor. It served as a boardroom until the opening of the new one in 1906. It now contains furniture and drawings by Mackintosh amongst others. The stone fireplace and panelling are original. When the room was first built it had windows on both sides, but those on the w were marooned inside the building when the staircase outside was added in 1907–9.

Starting again from the entrance hall, the main staircase rises up to the top-lit MUSEUM. On the mezzanine is a memorial portrait in marble of James Fleming (the Chairman of Governors at the time of the new building), by *George Frampton* and dated 1901: the polished steel surround is said to be by Mackintosh. The Museum was once filled with casts, of which only one remains stubbornly in place, part of a portal (the Ancestors of Christ) from Chartres Cathedral. The staircase to the Museum is framed at its four corners by attenuated columns with flat caps. These meet, but do not support, the elaborate timber trusses above. The trusses have heart-shaped frets cut through them and are jointed using pegs, which are left projecting.

At the end of the corridor to the w, passing three pairs of cosy built-in timber window-seats, is the LIBRARY. Although double-height and with a gallery, it is only a small room. The use of dark stained timber gives it a decidedly Japanese character, although the eye is distracted by the overwhelming array of timber detail. Nevertheless, at almost every point in this room one can find infinite pleasure in the subtleties of Mackintosh's hand. This is justly considered one of the finest rooms in Glasgow. Above the library is the FURNITURE GALLERY, conceived as the Composition Room. There are twisted iron hangers in the centre of the room which carry the floor (and the ceiling of the library below). Outside, at the top of the staircase, is a wrought-iron grille (there is a similar one at the top of the E staircase). The design shows Mackintosh's desire to reflect Arts and Crafts ideals: the ends of some bars are shaped in a variety of ways to mimic a craftsman's natural inventiveness.

The School of Art was extended on the neighbouring block to the N by the construction of the NEWBERY TOWER, 1970, by *Keppie, Henderson and Partners*. The BOURDON BUILDING, by the same architects, spans Renfrew Street and spoils the view to the w. On the concrete deck, at the base of the Newbery Tower, are new dining rooms by *Gillespie, Kidd & Coia, c.* 1982, with a Post-Modern façade. Further away in Hill Street, the HALDANE BUILDING, a lumpy red sandstone former drill hall (Highland Light Infantry Volunteers) by *H. K. Bromhead*, 1897.

STOW COLLEGE, 43 Shamrock Street. 1929–32, by *Whyte & Galloway*. A spare framed building with cast-iron panels.

Former FREE NORMAL SEMINARY (now Dundas Vale Teachers' Centre), 4–38 New City Road. Built in 1836–7 as Scotland's first teacher training college, founded by the educational pioneer David Stow. The plan, with two long wings enclosing a recreation yard at the back, reflects Stow's ideas. The Roman style is characteristic of the building's architect, *David Hamilton*. The taller hipped roofs with dormers, added to the main block by *Campbell Douglas & Sellars* about sixty years later, reinforce the Baroque flavour given by the round-arched windows with keystones set between giant pilasters and by the tower which rises from behind the main block and is crowned by scrolls supporting the clock stage and a vase finial. – BUST of Stow by *Alexander Handyside Ritchie*, 1852.

ST ALOYSIUS COLLEGE, 45–7 Hill Street. Built in 1882–3 on the site of James Smith's neo-Greek Collegiate School of 1866, and incorporating some of its Doric portico in a tall narrow Venetian palazzo by *Archibald Macpherson* of Edinburgh. The loggia, which fills the centre and has arches 'boldly constructed' on consoles, screens not a grand saloon but a rather mean staircase. Flanking balustraded single-storey wings added in 1892. N wing with pretty colonnetted windows to Dalhousie Street by *Walter Watson*, 1902. Watson also designed the classical-fronted W wing, 1908–9, linked to the main school in 1926. – In the link corridor, a WAR MEMORIAL by *Jack Coia*, 1948. The statue of the Virgin and Boy Jesus is by *Mortimer*.

The ANNEXE at the corner of Scott Street and Buccleuch Street is a former villa, remodelled and enlarged in 1882 and 1887 by *Campbell Douglas & Sellars* as the Sick Children's Hospital. Over the entrance a roundel with Charity supported by cherubs. – STAINED GLASS on the main staircase (Suffer the Little Children) and in the former ward windows (nursery tales) by *Shrigley & Hunt*.

For the former Dispensary, *see* Description, below.

GARNETBANK PRIMARY SCHOOL, 231 Renfrew Street. By *T. L. Watson*, opened 1905. The façade, with its shallow bay windows within a huge pedimented aedicule, breaks out of the simplest Board school formula. Art Nouveau touches in the curving window heads and in the carving and stained glass of the janitor's house.

Former GARNETHILL PUBLIC SCHOOL, 83–7 Buccleuch Street. By *James Thomson*, 1878. Italianate, with a big square pilastered tower and projecting end bays (cf. Thomson Street; *see* Dennistoun, below). Three-storey E extension of 1886 by *W. F. McGibbon* with hefty square buttresses topped by consoles. (From 1899 to 1968 it was Glasgow High School for Girls: *see* Kelvinside, below.)

DENTAL HOSPITAL, 203–17 Renfrew Street. By *Wylie, Wright & Wylie*, 1927–31. Steel-framed and clad mostly in stone, but with cast-iron panels between the large windows in the centre bays. Art Deco zigzag on the panels and on the pylon-like end bays. Unhappily, the cast-iron is painted grey to match the spandrel panels of the curtain-walled extensions (opened in 1970) facing Sauchiehall Street.

ROYAL BEATSON MEMORIAL HOSPITAL, 132–8 Hill Street. The Glasgow Royal Cancer Hospital of 1906–12 by *James Munro & Sons* in a dreary neo-Baroque style. It was reconstructed from the nurses' accommodation of the earlier hospital (opened in 1896), itself converted from two of Hill Street's villas. Many additions, including the former McAlpin Nursing Home of 1908 (No. 121) by *John Baird & James Thomson*, similar in style but of red sandstone.

DESCRIPTION

One of the first buildings to appear on this high and windy hill was the Egyptian-style observatory which stood s of what is now Hill Street. It was designed by *Thomas Webster* for the Glasgow Society for Promoting Astronomical Science soon after its foundation in 1808, but enthusiasm was short-lived and the enterprise failed in the 1820s. Development of the hill with houses also began in the first decade of the century. In 1807 four houses faced Sauchiehall Street (*see* Commercial Centre, above); by 1821 there were over twenty along the grid of streets continued from Blythswood without regard for Garnethill's exceptional steepness. Almost all of the earliest houses have gone or have been incorporated into later buildings.

In HILL STREET two are recognizable: Nos. 122 and 125, both of three bays with Roman and Greek doorcases respectively. (There is another villa and one house of a terrace to the s at Nos. 478 and 518 Sauchiehall Street, *q.v.*, and another villa s w in Renfrew Street.) Also in Hill Street, two of the blocks of tenements that succeeded the less lucrative detached houses. These two were the first of them and have large and expensive houses. PEEL TERRACE (Nos. 102–12), 1841–2, has a handsome but unsophisticated façade of four almost equal storeys plus basement, and eighteen very narrow and monotonously repeated bays. Alternating pediments are crowded together over the first-floor windows and cornices over the second-floor ones. BREADALBANE TERRACE, opposite, is slightly later and more skilfully designed to look like a terrace of individual houses. Its w end (Nos. 97–101 designed as a group with a recessed centre) dates from 1845–6; the e end (Nos. 103–113b) from 1855–6. All the main door flats, which include the basements, have Doric-columned porches. The top-lit common stairs to the upper houses (including the attics) are at the back, hence false windows over the close entrances. There are some full-height bay windows at the back as well. The decoration is rich and Italianate, with friezes of linked circles under windows and over porches, and brackets to the pedimented first-floor windows, more exuberant at the w end.

Similar but generally cheaper tenements (like those in Rose
Street) spread across the rest of Garnethill as its surroundings
became more built up making the area less desirable. On the
W and N fringes, the red sandstone middle-class tenements
date from the turn of the century. S of Hill Street at Nos.
347–53 RENFREW STREET are the most opulent examples –
ALBANY MANSIONS of 1897 by *J.J. Burnet* which form
the back of his Albany Chambers in Sauchiehall Street (*see*
Commercial Centre, above). More standard are the bay-
window ones, N of Hill Street, in BUCCLEUCH STREET,
where the two-apartment-and-bathroom house at No. 145
(open to the public as the National Trust for Scotland's TEN-
EMENT HOUSE) still has the complete interior fittings and
furnishings of 1911.

From the second half of the C19, public buildings, especially
educational and medical institutions serving a wide area (*see*
above), intruded, and commercial buildings spread on to the
S slopes from Sauchiehall Street. On the E edge, in ROSE
STREET, No. 6 is a former department store of *c.*1925 by
E. G. Wylie in the same stripped classical combination of stone
and cast-iron as the Dental Hospital (*see* Public Buildings,
above). Further N on the corner of Renfrew Street, the former
COSMO CINEMA (now Glasgow Film Theatre) by *W.J.
Anderson II* of *John McKissack & Sons*, 1938–9. It was the
'art cinema' in George Singleton's chain, modelled on Lon-
don's most famous 'art cinema', the Curzon. Dudok-inspired
brown brick, with a stepped tower over the entrance. Its
lighted glass canopy was replaced in the mid-1960s by *Gillespie
Kidd & Coia*, who rebuilt the offices towards Renfrew Street.
Interior remodelled by *Notman & Lodge*, 1967.

   Round the corner at the E end of RENFREW STREET,
FLEMING HOUSE (1960–3, by *Robert Bluck Associates*),
raised on a podium above street-level shops, is full of the jolly
curves and coloured claddings popular in the 1950s and early
1960s.

N of this, on the far slope of the hill, most of the distinctly artisan
tenements (really part of Cowcaddens) were cleared in the path
of new roads. Some have been rebuilt in red brick during the
1980s. A few older buildings survive: the former Free Normal
Seminary (*see* Public Buildings, above); the simple Scots
Renaissance former DISPENSARY of the Sick Children's
Hospital by *James Sellars*, 1884–8, in WEST GRAHAM
STREET; and, answering its modest tower with a prominent
Edwardian Baroque one, *Neil C. Duff*'s former GLASGOW
(now Trustee) SAVINGS BANK of *c.*1906 on the gushet of
NEW CITY ROAD and Shamrock Street.

THE WEST END

WOODLANDS AND FINNIESTON

An area of great contrasts, embracing the most sophisticated of residential developments on Woodlands Hill, the more sedate ones to its N, and those of Finnieston, shattered by industry and cheek-by-jowl with the housing schemes of Anderston.

CHURCHES

ANDERSTON KELVINGROVE CHURCH AND COMMUNITY CENTRE, 759 Argyle Street. By *Honeyman, Jack & Robertson*, 1970–2. The bold, black pyramid roof over the hall church is a dominant landmark and closes the S end of Elderslie Street. To it are attached a series of uncomfortably-angled lower blocks, and yet the whole makes a clear statement of function and provides a much needed focus. Inside, everything is simple, with light wood fittings in the church.

CHRISTIAN SCIENCE CHURCH, La Belle Place. *See* Public Buildings, below: former Queen's Rooms.

GAELIC CHURCH, Grant Street. An elementary Gothic box of *c.* 1862, with simple lancet windows in the pinnacled gable. Manse linked to the l.

Former FINNIESTON PARISH CHURCH (built as a Free Church; now in secular use), Derby Street. Elegant and late Greek Revival church of 1879–80 by *James Sellars*. A temple-fronted rectangular church on a corner site. On the E front, a Greek Ionic portico. Rising behind it, an attenuated octagonal lantern, a free rendering of the Choragic monument of

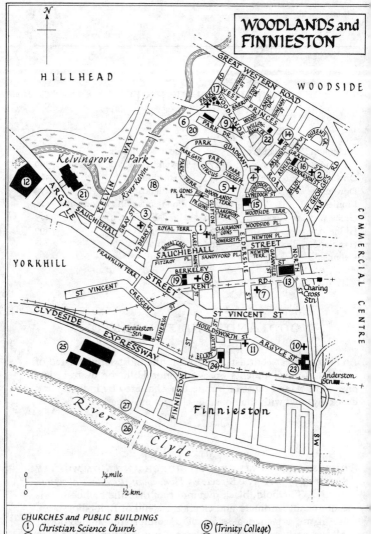

WOODLANDS and FINNIESTON

HILLHEAD

WOODSIDE

GREAT WESTERN ROAD

Kelvingrove Park

River Kelvin

PARK QUADRANT

PARK DR.

PARK CIRCUS

PARK GATE

PARK CIRCUS

PARK TERR.

WOODLANDS TERR.

CLAREMONT TERR.

ROYAL TERR.

CLAIRMONT GDNS.

WOODSIDE TERR.

WOODSIDE PL.

NEWTON PL.

SAUCHIEHALL STREET

FITZROY PL.

SANDYFORD PL.

NEWTON TERR.

GRANVILLE ST.

SOMERSET PL.

BERKELEY STREET

KENT ST.

ST VINCENT CRESCENT

ST VINCENT ST.

CLYDESIDE

Finnieston Stn.

CLYDESIDE EXPRESSWAY

MINERVA ST.

HOULDSWORTH ST.

ARGYLE ST.

ELLIOT ST.

Charing Cross Stn.

Anderston Stn.

YORKHILL

FRANKLIN TERR.

ARGYLE SAUCHIEHALL

KELVIN WAY

GRAY ST.

BERRY ST.

CLAREMONT ST.

FINNIESTON ST.

River Clyde

Finnieston

M 8

COMMERCIAL CENTRE

WOODSIDE

WEST PRINCES ST.

WOODLANDS RD.

PARK RD.

WILLOWBANK ST.

ARLINGTON ST.

GRANT ST.

ASHLEY ST.

CARNARVON ST.

ST GEORGE'S RD.

QUEEN'S CR.

WOODLANDS DR.

LYNEDOCH ST.

NORTH ST.

| 0 | ¼ mile |
| 0 | ½ km |

CHURCHES and PUBLIC BUILDINGS

1. Christian Science Church
2. Gaelic Church
3. (Finnieston Parish Church)
4. St Jude's Free Presbyterian
5. (Park Church)
6. St Silas English Church
7. St Vincent Church
8. (Trinity Congregational)
9. Woodlands Methodist
10. St Patrick (R.C.)
11. Anderston Kelvingrove Church
12. Kelvin Hall
13. Mitchell Theatre and Library
14. Arlington Baths Club
15. (Trinity College)
16. Woodside Public School
17. (Woodlands Public School)
18. Kelvingrove Park
19. Woodside Secondary
20. Queen's College
21. Glasgow Art Gallery and Museum
22. Willowbank School
23. St Patrick School
24. Finnieston Primary
25. Scottish Exhibition Centre
26. Clyde Tunnel
27. Finnieston Crane

Lysicrates, set on a square base. Symmetrically arranged side elevation with a row of tall pilasters at gallery level framing wide tripartite windows. Much of the interior remains intact. In the vestibule, a flat coffered ceiling and stairs to the gallery, which is set behind an elliptical Ionic screen. Generous semicircular pulpit and carved backboard.

Former PARK CHURCH, Lynedoch Place. *See* Perambulation 1, below.

ST JUDE'S FREE PRESBYTERIAN CHURCH (formerly Woodlands United Presbyterian), 133 Woodlands Road. 1874–5, by *John Burnet Snr* (who was assessor for a competition, but decided no scheme was satisfactory and made designs himself, taking the best features from the submitted designs). A carefully composed church with spacious halls on a tightly constrained corner site. Freely based on northern French Gothic in a manner anticipated by Leiper at Dowanhill Church (*see* below). The tall, unbuttressed tower and spire, with a porch in the base, rise from the NW corner of the church. Unusually gabled gallery windows punctuate the long elevations. Extending from the E end, an imposing range of domestic Gothic halls, with a bold candle-snuffer roof on the tourelle that marks the transition to an octagonal hall.

Inside, an impressive hall church with wide galleries supported on mighty cast-iron columned arcades. Excellent woodwork in the decorative flat-panelled ceiling and in the well-detailed pews (the long front four pews have hinged tops for communion use), pulpit and empty organ case.

ST PATRICK (R.C.), North Street. 1898, by *P. P. Pugin*. Functional Dec, without a tower, in an unrelenting red sandstone. Inside, a tall nave with wide-arched arcade and timber trussed roof. Elaborate canopied marble reredos and some stencilwork to chancel roof; carved altarpieces in side chapels. E organ gallery. – STAINED GLASS. Apse windows by *Eardley* of Dublin, *c.* 1911. – Large, unattractive W window by *John Hardman Studios*, 1951.

ST SILAS ENGLISH CHURCH (Episcopal), Eldon Street. Muscular E.E. by *John Honeyman*, 1864, with carved stonework by *Thomas Earp*. Nave and aisles but no tower. The door and powerful rose window above are emphasized by boldly carved ballflower decoration. Inside, a ponderously arcaded nave and wide aisles. – REREDOS with a blind cusped arcade. – PULPIT, quatrefoil on squat colonnettes with carved leaf capitals. – STAINED GLASS all *c.* 1880. – Mural MEMORIAL to Archibald Campbell of Blythswood, NW wall.

Former ST VINCENT CHURCH, 69 Kent Road. Designed for the United Presbyterians, but now in secular use. Slotted into the street frontage between tenement blocks; handsome, restrained Dec design of 1864–5 by *Alexander Watt*. Pinnacled gable front to the street with three Gothic doors, large Geometric-traceried window above and, in the gablehead, a circular frame with a watchful angel.

SANDYFORD-HENDERSON MEMORIAL CHURCH. See p. 295.

TRINITY COLLEGE CHURCH. *See* Public Buildings, below: Trinity College.

Former TRINITY CONGREGATIONAL CHURCH (now Henry Wood Hall), 71–3 Claremont Street. By *John Honeyman*, 1864; converted in 1978 by *John Notman & G. S. Calder* for the Scottish National Orchestra Society. Dec church, with prominent tower and elegant broached spire with restrained lucarnes, at the angle with Berkeley Street. Main entrance through the tower under a cusped arch. The stair turrets, which originally served galleries, are tucked into the angles created by the double-gabled transepts. Geometric tracery used consistently in all windows. Inside, the fittings have been removed and the transepts made one with the area devoted to the orchestra. Pseudo-hammerbeam roof with delicate pierced fretwork decoration. – STAINED GLASS. Two tall N windows depicting the Origins and Inspiration of the Protestant Religion by *Stephen Adam Studio*, 1905.

WOODLANDS METHODIST CHURCH, Park Drive. By *David Barclay*, 1909. Its cruciform plan is uncomfortably constrained by the slope of Woodlands Hill, and the tower is incomplete. Stylized Perp tracery. Inside, plain halls at ground level. A wide stair with good Art Nouveau tiles leads to a spacious but dull church. Simple fittings. – STAINED GLASS. E window, early C19 adapted to fit the tracery. – Two N windows by *Guthrie & Wells*, c.1920. – W window by *George Benson*, c.1920. – ORGAN presented in 1876 to 'the New Church', Cathedral Street; moved here in 1909.

PUBLIC BUILDINGS

KELVIN HALL, Argyle Street. 1926–7. Designed as an exhibition hall by *Thomas Somers* (City Engineer) to replace the hall that burnt down in 1926, and superseded by the Scottish Exhibition Centre (*see* below). In two distinct parts: the quasi-Durbar-style show front in red sandstone to Argyle Street (containing offices etc.) and the main hall. The show front consists of a long main block with tall twin towers terminating in lanterns surmounted by bronze globes (the symbol of the building's all-embracing and universal purpose) and pillared *porte cochère*. The flanking Doric colonnaded wings are stopped by massive but shorter domed towers topped by obelisks. Though shallower and more simply classical, in general massing this front follows the N side of Kelvingrove Art Gallery and Museum, which it faces across Argyle Street. The main hall has brick walls with stone facings and wide Deco-ish doorways. The ferro-concrete roof by *Considère Constructions Ltd* covers an area of 15,885 m² (171,000 sq. ft) supported by only twenty-two columns. Converted in 1984–8 by *Glasgow District Council Architect's Department* into a large sports complex and Museum of Transport, the latter entered through an incongruous skeletal high-tech portal which smothers the elegant lines of one of the original side doorways.

GLASGOW ART GALLERY AND MUSEUM, Kelvingrove Park. Its exotic towers and vivid colour dominate the s end of Kelvingrove Park, and loom large in the views along the main road. 1891–1901, by *J. W. Simpson & E. J. Milner Allen,* but owing its conception to a committee formed in 1886 to promote the erection of a combined art gallery and museum, with a concert hall and art college (both omitted from the final design; the latter was built in Renfrew Street). This grandiose scheme was prompted by the cramped conditions in both the McLellan Galleries (*see* Commercial Centre, Streets: Nos. 254–90 Sauchiehall Street) and in the museum then housed in Kelvingrove House (*see* Kelvingrove Park, below). To raise the capital, an International Exhibition was held in Kelvingrove Park in the summer of 1888. The £46,000 raised was then doubled by public subscription, though Glasgow Corporation eventually had to take over the financial responsibility. The competition was held in 1891, and the selection of English architects by the adjudicator, Alfred Waterhouse, caused a storm of protest equal to that provoked by Scott's appointment to design the university twenty years before. The foundation stone was not laid until 1897. The opening in 1901 was celebrated by another International Exhibition, the new building a solid red counterpoint to *James Miller*'s white and gold main exhibition hall. It officially became the Kelvingrove Art Gallery and Museum in 1902.

The extremely elaborate exterior of red Locharbriggs sandstone (cleaned *c.* 1986–8 by *Elder & Cannon,* to startling effect) clothes a simple plan. A main clearstorey-lit hall of Imperial proportions is flanked by smaller top-lit halls surrounded by galleries, side-lit for the museum on the ground floor and top-lit above for the art collection, a flexible and still useful arrangement. The style is Hispanic Baroque, the centre of the N front modelled closely on Santiago della Compostella, Obradoiro. Twin pinnacled towers flank a tall and pinnacled porch with square towers at either side. The wings are modelled with buttresses, and the advanced corner pavilions have large bay windows and are topped with steep cupolas reflecting the roof over the main hall. Terminating the whole composition, like symmetrical book-ends, are twin towers linked together on the E and W façades. The S front of the central block is much simpler than its counterpart on the N side, with a broad *porte cochère* flanked by towers.

The whole complicated picturesque arrangement is embellished with a rich programme of SCULPTURE. J. W. Simpson commissioned *George Frampton* in 1897 to supervise the external sculpture with the intention of integrating it with the architectural design. Frampton designed and executed only the free-standing and commanding bronze of St Mungo, bedecked 67 with the salmon, bell, and tree symbols of Glasgow, and attended by a musical maiden and her artistic sister (this prominent group sits in front of the N doorway), and the spandrels of the porch (the British Colonies saluting the arms of Glasgow; Love teaching Harmony to the Arts; and the Industries of Glasgow at the Court of Mercury), in which ethereal Della Robbia-inspired maidens are uneasily juxtaposed with conventional ornament round the arches. The figures on the corner pavilions are by *Derwent Wood* (Music, Architecture, Painting, Sculpture); *W. Birnie Rhind* (Science); *Johan Keller* (Religion); *E. G. Bramwell* (Literature); and *A. Fabrucci* (Commerce). These principal sculptures were originally accompanied by a bronze figure of Victory over the N porch and figures of Immortality and Fame over the tall flanking towers. On this side, there is also a plethora of decorative sculpture – all along the wings, in the tympana of the windows (the arms of the counties of Scotland), and on the piers between them (the names of great painters, sculptors, and architects).

The interior is almost as lavishly appointed, its white Giffnock stone exuberantly carved and modelled. The soaring arcaded five-bay, three-storey main hall was intended for the display of sculpture, but the organ at the N end and the names of composers in cartouches in the first-floor spandrels suggest that concerts were also planned. The Corporation's part in the scheme is clearly advertised by the enormous city arms carved in stone which fill the upper part of the S wall and are instantly visible when entering from the N. Prominently displayed on the arcade piers, the names of the Glasgow trades. The pattern of the marble floor mirrors the arrangement of the coffered barrel-vault above. Opulent and exquisite Art Nouveau light fittings, with inappropriate globes and lanterns replacing the original clusters of simple glass shades at the lowest level. The long two-storey side halls have large imperial staircases. In the spandrels of the first-floor arcade, gilded names of famous people. At the corners of the central block, four grand well staircases with coffered ceilings. In contrast, the galleries themselves are understated, a quiet background for the display of exhibits.

The gardens at the S entrance, with their semicircular-ended red sandstone walls, were created in 1914, when the carriage drive was altered from one with tight curves to an approach parallel to the building by *A. B. McDonald* of Glasgow's Office of Public Works. Planting redesigned 1988.

SCOTTISH EXHIBITION CENTRE, Finnieston Street, close to the site of the sturdily Scottish Stobcross House (home of the Andersons). Completed in 1987 by *James Parr & Partners*. This large and unprepossessing shed sits in acres of tarmac car park on the infilled Queen's Dock (constructed 1872–80; closed 1969), and a covered walkway links it to Finnieston Station like an umbilical cord. It makes nothing of its riverside site. Exhibition areas flank a central glazed concourse. It is accompanied by the tower-block FORUM HOTEL by *Cobban & Lironi*, 1988–9, dramatically faced in mirrored glass but with nothing to reflect except passing clouds. Only the dashingly angled bar and restaurant projection adds any excitement to this disappointing national centre.

On the w edge of the car park, the dock's former HYDRAULIC PUMPING STATION of 1877 by *John Carrick* (City Engineer), tiny beside its spreading neighbour but, with its Italian façade and accumulator tower disguised as a campanile, happily distinctive. Converted to a restaurant with a conservatory-like extension by *The Miller Partnership*, 1988. Behind it the transit sheds of Yorkhill Quays (*see* Yorkhill: Yorkhill Basin).

MITCHELL THEATRE (formerly ST ANDREW'S HALLS) AND LIBRARY, Granville Street and North Street. This substantial range of public buildings occupies an entire street block. The former St Andrew's Halls, built in 1873–7, was *James Sellars'* masterpiece. It fronts Granville Street and can only be seen in sharp perspective. The Schinkelesque composition of the main front is imposing and supremely self-confident. The boldly colonnaded upper storey rests on a heavy channelled masonry plinth, the upper part, into which the windows are punched, recessed to leave a base for the massive cast-iron lamp-standards. In contrast, the three central doors are set in a pronounced architrave and divided by Atlantes *in antis*. Giant plinths define the magisterial outer bays and support *John Mossman*'s dramatic figure groups. The effect of the colonnade is subtly modulated across the façade with the walls behind it in the outer bays less deeply recessed than those in the centre. The outer bays have attic storeys above the main cornice; in these, remarkably delicate caryatids and pilasters frame panels referring to the arts and inscribed 'RAPHAEL–WATT–M–ANGELO–NEWTON–FLAXMAN' (N) and 'PUR-CELL–BACH–HANDEL–MOZART–BEETHOVEN' (S). The monumental character continues for seven bays on each return elevation. Gutted by fire in 1962, the interior of the front part was reconstructed in 1972–80 by *Sir Frank Mears & Partners* to house the Mitchell Theatre, and the rear part of the building was rebuilt in an unflinching manner for the Mitchell Library, whose main entrance is now on Kent Road.

The original MITCHELL LIBRARY of 1906–11 by *William B. Whitie* (as the result of a competition) stands back to back with the theatre and library extension, a pompous Edwardian Baroque design with a bold central dome prominent in many views. Fussy detail on all the elevations. The seated figure sculpture on the parapet is by *John Miller,* the standing figures by *T. J. Clapperton,* both from London. The same civic confidence is reflected inside, especially in the oval marble and stone staircase which fits into the curve of the façade. Behind the staircase, a huge double-height reading room, with elaborate joinery, plasterwork and leaded glass, repeated in the equally grand reading rooms upstairs.

Former QUEEN'S ROOMS, La Belle Place (now the Christian Science church). 1857, by *Charles Wilson,* with sculpture by *John Mossman.* Its origins are clearly inscribed in the S pedi-

ment: 'ERECTED BY DAVID BELL OF BLACKHALL MER-
CHANT IN GLASGOW MDCCCLVII CHARLES WILSON
MQR ARCHITECT MOSSMAN SCULPTOR W T EDMISTON
WRIGHT WILLIAM YORK BUILDER'. It is one of Wilson's
most inventive buildings – a classical temple without a portico,
freely applied with Early Italian Renaissance ideas. All the
rectangular openings are linked by a continuous broad band;
above it, arched heads filled with sculpture and medallion
portraits over each, including David Hamilton representing
architecture. More bold carving in the deep processional frieze
representing the progress of the fine and useful arts. Despite
its modest scale, it has enormous presence and its themes are
continued on the adjoining tenements. The original interior
was gutted on conversion for the First Church of Christ Scien-
tist (planned in 1939 but not executed until c. 1948 by *A. M.
Gardner*).

ARLINGTON BATHS CLUB, 61 Arlington Street. 1869–71.
One of the earliest private swimming clubs in Britain, with a
slightly later Turkish bath adjacent. *John Burnet*'s original
building was single-storey. The s and the central blocks were
raised by *Andrew Myles*, 1893, the N part by *Benjamin Conner*,
1902. Inside, there are still many of the original fittings, including a large cast-iron ventilator over the main pool and coloured
glass set into the concrete ogival roof of the Turkish bath.

QUEEN'S COLLEGE (College of Domestic Science), 1 Park
Drive. The original building c. 1905 by *Cowan & Watson*,
powerful red sandstone with Renaissance detailed porches and
carved cornucopia over windows. Extended to the w, raised
on *pilotis*, c. 1950, and at rear in 1976 by *Building Design
Partnership*.

3 Former TRINITY COLLEGE, 31 Lynedoch Street. A vital
ingredient of the Glasgow skyline and a highly inventive composition, built in 1856–7 as the Free Church College to designs
by *Charles Wilson*. Three towers, all with novel, very elongated
round-arched openings, dominate the design. At the w end,
the dominant one, like an ecclesiastical lighthouse, closes the
vista at the E end of Woodlands Terrace. In height and outline,
though perhaps in nothing else, it is Lombardic in origin, and
has a stylistic affinity with Thomson's contemporary tower on
the Caledonia Road Church. The two towers at the E end mark
what was the original college church (destroyed by fire in 1903
and rebuilt as the college library by *Colin Menzies*, with a
concrete shell vault) and flank its pedimented centrepiece with
its suggestions of Wren. They rise, pencil-straight, to their
cornices and finialled parapets. The crisply classical two-storey
linking range, with its deeply modelled round-headed
windows, is reminiscent of Leo von Klenze's work of the 1820s
in Munich. Except for the galleried hall, the imperial stair
and the large memorial window to Professors Candlish and
Drummond, 1898, by *Guthrie & Wells*, designed by *David
Gauld* under the direction of *Sir J. J. Burnet*, the interior was
destroyed in the conversion to flats by *James Canning Young*

Partners for *Windex* in 1985–6. The rear hall still awaits attention in 1989.

ANDERSTON PRIMARY SCHOOL, Port Street. 1972, by the *City Architect*. A collection of low, single-storey linked blocks overlooking the Clydeside Expressway, built on the site of the Houldsworths' mansion.

WILLOWBANK SCHOOL, Willowbank Crescent. 1899–1901, by *Alexander Petrie* for the Glasgow School Board. A handsome symmetrical elevation with giant pilasters to the upper floors and recessed boys' and girls' entrances.

Former WOODLANDS PUBLIC SCHOOL, Woodlands Road, filling a prominent corner site. By *Robert Dalglish*, 1882, for the Glasgow School Board. Unusually, in a Jacobean style. Symmetrical elevations with a pseudo-arcaded angle tower crowned with strapwork pediments. Large Italianate extension (1896) to the W.

WOODSIDE PUBLIC SCHOOL (Albany Annexe; formerly Albany Academy), Ashley Street. A handsome school in the manner of a Renaissance villa and probably designed by *H. & D. Barclay c.* 1875. S extension of 1902.

WOODSIDE SECONDARY SCHOOL, Berkeley Street. By the *City Architect*, 1968. A utilitarian series of linked concrete and glass boxes, taller at the central entrance and with a glass-walled hall.

KELVINGROVE PARK occupies the valley where the River Kelvin flows between Gilmorehill and Woodlands Hill. It takes its name from the Kelvingrove estate which, together with the Woodlands estate, formed the nucleus of the park which now extends to 34 ha (85 acres). The initial plan which *Charles Wilson* presented to the Town Council in 1851 prompted the acquisition of the land. How far *Sir Joseph Paxton* was involved is not clear: he was commissioned to provide a plan and presented it in 1854, although work had already begun in the previous year. The Winter Garden he proposed was not built, and the lake was not formed until 1872 and then to a different design. Charles Wilson and the surveyor *Thomas Kyle* appear to have been the principal designers. The original Pleasure Grounds, with walks amongst trees and statues, are laid out on the steep slopes. More recent facilities for bowling, tennis and so on are concentrated at the flatter S end close by the Kelvingrove Art Gallery and Museum (*see* above), and in one small area at the extreme N end.

At Park Gate, the fine bronze equestrian STATUE of Lord Roberts by *Harry Bates*, with exotic attendant figures of Victory and War and a frieze of soldiers rendered with the fluidity of the New Sculpture, leads dramatically in. It is an exact replica (except for the inscription) of the monument erected in Calcutta in 1898 and was unveiled in 1916. Roberts looks out over the valley of the Kelvin towards the university. – Further S down the hill, one of the park's focal points, the richly carved and detailed Scottish Gothic STEWART MEMORIAL FOUNTAIN of 1871–2. The architect was *James Sellars*, the

sculptor *John Mossman*. Large granite basin, flying buttresses
in Dalmeny freestone, serpentine marble pillars and bronze
reliefs portraying Lord Provost Stewart and scenes commemorating the water supply from Loch Katrine which he
instigated. On top a two-metre-high (7-ft) bronze statue of the
Lady of the Lake. Restored in 1988 by *Page & Park*. – NE of
the fountain is a finely modelled and peculiarly Victorian piece
of STATUARY, representing a Royal Bengal tigress bringing a
peacock to her young (1867, by *Auguste-Nicolas Cain*, from a
sketch by *Rosa Bonheur*), a gift of W. S. Kennedy of New
York. – At the extreme E end of the park, by La Belle Place
(and visible from the fountain), the CHILDREN'S SHELTER
AND CONVENIENCES of brick with a steep tiled roof: 1913,
by Glasgow's *Office of Public Works*. – To the S, the entrance
GATE from Kelvingrove Street, 1897. Elaborate wrought-iron
gates and ashlar gatepiers, the principal ones originally topped
with lamps, the lesser ones with squat truncated obelisks. – W
of the Stewart Memorial Fountain and at the bottom of the
slope lies the LAKE, fed by the overflow from the fountain. –
To the S, the roller skating area, flanked by playgrounds,
marks approximately the location of Kelvingrove House, an
important classical mansion of 1782, possibly designed by
Robert Adam. It was destroyed to make way for the International Exhibition of 1901.

From here, the Kelvin flows down through the park from
the N, spanned by the FOOTBRIDGE and the majestic Prince
Albert Bridge, now known as the PRINCE OF WALES
BRIDGE (*see* Crossings of the Clyde and Kelvin, below). –
Close to the last bridge, the HIGHLAND LIGHT INFANTRY
MEMORIAL to those killed in the South African War. An
effective portrayal of a soldier guarding the bridge from a rock
by *Birnie Rhind*, 1906. – This statue faces, across the bridge,
a MONUMENT of *c.* 1883 to Carlyle, who rises from a massive
block of stone. – To the N, on this bank, lies the muddle of the
Park Nurseries, largely screened by vegetation. – W of the
Kelvin, the KELVIN WAY, the road cut through the park in
1914–26. – To the SE, the BAND STAND of 1924 built by the
Public Parks Department in red brick and render, with Ionic
columns flanking the shallow proscenium. On the tiled roof, a
squat domed cupola with an elaborate finial. Brick pay booths
of 1925. – W of Kelvin Way, the magisterial STATUE of Lord
Kelvin in academic robes, with the university as an appropriate
backdrop: 1913, by *Archibald Macfarlane Shannon*. – A little
to the SW, a bronze STATUE of Lord Lister, also in academic
dress: 1924, by *G. H. Parkin*. – Further to the W, the SUN-
LIGHT COTTAGES erected by *James Miller* for the 1901
exhibition as replicas of those at Port Sunlight and given to
the city by Lord Leverhulme after the exhibition closed. They
teeter on a steep bank above the Kelvin, their red brick, half-
timbering and elaborate bargeboards providing a picturesque
taste of an idealized England. – Further W still, close by Partick
Bridge (*see* Crossings of the Clyde and Kelvin), the OLD

MEN'S SHELTER of 1935, designed by the *Public Parks Department*.

Back on Kelvin Way, s of the Kelvin Way Bridge (*see* Crossings of the Clyde and Kelvin) and to the E, the BOWLING AND TENNIS PAVILION, also of 1924 by the *Public Parks Department*. An elegant design in brick, render and tile, with an octagon flanked by wings with hipped roofs and verandas. – To the w, the small BOWLING PAVILION of *c.* 1922, overshadowed by the picturesque mass of the Art Gallery and Museum. – Beyond it, by the Partick Bridge, is *I. Lindsay Clark's* WAR MEMORIAL of 1924, a convincing portrayal of a group of soldiers going 'over the top'. – The s end of the leafy Kelvin Way meets the urban mêlée of Argyle Street.

BELL'S BRIDGE, HARBOUR TUNNELS. *See* under Clyde, Crossings of the Clyde and Kelvin, below.

PARTICK BRIDGE. *See* under Kelvin, Crossings of the Clyde and Kelvin, below.

PERAMBULATIONS

1. Woodlands Hill

The development of Woodlands Hill represents the finest piece of town design in Glasgow, in planning and in architecture. Its dramatic skyline, dominated by the triple towers of the Free Church College and the tower of the demolished Park Church, is the most powerful image of the West End. The planning is full of surprises: a series of giant terraced platforms, starting with Sauchiehall Street, rises up the southern slopes of the hill and is linked by gentle curves and well-graded steps up to the crest, which is proudly defined by the boldest of terraces. The best secrets are kept to the end – the very heart of the summit is laid out with the subtlest of oval plans and lined with the most refined of terraces. The ultimate surprise is revealed at the w end of Park Circus, which opens on to a high platform perched on a rocky outcrop overlooking Kelvingrove Park and presenting views of the towers of Glasgow University on the next hill.

The development of the hill was not a single piece of monumental planning; the effect is cumulative and began low down on the southern slopes, which were laid out by the Edinburgh architect *George Smith* in the 1830s and 1840s. Also in the 1840s, *John Baird I* repeated the pattern with more westerly terraces, but the real magic was conjured by *Charles Wilson*. In 1854 *Joseph Paxton* was commissioned to design the West End (Kelvingrove) Park, and, for the site once designated for the university, the City asked Wilson to complete the already prestigious residential development. This he did with great flair, his bold outward-looking terraces in Park Terrace and Park Quadrant contrasting with the elegant and restrained inner terraces, which capture the privacy of an architectural interior.

The tour starts at Charing Cross on the w side of the chasm of the inner-city motorway. First we see the CAMERON MEM-

ORIAL FOUNTAIN, a drinking fountain by *Clarke and Bell,* 1896, erected in memory of Charles Cameron MP, standing with a drunken list at the junction of Sauchiehall Street and Woodside Crescent. Tiered and elaborately Baroque, in granite and Doulton ware, with a refined bronze medallion portrait of Cameron by *G. Tinworth.* Woodside Crescent (originally Britannia Place) begins the ascent of Woodlands Hill with, on the E side, replacing the lowest houses of the crescent, the disturbingly-angled FOUNTAIN HOUSE by *Walter Underwood & Partners,* 1981. This shiny glazed office block, with the appearance of an incomplete Rubik's cube discarded in frustration, shows no respect for the elegant late Georgian domestic scale of its neighbours.

Terraces step up Woodlands Hill from Sauchiehall Street. Off the lower end of the crescent, WOODSIDE PLACE of 1838, by *George Smith,* can be seen to the W. It forms part of the first level. Greek Doric porticoes emphasize the end and centre pavilions of this long, restrained terrace. Nos. 1 and 2 have been completely rebuilt inside; at No. 17, a wall plaque marks the residence of the eminent surgeon Joseph Lister. The houses of WOODSIDE CRESCENT, begun in 1831 by George Smith, now start at No. 6 (which has a surprising Tudorish rear elevation, prominently bay-windowed) and curve up the hill, with bold Greek Doric porticoes at Nos. 14 and 15, similar to those in Woodside Place. In the door of No. 13, colourful, late C19 Glasgow Style stained glass.

Woodside Crescent curves W into WOODSIDE TERRACE, the most dramatic of George Smith's terraces. The E part was built in 1835; the W followed in 1842; in both, Smith developed the use of sturdy Greek Doric porticoes, not found elsewhere in Glasgow. These three terraces all have spearhead cast-iron railings of a pattern unusually restrained for Glasgow.

From the W end of Woodside Terrace, the route W down across the gardens leads past Nos. 2–13 CLAIRMONT GARDENS, 1857–8. Elaborately sculpted first-floor oriels make their first appearance here in the front elevation of a terrace block, initiating a feature which was to find popularity in the 1880s in Hillhead and Hyndland. Inside, the plasterwork is similarly elaborate – of almost Moorish form. To the W, beyond Clifton Street, *Charles Wilson*'s remarkably original and striking former Queen's Rooms (*see* Public Buildings, above) and Nos. 2–5 LA BELLE PLACE, the short tenement of 1856–7 that he cleverly related to it, using similar Italian Renaissance decoration but on a reduced scale to enhance the importance of the Rooms themselves. Like the Rooms, this tenement was also designed for the speculator David Bell. ROYAL TERRACE to the W, begun in 1845, completes the lowest terraced step on the south-facing slopes of Woodlands Hill.

Back now to Clifton Street and onwards uphill to Claremont Terrace and Park Gardens. A glance to the E reveals the gently curving CLAREMONT TERRACE by *John Baird I.* It began with No. 6, built in 1842 as a free-standing mansion house (now known as BERESFORD HOUSE). This has a symmetrical façade, with an excellent anthemion cast-iron balcony across the five long first-floor windows. The Ionic columns of the doorpiece and the ironwork design are both repeated in the flanking terrace houses, begun in 1847. Most of these houses have original details inside, including columned screens in the halls and ornate cast-iron balustrades to the stairs. Inside No. 7 much of the plasterwork survives, along with a French style of decoration in some rooms and, in the hall, a painted ceiling with cherubs in scrolled panels.

Returning w across Clifton Street, we come to PARK GARDENS of c. 1855 by *Charles Wilson*, a short terrace extending between two broad flights of steps which lead to the uppermost level of Woodlands Hill. Wilson's terrace is composed of surprisingly narrow houses, each with storeys nearly identical in height. The E elevation, facing on to Clifton Steps, is altogether more generous than the main front, and echoes the design of the w façade of Claremont Terrace. To the w, at the foot of the steps to the upper terrace, the massive retaining wall incorporates a virtually subterranean mews (only accessible from Clifton Street), PARK GARDENS LANE, one of the few unspoilt mews in the city. Nos. 1 and 2 at the E end were substantially remodelled in 1906 by *J. J. Burnet* to form an unusual house with striped tiled walls set deeply into the outer frame and with a broad balcony along the first floor. The w elevation of the terrace looks on to the upper terraced paths of Kelvingrove Park.

The three monumental stairways that rise from this level (the w one of 1853–4, the two E ones of c. 1855 from Clifton Street and Elderslie Street) to Park Terrace and Woodlands Terrace are part of *Charles Wilson's* overall design for the upper slopes of Woodlands Hill, laid out in 1854. At the top of the grandest flight at the w end of Park Gardens, two bold pavilions (No. 1 Park Terrace and No. 24 Woodlands Terrace) herald Park Circus. They grandly terminate two terraces, Nos. 2–21 PARK TERRACE and Nos. 18–23 WOODLANDS TERRACE, both by Wilson, of 1855, and both inspired, at least at their roofs, by the French Renaissance models of the reign of François I, an unusually dramatic design for the date. The E terrace adjoins another earlier one (Nos. 1–17), 1849–51, by *John Baird I*, the curve in the road reducing the impact of the change in style. In 1904 Nos. 14 and 15 were extended and altered by *James Salmon Jun.* and given distinctive Glasgow Style intertwined metalwork and numbers over the doors. Inside, much of the joinery, door furniture and leaded glass survives.

Now to return to Park Street South (opposite the head of the westerly steps) and to continue w, following the curve round the brow of the hill to Park Gate. This upper level affords extensive views s over the remnants of the Clyde shipyards towards the Renfrew Hills. At the w end of the hill, by the entrance to Kelvingrove Park, the University buildings on Gilmorehill fill the horizon. From this platformed terrace overlooking the Park, a brief excursion NE takes in PARK QUAD-

RANT, also by *Wilson*, 1855–8 (and, unusually for this area, designed as a tenement), which carries a modified French Renaissance style round the hill to the N.

Behind lies PARK GATE, 1857–9, again designed by *Wilson* (where No. 4 has particularly elaborate plasterwork and an excellent cast-iron stair balustrade). Park Gate provides a short transition between the flamboyant outer terraces and the restrained and measured symmetry of PARK CIRCUS, the heart of Wilson's masterly planned scheme. Designed in 1855 and built in 1857–8, it demonstrates his subtlety and invention. The long NE section is carefully articulated with the flat centre sections, slightly projecting, and linked to the gently curved quadrants. It is complemented by the two S segments, divided by Park Street South. Superficially it perpetuates the proportions of late Georgian terraces, but in the treatment of the masonry and the cast-ironwork, and particularly in the handling of the ground floor as a restrained plinth to the upper storeys, it strikes a new line in terrace design. Despite their conversion to offices, these houses have kept much of their handsome plasterwork and many of their columned screens (Ionic in the halls, Corinthian in the main rooms) and cast-iron balustraded staircases.

The most remarkable house is No. 22 Park Circus, on the SW corner with Park Street South, built in 1872–4 to Wilson's design by *James Boucher,* who fitted it out with the richest interior in the Circus, indeed as rich as any in Glasgow. Especially fine are the arcaded ground-floor corridor with saucer domes and the similarly treated main stair, which leads up to an astonishing upper hall with Corinthian columns and galleries and a scalloped and glazed dome made in cast-iron by *Macfarlane*'s Saracen Ironworks. To this, in 1897–9, *James Salmon* and *J. Gaff Gillespie* added some of their best interior work – an elaborate Art Nouveau billiard room and a panelled and domed anteroom, both with richly embossed wallpapers. Into Boucher's principal rooms they introduced some remarkably sympathetic yet distinctively Glasgow Style chimneypieces. The magnificent woodcarving was probably by *Derwent Wood*, possibly by *Hodge* and *Keller* as well. At the rear, and little-noticed, a striking cast-iron conservatory made by *Macfarlane*'s, with delicately embossed metal end walls, a lacy arcade (now infilled) and a roof with a scalloped pattern of glazing bars.

Inside No. 18, an expensively panelled drawing room and richly decorated hall by *William Leiper* for John Anderson, 1891. At No. 19 (now occupied by the Franciscan Sisters) *Jack Coia* converted a former operating theatre into a small oratory for the Archbishop (1955). It is simply conceived, with excellent fittings and Stations of the Cross by *William Crosbie*.

PARK CIRCUS PLACE (designed 1855–6, built in 1872–3) leads E out of the Circus and continues Wilson's scheme. Nos. 8 and 17 have excellent original interior work, No. 15 a billiard room by *John A. Campbell*. The street gently slopes down the hill to LYNEDOCH PLACE. On its SE corner stands the tower of the former PARK CHURCH of 1856–8 by *J. T. Rochead*, a striking adaptation of West of England Perpendicular. The tower is very tall and an important landmark, but regrettably it lacks its church, which in 1968, despite much protest, was replaced by a reinforced-concrete office block, designed for the Bank of Scotland by *Derek Stephenson & Partners* in a misplaced endeavour to ape traditional Glasgow bay windows. Any virtue this idea might have had is denied by the monotonous nature of the material. Opposite, Nos. 1–12 (of 1869) close the vista from the Circus. Down the hill in LYNEDOCH STREET, first the former Free Church College (*see* Public Buildings, above: Trinity College), then two terraced houses of individual design. No. 27 looks earlier than its date of 1882: built as a manse and the only house in the street with a bay window. No. 25, *c.* 1870, has bold Thomsonesque incised decoration. Nos. 21 and 23 (basement) are related to the scheme *George Smith* designed for these streets in 1845. E of Lynedoch Terrace there is an irregular astylar terrace (Nos. 1–19) partly stepped on the slope and all apparently designed by Smith *c.* 1845. Opposite, LYNEDOCH CRESCENT completes Smith's layout.

2. St George's Road to Kelvin Bridge

The small triangle formed between St George's Road, Woodlands Road and Great Western Road demonstrates clearly the well-mannered urban domestic development that resulted, not from great enterprises, but from small-scale schemes, similar to those in Hillhead. At the E end, traces of grandeur are found in *John Bryce*'s Queen's Crescent of 1840, a design once carefully integrated with Clarendon Place and with West Princes Street and Baliol Street. Towards the tapering W end of the triangle, the domestic character is completed with late C19 tenements which line spaciously planned streets or long narrow tree-filled gardens.

N of Charing Cross, the gushet between St George's Road and Woodlands Road is dominated by ST GEORGE'S MANSIONS of 1900–1, designed by *Burnet & Boston* for the City Improvement Trust, with two additional blocks facing Woodlands Road. They are substantial red sandstone tenements of spaciously planned flats over a cast-iron framed ground floor linked to the back court conceived as a saloon serving the shops. The powerful corner block once answered, somewhat lumpishly, J. J. Burnet's dashing Charing Cross Mansions (*see* Commercial Centre, Streets, above: Sauchiehall Street), but any planned relationship has been swept into the fast lane of the motorway. The main interest of these tenements, besides their size, is in the ogee-roofed turrets, in the bold French Renaissance-style roof, with its cast-iron balustrade, and in the architects' hallmark – an aedicule framing the centre light of the canted windows, here at second-floor level.

Woodlands Road leads w and, off the e side, opens BALIOL
STREET, flanked by two small-scale ranges of surprisingly
old-fashioned late-Georgian-style tenements, the NW one of
c. 1850, the SE of a decade or so later. The two blocks (1865)
at the NE end of the street return into CARNARVON STREET,
but there the conservative development stops. Carnarvon
Street ends at ASHLEY STREET, a characterless open area
now devoid of its former restrained tenements and part criss-
crossed by tarmac paths, part planned for development. At the
junction is the Albany Annexe of the Woodside Public School
(*see* Public Buildings, above). Opposite and e of the school,
the remnants of a group of paired villas of c. 1850, each with
a Doric doorpiece, the penultimate one replaced by the pedimented red sandstone former CONGREGATIONAL CHURCH
and hall of c. 1900 by *Eric Sutherland,* converted to offices by
Weddell & Thomson in 1949. Past the school, the Arlington
Baths Club (*see* Public Buildings) is revealed to the w across
the open space. Intended to be seen in perspective, it is now
exposed in a confusing full-frontal view. To the N along Ashley
Street, more gaps where mid-c 19 tenements, originally part
of the planned development to which Queen's Crescent (*see*
below) belonged, stood until the early 1980s.

To appreciate what has gone, we must turn r. into WEST
PRINCES STREET to see the 1850s terraces which face
Queen's Crescent and then continue on both sides of the street
to the SE. Despite their neglected and gap-toothed condition,
they still form a recognizable continuation of *John Bryce*'s late
Georgian QUEEN'S CRESCENT of 1840. The crescent (which
in 1989 stands sadly neglected) has two plain but dignified
segments opening at the centre into Melrose Street and the
once handsome St George's Cross. Here and there, cast-iron
railings of a particularly strong design remain. In the centre
of the communal gardens, a tall, tiered stone fountain with
dolphins of c. 1870.

To the NW, West Princes Street is lined with a succession
of sedate, mainly red sandstone tenements, some with tiled
closes and with stained glass in the upper sashes of the
windows, but none of them individually distinguished. On the
s side, at No. 26, a crude former DRILL HALL AND OFFICES
by *George Bell* of *Clarke & Bell,* 1895–7. The overbearing red
Ballochmyle sandstone frontage makes the only break in the
ranks of middle-class tenements. The sturdy tenement tradition continues further w, where the street crosses
DUNEARN STREET, WOODLANDS DRIVE, BAR-
RINGTON DRIVE and MONTAGUE STREET. A glance up
and down these streets reveals a more spacious layout, with
shady narrow central gardens filled with tall trees, owing something to c 19 Continental town planning. These robust tenements, mainly of the early c 20, were the subjects of major
environmental improvements in the mid- and late 1970s, initiated by the Woodlands Residential Association in consultation
with *Arthur Ellams* (*Builders*) and the District Council.

West Princes Street dog-legs to the r. and l. at Park Road. From the w extension, there is a good view of the terraced layout of Hillhead rising up on the slope beyond the River Kelvin. Towards the s end of PARK ROAD, at Nos. 78–104, an unusual tenement of *c.* 1890 (possibly by *H. K. Bromhead*) with strong Thomsonesque details. Next a striking brick block of sheltered housing, designed by *Graham C. McWiggan,* 1987, for the Charing Cross and Kelvingrove Housing Association, happily respects the scale of its c 19 neighbours. Its restrained Post-Modern broken pediment and tripartite door are adapted from Nos. 78–104. The river front of this scheme is equally good, with continuous glazing to the communal sitting room.

At the junction with ELDON STREET, the muscular St Silas English Church (*see* Churches, above). Further E along Eldon Street, the former Woodside Public School; and opposite, set on the N slope of Woodlands Hill, the rear of Queen's College (the Dough School), which faces Park Drive (*see* Public Buildings). Now to return E along WOODLANDS ROAD, past Park Avenue and the unremarkable Woodlands Church (*see* Churches). On its N side, 1860s tenements of yellow sandstone. To the N, in WILLOWBANK STREET, two notably handsome blocks of tenements of 1863–4 (Nos. 9–21 and 2–30) and, at the N end of the street, Willowbank School (*see* Public Buildings). Back in Woodlands Road, grassy slopes on the s side sweep up to Park Quadrant, silhouetted against the skyline on the brow of Woodlands Hill. Further E, at Woodlands Gate, St Jude's Free Presbyterian Church (*see* Churches) catches the eye as it stands sentry over the northern entrance to Woodlands Hill.

3. Charing Cross to Kelvingrove Park

The development of this residential area followed rapidly after that of the Blythswood estate (*see* City Centre, Introduction, above) in the early c 19. It is spaciously planned with terraced houses and substantial tenements, and with St Vincent Crescent (*see* below) as its most striking set-piece.

w of Charing Cross, SAUCHIEHALL STREET opens out into a boulevard partly lined by trees, though successive road-widenings have gradually encroached into the gardens between the private carriage drives and the public street. The terraces along Sauchiehall Street blazed the trail for their more dramatic successors in Great Western Road: the simple classical pattern adopted here is definitely more conservative than the inventive designs of the later terraces. Tenements dominate both the w end of Sauchiehall Street and Argyle Street to the s w. Starting at the E end, at the junction of Sauchiehall Street and NORTH STREET is a tenement by *Charles Wilson,* built in 1853, two years before the Woodlands Hill terraces were laid out. The subtle grouping of the windows and the shell-heads over the central first-floor windows distinguish it. At No.

523 the coolly suave PELICAN BLONDE CAFÉ, by *McGurn, Logan, Duncan & Opfer, c.* 1986. On the N side of Sauchiehall Street, NEWTON PLACE (originally Caledonia Place) of 1837, the first of the terraces that *George Smith* designed for Woodlands Hill (*see* Perambulation 1, above). It is exceptionally long (eighty-one bays), with taller end and central pavilions, its severity only slightly modified by the cast-iron balconies to the first-floor windows. Opposite the W end of Newton Place, NEWTON TERRACE, *c.* 1864–5, with the end and central bays broken forward as pavilions and fashionable canted bays introduced at the ends. Still on the S side, SANDYFORD PLACE by *Brown & Carrick*, 1842–56, a composite terrace with two-, three- and four-storey sections; Nos. 3–6 were altered for the Glasgow Eye Informary by *Burnet, Tait & Lorne* in 1938.

On the N side of the street, SOMERSET PLACE, begun in 1840 by *John Baird I,* also has end and central pavilions, the one at the E end rebuilt *c.* 1962 by *Robert Bluck, Drummond Associates* in a timid style that is not facsimile nor even in character. The centre and W pavilions have Ionic-columned doorpieces. Beyond Clifton Street, *John Drummond & Partners'* CLIFTON HOUSE, 1968, bland four-storey and basement offices, occupies the whole street block as far as Claremont Street and replaces a terrace which continued the theme of Somerset Place. From here an excursion S down CLAREMONT STREET takes in, on the W side, the former Trinity Congregational Church (*see* Churches, above), now the Henry Wood Hall; and, at the end of the street, facing BERKELEY STREET, the extensive Woodside Secondary School (*see* Public Buildings).

We must continue now along the final boulevard section of Sauchiehall Street. On the N side, ROYAL CRESCENT by *Alexander Taylor,* 1839–49, its shallow curve and curious assemblage of applied detail (originally the centre was pedimented) resulting in a complex series of rhythms and an awkward composition. The final terrace on the S side of the street is FITZROY PLACE of 1847, an early work of *John Burnet Snr* on the site of the first Botanic Garden (instituted in 1817). It is of two storeys, with the end bays raised. Later alterations include the front door, and the stained-glass panel of No. 10, designed by *John Nisbet*. The brightly coloured peacock in a butterfly frame was immaculately executed by *Oscar Paterson, c.* 1905.

At this point Sauchiehall Street veers to the NW. Marking the SW corner, a handsome tenement block (Nos. 901–3, the Kelvin Park Lorne Hotel) by *Charles Wilson,* 1853, with considerable use of applied pilasters and a central Corinthian-columned portico. The adjoining C20 hotel extension takes no account of its polite neighbours but thrusts its crude concrete façade on to the street, which has not been improved by a glass conservatory (by *F. Timpson,* 1985), its curved shape reminiscent of a synthetic ice-cream. Next, a diversion N into

DERBY STREET to see the former Finnieston (or Kelvingrove) Parish Church (*see* Churches), converted to a recording studio. W of Derby Street, in BENTINCK STREET, Nos.
34–56, a striking tenement of *c.* 1880 in the manner of *James
Sellars,* cleverly articulated with alternate flat and full-height
canted bays. Gray Street leads back to Sauchiehall Street,
where, lining the W end, a series of decent but unexceptional
tenement blocks of the 1860s and 1870s (like Ardgowan
Terrace, Nos. 993–1037) continues unbroken on the S side
until the junction with Argyle Street; on the N side is the
Bowling Green (*see* Public Buildings: Kelvingrove Park).

From Sauchiehall Street the short SW stretch of Gray Street
continues to ARGYLE STREET, which is lined with plain
but handsome tenements dating from the 1840s to the 1880s.
Opposite the junction with Gray Street is the street's most
impressive example, the long four-storey FRANKLIN
TERRACE (Nos. 1185–1263), *c.* 1845, demolished above the
shops at the E end. Its length is counteracted by the shallow
stepping down of the blocks; and subtle variety in the detailing
of the first-floor windows prevents the equal heights of the
upper storeys from becoming monotonous. Just into Kelvinhaugh Street off the S side, appears the W front of the
Sandyford-Henderson Memorial Church (*see* Yorkhill, below:
Churches).

Further E along Argyle Street, two terraces on the S side, which
flank and return into CORUNNA STREET, announce the
extraordinarily grand piece of town planning centred on ST
VINCENT CRESCENT, a massively long and striking serpentine tenemented terrace by *Alexander Kirkland,* laid out in
1849 as part of a new suburb of Stobcross. Nos. 31–70 were
built in 1850, followed by the E ranges, completed by 1855.
The only gap is at No. 23, demolished in 1913 for the North
British and Caledonian Partick line. Originally an extensive
pleasure garden extended over two acres in front, but this
succumbed to the invasion of industry. A few minor variations
occur in different sections of the terrace, but the overall
impression is of a totally unified, classically detailed design,
with Doric-pilastered doorpieces or porches, emphasized first-
floor windows and a balustraded parapet. The terrace curves
into MINERVA STREET, built in two sections, the W part in
1858, the section joining Argyle Street, where it is proclaimed
by giant Corinthian columns framing the first and second
floors, in 1856. Opposite stood, until it was demolished, 35
another range by Kirkland, at Nos. 1–21 Minerva Street. Also
in Minerva Street, at No. 41 (and extending E to Finnieston
Street), the POSTAL AND ENGINEERING GARAGE, 1936,
and the former CRANSTONHILL LABOUR EXCHANGE,
1937–8, by *J. Wilson Paterson* – an unappealing concrete building with a coarse Gibbsian surround at the entrance, of the
type put up by Glasgow's *Office of Public Works* in many
suburbs.

Looking W along Argyle Street to Corunna Street, there are more restrained mid- and late C19 tenements. At Nos. 1067–73, the shabby former KELVIN CINEMA with its low, parasol-roofed octagonal turret, of 1929, by *A. V. Gardner*, reconstructed in 1935 by *Gardner & Glen*. E of Minerva Street the continuity of tenement building has been lost; a realignment of roads has severed Argyle Street at the point where it formerly joined St Vincent Street, leaving uncomfortable gaps. The few new buildings make no attempt to capitalize on these pivotal sites, a trick never missed in the C19.

4. S of Charing Cross: Finnieston and Anderston

In the early C19 Finnieston was a village, a retreat for Glasgow merchants. But even by 1805 industrialization was beginning; in that year Houldsworth's spinning mill in Cheapside Street attracted the attention of an Irish banker who recorded it in his diary. As the commercial development of the Clyde gathered momentum more industry appeared, at first engineering or allied works, followed by the storage and manufacture of foodstuffs. This development was combined with the building of tenements and a number of churches. From the mid-1960s, C19 industry and housing began to vanish as part of a comprehensive redevelopment scheme that incorporated the construction of the Clydeside Expressway and which stretched to the E into Anderston (*see* also Commercial Centre, Streets: Argyle Street). There are few C19 remnants: a large 1960s housing scheme and late C20 industrial premises cover most of the area.

First a lengthy excursion from Argyle Street (where our last perambulation ended) down FINNIESTON STREET, virtually denuded of its original industrial character. We pass the second phase of *Holmes & Partners'* large flatted factory development, the CLYDEWAY INDUSTRIAL CENTRE, completed *c.* 1969 and built of brick with jaunty pillarbox-red window-frames banding it. A trip further S involves a battle with the contortions imposed by road engineers, but will reveal the north ROTUNDA of the FINNIESTON or GLASGOW HARBOUR TUNNEL (*see* Crossings of the Clyde and Kelvin, below), whose twin can be clearly seen across the river in Govan. On the quay, the FINNIESTON CRANE, commissioned in 1926 and completed in 1931 for the Clyde Navigation Trust by *Cowans, Sheldon & Co.* of Carlisle. This 175-ton (178-tonne) giant cantilever quayside crane is a prominent and potent symbol of Glasgow's industrial past. It is surprising that the contract did not go to the local firm of Sir William Arrol, which had more experience in the field of giant cranes.

To the W, on the infilled Queen's Dock and the Dock's former pumping station, lies the Scottish Exhibition Centre (*see* Public Buildings, above). Back at the N end of Finnieston Street, turn into HOULDSWORTH STREET. On the N side is the MINERVA CENTRE, 1987–8, which incorporates in heavy disguise parts of David Carlaw's engineering works of 1897 (*Robert Brown*), 1905 (*Burnet, Boston & Carruthers*), and 1916 (a substantial ferro-concrete (*Hennebique*) range). A light-well has been carved through the 1905 section, and the whole, both new and old, is faced in neat buff brickwork. Triangular Meccano-like balconies, suspended from projecting dormerheads, hark back to industrial loading bays. On the s side of the street, at the junction with Elliot Street, No. 10 of 1870 was built for the former GLASGOW SAW AND FILE WORKS. Its arcaded polychrome brick façade was mirrored on the other side of Houldsworth Street until the E part of the Minerva Centre took its place. At No. 34 ELLIOT STREET, the brick-built former ANDERSTON BRASS WORKS, 1870–83, reconstructed as a paint works in 1914. Next, the boldly arched elevation of the former CRANSTONHILL IRON FOUNDRY, *c.* 1854 (No. 58). To the s, the rear of the flatted factory complex we saw in Finnieston Street.

At the NE end of Houldsworth Street is the start of the massive ANDERSTON HOUSING SCHEME, begun by the S.S.H.A. in 1965. A wall of multi-storey blocks of two-storey maisonettes, interrupted by lift towers, overlooks St Vincent Street. These reinforced concrete blocks faced with textured panels have heavily screened balcony access corridors, and rows of square, carefully balanced windows alternate to give a rhythmic pattern reminiscent of Rietveld's designs; unfortunately, constant repetition reduces the impact. s of St Vincent Street, lower flatted blocks and one large seventeen-storey block, with windows wrapped round the angles. Set back from Houldsworth Street, at the junction with ELDERSLIE STREET, is ELDERSLIE COURT by *Thomas Smith Associates* (Edinburgh), 1983, a low-rise, restless red-brick composition with varied heights and roof pitches. The Anderston Kelvingrove Church and community centre (*see* Churches) closes Elderslie Street, with the low red-brick box of the SALVATION ARMY HEADQUARTERS (SCOTLAND), by *Glynn & Duff*, 1972, to the r.

At this point Houldsworth Street joins the marooned section of ARGYLE STREET, with, on the N side, the former Anderston Cross branch of the GLASGOW SAVINGS BANK, 1899–1900, by *James Salmon Jun. & J. Gaff Gillespie*, with sculpture by *Albert Hodge*. This strikingly individual design originally occupied a prominent corner but has been left stranded by the comprehensive redevelopment, which has removed all its complementary neighbours. The favourite Glasgow method of turning a corner with a turret has been ingeniously adapted. The composition of the dramatic corbelled angle combines elements of Leiper's Sun Life Building (*q.v.*) with the sinuous Art Nouveau of the Glasgow Style, seen especially in the flower-like dome, and exploits Albert Hodge's sculpture to the full. Above the doorway is a bust of Henry Duncan, founder of the Savings Bank movement, shown tapping his left forefinger against his forehead and clutching his moneybag in his r. hand. Hodge's medieval men and maidens round the doorway, with its gleaming mosaic-clad domes, and his fine chimneypiece 81 inside are some of the finest examples of architectural sculpture in the city. The combination of Corennie granite and red Dumfries-shire sandstone, the variety of the window shapes and mouldings (the groups of slots high up in the turret being particularly unusual), and the richness of the surface ornament make this building a major example of Glasgow's particular type of Art Nouveau. E of the bank, the C19 pattern of streets is sucked into the complex of roads feeding Kingston Bridge. N of Argyle Street, in the shadow of the bridge, is St Patrick's R.C. Church (*see* Churches, above) and associated school.

A pause at St Vincent Street on the route N from here brings into view both public and private housing. On the S side, the wall of the Anderston Housing Scheme (*see* above). On the N side, a speculative tenement development by *Barratt*, 1985–7, with crisp semicircular oriels and round-arched dormers. They are now related to the former Wylie & Lochead cabinet works by *James Sellars*, begun in 1879 and converted to flats as part of the Barratt scheme; to KENT ROAD, a tall elevation with large lunettes along the top floor. Opposite, on the N of Kent Road, the Mitchell Theatre and Library (*see* Public Buildings, above), and, to the W, the former St Vincent Church (*see* Churches). Opposite the church, Nos. 48–88 (formerly Walworth Terrace), a long terrace of 1858–60 and significant for the early introduction of paired oriels punctuating the elevation. Then on the NW corner of Kent Road and Elderslie Street, *James Sellars'* former stables and workshops for John Wylie, 1870–3, their large but squat corner pavilions with strong echoes of Palladio. From here we can return N via Elderslie Street to Sauchiehall Street, where the last perambulation started.

YORKHILL

The hospitals clustered on Yorkhill are prominent in the view from the river. The first hospital (since replaced) was built in 1916 on the site of the mansion of Yorkhill, erected about a century before on a parcel of the lands of Overnewton, which lay between Kelvinhaugh and the old road to Dumbarton. In 1813 Andrew Gilbert bought the house, its grounds and some adjoining land and called the whole estate Yorkhill. What little remained of the Overnewton lands was built over with tenements between the late 1860s and 1900. This development was stimulated by the westerly spread of the city and by the growth of the riverside Kelvinhaugh, already an established industrial settlement, with smithy, boat-building yards and a cotton mill which had opened in the early 1840s. The Yorkhill Quay was constructed after 1868, and tenements and industry then spread along the riverside. Most was swept away when the Clydeside Expressway split the neighbourhood apart in the early 1970s.

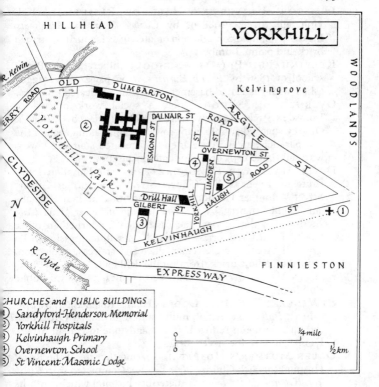

CHURCH AND PUBLIC BUILDINGS

SANDYFORD-HENDERSON MEMORIAL CHURCH (formerly the Sandyford Church) 13 Kelvinhaugh Street. Begun in 1854 to the designs of *J. T. Emmett*, but completed in 1856 by *John Honeyman*. The Geometrical tracery and E.E. doorways, shafted and with stiffleaf capitals and lots of dogtooth, are no doubt signs of Emmett's superior archaeological accuracy. The ashlar, though painted, is of the same high standard as his former Independent Chapel in Bath Street. Inside, a broad nave and aisles divided by arcades on quatrefoil piers, but just a flat beamed ceiling. Later chancel. – STAINED GLASS. In every aisle window, contemporary glass by *Ballantine & Allan*, 1857, with dense Gothic Revival geometric and floral patterns in deep colours. – Chancel window adapted for its new position by *W. & J. Kier*, 1866. – N gable windows with the Raising of Lazarus and SS. Peter and Paul by *William Wailes*, 1859. Altogether, an interesting demonstration of the tentative use of stained glass, of figurative subjects, and of memorial windows (see the early one to A. R. MacDuff † 1857), instigated by the artistically enlightened minister, the Rev. J. R. MacDuff.

GLASGOW UNIVERSITY HALL OF RESIDENCE, Kelvinhaugh Street. 1988–9, by *Cooper Cronmar Architects*. Pleasantly simple combination of late 1980s favourites; striped brick and painted timber.

KELVINHAUGH PRIMARY SCHOOL, Gilbert Street. Board school of 1886 by *Frank Burnet*. A big palazzo in stugged ashlar with rusticated basement and wide rusticated pilasters.

OVERNEWTON SCHOOL (now a social work office), 50 Lumsden Street. An early Board school of 1876–7 by *J. Burnet*. Of grey snecked rubble, with rows of gables along each of the two parallel ranges. At each end, castellated staircase towers with tall slated caps of Continental inspiration.

DRILL HALL AND HEADQUARTERS (15th Battalion Parachute Regiment T.A.), Gilbert Street. The former Gilbert Street Volunteer Headquarters of the 6th Battalion of Highland Light Infantry, by *William McNab* of *Leiper & McNab*, 1900–1. On the corner, the castellated Tudorbethan office block of hard red brick with red sandstone dressings. To Yorkhill Street, a big circular office and staircase projection, striped in yellow brick, fronting the drill hall.

KELVIN HALL. *See* Woodlands and Finnieston, above: Public Buildings.

ST VINCENT MASONIC LODGE, Haugh Road. 1904, by *Sinclair & Ballantine*. A tall, muted and unorthodox Edwardian Baroque façade in red rock-faced sandstone to Haugh Street. Domed apse to the street corner.

QUEEN MOTHER'S HOSPITAL, sharing the site of the Royal Hospital for Sick Children (*see* below). Completed in 1964 by *J. L. Gleave & Partners*. A maternity hospital which, with its greater range of materials and stylistic motifs and its more fragmented plan, is clearly earlier than its sleeker neighbour.

ROYAL HOSPITAL FOR SICK CHILDREN, Dalnair Street. 1968–71, by *Baxter, Clark & Paul*. A forbidding slab with large blank areas of blue-black engineering brick contrasting with bands of pinky-bronze glazing and white mosaic cladding. Long low yellow brick outpatients' wing.

YORKHILL BASIN, Ferry Road. A large rectangular basin at the end of Yorkhill Quays, built *c.* 1907 for the Clyde Navigation Trust and lined with long single-storey transit sheds, now quite a rare sight in Glasgow. The adjoining wharf was authorized in 1868.

DESCRIPTION

The tenements of Overnewton survive and have been rehabilitated (1980–8). This homogeneous group of simple flat-fronted cream sandstone tenements, with straight cornices on consoles over the first-floor windows, is centred on OLD DUMBARTON ROAD with its row of shops. They date from the late 1860s to the 1880s. To the S, some of them face OVERNEWTON SQUARE, one of the first three squares to be laid out with

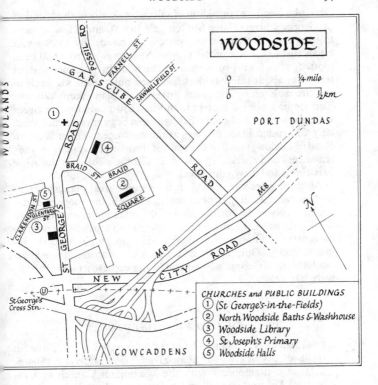

WOODSIDE

0   ¼ mile
0   ½ km

PORT DUNDAS

CHURCHES and PUBLIC BUILDINGS
① (St George's-in-the-Fields)
② North Woodside Baths & Washhouse
③ Woodside Library
④ St Joseph's Primary
⑤ Woodside Halls

walks and shrubs by the City Improvement Trust in 1866 (cf.
Cathedral Square, the only other to survive).
Just W of it, in LUMSDEN STREET, the former Overnewton
School (*see* Public Buildings, above) and the former halls and
church house of the Henderson Memorial Church (1878, by
John Burnet), which was burnt down in 1938. Further W still,
on the slopes round the hospitals in DALNAIR STREET,
ESMOND STREET etc., larger and later red sandstone ten-
ements designed by *Burnet, Boston & Carruthers* for the Over-
newton Building Company, 1906–9.

WOODSIDE

Woodside, nudged by the road network to its S, lacks personality,
and from its medley of buildings it is hard to guess that two
major attempts have been made to plan it. The first grandiose
plans for it were made in the late 1830s. Some building had
been done in the late 1820s along the road to Strathblane (now

Garscube Road): a sprinkling of villas, especially at the N end of St George's Street (later St George's Road), and a few terraces to its E along Kelvin Street (since obliterated). By 1838 a vast circus just to the NW of the present St George's Cross had been plotted, plus a grid of streets to the N of it, but only a short terrace of about thirty houses had been built at the SW angle of the circus. Even by the 1860s little of this plan except Windsor Terrace had been completed, and in 1879 plans for the circus were abandoned and even what had been begun was demolished; only Clarendon Place survives at the entrance to Great Western Road (*see* below) to tell of the scale of the plan. Instead, by *c.* 1865 tenements had sprung up SW of St George's Road in the angle between it and New City Road.

All these were swept away in the second great plan, the comprehensive redevelopment of the area during the 1960s and 70s, which involved the construction of the huge motorway junction. Woodside was the last Comprehensive Development Area to be designated in Glasgow (in 1964), and its housing reflects changing attitudes. Only a few C19 and early C20 buildings (particularly in St George's Road and in the earliest streets SW of it) were left intact.

CHURCH AND PUBLIC BUILDINGS

ST GEORGE'S-IN-THE-FIELDS (converted to housing in 1988–9) 485 St George's Road. By *H. & D. Barclay*, 1885–6. Almost contemporary with the Wellington Church in University Avenue (*see* Hillhead, below: Churches), but much less pure in its use of the Greek temple form. Nevertheless it is very grand. The body of the church is both wider and higher than the hexastyle Ionic portico: the gable-end forms almost a second pediment behind the first, its Thomsonesque decoration conflicting with the extremely naturalistic High Victorian sculpture in the portico's tympanum (Christ Distributing the Loaves and Fishes, by *William Birnie Rhind*).

WOODSIDE HALLS, 36 Glenfarg Street. Opened in 1925. Of the Wrenaissance type, in hard red brick with stone dressings, designed by the Corporation's *Office of Public Works* at that time. Modified internally in 1964.

NORTH WOODSIDE BATHS AND WASHHOUSE, Braid Square. 1880–2, by *John Carrick* (City Architect). A long two-storey building with simple classical detailing, set across the middle of Braid Square.

WOODSIDE LIBRARY, 343 St George's Road. 1902–5. *J. R. Rhind*'s grandest and most classical branch library, its entrance marked by a big segmental pediment and, on the skyline, a sculptured group of a woman reading to her children. Fluted Ionic columns flank the doorway in pairs and form a colonnade screening the windows along the rest of the flat façade.

ST JOSEPH'S PRIMARY SCHOOL, 39 Raglan Street. 1975, by the City of Glasgow's *Department of Architecture and Civic*

Design. A neat red-brown brick cube with a glazed central bay revealing the staircase, and a curtain wall along one side.

ST GEORGE'S CROSS MOTORWAY INTERCHANGE. Early 1970s. An impressive piece of engineering by *Scott, Wilson, Kilpatrick & Co.*, with *W. A. Fairhurst & Partners*. The thick planting and other landscaping were designed by *William Holford & Associates*. There are some Piranesian effects as the road flies over New City Road and the pedestrian underpass.

PERAMBULATION

ST GEORGE'S CROSS is a broad and formless road junction, flanked by the swooping and thickly planted carriageways of the inner ring road's western interchange (*see* above, and Great Western Road, below: Perambulation 1). CLARENDON PLACE of the late 1830s, with its monumental portico raised above a podium of shops, heralds the entrance to Great Western Road (*see* below). It is the only relic of the great circus planned here in the 1830s, contemporary with the similar Queen's Crescent (*see* Woodlands and Finnieston, above: Perambulation 2), whose long curved back is exposed to the S. On the SE side of the Cross, red brick flats of the mid-1980s by *Barratt*'s own architects, their canted bay windows weakly playing on the tenement theme.

ST GEORGE'S ROAD is a quiet backwater between two main roads. On the W side was the decaying Second Empire-style façade of the former METROPOLE THEATRE of 1910 by *W. B. Whitie*, with a neo-Baroque interior (all, sadly, demolished in 1989). Past Woodside Library (*see* Public Buildings, above), a solitary remaining villa (Nos. 361–5) of the 1830s, with a Greek Doric colonnade supporting a cast-iron balcony under pedimented first-floor windows. Due W, the grid of streets laid out in the 1830s still exists, though the buildings are of later dates, e.g. Woodside Halls (*see* Public Buildings) and, in CLARENDON STREET at No. 37, the very tall reinforced-concrete CITY BAKERY, 1924–8, with Baroque embellishments on its red brick face.

A broad band of housing, stretching from just N of here S to the M8, has been completely rebuilt. The architects were *Boswell, Mitchell & Johnston*. Belonging to the first phase of this comprehensive redevelopment, the three aggregate-clad slab blocks (1964–6), their end walls reclad by the *District Council's Architect's Department*, *c.* 1984, in stripes of red and blue that sing out across the city. Below them, along North Woodside Road, along St George's Road, and linked by bridges round the pre-existing Braid Square, deck-access blocks of five to eight storeys (1970–4), heavily modelled in pink brick in a pioneering attempt to return to the colour and some of the forms (e.g. the oriel windows) of the turn-of-the-century tenement. Between Braid Square and St George's Road, a retreat to low-rise by the S.S.H.A. Nothing of C19 Glasgow about the folksy pitched pantiled roofs, diagonal timbering and fenced gardens.

In POSSIL ROAD to the E, little of interest. At the N end, on the corner of Farnell Street, TOWER BUILDINGS (Nos. 2–14) of 1875, with a noticeable corner tower crowned in cast-iron. Just to the E in SAWMILLFIELD STREET, the former Corporation CLEANSING DEPARTMENT DEPOT of 1899 by *A. W. Wheatley* (engineer). Red and white brick with a Greek key pattern. Behind it loom the warehouses of North Spiers Wharf (*see* Port Dundas, below) high up by the canal.

GREAT WESTERN ROAD

Great Western Road was formed as a result of an Act of Parliament passed in 1836 authorizing the making and maintenance of a turnpike road from St George's Cross to Anniesland Toll. The road was to provide a new route into the city; it was also a response to the relentless pressure to develop residential suburbs W of Blythswood, away from the industry to the S and E and from the overcrowded city centre. It forged its way in a straight line NW through the estates of Woodlands, Hillhead and Kelvinside, drawn as though by magnetism towards the West Highland hills. So powerful is the linear attraction that our perambulation, divided into two sections, follows the road without deviation.

Great Western Road was never conceived as a formal setpiece and yet, beyond the first section, with tenements of urban character mainly built up to the line of street, it becomes one of the grandest suburban boulevards in Britain. Despite the fact that it passes across the estates of a number of landowners who never adopted an overall plan, there is a remarkable uniformity of design. With the high-level bridging of the Kelvin in 1840, the way was open to development even further W, encouraged by the transfer of the Botanic Gardens from the W end of Sauchiehall Street to S of the Kelvin at Hillhead (*see* Public Buildings, below).

CHURCHES

LANSDOWNE PARISH CHURCH, 416–20 Great Western Road. The most striking Gothic Revival church in Glasgow: designed by *John Honeyman* and built for the United Presbyterians in 1862–3, with fine carved stonework by *John Mossman*. E.E., but an individual conception, with a bold rhythm of tall lancets raised above the narrow aisle of the fourbay nave, stepped around the elaborately detailed W porch, and grouped as triple lights over the blind arcade of the S transept. The strongly articulated W front is prominently raised above the E bank of the River Kelvin. Cruciform plan, with an apsidal chancel tucked behind the tower and spire. The steeple is the *tour de force*, inspired more by early French

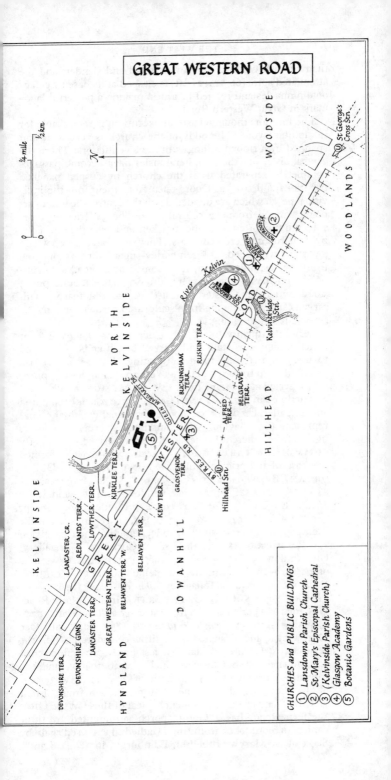

than English Gothic. The tower is tall and slender, and the attenuated spire (66·5 m; 218 ft) is clasped at its base by octagonal pinnacles and refined lucarnes, making a powerful landmark in Great Western Road.

The interior, though chaste in execution, is remarkable for its unique layout. The body of the church is very wide and spanned by a ribbed ceiling with huge ventilators. There is a central aisle, but the peripheral aisles have become passages completely separated from the church by cusped panelled partitions and coving. Doors open from them into the individual pews, which are divided down the centre, the inner part being entered from the central aisle. The galleries on three sides are supported by timber brackets and, over the transepts, by cast-iron clustered columns. They are reached by s w and N W stairs with good cast-iron barley-sugar balusters, opening from the vestibule. The apse is framed by a broad arch supported on massive stone piers (the original elaborate pulpit stood under it). Clustered wall-shafts of red marble with carved capitals springing from sculptured corbels carrying the rib-vaulted apse ceiling.

Very high-quality PEWS, the elders' seats along the front bench designed as stalls with carved bench ends. – Panelled PULPIT of 1910 and fixed oak seating. The decorative oak panelling with traceried detail like embryo canopies was probably inserted at the same time. – WAR MEMORIAL designed and sculpted in 1923 by *Evelyn Beale*. Three panels of coloured and gilded relief work set above the panelling in the apse represent the Saviour with outstretched arms welcoming figures from different branches of the war service. – The hefty COMMUNION TABLE of 1910 in a variety of marbles formed the base of the original pulpit. – FONT from 1910. Dull. – ORGAN. By *Norman & Beard*, 1911. In a carved case. – STAINED GLASS. Three apse windows and w window by *Henry Hughes* of *Ward & Hughes*, London. – Transept windows by *Alfred Webster*, 1913, excellent jewel-like examples of this artist's varied style, depicting the Crucifixion and Resurrection (s) and the Life of Christ (N). – N gallery. One window by *Gordon Webster*, 1966, and an adjacent window of *c.* 1929. – In the vestibule, a medallion portrait of Rev. John Eadie set in Ruskinian foliage by *John Mossman*, 1876.

ST MARY'S EPISCOPAL CATHEDRAL, Great Western Road. Designed as a parish church by *Sir George Gilbert Scott,* 1871–4, with a spire by *John Oldrid Scott*, 1893. E.E. with Dec borrowings, and designed with little consideration for the restricted street site. In plan it is less tautly constrained than Lansdowne Parish Church, which lies to the w, and the robustly overscaled tower has none of the soaring verticality of that near neighbour. The w front, hidden from distant view by a late classical tenement typical of those in the Great Western Road, has a Gothic porch surmounted by three gablets (a motif taken from Elgin Cathedral and used again by Scott at St Mary's Cathedral, Edinburgh, in 1874). Lancet windows, four at the W end and three at the E, are set in the gables with vesicas at the apex. Above the buttressed aisles rises the clearstorey, lit by cusped circular windows linked under a blind arcade, a pattern that Scott had used before at All Saints, Sherbourne, Warwickshire, in 1862–4. The massive buttressed tower, positioned between the S transept and the chancel, is correctly detailed at each stage, with saints in niches set into the buttresses and bold diapered masonry in the spandrels of the topmost stage, a model repeated from All Souls, Haley Hill but which ultimately derives from Lincoln Cathedral. The tiny bartizans at the angles of the parapet are left stranded as John Oldrid Scott's altogether more swanky spire soars away from them; only the unusual angle lucarnes seem to acknowledge their existence.

The interior is grand though predictable and uninspired. The tall nave is divided from the aisles by five-bay arcades, and the open timber roof springs from corbelled colonnettes attached above the spandrels of the arcade. Wide chancel arch and delicate wrought-iron chancel screen of 1894. In the N chancel aisle, ST ANNE'S CHAPEL, with a triptych by Miss *Hale*, 1902, showing the Deposition and with flanking panels all copied from works in the National Gallery, London, over the plain marble altar. The chapel is separated from the chancel by an oak screen, and from the aisle by a wrought-iron one. – REREDOS by *Sir Robert Lorimer*, replacing the original one by *Farmer & Brindley* (now on the N aisle of the nave and rather good). Familiar vine carving to the frames and central canopy. It houses a triptych by *Phoebe Traquair* depicting scenes from the life of the Virgin; the centrepiece is a particularly striking composition of the three Marys at the Tomb. – The octagonal ashlar PULPIT, of Caen stone on a granite pedestal with polished granite colonnettes, and the FONT, also octagonal on colonnettes, were designed by *G. G. Scott* and executed by *John Mossman*. Over the font, a very elaborate carved oak cover on a counterbalance. – STAINED GLASS. An extensive series including an E window by *Clayton & Bell* (centre light, 1871: the Ascension; side lights, 1872: the Nativity and the Resurrection). – N and S chancel windows by *Ward & Hughes*, 1872, although the upper part of the S window looks later. – S and N transepts by *Ward & Hughes*, 1873 and 1875. – Six handsome nave windows depicting the call of the Apostles by *Hardman*, 1872 and 1876. – Four-light W window by *Clayton & Bell*, 1877 (Christ commissioning the Apostles). – W aisle windows by *Ward & Hughes*, 1877. – MEMORIAL BRASSES. Chancel S wall. Panel to Edward Kempe Oldham † 1873, executed by *Lavers, Barraud and Westlake*. – Chancel floor, Bishop Archibald Ian Campbell, a medieval-style canopied brass.

Former KELVINSIDE PARISH CHURCH (now Bible Training Institute), 731–5 Great Western Road. A bold Geometric church on a constricted site, designed by *J.J. Stevenson* of *Campbell Douglas & Stevenson* in 1862, and altered in 1886 with the installation of the organ recess. Further additions of 1929 by *Jeffrey Waddell*. The tall campanile tower with its pyramidal spire (which had lucarnes until *c*. 1965) marks the transition of Great Western Road into a true boulevard. (It is built over old coal workings, and the foundations consist of iron columns slipped through bores in the rock to the bottom of the old coal waste.) The tower projects from the N W angle, and anchors the subtly articulated w elevation. The unusual apsed w end continues the full height of the nave, with the porch raised up in the centre, and owes something to Charles Wilson's beautiful unexecuted classical scheme. All the restrained Geometric motifs, including diminutive blind arcades and pastry-cutter rose windows, distributed throughout the church, are united in this elevation. The interior has Italian Gothic arcades with cast-iron columns, now floored over at gallery level. – Relief MEMORIAL by *A. Macfarlane Shannon*. – Two busts, one of John Campbell, Lord Overtoun, the other of Margaret Somerville; 1898, by *Derwent Wood*. – To the E of the church, a low office range posing as a transept but domestically dressed.

PUBLIC BUILDINGS

GLASGOW ACADEMY, Colebrooke Street. By *H. & D. Barclay*, 1878, an upmarket version of their handsome classical Board school designs, here using Greek detail. It is a solidly reassuring square block set back from Great Western Road and raised above it on a podium in a self-confident manner. Of polished yellow sandstone, with wide channelled pilasters marking the end bays and defining the angles of the five shallow advanced central bays of each elevation. On the main elevations, central hexastyle Ionic colonnades in front of recessed first-floor windows. Greater drama is given to the w elevation by the wide flight of steps ascending to the massive pedimented doorpiece set in boldly ramped architraves. The windows are unified by similar architraves. The grand effect of the heavy bracketed cornice has unfortunately been reduced by the insertion of flat-roofed dormers. Inside, an imposing central assembly hall rising from the basement to the upper floor (now used as a library). At ground-floor level, an excellent cast-iron balustrade, a fine vestibule screen with etched glass, and a doorpiece with ramped architrave and stylized scrolled pediment. – WAR MEMORIAL set into the boundary wall on the corner of Colebrooke Street and Great Western Road. By *A. N. Paterson*, 1924. A memorial plaque flanked by ashlar piers with wreathed dates commemorates the school's foundation in 1848 (in Elmbank Street; *see* Commercial Centre) and its reconstitution in 1923.

To the N, a two-storey pedimented building of 1903, also by *H. & D. Barclay*, built as laboratories and art room. The unconventional triple-light first-floor window has the ring of Post-Modernism before its time. To the N again, the CEN-

TENARY MEMORIAL BUILDING of 1946, a low brick building with large collegiate Tudor mullioned-and-transomed
windows to light a stripped classical assembly-hall-cum-
theatre. Opposite, on the W side of Colebrooke Street, a two-
storey terrace with canted windows of *c.* 1870, converted to
school use.

BOTANIC GARDENS, 703 Great Western Road. Moved from
the W end of Sauchiehall Street in 1839–42, in the search for
purer air, to a 25-acre (10-ha) site N of Great Western Road,
where they were an added lure to the developers of the high-
class residential West End estates. The gardens remained a
private institution until 1891. Entered at the corner of Great
Western Road and Queen Margaret Drive through handsome
wrought-iron gates, past half-timbered lodges, all by *A. B.
McDonald* (City Architect), 1894. The gardens' great ornament is the KIBBLE PALACE, a dramatic giant glass mush-
room, probably the work of *Boucher & Cousland* (Cousland is
known to have made a wire model), the architects for John
Kibble's Coulport House, Loch Long, for which the conservatory was originally designed in 1863–6. In 1871 Kibble
offered it to Glasgow Corporation to be re-erected as a palace
of art and concert hall in Queen's Park. In 1873 it was
reassembled here instead, the central dome (under which there
was a sunken orchestra pit) was enlarged to 146 ft (44 m) diameter, and a large entrance foyer with nave, transepts and a
central crossing dome was added. As first built, it was supported on twelve twisted cast-iron columns; when it was re-
erected twenty-four more were added which, together with
leafy cast-iron brackets, support the spreading circle and gentle 44
dome. It is still used as a conservatory, quintessentially Victorian, with lush plants and the erotic sculpture (by *Hamo
Thornycroft, Goscombe John* and others) that the Victorians
excused as art. – CURATOR'S HOUSE, by *Charles Wilson*,
1840, a restrained, mildly Italianate villa. – Extensive GLASS
HOUSES of 1883 using cast-iron, cedar and glass to produce a
long range with end and central pavilions. The gardens were
extended in 1892–3, when the elegant cast-iron balustraded,
plate girder footbridge was thrown across the Kelvin to bring
the wooded N bank into the gardens. Further extended in 1900
at the Kirklee (w) end.

GREAT WESTERN BRIDGE. *See* Crossings of the Clyde and
Kelvin, below.

PERAMBULATIONS

1. St George's Cross to Byres Road and Queen Margaret Drive

The start is not promising. The St George's Cross motorway
slipway slides off its elevated section, reaching ground level
some 20 yards or 18 metres W of what was the Great Western
Road's original beginning, leaving shipwrecked the dramatic

remnant of CLARENDON PLACE (*see* Woodside, above). This was conceived as part of a grand unified scheme to mark the junction of Great Western Road, New City Road and St George's Road, but the scheme was abandoned, leaving Clarendon Place as a lone trumpet instead of part of a triumphant fanfare. A late C 19 figure group of St George and the Dragon, donated to Glasgow by the Co-Operative Wholesale Society, was resited in front of Clarendon Place in 1988.

Once past this junction, and the classically detailed w pavilion at the entrance to Queen's Crescent on the s side (*see* Woodlands and Finnieston, above: Perambulation 2), Great Western Road makes a somewhat pedestrian beginning. Development was very slow in starting; apart from terraces in Burnbank Gardens just to the N (*see* North Kelvinside, below: Description), in Holyrood Crescent and in Lansdowne Creascent (*see* below), nothing was built E of the Kelvin until the early 1870s, despite the flourishing development w of the river. Then, during the 1870s and 1880s, between Cromwell Street and Melrose Street at the E end and North and South Woodside Streets at the w end, the street was lined with traditional four-storey tenements, the earlier ones in yellow sandstone, the later ones in red Ayrshire or Dumfries-shire sandstone. Some of these tenements have shops at the ground-floor level and all have simple architraves to the upper windows. Further w, a glance down Rupert Street on the s side, gives a glimpse of Woodlands Hill and the Gothic pinnacled tower of Park Church, commanding the brow (*see* Woodlands and Finnieston, above: Perambulation 1). The serried ranks of tenements are interrupted only by two tall spires, both striking landmarks on the N side of the street: first that of St Mary's Cathedral and then, more piercing in outline, that of the Lansdowne Church (*see* Churches, above). The straight line of tenements is broken on this side by HOLYROOD CRESCENT, a curving terrace of *c*. 1860, and again by LANSDOWNE CRESCENT, not a crescent at all but a cul-de-sac shaped like a hockey stick, with, on its E side, a curving, two-storey terrace of *c*. 1852 hooked round to the NW and interrupted by three-storey pavilions. It has wide basement areas and oversailing steps to the main doors, which have either cornices on consoles or ramped architraves, and to the close doors with Roman Doric pilasters. At No. 2, the lower sashes on the ground floor have textured and coloured glass panels inset with Glasgow Style floral designs and lettered '*J McDonald BDS Dental Surgeon*'. The two pavilions flanking the entrance to North Woodside Road are of *c*. 1875. On the w side, the terrace is of *c*. 1855–6, with subtly varied details including tripartite first-floor windows. Back in Great Western Road, Lansdowne Church stands guardian over the Kelvin gorge.

The road now crosses the impressive GREAT WESTERN BRIDGE (*see* Crossings of the Clyde and Kelvin, below). On the far w side of the bridge, set back and raised up on the N side is Glasgow Academy (*see* Public Buildings, above).

Opposite it, at Nos. 445–59, is CALEDONIAN MANSIONS, designed in 1895 by *James Miller* in a delightfully playful manner. This set of commercial and residential chambers was originally associated with Kelvinbridge Station (demolished), which, like the mansions, was designed by Miller for the Caledonian Railway Company. The street block bears no resemblance to traditional Glasgow tenements, but has its origin in the Arts and Crafts movement and imaginatively combines traditional Scottish details into a self-consciously asymmetrical composition. At the angles, tourelles corbelled out at first-floor level with broad ogee domes and finials. Between them, a façade full of surprises, breaking forward and back with a restless variety of window designs, oriels and dormers among them. This originality extends to all the façades: at the rear, the first-floor access balcony adds particular verve.

Further W on this side, the single-storey HILLHEAD SAVINGS BANK (No. 471, on the W side of Otago Street) by *Eric Sutherland*, 1940–2, is a disturbing hiccup in a district where corners are usually given more forceful treatment. However, it retains its etched glass panels and Art Deco lamp-standards, and the banking hall is almost intact. Opposite, on the N side, uncharted mineworkings have caused the demise of several tenements and put others at risk. Only one building deserves comment – the Art Deco Nos. 508–10, now a pub but designed in 1929 by *James Lindsay* as a high-class baker's shop and restaurant for the Hillhead baker Walter Hubbard. It was probably the first building in this neighbourhood whose height was dictated by the uncertain nature of the subsoil, and defies the general scale of the area with its two low storeys. It is, roguishly, faced in glazed terracotta with linear Deco designs in the glazing and in the railings of the rooftop balcony. On the S side, at the W corner with Bank Street, one of the most striking (though distinctly odd) landmarks of Great Western Road, at No. 499, the former COOPER'S BUILDING by *R. Duncan*, 1886. The culmination of its flamboyant French Renaissance façade is the clock tower, with the entrance at its base. Above the main eaves, unlikely architectural motifs are united in an exciting confection of exaggerated round-arched and pedimented windows, clock faces set in panels with linking swags at cornice level, a cast-iron balcony, classically detailed lucarnes set into a truncated conical roof with fish-scale tiles and a crowning cupola strongly reminiscent of a stone Coca Cola bottle. At Nos. 519–29, a terrace of *c.* 1885 by *James Thomson* in the manner of his namesake Alexander Thomson; on the corner with Oakfield Avenue, another tenement of *c.* 1885 in the same Thomsonesque idiom.

At the point where Great Western Road is crossed by Oakfield Avenue and Hamilton Park Avenue, its character changes. Here, urban buildings right on the street front give way to a spacious and altogether more opulent layout of terraces. These are set back, with their own service roads and narrow communal gardens: in the summer, their trees make it impossible to appreciate the composition of the terraces. At the E end, these gardens are little more than ribbons of trees. An extraordinary unanimity among the landowners led to conditions being embodied in the feu charters which dictated the consistent appearance of this residential development. Much of the W reaches of Great Western Road crossed the Kelvinside Estate, which was acquired in 1840 by Matthew Montgomerie, John Park Fleming and J. B. Neilson, who formed the Kelvinside Estate Company. Montgomerie resolved to make the suburb the best residential district of the city, and, to this end, *Decimus Burton* was appointed estate architect. Burton's credentials for devising superior residential developments were impeccable; he had worked with Nash in Regent's Park, London, and his own designs included the Calverley Estate at Tunbridge Wells. He envisaged terraces lining the road, with villas spaciously dispersed in sylvan glades behind. This scheme, although forming the basis of the present layout, was too profligate with land and was revised and extended in 1859 by *James Salmon*. Among the terraces in Great Western Road, four are architecturally outstanding: the E part of Buckingham Terrace, Grosvenor Terrace, Kirklee Terrace and Great Western Terrace.

W of Hamilton Park Avenue, we come first (though neither of them was among the first terraces to be built) to Belgrave Terrace on the S side and Ruskin Terrace on the N, both set quite high above the road. BELGRAVE TERRACE, 1856, by *Thomas Gildard & R. H. M. Macfarlane*, is composed of a long, two-storey central section over a basement with three-storey end pavilions, Italianate in spirit. The third storey is a bold attic with arched windows paired in the outer bays; the eaves, broader than along the two-storey section, are capped with diminutive antefixae. Much of the ironwork and the pierced balustrade over the two-storey range are missing. Facing Belgrave Terrace on the N side, the longer but less consistent RUSKIN TERRACE (formerly St James Terrace), *c.* 1855–8. The segmental pediments at the E end bear comparison with the first-floor windows of the Bank of Scotland in George Square (*see* Merchant City, above: Streets) of 1867–70 and so suggest the authorship of *J. T. Rochead*, but there are also distinct hallmarks of *Charles Wilson*'s style, particularly in the treatment of the masonry. As executed, the terrace is in two differing halves, the E section more sophisticated in detail, the W part longer, plainer and a storey lower, except for the W pavilion. The reason for what appears to have been a change of plan is not obvious, but overstretched finances and a glut of terraced property in the West End could account for the reduction in quality. The original intention seems to have been a unified composition of fifty-two bays, with perhaps three six-bay blocks at the centre, creating something of the effect achieved later at Great Western Terrace (*see* Perambulation 2, below). The part built forms a near symmetrical unit with end pavilions. The E pavilion's bookend position is reinforced by the fall in the land, which makes its E elevation a full four storeys, with a grandiose balustraded perron. The W pavilion of this grander section repeats the same details except for an additional bay and the double central doors. The subtly balanced range between them is of three storeys, with paired pedimented windows above the pillared porches. The whole of this E section of the terrace is unified by the channelled masonry treatment of the ground floor and by the stylized Ionic pilasters which divide each bay. The pilasters themselves are composed of unusually rusticated ashlar blocks. The W section of the terrace is relatively commonplace, with simple Corinthian pilasters at the doorpieces.

Next to the W, BUCKINGHAM TERRACE is also in two indi- 52 vidual parts. As at Ruskin Terrace, the W range (1858) is plainer than the E (1852). Both are by *J. T. Rochead*. The E block is an exceptionally long terrace, with no central emphasis but with a strongly horizontal ground floor forming the plinth from which the shallow first-floor balcony projects. The design of the first floor is full of imagination, using that much-favoured Glasgow feature, the canted bay window. Here each one (which forms the central window of a three-windowed drawing room) is very shallow and is linked to the next by handsome cast-iron work. The tall, narrow proportions of the first-floor windows, the pitch of the roofs and the relentless march of chimneystacks are all carefully modulated to give punch to the perspective view. The W half of the terrace has none of the subtlety of the E part: canted bays appear at the centre but rise from basement to first floor. The end pavilions, very similar to those of Belgrave Terrace, incorporate large triple-light windows. Even the simply canted gushet at the W end gives no hint of the ingenious ways Glasgow architects often found to turn corners.

Opposite the E part of Buckingham Terrace stands the much mutilated ALFRED TERRACE, built *c.* 1870 and originally raised up above the street in the manner of Great Western Terrace (*see* below), with a carriage drive and terrace in front. It was substantially altered by *John Burnet, Son & Campbell* in 1892, when the carriageway was removed and the raised terrace was built instead, with shops below it. The dull bay-windowed houses are set well back behind a much-depleted Granolithic balustrade, and their front steps, instead of rising from the pavement, are truncated by the higher level of the later terrace. At the SE corner with Byres Road, the Bible Training Institute, formerly Kelvinside Parish Church (*see* Churches, above).

2. W *from Byres Road and Queen Margaret Drive*

At the junction with Byres Road and Queen Margaret Drive, Great Western Road becomes a handsome tree-lined boulevard. The Botanic Gardens (*see* Public Buildings, above), laid out in 1840, must have underlined the benefits of pure air and fine views, always attractive to the potential West End resident. Kirklee Terrace was the first terrace to be planned, originally as a near, though not immediate, neighbour of the then smaller Gardens.

To begin with, the terraces are only on the s side, facing the Botanic Gardens. First on this side, GROSVENOR TERRACE, 1855, the most surprising of all the terraces, one of the city's great architectural set-pieces, and *J. T. Rochead*'s most original work. Its inspiration is clearly Venetian, possibly Sansovino's Procuratie Nuove. What makes this three-storey terrace so striking is the relentless repetition of the semicircular-headed windows and the attached columns which obey the classical hierarchy of Doric, Ionic, Corinthian. The eighty-three bays are identical; the only modulation in the entire length is in the end ten bays, which are very slightly advanced, halting the illusion of horizontal lines disappearing into infinity. The E end, converted into the Grosvenor Hotel in 1971, was seriously damaged by fire in 1978. Its main façade has been successfully re-created by *T. M. Miller & Partners* using a reinforced-steel and concrete frame, clad with glass-reinforced concrete (an early use of GRC on such a large scale). The rear is now unmistakably late C20 – an acceptable compromise – and the interior too bears the hallmarks of expensive 1980s taste and comfort. In many of the original houses at the w end of the terrace, the ground-floor windows have anthemion-etched glass. Inside, classically screened halls, top-lit stairs and exuberant plasterwork.

Further w, KEW TERRACE, 1849, is the second of this series of terraces. By *James Brown* in collaboration with *J. T. Rochead*, its composition of end and central pavilions, with linking two-storey sections, harks back to the terraces built earlier at the w end of Sauchiehall Street and across the lower slopes of Woodlands Hill (*qq.v.*). No. 6 has an elaborate door of *c.* 1900, No. 8 a bold Burges-style chimneypiece. Next come the two long ranges of BELHAVEN TERRACE, 1868–9, and BELHAVEN TERRACE WEST, 1870–4, by *James Thomson*, altogether more ponderous. Thomson has picked up the canted-bay theme of the w section of Buckingham Terrace (*see* above) and used it in every other bay, reversing the pattern at the centre to form a symmetrical composition. The only variation occurs in the mullion detail of the first-floor canted windows in the end and centre pavilions. These houses are grander than their earlier counterparts, and round-headed attic windows pop up above the main cornice like giant antefixae. A number of houses still have their screened halls and, at the principal rooms, their cornices which return into the bay windows as pelmet boxes. Five houses of the w terrace were converted into Glasgow University's DALRYMPLE HALL in 1965 by *W. N. W. Ramsay*. Some of the doors have been closed off but otherwise the exterior remains. Inside there are some unsatisfactory subdivisions; at the rear a dining hall, also by

Ramsay, has been cleverly sunk so that from the mews only a low roof is visible.

Opposite Belhaven Terrace, raised self-confidently above the road, is KIRKLEE TERRACE (originally known as Windsor 51 Terrace), begun in 1845 but not completed until 1864, when the last house was sold. It is an early domestic work by *Charles Wilson*, and there is no sign outside that it was nearly twenty years in the making (the E end pavilion and four houses were the first to be built, 1845–8). For much of the year, the terrace is obscured by the trees in the sloping south-facing pleasure gardens and can be seen only in sharp perspective. The terrace forms a grand palazzo emphasized on the first floor by solid balconies, pierced with panels of interlinked circles and supported by consoles, and by strongly projecting cornices, also carried on consoles, over the windows. Crowning the whole elevation, a bold cornice (with a geometrically patterned frieze in the end and centre bays), and, above that, distinctive low-pitched roofs. Every element is carefully composed and balanced, and the masonry detail in particular shows the influence of Wilson's then recent visit to France. The end pavilions are counterbalanced by solid recessed bays, a stroke of architectural imagination that lifts the design above those of most of the other terraces, for these bays, as well as being aesthetically important, serve the practical function of providing the outermost houses with an extra bay. The overall effect has been created by the precise regularity of every feature, so it is regrettable that misguided historicism has led to the original simple four-pane glazing pattern being replaced in one house by twelve-pane windows. To the rear, one of the few mews to survive in the West End, albeit much altered to suit modern domestic needs. It nestles neatly into the restricted site, which falls away to the N. Just beyond, at the corner of Kirklee Road, is a villa, No. 15 Kirklee Terrace (*see* Kelvinside, below: Perambulation).

LOWTHER TERRACE lies W of Kirklee Road. First, a 1950s intruder (No. 5), a long five-storey block of plain flats faced with concrete panels and with vertical strips of staircase window, built for the Ministry of Defence as married quarters. The rest of Lowther Terrace is exceptional, for it comprises three individually designed town houses (Nos. 8, 9 and 10) in a composition more reminiscent of London's Cadogan Square than anything Scottish. (Linked internally *c.* 1948 by *Wright & Kirkwood* as an old people's home for the Church of Scotland.) The houses are built in a combination of Giffnock and Bishopbriggs stone and, unusually, have Westmoreland slate roofs. No. 8 (1904) and No. 10 (*c.* 1900, with additions in 1904 and after 1909) are by *James Miller*. No. 9 is by *A. G. Sydney Mitchell*, 1904–6. Each is a different interpretation of Jacobean Renaissance style, elaborately modelled with shaped gables, pilasters and turrets. No. 10, built for J. Cargill, was extended to the W in 1904 when a conservatory-cum-wintergarden, an inner hall and a billiard room were added. Later the conservatory was converted into a room; subsequently together with the billiard room, it was raised to two storeys, which permitted the enlargement of the first-floor drawing room. Some excellent interior work, including an oak-screened outer hall and an inner hall with an elaborate chimneypiece, its stone overmantel carved with bas-relief baluster designs. In the billiard room (now chapel), banded plasterwork on the barrel ceiling. The large staircase window is inset with simple coloured-glass panels of genre scenes by *Oscar Paterson*. The stair itself is late C17-style, with wineglass balusters and a broad moulded handrail. On the first floor, in the double drawing room, a convincing reproduction of mid-C18 decoration, which must post-date 1909. Good Romantic landscapes on canvas set into the overmantels. Inside No. 9, a well-fitted library and good plasterwork in the original first-floor drawing room. At No. 8 the interior decoration is of a simpler, more formal type.

There is no direct carriage or pedestrian access between Lowther Terrace and the next terrace to the W, REDLANDS TERRACE (1924–5, by *J. McKellar* and *George Gunn*), a design of no merit and not appropriate in scale, but offering a good view of Great Western Terrace opposite.

54 GREAT WESTERN TERRACE, designed in 1869 by *Alexander Thomson*, is the most monumental and original of all the terraces. (The w houses were not built in Thomson's lifetime and were completed by *J. J. Burnet*.) It stands upon a platform contained at either end by railed walls with steps and ramps, and with a single carriage road to the terraced forecourt, skilfully modified by *W. Whitfield* of *William Holford & Associates* when Great Western Road was made an expressway.

Thomson resolved the visual problems of the long terrace better than any of his contemporaries by abandoning the concept of end and central pavilions for a formula which places two three-storey pavilions not at the ends but six bays in from each end. This creates the illusion that the lower sections thread straight through the taller blocks, which act as props to counter any sense of sagging. It is the severest of all Thomson's terraces, and indeed of all the terraces that line Great Western Road. The windows are punched in the walls. There is no decoration in the frieze; carved detail is found only in the four Greek Ionic columns to each pair of doors, and in the bold main cornice, but even this is restrained. More pronounced decoration is employed in the magnificent cast-iron work. Here, unlike in Thomson's other terrace designs, there is a weighty massing of the masonry and not a daring display of glass. Internally, there is considerable variety, but the most impressive spaces created by Thomson are the grand imperial stairs, the galleries round rectangular- or circular-domed light-wells, and the powerful cast-iron work, e.g. in Nos. 4 and 11. Common to all the houses is restrained but bold plasterwork, with repetitive rosettes, on cornices and ceilings; and a number of entrance halls still have their impressive Ionic-columned

screens. No. 4 has the best-preserved of Thomson's interiors.
A bold Ionic screen divides the front hall from the galleried
central hall: off this is the stair compartment. Both the staircase
and the galleries display Thomson's ironwork at its best, with
designs combining scrolls and stylized anthemia with rosettes:
the newels have the look of bamboo, foreshadowing the exaggerated naturalism which dominates the Glasgow Style. Two
rooms break from Thomson's classicism with a strong flavour
of the Aesthetic movement, a nearly contemporary scheme
designed by an English architect called *Middleton*. The E front
room and the rear sw room are decorated in a style that
suggests the work of *Daniel Cottier* (who had successfully
collaborated with Thomson at Queen's Park Church, where
he worked on wooden panels because of a strike among plasterers). These delicate and brightly coloured stencil designs
are on wooden panels, both above the picturerail and in the
ceilings. There are also intricately worked chimneypieces and
door architraves with carved panels and linear designs, and
the whole effect is of great richness. During the 1890s and
early 1900s, Great Western Terrace was altered and added to.
At No. 3, *A. N. Paterson* added a barrel-vaulted billiard room
and service rooms for W. N. Mitchell. No. 8 (BURRELL
HOUSE), as its name suggests, was transformed for Sir
William Burrell by *Robert Lorimer*, who was instructed to
'chip away the ginger-bread' and 'make the house very simple
as he [Burrell] has such lovely contents'. Although much of
Lorimer's work has been removed or altered, the imperial
staircase, a reworking of the original, is Jacobean in character,
with twisted carved balusters and panels of vines and fabulous
beasts commanding the newel posts. The balcony front is
now concealed behind a partition. In the hall, a 'medieval'
chimneypiece made up from carved masonry piers, and an
Italian *cassone* (with murky panels of the Crucifixion) makes a
curious overmantel. Some of the oak linenfold and plainer
panelling which originally lined the house is still in position,
but the stair window of 1892 by *George Walton* has gone. At
No. 10, *A. N. Paterson*, as late as 1917, based his alterations
on Thomson's original designs.

Further w, LANCASTER TERRACE, *c.* 1875–6, an incomplete
composition of three villas linked together to form a terrace,
is chiefly remarkable for the powerful term-pilasters flanking
the doors. WESTBOURNE HOUSE (No. 985), an Italianate
villa of *c.* 1873 has a tower and bold semicircular bays in the
manner of *Robert Turnbull*, Alexander Thomson's partner
from 1873 until the latter's death in 1875. Though it adopts
some of Thomson's vocabulary, this design is fussier than his.
It makes a picturesque statement on the corner with Hyndland
Road and provides a contrast with Thomson's Westbourne
Terrace to the s (*see* Kelvinside, below: Perambulation).

Back on the N side of Great Western Road, LANCASTER CRES-
CENT, built on part of the Redlands estate, curves eastward
from the junction with Hyndland Road. Its nine fairly small

houses, linked in a terrace, were designed by several different architects *c.* 1898. No. 1, by *Henry Higgins*, set obliquely at the end of the terrace, has term-pilasters like Lancaster Terrace. No. 2 is by *James Miller*, with a dwarf-galleried fanlight and leaded glass in the oak panelled door, and an excellent romantic townscape by the *Oscar Paterson Studio* spanning the large mullioned stair window. *J. L. Cowan* did Nos. 3–7 and *J. C. McKellar* the plainer Nos. 8 and 9 of 1907. Standing alone at the top of the curve, REDLANDS HOUSE, a stylish Italianate villa of *c.* 1871 built for James Mirrlees (owner of the Redlands estate) by *James Boucher*, with remarkably fine masonry and much use of cast-iron. Various much later excrescences above the cornice. Porch and rear additions (including an artist's studio) by *James Salmon*, 1922–3, when it was converted into Redlands Hospital for Women. The enormous, originally glazed porch, with Doric columns, encloses the steps spanning the basement area and a tripartite doorpiece with etched glass. The tripartite theme is variously repeated in the shallow projecting windows.

The last two terraces are again on the S side. Nos. 1–5 DEVONSHIRE GARDENS, *c.* 1870, on a larger scale and more ponderous than the terraces further E, employs the gamut of the projecting bay-window designs already seen. The composition's weightiness is emphasized by the French pavilion roofs with decorative ironwork over the end bays. William Burrell lived at No. 4 before moving to Great Western Terrace and the house still has a fragment of a good stained-glass window by *G. Walton & Co.* At Nos. 1–9 DEVONSHIRE TERRACE, *c.* 1883, *James Thomson* elaborates on all the details noted in Belhaven Terrace (*see* above); in particular, he has turned the surprised, wide-eyed dormers into miniature triumphal arches. Here, then, the extraordinary cavalcade of terraces ends the long march W.

On the N SIDE of the road their place is taken by a self-conscious string of smug villas sporting an assortment of bay windows, columned porches and balustrades. They increase in grandeur as they progress W. On the NW corner with Great Western Road, No. 1 CLEVEDEN ROAD has a spacious compartmented conservatory and an unusually elaborate interior with an Italianate arcaded hall. Its heavily decorated arches are supported on slender, paired black marble colonnettes. In the billiard room, Edwardian sporting scenes set into frames below the semicircular windows, in their turn set into the cove of the timber ceiling. No. 994 (RAVELSTON), *c.* 1875, by *John Gordon*, makes a display of tripartite openings. Set back to the W, a tall wing with study and private chapel added in Tudor style by *H. O. Tarbolton* for Bishop Reid, 1910. No. 996 (AVERLEY) dates from 1875–6 but has later interiors designed by *William Leiper*, with elaborately panelled rooms and plaster ceilings by the *Bromsgrove Guild*. No. 998, now ST MUNGO'S ACADEMY CENTENARY CLUB, is an Italian Renaissance palace of 1877 by *James Boucher*, complete with its service wing and stables. It was built for James Marshall of the Saracen Iron Foundry and capitalizes successfully on its prominent site. The rusticated ground floor forms a podium for the pilastered *piano nobile*. The quality of the masonry and carved detail is particularly notable. At the w end, a pretty cast-iron veranda opens on to the small terrace garden, the relic of a major conservatory. The interior is as lavish as only *nouveaux riches* could make it; the elaborately columned entrance hall opens on to an extravagantly proportioned imperial stair, with a dramatic sculptured arch at the head of the main flight framing a large three-light window with contemporary Neoclassical personifications of Art, Science and Literature, possibly by *W. & J.J. Kier*. But the drawing room is the *tour de force*: the effect of a symmetrical room with square alcoves at either end is cleverly created by the introduction of columned screens, and by an elegant cabinet made out of an otherwise redundant space. All this is unified by an icing-sugar confection of very French plasterwork. More ponderous but equally handsome is the billiard room, with its embossed leather wall panels. After this glamour, No. 1000, *c.* 1887, seems a cramped design; despite its conversion into the HOMEOPATHIC HOSPITAL, the interior is remarkably intact, including the charming tiny, galleried smoking room in the rooftop tower. No. 1012 is a grander, later version (from 1893) of Nos. 994 and 996, with bay windows of every shape and a vast area of glass. The bold bays have influenced HUGHENDEN GROVE, 1984, by *Cockburn Associates,* the three simple but stylish brick blocks of flats to the w. They capture the scale and massing of the earlier villas in a way that the neighbouring, nearly contemporary and self-conscious flats by *Coleman, Ballantine & Partners* completely fail to do.

Opposite these late C20 blocks, *J.J. Burnet*'s former KELVINSIDE RAILWAY STATION of 1896, one of five stations for the Lanarkshire and Dumbartonshire Railway. It was designed like a villa to harmonize with its neighbours. The shallow hipped roof and overhanging eaves owe much to Frank Lloyd Wright, whose work Burnet had seen. The station lay astride the low-level railway and was closed in 1942. In 1980 *Project Design Partnership* successfully and sensitively converted it to a restaurant. Beyond here, the Great Western Road enters Anniesland and is described with the rest of that district (*see* below).

KELVINSIDE

This grand residential suburb was conceived in 1840 and laid out on the Kelvinside Estate (*see* Great Western Road, above: Perambulation 1).

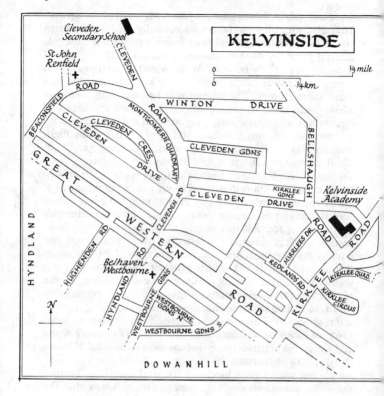

KELVINSIDE

CHURCHES

BELHAVEN-WESTBOURNE CHURCH, 52 Westbourne
Gardens, 1880-1. Designed as Westbourne Free Church by
John Honeyman. A small-scale Renaissance-style church, it has
a pedimented frontispiece, with superimposed orders of paired
columns, Ionic below, Corinthian above, composed on the
lines of the portico of Wren's St Paul's Cathedral. It screens
large arched windows and a central door. Flanking, blind bays
defined by paired pilasters, with half pediments reflecting the
slope of the main one. This pilastered and arcaded treatment
continues across the church hall to the l. Set back at the outer
angles of the church, pilastered bellcotes with ogee domes.
The masonry, channelled and banded with finely cut capitals,
is immaculate.

Inside, an open hall with a central bank of pews and side
aisles. Shallow side galleries, supported on carved consoles,
are linked by curved E angles to the deep E gallery. At the w
end, engaged columns and pilasters frame the organ gallery
and the windows. Above the cornice a ribbed cove flows into

the elaborately ornamented coffered ceiling. – The FURN-
ISHINGS include the richly carved Baroque communion table,
pulpit and elders' chairs. – ORGAN, 1892, with case by
Keppie. – STAINED GLASS. – E end of S gallery. War Memorial
window by *Douglas Strachan, c.* 1920. – Also by Strachan,
centre window of the N gallery, 1920. – In the W gallery,
three windows by *Margaret Chilton* executed by Chilton and
Marjorie Kemp, 1951–2.

ST JOHN RENFIELD, 22 Beaconsfield Road. 1929–30, by *James
Taylor Thomson.* A medieval-inspired church, but with the
imprint of Pearson in the tall, bold profile. It stands proudly
on the steep SW slope of the street surveying the spacious
surburb it serves. This church bears a strong similarity to
Leslie Graham Thomson's Reid Memorial Church in Edinburgh, of precisely the same date. Which design was published
first? Perhaps both owe the origin of their tall clearstorey
windows and the low passage aisles to Giles Gilbert Scott's
Lady Chapel at Liverpool Cathedral, although L. G. Thomson's time with Bertram Goodhue may have introduced him
to the simplified Bodley-derived style practised in the United
States. The church is built in neatly stugged ashlar on a constrained cruciform plan, the transepts barely projecting outside
the main rectangle of the church and a shallow chancel at the
N (liturgical E). The crossing is marked by an ornate open-
work *flèche.* The windows, in strongly defined bays, have
two-light cusped tracery with oculi at their heads, and the
S (liturgical W) window has prominent and austerely plain
buttress-like mullions and tracery of a type much favoured by
Bodley. Although much of the detail looks back to the late C19
Gothic Revival, the lack of detail at the coping is uncom-
promisingly C20. Inside, the walls are in polished sandstone
with a low arcade of depressed arches (also found at the Reid
Memorial Church). The fittings include a carved oak communion table, reredos, choir stalls and pulpit. – STAINED
GLASS. E window by *Douglas Strachan, c.*1932, a memorial
to Alexander Osbourne. The single leaded lights are by *Gordon
Webster,* 1967–70. – Linked to hall and house at N.

PUBLIC BUILDINGS

QUEEN MARGARET HALL, Bellshaugh Road. Student accommodation by *W. R. N. Ramsay* for Glasgow University, in two
phases, the first (1964) an open courtyard arrangement of four-
and five-storey blocks, concrete-framed, the exposed grid filled
with brick panels, set into the slope, the lower storey partially
supported on piers. Mannered timber oriels at the top floor on
the west-facing elevations. To the N, phase two, a monotonous
twelve-storey tower with similar detailing.

HALLS OF RESIDENCE (Glasgow University), 24–30 and 20–
22 Winton Drive. Nos. 24–30, completed 1987 by *Laing,
Bremner & Garnet,* four-storey L-plan blocks linked in pairs

with a central archway to each. Built in warm sandy brick,
used effectively in vertical detailing to the window. LISTER
HALL (Nos. 20–2), 1974–5, by *Walter Ramsay*, in the manner
of Coia, is a four-storey L-plan range, concrete-framed, with
arched parking bays in the east-facing elevation; on the N, a
curved stairwell with scooped-back wallhead and two
mannered, jettied windows.

CLEVEDEN SECONDARY SCHOOL, Cleveden Road. By
W. N. W. Ramsay and *Wright Construction* for Glasgow Corporation, 1965–9. A long four-storey classroom spine with
windows in set-square form producing a striking effect. At the
centre a cross-spine with gym and swimming pool to the front,
assembly hall and dining room to the rear.

KELVINSIDE ACADEMY, Bellshaugh Road. By *James Sellars*,
1877–9. Imposing post-Thomson Grecian. In its composition,
however, it looks back to Thomas Hamilton's Royal High
School, Edinburgh. The long, well-balanced façade, in
Wishaw freestone, is massed around the centrepiece of an Ionic
tetrastyle temple front, raised up on a plain podium into which
the main entrance is cut. Above the door, a frieze of bayleaves
and a helmeted bust. The cast-iron lamp-standards flanking
the entrance are also decorated with entwined bayleaves. The
starkly simple outer pavilions are linked to the centre by
slightly recessed wings: the colonnades of Hamilton's design
have been reduced to barely discernible pilasters along the first
floor. Throughout all this the conception of windows as just
voids in the wall, borrowed from Thomson, is extremely clear.
The wings and pavilions are of identical height, but the carefully judged advancing of the pavilions and the raising of
their parapets give them authority. The influence of Hamilton
appears again in the pedimented stone gateways, rather oddly
inserted into the handsome cast-iron railings: the magnificent
cast-iron gates well demonstrate the skill of Glasgow's iron-
founders. To the W a low pedimented range, formerly the
gymnasium. The interior is predictably austere, with the hall
behind the portico flanked by classrooms. Some unusual line-
etched glass, copying Flaxman's illustrations of Homer's *Iliad*
and *Odyssey*, appears in internal windows.

KIRKLEE BRIDGE. *See* Crossings of the Clyde and Kelvin,
below.

PERAMBULATION

This perambulation starts at the junction of Hyndland Road and
Great Western Road (described above). Immediately s of the
latter, on the E side of HYNDLAND ROAD, is *Alexander
Thomson's* WESTBOURNE TERRACE (now known as Nos.
21–39 Hyndland Road), 1871. Though not so dramatically
sited as Great Western Terrace (*see* above), this long astylar
terrace is full of invention. It is set back behind a wide basement area enclosed by low walls topped by bold cast-iron

railings identical in design to those of Great Western Terrace. Similar railings guard the two short flights of shallow steps leading to each door. The whole effect is that of a stepped plinth. In its horizontality and in the use of bay windows, the elevation bears the stamp of Rochead's earlier Buckingham Terrace (*see* Great Western Road above: Perambulation 1), but the elements of the composition are different. The ground floor has become a plain plinth, pierced by three-light windows and recessed porches with Ionic columns *in antis*. The two storeys above are set back between the slightly projecting block-like end bays. For the first and only time in a terrace design, Thomson used canted windows, so popular in Glasgow, on the tall first floor and combined them with plain single windows punched into the solid-looking walls. The upper floor differs again, with a continuous band of small, plain windows stretched along its whole length. Opposite, Nos. 10–20 (formerly known as MONTAGUE TERRACE) date from *c.* 1883 and are probably by *H. & D. Barclay*. Compared with Westbourne Terrace, the façade looks cluttered. At the rear, a mezzanine, which originally provided service accommodation, is clearly visible. Corinthian screens survive in the entrance halls, which open into top-lit stairwells.

w of, and parallel to, Hyndland Road is HUGHENDEN ROAD. At the s end on the e side, Nos. 1–7 HUGHENDEN TERRACE, designed by *H. & D. Barclay, c.* 1881, look similar to those just passed at Nos. 10–20 Hyndland Road. Adjoining the N end of the terrace, a villa of 1907 by *Burnet, Boston & Carruthers* (No. 25), built high up on an artificial platform with a terraced garden in front. In complete contrast to the uninspired elevation is the high quality of the decorative work inside, which includes many Art Nouveau fittings. Particularly noteworthy is the Art Nouveau stained glass in the door and in panels adjacent to it. Also in Hughenden Road, the tall KELVINSIDE POWER STATION, in 1892 one of the city's first two electric power stations, brick-built and much altered.

Returning now to Great Western Road and continuing w, we reach BEACONSFIELD ROAD off the N side. On the e side, a block of flats that really belongs to the final stretch of our perambulation along Great Western Road (*see* above). Further up, prominently positioned high above the road, is St John Renfield (*see* Churches, above). On the brow of the hill, KELVINSIDE HOUSE (formerly Beaconsfield), a large asymmetrical Italianate villa of *c.* 1874 with a three-storey tower and extensive Baronial additions of 1894 by *James Thomson*, embellished with strapwork, embattled parapets and corbelled oriels. The school entrance block dates from *c.* 1955: its curved canopy complements the shallow flight of steps, and portholes flank the wide door.

At the junction of CLEVEDEN ROAD and Winton Drive is Cleveden Secondary School (*see* Public Buildings, above). Beyond it, Cleveden Road leads over the hill into Kelvindale (an unassuming speculative scheme of the 1920s by *Mactaggart*

& Mickel), but opposite the road junction, rounding the convex curve of Cleveden Road, is the long, three-storey MONTGOMERIE QUADRANT (Nos. 17–25e), 1882–6, by *Alexander Thomson*, more imposing in its siting than in its constricted detailing, though it has handsome panelled iron-work to the balconies and railings. To the NE, WINTON DRIVE is lined with a variety of typical late C19 two-storey villas, mainly classical in inspiration. Among these, WINTON HOUSE (No. 9), *c.* 1880, is by *Robert Turnbull* of *Thomson & Turnbull*, in Thomson's manner and with boldly carved doorcases inside. The semi-detached villas are mainly of *c.* 1900 by *D. Woodburn Sturrock*, with whom *Basil Ionides* collaborated at the W pair on the S side. Right at the E end on the S side lies Queen Margaret Hall, a hall of residence of Glasgow University (*see* Public Buildings, above). Back in Cleveden Road, a large and disjointed Baronial composition of *c.* 1890 (Nos. 24–22) fills an obtuse angle. CLEVEDEN GARDENS follows and runs E with substantial detached and double villas on the N side. No. 5, a typical villa of the period around 1880, boasts bold window bays and a large central top-light dominating the roof. No. 15 by *A. N. Prentice*, 1902–6 is a small and unusual Wrenaissance villa of 1904, built of finely dressed ashlar, with boldly arched ground-floor windows, understated pilasters defining the front elevation, and a glazed cupola on the ridge. It faces a terrace of ten houses (Nos. 10–20) stepped in pairs and articulated by two-storey bow windows. Back once more in Cleveden Road, the four-storey Italianate tower of Early Renaissance origin, No. 16, *c.* 1883, makes an impact on the corner. Inside, a generous entrance hall with a powerful Corinthian screen, compartmented ceiling, elaborately carved doorcases and, in one section, an original deep frieze, painted with botanical subjects and rural labours set within Renaissance-style painted frames. In the large stained-glass window, a figure of Plenty surrounded by panels again on a Renaissance theme: it may be by *Stephen Adam*. Further on, at Nos. 4–8, a bulky asymmetrical villa of *c.* 1893 with Jacobean decoration, and No. 5 by *John Gordon*, *c.* 1877, a bold exercise in the Renaissance tradition but with a dull 1970s rear wing. The tower, with an arcaded belvedere top, offers views to the S. On the N wall, two Ruskinian heads in scrolled cartouches crane to examine each other. An archway leads to the (altered) service and stable court. Next door, the classical No. 3, *c.* 1874, with a conservatory on the NE side and a ward (1985) to serve the old people's home by *Thomson, McCrea & Sanders*. No. 1 brings us back to Great Western Road and is described there (*see* above).

Retracing our steps a short way up Cleveden Road we come on the W side to Cleveden Drive leading to CLEVEDEN CRESCENT, designed in 1876 by *John Burnet*, possibly with help from his son, *J. J. Burnet*. This symmetrical composition of fourteen substantial two-storey houses linked into a terrace follows the contour of the hill. Two matching houses stand in the centre on the brow, with two ranges, each of three houses, stepping up to the centre and returning at the outer ends to form pavilions. These pavilions (No. 1 Cleveden Crescent and No. 61 CLEVEDEN DRIVE) face Cleveden Drive and have prominent full-height square bays rising to shallow segmental pediments in the attic.

The w end of CLEVEDEN DRIVE is dominated by large and varied villas, built, between 1880 and 1900, with an eye to the views s. No. 60, c. 1893, a plain symmetrical design with strongly transomed and mullioned-and-transomed windows, has, at the rear, two full-height projecting bays linked by a balcony. At No. 58, the south-facing wing by *J. L. Cowan* is richly fitted out in a Renaissance idiom, with Corinthian columns in the hall and heavily ribbed plaster ceilings. The billiard room has Corinthian pilasters and a coved ceiling; in the library, original fittings in the manner of *Wylie & Lochead*. Inside No. 56 (designed by *John Gordon, c.* 1887) an interesting variety of stained glass: Glasgow Style in the inner screen of the front door and painted in the cupola of the attic billiard room. The staircase window has figures of Patience, Charity and Temperance in the Japanese-influenced manner popularized by *Cottier*. No. 54 (built *c.* 1893) has more stained glass in the very large window on the imperial stair: it depicts a big figurative group in a Renaissance architectural setting. Next, a French-inspired villa of *c.* 1887; then, at No. 50, a Gothic one (cf. No. 8 Sydenham Road; *see* Downanhill, below: Perambulation 1), with a heavy Gothic entrance hall, a hefty columned staircase and some unusually good stained glass depicting the opening scenes of Tennyson's *Lady of Shalott*: could it be by *Stephen Adam Senior*? Other windows suggest the work of *Oscar Paterson*. Most notable among the houses along this stretch is No. 48, STONELEIGH, designed by *H. E. Clifford*, 1900–6, for a Glasgow stockbroker, Joseph Turner, as a handsome neo-Tudor house on the lines, not of an urban villa, but of a small North of England country house, with the main rooms and the kitchen on the ground floor. The house is dramatically sited, and the s elevation is specifically planned to take advantage of the views. The N side (mainly devoted to service accommodation) combines elements of the Scottish tower house with ideas from English houses of the c16 and c17. This house was much admired by Herman Muthesius. It was converted for an old people's home in the mid-1950s, but the interior is remarkably intact. The open hall, familiar from English Arts and Crafts houses, virtually removes the need for corridors: it is oak-beamed and leads to an imperial stair with scrolled balustrade. The drawing room joinery is all of satinwood, with mother-of-pearl inlay. All the stained glass was made by the *Bromsgrove Guild* and designed by *Henry J. Payne* and *Mary Newill*. In the dining room, scenes from Sir Galahad's pursuit of the Holy Grail, in a Pre-Raphaelite manner; in the stair window, three mysterious but carefully detailed merchant ships encircling the deck-like landing, probably by Payne; and in the hall, black-on-white cameo panels of fairy tales, probably by Newill in the style of Burne-Jones woodcuts.

Cleveden Drive continues E of Cleveden Road, with, on the s side, an unusual terrace (Nos. 28–40) by *J. C. McKellar*, 1904–5. The pairs of houses at Nos. 30–2 and 36–8 mirror each other either side of the pivotal No. 34. The end houses are larger, and a corbelled angle turret gives further distinction to No. 40. Along the opposite (N) side of the road, mainly class-ically detailed double villas, with detached houses further E, including the bowed and gabled No. 3, *c.* 1875. In its oak front door, an exceptionally fine and large stained-glass panel, possibly by *Oscar Paterson*. At the SE end, Nos. 2–10 were designed by *Thomas Smellie* of Kilmarnock, *c.* 1902, and have distinctive rock-faced masonry. The terrace re-uses the idio-syncratic formula of J. A. Campbell's terrace close by in Kirklee Road and Mirrlees Drive (*see* below).

At its E end, Cleveden Drive joins BELLSHAUGH ROAD. Just to the N, set back from the road on the W side, is KIRKLEE GARDENS, a truncated astylar terrace of 1877–8 by *James Thomson*. Each five-bay house (unusually large for a terrace) has a central entrance with long narrow side lights. At the s end (and presumably intended to be repeated at the N one), two taller houses forming an end pavilion, each house with segmental pediments and balconies to the three central first-floor windows.

s of Kirklee Gardens, past Kelvinside Academy (*see* Public Build-ings, above), Bellshaugh Road joins KIRKLEE ROAD. To the s runs a long terrace (Nos. 7–23), the most interesting section of an unusual residential development designed by *John A. Campbell*, and built between 1900 and 1909 on the Mirrlees estate, which had been laid out for feuing by *James Thomson* in 1900. Campbell's commission came three years after he had left Burnet's practice and set up on his own account: his architectural pedigree shows in the design. Nos. 7–23 Kirklee Road, with No. 2 REDLANDS ROAD (the s house of the terrace), were the first houses to be built after 1900. Nos. 7–21 are arranged as four symmetrical pairs of two-storey houses with no basements – and, originally, with no attic windows either. A vigorous rhythm is established across the elevation by the pairs of full-height canted bay windows, which break the eaves and are linked across the intervening bays by first-floor balconies; but most strikingly novel are the wide-arched mullioned-and-transomed windows along the ground floor. The symmetry is dramatically broken by the end houses (No. 2 Redlands Road and No. 23 Kirklee Road), which have tall gable ends to Kirklee Road and Scots Renaissance details on the bold angle turrets. No. 3 Kirklee Road and No. 1 Redlands Road, built *c.* 1902, continue the same theme. Campbell also designed Nos. 3–13 and 14–18 MIRRLEES DRIVE, *c.* 1906, smaller but similar in concept.

Back on the E side of Kirklee Road, opposite Kelvinside

Academy, Nos. 1–7 KIRKLEE QUADRANT are all that was built, *c.* 1870, of an intended large curved terrace of houses. It degenerates at Nos. 8–12 into a gaunt and over-scaled tenement range, with all the storeys of equal height. To the s, past a pair of double villas of the 1870s, KIRKLEE CIRCUS opens from the E side. It is really an oval, a picturesque cul-de-sac with bushy evergreens in the central garden, closed by the W boundary of the Botanic Gardens. On the N side, detached houses: No. 18 has the tough Gothic detailing noticed already at No. 50 Cleveden Drive (*see* above). All along the s side, a shallow crescent of paired houses of the 1870s (Nos. 1–12) steps gently up the hill. Back in Kirklee Road, on the angle with Kirklee Terrace on Great Western Road, stands a substantial mid-C19 villa (No. 2a Kirklee Road and No. 15 Kirklee Terrace), extensively remodelled by *J. J. Burnet, c.* 1900. The Baronial tower and the elaborate porch of wrought-iron and glass make for a picturesque informality in marked contrast to the neighbouring terraces along Great Western Road. The interior is equally decorative, with details (particularly the chimneypieces) derived from R. Norman Shaw.

Now for another excursion s of Great Western Road, this time just beyond Belhaven Terrace to WESTBOURNE GARDENS SOUTH. On the E side, a gently curving terrace of *c.* 1879 (Nos. 20–7), based on a design by *Alexander Thomson,* with end pavilions distinguished by shallow Ionic porches and widely spaced second-floor windows which contrast with the regularly and closely spaced second-floor ones of the central section. The whole terrace is fronted by simple arcaded cast-iron railings. The street then opens into the spacious triangle of WESTBOURNE GARDENS. To the E, the gentle curved end of the N terrace (Nos. 1–18), built *c.* 1872 with first-floor oriels which suggest that *James Thomson* was the architect. The rhythm is broken by the taller No. 12, which must originally have been intended as the E end pavilion of a straight terrace to which Nos. 13–18 were quickly added: No. 18 now takes up the position of the W pavilion, although it can never be seen together with No. 1. That has a single-storey extension of 1905 by *David Barclay* facing the Belhaven-Westbourne Church (*see* Churches, above). Adjoining the church hall to the s, a refined Thomsonesque terrace (Nos. 49–51) of *c.* 1875, possibly the 'terrace behind Westbourne Terrace' mentioned in a letter from Alexander Thomson to George (Thomson), but it may have been altered in execution after his death. Each of the three two-storey houses, with shallow bay windows, is linked by an Ionic porch with delicate cast-iron balustrading (missing at No. 49). s of Westbourne Road, unusually bold cast-iron railings at Nos. 42–7, also of *c.* 1875. Adjoining their s gable, a small block of service flats, 1942, by *Wylie, Shanks & Wylie.* Along the s side of the triangle, a freely Gothic terrace of *c.* 1876 (Nos. 28–41), the only one of its kind in the West End. The end pavilions, canted bay windows and tripartite doorpieces, familiar from the classical terraces, are all transformed by colonnettes, hoodmoulds and gabled dormers. Perhaps this shows the influence of Professors' Square on Gilmorehill (*see* Hillhead, Glasgow University, below: Perambulation 1).

NORTH KELVINSIDE

North Kelvinside is bounded on the SW and NE by the River Kelvin and the Forth and Clyde Canal, and comes S in a wedge almost to the Great Western Road and St George's Cross. It remained a rural area until the early years of the C19, when industrial development began, encouraged by the opening of the Forth and Clyde Canal and of the Firhill Timber Basin (1788) and by the power of the Kelvin to drive mills. Only fragments of the past industrial prowess remain; an isolated example is the former Kelvinbridge Artistic Stationery Works at Nos. 24–8 Herbert Street by *Thomson, Turnbull & Peacock*, 1898.

After the Botanic Gardens opened in 1842, middle-class housing appeared on the south-facing hillside overlooking the Kelvin and then slowly extended over the hill with villas, e.g. the houses in Kelvinside Gardens, and handsome tenements, e.g. those in Wilton Street and Wilton Gardens. Further E, tenements were more tightly packed, although those fronting Maryhill Road were always grandest. These, along with virtually all the other buildings that once lined the southern stretch of Maryhill Road, were demolished in 1978, when, as part of the second phase of comprehensive redevelopment in the city, the concept of the Maryhill Corridor was adopted. It involved a swathe of demolition through North Kelvinside and Maryhill; the replanning follows the old street pattern quite closely but not the former urban scale. By the end of the 1980s large areas had been rebuilt with housing schemes expressing the reaction to the high-rise developments of the 1960s. The height of buildings has been restricted to eight storeys, and many schemes incorporate a variety of building heights and types of accommodation. Flats, maisonettes, terraced and sheltered housing all appear, in a well integrated fashion. In place of stone, brick of various colours and textures dominates the area, set off by liberal landscaping. The imposing presence of tenement-lined urban streets has been entirely lost, most obviously in the wide main thoroughfares, where the new suburbia looks least happy. Tenements, where they survive, are (in 1989) being rehabilitated and look remarkably solid beside all the pretty brickwork. The latest scheme (in 1989) at Shakespeare Street has taken its scale from neighbouring turn-of-the-century tenements and treats C19 details in a Post-Modern way. Will this be the key to future developments on the sites that still remain vacant at the time of writing?

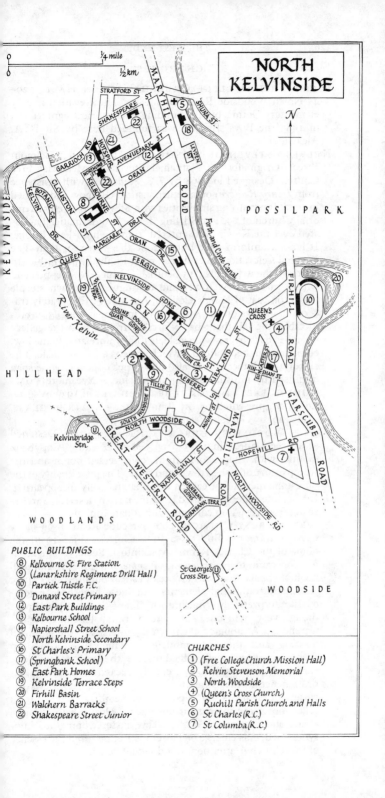

NORTH KELVINSIDE

¼ mile
½ km

N

POSSILPARK

KELVINSIDE

HILLHEAD

WOODLANDS

WOODSIDE

Kelvinbridge Stn.

Kelvinbridge Stn.

St George's Cross Stn.

GREAT WESTERN ROAD

MARYHILL ROAD

GARSCUBE ROAD

FIRHILL ROAD

River Kelvin

PUBLIC BUILDINGS

⑧ Kelbourne St Fire Station
⑨ (Lanarkshire Regiment Drill Hall)
⑩ Partick Thistle F.C.
⑪ Dunard Street Primary
⑫ East Park Buildings
⑬ Kelbourne School
⑭ Napiershall Street School
⑮ North Kelvinside Secondary
⑯ St Charles's Primary
⑰ (Springbank School)
⑱ East Park Homes
⑲ Kelvinside Terrace Steps
⑳ Firhill Basin
㉑ Walchern Barracks
㉒ Shakespeare Street Junior

CHURCHES

① (Free College Church Mission Hall)
② Kelvin Stevenson Memorial
③ North Woodside
④ (Queen's Cross Church)
⑤ Ruchill Parish Church and Halls
⑥ St Charles (R.C.)
⑦ St Columba (R.C.)

CHURCHES

Former FREE COLLEGE CHURCH MISSION HALL, 329–
45 North Woodside Road. Of c. 1879. The elevation is only
elementary Gothic, but the building has historical significance:
in 1883 the Boys' Brigade was founded here by Sir W. A.
Alexander.

KELVIN STEVENSON MEMORIAL CHURCH, Belmont
Street. Originally the Nathaniel Stevenson Memorial Free
Church. Designed in 1898 by *J. J. Stevenson* (with assistance
from *Henry Redfern*) on a return visit to Glasgow and opened
in 1902. It has strong similarities with Stevenson's Peter Memorial Church of 1901 at Stirling. Large and dramatically situated over the Kelvin, it is entered from the high-level bridge.
It lacks a uniform style but is none the worse for that. The
very tall s elevation takes its cue from English c 14 Gothic. In
contrast, the w front is c 15 Scottish Gothic, crowstepped and
with a massive NW tower and distinguished crown steeple
(based on that of King's College, Aberdeen). Elaborately traceried windows on the N side. The interior is equally unpre-
dictable: the tall three-bay N arcade, from which the gallery
stretches back over a wide aisle, is totally unrelated to the low,
elliptically arched s arcade, which screens a passage aisle. The
elaborately timbered roof also plays tricks, its very wide span
disguised by unusual boxing at the side. – Sycamore COM-
MUNION TABLE and oak ELDERS' CHAIRS of 1939 by *A. G.
Lochhead,* presented by Sir John Reith. – STAINED GLASS.
Mid-c 20, by *Gordon Webster*.

NORTH WOODSIDE CHURCH, 94 Raeberry Street. Designed
as a Free Church in 1875–6 by *Corrie & Craig*. Copybook
Gothic, with a tall gabled front, compressed porch and the
stump of an unfinished tower and spire. The poor quality of the
sandstone means that carved detail is gradually disappearing.
Inside, side galleries divided from the nave by a series of arches
rising from cast-iron columns with foliate capitals.

QUEEN'S CROSS CHURCH, 866 Garscube Road. 1896–9, by
C. R. Mackintosh. Built as a Free Church; since 1977, the
home of the Charles Rennie Mackintosh Society. The commission came to *Honeyman & Keppie* and gave Mackintosh
his first chance to design an ecclesiastical building. There are
still many traditional elements, but these have been ingeniously interpreted by Mackintosh. The site was a prominent
though very tight one, surrounded by tall tenements and a
warehouse. Although the church is quite small, the powerful
massing and the rich modelling, which produces deep
shadows, gave it a well-judged place in the street scene. Now,
surrounded by smaller, less closely packed brick houses, its
prominence is exaggerated. Instantly striking outside is the
variety of elements, not a confused assemblage but a careful
reflection of the internal arrangement. Although the design,
inside and out, at first sight seems austere, numerous idiosyncratic details emerge on closer inspection – and the essence
of this church is attention to individual detail.

The design is based on an open hall and owes much to Richard Norman Shaw's Harrow Mission Church in Latimer Road, Hammersmith, London, of 1887–9. At the important s w angle is a short but tapering tower derived, it seems, from the incomplete medieval one of Merriott Church in Somerset which Mackintosh had sketched in 1895. Each section of the s elevation, though treated individually, is cleverly related to the whole façade. Adjoining the tower to the E, two two-storey gabled bays, a form familiar in Glasgow's Gothic Revival buildings. The large Perp windows light the w gallery and, below them, a low passage aisle ingeniously links the two entrance vestibules. It is clearly expressed as it crosses the next two recessed bays. Here the flying buttress is a clue to the construction of the roof; no other indication of tie-beams appears on the exterior because their thrust is absorbed into cross walls of the two-storey sections. The origins of the easternmost bay lie in the two-storey medieval porch, an idea more readily appreciated in Mackintosh's delicate drawing than in the executed porch with its bold vertical accent. The curious Art Nouveau details have no historical precedent.

Inside, the wide timber barrel-vaulted hall is spanned undisguisedly by rolled-steel tie-beams (about 50 ft or 15 m wide), although against the dark stained wood their honest exposure is not immediately apparent. The two galleries, one at the E end and the other over the s w projection, are boldly cantilevered with pendant details which foreshadow those used in the School of Art Library. Below the E gallery, a timber screen (by *Thomas Howarth*) partitions a former schoolroom (1939–45). The organ gallery (lacking an organ) is hollowed out of the tower. – Mackintosh designed the FURNISHINGS and most of them survive. At the w chancel (rood beam to be replaced 1989), a shallow, panelled recess, with a slight central emphasis, for the COMMUNION TABLE. – A circular, canopied wooden PULPIT clasps the N w angle of the recess and is delicately carved with sinuous low reliefs based on floral motifs. Incorporated is a seat, upholstered in green and crowned by a stylized dove. – STAINED GLASS. In 1960 *Gordon Webster* inserted three coloured lights into the w window below the flowing tracery. – To the N w, the HALL, with a characteristic open-trussed roof and tall dado panelling.

RUCHILL PARISH CHURCH AND HALLS (formerly Ruchill United Presbyterian Church), Ruchill Street. The church, by *Neil C. Duff*, 1903–5, is neo-Perp with a solid, buttressed s w tower attached to the w gable, all of it built in red Locharbriggs stone. Adjoining the tower to the s, a Gothic porch which provides access to the church (l.), the halls (r.) and the courtyard between them. Inside, a wide nave and arcaded aisles. One arcade continues up to frame the s gallery, which is lit by triple-light windows with cusped lintels. Organ in the apsidal E end. Delicate Art Nouveau stained glass.

The HALLS, of 1899, are by *C. R. Mackintosh* and were originally mission halls for Westbourne Free Church. Small, of one and two storeys, and Art Nouveau. The interest of the street elevation is in the use of curved details in various planes. At the N end, a rounded stair compartment, now linked to a later porch. The street front and the raked buttressing to the side elevations are of yellow sandstone; otherwise the walls are harled. Careful planning allows maximum flexibility of use inside, but all is quite simply detailed, with deeply corniced panelling, open timber roofs with bolted collar- and tie-beams and curved bracing, and a few inset decorative glass panels and fretwork details. The caretaker's house with a turret stair closes the tiny courtyard.

ST CHARLES (R.C.), Kelvinside Gardens. By *Gillespie, Kidd and Coia*, 1959–60. A long church on a steep hillside, its design derived partly from Auguste Perret's church at Raincy and partly from the top-lit halls of engine works. The main entrance is at the E end, in a confined space where the steps from Melrose Gardens join the cul-de-sac of Kelvinside Gardens East. The wide door is in a substantially glazed gable, seen most readily in perspective. A second entrance facing the piazza to the N has been almost lost in a depressing extension which destroys the impact of the circular sacristy and the dramatic Scandinavian-inspired cloche, the latter a prominent landmark with a delightful weathervane. Inside, tall concrete columns, swelling at the top to support the fanfold vault, encircle the nave and apse. Between the columns, brick panels below a narrow clearstorey (except in one bay at the W (liturgically E) end), which makes the roof appear to float over the church. Chapels project from the side aisles, and above the aisle runs a broad concrete beam which provides a base for *Benno Schotz*'s ingenious STATIONS OF THE CROSS, a frieze of modelled terracotta figures for which the architect of the church (*Jack Coia*) and the sculptor himself were models. – Schotz also designed the SANCTUARY LAMP. – The ALTAR of Mexican onyx has a daringly cantilevered concrete baldacchino. The seating, designed by the architect, attempts to fulfil a particular request for comfort.

ST COLUMBA (R.C.), Hopehill Road. 1937, by *Gillespie, Kidd & Coia*. Large and effective, although built on a tight budget. Adjoining to the S, an equally good two-storey presbytery with a boldly carved hoodmould over the door. The W front of the church looks imposing. The enormous central screen-wall, clasped by two low curved projections for baptistery and staircase, is Italian Romanesque in inspiration. It is dominated by a tall glazed cross flanked by two arcaded panels. The triple arches of these panels are echoed in the three entrances, boldly framed in stone. The centre one is carved with the paschal lamb and other symbols and with a bishop attended by angels. Inside, the full height can be appreciated, the severely simple concrete portal frames giving the nave a dramatic appearance. Light comes from clearstorey windows. – On the brick walls below, painted panels of the STATIONS OF THE CROSS by *Hugh Adam Crawford*, transferred from the Catholic Pavilion at the Empire Exhibition. – In the sanctuary, which is plastered in contrast to the rest of the church, light floods from the side windows and concentrates on the marble REREDOS carved with a crucifix by *Benno Schotz*. – The stone PULPIT is, unusually, brought well forward into the nave.

PUBLIC BUILDINGS

KELBOURNE STREET FIRE STATION, 35 Kelbourne Street. 1936, by *Thomas Somers*. A large red brick courtyard range of firemen's housing and a fire station with a tall drying tower.

WALCHERN BARRACKS (Territorial Army; originally drill halls for the Glasgow Highlanders' Territorial Division), Garrioch Road. By *John Laird & Son*, 1938–9. Low Z-plan white-walled range with curved entrance in the s angle and functional drill halls to rear.

Former LANARKSHIRE REGIMENT DRILL HALL, Jardine Street. 1894. Red brick, with a surprisingly frivolous double-gabled, timber-framed upper floor.

PARTICK THISTLE FOOTBALL CLUB, 80 Firhill Road. 1927. In the centre of the long stand façade, the office and club members' entrance are given desultory emphasis.

DUNARD STREET PRIMARY SCHOOL. By *H. B. W. Steele & Balfour*, 1900. A dull red sandstone Board school.

EAST PARK BUILDINGS, Avenuepark Street. Built in 1888 as East Park Board School. The emphasis is on the central bays.

KELBOURNE SCHOOL, Hotspur Street. An 'open-air' school of 1914. Red brick, with timid Arts and Crafts detail in stone.

Former NAPIERSHALL STREET SCHOOL, 40–50 Napiershall Street. Plain three-storey red sandstone Board school of *c*. 1900, with excellent cast-iron railings and lamp-standards.

NORTH KELVINSIDE SECONDARY SCHOOL, Oban Drive. Three buildings stepping up the hill. The earlier ones (of 1914 and *c*. 1920) are of solid red sandstone: the latest (*c*. 1965) is a functional building of brick with concrete banding, quite respectably detailed.

ST CHARLES'S PRIMARY SCHOOL, 13 Kelvinside Gardens. Dull red sandstone range of 1901, and a substantial addition of 1932–3 by *William McCaig*, architect to the City's Education Department, possibly in collaboration with *Weddell & Inglis*.

ST COLUMBA'S ROMAN CATHOLIC SCHOOL, Callander Street. By *John McNab*, *c*. 1950, with subsequent additions.

Former SHAKESPEARE STREET SCHOOL, Shakespeare Street. By *McWhannell, Rogerson & Reid*, *c*. 1915.

SHAKESPEARE STREET JUNIOR SCHOOL, 75 Hotspur Street. An imposing red sandstone school of *c*. 1905 with a bold Baroque columned centrepiece, built for the Maryhill School Board as Garrioch Street School.

Former SPRINGBANK SCHOOL, Hinshaw Street. 1884. Sturdy yellow sandstone former Board school with large pil-

astered first-floor windows; now a landmark in a sea of late
C 20 red brick building.

EAST PARK HOMES FOR INFIRM CHILDREN, 1092 Maryhill
Road. Established in 1874, but the earliest surviving building
is of 1888, gabled and with a pretty attached tower and spirelet.
Much altered and extended by *John Fairweather*, 1932 and
1939, and by *John Fairweather & Son*, 1947.

KELVINSIDE TERRACE STEPS AND RETAINING WALL.
Probably designed in the early 1870s by *Alexander Thomson*.
Monumental retaining walls with steps at the w end, originally
linked to the (demolished) Queen Margaret Bridge of 1870.
Facing the bridge, the wall is crowned with a stumpy columned
screen bearing all the hallmarks of Thomson.

FORTH AND CLYDE CANAL AND FIRHILL BASIN. The
canal was extended from Maryhill to Hamiltonhill in 1777. In
1788 the Firhill Timber Basin was constructed by widening a
bend, with a second basin made on the inside of the bend in
1849. Further up the canal, spanning the w end of Bilsland
Drive an AQUEDUCT of 1879, very like those in Maryhill and
Possilpark.

QUEEN MARGARET BRIDGE, KIRKLEE BRIDGE. *See* Crossings of the Clyde and Kelvin, below.

DESCRIPTION

There is much familiar mid-to-late C 19 HOUSING in the area,
and a good cross-section can be seen in the following streets.
On the SE edge, just w of Maryhill Road, in BURNBANK
GARDENS, five unusual Venetian Gothic terraced houses of
c. 1860. Some way to the NW, WILTON CRESCENT, an
unusual Wilsonesque terrace of houses of *c.* 1855 (with later
Glasgow Style railings at No. 87), faces WILTON GARDENS,
composed of bay-windowed tenements of *c.* 1870 on the N
side of the central gardens. This tenement form, with some
variations, can be seen in the streets to the w. From the s side
of WILTON STREET, two refined quadrant blocks of *c.* 1860
turn into Belmont Street. To the E and w, along the banks of
the River Kelvin, the terraced housing of *c.* 1865 in DOUNE
GARDENS gives way to the larger tenement ranges of DOUNE
QUADRANT and KELVINSIDE TERRACE, both built in the
1870s. Further w, beyond Queen Margaret Drive, in KELVIN
DRIVE, another terrace of houses dating from *c.* 1865, this
time a row of twelve with generous canted bays and tripartite
doors. At No. 8, the elaborate cast-iron-columned balcony
looks more reminiscent of New Orleans than Glasgow. On the
turn of the terrace into BOTANIC CRESCENT, two houses
sporting large bowed windows, and at No. 13 pretty patterned
slatework. The crescent itself is of standard bay-windowed
houses, turning to tenements at the later w end. At the corner
in Kelvin Drive, a handsome Italianate villa of *c.* 1860 with a
tower and a substantial two-storey bowed window overlooking

the Kelvin. The large, late C 19 red sandstone tenements with bowed dormers further N in GARRIOCH ROAD are reminiscent of those in Hillhead Street (*see* Hillhead, below: Perambulation). Off to the r. in CLOUSTON STREET, earlier tenements of *c*. 1865 have Wilson's favourite shell-head motif. On the NE side, on the corner with Sanda Street, a handsome tenement covered with Thomsonesque details.

E and W of Maryhill Road, a number of C 20 HOUSING SCHEMES can be clearly identified. Our description takes us from S to N and starts with the earliest, BURNBANK GARDENS, developed in four phases by *Eason & Jardine* for Glasgow District Council. The first phase, of 1965–6, with an L-plan block on the corner with Napiershall Street, set the pattern of five-storey deck-access, two-apartment blocks with stairs at either end. The ground floors are stone-clad, the walls above rendered. A similar block followed at the E end of the street in 1970, and the two were linked by a lower old people's hostel. The final block at the E end, in BURNBANK TERRACE, is of 1971–2. Originally flat-roofed, all the blocks now have oversized pitched roofs and some weak Post-Modern casing to the lift-shafts.

The NORTH WOODSIDE ROAD, MOUNT STREET, RAE-BERRY STREET scheme of the mid-1980s is a mixed development of three-storey flats and two-storey terraced houses, all in buff brick, with uncomfortably exaggerated window margins.

The DONCASTER STREET scheme fronts Maryhill Road between Trossachs Street and Hinshaw Street: 1980–2, by Glasgow's *Department of Architecture* (project architect *Alan Martin*). A courtyard development of three-storey blocks in a smooth red brick with a shallow version of the traditional canted oriel. Above the entrances, the linking corridors are faced with a scooped parapet inspired by Mackintosh.

Between MARYHILL ROAD, KIRKLAND STREET and RAEBERRY STREET, a large and pleasing scheme designed and built between 1981 and 1985 by the S.S.H.A., which involved an interesting experiment in tenant participation. Two-storey houses and three-storey flats in good-quality red brick with projecting bays, simple bracketed porches and deep eaves. The surrounding retaining walls and arched entrances to rear gardens add distinction.

A good way past Queen's Cross, in LEYDEN STREET, a private block of four-storey flats on a Z-layout by *Honeyman, Jack & Robertson* for Taylor Woodrow Homes (Scotland), 1985–6, which, although only four storeys high, shows no respect for the rehabilitated tenements of *c*. 1900 lying to the E. On the ground floor, an arresting banded combination of straw-coloured and red textured bricks.

On the opposite side of Maryhill Road, the ORAN STREET scheme, completed by Glasgow's *Department of Architecture* in 1986. Most striking is the continuous wall of red brick housing which fronts Maryhill Road and Queen Margaret

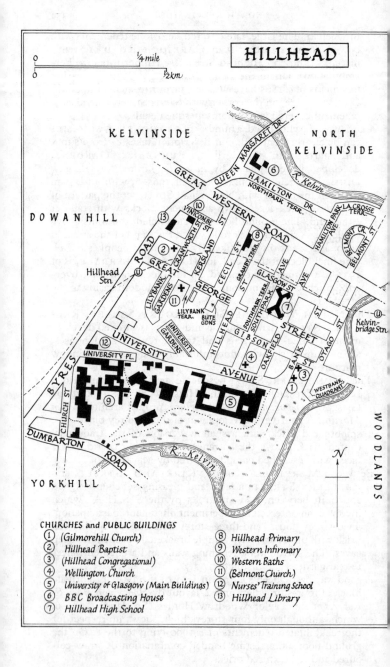

HILLHEAD

¼ mile
½ km

KELVINSIDE

NORTH KELVINSIDE

DOWANHILL

R. Kelvin

GREAT WESTERN ROAD

QUEEN MARGARET DR.

HAMILTON DR.

NORTHPARK TERR.

HAMILTON PARK AVE

LACROSSE TERR.

BELMONT CR.

BELMONT ST.

Hillhead Stn

GREAT WESTERN ROAD

VINICOMBE ST.

CRANWORTH ST.

KERSLAND

CECIL ST.

GRANBY TERR.

GLASGOW ST.

AVE

AVE

ST.

ST.

OTAGO ST.

LILYBANK GARDENS

GEORGE

HILLHEAD ST.

SOUTHPARK TERR.

SOUTHPARK AVE

STREET

LILYBANK TERR.

BUTE GDNS

UNIVERSITY GARDENS

GIBSON

OAKFIELD

BANK ST.

WESTBANK QUADRANT

Kelvinbridge Stn

BYRES ROAD

UNIVERSITY

UNIVERSITY PL.

AVENUE

CHURCH ST.

DUMBARTON ROAD

R. Kelvin

YORKHILL

WOODLANDS

N

CHURCHES and PUBLIC BUILDINGS

① (Gilmorehill Church)
② Hillhead Baptist
③ (Hillhead Congregational)
④ Wellington Church
⑤ University of Glasgow (Main Buildings)
⑥ BBC Broadcasting House
⑦ Hillhead High School
⑧ Hillhead Primary
⑨ Western Infirmary
⑩ Western Baths
⑪ (Belmont Church)
⑫ Nurses' Training School
⑬ Hillhead Library

Drive. Blue brick emphasizes the large round-arched, glazed entrances to the three-storey flatted blocks and some of the window details. Dashing bright blue railings and globe lamps in cages.

In SHAKESPEARE STREET, CRAIGEN COURT, of 1987–8, by 121 *Ken MacRae*, in association with *McGurn, Logan, Duncan & Opfer*, forms two-thirds of a circle and very successfully translates the traditional tenement theme without banal pastiche. The front has storey heights to correspond with its rehabilitated tenement neighbours of *c*. 1900, and only at the rear have two additional storeys been inserted. A variety of textured building materials is used to make a polychromatic pattern, most distinctive the simulated channelled granite facing the ground floor and the red margins round the gallery-like arrangement of grouped third-floor windows *à la* Thomson.

E of Maryhill Road, overlooking the canal just off Ruchill Street, the GLASGOW RUBBER WORKS (Nos. 125–9 SHUNA STREET), with a range of handsome, simply detailed buildings of 1895–1914 by *George Simpson*.

HILLHEAD

Hillhead is a neat enclave contained within the eastern loop of the River Kelvin, with its western boundary following Byres Road. In the early years of the C 19, Gilmorehill House occupied an elevated site in the S of the district, with views over the Kelvin and the Clyde. In 1863, the house and about 43 acres (17.5 ha) were bought, together with Donaldshill to the W, for the new Glasgow University buildings and for the Western Infirmary. (These institutions now dominate the S part of Hillhead.) N of University Avenue, Hillhead itself was mainly in one ownership. A plan for developing the area was drawn up by *David Smith* in 1830. In 1833, a part of the eastern Hillhead estate was advertised for sale, but clearly Walter Gibson, the owner, was over-optimistic, and it was not until the 1850s that building of residential property began in earnest. The estate was laid out on the grid plan which still distinguishes the district. Building over the hill continued slowly, and by 1869, when Hillhead was given burgh status, most of the area E of Hillhead Street and from Great Western Road at the N had been covered. By 1891, when Hillhead was absorbed into Glasgow, it was a flourishing urban area. The land was developed with a mixture of terraced housing, tenements and a few detached and semi-detached villas. Here, in comparison with the other West End areas, there is a greater concentration of mid-C 19 tenements, mostly of three storeys plus basements, with two floors to each apartment, making them quite spacious.

CHURCHES

Former BELMONT CHURCH (now Laurel Bank School), 121 Great George Street. 1893–4, by *James Miller* for the Established Church. A straightforward cruciform Gothic church with an apse but no tower, and making ample use of grouped lancets. Interior converted to assembly and dining hall. It was aisleless, a simplified version of Burnet's Barony Church (*see* Townhead, above).

Former GILMOREHILL CHURCH (built as Anderston Free Church), University Avenue. Now the Gilmorehall, used by Glasgow University as an examination hall. By *James Sellars*, 1876–8. Normandy Gothic. The tower which should have closed the vista at the E end of University Avenue was never completed. Built on a rectangular plan, with low projecting buttressed aisles and a lower gabled hall to the N. The five gabled clearstorey windows closely resemble those used by John Burnet Snr at St Jude's, Woodlands Gate (1874–5). Nothing of interest remains inside: the nave has been ceiled over above the arches of the aisle arcades.

HILLHEAD BAPTIST CHURCH, Cresswell Street. A neo-Greek design of 1883 by *T. L. Watson*, based on his Adelaide Place Baptist Church (*see* Commercial Centre, above), but stylistically borrowing from Sellars' Finnieston Church (*see* Woodlands and Finnieston, above). A tall rectangular church with the ground floor acting as a podium for a restrained, Ionic-pedimented temple front as the centrepiece. To the r., a single-storey pilastered and pedimented hall. The simple classicism continues with the paired pilastrade along the Cranworth Street elevation: it frames the recessed gallery windows which themselves have pilastered reveals. At the W end, a lower pedimented bay fronts the caretaker's house. Handsome pilastered and galleried interior, with a compartmented and coffered ceiling. The apsidal recess, with the organ, at the S end is framed by a pedimented aedicule.

Former HILLHEAD CONGREGATIONAL CHURCH, University Avenue. Now Glasgow Christian Fellowship. By *H. & D. Barclay*, 1895, possibly based on a design by *Bruce & Hay*. A bulky French Gothic church filling a sloping corner site without distinction. The interior has been extensively altered.

WELLINGTON CHURCH, University Avenue. A dramatic and very late Greek Revival temple by *T. L. Watson*, 1882–4. Built for a United Presbyterian Church congregation. It is raised high above the street on a podium with steps (an idea borrowed from University College, London) ascending to the mighty hexastyle Corinthian-columned portico. Similar columned screens *in antis* line the side walls. Inside, galleries round three sides with gallery stairs at the S end and half-domed organ recess to the N. Two malleable iron lattice girders spanning N to S of the church support three arched sections of the roof: the sides are coved to create a plaster wagon roof. – ORGAN

by *Forster and Andrews* of Hull, 1884. – WAR MEMORIAL
by *Sir J. J. Burnet*, 1920–1.

UNIVERSITY OF GLASGOW

The present university buildings on Gilmorehill have been long
overshadowed by the reputation of their predecessors, which
stood round College Green off the High Street. The buildings
of the Old College comprised some of the most remarkable C 17
architecture in Scotland and their loss was a tragedy. In the
1840s, the Superintendent of Police described the old buildings
as 'situated in an old and decayed part of the city where the very
poorest of the population reside or where, as is usual in such
localities, there is a very large number of whisky shops, little
pawns or houses in which disreputable persons of both sexes are
harboured, crimes and disorder are a common daily occurrence.'
This was not, it was generally thought, a seemly place for a seat
of learning, though Lord Cockburn, the staunch defender of
Scotland's architectural riches, disagreed and accused the university's professors of selfishness in planning to move from such
architecturally distinguished buildings which it was possible to
restore. Funds for restoration seem to have proved the stumbling
block: the only way the university could realize capital was to sell
the College Green buildings and build on a new site.

By the 1840s the High Street site had caught the eye of the
railway builders. In 1845 the Glasgow Airdrie and Monklands
Railway Company made an offer for the site, in return for which
the company would build a new university in the fashionable
West End. An Act of Parliament allowing the college to dispose
of its buildings received the royal assent in 1846 and an agreement
was drawn up. The company purchased the lands of Woodlands
in 1847 and commissioned the Glasgow architect *John Baird I*
to draw up plans. He submitted three sets in so many years. The
professors, however, having sought advice from W. H. Playfair
(who declined to help) and consulted Barry and Pugin, found
fault with them all. They then, under pressure from the Treasury,
commissioned *Edward Blore*, an architect with considerable
experience of designing public buildings, to produce a less costly
design. Unfortunately, by 1849, when a compromise scheme had
been agreed upon, the railway company was unable to honour its
part of the deal and the university had to remain in the High
Street.

In 1863 a subsidiary of the North British Railway Company
made the university an offer of £100,000 to buy the High Street
site for a goods yard, and a second Act was passed to allow the
university to sell. Woodlands, of course, had by then been built
over with Charles Wilson's magnificent residential scheme, so a
new site was purchased at Gilmorehill for £65,000, and the
additional site of Donaldshill was acquired for a new infirmary.
But the university's troubles were not yet over. The Removal
Committee, which was dominated by Professor Allan Thomson,

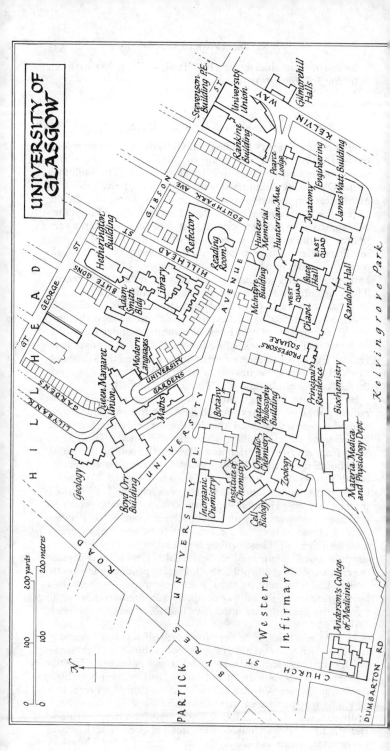

UNIVERSITY OF GLASGOW

a 'committee man' closely connected with the London establishment and with a particular interest in the Gothic Revival,
decided to side-step the competition system and offer the commission to *George Gilbert Scott*, whose Foreign Office scheme
was then being built. The choice of an English architect was
greeted with derision by the Glasgow architectural establishment, most particularly Alexander Thomson. (Their views
and criticisms of Scott's scheme were published in the *Pro-
ceedings of the Glasgow Architectural Society*.) The university was
undeterred, and Scott, heavily dependent on *Baird*'s first set of
plans for Woodlands Hill, devised a traditional collegiate scheme
round two courtyards, with the western side of the w court left
open (until filled by *Sir J. J. Burnet*'s chapel and west wing in
1923–9) to look across an open green towards the residential
ranges of Professors' Square.

For other university buildings, *see* Anniesland and Jordanhill;
Maryhill; and Knightswood, below.

PERAMBULATIONS

The university buildings are described in three perambulations:
the main university buildings; the main departmental buildings;
the buildings N of University Avenue. (*See* map.)

1. The main university buildings

The first perambulation starts towards the E end of University
Avenue at the PEARCE LODGE of 1885–8 by *A. G. Thomson*,
which, with its Baronial guise, gives a tantalizing reminder of
the Old College; through the generosity of the engineer and
shipbuilder Sir William Pearce, fragments of the C17 Old
College entrance front on the High Street were saved and
incorporated into this new entrance lodge. The fragments
include one panel dated *ANN. DOM 1658* and another
inscribed with *CR2* and two crossed swords. The boldly rusticated arched entrance, the elaborately sculpted pedimented
panel, the supporting bas-relief urns and the gable head with
three diamond flues at the apex all echo the old main entrance.
The two bays to the N and the two wrapped round to the S,
each with a heavily corbelled balcony and strapwork window
heads, are copied from the Old College, though the proportions
are not, nor is the Baronial stair turret. Once through the
archway, or past the powerful drum GATEPIERS (also by *A. G.
Thomson*, 1889), the first building we come to on the r. is the
ENGINEERING BUILDING of 1901 by *Sir J. J. Burnet* and
J. Oldrid Scott, a powerful block reflecting many details from
Old College. It was extended S in 1908, but to plans approved
in 1901, by *J. J. Burnet*, and again in 1920 with an arcaded
range, heightened by two storeys in 1952 by *J. Keppie, Henderson & Gleave*. Next, the JAMES WATT ENGINEERING
BUILDING by *Keppie Henderson & Partners, 1957–8*, replac-
ing one of Sir G. G. Scott's buildings (it was an interpretation

of the Abbot's Kitchen at Glastonbury). The building steps round the corner at the E edge of the flat top of Gilmorehill, and has a powerful presence at the E end of Scott's long S façade. The south-facing walls are of Portland stone, with at the SW end, a massive bas-relief by *Eric Kennington* (who died while the work was in progress in 1957), depicting Science. The E elevations are glass and steel screens with a version of the favourite Glasgow eaves gallery on the E side. Though the materials make some concession to the neighbouring buildings, the size of the building does not and its bulk now dominates the dramatic view of the university from Park Terrace.

The MAIN BUILDINGS comprise two quadrangles forming a rectangle of 600 by 300 ft (180 by 90 m). *Sir George Gilbert Scott*, taking his cue, as he had been instructed, from the earlier designs by Baird and Blore (*see* above), was responsible for the N, S and E fronts and for the tower of 1864–70. Just as Glasgow's own architects had failed to win the commission to design the university, so local contractors were passed over in favour of one that Scott often used, *John Thompson* of Peterborough. *J. Oldrid Scott* completed the 100-ft (30·5-m) tower and spire in 1887–91 (Sir G. G. Scott had planned a lead-covered spire). The stone is local, with good-quality Kenmure freestone for the dressings. In some windows there are a few columns of red sandstone (unusually, Old Red Sandstone from Bonhill). The columns flanking the great S door are of pink Ross of Mull granite. Inside, iron construction is remarkably frankly used, as it had been at Scott's St Pancras Hotel, London. For the S FRONT he used what he claimed was his own interpretation of Scottish Gothic – 'a style which I may call my own invention, having already introduced it at the Albert Institute at Dundee ...' – although a strong Flemish influence is equally apparent (the Cloth Hall at Ypres must be the source for the very long S façade with its central ventilating tower). Neither the impact of the whole façade nor its lack of symmetry can be accurately experienced on Gilmorehill itself, as the ground falls away quickly to the S and E, allowing only a sharp perspective view. The compelling impression is of great size with plenty of Gothic detail, dominated by the mighty central tower and fanciful open spire. The tower, although infinitely larger, is distantly related to those often attached to tolbooths; the spire recalls that of Regensburg Cathedral, with a corona similar to that on the Tron Steeple (*see* Merchant City, Churches, above: Tron Kirk) clamped over it. The corbelled angle turrets on the larger end blocks take up the Baronial theme which is also used, more convincingly, in the Bute Hall. In front of the E range, a TERRESTRIAL GLOBE, a great stone globe with a slate dial, traditionally known as Lord Kelvin's Sundial and possibly made by him.

Passing through the main entrance, the central vaulted passage opens into one of the unsung achievements of the Gothic Revival and Scott's supreme achievement for the university –
48   the open-columned and vaulted undercroft of the RANDOLPH

AND BUTE HALLS. Substantial gifts from Charles Randolph and the third Marquess of Bute allowed Scott to expand his preliminary thoughts of 1865–6 and elevate the halls (an idea developed in his Bombay University building). Scott died shortly after the drawings were completed, and the execution of the work fell to *J. Oldrid Scott* and *Edwin Morgan* (1878–84). The forest of clustered and cylindrical columns supports the tall buttressed hall; the tracery of the windows is a variant of that in the triforium and clearstorey at Lincoln Cathedral. The elevations are clasped by circular tourelles with galleried tops. To enter the Halls, one must return to the main entrance and take the PRINCIPAL STAIRCASE, carried on decorative cast-iron beams and with an elegant balustrade and ribbed vault. The two memorial tablets in the Italian Renaissance manner (one to Lord Sandford, one to Professor Veitch) are by *J. Oldrid Scott*, 1896. A turn l. and then r. leads into the 47 Randolph Hall, an anteroom in the form of a transverse hall with a stencilled barrel-roof and walls patterned with fleur-de-lis. Separated by a screen but part of the same space is the N–S-orientated Bute Hall, large and aisled, with clustered cast-iron columns, stencilled with fleur-de-lis, supporting the arcaded gallery and panelled roof. The restoration of the halls in 1986 has revealed one of the richest Victorian interiors in Glasgow. The columns and the canopied niches and quatrefoils in the spandrels are coloured Crichton Stuart blue (for the Marquess of Bute) and gold. In the Randolph Hall, the gable wall with blind arcading is stencilled with red fleur-de-lis, the wall carrying the organ in the Bute Hall with blue stylized thistles. The STAINED GLASS is equally lavish and includes, in the centre W windows (upper and lower), of 1893, literary figures by *Burne-Jones* (except for Milton and Shakespeare, by *Henry Holiday*) to designs, with the exception of Virgil, made twenty years before for Peterhouse, Cambridge. – Centre window by *Burne-Jones*. – Centre E by *Henry Holiday*, 1903. – The memorial window to Principal Caird is by *Henry Dearle* of *Morris & Co.*, 1901. – *Douglas Strachan* added two windows at the N in 1907. – In 1970, *Gordon Webster* provided the window with the arms of the former rectors. – MEMORIAL TABLET to Sir William Ramsay, 1917, by *Sir J. J. Burnet*. – Opposite the Randolph Hall, in the centre of the S front, the SENATE ROOM, like a chapter house and oak-panelled. Its elaborately carved chimneypiece was spikily recast with a complex timber canopy by *Ivor G. Dorward* of *J. L. Gleave & Partners*, 1969. At the SW corner of the S front, the HUMANITY CLASSROOM remains in its original C19 form.
Facing the E quadrangle, the elevations are a restless combination of Gothic and Baronial. On the N side, the HUNTERIAN STAIR, an exuberant creation of structural cast-iron and with a magnificent scrolled wrought-iron balustrade in C17 style and a timber coffered ceiling. It leads to the N end of the Bute Hall and to the HUNTERIAN MUSEUM. The museum entrance hall is gracefully arcaded and apsed with an elaborate

timber wagon roof. Statues of Adam Smith by *Hanns Gasser* (1867) and of James Watt by *Francis Chantrey* (1823) hold pride of place. To the r., in the main galleried exhibition hall, Scott (following in the tradition of the Oxford Museum) made dramatic use of decorated cast-iron structural members with both clustered and diapered paired shafts. The gallery is cantilevered, with ingenious display cabinets fixed to the handrail. To the l. of the apsed centrepiece, the equally handsome former LIBRARY, where the elaborate ironwork and roof structure, partially obscured in the late 1960s by partitioning, await restoration in 1989.

Back to the w quadrangle, which has a sculpture (Three Squares Giratory) by *George Rickey*, 1972. Gilmorehill House remained on the site of the w quadrangle to serve as offices for the architects and contractors during the first phase of building: it was not demolished until 1872. The court was open to the w until the 1920s but is now dominated by *Sir J. J. Burnet*'s WAR MEMORIAL CHAPEL (1923–7), Scots Gothic, straddling the simplified Gothic w courtyard range, and in harmony with Scott's buildings. The skeleton structure of reinforced concrete is faced inside and out with stone. Tall nave with delicate open-work *flèche* and shallow chancel, its E end owing much to Burnet's own Barony Church of 1886–90 (*see* Townhead, above: Churches) and perhaps to Sellars (cf. St Luke's Orthodox Cathedral; *see* Dowanhill: Churches). The interior is very chaste, with every aspect skilfully integrated. The tall single space is divided according to function with the centre part arranged in the collegiate manner with opposing choir stalls. *Archibald Dawson* was responsible for the sculpture, including the small grotesques on the w front and the naturalistic decoration of the STALLS. – PULPIT with Scottish saints, worked by *Walter Gilbert*. The shallow chancel is simply arcaded with memorial tablets below the three identical-height lancets. In the central niche, a figure of St Mungo. – Ten of the STAINED-GLASS windows, installed in 1931, are by *Douglas Strachan* in a cycle intended to depict the whole of human life as a spiritual enterprise. – w window also by Strachan, with four Scottish saints. – Faculty windows on the N side by *Gordon Webster*. – E window by *Lawrence Lee* (London), 1962. – Further window by *Keith New*, 1966, depicting Science and Philosophy. – Incorporated into the w range s of the chapel is another fragment salvaged from the Old College, THE LION AND UNICORN STAIR (by *William Riddell*, 1690). This heavily balustraded stair, with sedant sculptures of the beasts, was originally resited to serve as an entrance to the main buildings from Professors' Square. With the completion of the w wing in 1929, the stair was altered to make a r. turn into the new wing.

PROFESSORS' SQUARE was completed in 1870 by *Sir G. G. Scott*. Sombre pared-down Gothic around three sides of the square, designed as residential accommodation but now used for departmental purposes, except for the Principal's Residence at the s end. (Lord Kelvin lived in No. 11 during his long association with the university.) We leave the square at the NE via the MCINTYRE BUILDING AND GATEWAY. The gateway, of 1908 by *Sir J. J. Burnet*, forms the remarkably insignificant main entrance to the university, which seems always to have been schizophrenic about which was its chief entrance. To the r. of the gateway, the McIntyre Building, formerly the Students' Union, is an exercise in English collegiate Gothic built in three stages by *Sir J. J. Burnet*. The main gabled hall at the E end was completed in 1886 together with the squat tower and linking range; it was extended on the w in 1893 and again with the s block in 1908. Reconstructed in 1931 after completion of the new Union (*see* Perambulation 3, below) by *T. Harold Hughes*. E of the McIntyre Building, another entrance and the HUNTER MEMORIAL, a cenotaph of 1925 to William and John Hunter by *Sir J. J. Burnet*, with sculpture by *George Henry Paulin*, laid out in front of the apse of the Hunterian, with the QUINCENTENARY GATES of 1954 on the same axis, opening on to University Avenue. Looking to the E, we see *J. J. Burnet*'s ANATOMICAL BUILDING, 1900–1, a Scots Renaissance block slotted in between the E range of the main buildings and the Engineering Building. Extended at the NW by *Dorward, Matheson, Gleave & Partners*, 1977.

2. The main departmental buildings

Every inch of the main site on the s side of University Avenue has been put to use, and new buildings are still being squeezed in, making it difficult to appreciate the architecture. Starting from the s front of the Principal's Residence and heading w, the first building on the l. is the BIOCHEMISTRY BUILDING by *Richard De'ath* of *Keppie & Henderson*, 1963–4, a blocky ashlar-faced and glass range built over *Jack Coia*'s BOILERHOUSE of 1952. Coia consciously specified a rock-faced masonry skin over the concrete frame in deference to the neighbouring MATERIA MEDICA and the PHYSIOLOGY DEPARTMENT BUILDING, 1903–7, by *James Miller* as the result of a competition; the contorted Scots Renaissance design harks back to the Old College. The Physiology Building at the w is stepped down the slope with a crowning cupola to the lower w building.

Across the only open space in this tightly knit area, facing the Materia Medica, is the NATURAL PHILOSOPHY BUILDING, also by *James Miller*, 1906. Its two pilastered blocks are linked by a gabled Jacobean centrepiece with a set-back decorative cupola. The elaborate strapwork decoration over the door and first-floor window recalls Board school architecture. *Basil Spence & Partners* are responsible for the three restrained, extensive, Portland stone-faced extensions made in 1947–52 (N, research, to house the synchrotron), 1959 (W, teaching, with cantilevered, reinforced-concrete lecture theatre; E, in the courtyard), and 1966. To the w, also fronting the green, the far more remarkable ZOOLOGY BUILDING, by *Sir J. J. Burnet* (*Burnet, Son & Dick*), 1923. It seems to be a compromise between his earlier Edwardian style and his later functionalism. The functions of the various parts of the building are clearly expressed in the massing and the detailing, a classic example of Burnet's precept of designing from the inside out. The w and s sides are distinguished by the powerful channelled masonry (found in earlier Burnet buildings, e.g. the Glasgow Savings Bank banking hall; *see* Merchant City, Streets, above: Ingram Street), blank walls, the courtyard screen and the stepped windows, following the rake of the lecture theatre; the N is strongly vertical and well glazed to light the laboratories.

To the N of the Zoology Building, the butterfly-plan INSTITUTE OF CHEMISTRY by *T. Harold Hughes* with *D. S. R. Waugh*, 1936–9, completed 1950–54 by *Alexander Wright & Kay*, and with the addition of the timber upper storey (the original design planned for an additional floor) over part of the building by *Alexander Wright & Kay*, 1963 and 1966. The first building to break with the conventional use of masonry, it has a very carefully detailed brick facing using small 'Roman' bricks between bands of concrete over the reinforced concrete frame. The three blocks are linked by tall shallow curved stairwells reminiscent of Mackintosh's Scotland Street School (*see* Gorbals, below: Public Buildings), but more clearly influenced by Erich Mendelsohn's German Metal Workers' Union building in Berlin (1929). Each block is restlessly articulated to suit the internal needs (the elephant trunk extractors add to the movement). The only concession to the Zoology neighbours is the amusing incised frieze on the s wall depicting the origin of species; also on this block, a plaque to Joseph Priestley. Many of the original internal fittings exist, including the vertiginous main lecture theatre. The Inorganic Chemistry block facing University Avenue was the last to be completed and has a memorial plaque to Joseph Black on the N wall. Immediately E, the headquarters of Glasgow University's OFFICERS' TRAINING CORPS (*c.* 1900) by *H. & D. Barclay* under the supervision of *Colin Sinclair*. Fronting University Avenue, N of Natural Philosophy, the BOTANY BUILDING of 1900 by *J. Oldrid Scott* and *J. J. Burnet* combines Scottish Renaissance and Baronial details and uses corbelled turrets freely.

Three more departmental buildings which belong to this group but are divorced from it are on the corner of the Western Infirmary site facing Dumbarton Road. ANDERSON'S COLLEGE OF MEDICINE, 1888–9, by *James Sellars* but completed after his death by *John Keppie*, with sculpture by *Pittendrigh MacGillivray*. A bold exercise in restless Italian-cum-Scots Renaissance detail, with an elaborately modelled entrance and large arched windows to the E elevation. – To the w, on the corner of Dumbarton Road and Church Street, DEPARTMENT OF GENETICS, 1966, by *Basil Spence &*

Partners in association with *Peter Glover*, 1961–2. A tall, starkly angular reinforced cantilever frame, clad partly in green riven slate and partly in grey mosaic which is falling off. Immediately to the N in Church Street, the INSTITUTE OF VIROLOGY by the same architects but of 1961, and equally shabby now.

3. The buildings N of University Avenue

Opposite the Chemistry Building on the N side of University Avenue, there are a number of departmental buildings but very little evidence of any overall plan for the area, although this was not the intention. *Sir Frank Mears* in 1951 provided a plan which was not adopted. Had it been used it would have given a pleasant, though rather dull, series of courts. Now, however, the buildings appear to fill sites at random, like pins stuck haphazardly into a pincushion. The hilly nature of the area provides a necessary foil to this apparent lack of cohesion. The first building on the N of the street (when heading E) is the BOYD ORR BUILDING by *Ivor G. Dorward* of *Dorward, Matheson, Gleave & Partners*, opened in 1972, a massive reinforced-concrete building clad with bands of glass and aggregate panels on a powerful grid module and capped by a copper-faced shaped roof. It provides eleven floors of teaching accommodation with lecture theatres projecting at ground level to the E. E of it, the lower but similar MATHEMATICS BUILDING by *J. L. Gleave & Partners*, 1969; three linked blocks, with the lecture building at the centre flanked by the administrative department and the library. The whole façade is united by pre-cast concrete panels with aggregate finishes in unwelcoming dark grey. Turning sharply to the l. at the SE end of the Mathematics Building into University Gardens (for the original houses, *see* the Hillhead Perambulation, below), at the N end stands the dull QUEEN MARGARET UNION by *Walter Underwood & Partners*, 1968, which looks like a stack of television screens to which the boldly jettied lecture theatre is attached. To the rear of the Union Building and past the back of the Boyd Orr Building, we come to Lilybank Gardens and, on the l., the GEOLOGY BUILDING by *Dorward, Matheson, Gleave & Partners*, 1980. It reflects the shift in fashion from exposed concrete and aggregate panels to facing-brick, and it is well-mannered and carefully tailored to step round the curved site with canted projections. The horizontal strips of windows are neatly sandwiched between sensibly broad and subtly detailed brick bands. In front, an appropriately solid piece of rock (xenolithic Ballachulish granite), part of a demolished railway bridge. Back in University Gardens, on the NE side is the MODERN LANGUAGES BUILDING, 1958–9, the first of a number of commissions from the university for *W. N. W. Ramsay*. Now up the dank concrete steps to its r. to the top of the hill. To the l., Lilybank House (*see* the Perambulation, below) and, to the E of it, the ADAM SMITH BUILDING by *David Harvey, Alex Scott & Associates*, 1967, a large utilitarian range composed of a series of linked concrete-framed blocks faced with rugged reinforced dark grey pebble-studded panels. It stretches randomly along the top of the hill and, at the S end, sits on an ill-kempt and crumbling platform. Diverting into Bute Gardens, on the E side the low, unassuming brick HETHERINGTON BUILDING, originally known as 'Basic Arts', by *Gillespie, Kidd & Coia*, completed 1983. The façades are punctuated by V-section windows set in full-height timber panels.

115 To the SE, the towered UNIVERSITY LIBRARY AND HUNTERIAN MUSEUM AND ART GALLERY EXTENSION by *William Whitfield*. The main library was completed in 1968; the art gallery dates from 1971–81. This very prominent building, the C20 landmark to match the Scotts' tower, can be seen from many parts of the city. Consciously or unconsciously, the positioning of the towers competes with Trinity College and, from a distance, underlines the image of an Italian hilltop town at Gilmorehill. It is most rewarding to approach this complex from the S end of Hillhead Street. The first impression is of a series of stepped projections of unrelenting bush-hammered concrete and a bold round tower like the funnel of a liner. Closer to, the first element to attract attention is the bizarrely suspended MACKINTOSH HOUSE, sealed into the Art Gallery. It is a re-creation of the house at 78 Southpark Avenue which Mackintosh had recast internally for himself after he had moved there in 1906 and which was demolished by the university in 1963. Here, an elevation designed to recall the level and the spirit of the mid-C19 terrace (Mackintosh only altered the side elevation of the original house, and windows corresponding to those he inserted appear on the S gable) is uncomfortably hoisted on to a pedestal, giving the Glasgow hero a leg-up to heaven but creating a front door that leads nowhere and an architectural enigma for the uninitiated. To see inside, it is necessary to approach it from the rear, through the lobby of the new art gallery. The interior re-creation is as close as it was possible to make it; before the Southpark Avenue house was dismantled, everything was photographed and specimens of Victorian mouldings were kept to assist in the reconstruction. Some licence was taken with the hall, but the dining room and studio-drawing room are re-created and furnished as accurately as possible. The dining room, which combines dark walls with a white frieze and ceiling, is characteristic of Mackintosh's domestic dining rooms. In the studio-drawing room, we see that he removed all the house's Victorian detail or disguised it (for instance, the screen-wall was inserted to reduce the height of the E window) to create a pure, plain space on to which he stamped sparse but jewel-like decoration. The bedroom above received similar treatment. Also on display, a re-creation of the bedroom he designed later and very differently for No. 78 Derngate, Northampton, with its migraine-inducing striped decoration of 1919.

In the foyer of the gallery the rough-hewn exterior detail

continues. It makes a fit setting for the vast and rugged cast-aluminium doors by *Eduardo Paolozzi*, 1977, so powerful that their true function (as entrance to the main gallery) can easily be misinterpreted. The galleries themselves are, in contrast, understated and provide a sensitive setting for the university's impressive art collection, including the famous paintings and drawings by Whistler. In the sculpture court, the cupola, detailed by *C. R. Mackintosh*, which crowned Pettigrew and Stephen's warehouse (1896–7) in Sauchiehall Street until the 1970s.

To the N, the Library towers over the gallery, faced in pre-cast concrete cladding units with exposed Shap granite aggregate and with a rigid pattern of windows. This is a building which needs to be seen from all sides; the rear is a dramatic progression of restless angled façades emphasizing the fortified nature of the building.

On the other side of the paved, pedestrianized street, the refreshingly simple and discreet student REFECTORY (THE HUB) by *Frank Fielden & Associates* (in association with *W. V. Zinn & Associates* and the co-ordinating architect, *J. L. Gleave*). Its low rectangular shape, faced with natural and enduring materials, including exposed granite and flint aggregate, vies neither with the Library nor with the Reading Room, and, set behind the latter, can barely be noticed. The cleverly conceived READING ROOM, by *T. Harold Hughes & D. S. R. Waugh*, 1939–40, set back from University Avenue and surrounded by well-matured trees and landscaping, is also remarkably unassuming (but intended to be the centrepiece of a never built quadrangle with a clock-tower). The low domed rotunda of reinforced concrete is clad in bands of small yellow bricks, with tall metal windows and doors. The only emphasis is the prominent entrance at the head of shallow steps, a sparsely decorated triumphal arch attached to the S, with a giant archway framing the door and enormous window lighting the stair. The galleried interior retains its original fittings.

E of Southpark Avenue, the Wellington Church (*see* Churches, above). On the E side of Oakfield Avenue, first the RANKINE BUILDING of 1969 by *Keppie, Henderson & Partners*, a grim five-storey block with boldly projecting concrete beams and crumbling terrazzo facing. To its N, by *A. Graham Henderson* of the same firm, the STEVENSON PHYSICAL EDUCATION BUILDING, 1960, a timid glass-walled design with a wavy roofline and random balconies to little purpose. Immediately to the E, on the curve of University Avenue, the UNIVERSITY UNION, firstly the extension of 1965 by *Keppie, Henderson & Partners*, joined to the E gable of the main range of 1929–31, by *A. McNaughton* of *Arthur & McNaughton*, who won the competition with this solid late interpretation of Baronial. There are backward glances at both Burnet and Mackintosh in the drum towers, strapwork window heads, eaves balcony and shallow gable-end oriels. On the other side of University Avenue, two drum gatepiers announce the entrance to that

spacious parkway KELVIN WAY. Their banded vermiculation and wrought-iron lamp brackets are so closely
related to the gatepiers by *A. G. Thomson* at Gilmorehill that
they surely must be by him. (A similar pair stands at the s end
of Kelvin Way.) The Gilmorehall, formerly Anderston Free
Church, faces the Students' Union, and next to it, on the
corner with Gibson Street, is the former Hillhead Congregational Church (for both, *see* Churches, above).

PUBLIC BUILDINGS

BBC BROADCASTING HOUSE, 20 Queen Margaret Drive.
Part of it is NORTH PARK HOUSE, built for two Glasgow
merchants, John and Matthew Bell. This Renaissance palazzo
was begun by *J. T. Rochead*, 1869, and completed by *John
Honeyman*. Additions were made by *James Miller*, in association with *M. T. Tudsbery* (Chief Engineer to the BBC), in
1936–8 and later. Inside, a double-height Doric-columned
and galleried entrance hall, elaborate plaster decoration and
compartmented barrel-vaulted ceiling. The house later became
Queen Margaret College, to which *John Keppie* with *Charles
Rennie Mackintosh* added the MEDICAL BUILDING in 1895.
Although the building has been partially demolished and substantially altered, the stairtower, with its open-arched belfry
and bell-cast roof, survives, and so does the balustraded porch.
The extent of Mackintosh's part in the design is uncertain,
but there is no doubt that the perspective published in the
British Architect is in his hand. On display in the foyer of the
studios, a bust of Hugh MacDiarmid by Benno Schotz, 1958.

HILLHEAD PUBLIC LIBRARY, 348 Byres Road. By *Rogerson
& Spence*, 1972, built on the site of Hillhead Burgh Buildings.
Bold vertical aggregate-faced panels between narrow glazed
strips and over the entrance a huge decorative balcony.

HILLHEAD HIGH SCHOOL, Oakfield Avenue. A very large
example, one of the best surviving, of the once common open-
gallery-access butterfly-plan 1930s Glasgow Corporation
schools. By *E. G. Wylie* of *Wylie, Shanks & Wylie*, 1928–31
(competition 1921), in bright red brick with decorative patterns and, unusually, four two- to three-storey classroom
wings splayed from each angle of the central block. The classroom corridors and all the angle staircases were originally open
to the icy blasts, and even now are only partially filled. Solemn
classical detail on the central block and end elevations, and
to Southpark Avenue a grand gatehouse firmly guarding the
entrance. It seems to have been built for the War Memorial
Trust by *W. Hunter McNab & Son*, 1931. The boundary walls
and in particular the ironwork to the gates and railings are
strongly influenced by Mackintosh.

HILLHEAD PRIMARY SCHOOL (formerly Hillhead High
School), Cecil Street. By *H. & D. Barclay*, completed in 1883,
with an added attic of 1908 by *Samuel Preston*. Built on a

constricted and sloping site. The main s part has a pedimented centrepiece with Ionic columns *in antis* above the pilastered entrance and Thomsonesque caryatid pilasters. The flanking bays repeat the theme of Ionic columns from the first floor.

WESTERN INFIRMARY, Church Street and Dumbarton Road. The siting of this infirmary, to serve the western district, was linked to the removal of the University to Gilmorehill. After abortive attempts in 1846, *John Burnet Snr* was commissioned to produce plans in 1867. In 1871, on a reduced plan, the severe Baronial-style hospital (now hidden behind the eleven-storey main infirmary building) was begun on the present site and opened in 1874. The Freeland bequest provided the E range in 1881, completing the symmetrical composition. The turretted centre was based on gables of Glamis Castle. In 1897 *J. Burnet & Son* added a three-storey operating block with large windows (due for demolition in 1989) in the SE angle of the Baronial block. Inside G Wing, the small ALEXANDER ELDER MEMORIAL CHAPEL, by *John Burnet, Son & Dick*, 1926, in a confused Norman style with the stone details mechanically carved. A wide round arch frames the shallow chancel, and the two chancel windows are elaborately arched. There is, however, some notable STAINED GLASS, designed by *R. Anning Bell* and executed by *J. & W. Guthrie*. Numerous additions followed until in 1988 the rear projections were almost totally demolished. – Buildings fronting Church Street from the N – PATHOLOGICAL INSTITUTE by *J.J. Burnet*, Scots Renaissance of 1894–6, very plain except for an elaborate aedicule window in the street gable. Extended 1933–5. – Continuing the Scots Renaissance style, the OUTPATIENTS AND DISPENSARY by *J.J. Burnet*, 1902–5. – *Norman A. Dick* was architect for the next two buildings. The GARDINER MEDICAL INSTITUTE, 1937–8, a tall, sparingly detailed building (apparently *T. Harold Hughes* planned for a mirror-image building on the other side of the Tennant Building to form a symmetrical composition, but this was not completed because of the war), and the TENNANT MEMORIAL BUILDING, 1933–6, has sculpture, including barley-sugar columns with the 'owl' order and figures of light and darkness over the door, all by *Archibald Dawson*.

Returning into the heart of the complex, the huge, square, eleven-storey ACCIDENT AND EMERGENCY DEPARTMENT by *Keppie, Henderson & Partners*, 1965–74. The balconied elevations, with grids of concrete clad in white Skye marble aggregate above a blue engineering brick plinth, are very like those of the earlier Gartnavel Hospital by the same architects. The plan here is not linear, but a grid of four wards on each floor. To the E, overlooking the Kelvin, the former STAFF NURSES' HOME (now ADMINISTRATION), 1948, by *Robert Love*, with a semicircular glazed stairtower and wrap-round windows to the canted ends in the manner of T. S. Tait.

For Anderson's College of Medicine and the Institute of

Virology, *see* Glasgow University, above, Perambulation 2. At No. 120 University Place, the dull NURSES' TRAINING SCHOOL, 1971, and NURSES' HOME, 1970, by *Keppie, Henderson & Partners*.

WESTERN BATHS CLUB, Cranworth Street. By *Clarke & Bell*, 1876–81. A private swimming club, unusually complete inside and out. The façade is composed like a Palladian villa but dressed up in Venetian Gothic. The two-storey central entrance and clubroom block has an arcaded porch and opens into a columned hall and imperial stair. To the rear, a tall gabled building housing the swimming pond. It has a handsome cast-iron roof with pierced spandrels, and a gallery on one side with decorative cast-ironwork to the screens concealing the changing rooms below.

GIBSON STREET-ELDON STREET BRIDGE, QUEEN MARGARET BRIDGE. *See* Crossings of the Clyde and Kelvin, below.

PERAMBULATION

This perambulation also starts in BYRES ROAD, this time at the junction with University Avenue. On the NE corner a three-storey late classical curved tenement of *c.*1862, its simple dignity contrasting with the more commonplace four-storey blocks on the W side of the street. Extending E, the truncated Nos. 5–27 ASHTON ROAD, twelve houses of *c.*1862, with bowed first-floor oriels in the style of *James Thomson*'s Dowanhill development (*see* below). They are all that remain of ASHTON TERRACE and now face University Avenue across a triangular open space, part of the complete transformation of the W end of the Avenue in the 1970s. On the S side, the dull parallel blocks and lower linking ranges of the Western Infirmary's Nurses' Training School and Nurses' Home (*see* Public Buildings, above), purposely defying the existence of the street pattern. Behind, the Baronial ranges of the Western Infirmary (*see* Public Buildings, above). Further E, past the Boyd Orr Building (which brutally cuts through the E end of Ashton Terrace) and the Mathematics Building (for both, *see* Glasgow University, above: Perambulation 3), we reach UNIVERSITY GARDENS. With the exception of Nos. 1 and 12 (*see* below), the houses on the E are by *Sir J.J. Burnet* and date from 1882–4: all are occupied by departments of the university. Of the SW side, Nos. 11 and 13 at the SE are all that remains, their bold cliff-like S elevation with a substantially glazed top floor like the bridge of a liner. Turning l. into the Gardens, the porticoed terrace theme resumes for their front elevations. To their NW lies a bridge which crosses to the main entrance of the Mathematics Building, but we leave the purpose-built university buildings to the NW (*see* Glasgow University: Perambulation 3) and follow the steps in the centre of the central garden to Nos. 12 and 14, individually designed houses tacked on to the end of the longer, already existing terrace. No. 14 was finished in 1904 and is also by *Burnet*. Its façade is asymmetrical but cleverly balanced and sparingly detailed, with a solid balcony (the unusual cast-iron guard rail exploits a detail found inside the terrace houses) dying into the generous N W canted gabled bay. Inside, more excellent Glasgow Style work, including decorative glass. No. 12, by *J. Gaff Gillespie*, 1900, is an exceptionally resourceful design with a canted entrance bay which rises into a broad octagonal turret with a bell-cast roof, cleverly set within the elevation. The very complete and fine interior fittings and decoration demonstrate the powerful influence of Mackintosh and Art Nouveau. *Oscar Paterson* provided the stained glass. Nos. 9 and 10 adjoin Burnet's main terrace (originally called SAUGH-FIELD TERRACE) but lie at approximately 150° to its gentle curve. They are restrained, except for the excellent neo-Baroque doorpieces. Inside No. 9, a large stairwell divided from the hall by a carved Jacobethan screen with animals poised on the newels. No. 10 has a columned staircase, also of timber. Burnet's inventive terrace (Nos. 2–8) is full of subtle asymmetry. The wide canted bays like pavilions and the inter-mediate first-floor canted windows rising from the balustraded balcony articulate the façade boldly. (Note the use of concrete in the balcony rail.) The arresting batter to the ground floor E of the centre upsets the vertical rhythm and, together with the elaborately jettied dormers, gives the elevation even more movement. Many of the original panelled interiors survive: at No. 2, there are fretwork cast-iron balusters and carved pendants; at Nos. 3, 4 and 5, columned hall screens, and No. 4 has extensive panelling; at No. 6, a lavish marble bathroom; at No. 7, decoratively carved chimneypieces; and at No. 8 an Edwardian Baroque entrance hall. No. 1, by *Robert Ewan*, 1902, is a weighty book-end block at the S E angle with Hillhead Street. It has a pavilion roof on the angled projection at the corner.

To the N, within the pedestrianized area of HILLHEAD STREET and past a pair of isolated Post-Modern gatepiers, the University Library and Hunterian Art Gallery (to the l.) and the Reading Room (to the r.); set back behind a low wall with another set of gatepiers is The Hub (for them all, *see* Glasgow University: Perambulation 3). Beyond, a secluded domestic layout takes over. On the r., after the plain Nos. 41–51, is FLORENTINE HOUSE (53 Hillhead Street), built *c.* 1840 and one of the earliest buildings on the Hillhead feu. This small-scale but elegant villa, with simple late Georgian details and carefully executed ashlar, is set back in its own garden. Opposite, tall tenements of *c.* 1890 (Nos. 50–68) with bold bowed bays, some of them capped with curved dormers and some still with good panelled cast-iron railings, similar to tenements in Garrioch Road (*q.v.*). Similar tenements opposite.

Turning E into GIBSON STREET, the road descends steeply to

the E slicing through the main N-to-S layout of terraces. At SOUTHPARK AVENUE, on the NW corner, a handsome double villa of around 1850 with a central Doric portico serving both houses. To the NE, the terraced Nos. 53–63, of 1867–70, have oriels on the first floor in the manner employed by James Thomson in Dowanhill (*see* below). To the SE are Nos. 65–73, *c.* 1852, with raised ground floors. Further down Gibson Street, where Oakfield Avenue crosses, on the SW corner there is a long terrace (formerly Oakfield Terrace), *c.* 1855, in two parts (Nos. 62–70 and 72–80 Oakfield Avenue), with a return elevation to Gibson Street (No. 63). Channelled rustication gives the ground floor a strong horizontal emphasis. At No. 80, *J. J. Burnet* made additions for himself in 1881. To the NE, Nos. 57–69 Oakfield Avenue is a conventional terrace of *c.* 1868, very similar to Southpark Terrace (*see* below). Further down Gibson Street on the S side stand the university's Stevenson Physical Education Building and the Students' Union (*see* Glasgow University: Perambulation 3). Gibson Street now crosses the junction of University Avenue and Bank Street. On the SE corner, the former Hillhead Congregational Church (*see* Churches, above). Beyond the junction on the N side, a range of plain but stylish late Georgian tenements of *c.* 1850 stretches from Bank Street to Otago Street, growing larger in scale towards the E. On the S side, later tenements of *c.* 1874 (Nos. 39–47) return into the S part of Otago Street (Nos. 94–106) in a Thomsonesque style. At the foot of Gibson Street, the view N from the Gibson Street-Eldon Street Bridge (*see* Crossings of the Clyde and Kelvin, below) catches the untidy backs of buildings fringing the Kelvin in the N part of Otago Street. On the S side of the street, at the E end, a curved, simply domed angle to No. 3 returns into WESTBANK QUADRANT, a long bay-windowed tenement range with a picturesque view over the Kelvin gorge. The two eastern blocks are by *John Burnet*, 1877 (E), 1886 (central), that at the W end, on the corner with Otago Street, by *P. McNaughton, c.* 1880.

Returning to OTAGO STREET, our route goes N again past more three-storeyed symmetrical tenements of *c.* 1850 on the W side. They are remarkably spacious, often with two floors to each house. There are more in Great George Street and in Bank Street, the latter with some similar terraced housing as well. All of this housing continues the same refined late classical tradition, with boldly corniced main doors and plain close entrances cut through the unusual channelled rustication. Going E along Otago Street, at the foot of GREAT GEORGE STREET on the N side, a pair of classically detailed villas (Nos. 2, 4 and 10, with 63 Bank Street, divided into flats): their doors, which are of conventional size, fit uncomfortably into exceptionally tall doorpieces. Then No. 49 Otago Street, a simple picturesque villa of *c.* 1840, dwarfed by its neighbours. Off the W side of Otago Street, in COWAN STREET, well-mannered but unexceptional four-storey tenements built 1877–87. After the kink in Otago Street, there are two more

1. The River Clyde with Govan in the foreground

2. Commercial Centre: St Vincent Street

3. The West End: Woodlands Hill and the northern suburbs

4. The M8: Baillieston Interchange

5. Townhead: Glasgow Cathedral from the south-east,
thirteenth century, tower fifteenth century

6. Townhead: Glasgow Cathedral, capital in the north choir arcade,
second half of the thirteenth century

7. Townhead: Glasgow Cathedral, the crypt,
second half of the thirteenth century

8. Townhead: Glasgow Cathedral, pulpitum,
early fifteenth century, and altar platforms, 1503

9. Townhead: Bishop's Castle, fifteenth and sixteenth centuries, and Cathedral (engraved by Swan)

10. Townhead: Provand's Lordship, 1471, extended 1670

11. Pollokshields: Haggs Castle, 1585–7,
remodelled in the nineteenth century

12. Pollokshields: Haggs Castle, doorway, 1585

13. Merchant City: Tron Steeple, *c.* 1592, spire 1630–6, archways 1855

14. Merchant City: Tolbooth Steeple, by John Boyd, 1625–7

15. Pollok Park: Pollok House, garden front, 1747–52,
and wings by Sir Robert Rowand Anderson, c. 1904–8

16. Pollok Park: Pollok House, dining room overmantel, 1747–52

17. Merchant City: Hutchesons' Hall, by David Hamilton, 1802–5

18. Merchant City: Trades' Hall, by Robert Adam, 1791–4

19. Calton and Camlachie:
tenement at No. 394 Gallowgate, 1771

20. Gorbals: Laurieston House,
Carlton Place, staircase hall, c. 1804

21. Commercial Centre: Buchanan Street with St George's Tron, by William Stark, 1807–9

22. Calton and Camlachie: St Andrew's Parish Church, by Allan Dreghorn and Mungo Naismith, 1739–56

23. Saltmarket and St Enoch: Justiciary Courts, portico, by William Stark, 1809–14

24. Commercial Centre: St Vincent Street from the south side of Blythswood Hill (engraved by Swan)

25. Merchant City: former Royal Exchange, a mansion of 1778–80, remodelled by David Hamilton, 1827–32

26. Saltmarket and St Enoch: St Andrew's Roman Catholic Cathedral,
by James Gillespie (Graham), 1814–17

27. Merchant City: former Royal Exchange, newsroom,
by David Hamilton, 1827–32

28. Townhead: The Necropolis, Monteath Mausoleum, by David Cousin, 1842

29. Townhead: The Necropolis, opened 1833 (a nineteenth-century photograph)

30. Clyde crossings: South Portland Street Footbridge, by Alexander Kirkland and George Martin, 1851–3

31. Clyde crossings: St Andrew's Footbridge, Glasgow Green, by Charles O'Neill and Neil Robson, 1854–5

32. Shettleston and Tollcross: Tollcross House,
by David Bryce, 1848 (a nineteenth-century photograph)

33. Pollokshields: The Knowe, Albert Drive,
by Alexander Thomson, begun in 1852

34. Woodlands and Finnieston: Park Circus, Park Terrace,
Park Quadrant, by Charles Wilson, 1850s

35. Woodlands and Finnieston: tenements in Minerva Street,
by Alexander Kirkland, 1856

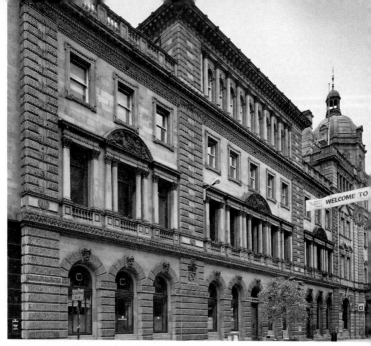

36. Commercial Centre: former Commercial Bank, Gordon Street, by David Rhind, 1853–7

37. Commercial Centre: former Commercial Bank, Gordon Street, relief by A. Handyside Ritchie, 1853–7

38. Commercial Centre: Royal Faculty of Procurators' Hall, Nelson Mandela Place, by Charles Wilson, 1854–6, reading room

39. Saltmarket and St Enoch: former Gardners' warehouse, Jamaica Street, by John Baird and R. McConnel, 1855–6

40. Commercial Centre: St Vincent Street Church,
by Alexander Thomson, 1857–9, from the north-west
41. Queen's Park: Nos. 1–10 Moray Place,
by Alexander Thomson, 1859–61
42. Commercial Centre: St Vincent Street Church,
by Alexander Thomson, 1857–9, interior

40

42

41

43. Rutherglen: former Town Hall, by Charles Wilson, 1861–2, extended by Robert Dalglish & John Thomson, 1876

44. Great Western Road: Kibble Palace, Botanic Gardens, 1863–6, modified in 1873

45. Port Dundas: North Spiers Wharf, City of Glasgow Grain Mills and Stores, *c.* 1851–70, and Canal Offices, *c.* 1812

46. Broomielaw: former tobacco warehouse, James Watt Street, John Baird, 1854, raised *c.* 1870, reconstructed later

47. Hillhead: Glasgow University, by Sir G. G. Scott,
designed in 1864, Randolph and Bute Halls, interior

48. Hillhead: Glasgow University, by Sir G. G. Scott,
designed in 1864, Randolph and Bute Halls, undercroft

49. Dowanhill and Dowanside: Crown Circus, by James Thomson, 1858, and Dowanhill Church, by William Leiper, 1865–6

50. Dowanhill and Dowanside: Dowanhill Church, by William Leiper, 1865–6, roof trusses

51. Great Western Road: Kirklee Terrace,
by Charles Wilson, 1845–64

52. Great Western Road: Buckingham Terrace,
by J. T. Rochead, east section, 1852

53. Great Western Road: Grosvenor Terrace,
by J. T. Rochead, 1855

54. Great Western Road: Great Western Terrace,
by Alexander Thomson, 1869

55. Commercial Centre: Ca' d'Oro, Gordon Street,
by John Honeyman, 1872

56. Commercial Centre: Stock Exchange, Buchanan Street,
by John Burnet, 1875–7

57. Dowanhill and Dowanside: Belmont Hillhead Parish Church, by James Sellars, 1875–6, interior

58. Queen's Park: Crosshill Queen's Park Church, by Campbell Douglas & Sellars, 1872–3

59. Queen's Park: Camphill Queen's Park Church, by William Leiper, 1875–83

60 and 61. Merchant City: City Chambers,
by William Young, 1882–90; south staircase (*below*)

62. Merchant City: City Chambers,
by William Young, 1882–90, Banqueting Hall

63. Broomielaw: former Clyde Navigation Trust,
by J. J. Burnet, Reception Room, 1882–6

64. Townhead: Barony Church,
by J. J. Burnet and J. A. Campbell, 1886–9, interior

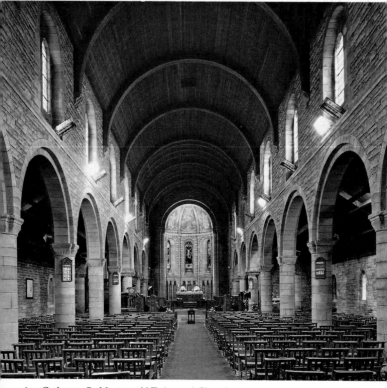

65. Cathcart: St Margaret's Episcopal Church,
by P. Macgregor Chalmers, designed in 1895, interior

66. North Kelvinside: Queen's Cross Church,
by C. R. Mackintosh, 1896–9

67. Woodlands and Finnieston:
Glasgow Art Gallery and Museum, Kelvingrove Park,
by J. W. Simpson & E. J. Milner Allen, 1891–1901,
St Mungo by George Frampton, *c.* 1897

68. Calton and Camlachie: former Templetons' Factory, Glasgow Green, by William Leiper, 1888

69. Saltmarket and St Enoch: former Underground Station, by James Miller, 1896

70. Townhead: City Improvement Trust tenements, High Street,
by Burnet, Boston & Carruthers, 1899–1902

71. Hyndland and Partickhill: tenements in Lauderdale Gardens,
by John McKellar, 1890–1914

72 and 73. Garnethill: Glasgow School of Art, by C. R. Mackintosh, main entrance, 1896–9 (*above*); Museum, 1896–9 (*below*)

74 and 75. Garnethill: Glasgow School of Art, by C. R. Mackintosh, west elevation, 1907–9 (*above*), Library, 1907–9 (*below*)

76. Commercial Centre: Mercantile Chambers, Bothwell Street,
by Salmon, Son & Gillespie, 1897–8
77. Commercial Centre: Mercantile Chambers, Bothwell Street,
1897–8, Mercury, by Derwent Wood
78. Commercial Centre: offices at the corner of Hope Street
and West George Street, by John A. Campbell, 1902–3

76

77

78

79 and 80. Commercial Centre: the Hatrack building, 142a–144 St Vincent Street, by Salmon, Son & Gillespie, 1899–1902; oriel (*below*)

81. Woodlands and Finnieston: former Glasgow Savings Bank, Anderston Cross,
by Salmon, Son & Gillespie, 1899–1900, sculpture by Albert Hodge

82. Govan: former British Linen Bank,
Govan Cross,
by Salmon, Son & Gillespie, 1897–1900,
sculpture by Derwent Wood

83. Pollokshields: former Miller
& Lang printing works,
Darnley Street, stained glass,
by W. G. Morton, 1901–3

84. Govanhill: Annette Street Primary School,
by H. & D. Barclay, 1886

85. Gorbals: Scotland Street School,
by C. R. Mackintosh, 1904–6

86. Calton and Camlachie: fountain, Glasgow Green,
by A. E. Pearce of Doulton & Co., 1888

87. Dennistoun: fountain, Alexandra Park,
designed by D. W. Stevenson, cast by the Saracen Foundry, 1901

88. Govan: Pearce Institute, by Sir Robert Rowand Anderson, 1902–6

89. Govan: Elder Library, by J. J. Burnet, 1901–3

90. Commercial Centre: Lion Chambers, Hope Street,
by Salmon, Son & Gillespie, 1904–7

91. Commercial Centre: Lion Chambers, Hope Street,
by Salmon, Son & Gillespie, 1904–7, detail

92. Woodlands and Finnieston: memorial to Lord Roberts, Kelvingrove Park, by Harry Bates, unveiled 1916

93. Merchant City: Duke of Wellington (outside the former Royal Exchange), by Baron Marochetti, 1844

94. Merchant City: William Gladstone, George Square,
by W. Hamo Thorneycroft, 1899–1902

95. Woodlands and Finnieston: memorial to Lord Roberts,
Kelvingrove Park, by Harry Bates, unveiled 1916, War

96. Scotstoun: North British Diesel Engine Works,
by Karl Bernardt and J. Galt, 1912–13 (photograph of 1915)

97. Commercial Centre: Central Station, concourse of 1899–1905,
modified in 1988

98. Commercial Centre: former North British & Mercantile Building,
St Vincent Street, by Sir J. J. Burnet, 1926–9

99. Commercial Centre: former Union Bank, St Vincent Street,
by James Miller, 1924–7

100. Knightswood: cottage flats
by Glasgow Corporation, 1920s

101. Possilpark and High Possil: tenements
by Glasgow Corporation, 1920s

102. Partick: Crathie Court, Crathie Drive,
by Glasgow Corporation, 1946–54

103. Pollok: tenements
by Glasgow Corporation, late 1940s

104. Dennistoun: St Anne (R.C.), by Gillespie, Kidd & Coia,
1931–3, sculpture by Archibald Dawson

105. Knightswood: St Ninian's Primary (former Cloberhill) School,
by Keppie & Henderson, 1929–32

106. Bellahouston and Dumbreck: former Palace of Art, Bellahouston Park, by Launcelot Ross, 1938 (contemporary photograph)

107. Commercial Centre: former Beresford Hotel, Sauchiehall Street, by Weddell & Inglis, 1937–8 (contemporary photograph)

108. Anniesland and Jordanhill: Kelvin Court, Great Western Road, by J. N. Fatkin, 1937–8

109. Dowanhill and Dowanside: Notre Dame High School, by T. S. Cordiner, designed in 1939, completed 1953

110. Maryhill: Immaculate Conception,
by T. S. Cordiner, 1955–6

111. Drumchapel: St Benedict,
by Gillespie, Kidd & Coia, 1964–70

112. Gorbals: flats in Hutchesontown,
by Sir Basil Spence, 1960–6
113. Springburn: Red Road flats,
by Sam Bunton & Associates, 1962–70
114. Maryhill: Wyndford,
by Harold Buteux
(Scottish Special Housing Association), 1960–9

112

114

113

115. Hillhead: Glasgow University Library,
by William Whitfield, completed in 1968

116. Gorbals: Sheriff Court of Glasgow and Strathkelvin,
by Keppie, Henderson & Partners, 1980–6

117. Commercial Centre: Scottish Amicable Life Assurance,
St Vincent Street, by King, Main & Ellison, 1973–6

118. Pollok Park: Burrell Collection
by Barry Gasson Architects, 1972–83, covered courtyard

119. Merchant City: Ingram Square, restored and with new buildings, by Elder & Cannon, 1984–9

120. Townhead: Strathclyde University, Murray Hall, by G. R. M. Kennedy & Partners, 1983–4

121. North Kelvinside: Craigen Court, Shakespeare Street, by Ken MacRae with McGurn, Logan, Duncan & Opfer, 1987–8

122. Govan: Elderpark housing, Langlands Road, by Simister, Monaghan, McKinney, MacDonald, 1984–6

123. Commercial Centre: Princes Square, Buchanan Street, *c.* 1854, transformed by Hugh Martin & Partners, 1985–7

industrial buildings on the E side, of 1887–97, with plain red and yellow sandstone street elevations but, more remarkably, bold repetitive red and yellow brick façades towards the river; cast-iron columned interiors.

Where the street kinks, a turning W leads into GLASGOW STREET, where the small-scale, late Georgian tenement tradition continues into Bank Street (see above). OAKFIELD AVENUE, formerly Wilson Street, is the next to cross Glasgow Street. Here both the tenement form and the terraced house are found. At the SE angle, Nos. 57–69 (see above), and beyond, opposite Hillhead High School (see Public Buildings, above), a striking terrace (Nos. 41–53) by *Alexander Thomson*, 1865, in which he adapts the Schinkelesque temple-fronted centrepiece of his South Kensington Museum competition design of the previous year to pilastered and pedimented end pavilions. The intervening bays have paired pilastered porches tied into the façade by an all-embracing incised Greek key (or, more descriptively, 'T') band. The incised detail, in a variety of Greek key and anthemion patterns, is essential to the unity of the elevations. Niches are cut back between the first-floor window heads and sealed with carved anthemia, a detail taken from his demolished Queens Park Terrace. Though the whole façade would have greater drama without the mansarded attic, it illustrates the potential inherent in terrace design. Much good but conventional interior detail survives. Adjoining to the N, seven three-bay houses on a smaller scale, with a variety of door detail. They are taller at the return to Glasgow Street. N of Glasgow Street, where Oakfield Avenue drops down to Great Western Road, a long tenement range of *c.* 1859 (Nos. 7–23), with tall end blocks and a lower three-storey central section.

Back in Glasgow Street, the boundary wall of Hillhead High School (see Public Buildings) guides us W to SOUTHPARK AVENUE. To the S, set back opposite the school, lies SOUTHPARK TERRACE, a long three-storey terrace of 1862 with advanced blocks at the ends and centre. Over the first-floor windows, cornices with rosettes in the frieze. (It is closely related to Nos. 57–69 Oakfield Avenue: see above.) Nos. 14 and 15 have been converted to TURNBULL HALL, a university residence; in one entrance, etched glass has replaced the door. At the rear, the uninspiring TURNBULL HALL CHAPEL by *Jack Coia*, 1955, finished in Sol brick with a large W window and a cross above the W door, which penetrates the window. Inside, the chief interest is in the variety of timber – mahogany pews, sycamore details to the stepped altar platform, walnut-faced altar and a ten-panel canopy above. In the link to the house, a metal relief of the Madonna by *Mortimer*.

Further still up Glasgow Street, at the junction with HILLHEAD STREET, GRANBY TERRACE (Nos. 2–28 Hillhead Street) lies straight ahead. It seems from the detailing at the S end that this exceedingly long terrace of houses and tenements of 1856 by *William Clarke* (who lived in this block) was to have been even longer. The grouping of the windows – 1–3–3–1 etc. throughout the central section – breaks with Georgian symmetry. The single windows light the stairs above the street doors. No. 14 has unusual stained glass with female busts in the upper lights of some rear windows, and a perspective view of an empty street by *Oscar Paterson* in the front door, *c.* 1905. Turning s on the E side, another long terrace of *c.* 1870 (Nos. 17–39), with taller end blocks and bay-windowed houses to the centre. Opposite, more bay-windowed tenements.

Leaving Hillhead Street, Great George Street continues w, passing, on the l., the return of Nos. 50–68 Hillhead Street (*see* above). BUTE GARDENS is the cul-de-sac off the w side, with a two-storey terrace, *c.* 1887, indicating the appearance of the generous terrace (demolished) opposite, the site of the Hetherington Building (*see* Glasgow University: Perambulation 3). On the N side of Great George Street, a series of short tenement blocks is interrupted by CECIL STREET, lined on its E side by tall tenements of *c.* 1880, with stumpy Thomsonesque pilasters to the door and window heads dying into the walls. They adjoin Hillhead Primary School (*see* Public Buildings, above) to the N. On the w side, a miscellany of pattern-book terraced houses, all with bold bay windows and some with gables to the street.

Back in Great George Street and further w, the next street to join it is KERSLAND STREET, with some red and some yellow tenements of 1880–1905, the bold w corner block by *John Nisbet*, superseding a scheme by *Burnet & Boston*. Back again in Great George Street, on the s side is LILYBANK TERRACE (now occupied by Lilybank School) by *David Horne*, 1881–3, with wide canted bay windows and a serrated roofline of weighty mansarded and pedimented dormers. In front of the basement areas, excellent circled cast-iron railings and, at No. 1, truncated lamp-standards. Opposite this terrace, the former Belmont Church (*see* Churches), now the school hall.

From the s end of Lilybank Terrace, an excursion up the hill behind leads to the back of LILYBANK HOUSE and thence, keeping l., to the entrance front. This restrained but elegant villa of *c.* 1850 is in the manner of *David Hamilton*, with an asymmetrical addition to the s by *Alexander Thomson*, 1863–5. This extension includes the prominent pedimented tetrastyle Greek Ionic portico and very handsome Grecian interior detailing. To the N, a further addition, two-storey but small in scale, by *Honeyman and Keppie*, 1895. After completing the circuit of the house, we can return via Lilybank Terrace to Great George Street and continue w to LILYBANK GARDENS, the seventeen remaining houses of a terrace, apparently one composition but actually the work of a number of architects and with minor variations. No. 1 is a three-storey corner block by *John Cunningham*, 1883. The lower two-storey houses, mainly with mansard roofs and some handsomely detailed doors, are also by Cunningham (Nos. 2–5), 1880; by *A. G. Robertson* (Nos. 6–9), 1880; by *Lindsay & Benzie*

(Nos. 10–15), 1881–3; and by *David Wylie* (Nos. 16–17), 1893.

Opposite Lilybank Gardens, in CRANWORTH STREET, more bay-windowed red sandstone tenements, those on the w side adjoining the Hillhead Baptist Church, which faces Cresswell Street (*see* Churches, above). Beyond Cresswell Street, on the w side, the Western Baths Club (*see* Public Buildings), and adjacent at the N end of Cranworth Street, but facing VINICOMBE STREET, the SALON CINEMA, an early cinema (originally the Hillhead Picture House) by *Brand & Lithgow*, 1913, with alterations by *Burnet & Boston*, 1940. Low and restrained, with pilasters and emphasis to the corners, provided on the w by a dome and swagged plaster decoration over the door. Inside, an arcaded foyer and shallow-arched balconied auditorium with pilasters and swags. Opposite the BOTANIC GARDENS GARAGE by *D. V. Wylie*, 1912, a boldly arched green and white tiled front and an unusual steel-trussed roof and extensively glazed rear wall, crowned with shaped gables. Near the SE corner with Byres Road, an ELECTRICITY SUBSTATION of 1912, attributed to the electrical engineer *W. W. Lackie*. On the NE corner, an example of a disastrous Glasgow habit of demolishing tenements above the lowest storey, in this case leaving just a cast-iron-columned ground floor and giving it a ridiculous slated hat.

Now for an excursion, via Byres Road, N of Great Western Road into QUEEN MARGARET DRIVE. Here, the scale of the residential development becomes more spacious and substantial than in Hillhead proper. To our r., the w end of Buckingham Terrace (*see* Great Western Road, above: Perambulation 1) and, beyond it, the curving tenement block of Nos. 10–18 and 71–85 HAMILTON DRIVE, an imposing four-storey corner block of 1884, probably by *H. K. Bromhead*. Beyond Hamilton Drive, the BBC's Broadcasting House (*see* Public Buildings, above) and Queen Margaret Bridge (*see* Crossings of the Clyde and Kelvin, below). On the s side of Hamilton Drive, three terraces set up above the road and screened by shrubs and trees. Nos. 53–67, by *Robert Crawford*, 1857–9, are of two storeys, with one three-storey pavilion at the w end. A similar terrace (Nos. 1–33) at the E end of the Drive is also by Crawford but has pavilions at both ends. Between them, on the site of Northpark House, *Alexander Thomson*'s NORTHPARK TERRACE, begun in 1866. (Thomson was involved in a layout for this area but it does not appear to have been adopted.) The whole terrace can only be seen in very sharp perspective, and its repetitive severity implies that it could recede into infinity. The flatness of the façade is broken only by the blocky porches, weightier than those of Thomson's terrace in Oakfield Avenue (*see* above), though the stepped detail of the first-floor windows is echoed from that terrace and in part reversed. The pilastered upper floor is a more repetitive version of that at Moray Place (*see* Queen's Park, below: Perambulation 1). This is not Thomson at his most inventive or theatrical, but the design demonstrates clearly his mastery in relating detail to the mass in a continuous terrace. On the N side of Hamilton Drive, Nos. 2–36, a well-mannered terrace of *c*. 1859–60. Along the E side of HAMIL-TON PARK AVENUE, a regular-bayed range of two-storey houses. It continues in a simplified pattern into LA CROSSE TERRACE, which almost cascades into the Kelvin Gorge to its N. The footpath leads to the E part of the terrace and thence to BELMONT STREET. To the s, on the E side of the street, is a terrace of *c*. 1865. (The s terrace was a victim of settlement caused by old uncharted mineworkings.) The w side of the street opens into the charming BELMONT CRESCENT, 1869–70, probably with elevations by *John Honeyman*, a generous semicircular terrace of houses with a centre pavilion; the end pavilions, which collapsed during construction, are to be reinstated (1989). Looking E from the Crescent, we can see Glasgow Academy (*see* Great Western Road, above: Public Buildings).

DOWANHILL AND DOWANSIDE

Dowanhill rises up sharply to the w of Byres Road and to the s from Great Western Road. To the s, it slopes down to Partick with a prominent terrace occupied by Crown Roads North and South and by Crown Circus. These southern slopes make up Dowanside. The Buchanans' Dowanhill estate of around 100 acres (40 ha) was one of the largest in the West End. By 1850, when the estate was acquired by T. L. Paterson, the area was recognized as a potentially desirable suburb, and the presence of the Observatory (1841), commemorated by the name of Observatory Road, underlined the purity of the air, an essential ingredient for a successful suburban development. Between 1850 and 1905, the hill was transformed into a desirable residential quarter following an estate plan devised by *James Thomson* in 1850. Some of the earliest purpose-built suburban villas in the West End appeared around the brow of Observatory Hill, and terraced houses were built in Crown Circus and its vicinity. Terraced housing continued to be built in the 1860s and early 1870s, mainly in the eastern part of the estate: all these developments have classically derived elevations. More villas appeared to the w, in a greater variety of styles, including classical, Italianate and Tudor. The area also has some unusual and picturesque late C19 terraced and tenemented developments, easily distinguished by the red sandstone frontages (grey at the rear) and the liberal use of coloured glass in windows and doors.

CHURCHES

BELMONT HILLHEAD PARISH CHURCH, Saltoun Street. A dramatic interpretation of the Sainte Chapelle in Paris. The

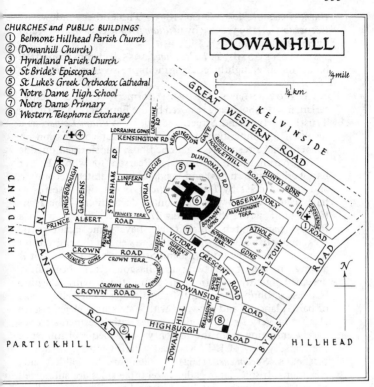

CHURCHES and PUBLIC BUILDINGS
① Belmont Hillhead Parish Church
② (Dowanhill Church)
③ Hyndland Parish Church
④ St Bride's Episcopal
⑤ St Luke's Greek Orthodox Cathedral
⑥ Notre Dame High School
⑦ Notre Dame Primary
⑧ Western Telephone Exchange

DOWANHILL

competition for this church of 1875–6 was won by *James Sellars*, but the design is said to have been much influenced by *William Leiper*. A tall apsed church, ringed round by identical French gabletted windows of combined lancets and roses, and with a slender *flèche*. The w front, which seems to derive from William Burges's St Finbar's Cathedral in Cork (then being completed and given much publicity), is difficult to see except in sharp perspective because of the wooded gardens in front, but it is full of carving. Most original are the guardian angels, closely related to Burges's symbol of St Matthew the Evangelist, which appear in low relief in the spandrels above the large rose window. The whole elevation is anchored by solid buttress turrets with octagonal spires. The Parisian influence continues inside, to great effect. Elongated columns between the windows support the wooden groin vault. At the w end, a gallery with an ORGAN by *H. Willis & Son*, 1876 (restored 1930). The interior was recast *c.* 1921 by *P. Macgregor Chalmers*. The blind arcading along the apse wall frames war memorials. – COMMUNION TABLE of Rochette marble by *Macgregor Chalmers*. – Good STAINED GLASS by

Burne-Jones for Morris & Co., 1893. – Three other windows: by Cottier & Co., 1893–1903; by William Meikle & Sons, 1917; and by Sadie McLellan, 1958.

SESSION ROOM by T. J. Beveridge, 1955. It clamps around the base of the apse, slightly reducing the impressive verticality of the Eend.

Former DOWANHILL CHURCH (formerly United Presbyterian; now (1989) being restored by the Four Acres Charitable Trust), 93 Hyndland Street. 1865–6, by William Leiper, as a result of a competition: his first important commission. A conventional Presbyterian galleried box, transformed outside by the soaring tower and spire à la Pearson (for whom Leiper had worked in London) and inside by the painted decoration and stained glass by Daniel Cottier (Andrew Wells seems to have been involved with the painted decoration). 'The architect's aim,' wrote the Building News, 'has been to build a Presbyterian church which might have some claim to be reckoned artistic.' The steeple is at the s end of the church and dominates the view up Hyndland Street; at 195 ft (60 m), it is among the finest surviving in Glasgow. It is beautifully designed, gently tapering in four stages with clasping buttresses, blind lancets in the third stage, a tall belfry stage of paired lancets, and crowned with a strikingly elegant spire clasped by very French angle lucarnes with intermediate ones barely emerging from the masonry. The medieval influence (perhaps by way of J. T. Rochead's Park Church, 1858, and Nesfield's Specimens, 1862) is seen in the gabled side elevations. Inside, large galleries on three sides are supported on cast-iron columns with blind, cusped arcading to the gallery fronts. Over all a hammerbeam roof, with the spandrels filled with fretted decoration, and derived from E. W. Godwin's roof to the Great Hall in Northampton Town Hall, published in The Builder in 1863. But it is the comprehensiveness of Cottier's decoration in the stained glass, composed of vigorous geometric and foliage patterns framing stirring full-length figures (David and Miriam) or heads of Biblical figures, and the stencil work (which it is planned to reveal), which make this church so striking. The PULPIT is unusual, set into a shallow recess provided by the tall arched N end; it is a tabernacle with a bowed front but no access from the body of the church. It is here that the quality of the painted decoration can be glimpsed: a convincing painted draped curtain along the back, and the roof of the diminutive flanking arcaded passages spangled with stars. In the s gallery, a powerful ORGAN.

To the NW, a handsome two-storey range of church halls.

HYNDLAND PARISH CHURCH, 79 Hyndland Road. 1885–7, by William Leiper. Dec to a liturgical plan, but the composition spoiled by the unfinished tower now forming nothing more than a porch, albeit elaborately cusp-arched and with delightful carved details (tympanum carving never executed). Built in Ballochmyle stone with handsomely traceried windows (three-

light to the three large aisle windows to E and W; four-light in
the gable ends). Inside, a straightforward plan with nave,
chancel, transepts and arcaded aisles, walls plastered only in
the aisles and a good timber roof. Throughout, excellently
carved capitals and corbels by *McCulloch* of London. – COM-
MUNION TABLE. Polychrome marble on a dais with delicately carved wooden reredos flanked by figures of saints in
niches. Chancel lined with elders' stalls. – PULPIT also
marble, with ashlar and alabaster, and elaborately carved. –
ORGAN. *Henry Willis*, 1887; in N transept. – Former LADY
CHAPEL in S transept, converted to memorial chapel by *I. J.
Ballantine*, 1966. – STAINED GLASS. Original clear glass with
ornamental leadwork designed by Leiper and executed by
Guthrie, now mainly superseded. – E window *Douglas
Strachan*, 1921, as War Memorial; aisle windows by *David
Hamilton*, c. 1930; *Gordon Webster*, 1960 and 1963 (two in N
and S aisles); *William Wilson*, 1962; and *Sax Shaw*, 1969.

Attached to the S W angle, two-storey halls by *A. N. Paterson*,
1913. Three small stained-glass windows in lower hall by *J.
& W. Guthrie* depicting the architect and craftsmen.

NOTRE DAME CHAPEL. *See* Perambulation 1, below.

ST BRIDE'S EPISCOPAL CHURCH, 69 Hyndland Road and
Kingsborough Gardens. Designed in 1903 (foundation stone
laid 1906) by *G. F. Bodley*, who built the chancel (1904), the
nave (dedicated 1907) and part of the N aisle, but did not
complete the planned three aisles, the tower and spire planned
for the SW angle. In 1910 *H. O. Tarbolton* was called in to
report on defects discovered in the nave and to complete the
church; this included partially rebuilding the nave, adding the
two N aisles and tower at the NW angle (to a design reminiscent
of Bodley's St Chad's, Stoke on Trent, 1904), all done 1913–
16. He also made considerable later embellishments. The
exterior is dominated by Tarbolton's solid Dec crenellated
tower (with bells) at the NW, with a niche containing a statue
of St Bridget of Kildare by *R. Bridgeman & Sons* (Lichfield);
it is linked to the nave gable (Bodley's porch not built); the
rendered S wall marks the unbuilt S aisle. The interior scheme
is mainly Bodley's, a refined Dec design with slender arcades
of quatrefoil piers and pointed arches embracing nave and
chancel. The chancel is marked off only by a low screen and
painted rood beam fitted into the curve of the arched timber
roof. Carved woodwork and fittings by *Scott Morton & Co.* –
LADY CHAPEL in the N aisle. Marble altar with panels of
mosaic work, on N wall a deep recess for recumbent figure, on
wall to S of the altar a niche with figure of Our Lady and Child
by *Eric Gill*, 1915. – STAINED GLASS. In N aisle by *Karl
Parsons* (London) of the late 1920s; other glass by *Herbert
Hendrie* and *Edward Woore*. A number of pictures and pieces
of furniture given to the church by Bishop Reid.

ST LUKE'S GREEK ORTHODOX CATHEDRAL (formerly
Belhaven Church), Dundonald Road. Built for a United Presbyterian congregation. By *James Sellars*, 1876–7. A powerfully

vertical and inventive design in Normandy Gothic by way of J. L. Pearson and of R. Norman Shaw's church in Lyons (1865). On the main front, the buttress turrets are carefully integrated into the design and flank tall lancets, inspired by Dunblane Cathedral. Below, a low arcade, with the entrance to the r. in the link between the hall and the body of the church. The interior has arcaded aisles and a gallery at the N (liturgically w) end; originally it was elaborately stencilled. The organ is in the apse with, in front of it, a modern Byzantine iconostasis. – Vibrant STAINED GLASS by *Stephen Adam*, 1877.

Former ST PETER'S SEMINARY CHAPEL, Partickhill Road. *See* Hyndland and Partickhill, below: Perambulation 2.

PUBLIC BUILDINGS

NOTRE DAME TRAINING COLLEGE. *See* Perambulation 1, below.

HYNDLAND SECONDARY SCHOOL. *See* Hyndland: Perambulation 1.

109 NOTRE DAME HIGH SCHOOL, 160 Observatory Road. The best example of functional Scandinavian influence in Glasgow. By *T. S. Cordiner*, designed in 1939, left unfinished until 1949, and completed in 1953. Skilful use of narrow bricks, concrete and ashlar, with minute attention to detail and excellent sculpture on the tall main entrance pavilion and scattered randomly over the other elevations. At the rear, a free-standing niche with a figure of Our Lady. The main front is dominated by the emphatic entrance tower with pitched tile roof supporting an elaborate plinth and cross. Low two-storey flanking classroom blocks with horizontal metal-framed windows. The rear is equally original, with a long elevation opening on to a carefully designed terrace and the emphasis firmly on fresh air in the classroom. Consciously asymmetrical gable ends with witty connotations of the Arts and Crafts movement. Every aspect of the design has received careful attention, from the handsome entrance to the cleverly contrived rear access steps, with fragile curved canopy, and the bicycle shelter. Within, the planning is functional but with decorative ironwork in screens to the stairs and in the practical door furniture.

NOTRE DAME PRIMARY SCHOOL (formerly ST PETER'S GIRLS' PRIMARY), Victoria Crescent Road. An austere red ashlar Board school, by *James Cowan*, 1898.

WESTERN TELEPHONE EXCHANGE, 24 Highburgh Road. By *Leonard Stokes* with *Colin Menzies*, 1907. A polychrome ashlar building, transferring an English brick technique to stone, with questionable success. Paired orieled bays with eyelets let into the raised parapet above.

PERAMBULATIONS

1. Dowanhill

The perambulation leads W from the N end of Byres Road. On entering OBSERVATORY ROAD we see, immediately ahead, the dazzlingly clean vertical E end of Belmont Hillhead Parish Church (*see* Churches, above). Curving up to the N, GROS-VENOR CRESCENT, 1880–3, a serpentine terrace of houses with fanciful bowed oriels on the first floor. Continuing up the hill, the houses of Nos. 1–20 HUNTLY GARDENS, a typical three-storeyed bay-windowed terrace of 1872–8, rise in pairs, with good circled cast-iron railings and solid gatepiers with the remains of lamp-standards at the W end. On the other, S side of the communal gardens are Nos. 21–34 (this section of Huntly Gardens is also known as Observatory Road), 1878–84, each house stepped up the hill, the five top houses (Nos. 30–4) with decorative ironwork and continuous glazing at ridge level, probably intended to light billiard rooms. No. 26 was refitted in the Glasgow Style by *John Ednie*, 1907. At the top of the gardens, No. 1 HORSLETHILL ROAD, a simple late Georgian classical villa with an E addition, closes the head of the communal gardens in an unusually bland manner. The column-screened hall has striking stained glass in the staircase window, probably by *Daniel Cottier*.

Horslethill Road wraps round the lower N slopes of Dowanhill. On the N side is ROSSLYN TERRACE (Nos. 1–16), a restrained, small-scale, bay-windowed terrace of 1873–5, with taller houses at the lower W end of the slope. On the S side, a series of much enlarged villas built in the 1870s, including HORSLETHILL HOUSE, with a substantial curvilinear conservatory and Glasgow Style fittings of *c.* 1900, and, at the W end, a large double villa of *c.* 1875 (No. 11), with the elevations stepping and curving restlessly around the prominent, sloping corner site.

Diverting W from the circuit of the hill, KENSINGTON GATE by *David Barclay* of *H. & D. Barclay*, 1902–3, a delightful serpentine terrace (seen to best effect from above the gardens in Victoria Circus) of red sandstone houses, the front elevations tightly compressed into the curve with distinctive five-light bowed windows capped with bowed dormers, and diminutive baroque entrances, some with elaborate stained-glass panels. Built on a sloping site, some houses have unusually deep basements with galleried interiors, and all have more generous rear elevations, opening into gardens. This piece of picturesque planning continues into KENSINGTON ROAD (Nos. 2–8) and around the corner into LORRAINE ROAD (Nos. 3–9). At Nos. 2–4 Lorraine Road, another design by *David Barclay*, this time a symmetrical double villa of 1899. Kensington Road extends W from Kensington Gate, and along the S side lies a series of villas, the most remarkable of them No. 5, built in the mid-C19 and with an E extension and refitting done in a Thomsonesque manner by *Alexander Skirving*, 1893. On the N side, with its own carriage road and gatepiers, LOR-RAINE GARDENS, by *James Thomson* (cf. Belhaven Terrace; *see* Great Western Road, above: Perambulation 2), completed in 1890, an astylar, bay-windowed terrace of ten houses. At the NW end of Kensington Road, a blunt, cubic, seven-storey brick flatted block by *Notman & Lodge*, 1966–7, for Strath-clyde Housing Society Ltd.

SYDENHAM ROAD was originally laid out with mid-C19 villas in generous grounds, but some have been replaced by denser development. At No. 2 (set back and virtually in Kingsborough Gardens), a small-scale flatted scheme by *Powell & Anderson*, 1963; at No. 6, more skilful infill with a restrained, stepped block of brick flats by *John Hepburn*, 1968. On the large site at the corner with Linfern Road, BRITISH TELECOM's head-quarters, a large, intrusive brick office block of 1970–1 by *Covell Matthews & Partners*, destroys the domestic character of the area. Of the surviving villas, Nos. 1, 3 and 4 are Italian-ate, by *Boucher & Cousland*, c. 1865. No. 1 with a conservatory and a distinctively Thomsonesque bowed-and-arcaded bay window. No. 8 is by *J. Thomson*, a Tudor Gothic villa of 1859 with elaborate bargeboards and a picturesque low S wing with arcaded loggia and octagonal top-light. No. 10, also by *Boucher & Cousland*, c. 1858, is large, gabled and rigidly corseted. Turning into PRINCE ALBERT ROAD, more villas line the N side. The two buildings at the E end are double villas; the most interesting, No. 8 with No. 7 Sydenham Road, c. 1868, neatly turns the corner, giving two integrated but individual houses. On the S side and set back is Prince's Terrace (*see* Dowanside, below). HOLMHURST at the E end, on the promi-nent corner with Victoria Circus, is Italianate, c. 1865, with a rear extension and a studio added c. 1894, possibly by *David McSkimming*.

Prince Albert Road continues E into VICTORIA CRESCENT ROAD (for the E part of this street, *see* Perambulation 2, below). On the l., the steep slope of the upper part of Dowanhill, with an extensively altered group of buildings which all belong to the NOTRE DAME TRAINING COLLEGE. On the r., Notre Dame Primary School (*see* Public Buildings, above), and, set back, a mid-C19 bay-windowed villa which formed the original college. That was altered and added to by *Pugin & Pugin* with *Bruce & Hay*, 1909. These buildings are linked at the W to the former CHAPEL of the College of Notre Dame, also by *Pugin & Pugin*, 1900 (now converted to offices). It has kept its open roof but has lost the ecclesiastical fittings and the stained glass by the Irish Art Nouveau artist *Harry Clarke*. To the W of the chapel, the low, characterless, L-plan, prefabricated extension of 1963 by *Gillespie Kidd & Coia*.

VICTORIA CIRCUS continues the circuit of the hill northwards, with more substantial mid-C19 villas in spacious grounds on either side. Some of these have been replaced – No. 11, c. 1980, by a bulky and poorly detailed block of flats; and No. 8, in

1976, by sheltered housing (Rament Lodge Court) designed by *William Nimmo & Partners*. It is a strongly articulated block with the common room boldly defined in a prominent octagon. One of the more notable villas, No. 6 (Italianate, *c.* 1855) was altered in 1897 by *Joseph Cowan*, with the addition of service accommodation, and again in 1900 by *George Simpson*, who made a further two-storey addition. Opposite, the restrained, classical, villa at No. 7, given added severity by the lampblack treatment of the masonry. It retains its detached mews. In 1899 *A. N. Paterson* undertook a thorough-going remodelling of No. 5, ELSTOW, transforming a standard villa into a fashionable suburban mansion. He added the boldly gabled storey, the elaborate Jacobean porch, and created a schoolroom and a billiard room within the old house. Bold canted bay and bowed windows project from the front elevation, the latter with a galleried top floor and semi-domed roof. No. 2, a dignified Victorian villa of *c.* 1865 on an exposed corner, has been cruelly encased on the s and w by an ugly low brick extension. Turning the corner into DUNDONALD ROAD, on the s we see St Luke's Greek Orthodox Cathedral (*see* Churches, above). Curving up the hill, a tall terrace of 1897–8 (Nos. 15–25, with a gap at No. 17), its attic windows deeply recessed between elongated brackets beneath. The terrace continues up the hill with plenty of applied detail, but less originality. On the brow of the hill, more villas, most notable the picturesque FERN TOWER (No. 1), 1874, Italianate with boldly arched windows.

At the head of the short spur of OBSERVATORY ROAD which leads off to the r., Notre Dame High School, a masterly exercise in Scandinavian manner (*see* Public Buildings, above). Opposite the cul-de-sac of Observatory Road, sloping down the hill are, to the l., MARCHMONT TERRACE (*c.* 1870), linked to the NW end of Huntly Gardens, and, to the r., BOWMONT TERRACE (*c.* 1880), the latter with neat V-channelled masonry and a standard bay-windowed front, and Nos. 11–15 BOWMONT GARDENS, 1875–80, to the sw. Facing it, the remainder of Bowmont Gardens, Nos. 1–7, *c.* 1880, raised up on a terraced platform. The doors of Nos. 2–6 were converted to windows when the houses were adapted for the Notre Dame Training College, probably in the 1930s. The ground falls steeply to ATHOLE GARDENS, a long rectangle, with its gently curved high w end reflecting the curve of Bowmont Gardens above and lined with bay-windowed terraced houses. Although of the same date (*c.* 1878–80) as the other terraces in the area, the elevations display a more powerful Thomsonesque influence. Nos. 1–19 have original anthemion-pattern cast-iron railings, Nos. 7–19, lotus capitals to columned doorways, dwarf pilasters dying into the walls and incised lintels above the second-floor windows. Along the w side of the gardens, a carefully modulated terrace of *c.* 1880 with taller end houses and regularly stepped intermediate houses. The groups of second-floor windows are linked as if to form a continuous strip of windows between pilasters, but, because of the hill, each group steps up to the next. Most of the fleur-de-lis railings have gone, but bold angle piers with lamp-standards remain at the E end.

2. Dowanside

Dowanside occupies the s slopes of the Dowanhill estate, and, together with the hilltop development, forms a solidly bourgeois enclave which changes below Highburgh Road into an area primarily occupied by tradesmen. Dowanside is dominated by terraced houses and tenements built in the second half of the C19 and illustrates the transition from classically derived elevations with lofty interiors to the Free Style smaller-scaled essays of the late years of the century, with greater emphasis on individual decorative treatment. The architect *James Thomson* was responsible for planning the layout of the estate and for the elevations of the earliest buildings.

Our route leads W from about halfway down Byres Road. Off it, HIGHBURGH ROAD is flanked by three-storey tenements with highly decorative ironwork. Turning N into CALEDON STREET, *Leonard Stokes*' Western Telephone Exchange (*see* Public Buildings, above). At the N end of Caledon Street, a curved tenement of *c.* 1872. On the other side of the road, the slightly later Nos. 2–14 DOWANSIDE ROAD, *c.* 1880, with Nos. 6–34 VICTORIA CRESCENT ROAD, also of *c.* 1872, the latter with cheerful bowed first-floor oriels. Nos. 38–52 form an earlier terrace of *c.* 1860 with end pavilions, whose effect is somewhat reduced by the curve of the road and the slope. In the gardens formed in the wedge between these two streets is the WILLOWBANK BOWLING CLUB with a picturesque club house of 1896 by *P. Macgregor Chalmers*. A small stained-glass window appropriately depicts Drake playing bowls on Plymouth Hoe: 1897, by *Norman Macdougall*. Perched on a platform overlooking the bowling green to the W, KING'S GATE, *David Barclay*'s extraordinary terrace of four linked, paired villas of 1902, Nos. 33–7 Victoria Crescent Road at the N end. The l. villa of the southern pair is entered from Dowanside Street (Nos. 48 and 48A). At the s end but detached, No. 50 Dowanside Street, by *Alexander Wingate* of 1906. These houses are the grandest to be found in the unusually cohesive and late piece of speculative development, which dominates the E part of Dowanside. It combines terraced housing with tenements, on the slopes below Crown Circus. The overall scheme was designed by *David Barclay* of *H. & D. Barclay*, in collaboration with *G. S. Kenneth*, between 1898 and 1912, and is unified by the use of particularly distinctive detailing on the bowed windows, by elaborate door-pieces and by a profusion of stained and painted glass in the fanlights and upper sashes, using every variation of Glasgow Style Art Nouveau. Tenements appear in BEAUMONT GATE, on the E side of DOWANHILL STREET (Nos. 78–104) and fronting Highburgh Road between these two streets (Nos. 28–40). The terraced housing is at the W end of Dowanside Road, and also on the W side and at the N end of Dowanhill Street. At No. 91 Dowanhill Street, the bow window on the S elevation has become a miniature conservatory. The last and very restrained part of the scheme is at Nos. 5–9 CROWN ROAD SOUTH, 1908–12. The brick-built block of flats at No. 11 is by *Jenkins & Marr*, 1987.

At the head of Dowanside Street, raised up on the crown of the hill, another unusual and earlier residential development, laid out by *James Thomson* in 1858 – the remarkable convex CROWN CIRCUS and the two long terraces, Nos. 1–17 CROWN TERRACE and Nos. 1–14 CROWN GARDENS, which create an elongated U enclosing a communal garden. Crown Circus, of 1858 (although difficult to appreciate fully, particularly in summer), is a descendant of John Baird's Claremont Terrace of 1847 (*see* Woodlands and Finnieston, above: Perambulation 1). Baird's Greek Doric porticoes are translated here into a continuous colonnade of Roman Doric columns with full entablature, but the two centre houses, where the ground-floor windows are pulled forward and flanked by pilasters with bay windows above, herald Alexander Thomson's more audacious Westbourne Terrace of 1871 (*see* Kelvinside, above: Perambulation). The bold convex curve is anchored by end pavilions, which in turn relate to the long N- and S-facing terraces. Crown Terrace, on the S and built in two sections between 1873 and 1880, is an opulent piece of Victorian drama with expansive views over the Clyde. It is confidently decked out with pilasters, console-bracketed windows, cornices and pedimented dormers, the latter grander in the centre pavilion. The W section is simpler, with end pavilions and a rhythmic use of arched dormers. (In SYDENHAM LANE, lying between the two terraces, No. 12, of the early 1880s, is an unusual mews property with an extensive use of large exposed cast-iron beams.) Crown Gardens, 1873–4, is a restrained version of the Circus, a consoled balcony with a cast-iron balustrade replacing the colonnade. At the E end, it is linked to the Circus by an archway reminiscent of the screens to mews in London's Belgravia. Unrelated but no less impressive is the large double villa of *c.* 1889 (WESTDEL and ROYSTON) at the junction with QUEEN'S PLACE. The asymmetry, reflecting the work of J. J. Burnet, contrasts with the regularity of the neighbouring terraces. *A. N. Paterson* extended Westdel in 1896 and again in 1902 (including the conical roof over the front cloakroom extension), and *C. R. Mackintosh* designed a bedroom, bathroom and other fittings (now in the Glasgow University collection) *c.* 1901. At the N end of Queen's Place and to the r., QUEEN'S GARDENS is a fragmented terrace of 1882–93 by *James Thomson*, with bay windows and terminal pavilions; a flatted brick block of *c.* 1960, with wide windows characteristically angled at one side, now fills the bombed site at Nos. 2–4. To the N, the severe PRINCE'S TERRACE, by

James Thomson, 1868–72, set back from PRINCE ALBERT ROAD, with its own service road and tall gatepiers supporting cast-iron lamp-standards. There are twelve houses in all, the centre two with paired central doors and flanking bay windows. A rhythmic succession of round-arched dormers completes the composition, which is fronted by very solid but elegant, simply arched cast-iron railings. No. 1 (1868–9) was refitted towards the end of the century for William Henderson, a leading shipping magnate closely associated with the Anchor Line; perhaps *James Miller*, who was designing for the line at the turn of the century, could have had a hand in the interior, which has all the opulence of a great liner, with high-quality woodwork to screens, doors and panelling. It also has an unusual double-glazing system, with leaded secondary windows ingeniously constructed. Very elaborate stained glass is set in the inner door, some possibly C 16 or C 17 signed '*Henri Goltzias artefeci*'. Further along the terrace to the r., Nos. 6 and 10 have good leaded glass in the doors and upper sashes.

Further W in Prince Albert Road is a substantial and intrusive housing scheme by the City Architect, *A. G. Jury*, 1964–8. Despite a self-conscious use of areas of imitation stone, it bears no relation to its well-mannered neighbours, whose congruity depends on scale and materials. To the S, down PRINCE'S PLACE beyond the E side of the housing scheme, more houses of *c.* 1880, in the manner of *David Barclay* and similar to those in Dowanhill Street (*see* above). Opposite, in the shallow crescent of PRINCE'S GARDENS, 1891–3, the bowed windows give a foretaste of the same theme adopted more convincingly by David Barclay at Dowanhill. Back N again beyond Prince Albert Road, KINGSBOROUGH GARDENS has a series of houses in short linked groups on two sides of a tapering garden. Nos. 42–54, *c.* 1900, and No. 40 by *G. S. Kenneth*, 1902, are small-scale houses in the manner of David Barclay, but with particularly notable overhanging eaves projecting like Chinese parasols over the bay windows. On the W side of the garden, the long range of small-scale red sandstone houses (by *D. Woodburn Sturrock*, 1899–1901) look similar to those on the E side of the Gardens, but are distinguished by conical roofs over the bays. Nos. 22–38, of 1878–82, the earliest houses in the Gardens, are in an unimaginative Baronial style: at No. 34, of the interiors done *c.* 1900 by *C. R. Mackintosh*, some fragments of panelling and hall furnishing remain. At the N end of the Gardens, Nos. 10–16 forms an unfinished Frenchified range of *c.* 1885, its pavilion roofs now lacking their decorative brattishing. A turn W past St Bride's and Hyndland Parish Churches (*see* Churches, above) leads on to Hyndland Road.

HYNDLAND AND PARTICKHILL

Hyndland, owned by the Stirling Crawford family, was first offered for sale in 1877, but its westerly position and the extent of house-building in the more desirable areas to the E meant that demand for the Hyndland building land did not materialize until the development of rail and tram routes late in the century. Hyndland was laid out on a spacious grid pattern, with streets lined, between 1890 and 1914, with some of the largest and grandest tenements in the city.

Partickhill was developed in an entirely different manner. Unlike Hyndland, its relatively isolated position w of Dowanhill did not deter the developer. Of all the West End developments it is the least formal, with random villas, semi-detached houses and short terraces around the crest of the hill in well-wooded grounds. It appears to have been laid out for building in the 1830s and 1840s, probably by the architect *Alexander Taylor*. The sites on the outer circumference of Partickhill Road offer dramatic views to the s and w over the city and beyond. Partickhill Road curves around the hill, the summit itself remaining a remarkably secluded and somewhat neglected open space. The generous size of the villas' plots proved attractive to developers during the 1980s, and several housing schemes have appeared. At the time of writing, new building has not greatly disrupted the sylvan qualities of the hilltop, but they are increasingly fragile.

PERAMBULATIONS

1. Hyndland

This perambulation begins in HYNDLAND ROAD opposite and just s of St Bride's and Hyndland Parish Churches (*see* Dowanhill and Dowanside, above: Churches), on the eastern flank of a grid-like development of substantial tenements, mainly of four storeys with bay windows and corner turrets. None is particularly imaginative, but the overall effect is of a solidly respectable middle-class quarter. These tenements were built between 1890 and 1914 by six builders (and many have stained-glass panels by the *Oscar Paterson Studio*). Those lining the w side of Hyndland Road are by *John Smart*. QUEENSBOROUGH GARDENS leads w from Hyndland Road and bisects the other tenemented streets, so giving a representative impression of the development. FALKLAND STREET, LAUDERDALE GARDENS, POLWARTH STREET 71 and AIRLIE STREET (between Clarence Drive and Queensborough Gardens) are by *John McKellar*. *John Nisbet* was responsible for the blocks in the NW quadrant, *Andrew Mickel* for those in the sw one. In Lauderdale Gardens, a good red sandstone example (1937) of the typical neat interwar ELECTRICITY SUBSTATION. To the w of Clarence Drive, between Lauderdale Gardens and Airlie Gardens, the two

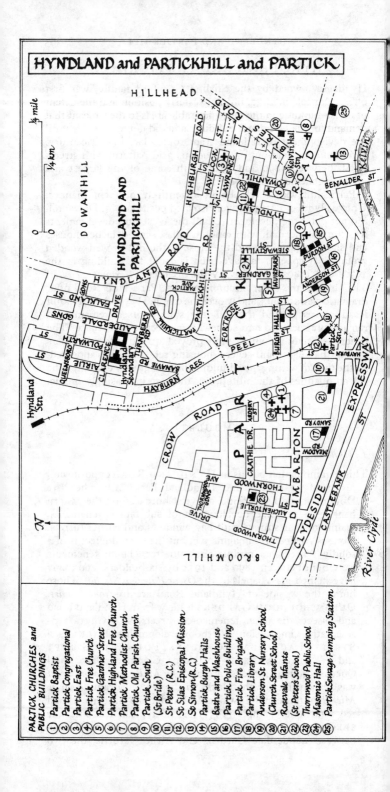

HYNDLAND and PARTICKHILL and PARTICK

PARTICK CHURCHES and
PUBLIC BUILDINGS

① Partick Baptist
② Partick Congregational
③ Partick East
④ Partick Free Church
⑤ Partick Gardner-Street
⑥ Partick Highland Free Church
⑦ Partick Methodist Church
⑧ Partick Old Parish Church
⑨ Partick South
⑩ (St Bride)
⑪ St Peter (R.C.)
⑫ St Silas Episcopal Mission
⑬ St Simon (R.C.)
⑭ Partick Burgh Halls
⑮ Baths and Washhouse
⑯ Partick Police Building
⑰ Partick Fire Brigade
⑱ Partick Library
⑲ Anderson St Nursery School (Church Street School)
⑳ Rosevale Infants
㉑ (St Peter's School)
㉒ Thornwood Public School
㉓ Masonic Hall
㉔ Partick Sewage Pumping Station

blocks of HYNDLAND SECONDARY SCHOOL (formerly Hyndland Public School), 1910, by *H.E. Clifford* for the Govan Parish School Board. A bold red sandstone school with Mannerist details to the first-floor windows of the main w elevation. To the E, a substantial extension by *Denny & Bain* for Glasgow Education Authority, 1928–9; U-plan with open-gallery access round the courtyard.

More tenements in CLARENCE DRIVE; the corner block on the SE angle of the junction with Hyndland Road is by *Alexander Adam*. To the S of this, in Hyndland Road, at No. 162, the little ROYAL BANK OF SCOTLAND by *James McLachlan*, 1934, with Egyptian-inspired Deco ornament.

2. *Partickhill*

As Hyndland Road swings E, a turning W leads into TURNBERRY ROAD. At the corner, on the S side, a large tenement by *Hugh Barclay* and *John Baird*, 1874. Next Nos. 7–11 (probably by *Hugh Barclay*, 1874), a tall stern terrace, the ground floor raised up, with good ironwork to the steps. Beyond it, a series of detached or semi-detached villas: Nos. 13 and 15 are a pair by *Hugh Barclay*, 1874; No. 19, a Thomsonesque villa with the front door on the side elevation to face the wide unadopted drive leading to the top of Partickhill. The summit is a forgotten and surprisingly wild space which presumably never became a formal communal garden because all the surrounding houses had substantial private grounds. Back to Turnberry Road, opposite No. 19, the quiet backwater of TURNBERRY AVENUE, with a variety of classical and Tudor Gothic detached and double villas of *c.* 1870. Further down Turnberry Road, past where Partickhill Road turns off S, more villas of *c.* 1870 line the N side, one of them Tudorish with jaunty pennant weathervanes. These villas back on to the two blocks of Airlie Street School (*see* Perambulation 1, above).

BANAVIE ROAD (off to the S) gently takes up the curve of Partickhill. Nos. 1–37, 1869, were built by *Thomas Binnie*, who was also the speculator. The three S houses were the last to be completed (in 1873). This long terrace, attractively small in scale, has a subtly emphasized centrepiece. (The architect William Leiper lived at No. 11.) Opposite, more villas on the upward slope of the hill, No. 6 with brightly coloured glass to the upper sashes. Then, after three single-storey houses, No. 72 PEEL STREET, mildly Italianate in Charles Wilson's manner, with an excellent Regency-style cast-iron veranda. Further down the hill, Banavie Road joins, on its W side, the curving tenemented HAYBURN CRESCENT, *c.* 1875, mainly by *John Cunningham*. The crescent theme continues at Nos. 53–63 PEEL STREET, 1875, by *H. & D. Barclay*, a tall terrace with carved foliate details in the shell-heads of the first-floor windows. The simple Italianate style of the villas already passed recurs in the houses set up on the S slope of Partickhill (e.g. No. 46 FORTROSE STREET, *c.* 1860).

At the junction of Fortrose Street and Peel Street, where two
blocks of flats by *Jenkins & Marr* (1989) are tightly packed,
PEEL LANE, a steep footpath between high walls, leads up
to Partickhill. Sadly, the walls have been cut down at the top
on the l., revealing a dreary row of garages belonging to two
dull brick infill blocks at No. 65 PARTICKHILL, which make
a poor substitute for the villa they replaced. This leafy crown
of Partickhill and the informality of the villa development are
in marked contrast to the rigidity of the Hyndland tenements.
PARTICKHILL ROAD curves w and N round the hill. On
the l. side, at Nos. 67–9, a pair of houses with a tripartite
arrangement of windows similar to that just seen in Banavie
Road. No. 71 is an austere Thomsonesque villa of *c.* 1885 with
a prominent arcaded central cupola lighting the former billiard
room; flanking this house (converted to flats) are two low
ranch-style houses of 1983. At the sharp angle junction with
Turnberry Road, No. 33, a brick and slate-hung block of
flats, combining ideas from Mackintosh with some from Frank
Lloyd Wright. It has powerful horizontals and low-pitched
set-back roofs, but the overall linear effect is spoilt by the
wide arched garage entrance. Returning on the uphill side of
Partickhill Road, at the N end, ST JOHN'S COURT (Nos.
76–8) by *Boswell Mitchell & Johnstone*, 1972, is an L-plan
development of flatlets for the St John's Housing Association.
The simple brickwork, ample glass and monopitch roof recall
Scandinavian precedents, but the size of the scheme is out of
character with the neighbourhood's villas. No. 74 is a Boucher-
style Italianate villa; No. 64, the earliest house on the hill, a
simple three-bay house, remodelled and joined to another pair
(of which only No. 66 survives) *c.* 1845: all possibly by *Charles
Wilson*. To the E, a large development of 1969 by *Hugh Wilson
& Lewis Womersley*, comprising two plain three-storey blocks
of flats and two groups of patio houses set back behind Nos.
52 and 56 on the brow of Partickhill. The best house on the
hill is No. 56, *c.* 1841, a restrained but elegant and unaltered
villa with an Ionic portico; all its ancillary buildings are
screened by a handsome pedimented archway and gates.
Opposite, at No. 53, a gabled villa of the 1870s and a terrace
of five houses (Nos. 51–9), possibly by *Robert Turnbull, c.* 1888.
Their tripartite windows are surprisingly old-fashioned. At
No. 52, an unusual turreted porch and a sympathetically
designed w addition. The last villa, No. 50, *c.* 1870, is fashionably bay-windowed.

Where the road descends to the E, it is lined with bold red
sandstone tenements of 1887–1900, their interiors spaciously
planned: on the s side, six blocks of 1896 by *Adam Short*, the
easternmost block, also of 1896, by *John Cunningham*. These
tenements continue in NORTH GARDNER STREET, those at
the N end by *John Kennedy*, 1888, those on the w side by
Thomas Band, 1905, for the Partickhill Building Company.
More of similar type down the vertiginous GARDNER
STREET, which leads off Partickhill Road to the s: at the NE

corner they are by *William Tait*, 1887. The easternmost house in Partickhill Road is the former WELLPARK HOUSE (No. 10, formerly St Peter's Seminary), *c.* 1869, with an institutional-looking Jacobean-style front. Behind, a simple timber chapel of 1877 by *W. & R. Ingram*. Opposite, more tenements, this time by *Adam Short*, 1896, and at the E end of the street by *John Cunningham*, 1894–6. Where Partickhill Road meets Hyndland Road and Hyndland Street, Dowanhill Church (*see* Dowanhill and Dowanside, above) provides the most dramatic piece of townscape in the area, proudly dominating the view from the S up Hyndland Street. E of the church, a smart quadrangular block of classically detailed terraced tenements with corner pavilions, dating from *c.* 1858–64 (Nos. 36–52 LAWRENCE STREET, 45–9 DOWANHILL STREET, 29–47 HAVELOCK STREET, and 86–90 HYNDLAND STREET). This development is the last middle-class one on the lower slopes of Dowanhill: the lowest ones to the S are densely packed with working-class tenements (*see* Partick, below). To the N of Dowanhill Church, in Highburgh Road, an unusual Tudor-style terrace (Nos. 65–73) by *P. Macgregor Chalmers*, 1899.

PARTICK

Partick is bounded to the N by the affluence of Partickhill and to the S and E by the Clyde and the Kelvin, the sources of its prosperity. It is first mentioned in 1136, when David I granted land at 'Perdyc' to the church of Glasgow on its dedication to St Kentigern. It was not until the 1840s, with the rise of shipbuilding, that Partick changed radically from a small village; its population doubled between 1851 and 1861. Although overshadowed, the traditional industry of milling continued and has outlived most of the shipyards. Partick became an independent burgh in 1852 and managed to maintain its independence from Glasgow until 1912. The Clydeside Expressway, a barrier between Partick and the Clyde, has cut a desolate swathe through its industry and housing. The remaining buildings reflect a strong working-class society and are mainly later C 19 and C 20.

CHURCHES

PARTICK BAPTIST CHURCH, Crow Road. By *Miller & Black*, 1927. Dressed sandstone front and first bay, the remainder roughcast in debased Collegiate Perp. Simple rectangle with U-plan galleries, vestry etc. to the W. Plain interior.

PARTICK CONGREGATIONAL CHURCH, 37 Stewartville Street. Built 1910. Façade based on the E front of Dunblane Cathedral. An aisleless galleried rectangle, with halls to the W, elaborately decorated inside by *Milne & Kilgar*, 1914. – STAINED GLASS. One large three-light window and one two-light window by *William Meikle & Son*, *c.* 1930. – Two-light window in the N wall by *Gordon Webster*, 1951.

PARTICK EAST CHURCH, 20 Lawrence Street. Formerly United Presbyterian. By *J. B. Wilson*, 1897. Well-detailed Scots Late Gothic in red rock-faced rubble. An octagonal staircase turret links the church with the hall and vestries to the W. Galleried and aisled interior, with the organ chamber recess to the N.

PARTICK FREE CHURCH, Crow Road. 1910, by *A. Petrie & Sons*, in an uninspired Scots Late Gothic style. This white freestone rectangle has a simple gabled elevation to the street with a debased Perp window. Very austere interior, with an E gallery. Vestry and hall behind.

PARTICK GARDNER STREET CHURCH, Gardner Street. Designed as Partick Gaelic Church by *H. & D. Barclay*, 1904. Red rock-faced sandstone in anaemic Glasgow Style Gothic. The diminutive octagonal corner entrance tower lacks the presence of the surrounding tenement's bay windows. Simple galleried interior.

PARTICK HIGHLAND FREE CHURCH, Dowanhill Street. Small Early Gothic sandstone rectangle of *c.* 1880 with a gallery at the W end.

PARTICK METHODIST CHURCH, Dumbarton Road. Simple rectangle of 1880 by *William F. McGibbon*. He also inserted a gallery in 1901. Dressed sandstone with a sophisticated E.E. S front. The W spire was removed in 1904 by *Watson & Salmond* and replaced by the curved parapet. Plain interior. – STAINED GLASS. One window by *Abbot & Co.* (Lancaster), 1957. – Series of halls at the back (N), by *W. F. McGibbon*, 1882.

PARTICK OLD PARISH CHURCH, Church Street. 1879. Simplified French Gothic in ashlar. Slender spire. Rose window in the street elevation (E). Otherwise, an aisled rectangle to which *Steele & Balfour* added a new bay and chancel with an organ chamber in 1896. Their new fittings include specially designed oak choir stalls, communion table, carved pulpit and a marble and onyx font. – STAINED GLASS. An important late C19 and early C20 collection. S aisle from E to W: Charity, in muted colours, by *Stephen Adam*, 1895; The Good Shepherd, a strong design by *J. T. Stewart*, executed by *J. L. Kilpatrick* for *Meikle & Sons*, given 1901; Resurrection and Ascension by *James Steel & Co.*, undated; Queen Victoria Memorial window, *c.* 1901, made by *William Meikle & Sons* and perhaps designed by *J. T. Stewart*; and The Feeding of the Five Thousand (dedicated to George Peebles † 1900), an extravagant, overcrowded display in the descriptive use of lead lines and coloured and textured glass, also by *J. T. Stewart* for *William Meikle & Sons*. – N aisle from E to W: two windows (The Faithful Servant and St Mary Magdalene's Communion) by *J. T. & C. E. Stewart*, both *c.* 1905, simpler and more harmonious than Stewart's work in the S aisle; Sacrifice of Isaac by *David Gauld*, 1896; Christ Walking on the Water, a dramatic composition by *Robert Anning Bell*, 1896; and one window by

Gordon Webster, 1938. – The E and W windows look contemporary with the church. Two-storey halls of 1896 behind.

PARTICK SOUTH CHURCH, 259 Dumbarton Road. Built in
1988 by *Fleming Buildings*. Ineffectual timber-framed church
clad in buff brick on the site of *James Hamilton*'s St Mary's
Church of 1864. Square with a shallow E apse. The lower
block to the W and N contains vestry and halls. Standard
contemporary interior fittings. To the S, Gothic mission halls
by *Baldie & Tennant*, 1885.

ST BRIDE, 19 Rosevale Street. Disused. 1897, by *Peter Macgregor Chalmers*. A simple Gothic church in red snecked
rubble. Nave with a single galleried N aisle and a deep chancel
to the E.

ST PETER (R.C.), 46–50 Hyndland Street. 1903, by *Peter Paul
Pugin*. This substantial church is linked to the large presbytery
by what was originally a two-storey baptistery. In style it
is simple Gothic, built of red rock-faced sandstone with a
prominent slated roof. Bright, clearstorey-lit nave with aisles.
Semicircular E apse and a gallery. Red sandstone piers support
the single nave arcade. Elaborate carved REREDOS, with
stained-glass windows behind it.

ST SILAS EPISCOPAL MISSION CHURCH, 14 Hayburn
Street. 1874, by *John Honeyman*. A plain Gothic sandstone
mission church with a gabled S porch. Derelict in 1989.

ST SIMON (R.C.), Partick Bridge Street. Known as St Peter's
(R.C.) until 1903: now the church of the Polish community. By
Charles O'Neill, 1858. Plain aisleless simple Gothic sandstone
rectangle, with a semicircular apse to the E and a W gallery
with an organ. Renovated in 1956–7 by *Gillespie Kidd & Coia*,
with new marble fittings including the altar (with a panel by
Mortimer depicting Christ comforted by His Mother), pulpit,
font, dado and altar rail. – PAINTING. Copy of the 'Black
Madonna' above the Lady altar, a gift from the Polish army. –
Contemporary sandstone PRESBYTERY to N, with an empty
niche above the door.

PUBLIC BUILDINGS

PARTICK BURGH HALLS, Burgh Hall Street. Exuberant, in
François I style and built of finely detailed ashlar, the halls
rather incongruously overlook the West of Scotland Cricket
Ground. The design, by *William Leiper*, 1865, was displayed
at the 1867 Paris Exhibition among work chosen to show the
'Progress of British Architecture'. It was built in 1872 and
reflects the burgh's increasing civic pride. The principal three-
bay block, of two storeys crowned by a steep, elaborately
crested mansard roof and elegantly attenuated cupola, contains
the hall itself. Over the ground-floor windows, three carved
roundels of *Misericordia, Veritas* and *Judicia* by *William
Mossman*. The first-floor window of the advanced central bay
is placed within a heavily moulded arch and topped by a

pediment. The single-storey entrance to the w repeats the arch-and-pediment motif. A more utilitarian three-storey wing to the E, which contains offices and the lesser hall, has pedimented, shallowly projecting bays and a pyramidal roof with a small cupola repeating elements from the main block.

The interior, though extensively altered and modernized by the Corporation in 1936, 1966 and 1971, retains the large galleried hall, with open, semicircular, bound couples supporting the roof, and the marbled principal staircase. There is decorative stained glass throughout, incorporating the burgh coat of arms, which reflects some of the original opulence.

BATHS AND WASHHOUSE, 71–3 Purdon Street. By *John Bryce* (Burgh Surveyor), 1912. An effective combination of red brick and yellow sandstone dressings: inside, white glazed tiles. Still in use.

PARTICK FIRE BRIGADE, ELECTRICITY GENERATION and CLEANSING DEPARTMENT. All three services are housed on the same block between Sandy Road and Meadow Road, bounded to the s by Beith Street and overshadowed by the expressway. – PARTICK CLEANSING DEPARTMENT, 24 Sandy Road. By *John Bryce*, Burgh Surveyor, *c.* 1905. Red brick buildings, including refuse destructor and walled compound. – PARTICK FREE FIRE BRIGADE STATION, 120–4 Beith Street. By *James Miller*, 1906. Queen Anne-style block of red brick with sandstone dressings on an L-plan; now converted into housing. Elegant campanile for hoses behind it.

PARTICK POLICE BUILDING, Anderson Street. By *Charles Wilson*, 1853. Diminutive, well-detailed two-storey five-bay palazzo, with rusticated ground-floor and pedimented first-floor windows. Single-storey windowless wing to the E, the courtroom surmounted by a stone balustrade and rooflight. At the time of writing, stranded in a derelict wasteland.

PARTICK LIBRARY, 305 Dumbarton Road. Designed by Glasgow's *Office of Public Works* in 1925 but not opened until 1935. Renaissance. Single-storey, ashlar, with a balustraded parapet, and placed diagonally to the street for maximum effect. Granite-shafted Doric columns flank the doorway; Glasgow's coat of arms is prominent on the principal bay window. Brick rear elevation. The interior, originally in three departments, was modernized by the *City Architect's Department*, 1963–6. Shallow rear extension, with lions' heads along the stringcourse, housing offices and so on.

CHURCH STREET SCHOOL (formerly Partick Academy, now an adult education centre), Church Street. 1903, by *Bruce & Hay* for Govan Parish School Board. A red sandstone Italianate block in a commanding position facing N up Byres Road. Swimming pool and workshops of 1904 by the same architects in a separate block to the rear.

ANDERSON STREET NURSERY SCHOOL, Anderson Street. *c.* 1860. Two-storey, of snecked sandstone. The steep gable, with its prominent asymmetrically placed chimneystack, looks rather rustic. Over the pair of first-floor windows, a semi-circular arch inscribed with the school's name. The main block contained an upper and lower hall with the school house forming an outshot to the s. It is now the only C19 building left on the w side of Anderson Street.

ROSEVALE STREET INFANT DEPARTMENT, Rosevale Street. Disused in 1989. By *Samuel Preston*, 1904. Severe grey sandstone T-plan school with a symmetrical E elevation. 'Infant Department' is carved on the central gable. Next door was an earlier Board school of 1874.

Former ST PETER'S PUBLIC SCHOOL, Stewartville Street. Large red sandstone Board school of the 1890s, in Renaissance Free Style incorporating Dutch gables, crowsteps and a classical porch. Converted into forty-six flats by *Robertson, Graham & Partners*, 1982–6.

ST PETER'S SCHOOL, Dowanhill Street. Severe rock-faced red sandstone school by *James Cowan*, 1898, with an equally severe extension along Chancellor Street by *Walter R. Watson*, 1912.

THORNWOOD PUBLIC SCHOOL, Auchentorlie Street. By *Andrew Balfour*, 1900. A three-storey square block in red Locharbriggs sandstone. Unsympathetic grey brick primary school added to the s.

MASONIC HALL, Ardery Street. 1910, by *Brand & Lithgow*. Designed as the mission hall of St Silas's Episcopal Church, containing a classroom and large hall. Red brick with sandstone dressings; drastically altered to form the Masonic Hall.

PARTICK SEWAGE PUMPING STATION, 35 Dumbarton Road. 1904, by *A. B. McDonald* (City Engineer), and apparently derelict in 1989. Baroque with Glasgow-Style flourishes in red sandstone, it takes advantage of a prominent site w of Partick Bridge with an exuberant silhouette. The boilerhouse, which once supplied steam to the Kelvin Hall via a surviving roofed lattice girder bridge, has now gone from the rear.

KELVIN HALL STATION, Benalder Street (formerly Partick Central). All that remains of this Lanarkshire & Dumbartonshire Railway station is a diminutive (and disused) booking office of *c.* 1896, now stranded on the contemporary Old Partick Bridge. It served the island-platform station below.

DESCRIPTION

The majority of Partick's housing stock consists of late C19 tenements, good-quality but unexceptional. They stretch northward from Dumbarton Road. The area s of the main road has largely been cleared for the expressway and for redevelopment schemes that are still unrealized in 1989. DUMBARTON ROAD affords a few surprises, especially the Georgian Survival-style block of *c.* 1850 in yellow sandstone at Nos. 360–92. Its chaste classicism contrasts markedly with

Burnet & Boston's heavily modelled and turreted red sandstone block of 1885 opposite at Nos. 385–93.

Two handsome pub fronts brighten the scene, especially at No. 59 the EXCHEQUER (formerly the Roost Bar), 1899–1900, by *James Hoey Craigie* of *Clarke and Bell*. Fine repetitive Art Nouveau frontage on an earlier building that was later extended; original but simple interior. The tenement above has been removed, leaving the pub, now single-storey, stranded – a common sight in Glasgow. Much later in date is the THORNWOOD (Nos. 722–4), 1939, by *James Taylor*. Art Deco Vitrolite exterior in primrose and black with a neon-illuminated fascia. Contemporary dark walnut veneered interior. All this forms the ground floor of a red sandstone tenement of the 1890s.

102 The most important C20 housing development is CRATHIE COURT on CRATHIE DRIVE. Designed in 1946 and built in 1952–4 under the direction of *Dr Ronald Bradbury*, Director of Housing, it was an experiment in building high-rise flats. The single U-plan block of six to eight storeys consists of eighty-eight single-person flats with balcony access. In this extremely sophisticated building, different masses and materials interact in the manner inspired by International Modernism to create a dramatic and popular high-rise housing scheme. The area to the NW of Crathie Court was developed at the same time. THORNWOOD DRIVE and THORNWOOD GARDENS have four-storey tenements in buff brick, with balconies and porthole windows of the kind then being built at Pollok etc. (*see* below).

S of Dumbarton Road are a few fragments of Partick's once thriving industry. There are two descendants of Partick's ancient mills. In BENALDER STREET, BISHOP MILLS lies on the site of the medieval 'Mill of Partick'. A handsome rubble building, built for William Wilson in 1839, with elaborate stone wheatsheaf finials on the gables, clumsily converted into twenty flats in 1987 and surrounded by a manicured swathe of grass in place of the wheel and the mill lade. Its near neighbour in SCOTSTOUNMILL ROAD are the SCOTSTOUN FLOUR MILLS, the last mill still operating in the area, though now largely housed in the industrial sheds round St Simon's Church. *J. W. & J. Laird* designed the oldest surviving buildings – the slender red brick tower with corbelled crenellated parapet and the attached five-storey painted brick block of 1909 on Thurso Street.

Closer to the Clyde in CASTLEBANK STREET, all that remains of the former MEADOWSIDE YARD of the shipbuilders D. & W. Henderson (founded *c.* 1845) is the now engulfed red brick and stone office block at No. 165: 1895, by *Bruce & Hay*, in a restrained French style, its only accent the advanced entrance bay shorn of its roof cresting. Further W along Castlebank Street loom the MEADOWSIDE GRANARIES, Partick's most dramatic structure by far, but which, sadly, closed in 1988. The first granary of thirteen bays and thirteen storeys was

built in brick for the Clyde Navigation Trust in 1911–13 by
the engineer *William Alston*. Extended E and W in 1936–7,
creating a colossal thirty-four-bay, thirteen-storey building.
In 1960 and 1967 two more granaries were built to the W for
what was by then the Clyde Port Authority.

BROOMHILL

0 ¼ mile
0 ½ km

JORDANHILL

Jordanhill Stn

CROW RD

DRIVE

⑧

ABBEY DR.

②

BEECHWOOD DR

MITRE ROAD

CROW

RANDOLPH

WOODCROFT AVE

NASEBY AVE

ESSEX

⑨

⑩

WESTLAND

VICTORIA

PARK

DRIVE

AVE

⑤

③

ROAD

Fossil Grove

Victoria Park

DRIVE NORTH

VICTORIA PK. GDNS N

①

Victoria Pk. Gdns S

BALSHAGRAY

MARLBOROUGH AVE

ROAD

CLYDESIDE

Lake

④

BROOMHILL DR.

PARTICK

WHITEINCH

BROOMHILL CR.

BROOMHILL TERR

BROOMHILL DRIVE

⑥

to CLYDE TUNNEL

EXPRESSWAY

⑦

CHURCHES and PUBLIC BUILDINGS
① Broomhill Trinity Congregational
② Balshagray Parish Church
③ Broomhill Church
④ Church of the Nazarene
⑤ Our Lady of Perpetual Succour (R.C.)
⑥ Victoria Park Parish Church
⑦ Balshagray Public School
⑧ St Thomas Aquinas Secondary
⑨ Westercraigs
⑩ Whiteinch Homes

N

SUBURBS NORTH OF THE CLYDE

BROOMHILL

Victoria Park was laid out in 1886–7 as a public park for the burgh of Partick. On the E side of the park, 'Broomhill, with its drive, terrace and avenue' and 'select appearance', was laid out *c.* 1870 on the W edge of Partick. Balshagray Avenue, which overlooked the park, was in origin the avenue to the C17 Balshagray Mansion (demolished). The N part of Broomhill (around Randolph Road) was developed immediately after the park opened (1890–1910), the area immediately N of the park even later (after 1910). Today Broomhill is cut off from the park by the approach to the Clyde Tunnel, and the imposing villas on the hill itself have been replaced by tower blocks.

CHURCHES

BALSHAGRAY PARISH CHURCH, 218–30 Broomhill Drive. 1907–12, by *Stewart & Paterson*. Slightly raised across the junction of Broomhill Drive and Crow Road, its long, low, towerless N elevation, with gabled transept balanced by a NW porch, facing up Crow Road. Droved red sandstone in Free-Style Gothic, with very fanciful tracery. – STAINED GLASS. Scottish Industries by *Sadie McLellan*, 1950.

BROOMHILL CHURCH, 64–6 Randolph Road. A former United Free Church, 1902–3, by *Stewart & Paterson*. A large red sandstone church, its big engaged corner tower with a short recessed tiled spire. Conventional Geometric style. Inside, low aisles and a tall clearstorey, galleries in the E transept and at the W end. – STAINED GLASS. A contemporary highly coloured, pictorial rendition of 'Suffer the Little Children' and other Gospel scenes, probably by *David Gauld*. – Large halls and church house of 1899 round a courtyard to the N.

BROOMHILL TRINITY CONGREGATIONAL CHURCH, 30–2 Victoria Park Gardens South. By *J. J. Burnet*, 1900–8. One of a series of Burnet churches, beginning with Corrie and Shiskine on Arran (1887–9), in which Arts and Crafts features meet the Scottish Baronial, Romanesque and Gothic styles in variations on the same composition, and with strange juxtapositions of scale. Stolid Baronial tower to the street, with a delicate late Gothic dedicatory carving within a tall Romanesque window, and oversized bell-openings. Attached to the tower, the domestic-looking vestibule and, also oversized, a half-timbered porch. In comparison, the conventional Gothic nave, deep chancel, E aisle (with choir at the N end) are all low. So is the long hall at r. angles to the church, with, again, an English domestic flavour, particularly in the unbroken band of windows.

The distinction of parts is less obvious inside: the interior is opened as far as possible into a single space. The Arts and Crafts feeling is concentrated in the chancel – in its carving (see the delightful band of text, 'All ye Works of the Lord magnify Him forever', entwined with birds and beasts in a Celtic interlace) and in the STAINED GLASS (individual figures of Christ and Saints) by *Wm. Meikle & Sons*, though this is later (World War I memorial). – Nave N wall, two windows by *Gordon Webster*, 1951. – Plain marble reredos installed in the 1960s. – WAR MEMORIAL by *Burnet*, 1920–1.

CHURCH OF THE NAZARENE, Broomhill Drive, at the corner of Norby Road. 1969–72, by *N. N. Gilkinson*. An octagonal hall church in pink snecked rubble with a token spirelet.

OUR LADY OF PERPETUAL SUCCOUR (R.C.), 17 Mitre Road, Broomhill. 1962–5, by *Charles Gray*. A boxy church in pink sandstone rubble relieved by a dramatic concrete A-frame forming the entrance. In the upper part of it, over the open porch, a mosaic of Christ. Two *dal-de-verre* windows in the narthex.

VICTORIA PARK PARISH CHURCH, Broomhill Drive. By *Robert Rogerson & Philip Spence*, 1968–70, replacing a church of 1877 by Leiper which was demolished to make way for the Clyde Tunnel. It fits into the side of the hill crowned by Broomhill's tower blocks (*see* Perambulation, below): the changes of level mean flights of steps up to the church and to the generous foyer linking church and hall, and an unusual plan. The entrances are to halls and ancillary rooms, including a small chapel. Blue engineering brick and exposed concrete inside and out. The church lies above, its broad chancel cantilevered over the NW door, the choir gallery sheltering the rear entrance. Otherwise the church is one restfully spacious volume under a shallow timber monopitch with lots of diagonal bracing. – Disappointing furnishing except for two *dal-de-verre* STAINED-GLASS windows by *Gordon Webster*, 1970.

PUBLIC BUILDINGS

BALSHAGRAY PUBLIC SCHOOL (now Anniesland College, Balshagray Annexe), 722–36 Dumbarton Road. 1904, by *Bruce & Hay*, for Govan School Board. Huge, with a Roman *gravitas* to the main façade. Extra storeys fitted under hipped roofs on the end elevations. Well-preserved galleried central hall of the usual type but on a very large scale.

ST THOMAS AQUINAS SECONDARY SCHOOL, 80 Westland Drive. A big, prominently sited brick school of 1951–3 by *William Baillie & Son*.

THORNWOOD PUBLIC SCHOOL. *See* Partick, above: Public Buildings.

WESTERCRAIGS (Church of Scotland Home for Girls), 21 Westland Drive. 1890–1 by *Simon & Capper*, the design amended by *S. Henbest Capper*. Designed as an orphanage in a friendly neo-C17 Scottish style, with a big stepped, very Victorian staircase window. Positively coloured in purplish Bothwell Park rubble, with rich red dressings from Ballochmyle and a green Westmoreland slate roof.

WHITEINCH HOMES, 19 Westland Drive. Built *c.* 1890 like English C17 almshouses, with shaped pedimented gables, cartouches and swags. Three ranges of lodgings, with internal corridors round a courtyard. Central entrance passage with wrought-iron gate, and a long, arched staircase window towards each end.

VICTORIA PARK. Laid out on the Scotstoun estate 1886–7, extended 1894–1909. – FOSSIL GROVE. Ten fossil roots and stems of trees were found when a path was cut through the

whinstone quarry in the SW corner of the park, and were
protected with a glass-roofed building. A prosaic setting for
an eerie relic. A Middle Bronze Age CIST CEMETERY was
discovered in the layers above the fossils. – GATES commemorating Queen Victoria's Jubilee, 1887, by *Walter Macfarlane & Co., Saracen Foundry*. – CLOCK by the lake, given
by Gordon Oswald of Scotstoun, who gave the land for the
park. – BANDSTAND AND SHELTER. 1908, by *John Bryce*,
Burgh Surveyor, with a brick bow of 1930. – WAR
MEMORIAL, with a good figure of Victory by *F. W. Doyle
Jones*, 1922, above a granite cenotaph.

PERAMBULATION

Broomhill is divided from Victoria Park by the expressway
approaches. The terrace of bay-windowed villas on BAL-
SHAGRAY AVENUE now faces what was the park's main
entrance across a gulf of tarmac. Those at the N end were built
soon after the park opened in 1887, those at the S end (by *John
Smellie*, builder) in 1892. Behind, in BROOMHILL AVENUE,
TERRACE and DRIVE, a superior tenement development
begun on the W edge of Partick by the *Victoria Park Feuing
Co. Ltd* in 1871, fifteen years before what is now called Victoria
Park was even begun. Cream sandstone tenements of ambitious
High Victorian design. The details are French Empire: big
mansards with pedimented dormers over the corner pavilions
and shell tympana over the first-floor windows, with a bold
bracketed cornice above them. Prominent pyramidal slate caps
to the full-height bay windows (except for the elaborate mansarded dormers with steep pediments, tiny bartizans and decorated gables at the later INVERCLYDE GARDENS (Nos.
137–59 Broomhill Drive), 1902). The tenements on Broomhill
Avenue are later (1885, by *John Smellie*) and have balustraded
bays.
The S.S.H.A.'s BROOMHILL SCHEME, 1963–9, by *Harold
Buteux* (Chief Technical Officer), rises from the heart of this
Victorian suburb. In place of six large villas on the steep
hill, five eighteen-storey tower blocks provide 'dramatic and
envigorating contrast'. They were built to house those displaced by the Clyde Tunnel's construction. Mature trees and
grassy slopes surround the blocks, whose concrete frames and
grey and white mosaic panels form a restless pattern. On the
W side of Broomhill Drive, three eight-storey white mosaic-
clad blocks, with no frills, and four-storey tenements try to
mediate between the towers and the older housing. Tucked
into the side of the hill, Victoria Park Parish Church (*see*
Churches, above).
Between *c*.1888 and 1910, red sandstone villas and tenements
and their associated churches (*see* above) spread N into
WOODCROFT AVENUE and NASEBY AVENUE, for
example. Off Crow Road, the oval of MARLBOROUGH
AVENUE (with tenements of 1902 (N) and 1907 (S) by *Whyte*

& Kennedy) leads to a row of interesting houses at the w end, especially the Glasgow Style Nos. 1–24 (1903) by *William Baillie*, with tapering chimneys and Art Nouveau leaded and stained glass. Development did not spread w of Crow Road to the area N of Victoria Park Drive until after 1900. Here, among the substantial, mostly double villas, No. 55 MITRE ROAD, by *E. G. Wylie* of *Wright & Wylie* (1924), stands out. It is of cream snecked rubble with a wide swept roof in Scottish C17 style reduced to the barest essentials *à la* J. J. Burnet. At the back, a fine octagonal conservatory.

WHITEINCH

Originally an island (*inch*) in the Clyde, joined by silting to the N bank, Whiteinch became in the C18 a low-lying farm owned by the proprietors of Jordanhill (*see* Anniesland). Improvement began with the dredging of the Clyde in 1837, when the silt was used to raise the level of the land. Barclay Curle's shipyard opened in 1855, and the population soon rose from almost nothing to over 1,000, living in Northinch Street, Curle Street and South Street. Most of this industrial settlement has been rebuilt since 1960. At the w end of Whiteinch (which fell within the Scotstoun estate; *see* below), Gordon Oswald of Scotstoun built the first church (1874; *see* Perambulation, below) and in 1885 began to establish a planned development of workers' cottages, later known as Gordon Park. Tenements were built along the s fringe of the newly laid-out Victoria Park in 1900, joining up to Partick (to which burgh it belonged). Many of these were obliterated by the Clyde Tunnel approaches, which severed Whiteinch from Victoria Park.

CHURCHES AND PUBLIC BUILDINGS

Former GORDON PARK CHURCH. *See* Perambulation, below.
ST PAUL (R.C.), 1213 Dumbarton Road. 1957–60, by *R. Fairlie & Partners*, in red sandstone ashlar. Of basilican type, with low passage aisles. All the forms much simplified and rectilinear: no mouldings, no ornament except the statue of St Paul on the façade. Flanking the street façade with its tower, the PRESBYTERY (converted from Jordanvale House by *Cowan & Watson*, 1904) and HALLS (by *Walter R. Watson*, 1908) of the previous church. Inside, crushingly vivid STAINED GLASS in the wide curved sanctuary window and dingy abstract glass in the nave: by *Gabriel Loire* of Chartres.
WHITEINCH-JORDANVALE PARISH CHURCH, 25 Squire Street. 1912–13, by *P. Macgregor Chalmers*, in snecked red sandstone rubble. Minimal Scots Romanesque, with blunt forms and no tower. The interior, as with many of this architect's churches, is more interesting. The nave arcades have

WHITEINCH

SCOTSTOUN

Victoria Park

BOWLING GREEN RD.

DUMBARTON

PRIMROSE ST
WESTLAND DR.
CLYDESIDE
VICTORIA PARK DR.
Gordon Park
LIME ST
ELM ST
VICTORIA PK. ST
VICTORIA PARK DR. SOUTH

MEDWYN

INCHLEE ST
GLENDORE ST
EXPRESSWAY
BALSHAGRAY AVE.

ROAD

FORE ST
EDZELL ST
SQUIRE ST

SOUTH STREET

River Clyde

TUNNEL

CHURCHES and PUBLIC BUILDINGS
1a (Gordon Park Church)
1 St Paul (R.C.)
2 Whiteinch-Jordanvale Parish Church
3 Whiteinch District Library
4 (Whiteinch Burgh Halls)
5 Whiteinch Public School
6 Whiteinch Primary and Nursery Schools

0 ¼ mile
0 ½ km

N

unmoulded arches and cushion capitals carved with figurative medallions and foliage. Two apses, the chancel apse groin-vaulted and blind-arcaded with communion table, pulpit and lectern placed according to Early Christian usage.

WHITEINCH DISTRICT LIBRARY, 14 Victoria Park Drive South. 1923–6, by the *Office of Public Works, Glasgow*. Attractive single-storey stripped classical building in red sandstone ashlar, its hipped roof crowned with a cupola above the corner entrance. City arms over the door. Nice fittings and plasterwork.

WHITEINCH BURGH HALLS (now Whiteinch Work Centre), 35 Inchlee Street. 1894, with quite an ecclesiastical air and some C17 Scottish detailing. Towers flank a big window above the entrance. Buttressed side elevation, with triangular and segmental pediments rising above eaves level. Police and fire station to the s.

WHITEINCH PUBLIC SCHOOL (now Rosepark Tutorial Centre), 13 Victoria Park Drive South. 1914–17, for Govan School Board, by *Samuel Preston*, the Board's Master of Works. Large, and plain classical.

WHITEINCH PRIMARY AND NURSERY SCHOOL, Glendore Street. Late C19 Board school. A hint of the French Renaissance in the tall mansard. A similar but plainer grey ashlar block faces Medwyn Street.

WHITEINCH HOMES. *See* Broomhill, above: Public Buildings.

CLYDE TUNNEL. *See* Crossings of the Clyde and Kelvin, below.

PERAMBULATION

Whiteinch, like Broomhill, is cut off from Victoria Park by an approach to the Clyde Tunnel. Facing the park across it from VICTORIA PARK DRIVE SOUTH are tenements of 1900 by *G. S. Kenneth*. SE of them, a scrappy mixture of buildings, with one or two worth noting.

On DUMBARTON ROAD, just by the Clyde Tunnel entrance, at No. 150, the former AVENUE THEATRE of 1912, an entertaining cinema in French Empire style by *Thomas Baird*. The twin towers have swags and pyramidal roofs, the main keystone a rococo lady. Set back behind a green further w, SUMMERFIELD COTTAGES, a cheerfully painted stone terrace with pairs of shallow gables, some round-arched windows (all the windows have brick margins) and lead doorhoods. They were built *c.*1877 by Mr Corbett, son of Lord Rowallan, 'to prove that self-contained cottages could pay at a small rental'.

s of Dumbarton Road, in EDZELL STREET, more terraced cottages (and cottage flats), this time of 1986–7 by *David Simister* and *Alistair McEarchan* for *Simister, Monaghan, McKinney, MacDonald*, and refreshingly coloured in cream brick, grey tile and green-grey timber. Several imaginative touches, such as the concrete plaques recalling shipbuilding and looking forward to the area's regeneration: by *Brian Kelly*. Back on Dumbarton Road, opposite the N end of Edzell Street, is the simple Gothic façade of the former GORDON PARK CHURCH, built in 1874 by Gordon Oswald as Whiteinch United Free Church (architects *McKissack & Rowan*), to serve the industrial settlement. It pre-dates the small leafy enclave of semi-rural cottages that lies to its W, known as GORDON PARK. The cottages were begun in 1885 by Gordon Oswald for the workers on his Scotstoun estate. The first rows, of 1885, facing Dumbarton Road, are by *Alexander Petrie* and are simply one-storeyed with dormers. The subsequent ones, in VICTORIA PARK STREET, ELM STREET, LIME STREET, WESTLAND DRIVE and BOWLING GREEN ROAD, were put up between 1888 and 1895 by a builder, *George Anderson*. The later ones are two-storey villas in rock-faced red and white sandstone, many of them painted. All have gardens, back and front, and a network of back lanes. Along the S side of Dumbarton Road, tenements continue without a break into Scotstoun (*q.v.*). The boundary is Primrose Street.

SCOTSTOUN

Scotstoun House survived until *c.* 1960. It was built in the early C18 by the Walkinshaws, and lay at the centre of a large estate with a commanding view of the Clyde. In 1825 the Oswalds added a new front, designed by *David Hamilton*, but only four decades later, shipbuilding and Clydeside industries, spreading W from Whiteinch, began to destroy the estate's amenity. Connell's Scotstoun Yard was the first to open in 1861. In the following decades, Gordon Oswald began to develop the E end of his estate, which falls within Whiteinch (*q.v.*), with a church and cottages for his workers. In 1886 he sold a large parcel of land to the expanding burgh of Partick for Victoria Park (*see* Broomhill, above). The cottage development was continued commercially after 1895, encouraged by the arrival of the Lanarkshire & Dumbartonshire Railway and the continuation of the tram route beyond Whiteinch. Along the river, iron, engineering and shipbuilding industries and their associated tenements grew apace between 1890 and 1914. Yarrow's shipyard (the only one still functioning) was attracted from the Thames to Scotstoun in 1906.

The N part of the estate, apart from a scatter of villas round the Scotstounhill railway station, which opened in 1887, was untouched until the 1920s, when the Corporation bought it for a housing scheme. Scotstoun House was engulfed, but survived until tower blocks took its place.

SCOTSTOUN

0 ¼ mile
0 ½ km

N

KIRKTON AVENUE

CRESCENT RD

TALBOT TERR.

TALBOT RD

ANNIESLAND RD

ANNIESLAND ROAD

LINCOLN AVENUE

JORDANHILL

KINGSWAY

Scotstounhill Stn.

DANES

DUMBARTON

QUEEN VICTORIA DR.

DRIVE

NORSE AVE

SOUTH

STREET

VERONA AVE

EARLBANK

ORMISTON AVE

ROAD

AVE

LENNOX AVE

BROOMHILL

BALMORAL ST.

SOUTH STREET

HARLAND ST

ROAD

SCOTSTOUN ST.

WHITEINCH

River Clyde

① ✝

⑤

③ ✝

② ✝

④

⑥

⑦

⑤ₐ

CHURCHES and MAJOR BUILDINGS
① Corpus Christi (R.C.)
② Scotstoun East
③ Scotstoun West Parish Church
④ Scotstoun Primary
⑤ Victoria Drive Secondary
⑤ₐ North British Diesel Engine Works
⑥ Albion Motor Works
⑦ Yarrow's

CHURCHES AND PUBLIC BUILDINGS

CORPUS CHRISTI (R.C.), Lincoln Avenue, Scotstounhill. By *Peter Whiston*, 1969–72. Charmless grey harled box with copper-clad butterfly roof over church and day-chapel (s). Linked halls and manse.

SCOTSTOUN EAST CHURCH, 70–6 Earlbank Avenue. Added in 1904–6 by *H. E. Clifford* to the Eaton Hall by *J. B. Wilson*, which had opened in 1902 as the Scotstoun United Free Church. (Hall interior altered 1972.) Clifford's church is an unprepossessing, towerless neo-Perp design in red snecked rubble. W gallery and gallery over the aisle. Hammerbeam roof. – WAR MEMORIAL TABLET, 1920, by Clifford. – STAINED-GLASS window to Dr Eaton, 1924, by *Meikle & Sons* (Good Shepherd and the Cardinal Virtues).

SCOTSTOUN WEST PARISH CHURCH, 8–16 Queen Victoria Drive. By *James Chalmers*, 1905–6. Romanesque in style and as unarchaeological as his All Saints (Episcopal), Jordanhill (*see* under Anniesland). A large cruciform church in red snecked rubble, with a squat central tower. Many idiosyncratic details, such as the domestic dormers to the tower's octagonal tiled cap, and the tracery of the windows. Aisleless nave, galleries in the transepts, which open with tall broad arches, apsed chancel with a strong corbel course. Heavy symbolism inside and out: the Good Shepherd carved on the S gable, angels with symbols from the Book of Revelation on the tower, more stucco angels on the inside of the tower, the Burning Bush in the mosaic chancel pavement, and symbols of the Evangelists and the twelve tribes of Israel painted on the tower ceiling. – Oak PULPIT, FONT, and COMMUNION TABLE in Romanesque style. – STAINED GLASS by *Douglas Hamilton*, including (nave W side) memorial window to the Revd Cruikshank † 1948 (The Risen Christ). – E transept. Three windows of 1953 (SS Andrew, Ninian, Columba). – HALL. By *Stewart & Paterson*, 1928.

SCOTSTOUN PRIMARY SCHOOL, Earlbank Avenue. Handsome school of 1905 for the Renfrew Landward School Board, different in style from the Glasgow Board schools. At each end, a tower with a wooden cupola and raised porches with stumpy Ionic columns.

VICTORIA DRIVE SECONDARY SCHOOL, Larchfield Avenue. A Higher Grade school by *Kerr & Watson* of Johnstone, opened in 1909. Of red sandstone ashlar, mixed Baroque and French Renaissance in style, with Art Nouveau influence apparent in some of the sinuous details. Large concrete-framed addition by *Honeyman, Jack & Robertson*, 1962–8, with a glazed stairwell. Figurative marble and tile mural on the entrance wall.

PERAMBULATIONS

1. S of Dumbarton Road

DUMBARTON ROAD was, according to a speculator's advertisement in the *Glasgow Herald* of 1905, the dividing line in this district of 'masses and classes'. Along the S side, and in the streets to the S, grey and red sandstone tenements that merge imperceptibly into those of Whiteinch at Primrose Street, opposite the bowling green.

SOUTH STREET, best reached via Scotstoun Street, is the exclusive preserve of industry. First, the most interesting industrial building along this stretch of the Clyde: the NORTH BRITISH DIESEL ENGINE WORKS, built in 1912–13 as 96 part of Barclay Curle & Co.'s Clydeholm shipyard (now defunct). The main steel-framed shop, with its clean lines and distinctive curved roof, strongly resembles Peter Behrens' pioneering AEG turbine factory in Berlin of 1908–9, a likeness explained by the fact that the architect who provided the elevations, *Karl Bernardt*, had worked with Behrens on the German factory. The executive architect was *J. Galt*. Now sadly shrouded in corrugated steel. The most novel feature, the largely glass walling, has been replaced, except for a small section on the NW side, which can be seen from inside.

Nothing else of interest until HARLAND COTTAGES (Harland Street), four rows of cottage flats built speculatively in 1895. They have stone walls and brick window margins like Summerfield Cottages, Whiteinch (*q.v.*), but also scanty mock half-timbering. Further W still, the iron-clad sheds of the CLYDE-SIDE IRONWORKS, built for the Clyde Structural Iron Co. (iron roof and bridge builders), *c.* 1898, and the tall and much more impressive steel-framed sheds of Harland & Wolff's Scotstoun Works, the first part of which was built *c.* 1907 for the Coventry Syndicate by *Sir William Arrol & Co*. Both are part of the huge ALBION MOTOR WORKS (now Leyland Daf), founded in 1903. Long brick sheds on the N side of the street screen the one that remains from the two concrete-framed office blocks, with large expanses of glazing, designed in 1913 by the *Trussed Concrete Steel Co.* of the U.S.A.

Further W, the much rebuilt YARROW'S SHIPYARD (with nothing of architectural interest, except perhaps the Technical Office of 1919), which was founded here in 1906. Yarrow's continues for almost a mile right to Yoker, and incorporates the ELDERSLIE DRY-DOCKS. The first of these dry-docks was opened in 1904 by Shearer & Co., ship repairers (engineer *James Dear*), the second and third in 1933 and 1965 by Barclay Curle & Co. To the N, along DUMBARTON ROAD (in RIVERSDALE LANE, THORNDEN LANE and ARDSLEY LANE), the cottages that Yarrow's built to house its workers in 1905–6, originally intended to last five years.

2. N of Dumbarton Road

Along the N SIDE of Dumbarton Road, W from Westland Drive, the S fringe of a well-planted cottage estate, a continuation on a strict grid of the Gordon Park scheme S of Victoria Park (*see* Whiteinch) by the *Scotstoun Estate Building Co. (cottage and villa builders)*, established in 1895. The earliest ones, at the E end, are of the Whiteinch type of one storey with dormers or two storeys, some rock-faced with half-timbered gables and mostly painted. Those furthest W lack any embellishments (e.g. VERONA AVENUE, 1912). At the centre, in Earlbank Avenue, Scotstoun East Church; at the SW corner, on Queen Victoria Drive, Scotstoun West Church (*see* Churches, above). At the E edge, in LENNOX AVENUE, five much more austere blocks of C19 artisan cottage flats in red and cream brick, set in long gardens. Each flat opens either on to Lennox Avenue (Nos. 41–55, i.e. MONTGOMERIE GARDENS) or on to VANCOUVER ROAD (Nos. 4–18).

Queen Victoria Drive divides this planned estate from the more heterogeneous area of SCOTSTOUNHILL, which contains small pockets of inventively designed late Victorian and Edwardian villas near the Scotstounhill railway station (opened in 1887). At the N end of QUEEN VICTORIA DRIVE, Nos. 227–33, a row of four Edwardian bungalows, distinguished by the unusual dormers on their wide hipped roofs, semicircular in plan on the sides, semicircular in elevation on the front. Further W along ANNIESLAND ROAD, Nos. 583–85 (SHERWOOD and AINSLIE) are a self-consciously asymmetrical pair, dated 1891, with much half-timbering, 'Olde English' rather than Scottish vernacular. On the other side, the terraced stone villas at Nos. 702–8 have some curiously detailed timber bay windows, with square upper storeys jettied above polygonal lower ones.

TALBOT TERRACE (with its terrace of grey stone villas overlooking the railway cutting) leads to CRESCENT ROAD. Here DUNRONALD (No. 55) is another very English concoction of ill-assorted Arts and Crafts motifs: a half-timbered wing ending polygonally, a deep-eaved roof with big chimneys and so on. The site slopes very steeply; the next house, a classical stone villa, drops down to extra storeys at the back.

Crescent Road is the oldest section of several concentric crescents laid out in the 1930s with substantial semi-detached red sandstone villas. They centre on TALBOT PLACE, with Arts and Crafts-style pairs of houses set diagonally on the corners. S of Anniesland Road, the large Scotstoun Corporation housing scheme of the 1920s with houses and cottage flats like Knightswood's plainer ones.

SCOTSTOUN HILL itself is now crowned, in place of Scotstoun House, with six twenty-storey tower blocks, all of the familiar *Wimpey* type with glazed attics (1962–4). A string of five more in the grassy band between KIRKTON AVENUE and Crescent Road (1965–9); and two more further W in PLEAN STREET

(1964–5), neighbours of the former PARISH COUNCIL CHAMBERS (now clinic), with a crowstepped gable over the entrance (*c.* 1910, by *Halley & Neil*).

From Plean Street w along Dumbarton Road, red sandstone tenements go on and on to Yoker, those near Plean Street with some nice details (especially the eye-catching pair on the gushet), those further w progressively meaner.

YOKER

Yoker lies only partly within the present city boundary. The part that does belong to Glasgow was not annexed until 1926. The village of Yoker first appeared on a map of 1734, with houses on both sides of the Yoker Burn (coincidental with the present city boundary). Its *raison d'être* was whisky distilling, and a century later it was still remarkable only for its large distillery. By the 1860s it had other industries, but it grew most rapidly after 1877, when Napier Shanks & Bell moved their shipyard downstream from Govan, after 1882, when the main North British Railway line arrived, and after 1898, when the Rothesay Docks (across the boundary in Clydebank) opened.

YOKER OLD CHURCH, 2484 Dumbarton Road, on the corner of Hawick Street. By *Boston, Menzies & Morton* of Greenock, 1895–7. Of pink snecked Bredisholm rubble, low, broad and cruciform, in a Perp style with no frills, except the inventive tracery in the s window. Gabled halls, nearly as big as the church, by *H. D. Walton*, 1911–12.

YOKER SCHOOL (now Educational Resource Centre), 2418 Dumbarton Road, on the corner of Kelso Street. 1876. In Tudorbethan style. Much extended in 1902.

DESCRIPTION. The much redeveloped late C19 centre lies along DUMBARTON ROAD mostly between Hawick Street and Kelso Street. Here are the parish church and the Board school (*see* above). At Nos. 2452–72, the cheerful red and yellow stone ALEXANDRA TERRACE with steep-pitched gables and bargeboards, and further E the very similar GLEN-EAGLES COTTAGES. To the w, Mill Road (just over the boundary) turns into YOKER MILL ROAD, which with its high hedges is still a bit countrified. Along it and to the N, a few villas of *c.* 1900, e.g. LOURDES, a rural-looking house, all in red brick, with a crowstepped gable. Further E, the fringes of the Knightswood housing scheme (*q.v.*). By the river in BULLDALE STREET, the large single-storey engineering shop built *c.* 1901 for a brass and bronze founders, Bull's Metal & Marine Co. Round-headed windows flank the big arched doorway.

ANNIESLAND and JORDANHILL

N

Knightswood

Temple

Dawsholm Park

FULTON ST
SPENCER ST
9a
BEARSDEN ROAD
SUTCLIFFE RD
2
5
STRATHCONA DR
12
CROW
4
CRAIGEND ST
QUINN PL

GREAT WESTERN ROAD

ANNIESLAND
HELENBURGH DR
CHAMBERLAIN RD

Anniesland
6a
Anniesland Station

ANNIESLAND ROAD

Claythorn
HATFIELD DR
7
WHITTINGHAME DR

MUNRO ROAD
Jordanhill
3
WOODEND
DR
8
9
CROW ROAD
10
11

SOUTHBRAE DRIVE

SCOTSTOUN

BROOMHILL

CHURCHES and PUBLIC BUILDINGS
1 All Saints Episcopal
2 Anniesland Methodist
3 Jordanhill Parish Church
4 Temple Anniesland
5 (Temple Parish Church)
6 University of Glasgow (Garscube)
6a University of Glasgow
 Athletics Pavilion
7 Anniesland College
8 Jordanhill College
9 Jordanhill College School
9a Temple Primary
10 Gartnavel Hospital
11 Gartnavel Royal Hospital
12 Temple Gasworks

ANNIESLAND AND JORDANHILL

C 19 industry, Edwardian suburbs, and Corporation housing schemes meet round Anniesland Cross. The Great Western Road had reached Anniesland Toll by 1850 and went no further that century. For most of the C 19 the only buildings around it were farms, small mining, brick-making and quarrying settlements such as Temple and Claythorn, and Glasgow's lunatic asylum. In 1871 gasworks to serve the NW suburbs were founded at Temple, contemporary with the Corporation gasworks just to the N at Dawsholm. Industry (some of which still survives) then grew quickly in this area: sawmills opened by the Forth and Clyde Canal in 1874, and ironworks began in 1890. The arrival of the North British Railway in 1886 encouraged the middle classes to move to villas in Claythorn and imposing tenements round Anniesland Cross. The construction of Bearsden Road and the westward spread to Knightswood in the 1920s added a new aspect to Anniesland's character.

The suburb of Jordanhill developed more or less contemporaneously. Before that, it was a private estate owned by the Smiths, centred on Jordanhill House, which had been built c. 1782 to replace a C 16 mansion house. In the mid-C 19, the Smiths built an Episcopal church to serve the outlying settlements to the N and E. This was rebuilt more lavishly, and was joined by a parish church, in the first decade of the C 20, when residential development began in earnest. The W part of the estate, including the house (which survived until the 1960s), was sold in 1912 for Glasgow's new teacher training college.

CHURCHES

ALL SAINTS (Episcopal), 10 Woodend Drive, Jordanhill. By *James Chalmers*, 1904. N aisle of 1910. Of red snecked rubble, cruciform but without accents; the intended crossing tower was never built. The plain round-headed windows and the zigzag and the scalloped capitals on the two doorways are in Norman style. More scallops inside, where the arches of the nave arcades perversely overhang the short round piers on their tall pedestals. Thick vaulting shafts but a barrel-vault of timber. Raised chancel, with the choir under the crossing: the timber groin-vault replaced a roof of yellow glass after 1945. Only the s chancel aisle was completed (as the exterior walling on the N side makes clear).

Lavish FURNISHINGS. – REREDOS. A triptych by *Lorimer*, 1920–1, with luxuriant late Gothic foliage framing pastel panels in a fresco manner by *Phoebe Traquair* (Christ Seated in Glory, a subject designated in 1904 by Chalmers, who had strong views about the symbolism of his church). – FONT (in w apse). Gothic, heavily carved in marble by *Purdie & Howard* of Belfast, 1904. – PULPIT (similar to the font); LECTERN (by *Whippel* of London); and STALLS (by *Jones & Willis* of Birmingham), all 1904. – STAINED GLASS. E window in jewel colours by *Bacon*, 1911. – s chapel. A 1914–18 War Memorial designed by *Lorimer* and executed by *Robert William & Florence Camm*. – s aisle (from E). Window by *Gordon Webster*, 1957. – Memorial window to Alexander 'Greek' Thomson, designed by *James Chalmers*, 1904. It depicts 'The Architect inspired' with a vignette of the gateway of Glasgow's College that Thomson had fought to save. – N aisle (W end): 'Prophecy' in coloured and textured glass, given by Chalmers in 1910.

Behind the church, the original plain chapel-school (now hall) of 1861. Next door at No. 12 is the RECTORY, the W bay of 1861, the rest of 1905 and 1920.

ANNIESLAND METHODIST CHURCH, Bearsden Road and Sutcliffe Road. 1927, by *E. A. Sutherland*. Small and Romanesque.

JORDANHILL PARISH CHURCH, 28 Woodend Drive. 1900–5, by *James Miller*, in snecked red sandstone rubble. Squat and broad in a Perp style, much more conventional than his church in Dennistoun (*q.v.*). The absurdly short battlemented and pinnacled SE tower seems to lack a stage. A mock-hammerbeam roof spans a broad unadorned interior. Wide W aisle and s gallery, 1921–3. – ORGAN by *Lewis*, 1923. – At the N end, the MEMORIAL HALL, 1922–3, enlarged in red brick by *Alexander A. Macfarlane*, 1957–8.

TEMPLE ANNIESLAND CHURCH, 867 Crow Road. The first United Free church on this site (of 1898–9 by *Alexander Petrie*) is now the hall attached to the large red sandstone building by *Badenoch and Bruce* of Newcastle, 1904–5. Lancet-style, with a row of tiny lancets round the top of each canted gallery-staircase projection. Gloomy interior, with two tiers of attenuated cast-iron columns and a gallery round three sides. – ORGAN from Berkeley Street United Free Church.

Former TEMPLE PARISH CHURCH, 957 Crow Road (closed in 1984). By *Henry Higgins*, 1891–2. Rock-faced red sandstone. Cruciform, with a W tower, with tiled pyramidal cap, preceded by a gabled porch. Lancets, except for the circular W window with star-like tracery. Inside, E. E. arcades, a W gallery, and a raised chancel railed off in wrought-iron.

PUBLIC BUILDINGS

UNIVERSITY OF GLASGOW (GARSCUBE SITE). VETERINARY HOSPITAL AND SCHOOL, Bearsden Road. The utilitarian red brick Hospital of 1957–8 is by *Gillespie, Kidd & Coia*; the Wellcome Laboratories of 1959–60 by *W. N. W. Ramsay*; and the more ambitious copper-roofed Veterinary School of 1964–70 by *Building Design Partnership* (*Preston*).

For other buildings on the Garscube site, *see* Maryhill, below.

UNIVERSITY OF GLASGOW ATHLETICS PAVILION, Ascot Avenue. By *J. M. Honeyman*, 1923–6, in domestic style.

ANNIESLAND COLLEGE OF FURTHER EDUCATION, Hatfield Drive. 1962–4, by *Ross, Doak & Whitelaw*. Four-storey teaching block with a slim exposed concrete frame. Not exciting, but neatly done.

JORDANHILL COLLEGE OF EDUCATION, Southbrae Drive. Sixty acres (24 ha) of the Jordanhill estate were purchased in 1912 for Glasgow's new teacher training college and associated demonstration school. Competition designs were submitted in 1913; the large and institutional-looking college, by *H. & D. Barclay*, opened in 1922. Red sandstone, with a centrepiece of Franco-Flemish inspiration; a big stepped gable, with some classical and some rather ecclesiastical details, between two big towers. Their copper spires echo the long-demolished Old College tower. Impressive entrance hall, with galleries through two storeys on Ionic columns of boldly jointed stone. They screen C17-style N and S staircases, lit by full-height bay windows in the towers. On axis with the hall, the former Council Chamber, with the examination hall above, bisecting the central courtyard.

Linked to the W side but assertively independent, the Brutalist HENRY WOOD BUILDING, 1967–8, by *Keppie, Henderson & Partners* (who designed all the 1960s buildings on the campus). Four-storey aggregate-clad block on tall *pilotis*, with shuttered concrete staircase towers. Slotted beneath, a brick wing with projecting lecture theatre.

Further W, two students' hostels: GRAHAM HOUSE, 1913, by *A. Balfour*, H-plan with thin classical detail; and DOUGLAS HOUSE, 1931, by *Balfour & Stewart*, larger, sparer and in shiny red brick.

N of the main building, the CRAWFURD BUILDING (for music and drama, with theatre and refectory), 1962–3. Well-tailored to the site of the C18 Jordanhill House, with many of the original trees, and more appealing than the same architects' Henry Wood Building. It is in a straightforward modern idiom but built with appropriately natural materials (rustic brick, stained timber, and copper roofs). SW extension of 1966–9 for the SCOTTISH SCHOOL OF PHYSICAL EDUCATION, with an externally dumb sports hall.

The other 1960s buildings on the S edge of the site are of no particular interest.

JORDANHILL COLLEGE SCHOOL, Chamberlain Road, on the far E side of the Jordanhill College site. Designed as the college's demonstration school by *Honeyman, Keppie & Mackintosh* in 1913, and completed in 1920 by *Keppie & Henderson*. An extremely long red sandstone ashlar façade, in an unimaginative stripped Baroque style. Three-storey centre of eleven bays, accented with a semicircular Doric portico and stubby bell towers. Two-storey wings of ten bays. At the back, a large clearstorey-lit gymnasium and hall. An influential plan.

TEMPLE PRIMARY SCHOOL, Spencer Street. By *Henry Higgins*, 1899, for New Kilpatrick School Board (*see* inscription). Gabled end bays and a wooden bell turret. Grey snecked rubble.

GARTNAVEL HOSPITALS, 1055 Great Western Road. GART-
NAVEL GENERAL. 1968–73, by *Keppie, Henderson & Partners*. A nine-storey slab of wards, with an exposed concrete
frame, rising from a podium containing operating theatres,
outpatients' and other services. The podium, like the slab's N
and S staircase towers, clad in bush-hammered concrete and
white marble aggregate.

GARTNAVEL ROYAL. 1841–3, by *Charles Wilson*. Built as
the City Lunatic Asylum on the elevated lands of Gartnavel
farm to supersede *William Stark*'s asylum of 1809 in Par-
liamentary Road. Early views show a silhouette like a towered
Tudor palace strung out along the ridge, a forbidding effect
destroyed by mature trees, later buildings and suburban surroundings. In Wilson's design the two houses were intended
to be linked by a Perp arcade and a shared chapel with a
prominent tower, but these were never built.

The WEST HOUSE was intended for 300 paying patients,
the west-facing wing for ladies, the other for men, separated
by the superintendent's house. The battlemented and turreted
façade is so long that its design of two-storey ranges and three-
storey pavilions is incomprehensible from close to. Inside,
the original arrangement was very enlightened (Wilson had
gleaned new ideas from England and France), with bedrooms
opening off one side of wide corridors used as dayrooms. To
the S, airing courts look towards the Clyde.

The more modest EAST HOUSE (for charity patients) has
three ranges with corner pavilions but lacks the conspicuously
expensive turrets. In its courtyard (W), the kitchens and later
laundry (1910–12, by *J.J. Burnet*).

Other alterations were made in 1847, when the capacity of
the East House was almost doubled; in 1877, when a recreation
hall (East House) and large dining rooms were provided; and
in 1883, when some sills were lowered to improve the view.

CHAPEL, to the N. 1904–6, by *J. Burnet & Son*. Domestic-
looking, rendered with brick dressings.

NURSES' HOME, to the S. 1931–8, by *J. Burnet, Son &
Dick*. Streamlined red brick with bands of metal windows and
a flat roof.

STAFF RESIDENCES, like a small village of rendered terraced houses and flats on the north-facing slope below the
hospital. Built in the 1970s.

GATE LODGE. 1898–9, by *J.J. Burnet*.

TEMPLE GASWORKS, Strathcona Drive. Two big gas-holders
of 1893 and 1900, built for Glasgow Corporation after they
purchased the Partick, Hillhead and Maryhill Gas Co. in 1891.

TEMPLE BRIDGE, Bearsden Road. An electrically operated
steel lifting-bridge (now fixed) of 1931–2 by *T. Somers* (City
Architect) and *Sir William Arrol & Co.* (engineers), spanning
one of two modified locks of 1790 on this stretch of the Forth
and Clyde Canal. Just to the W at Netherton, one of the
standard Forth and Clyde BASCULE BRIDGES of c. 1790.

PERAMBULATION

We start S of the Great Western Road in CLAYTHORN. Just after
the entrance to Gartnavel Hospitals, in WHITTINGEHAME
DRIVE (overlooking the boating pond), No. 11's C17 Scottish-
style exterior of 1908 by *John Ednie*, with unorthodox rus-
tication and whimsical details at the back, conceals fine
Glasgow Style joinery and stained glass. Just to the W in
GREAT WESTERN ROAD, and backing on to it in HATFIELD
DRIVE, rows of identical double villas in red sandstone by
Fryers & Penman, 1902–4. Big castellated bays and bal-
ustraded corner towers containing rooftop billiard rooms.

KELVIN COURT, next to the W along the main road, displays 108
a later style of bourgeois comfort. This private development
of luxury flats (by *J. N. Fatkin* of Newcastle, 1937–8), almost
unique in Glasgow, would be quite at home on one of London's
arterial roads. Two H-plan six- and seven-storey blocks of
brown brick, with separate garage blocks between. The backs,
with curved cantilevered balconies, are more streamlined than
the rectilinear fronts. On both sides, long glass-brick staircase
windows. Almost opposite, another hallmark of the period,
Glasgow's last super-suburban cinema, the ASCOT (now
County Bingo), with its monumental tiled semicircular towers
(1938–9, by *C. J. McNair & Elder*).

ANNIESLAND CROSS and rows of large-scale red sandstone
tenements with cast-iron parapets (by *H. Campbell*) lie beyond
the railway line. Those on the S side, ANNIESLAND MAN-
SIONS, 1907–13, incorporate the columned portico of the
ANNIESLAND HALL (a mission hall with hammerbeam roof
on cast-iron columns), hidden behind them. The main road
junction is inescapably marked by a twenty-two-storey slab of
Corporation flats, raised on a podium and linked to a lower
block facing Crow Road (1966–8, by *Jack Holmes & Partners*,
with cosmetic trimming of 1984–5).

Just to the NE, off Crow Road in FOULIS STREET, the maltreated C17 domestic-style offices of the former UNIVERSITY
PRESS (1903, by *A. N. Paterson*). Beyond them lies the industry of TEMPLE.

There is little to see of this C19 and early C20 industrial settlement. Near the top of CROW ROAD, the former Temple
Parish Church (*see* Churches above), faces TEMPLE
GARDENS, a row of coarse late C19 bow-fronted tenements,
built of the rubbly sandstone quarried locally at Netherton. A
parallel row of these faces BEARSDEN ROAD. Further N, two
timber-drying sheds (one with lattice stanchions supporting a
jettied upper storey) and a neat little 1930s office block by *J. A.
Laird* of *Laird & Napier* survive from the once extensive
TEMPLE SAW MILLS, founded in 1874 by Robertson, Dunn
& Co. Further W, facing FULTON STREET, the former
Temple Public (now Primary) School (*see* Public Buildings,
above) and, almost opposite, a row of curiously stark and sheer
late C19 tenements, their chimneys forming battlements.

w of Anniesland Cross, a big 1930s Corporation housing scheme stretches along Great Western Road and N of it, to Knightswood (*q.v.*). Tenements more monumental in design than usual, in long sweeps of rock-faced red sandstone with cantilevered curved balconies and a prominent attic storey with big box dormers.

s of Great Western Road, on the N edge of JORDANHILL, a small pocket of red and cream brick single-storey cottages behind the bus depot in MUNRO PLACE, GREENLEA STREET and CRAIGEND STREET. Built for the Jordanhill Co-operative Buildings and Land Society Ltd, *c.* 1877. More, similar cottages with gables, porches and some Gothic references in rows off the E side of CROW ROAD (Nos. 624–74, and FERN, ALBANY and AIGAS COTTAGES), built for workers of the Scotstoun estate nearly a decade later.

The heart of Jordanhill, between Crow Road and Jordanhill College, and especially around WOODEND DRIVE, comprises terraced and semi-detached stone villas of moderate size begun between 1905 and 1913. Those furthest N in HELENBURGH DRIVE have Art Nouveau detailing and stained glass. The rest of the Jordanhill estate was devoted to Jordanhill College (*see* Public Buildings, above).

KNIGHTSWOOD

Knightswood is Glasgow's third and largest interwar housing scheme, with thousands of two-storey cottages and cottage flats laid out in spacious crescents and circuses and along broad avenues over the slight undulations of the Knightswood estate. Early photographs show a monotonous scene of dun-coloured houses looking bleak without the pastels of later colour-washes and the mature planting of individual gardens.

The Corporation bought the farmland, sprinkled with exhausted iron and coal workings, from the Summerlee Iron Co. in 1921. The layout, designed on garden-suburb principles by *John Bryce* for Glasgow's City Engineer, was approved the same year. The first phase of 1,132 houses NE of the Great Western Road was begun in 1923; it was only a little smaller than the whole of the contemporary Mosspark scheme (*q.v.*). Later phases (1926–31) added nearly 5,000 more houses (6,126 in total), centred on a public park and with a community centre, conceived in 1935, sited rather distantly on its S edge. The first school (now St Ninian's Primary) and the first church (St Margaret) opened in 1932. The last phases, on the far W edge, were not completed until the 1940s.

The scheme started ambitiously in the first area with at least fifteen types of three-, four-, and occasionally five-apartment cottages and cottage flats, both semi-detached and terraced. Most are rendered with decorative brickwork, such as quoins and patterns of headers. Two of the cottage types also have alternative

stone and terrazzo fronts. Many houses have bay windows, often 100
shallowly canted and to full height; doorhoods on brackets; small
gables breaking the eaves line; and others of the simplified Arts
and Crafts elements recommended in the Government hand-
books for such houses.

Costs were drastically cut in the next phases (SE and SW of
the park, 1927–8; N and W of it, finished by 1929; S of Garscadden
Station, begun c. 1930; and round Kelso Street, begun c. 1940).
Here only eight of the original house types, mostly flatted and
larger cottages, were used, and all the brick and alternative facings
were excluded. But after 1930 some new house types with
fashionable motifs were introduced. In LESMUIR DRIVE, for
example, is a five-apartment cottage of c. 1936 with a balcony
over a Crittall-windowed bow and a long staircase window. Some
of the houses in the last, westernmost area are even more consciously Modern Movement in design, with smooth rendered
brickwork and flat roofs (cf. Penilee and Pollok). On KELSO
ROAD the houses have either shared recessed porches or external
access balconies on *pilotis*. In BEIL DRIVE and HAWICK
STREET is a third type with slightly projecting porches supported on *pilotis*. Some of these houses have, alas, had pitched
roofs added since.

The homogeneous mass of cottages is broken occasionally by
taller blocks of flats built to replace prefabs in the 1960s. At the
N edge of BANNER ROAD are four- and five-storey blocks.
Further W, more prominent rows of tall flats. Those on GREAT
WESTERN ROAD (1960–5, by *Sam Bunton & Associates*) are Y-
shaped, with coloured spandrel panels marking the service core.
In ARCHERHILL ROAD, five designed by the City Architect,
A. G. Jury, 1966–9, and in LINCOLN AVENUE, six characteristic *George Wimpey* blocks, 1962–5. Close to these towers,
small pockets of contemporary brick and render houses continue
the cottage theme.

CHURCHES

BLAWARTHILL CHURCH, Millbrix Avenue, Garscadden. By
J. Thomson King & Partners, 1960–4. A dull box with abstract
coloured stained glass, and a large cross facing Craggan Drive.

GOSPEL HALL, 361 Fulton Street. Originally church halls for
the Congregation of Christians, 1932, by *Miller & Black*. Dec
tracery in timber.

HOLY CROSS (Episcopal), 2064 Great Western Road. By *Spiers
Ltd*, 1937–9; completely remodelled in simple Gothic style by
Whyte & Nicol, 1947.

KNIGHTSWOOD CONGREGATIONAL CHURCH, Dunterlie
Avenue. By *Frank F. Macdonald*, 1933. Of reconstituted stone,
with nave and aisles. Trefoil- and ogee-headed windows. Leafy
capped piers inside. Hall of concrete blocks by *Lockhart W.
Hutson* of Hamilton, 1949–53, and manse with Gothic details.

ST BRENDAN (R.C.), 187 Kelso Street. 1947–9, a minimal
hall church by *T. S. Cordiner*.

St David, Boreland Drive, on axis with the community centre on Alderman Drive. By *A. Gardiner & Gardiner-McLean*, 1938–9. A traditionally planned church (cruciform with an entrance tower) but non-historicist in style and built of rustic brick, with, inside, concrete arches. Over the main door, a relief of the Burning Bush. Halls behind by the same architects, 1929.

St Margaret, 1996 Great Western Road. A welcome landmark at Knightswood Cross. By *Lorimer & Matthew*, 1929–32, executed by *J. F. Matthew* after Lorimer's death in 1929. The tall tower with crowstepped gables, piended roofs, and the sheer rough grey walls of Doddingston stone are familiar from Lorimer's Scottish castle style. Inside, the rough stone has a pinkish cast, enhanced by the tinted glass in the plain round-headed windows. The broad chancel, with its stained glass and low side lighting, is, in contrast, mysteriously dim. Exceedingly simple E aisle with piers dying into slightly moulded segmental arches and a panelled ceiling. All the details show typical Arts and Crafts-style care, e.g. the stone gallery stair with wrought-iron work in the curved NE projection. The only jarring note is the horrible screen of 1975 beneath the deep W gallery.

The FURNISHINGS of oak, designed by Lorimer and made by *Grieve & Co.* of Edinburgh, are appropriately simple, almost roughly carved by *Clow Bros.* – COMMUNION TABLE and REREDOS with Eucharistic symbols of vine, wheat and, on the reredos, angels bearing a crowned chalice and paten. (The PLATE was also designed by Lorimer.) – FONT of Iona marble attached to the wall E of the chancel arch. An angel tops the wooden font cover; carved into the wall behind, a dove. – LECTERN. Three angels sit on twisted pillars linked to the central support by tracery spandrels. – PULPIT, with a frieze of passion flowers. – AUMBRY and MINISTER'S CHAIR by *Cochrane* of Glasgow. – ORGAN rebuilt in 1977 by *Hill, Norman & Beard.* – STAINED GLASS. Chancel windows, 1950–7, in a sympathetic Arts and Crafts manner by *Alexander Russell* (The Risen and Ascended Christ). – In the porch, St Margaret, by *Herbert Hendrie*, *c.* 1930.

Well-intentioned HALL by *Thomas Beveridge*, 1961, and earlier HALL of red sandstone, 1924–5, by *Jeffrey Waddell*.

St Matthew, Beil Drive and Hawick Street. 1950–2, by *Honeyman, Jack & Robertson*. Tiny and domestic in style, with white render and a green pantiled roof.

St Ninian (R.C.), Knightswood Road, Knightswood Cross. 1956–9. Designed by *C. H. Purcell*, the last surviving member of *Pugin & Pugin*'s practice; completed by *S. Stevenson-Jones*. Traditional in character (Dec tracery), but large and monotonous in dreary pinkish brick with stone dressings. No tower or spire. Aisled interior in the same manner, with furnishing designed by Purcell. – The PRESBYTERY of 1927–30 in Baldwin Avenue looks late C 19.

United Free Church, 2144 Great Western Road. A rendered box with lancets and Y-tracery by *Stellmacs Ltd*, 1936.

PUBLIC BUILDINGS

KNIGHTSWOOD COMMUNITY CENTRE, Dunterlie Avenue. Library, health centre, swimming pool and community hall were planned for this site in 1937. Only the Community (now Youth) Centre (by *Thomas Somers*, City Engineer) was built in 1938. It faces Dykebar Avenue; Thirties Modern, i.e. flat-roofed and streamlined, with strips of metal windows and curved ends to the wings, and all in brick. To its N, the linked group of library, swimming pool and replacement community centre, not designed until 1963 (by *A. G. Jury*, City Architect) and not built until 1969–71. Many popular mannerisms of 1963, particularly the library's zigzag roof.

UNIVERSITY OF GLASGOW SPORTS PAVILION, 357 Garscadden Road. By *T. Harold Hughes*, 1936. Though the simple forms, colour-washed brick, horizontal bands of windows and asymmetrically set stairtower have an International Modern flavour, the bowed tea room with its cast-iron balcony and colonnade betray the same classical allegiances as Professor Hughes' University Reading Room (*see* Hillhead, University, above: Perambulation 3).

KNIGHTSWOOD SECONDARY SCHOOL, Knightswood Road. Designed by *Gillespie, Kidd & Coia* in 1938 but not begun until 1954. Cream brick with large windows on Scandinavian models.

BANKHEAD PRIMARY SCHOOL, Broadlie Avenue. A clear contrast between the still classically inspired interwar school (1933, by the *Corporation Education Office*) facing Broadlie Avenue, and the flat-roofed blocks (1941, by *John McNab* of the same office) stepped down Caldwell Avenue.

GARSCADDEN PRIMARY SCHOOL, Hurlford Avenue. 1930–1, by *J. B. Wilson, Son & Honeyman*. Of familiar type, with a two-storey central block (here classical) and long single-storey wings (originally with open corridors) bent back round three sides of the playground.

KNIGHTSWOOD PRIMARY SCHOOL, Knightswood Road. 1930–4, by *Ross & Buchanan*. Built as Knightswood Junior Secondary School. An imposing red sandstone ashlar stripped-classical classroom block raised high above Great Western Road. A long dog-leg hall block links it to the administration block facing Knightswood Road. Completely conventional in comparison with its neighbour, St Ninian's Primary.

ST BRENDAN'S PRIMARY SCHOOL, 170 Hawick Street. By *William Baillie & Son*, 1959–62. Stylish, with many motifs of the 1950s, particularly the patterned brickwork and boomerang-shaped block with a corner tower.

ST NINIAN'S PRIMARY SCHOOL, 2150 Great Western Road. Built in 1929–32 as Cloberhill Elementary School for 1,000 pupils. An outstandingly inventive interpretation of the standard contemporary Glasgow school design, which won *Keppie & Henderson* the R.I.B.A. Bronze Medal for Architecture of 1938. The simple neo-Georgian central office block and 105

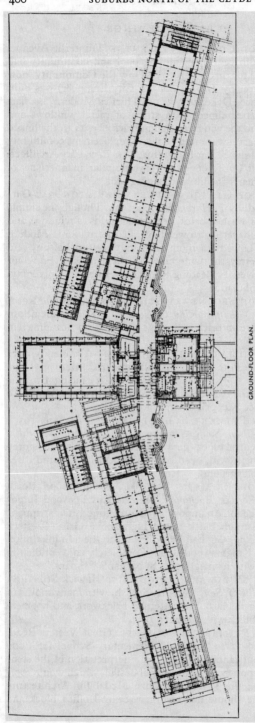

GROUND-FLOOR PLAN.

St Ninian's Primary (former Cloberhill) School
(Reproduced from *The Builder*, 1938)

pedimented hall behind are still of conventional type, but the long two-storey wings splayed out each side are linked to it by completely glazed stairwells, the glass walls canted out beyond the supporting concrete piers. The tall arches in the brick bays gave access to once-open corridors on both floors, from which classrooms opened by entirely retractable screens to make an open-air school.

BLAWARTHILL HOSPITAL, Dyke Road. Built in 1895–7 by *R. Bryden* as the Renfrew and Clydebank Joint Hospital. Stone administration block (N) and three red brick pavilions to its E and W. Altered and extended in similar style by *Stewart & Paterson*, 1903–4. Additions of 1931 (by *A. J. Merrilees*) and 1972.

KNIGHTSWOOD HOSPITAL, Knightswood Road. The original stone building (plus two pavilions) was built in 1875–7 by *Clarke & Bell* as the Partick, Hillhead and Maryhill Joint Hospital for Infectious Diseases. Extended (by nine pavilions) by successive City Engineers and Architects in 1887, 1922, 1937, and 1940. Laundry of 1966.

DRUMCHAPEL

The village of Drumchapel developed on the SE edge of the Garscadden estate *c.* 1870 when coalmining began in the vicinity. It was the decline of industry and the opening of the station in 1891 that stimulated the building of a dozen or so middle-class villas (none of especial note) in the Garscadden and Drumchapel Roads. A church was built in 1901 (replaced after the influx of worshippers from the adjacent Knightswood) and a school in 1905.

Garscadden House, built some time after 1664 by the Colquhouns and enlarged *c.* 1747, stood high above the Garscadden Burn. Its 'fantastical' South Gates (by *Charles Ross* of Paisley, 1789) lay just W of the village until the 1960s. By then both house and gates had been engulfed by Glasgow's third peripheral housing scheme, which the name Drumchapel now evokes. The estate was purchased in 1939 but the scheme was not planned until 1951. At its peak, in 1961, it housed 35,000 people in nearly 1,000 dwellings. Like the other schemes (Pollok, Castlemilk, Easterhouse) it was envisaged as a semi-independent township with its own centre (not begun until 1962) and industrial estate. Like them, it comprises several undifferentiated neighbourhoods of repetitive tenements, here laid out along the contours of a dramatic hilly site with wooded fringes. Like them also it has suffered problems, demolitions and depopulation.

CHURCHES AND PUBLIC BUILDINGS

CHURCH OF JESUS CHRIST AND THE LATTER DAY SAINTS, Kinfauns Drive. 1961–4, by *John Easton*. Long, low and painted white, with dark red sloping buttresses and a tapering tower with horizontal fins that looks more characteristic of the 1930s than of the 1960s.

DRUMCHAPEL OLD CHURCH, Drumchapel Road. 1936–9, by *Launcelot Ross*, replacing in a more central position the church of 1901. It was rebuilt in 1941–3 after the Clydebank blitz. It is a design of 'rural Scottish simplicity' with white harled walls, light stone dressings and a slate roof. The main E gable has a bellcote above a Venetian window. Low chancel with a wheel window. Partly gabled aisles with round-headed windows. Inside, white-plastered walls and rush-seated chairs.

DRUMRY ST MARY, Drumry Road East. 1955–7, by *Ross, Doak & Whitelaw*. Simple church with shallow-pitched roof, linked to the flat-roofed hall by a vestibule with a bell turret.

ST ANDREW, Kinfauns Drive. A dismal grey-harled hall church of 1956–8 by *H. Taylor*, Church of Scotland Home Board architect.

ST BENEDICT (R.C.), Drumchapel Road. 1964–70; one of *Gillespie, Kidd & Coia*'s most powerful compositions. All that is visible from the road is the great concave sweep of the copper roof, like a gigantic sail. The rest of the church, an irregular octagon with blank, grey-harled walls, is sandwiched between the clearstorey-lit, copper-roofed halls, at r. angles to the
III road, and the presbytery stepped up behind. The interior, approached obliquely through porch and narthex, is theatrical. The timber-lined roof, like the underside of a ship's keel, swoops over the auditorium on two big curving beams which rest on a rood-like cross beam spanning the church. All the light, coming from a clearstorey flush with the curve of the roof near its apex, is directed on the altar, which is set against a brick screen. No distracting decoration, only a pattern of soldier courses in the yellow brick walls and chunky timber furnishings.

ST LAURENCE (R.C.), Kinfauns Drive. 1954–7, by *R. Fairlie & Partners*, almost identical to St Augustine's, Milton (*see* Possilpark and High Possil). *Hacienda*-style, with white render and dark pantile roofs; a veranda of broad arches links the presbytery. Battered walls to the vestibule with a half-octagonal day chapel. Aisleless interior spanned by concrete arches.

ST MARK, Kinfauns Drive. 1955–6, by *Honeyman Jack & Robertson*. Rendered white, with a stone porch and short square tower. Wrought-iron cross on the gable wall. All along the outer wall, long windows angled out.

ST PIUS (R.C.), 4 Bayfield Terrace. 1954–7, by *Alexander McAnally*. A substantial sub-Romanesque composition in red brick and stone. Apsidal sanctuary and baptistery. Shallow transepts but no aisles. Tower with a tall copper cap.

SCHOOLS. DRUMCHAPEL SCHOOL (now Thomas Fortune Work Centre). The former village school of 1905, repeating the design (probably by *James Miller*) used to demonstrate good school architecture at the Glasgow International Exhibition of 1901.

The three big secondary and several primary schools are consistent in style and planning. They are composed of linked brick blocks of various heights with some curtain walling and some coloured cladding: e.g., KINGSRIDGE SECONDARY, 41 Achamore Road, by *Thomas Cordiner*, 1955–8 and 1967–9, strung out along the ridge; WAVERLEY SECONDARY, Summerhill Road, by the same architect; and PINEWOOD PRIMARY, 140 Drunmore Road, by *T. M. Miller*, both of *c*.1966. LADYLOAN SCHOOL, 57 Ladyloan Avenue, by *A. Buchanan Campbell*, 1955–7, is not of brick but of prefabricated timber on the 'Derwent' system.

DRUMCHAPEL HOSPITAL, Drumchapel Road. The main red sandstone block of *c*.1898, by *Robert Bryden*, is a branch of the Royal Hospital for Sick Children, now at Yorkhill (*q.v.*).

DESCRIPTION

KINFAUNS DRIVE is the main road looping through the scheme. On it are most of the churches, many of the schools (*see* above), and the ARNDALE CENTRE, by *Gerald M. Baxter*, a precinct of two-storey shops round a pedestrian mall, built in 1962–4 but still with many entertaining hallmarks of the Festival of Britain style. Covered walks in front of the flat-roofed shops, clad in green pebble aggregate and with lime green and turquoise in the curtain walling. Zigzag canopied walkway across the mall, and a timber 'wig-wam' supporting the sign. Behind, big extensions of 1971.

All around, following the contours of the hilly site, three- and four-storey tenements of the 1950s and early 1960s predominate (they comprise 87 per cent of the housing). Earliest are those with a common stair leading to long access balconies, e.g. those in TALLANT ROAD and CAROLSIDE AVENUE. Later, and in the majority, are the ones with recessed individual balconies, roughcast or of concrete blocks with brick plinths and balcony fronts. Small groups of contemporary semi-detached and terraced cottages leaven the mixture. Most are roughcast, but those almost opposite the Arndale Centre in KINFAUNS DRIVE are prefabricated of timber. Dominating all, from the high and now scrubby hill where Garscadden House once stood, GARSCADDEN POLICIES, three tall grey tower blocks (of eighteen to twenty-three storeys on a *Truscon* system), by *A. Buchanan Campbell*, 1965–71.

MARYHILL

Through the heart of Maryhill runs the Forth and Clyde Canal, which with its series of aqueducts and its stairway of elegantly constructed locks and basins is the district's most spectacular

MARYHILL

CHURCHES
1 Gairbraid Church
2 Immaculate Conception (R.
3 Maryhill High
4 (Maryhill Old Parish Church)
5 St George Episcopal
6 St Gregory

PUBLIC BUILDINGS
7 (Burgh Hall)
8 Public Library
9 Glasgow University - Garscube Site
10 (Gairbraid Public Sch.)
11 John Paul Academy
12 Wyndford Primary and St Gregory (R.C.) Primary
13 Forth and Clyde Canal

sight. Otherwise, Maryhill has little left that is architecturally significant to show for its short but interesting history.

The canal stimulated the industrial growth which had begun in the c17 with mills and a bleachfield by the Kelvin, followed by the establishment of calico printworks there *c.* 1750 and the opening of the turnpike from Glasgow to Garscube (1753). The canal reached Stockingfield in 1775 and was then extended s as the Glasgow branch, reaching Hamiltonhill in 1777. *Robert Whitworth* continued the main line w to Bowling in 1786, and his are the aqueducts that soon became famous with sightseers like Robert Denholm, who in 1804 marvelled to see 'square-rigged vessels ... navigating at a height of seventy feet above the level of the spectators'.

The printworks in Kelvindale became papermills, and coalpits were sunk round about (at Gilshochill and Garscube) by the proprietors of Gairbraid House, which lay to the s by the Kelvin. In 1790 a dry-dock opened on the canal just w of the turnpike, and three years later a local grocer, Robert Craig, feued land for a new town between Glasgow and Garscube (now Dawsholm) Bridge from Mary Hill, the mistress of Gairbraid, promising to name it after her. Little was built, however, until the 1820s, and the settlement was confined to a handful of cottages round the dock, known as Kelvindock or Drydock, where a chapel-of-ease (now Maryhill Old Parish Church) was built in 1826.

In 1841 the population was 2,552, and the setting still rural. About then, ironworks opened near by and iron boats were first built on the dock. Fifteen years later, work on the Loch Katrine pipeline and the Glasgow, Dumbarton and Helensburgh Railway raised the population temporarily to 6,000, so in 1856 the area became a police burgh. In the same year the Helensburgh Railway station opened at Maryhill Park, and the village spread N between dock and station. Industry, population and building work increased rapidly after 1870, with further growth N of the station and S towards Wyndford, where a new barracks had opened in 1869. In 1878 the seat of the burgh moved S to Wyndford Cross, and Gairbraid House 'stood naked and forlorn among the abominations of a new suburb' (J. Guthrie Smith). Although Glasgow became easily accessible by tram and train (Maryhill Central Station opened in 1896), Maryhill retained its independence until 1918, when its population was 18,318.

After 1918, Maryhill's decline was almost as swift as its rise. The old settlement of Kelvindock was obliterated by a slum clearance scheme in the 1930s, and by 1962, when the canal closed, the number of industries was down to thirty, the population below its 1860 level. Since then, the area has become a dormitory for 25,000 people (in 1983) as housing schemes have invaded farmland, and most of the C19 villas and tenements have been replaced in the comprehensive redevelopment of a long corridor stretching through North Kelvinside (see West End, above) and Maryhill.

The C19 town can now be identified only by a frayed ribbon of tenements along Maryhill Road, the middle-class homes of Maryhill Park, and two or three churches and public buildings.

CHURCHES

GAIRBRAID CHURCH, Maryhill Road, high up on the bank by the canal and thoroughly undistinguished. Built in 1871 for the United Presbyterians. In 1894 *Alexander Petrie* incorporated the sessions house (E), extending it N and S, and added vestries, hall and church officer's house to face Burnhouse Street. Grey and towerless, with E and W rose windows. A single bare space inside, with two boxy transepts and a W gallery. Chancel created by the big divided organ case, a Second World War memorial. Facing Maryhill Road, the original hall (made into the sessions house in 1894) and the severe gabled MANSE, also of 1871.

IMMACULATE CONCEPTION (R.C.), 2049 Maryhill Road. 1955–6, by *Thomas S. Cordiner*. A bold, almost Arts and Crafts-style silhouette, with steeply sloping mossy-tiled roof, 110 tall clearstorey and low passage aisles, surprisingly achieved by the use of a concrete A-frame exposed, like flying buttresses, above the aisles. The façade's sentimental mosaic (by *Jack Mortimer*) gives the date away. So does the jazzy mosaic of pink, blue and white diamonds behind the altar. The interior has been made as conventional as possible, with panelled ceiling and painted concrete.

PRESBYTERY also with an A-frame and an Arts and Crafts feel.

MARYHILL HIGH CHURCH, 7 Sandbank Street. Built as Maryhill Free Church. By *Charles Wilson*, 1846–8. Steeple 1859. Small, cruciform, and unarchaeological Gothic. In the S angle the steeple, its bell-stage on broaches topped by a ring of diminutive gables round the short spire. The interior is less intimate and more altered than Wilson's Rutherglen West Parish Church. Galleries in the three broad arms linked by a curve at the re-entrant angles on a single tier of plain cast-iron columns. Simple domical vault, with plaster ribs meeting in the centre. Ugly pews of 1907. – ORGAN (by *Abbot & Smith* of Leeds), 1912. – Session house and halls of 1907.

MARYHILL OLD PARISH CHURCH, 1956 Maryhill Road. Built as a chapel-of-ease in 1826; just a shell in 1989. Simple harled two-storey box. E projection with a Venetian window, the other windows modern. Pedimented and pilastered ashlar W front, distinctly C20 (in fact of 1924, by *Jeffrey Waddell*) in the squat proportions of its central door and window. Interior (stripped of its fittings) recast in 1893.

The CHURCHYARD has a selection of early to late C19 tombstones and, by the church door, the Trades Union Martyr MEMORIAL PILLAR, a cast-iron column with vase finial erected 'To the memory of George Millar ... mortally stabbed on the 24th of February 1834 by one of those put to the Calico Printing Trade for the purpose of destroying a Union of the regular workmen ...' – HALLS, N of Duart Street, by *Balfour & Stewart*, 1939. Brick and render.

ST GEORGE (Episcopal), 11 Sandbank Street. 1891–2, by *Alexander Petrie* of Maryhill. Low and towerless, of grey snecked rubble. Aisles with single and paired lancets between buttresses. At the W end, the porch (S) and baptistery (N). SE vestry open to the nave by a two-bay arcade. Apsidal chancel, open timber roof. – STAINED GLASS in many of the windows, including two by *Kempe*: Boer War Memorial, 1901 (SS Michael and Raphael, angels of War and Peace), and the memorial to Henry Jebb, 1896 (St John Evangelist); and three of 1947–50 by *Margaret Chilton* and *Marjorie Kemp*.

Next door, the former RECTORY, by *W. G. Johnson*, 1892, enlarged in 1898 by *Petrie*.

ST GREGORY (R.C.), Kelvindale Road. 1965–71, by *Thomas Cordiner, Cunningham & Partners*. Church, hall and presbytery linked formally round a garden. Ham-fisted treatment of the very prominent roof to admit indirect light into the interior. 'Crazy-paved' stained glass throughout.

PUBLIC BUILDINGS

Former BURGH HALL, 1513 Maryhill Road. 1876–8, by *Duncan McNaughtan*. It resembles a French *hôtel* (though less so now it has lost its very steep hipped roof and cupola) and looks proudly s down Maryhill Road. Very French Renaissance detail, including the shell-topped aedicule enclosing the clock. The French style continues behind in the equally tall but one-storey public hall. Giant Corinthian pilasters between long round-headed windows with carved spandrels and heads for keystones. Inside, only the roof trusses with turned posts left. The STAINED GLASS from the windows, with wonderfully graphic representations of twenty of the burgh's trades by *Stephen Adam*, has been taken to the People's Palace.

Towards Gairbraid Avenue, a wing that once housed the Police Department linked to the former Fire Station of 1892 by *A. B. McDonald* (Office of Public Works) and, next to that, the BATHS AND WASHHOUSE at the corner of Burnhouse Street: also by McDonald, 1896–8. The laundry, with its iron-truss roof, is now a sports hall. Along Gairbraid Avenue, a strip of windows divided by bulgy Ionic columns lights the swimming pond.

MARYHILL PUBLIC LIBRARY, 1508 Maryhill Road. 1902–5, by *J. R. Rhind*. This façade, squeezed by its neighbours, is smaller than those of many of Rhind's libraries but, even so, has a characteristically rich design, with coupled columns between the upper windows and a bookish matriarch and two children over the segmental pediment of the entrance bay. Two top-lit and columned reading rooms behind, and the original timber screens.

UNIVERSITY OF GLASGOW (GARSCUBE SITE). ACRE HOUSE (Marine Technology), Acre Road. C19 Italianate villa with a belvedere in a contemporary garden of evergreens. 1960s extensions.

HYDRODYNAMICS LABORATORY and ASTRONOMY BUILDING, Acre Road. Both by *Keppie, Henderson & Partners*, 1964–7, the first a simple rectangular block with aluminium cladding, the second a long brick block with cantilevered concrete arches over the windows and a pepperpot observatory tower with a copper dome at the NW angle. Simpler laboratory block behind.

WOLFSON HALL, Maryhill Road. By *Building Design Partnership*'s Preston office, 1961–5. In the grey brick and white weatherboarding popular at that time: the Scottish climate has taken its toll. Residential wings, two square and two long (the SE one an afterthought of 1965–9), are attached to the communal spine and raised dining hall with its dominating copper roof. Overall, an informal, even confusing composition on several different levels.

VETERINARY HOSPITAL. *See* Anniesland and Jordanhill, above.

WEST OF SCOTLAND SCIENCE PARK, Maryhill Road. Begun

in 1983 by Glasgow's two universities, the Scottish Development Agency, and the District Council. KELVIN CAMPUS (W side of Maryhill Road). Curved unobtrusively round the wooded perimeter of the Wolfson Hall site, three crescents of single-storey industrial units by the *Scottish Development Agency Design Team*, 1981–3. On the other side of the road, the TODD CAMPUS, with two identical buildings of pleasingly simple and almost perfectly symmetrical stepped shape, well set in a slightly undulating landscape. Red brick with grey profiled-steel roofs and grey-tinted glazing. By *William Gillespie & Partners* in association with the Scottish Development Agency Design Team, 1981–3.

Former GAIRBRAID PUBLIC SCHOOL, Gairbraid Avenue. 1898–9, by *T. L. Watson*. A stolid Italian palazzo in red sandstone with a heavily rusticated basement.

JOHN PAUL ACADEMY, Arrochar Street. Summerston's R.C. secondary school of 1980 by *Strathclyde Regional Council's Department of Architecture and Related Services*. The usual linked buildings of different heights in a very 1980s manifestation, i.e. of smooth red brick and with the dining hall at the SW corner of the long administration wing extended by a glazed lean-to.

WYNDFORD PRIMARY and ST GREGORY R.C. PRIMARY, Glenfinnan Drive and Wyndford Road, serving the Wyndford scheme (*see* Perambulation, below). Two schools on one campus, 1963–7, by *Jack Holmes*. Chunky concrete blocks of one and two storeys, interlocking, crown a steep, thickly-planted slope.

BELLCRAIG COMMUNITY EDUCATION CENTRE, Rothes Drive, Summerston. By *Strathclyde Regional Council's Department of Architecture*, c. 1980. Minimal red brick, but with Mackintosh-inspired black timber lattices on porches and windows.

FORTH AND CLYDE CANAL. The canal reached Stockingfield in 1775 and was then extended as the Glasgow branch S to Hamiltonhill (*see* Possilpark). On the first stretch, E of Stockingfield, at the far E end of Lochburn Road, a small segmental-arched AQUEDUCT of c. 1777, side by side by one of c. 1858 over the railway.

Robert Whitworth continued the canal W from STOCKINGFIELD JUNCTION in 1786. This branch starts with Whitworth's STOCKINGFIELD AQUEDUCT over Lochburn Road, further W. One semicircular ashlar arch with curved abutments. To the S, near Craigmont Drive, a late C19 SPILLWAY, with a three-arched culvert and a stone-lined drain leading to an older, arched drain. (Adjacent to it, the entrance to the TUNNEL of c. 1894 that used to carry the Lanarkshire & Dumbartonshire Railway under Ruchill.)

Further W, over Maryhill Road, another AQUEDUCT, this one a lumpish structure of 1881, built to replace an C18 aqueduct like the one in Lochburn Road. Just N of it, a simple canal hostelry.

w of Maryhill Road, an elegant flight of five LOCKS by Whitworth (1787–90) at the w end of the summit level of the canal. Between each one, large oval basins with masonry walls. Opening from the basin adjacent to Maryhill Road, the small dry-dock (KELVIN DOCK), constructed by the canal company *c*. 1790, that fostered the growth of the original village here (*see* above). It was last used for boat repair in 1962.

w of the locks, Whitworth's spectacular KELVIN AQUE-DUCT of 1787–90 spanning the Kelvin valley 70 ft (21 m) above the river. Four massive stone segmental arches, with elegantly curved ashlar spandrels, each 50 ft (15 m) long, and four piers with V-shaped cutwater buttresses, heavily rusticated. Just to the N, a two-span lattice-girder BRIDGE of *c*. 1871 carries the road over the Kelvin.

ANTONINE WALL (Balmuildy to West Millichen). This sector, *c*. 2·2 km in length, can be followed through the fields almost without a break, although in places the vestiges are so faint as to demand close scrutiny. (Permission of the relevant landowners and tenants should of course be sought before making such inspection.) The only two elements of the frontier which survive to any degree are the Ditch and Outer Mound, the Wall itself having long since been reduced by the plough to an inconsiderable grassy swelling in the contour of the ground. The line may be picked on the right bank of the River Kelvin, but the remains acquire greater stature N of Summerston farmhouse, where the Outer Mound is the most conspicuous element, bulking large on the outer side of the broad hollow that represents the silted Ditch. On Summerston Hill and on Crow Hill, to the w, the Wall-builders have so placed the frontier-works as to thrust the Rampart well back from the edge of the natural slope, which might have provided con-siderable protection in these parts. Instead, it is the Outer Mound that follows the crest, leaving any sentries on the curtain, disadvantaged by poor lines of sight, some 35 m to the rear. From the summit of Crow Hill there are magnificent views along the Wall to E and w and northwards up Strathblane into 'enemy territory'.

BALMUILDY, Roman fort, immediately SE of where the A879 crosses the River Kelvin. Little more than the level plateau occupied by the Antonine Wall fort can now be seen above the left bank of the Kelvin, but once it appeared as 'the ruins of an old city'. It was defended on all sides by multiple ditches and a stone wall and measured 140 m by 126 m, covering an area of 1·8 ha (4·4 acres). The wall, which was backed by an earthen rampart 6·1 m thick, was itself only 2·3 m thick but originally stood some 3 m high; at the NE and NW angles it was extended in short wings, as if the builders expected that it would be connected to an Antonine curtain of stone; in the event it was a turf wall that abutted it from E and w. The defences of the fort were equipped, at the gates and the s angles, with rectangular or subrectangular towers, also of stone and probably as much as 6 m in height. Excavation in 1912–14 concentrated on the defences and principal internal structures. The buildings of the central range, which were all built of stone, comprised the customary suite of headquarters building, commander's residence, granaries, and stores or workshops. Also of stone were a simple row-type bathhouse in the NE angle and a more sophisticated set of baths overlying the ditch-defences near the SE angle; the latter lay within an annexe that extended some way behind the Antonine Wall to the E. Little is known of the identity of the garrison who occupied the site between c. A.D. 140 and its evacuation in c. A.D. 163, since it is not mentioned on any of the numerous inscribed stones found on the site, and the excavation of the barrack areas of the fort failed to reveal either the exact number or the character and capacity of the timber-built barracks. The original construction of the fort was in the hands of the Second Legion, whose handsome stone building-records, dedicating the work to the emperor Antoninus Pius, are preserved, along with statues, altars, coins, pottery, and other artefacts recovered during excavation, in the Hunterian Museum at the University of Glasgow.

About 88 m NNW of the fort the Military Way, which provided lateral communications for the garrisons of the Wall, probably crossed the Kelvin by way of a bridge. Dressed stone blocks and fragments of timber recovered from the river-bed while it was being deepened have been hailed as relics of that structure. However, although the stones may well have formed part of abutments or cutwaters of such a bridge, dendro-chronological dating of the timbers has recently indicated a medieval origin.

Some 500 m to the NE of the fort, aerial survey has identified the cropmarks of a Roman temporary camp, larger than most of the Wall camps at 4·9 ha (12·1 acres). It seems likely that it represents an early stage in Antonine-period campaigning rather than one of the series of labour-camps used by builders of the Wall.

PERAMBULATION

MARYHILL's centre was transplanted s from Maryhill Cross to Wyndford Cross (the junction of Maryhill Road and Gairbraid Avenue) in the 1870s. It is still recognizable, with its Burgh Hall, library, baths, school, and church (see above). Although most of the area's C19 tenements have gone, a few, e.g. the row of 1892 by J. L. Cowan, with a little Baroque detailing (Nos. 1512–28), survive along this stretch of MARYHILL ROAD.

114 THE WYNDFORD HOUSING SCHEME lies to the sw within the stone boundary wall of the old Wyndford Barracks (1869–76) it replaced. A classic post-1945 mixed development with high-rise, medium-rise and walk-up flats for 5,000 people (152 p.p.a.). Laid out and built in 1960–9 by the S.S.H.A. (Chief

Technical Officer *Harold Buteux*) to encourage a sense of community. It is fostered by the enclosing wall, by the linked traffic-free squares and pedestrian walks, and by the lush shrubs and mature trees, all well maintained. Round the squares, traditional-looking blocks of flats and maisonettes in yellow brick with pitched roofs. In small groups, the thirteen squat and square blocks of eight to fifteen storeys, with patterned cladding in grey mosaic or terracotta tile and brick; and, on the SW edge, four twenty-six-storey blocks (begun in 1964) with long shared balconies. They overlook the two primary schools (*see* Public Buildings, above).

MARYHILL SHOPPING CENTRE (1980, by *CWS Ltd Architecture and Interior Design*) lies s of the scheme on the site of Maryhill Central Station (demolished 1966), set low (at platform level) and with its façade sloped back from Maryhill Road to disguise its bulk.

Just W of Wyndford Cross, in Burnhouse Street, access to the canal path and the stairway of locks (*see* Public Buildings). SANDBANK STREET starts just beyond the canal aqueduct and climbs eastward over Maryhill's highest hill, Gilshochill, passing the High Church, the Episcopal church (*see* Churches) and a few surviving villas of 1900–1. From the summit a panoramic view of the MARYHILL 'B' SCHEME, spread out like an architect's model down the precipitous slope and over the broad valley below. It is another mixed development (1966–71) but this time perfunctory and *Reema* system-built with a cluster of three tower blocks and thirteen stubby eight-storey blocks facing each other across the valley. Crossing the valley bottom, a single street (KILMUN STREET) of terraced flats, which leads back W to Maryhill Road and to what was once the centre of the village, with the Old Parish Church (*see* Churches).

MARYHILL PARK, the haphazardly mixed group of middle-class villas, terraces and tenements, lies beyond the railway line that crosses Maryhill Road. Caldercuilt Street is the only way to it. Overlooking the railway cutting, FALCON (originally ALBERT) TERRACE, a row of plain stone houses set behind long countrified gardens, begun in 1867. To the N, an extraordinary planned group of 1901 by *John Gordon* in DUNGOYNE STREET, BARRA STREET and CROSBIE STREET. Battlemented, almost completely circular bays mark the angles of a square block of terraced houses, their other details of Vanbrughian eccentricity. Facing them, more conventional semi-detached villas with deep eaves; built in 1908 by *D. Bennett Dobson & Co*. To the W, a row of yellow sandstone tenements (Nos. 9–21 Crosbie Street, also by *John Gordon*, 1903) that are just as queer, with classical motifs used in the unsystematic and quirky way that Post-Modern stylists call their own.

Off Crosbie Street, the oval PRINCE OF WALES GARDENS, lined with one- and two-storey pebbledashed cottages of 1920–2 by *Frank Southorn & Orr*, a rare scheme of the Scottish

Veterans' Garden City Association. Overlooking Maryhill Park (laid out in 1892) from SPENCE and WHITTON STREETS, individually designed Baronial villas of the 1890s.

Beyond the park to the NE lies Summerston (*see* below) and to the NW, the ACRE ROAD scheme of 1969–75 (four lonely stumpy towers of *Reema* construction by *Parry & Hughes*, with strict rows of four-storey slabs opposite); and a few outposts of Glasgow University (*see* Public Buildings, above).

SUMMERSTON is an isolated hilltop township developed on farmland beyond Maryhill Park by Glasgow Corporation in association with various private developers. It was completed *c.* 1975. In the valley to the S and linking it to the Maryhill 'B' Scheme (*see* above), the Township Centre, just a short row of shops, a domineering superstore, a pub, warehouses and a community centre, which shows the only – slight, admittedly – attempt at architecture (*see* Public Buildings, above). Round about, three-storey flats and two-storey terraced houses designed by the City's *Department of Architecture and Related Services* and laid out along the short pedestrian paths of the Radburn system. Grey harling, dark tiled roofs and broad black-painted window surrounds ape the Scottish vernacular, but the construction looks sadly flimsy.

POSSILPARK AND HIGH POSSIL

Public housing schemes now cover the hilly lands of Possil, but until the mid-C19 the hills were almost bare. The Forth and Clyde Canal reached Lambhill in 1774 and Hamiltonhill in 1777, where it stopped for nearly twenty years. Industry was concentrated round these northern and southern corners of Possil but spread no further until 1868, when the Lower Possil estate, with its late C17 mansion, was feued to Walter Macfarlane & Co. By 1878 Macfarlane had 'removed the house, felled the trees, erected on part of it a spacious foundry ... and laid the rest out as streets and dwelling houses' to form what was considered by Smith and Mitchell 'one of the finest and best conducted suburbs in Glasgow', Possilpark. Other industries (pottery, chemicals, iron and steel) followed, and by 1891 the population had grown to 10,000.

Corporation tenements of the most austere kind supplanted the C19 suburb in the 1930s and after 1945 spread round about, across High Possil as well. None of the industries survived the 1960s. Only Saracen Street, once an almost processional route N to the Saracen Foundry, retains any of its C19 character.

CHURCHES

COLSTON MILTON CHURCH, Egilsay Crescent. The original red sandstone and rendered church of 1950–2, by *Wylie*,

POSSILPARK

CHURCHES and PUBLIC BUILDINGS
① Our Lady of the Assumption (R.C.)
② Possilpark Church
③ St Matthew Episcopal
④ St Teresa of Lisieux
⑤ Trinity Possil
⑥ Possilpark Library
⑦ Parkhouse School
⑧ (Possil School)
⑨ Possilpark Secondary
⑩ Rockvilla School
⑪ St Cuthbert's Primary and Saracen Primary
⑫ St Teresa's Primary
⑬ Health Centre
⑭ Ruchill Hospital
⑮ Ruchill Park
⑯ Cowlairs Park

Shanks & Partners, is now the hall, attached to a flat-roofed church of dark brick with, in place of a tower, a tall concrete frame enclosing a cross: 1963–4, by *James Houston & Partners*.

OUR LADY OF THE ASSUMPTION (R.C.), 493 Bilsland Drive, Ruchill. 1953–6, by *T. S. Cordiner*. Stone façade, its centre rising into a short tower. No historicist references.

POSSILPARK CHURCH, 124 Saracen Street. 1889–90, by *Malcolm Stark*. Built as Rockvilla United Presbyterian Church. Simple Geometrical style. Absolutely plain interior, rearranged 1946–8. – STAINED GLASS. 1926, by *Guthrie & Wells & Co.* to a design by *Isobel Goudie* (Religion, Education, Temperance). – HALL in a similar style, with projecting polygonal porch by *Wright & Wylie*, 1917–19.

ST AGNES (R.C.), 644 Balmore Road, Lambhill. 1893–4, by *Pugin & Pugin*. Rock-faced Locharbriggs sandstone. Towerless and with Perp windows. Double porch on the entrance façade. Altar rails and pulpit, 1911; side altars, 1939. – STATIONS OF THE CROSS, 1906, from Bruges. – PRESBYTERY, 1888. – The former SCHOOL has a dark stone rear portion which was part of the school-cum-chapel of 1880. Enlarged 1886 and 1903.

ST AUGUSTINE (R.C.), Ashgill Road, Milton. 1954–6, by *R. Fairlie & Partners*, in Spanish Colonial style. White with a green slate roof. On the gable end, naively carved panels of St Augustine, loaves and fishes, chalice and water. Dull interior enclosed by concrete parabolic arches. A range of wide arches links church and presbytery.

ST MATTHEW (Episcopal), 200 Balmore Road. 1935–7, by *T. Harold Hughes*. Beige brick, aisles, long windows with triangular heads. Square bell turret.

ST MONICA (R.C.), Castlebay Street. 1970–4, by *Alexander McAnally*. Harled box with a steep monopitch. Slate-clad battered corner buttress supporting a slate cross.

ST TERESA OF LISIEUX (R.C.), 86 Saracen Street, sharing the grounds of the demolished C18 Craigbank House with the previous church (1920s, now church hall), PRESBYTERY (1934–5, by *A. McAnally*) and primary school (*see* Public Buildings, below).

The large extraordinarily eclectic brick church (also by McAnally, 1956–60) has a domestic flavour. Nave and passage aisles with windows 'semi-Norman in style'. Higher chancel and transepts under a green slate hipped roof. NW tower with a short aluminium spire and relief of St Teresa. On the N side a big semicircular bay window and a canted one (mortuary chapel). Confessionals and sacristies project from the hidden E side. Over the entrance doors, reliefs of St Mungo and St Andrew. Sub-classical interior, profligately embellished in marble by *Mortimer, Willison & Graham*, with stained glass (brilliantly coloured and childishly realistic) by *Guthrie & Wells* and metalwork by *Thomas Bogie & Sons*. Wooden organ gallery, Gothic surprisingly, with figures (like the other wooden sculpture) by *H. A. Heinzeller* of Oberammergau.

TRINITY POSSIL AND HENRY DRUMMOND CHURCH, Broadholm Street, Parkhouse. 1934–6, by *Stewart & Paterson*. Dark brick, with stark white pointing. Simple round-arched style. No tower.

LAMBHILL CEMETERY, Balmore Road. Opened 1881. 49 acres (20 ha) laid out geometrically. Entrance GATEWAY a triumphal arch in banded ashlar, with lodges concealed by the flanking walls. Good cast-iron gates. By *James Sellars*, whose memorial here (unveiled 1890) was designed by *John Keppie*: Egyptian-style in red and grey granite.

Adjoining to the S, the slightly later Roman Catholic ST KENTIGERN'S CEMETERY with many lavish monuments to the Italians of Glasgow.

WESTERN NECROPOLIS, Tresta Road, almost adjoining Lambhill Cemetery. Opened 1882. Near the entrance, the Scottish Burial Reform and Cremation Society's CREMATORIUM (1893–5, by *James Chalmers*). – STAINED GLASS. One window by *Harrington Mann* for *Guthrie & Wells*, 1950; another (S wall) by *Gordon Webster*, 1965. – REMEMBRANCE BUILDING, 1975.

PUBLIC BUILDINGS

POSSILPARK LIBRARY, 127 Allander Street. 1911–13, by *George Simpson*. Single-storey and top-lit, with cautious Baroque touches. Inside, panelling and fittings mostly intact and, in the reading room, contemporary PAINTINGS by students of Glasgow School of Art. Broadly modelled classical figures in sombre colours: Astronomy by *Alma Assefrey*; Geography by *Archibald McGlashen*; Poetry by *Tom Gentleman*; Commerce by *Robertson Weir*; Art by *Helen Johnston*; Science by *Josephine Cameron*.

CADDER PRIMARY SCHOOL. *See* Descriptions, below: Cadder.

CHIRNSYDE SCHOOL. *See* Descriptions: Milton.

LANGA STREET NURSERY SCHOOL. *See* Descriptions: Cadder.

PARKHOUSE SCHOOL FOR THE PARTIALLY HEARING, Buckley Street. The former Balmore Public School of 1929–32, by *J. A. Laird*. Handsome Wrenaissance block at the meeting of two streets; long splayed wings (the open corridors glazed in 1962–4 by *R. W. K. C. Rogerson*) and central hall behind. The C17 detail extends to the Tijouesque perimeter railings.

POSSIL SCHOOL, Bracken Street and Balmore Road. A very large school by *James Taylor Thomson*, 1930–4, converted to flats (*c.* 1985) by *Walter Underwood & Partners*. The severe classical frontispiece of red sandstone faces Bracken Street. Long red brick wings splay back round a courtyard high above Balmore Road. Their open corridors are now access balconies, with additional fancy ironwork.

POSSILPARK SECONDARY SCHOOL, Saracen Street. Prominent from the street, the curtain-walled classroom block and brick gymnasium of 1964–70 by *Wilson, Hamilton & Wilson*.

ROCKVILLA SCHOOL, Dawson Road, perched above Possil Road and reached by an arched gateway and flight of steps. 1874–7, by *John Honeyman*. Tudor with mullioned and transomed windows. In the centre of the front, a round staircase tower with conical cap and polygonal topknot. Tiny lights in its solid base, glazed with a fancy pattern above. Boys' and girls' staircases rise together inside it, separated by a glass screen.

ST AGNES PRIMARY. *See* Descriptions, below: Cadder.

ST AUGUSTINE PRIMARY AND SECONDARY SCHOOLS. *See* Descriptions: Milton.

ST CUTHBERT'S PRIMARY SCHOOL, Auckland Street. Designed in 1935 by *Weddell, Inglis & Taylor*; not completed until 1950. The plan typical of 1930s schools: central block and long wings, here turned back to follow the crescent, and with decorative brickwork and stucco panels. Sharing the site, SARACEN PRIMARY (1932–3, by *William McCaig*), wrecked by additions.

ST TERESA'S PRIMARY SCHOOL, 65 Killearn Street. 1961–3, by *A. Buchanan Campbell*. A striking white silhouette, with its funnel-like service tower, on the hilltop above the church. Very Corbusian. – SCULPTURE. Alice and the Red Queen by *Benno Schotz*, 1963, in the playground.

HEALTH CENTRE, Denmark Street. 1936–7, by *Thomas Somers* (City Engineer). A flat-roofed brick clinic influenced no doubt by Dutch work and possibly by Holden's London underground stations. Of one and two storeys, with a circular stair-tower, almost completely glazed.

RUCHILL HOSPITAL, 520 Bilsland Drive. The salubriously high land was acquired in 1892, and nearly half of it was opened that year as RUCHILL PARK (with, until *c.* 1914, the C17 and early C19 Ruchill House at its N end). Bilsland Drive was laid out at the same time. The hospital was designed by *A. B. McDonald* (City Engineer) in Flemish Renaissance style. A plaque on the gatehouse reads 'City of Glasgow Hospital for Infectious Diseases opened 1900. Foundation stone laid 1895'.

Flanking the entrance lodges, stone villas and cottages for non-medical officials. From the gate, steep flights of steps to the ENQUIRY BLOCK, flanked by the CLEARING HOUSE (W) and MORGUE (E), with a domed octagonal LABORATORY projecting. Behind on the central axis, the KITCHEN and DAY WORKERS' BLOCK (1910) and, at the highest point, the WATER TOWER like a Flemish bell tower, its top of intriguing complexity. To the E and W, strict rows of sixteen pavilions with bay windows, shaped end gables and pretty vents with timber balusters and ogee caps. All of red brick, with red sandstone and terracotta dressings. To the E, the BOILER HOUSE, with a red and black chimney, the LAUNDRY (1976) and other offices. To the W, the big

ADMINISTRATION BLOCK, the façade with semicircular bay windows and prominent chimneys facing the park. At the back, wings of staff accommodation.

The former PHTHISIS HOSPITAL (1910–14) lies to the N. Harled main block (built as a nurses' home) flanked by pavilions linked by spine corridors.

RUCHILL PARK. *See* Ruchill Hospital, above.

RAILWAY STATION, 441 Balmore Road, now offices. Built *c.* 1877 for the Lanarkshire & Dumbarton Railway. Red brick, with decorative timbering in the gables and moulded terracotta tympana over the windows.

FORTH AND CLYDE CANAL. OLD BASIN, Applecross Street, the Forth and Clyde Canal's E terminus at Hamiltonhill from 1777 until 1790. Lining the N bank, the long low CANAL WORKSHOPS of whitewashed rubble, with a clock on the splayed E corner. Behind them, a simple three-bay house, also of *c.* 1790, and the brick pavilion of the British Waterways Board (1984, by *Ian Burke & Associates*). Over the canal, a BASCULE BRIDGE of the standard Forth and Clyde type (cf. Port Dundas).

The CANAL AQUEDUCTS bridging the gulf of Possil Road can be seen from up here. One was built *c.* 1790 to continue the canal to Port Dundas: the one in current use was built *c.* 1880 and has a heavy segmental arch carrying the channel and lighter semicircular ones carrying the towpaths.

Much further N, LAMBHILL BRIDGE (an electrically operated rolling-lift bridge of 1934 by *Thomas Somers* (City Engineer) and *Sir William Arrol & Sons Ltd*) takes Balmore Road over the canal. Alongside it, at Nos. 21–5 CANAL BANK, a former canal stables and dwelling house of *c.* 1790. Ashlar-fronted and pedimented.

DESCRIPTIONS

Possilpark

SARACEN STREET is Possilpark's main street, still with some of its C19 tenements, and, at the S end, a number of churches and public buildings (*see* above). All around, monotonous and almost treeless streets with the most basic concrete-block tenements and cottage flats of the 1920s and 1930s.

W of Saracen Street is the HAMILTONHILL scheme, with its large contemporary school in Auckland Street (*see* Public Buildings, above). On the NW edge, in WESTER COMMON ROAD, a mixed development by the S.S.H.A. (Chief Technical Officer *H. Buteux*), 1967–9. Four system-built slab blocks banded in white and grey mosaic and grey-harled terraces of maisonettes. On the S edge off Ellesmere Street, the old Hamiltonhill terminus of the Forth and Clyde Canal can be reached: so can Rockvilla School below it in Possil Road (for both, *see* Public Buildings, above).

101 E of Saracen Street, the EAST KEPPOCH scheme, a strict grid of Corporation tenements (1932–4) with backcourts landscaped by *Brian Clouston & Partners*, *c.* 1980, and linked with COWLAIRS PARK, informally laid out with areas for sport, play and sitting. N of East Keppoch, at the E and W ends of the playground between SLOY STREET and FINLASS STREET, two arches which originally flanked the entrances to Macfarlane's SARACEN FOUNDRY of *c.* 1869 (demolished in 1967). Some of the tenements in this neighbourhood, and the Health Centre in Denmark Street (*see* Public Buildings), have more interesting consciously modern details.

Further N still, halfway down HAWTHORN STREET, a former Corporation TRAM DEPOT for electric cars (No. 240), 1900. Off the N side of the street lies HAWTHORN, a small scheme of cottage flats of the Mosspark and Knightswood type, built in 1925–7 and given street names evocative of a leafy southern English suburb. More, of a simpler slightly later type (1927–9), in PARKHOUSE, N of the railway line, and, between the two on BALMORE ROAD, the former VOGUE CINEMA, 1932–3, by *James McKissack*.

Cadder

A scheme of 850 houses begun by the S.S.H.A. (Chief Architect *T. O. W. Gratton*) in 1947 on the lands of Lambhill House. Three- to four-storey pebbledashed tenements, with pitched roofs and recessed stair windows over canopied doorways, a little more imaginative than contemporary Corporation house types. Some are laid out round squares S of SKIRSA STREET, others along the steep ridge, intermixed with a few four-in-a-block flats.

The schools (LANGA STREET NURSERY and ST AGNES PRIMARY, both in Tresta Road, and CADDER PRIMARY in Herma Street) are by *Honeyman, Jack & Robertson*, 1955–9, all with linked brick blocks in different arrangements, some with curtain walling and some with shallow-pitched roofs.

Milton

A Corporation scheme planned in 1949 and built in 1955–8 and 1967–9, with four-storey tenements at its centre in and around LIDDESDALE ROAD. Shared sheet-metal balconies painted in delicious 1950s favourites – lemon, turquoise and lilac. Round them, pitched-roofed cottages with no frills. Two schools on the same huge campus (ST AUGUSTINE'S PRIMARY, 1953, and SECONDARY, 1954, by *Frank Burnet*), just dull rendered blocks. CHIRNSYDE SCHOOL, Ashgill Road, is more interesting as an early post-World War II example: 1950, by *Ninian Johnston*.

On the N edge of the scheme, off either end of CASTLEBAY STREET, two groups of three high-rise blocks, each of them of two sheer towers with aggregate panels and coloured spandrels, by *John B. Wingate & Partners*, 1966–72.

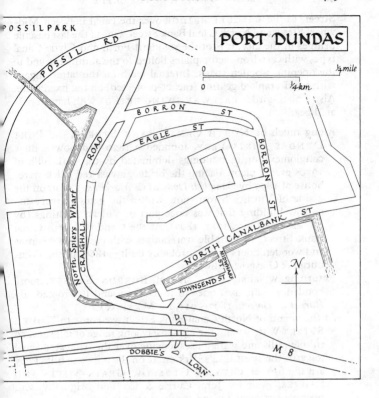

PORT DUNDAS

Port Dundas, the Glasgow terminus of the Forth and Clyde Canal, stands on a drumlin high above the city centre, with its long grey range of former mills and warehouses riding on the skyline.

The port, named after the chairman of the canal company, was built between 1786 and 1790, and then comprised an oval basin with a granary, and a link with Monkland Canal at the E end. Further basins were built, and Port Dundas quickly became industrial, with all sorts of processing – founding and engineering, distilling, sugar refining, chemical manufacture and so on. The canal is now interrupted, and most of Port Dundas Basin has disappeared under the M8, which cuts the port off from the once industrial area that spread s of it (*see* Cowcaddens, above).

The approach from the city centre is by either North Hanover Street or Port Dundas Road to Dobbie's Loan, which passes under the M8. Pedestrians can then go due N, via Townsend

Street, to the BASCULE BRIDGE over the canal between Mid-wharf Street and North Canal Bank Street. One of the last bascule bridges in the city, it is of the standard Forth and Clyde Canal type, with cast-iron sector-plates bolted to the abutments and to the opening wooden spans. Internal teeth on the latter engage with hand-cranked gearing (rachet-protected) on the fixed plate. Also a plate-girder RAILWAY SWING BRIDGE with hand-operated gear.

Along much of NORTH CANAL BANK STREET, the PORT DUNDAS DISTILLERY, founded *c*. 1820 and now a huge conglomeration of buildings dominated by the dark bulk of 1970s grains plant. Facing the bridge, a vast red brick warehouse of 1899 by *Campbell Douglas & Morrison*. E of it, off the E side of Vintner Street (now within the gates), a very tall narrow building that was once part of Vulcan Maltings (by *Russell & Spence*, from 1893). At the E end of North Canal Bank Street, two rubble warehouses with cast-iron columns and wooden floors inside, probably built *c*. 1860 for the Edinburgh & Glasgow Railway.

Returning W, along the E side of BORRON STREET, more bonded warehouses, one- to four-storey and flat-roofed. By *Burnet & Boston*, 1897–1911, for Mackie & Co.

At the W end of North Canal Bank Street, we come to NORTH
45 SPIERS WHARF and the immensely long range of tall snecked rubble mills and warehouses looking over the truncated canal towards the West End's Park estate on the opposite hill. They are the former CITY OF GLASGOW GRAIN MILLS AND STORES, built for John Currie & Co. and originally with twenty pairs of stones and 100-horsepower condensing engine. The six-storey N block dates from *c*. 1851, the rest from 1869–70. Inside, brick arches on cast-iron columns. At the N end of them, the even taller, ashlar-fronted red and white brick PORT DUNDAS SUGAR REFINERY of 1866, with lower red and white brick ranges round a courtyard to the N and facing Craighall Road. All these buildings being converted (1989) into flats, with very little alteration to the exterior, by *Nicholas Groves-Raines* (job architect *John Forbes*). At their S end, the CANAL OFFICES of *c*. 1812, like a two-storey, five-bay house, with steep central pediment and chimney, Doric porch, and aprons under the lower windows. The panelled end pilasters and Neo-classical husk-garland give away the date. It is to become the local inn. (Just to the N, on the E side of CRAIGHALL ROAD, a group of mid-C19 rubble and taller ashlar buildings, the former DUNDASHILL DISTILLERY (now a cooperage), founded *c*. 1811.) The towpath on the W side follows the canal NW to the earlier terminus at Hamiltonhill (*see* Possilpark), to the Firhill Basin (*see* North Kelvinside), and on through Maryhill (*q.v.*) to *Whitworth*'s fine locks and aqueduct.

ROYSTON

Royston is the relatively new name for Garngad, which was rechristened during redevelopment in the 1950s in an attempt to obliterate the memory of a notorious industrial slum, until 1891 just beyond the city boundary. Heavy industry had developed here, after the opening of the Monkland Canal, with the establishment in 1799 of Tennant's famous St Rollox Chemical Works (by 1835 the most extensive in Europe), and it increased after the arrival in 1831 of the coal-carrying Garnkirk and Glasgow Railway. Industry, including the chemical works, remained here until the 1960s, when the M8 and new housing (a Comprehensive Redevelopment Area was declared in 1964) swept it away and divorced Royston from its intimate neighbour Townhead.

CHURCHES

TOWNHEAD AND BLOCHAIRN PARISH CHURCH, 176 Royston Hill. 1865–6, by *J. J. Stevenson* of *Campbell Douglas & Stevenson*. Geometrical style, in grey snecked rubble. The extremely tall NE tower, holding its own with the surrounding blocks of flats, is a landmark on the hill above the M8, which now separates the church from Townhead. Its silhouette is almost as unusual as that of Camphill Queen's Park Church, probably also by Stevenson (*see* Queen's Park, below), tapering bluntly from the ground with stepped clasping buttresses up to where the spire starts with broaches disguised by aedicules. Tall nave, with round clearstorey windows and plate tracery, the bold foiled motif being repeated throughout the interior, in the spandrels of the two-tier arched roof trusses, on the gallery front and on the pulpit. Inside, the nave seems particularly high and narrow, flanked by galleries on cast-iron columns with waterleaf capitals and with the portrait heads of famous Protestants as stops to the upper arches. These plain, bold forms were originally a background for PAINTED DECORATION by *Cottier* (who had shared an Edinburgh office with the architects and did this as his first Glasgow commission). Only fragments of paint on the gallery fronts and columns and coloured window glass survive of this reportedly dramatic, almost Egyptian scheme, with large areas of red and blue figured in black. Cottier was assisted by *Andrew Wells*. – The only figurative STAINED GLASS (E window) is by *Morris & Co.*, 1866, one of their earliest ecclesiastical works in Scotland. Large simple figures in clear colours, with *Burne-Jones*'s drawing style especially evident. In the two pairs of lancets: Moses and the Golden Calf, by Burne-Jones; St Peter and St Paul Preaching, by Burne-Jones and *Morris* respectively; David and Goliath, by Burne-Jones and *Ford Madox Brown*; St John the Baptist and the Baptism of Christ, again by Burne-Jones and Morris. Also by Burne-Jones, the angels in the quatrefoils, and the Christ in Majesty in the rose. Angels in the rose by Burne-Jones and Morris. – ORGAN by *Willis*.

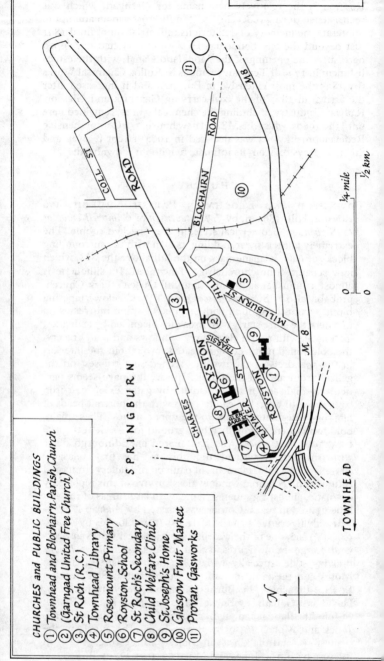

ROYSTON

CHURCHES and PUBLIC BUILDINGS
① Townhead and Blochairn Parish Church
② (Garngad United Free Church)
③ St Roch (R.C.)
④ Townhead Library
⑤ Rosemount Primary
⑥ Royston School
⑦ St Roch's Secondary
⑧ Child Welfare Clinic
⑨ St Joseph's Home
⑩ Glasgow Fruit Market
⑪ Provan Gasworks

Former GARNGAD UNITED FREE CHURCH, 15 Tharsis Street. 1895. Minimal Gothic with a bellcote.

ST ROCH (R.C.), 311 Royston Road. By *Walter R. Watson*, 1906–7. Minimal chapel with rendered walls, sash windows and, inside, cast-iron columns. Contemporary school and presbytery opposite, flanking the site intended for a more substantial church.

PUBLIC BUILDINGS

TOWNHEAD PUBLIC LIBRARY, 188–92 Castle Street. Now isolated from Townhead on the N side of the M8. 1907, by *John Fairweather*. Like Springburn Library, fairly simple, single-storey and top-lit from a dome. Red sandstone façade with rusticated pilasters and balustraded parapet. To the reading room, an ornamented pediment. Over the entrance and also at the other end, aedicule surrounds with figures. Inside, the dark panelling, desks and racks, plaster ceilings and tiled hall all survive.

ROSEMOUNT PRIMARY SCHOOL, Millburn Street. 1897, by *J. B. Wilson*. An Italianate Board school; two storeys with a central hall and a broad porch.

ROYSTON SCHOOL, 102 Royston Road. Built as St Rollox Public School in 1906 by *Duncan McNaughtan*. Its Scottish Renaissance style is given a severity familiar from Mackintosh's then recently completed Scotland Street School, but has many more literally historicist details. Three storeys towards Rhymer Street, four to Royston Road, with gabled hall and staircase projections, divided, internally, from the classrooms by an E–W spine corridor.

ST ROCH'S SECONDARY SCHOOL, 40 Royston Road. A big pink classical block of 1925–8 by *Thomas Baird* with a gymnasium as the centre stroke of the E-plan.

CHILD WELFARE CLINIC, Glenbarr Street. 1932–5, by *Thomas Somers* (City Engineer), in the same spirit as the early Corporation housing nearby.

ST JOSEPH'S HOME, 220 Royston Hill. A very plain grey stone H-shaped block of the 1880s. Towards the road an ugly red sandstone chapel, minimally Romanesque outside, almost classical within; by *Charles J. Menart*, 1910–14.

GLASGOW FRUIT MARKET, Blochairn Road. The fruit and vegetable and the poultry and fish markets moved from Candleriggs to this unremarkable building (by *Gotch & Partners*, begun 1969).

PROVAN GASWORKS, Royston Road. The two huge gas-holders, 85 m (280 ft) in diameter and painted a vivid blue (in 1989), are a memorable landmark in the route along the M8. They belong to a gasworks begun in 1900–4 for the Glasgow Corporation Gas Department by *William Foulis*, engineer, and greatly extended after 1919.

DESCRIPTION

The Corporation made the first of several attempts to eradicate the notorious slums of Garngad in 1918–20, when *Thomas Nisbet* (City Engineer) built a very long brick-and-render tenement block and several two-storey blocks of cottage flats round ROYSTON SQUARE at the w end of ROYSTON ROAD. A typical slum clearance scheme of 1931–5 swept away much more of the C19 property. Many local people were rehoused again in a scheme begun on derelict land in 1952 by *A. G. Jury*, then Director of Housing. As well as cottages and three- and four-storey tenements and a little square of shops characteristic of that date, three tower blocks (1958–61) by *Geo. Wimpey*'s own architects between Royston Road and CHARLES STREET, at twenty storeys, then the highest in Scotland. The design, with glazed attic storey, was repeated many times. By 1963 all the slums had been cleared, leaving a few solid red sandstone tenements of 1906–7 (by *A. V. Gardner*) just w of Royston School. Two later blocks by Wimpey in Charles Street, 1969–71. Also of that date, three twenty-five-storey blocks of the *Reema (Scotland) Ltd* system to the s in MILLBURN STREET. SE of Royston Hill (in KILBERRY, FORRESTFIELD, CARBROOK and KINTYRE STREETS), some of the earliest houses of non-traditional construction in Scotland, built in 1925 for the Scottish National Housing Trust Company, a forerunner of the S.S.H.A. (which has refurbished them) and constructed of steel by *W. J. Weir* and *Cowieson Ltd*.

To the E, another slum clearance scheme, begun in 1930 on the Germiston estate. Three *Reema* blocks were inserted in COLL STREET in 1967–70.

SPRINGBURN

Only the small maintenance depot at the St Rollox Works is an active reminder of Springburn's fame as a centre of railway locomotive building. At the height of its activity in the C19, three out of every four men employed in that industry in Britain worked in one of Springburn's manufactories. Yet the name Springburn does not even appear on Cleland's map of 1822, although familiar names like Balgray, Sighthill, Petershill, Barnhill, Cowlairs, Flemington, Mosesfield, Balornock, and Stobhill do. They convey the hilly character of the terrain with its numerous steep drumlins. Balgray Hill, 107 m (351 ft) above sea level, is the highest point in the modern city.

In 1817 a tiny stretch of the main road s of what is now Springburn Cross had been built up as Coburg Place by the owner of Petershill mansion. It remained isolated until, in the mid-1830s, a small settlement of weavers, miners and quarrymen grew up just to its N. In 1842 a chapel-of-ease opened to serve

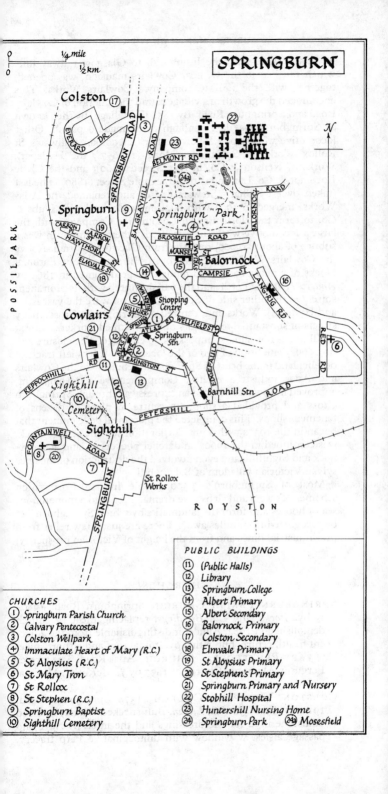

SPRINGBURN

0 ──── ¼ mile
0 ──── ½ km

Colston ⑰

EVERARD DR.

SPRINGBURN ROAD

③

BALGRAYHILL ROAD

㉒

㉓

Springburn ✠ ⑨

BELMONT RD.

㉔ᵃ

Springburn Park

④

BALORNOCK ROAD

CARRON PL. ⑲
CARRON ST.

HAWTHORN ST.

ELMVALE ST. ⑱

BROOMFIELD ROAD

MANSEL ST. ✠
⑮ SYDE ST.

Balornock

CAMPSIE ST.

LANGRIG RD.

⑯

WANNAN ST.
HILLKIRK ST.

⑤
Shopping Centre

⑭

Cowlairs

⑫
ATLAS RD. WELLFIELD ST.

SPRINGBURN ROAD

①
ATLAS ST. **Springburn Stn.**

㉑

AYR ST.

②
⑪

EDGEFAULD

RED RD.

✠ ⑥

FLEMINGTON ST.

KEPPOCHHILL RD.

⑬

Sighthill Cemetery ⑩

Barnhill Stn.

PETERSHILL ROAD

Sighthill

FOUNTAINWELL ROAD

⑧ ✠ ⑳

⑦ ✠

SPRINGBURN ROAD

St Rollox Works

R O Y S T O N

P O S S I L P A R K

N

PUBLIC BUILDINGS

⑪ (Public Halls)
⑫ Library
⑬ Springburn College
⑭ Albert Primary
⑮ Albert Secondary
⑯ Balornock Primary
⑰ Colston Secondary
⑱ Elmvale Primary
⑲ St Aloysius Primary
⑳ St Stephen's Primary
㉑ Springburn Primary and Nursery
㉒ Stobhill Hospital
㉓ Huntershill Nursing Home
㉔ Springburn Park ㉔ᵃ Mosesfield

CHURCHES

① Springburn Parish Church
② Calvary Pentecostal
③ Colston Wellpark
④ Immaculate Heart of Mary (R.C.)
⑤ St Aloysius (R.C.)
⑥ St Mary Tron
⑦ St Rollox
⑧ St Stephen (R.C.)
⑨ Springburn Baptist
⑩ Sighthill Cemetery

it. In the same year, the Edinburgh to Glasgow railway line, which ran just to the w, near Cowlairs mansion, was opened, together with the railway company's Cowlairs Works. This encouraged the growth of a village round the junction of Cowlairs Road and Springburn Road. By 1854 this village (by then known as Springburn) was large enough to be made a parish. Other locomotive works soon followed: the Caledonian Railway's St Rollox Works in Springburn Road (1856–7); the Hydepark Works of Neilson & Co. in Ayr Street (1860); and the Clyde Locomotive Co. Ltd opposite in Barcaple Street (1880). The last (taken over by Sharp Stewart & Co. and renamed the Atlas Works) merged in 1903 with Neilson & Co. and with Dubs & Co. to form the North British Locomotive Company, with the largest locomotive works in Europe. By then Springburn was a suburb of about 30,000, reached from Glasgow by tram. Above the Cowlairs Works, on Springburn Hill, stood four Baronial blocks of a never completed model village designed in 1863 by *Andrew Heiton* of Perth, and the parish church with its prominent spire. On the other side of Springburn Road were the vast Atlas and Hydepark Works and, centred on Springburn Cross, many streets of substantial tenements built for skilled workers.

All this is now almost impossible to envisage. The closure and (in 1969) demolition of two of the locomotive works left tracts of derelict land in the heart of Springburn, rebuilt with the Cowlairs and Atlas industrial estates. Comprehensive redevelopment, approved in 1973, also forced an expressway through Springburn Cross and provided a shopping centre in place of dozens of tenement shops. This completed the piecemeal development that began in the 1930s with a big Corporation scheme at Balornock, was continued in the 1960s on derelict pockets of land at Balornock and Sighthill, and even involved the destruction of the once sylvan Victorian villadom of Balgrayhill.

Most of Springburn's 3,500 people live in Corporation schemes. Towers and slabs give dramatic relief to a monotonous sea of houses and form the landmarks by which Springburn can be recognized from miles away. There are just a few relics from pre-industrial times and from the height of Victorian prosperity.

CHURCHES

SPRINGBURN PARISH CHURCH, Springburn Road. 1980–1, by *Stocks Bros Ltd Buildings*, replacing the C19 church demolished in 1982. Almost indistinguishable from the adjacent health centre, but with a pyramidal roof and a short spike.

CALVARY PENTECOSTAL CHURCH, Atlas Road. The former Ferguson Memorial Church of 1897 by *J. McKellar*. Minimal Gothic.

COLSTON WELLPARK CHURCH, 1378 Springburn Road. 1912–15, by *Clifford & Lunan*. Buff snecked rubble, with red sandstone used for the dressings and the interior. Nave and passage aisles. w window with unimaginative Perp tracery.

Arcades with pointed arches and capital-less piers. Tall chancel arch. Bold hammerbeam roofs. – ORGAN brought from the Tron Kirk.

THE IMMACULATE HEART OF MARY (R.C.), 162 Broomfield Road. 1950–2, by *Thomas Cordiner*. Brick, with a wheel window and sculpture of Our Lady on the gable end. The roof comes down low on the Syriam Street side. Triangular buttresses continue its line. A simple concrete-trussed interior, as might be expected.

ST ALOYSIUS (R.C.), Hillkirk Street. 1881–2, by *J.L. Bruce* of *Bruce & Sturrock*, retaining the E end of the church of 1855–6 by *Charles O'Neill*. Fully fledged E.E. style, but towerless. Gabled street elevation (s) of fine cream ashlar with a group of three shafted lancets flanked by empty niches. Below them, a partly blind arcade. Short transepts mask the aisles with (W) the gabled porch (with bust of St Aloysius) and gallery stair, and (E) the baptistery and organ chamber.

Inside, a wide and surprisingly bright nave lit from skylights in the open timber roof. Nave arcades with slender quatrefoil piers narrowly set. At the (liturgical) E end a greater concentration of more richly moulded and dogtooth-decorated arches, their clustered responds resting on corbels of foaming foliage and worldly-looking heads. The apsidal sanctuary was part of the old church but was much heightened in 1881–2. Marble panelling and altar rails of the late 1940s. – Elaborate pinnacled HIGH ALTAR in *Pugin & Pugin*'s usual taste, c. 1896. – ORGAN. By *Alexander Kirkland*, no date. – STAINED GLASS. s, NW rose, baptistery, and figurative Lady Chapel windows by *Hooper*; cathedral glass in the aisle lancets by *Adam*; all of 1881–2.

PRESBYTERY. The house of 1882 (*see* the datestone) was enlarged by *Joseph Cowan* in 1891–2 and given a rock-faced façade with mullioned windows and a gabled Gothic porch. – HALLS. 1937, red brick. No Gothic references.

ST MARY TRON PARISH CHURCH, 128 Red Road. By *Rogerson & Spence*, 1964–6. A little grey harled building, overwhelmed by neighbouring tower blocks. Ecclesiastically, it succeeds the Tron Kirk (*see* Merchant City, above: Churches).

ST ROLLOX, 155 Springburn Road. An insignificant brick replacement of 1982–4 for a church of 1892–4 by *John Hamilton*, burnt out and demolished in 1981.

ST STEPHEN (R.C.), Fountainwell Drive, Sighthill. 1970–2. An interesting and nearly successful design by *Thomas Cordiner*. A bold brown brick cube with chamfered corners, topped by a tapering lead-covered funnel which penetrates the roof, directing light on to the altar and acting as a rather clumsy altar canopy. The only other light filters from the roof along the edges of the suspended timber ceiling, or comes from a slot behind the altar and from lunettes very low down.

SPRINGBURN BAPTIST CHURCH, Springburn Road. By *R. B. Rankin & Associates*, c. 1980, replacing a church of 1891. A steep monopitch over the brick church, and another over the attached harled halls further down the steep slope up the Balgrayhill Road.

SIGHTHILL CEMETERY, 225 Springburn Road. Opened on this dramatic hill site in 1840. Gates and former chapel in exaggerated Greek style by *John Stephen* of *Scott, Stephen & Gale*, 1839. – On the main avenue, the MARTYRS' MEMORIAL, to John Baird, Andrew Hardie and James Wilson, leaders of the 1820 uprising.

PUBLIC BUILDINGS

SPRINGBURN PUBLIC HALLS, 46 Keppochhill Road. 1899–1902, by *William B. Whitie*. Red sandstone ashlar façade like an Italian Cinquecento church, with a tall central section like a nave, crowned by a big segmental pediment on Ionic columns. Smaller hall with corner entrance tower to the N. The main hall has a wide plaster barrel-vault, galleries and a large organ.

SPRINGBURN DISTRICT LIBRARY, 179 Ayr Street. 1902–6, by *W. B. Whitie*. Single-storey and top-lit throughout its interior (now also a museum). Red sandstone ashlar façade with a balustraded parapet. Entrance with Ionic columns *in antis*.

SPRINGBURN COLLEGE, 110 Flemington Street. 1909, by *James Miller*. Built as the offices of the North British Locomotive Company (founded 1903), and converted to a college of engineering in 1962–5 after the works closed. Four ranges round a courtyard, with the main façade, befitting the company's status, on a grand scale and expensively embellished. Even the glazing bars are shaped into little segmental pediments. Of three storeys plus an attic, with the projecting end and centre bays most elaborately treated in English Baroque style. The doorway is ingeniously symbolic with a cartouche composed of a recognizable type of locomotive, with chains and haulage gear as swags. Flanking the pediment, Speed with a flying cloak, and Science with globe, compasses and plans. Other elevations are utilitarian, the tiled courtyard ones especially so. Late C17-style decoration continues inside. Above the staircase (across the back of the entrance hall) three STAINED-GLASS windows, a War Memorial by *Wm. Meikle & Sons* (unveiled 1921), depicting Scottish regiments and their heraldry and three large figures (a woman at a lathe; a man at an anvil; and a Scottish soldier).

ALBERT PRIMARY SCHOOL, 10 Barclay Street. 1960s and brown brick like the adjacent Balgraybank flats, with a series of monopitches.

ALBERT SECONDARY SCHOOL, Mansel Street. A Higher Grade school of 1926–7 by *Wright & Wylie*, brightening up this drab area with jazzy abstracted classicism. Hard red brick with raised and grooved bands and inset coloured tile patterns. Grey concrete of the 1960s at the back.

BALORNOCK PRIMARY SCHOOL, Lang-rig Road. 1929–30, by *Lennox & Macmath*. Hard red brick with stone dressings in a similar style to Albert Secondary School. There is an Art Deco flavour to the stepped parapet and window lintels.

COLSTON SECONDARY SCHOOL, 15 Newbold Avenue. 1907–8, by *Duncan McNaughtan & Son* for the Maryhill School Board. Red sandstone front facing Springburn Road, with minimal late C 17-style detail in the gabled end bays. Much extended.

ELMVALE PRIMARY SCHOOL, 712 Hawthorn Street. A particularly handsome square red sandstone Board school of 1901 by *H. E. Clifford*, in a style touched by the American influence of H. H. Richardson and Louis Sullivan. Hipped roof with twin squatly domed bell turrets and wide up-tilted eaves cornice. Just below the eaves, bands of windows divided by stumpy columns with bell-like capitals. The unmoulded wavy parapet and window openings of the janitor's house owe more to Mackintosh or Salmon.

ST ALOYSIUS PRIMARY SCHOOL, Carron Street. 1966–7, by *A. G. Jury* (City Architect). Neat steel-framed cube with brick panels peeled down intermittently.

ST STEPHEN'S PRIMARY SCHOOL, Pinkston Drive, Sighthill. By the *City Architect*, 1971–2. The most distinctive of the small brick schools in this scheme. Lunettes along the low front block and three white-weatherboarded funnels along the taller back one.

SPRINGBURN PRIMARY AND NURSERY SCHOOLS, 48 Gourlay Street. The Gourlay Street Public School of 1873–5 by *David Thomson*. Grey stone with gabled wings, one of them projecting oddly in the middle of the front. Entrance in this angle, gabled with some strapwork. The block facing Crichton Street is by *Thomson & Menzies*, 1894–5.

STOBHILL HOSPITAL, Balornock Road. 1900–4, by *Thomson & Sandilands*. Built as a Poor Law hospital to supplement the Barony Poorhouse at Barnhill (demolished in 1988). It opened with nearly 2,000 beds in twenty-eight red-brick two-storey pavilions of no particular style. At the centre, the excessively tall clock tower, attached to the kitchen and stores, and its rival, the laundry chimney. To their E, fourteen wards in two groups, linked by spine corridors. Between them and the laundry, the CHAPEL, 1902, still looks ecclesiastical though now the assembly hall. Near the S end of the main avenue, the former ADMISSIONS BLOCK (Biochemistry Department); at the N end, the ISOLATION WARD.

w of the entrance, the Medical Superintendent's English-looking house (now the staff dining room), adjacent to the ADMINISTRATION AND STAFF ACCOMMODATION BUILDING (converted to a nurses' home in 1931 by *Thomas Somers*). Five plain storeys, with a little French Renaissance detail as a centrepiece. Behind are the four INFIRM WARDS, 1902; and, to their w, ten cottage WARDS FOR CHILDREN (1903; some enlarged since); and the workshop. Further N, the former NURSES' AND MAIDS' HOME, and the old MOR-

TUARY, like a bay-windowed villa. Outside the grounds (NW), gabled rows of workmen's cottages.

Nothing distinguished among the later buildings: RADIOLOGY DEPARTMENT, 1928 (E of the clock tower); five GERIATRIC WARDS, like elongated bungalows, 1953 (NW corner); PHARMACY, 1961, CLINICAL TEACHING CENTRE, 1968–9, and the bulky red brick theatre suite of 1968–70 by *Cullen, Lochead & Brown*, all E of the main wards.

HUNTERSHILL NURSING HOME (Marie Curie Memorial Foundation), 1 Belmont Road. 1974–6, by *Stanley Peach & Partners*, repeating their design for Edenhill Nursing Home, Hampstead, London. Two storeys of oriel windows in a band across this concrete-frame and glass building catch a view of the distant hills.

SPRINGBURN PARK, Balgrayhill Road. Laid out on the lands of Old Mosesfield and Cockmuir in 1892–5 by the City Engineer, *A. B. McDonald*.

MOSESFIELD, at the N end, was incorporated in 1904–5 as a museum and reading room (although, in 1989, in residential use once more). This modest, inaccurately Tudor villa of grey ashlar was built by James Duncan in 1838 to replace the C18 Mosesfield (built by James Moses) on a new site. Inscribed inside the porch: *David Hamilton Architect 1838*. Gables with strapwork finials, grouped chimneys and angle pinnacles of no historical precedent. Inside, a little simple Perpish detailing. To the r., an arched entrance to the service court.

WINTER GARDEN, S of Mosesfield. 1899–1900, by *Simpson & Farmer*, hothouse builders, in conjunction with *William Temple* of the Temple Ironworks. Funded by the Reids, proprietors of the Hydepark Works. Large but not elaborate; just an elegant arched cast-iron and glass roof on mild steel girders above low brick walls. Gallery all round on cast-iron columns. Four propagating houses at r. angles.

COLUMN, at the junction of the main avenues, originally part of a fountain in Balgray Pleasure Ground (where the sports hall now stands in Springburn Road). Mannerist Ionic capital with female heads, a unicorn on top.

STATUE, at the E end of the main avenue, by *Goscombe John*, 1903; a bronze figure of James Reid of the Hydepark Works holding plans and papers. On the plinth, reliefs of female figures with dedicatory inscriptions.

ELECTRICITY SUBSTATION, 136 Flemington Street. For Glasgow Corporation Electricity Department, 1906. A tall red brick block with round-headed windows.

SPRINGBURN STATION, Atlas Road. A neat little classical building of 1885 by *James Carsewell*, Chief Engineer of the City of Glasgow Union Railway.

QUEEN STREET STATION RAILWAY TUNNEL starts just W of Pinkston Road. Its entrance is as it was completed in 1842 (though the Queen Street end was cut back when the station was enlarged in 1878–80). A double-track tunnel on a 1-in-46 gradient, with a single ventilation point.

DESCRIPTIONS

The centre

Springburn Cross, with its familiar tenement arrangement, has been swept away in the path of a raised expressway that has scattered the neighbourhood and its churches and public buildings into a new pattern redolent of a 1960s New Town. The centre, deliberately moved N, now huddles in the declivity between this major road and the raised Atlas Road. It consists of just a short traffic-free stretch of the old Springburn Road (SPRINGBURN WAY), with only a few C19 buildings left on the W side. On the E side, the church, health centre, sports hall and shopping centre are all very dull stuff of the 1980s. Of the C19 buildings, the only one worth singling out is the Italianate Nos. 563–7 (TRUSTEE SAVINGS BANK), with a big bracketed cornice and some nice Quattrocento-style carving. Opposite, the entrance to a SHOPPING CENTRE of the usual inarticulate kind, totally enclosed in walls of brown brick and with only a short row of shops to bring it down to the scale of the street; by the *Cunningham Glass Partnership*, 1980–1. At the entrance, a polished granite CO-OPERATIVE DRINKING FOUNTAIN of 1902 by *Scott & Rae* of Glasgow, moved from outside the former Cowlairs Co-Operative Society, the long late C19 building further S, on the curve of the street beneath the expressway.

Further SW, a few other reminders of the old village, including the station, library, public hall, one or two schools, and the former North British Locomotive Company offices (*see* Public Buildings, above). On Springburn Road, the former FIRE STATION, 1893, like a plain tenement except for the city arms in the pediment. To the W, in KEPPOCHHILL ROAD, the long brick sheds of the former CORPORATION TRAM DEPOT (1893–4, by *William Clark*, with, behind, an electricity generating station built in 1898 for the experimental electrification of the Mitchell Street to Springburn route) and a wall of red sandstone tenements. To the E, at the E end of FLEMINGTON STREET, the lonely ornamental gateway (probably built in 1885) of the demolished HYDEPARK WORKS.

Springburn E of Springburn Road

Pass under the flyover N of the shopping centre and you are in BALGRAYHILL ROAD, once characterized by tenements at the start and C19 villas further up fringing open land, but now part of a big housing scheme of the 1960s which replaced ten big houses with almost 1,000.

There are a few earlier relics. At the bottom of the hill, on the corner with Barclay Street, a block of red sandstone tenements of 1903 by *Beattie & Morton*, with sinuous parapets, prominent chimneys and a corner tower with a curvaceous domical cap, all very Glasgow Style. Further up, just behind the cottage-revival-style houses of the 1980s, at No. 19 BROOMFIELD ROAD, is a fragment of pre-industrial Springburn: BALGRAY or BREEZE'S TOWER built c. 1820 by Moses McCulloch to catch the western panorama. It is a battlemented octagonal belvedere with a taller stairtower sitting on a battlemented one-storey block with bay windows and a little Gothick detail outside and within: all of harled rubble. Further N along Balgrayhill Road, a semi-detached pair of two-storey red sandstone villas (Nos. 140–2) with big canted bay windows. Nothing inside or out, except perhaps the generosity of the bays and the windows tucked up under the eaves, even hints that they are an early work of 1890 by *Charles Rennie Mackintosh*, whose client was his uncle.

Following the contours of the steep bank between Balgrayhill Road and Springburn Road, a long chain of six-storey blocks, their continuous decks at first- and third-floor levels opening into a complicated system of split-level homes, and linked by bridges and staircase towers in the manner of their much larger model, Park Hill Estate in Sheffield. At the N end, further up the slope, shorter parallel blocks, also linked. In sudden contrast, four sheer towers rise from the summit of the hill to twenty-five and twenty-six storeys, their height and slenderness accentuated by ribbed cladding (of the early 1980s) in diminishing shades of burnt orange and olive green, which conceals the dark and light grey bands of the *Reema* panel construction. This was Glasgow's first scheme incorporating deck-access blocks: 1964–8, by *A. G. Jury* (City Architect). It houses 3,000 people.

Springburn W *of Springburn Road*

HAWTHORN STREET, with its red sandstone tenements, is the main artery through the W part of Springburn, now almost divorced from the rest by the expressway. On either side of it, pockets of public housing.

To the N in CARRON STREET, some three-storey flats set round four fifteen-storey blocks for the S.S.H.A., by their Chief Technical Officer, *Harold Buteux*, 1961–4. Concrete-frame, clad in brown and yellow brick, except at the corners, which are formed by glazed balconies. Further W in CARRON PLACE, three nine-storey blocks, grey and dark grey concrete in a jazzy pattern. By *Concrete (Scotland) Ltd* for the Corporation, 1964–6. St Aloysius Primary School (*see* Public Buildings, above) is part of this development.

To the S of Hawthorn Street, beyond the slum clearance tenements of 1933, the FERNBANK scheme, poised like a fortress on the edge of a hill. Five- to six-storey deck-access blocks follow the contours of the hill and are linked by utilitarian concrete decks and slatted stairtowers. Built in a system of pinkish concrete panels by *Mitchell Camus Ltd*, 1971–6, on the site of Heiton's model village (*see* above). To be rehabilitated and, no doubt, disguised (1989).

OUTER AREAS

Balornock

Apart from a fringe of terraced villas and tenements (built speculatively between 1892 and 1899) which face Springfield Park from BROOMFIELD ROAD, Balornock consists of a large scheme of predominantly late 1920s Corporation houses. In the N part, round BALGRAYBANK STREET, plain concrete-block tenements. In the S, and on a freer layout with gardens, cottage flats, harled and with brick trim like those at Knightswood etc.

The RED ROAD FLATS, notorious for their height, their cost 113 and their problems, rise abruptly out of this sea of cottages and tenements, an island of awesomely tall, closely packed slabs and towers. Designed in 1962 by *Sam Bunton & Associates* for the Corporation, here is, according to Mr Bunton, housing that is no longer domestic architecture but 'public building without airs and graces'. Yet its very scale cannot fail to impress and the coloured steel cladding (added to some blocks in 1982) in red, blue and ochre gives a glamour originally lacking. Into the scheme's 8·7 ha ($21\frac{1}{2}$ acres) are squeezed nearly 4,700 (the population of a small town like Dingwall); for its date, though, this was not uniquely populous. The towers were, however, at that time the tallest residential blocks in Europe: two slabs of 26–28 storeys, four point blocks and two tower blocks of 31 storeys, constructed, for the first time in Glasgow, not with concrete but with a steel frame and asbestos cladding panels (since replaced).

The promised speed and cost-effectiveness of this system proved illusory: the first block took two years (1964–6), not twenty weeks, to complete, the whole scheme nearly seven. Economies meant underprovision of lifts and communal facilities. Bad planning, with a concentration of flats of the same size in individual blocks, led to vandalism in the two blocks with the largest flats. Declared unfit in 1980, they were converted for mostly student and executive use in 1981 (10 Red Road) and for the Y.M.C.A. in 1983 (33 Petershill Drive).

W of Red Road flats, off EDGEFAULD ROAD, four parallel stone terraces of one- and two-storey cottages (FOYERS, EASTCROFT, YOUNG TERRACES and EDGEFAULD PLACE) built *c.* 1872 by the Glasgow Workmen's Dwelling Company, possibly for local railway workers. Further N up Edgefauld Road, back into the housing scheme, then just to its S, two isolated point blocks of 26 storeys in WELLFIELD ROAD (1966–9, by *Reema (Scotland) Ltd*) overlook Springburn's centre from this steep slope.

Colston

A sandstone quarrying settlement that failed to develop as a
suburb. When the church was built (*see* Colston Wellpark
Church, above), the land around it, now mostly allotments,
was intended for housing, but only the handful of villas in
EVERARD DRIVE materialized.

Covering the hill, Colston Secondary School (*see* above) and a
compact scheme of British Iron and Steel Federation prefabricated houses of *c.* 1945.

Sighthill

A mixed development (1964–9) of ten twenty-storey slab blocks,
a five-storey deck-access block and some single- and two-
storey houses built on the 'soda wastes' of the St Rollox Chemical Works (*see* Royston) between Sighthill Cemetery (*see*
Churches, above) and the main railway line. A singularly
unpropitious site, since landscaped by *James Cunning, Cunningham & Associates* into SIGHTHILL PARK (*c.* 1987), with
broad sweeps of grass threaded through it and a mock henge
monument on the summit to the s. From a distance the scheme,
with its slab blocks ranged in parallel, resembles the Utopian
illustration that no doubt was in the architect's mind. Close
to, the Brutalism of the concrete construction by *Crudens
Ltd* and *Truscon* is revealed: hammered concrete panels, huge
pebble aggregate and slatted concrete screens to the drying
areas. (For the scheme's churches and schools, *see* above.)

Opposite, on the E side of SPRINGBURN ROAD, the ST
ROLLOX RAILWAY WORKS (Nos. 130–40), built for the
Caledonian Railway Company in 1856–7 but completely
rebuilt in the 1880s under the direction of *Dugald Drummond*
to the designs of *Robert Dundas*. Behind a long office block of
1887 along Springburn Road (Nos. 130–40), red and white
brick sheds with impressively large amounts of glazing supported on cast-iron columns. Just s of the works lies Royston
(*q.v.*).

CARNTYNE AND ROBROYSTON

Before the First World War these lands, which in the Middle
Ages formed part of the prebendal estate of Barlanark, with its
country seat at Provan Hall (Easterhouse), were all rough open
country, studded with partly silted lochs, such as the surviving
Hogganfield Loch, and scattered with small settlements at
Riddrie (a few villas), Smithycroft, Hogganfield (with a church),
and Provanmill (the site of the prebendal mill). There were a
number of farms, originally feued by the Town Council, which
had bought the estate in 1667, and a few country houses (Barlanark, Barmulloch, Carntyne, Gartcraig, Lethamhill), built after
the Council sold it again 100 years later. There was also a sprink-

ling of industry: clay pits and associated brick and tile works at Robroyston, bleachworks at Hogganfield, a distillery at Provanmill, and an abandoned colliery at Carntyne, where coal was in production from 1600 and which was one of Glasgow's chief sources of supply until 1875. Associated with the Monkland Canal (which ran through the area until it was drained in 1972) was a dock on the Blackhill Locks and Incline.

Public housing began to spread across the countryside in 1920, when the Corporation's first scheme (one of the first three in Glasgow) was begun at Riddrie. It was followed at the end of the 1920s by another at Carntyne to the S, in the 1930s by schemes at Blackhill and Provanmill, and after the Second World War by tenements and houses at Barmulloch, Cranhill, Ruchazie, Garthamlock and Barlanark. Beyond these schemes, right out to the N E city boundary, lie open farmland and country parks. To the E lies Easterhouse (*q.v.*), physically almost indistinguishable from the other schemes but conceived as a self-sufficient township.

CHURCHES

ALL SAINTS (R.C.), Broomfield Road. 1969–71, by *John Stewart*. Just a box, with a few crowsteps to jazz it up.

BALORNOCK NORTH CHURCH, 57 Northgate Road. 1949–50, by *Stewart & Paterson*. Hall rebuilt 1976.

BARLANARK GREYFRIARS CHURCH, Edinburgh Road and Hallhill Road. A hall church by *William Nimmo & Partners*, dedicated in 1956 and extended in 1968–70 with an octagonal conical-roofed addition.

BARMULLOCH CHURCH, Ryehill Road and Quarrywood Road. 1954, by *Noad & Wallace*. Small, grey and harled. Extension to hall by *William Nimmo & Partners*, 1964.

CRANHILL PARISH CHURCH, Bellrock Street. Polygonal yellow brick church of 1963–5 by *P. L. B. Borthwick*, its pleated roof topped by an open-work aluminium spire incorporating a crown motif. The two-storey halls were the original hall church of 1952–4 by *Wylie, Shanks & Wylie*.

GARTHAMLOCK AND CRAIGEND CHURCH, Porchester Street and Balveny Street. Unremarkable hall church by *Ross, Doak & Whitelaw*, dedicated in 1957.

HIGH CARNTYNE CHURCH, 358 Carntynehall Road. 1931–2, by *J. Taylor Thomson*. Much simplified Romanesque style, in New Cumnock brick, with Forest of Dean stone for the dressings and for the facing to the projecting vestibule, porches and window above them. Nave, passage aisles, transepts and raised chancel all with round unmoulded arches and much exposed brick. Large HALLS to the N, 1951–2.

Former HOLY TRINITY (Episcopal), 1014 Cumbernauld Road (now business premises). 1926–7, by *Whyte & Galloway*. Low and lancet-style, in red sandstone.

MILLERSTON UNITED FREE CHURCH, 1545 Cumbernauld Road. 1856. Small, lancet-style with a gabled porch and bell turret.

RUCHAZIE CHURCH, Elibank Street and Milncroft Road. Cheap hall church by *R. W. K. C. Rogerson*, dedicated in 1955.

ST BERNADETTE (R.C.), 361 Carntyne Road. Tiny harled gabled box of 1934 behind high walls. Very simple PRESBYTERY by *Gillespie, Kidd & Coia*, 1952–3.

ST CATHARINE LABOURE (R.C.), 90 Lamont Road, North Balornock. 1952–3, by *R. Fairlie & Partners*, in the Early Christian style preferred by this firm. Harled, with dun brick dressings and a shallow copper roof. Three arched doorways and, inside, a semicircular brick chancel arch and brick aisle piers.

ST ENOCH HOGGANFIELD, 860 Cumbernauld Road. 1927–30 by *Keppie & Henderson*, in red rock-faced sandstone. Looks more of 1900 than 1927, with Art-Nouveauish tracery and a short, slightly battered w bell tower. w aisle with three octagonal piers. Two arches on a circular pier screen the gated E transept. w gallery. Open timber roof and Art-Nouveauish chancel screen furnishings. In the w aisle, the memorial stone (dated 1780) from the St Enoch's Church that stood in St Enoch Square (*see* Saltmarket and St Enoch, above: Streets) until the 1920s. This church is, indirectly, its successor.

ST JUDE (R.C.), 159 Pendeen Road, Barlanark. 1954–6, by *T. S. Cordiner*. Aisleless brick church, with the baptistery in the angle formed by the projecting vestibule. Contemporary presbytery.

ST MARIA GORETTI (R.C.), 259 Bellrock Street, Cranhill. 1954, by *T. S. Cordiner*. A simple brick church with a shallow-pitched copper roof, a slightly angled wall to the sanctuary (richly furnished with marble) and an attached presbytery. Greater presence is given by the church hall neatly grafted on to the E end by *Gillespie Kidd & Coia* in 1966–9. Half an octagon with characteristic stepped brickwork round the entrance and a dramatic top-lit timber roof inside.

ST PAUL PROVANMILL, 48 Greenrig Street. 1948–51. A rare Church of Scotland commission for *T. S. Cordiner*. Brick with shallow-pitched copper roof. Additional halls of 1964.

ST PHILIP (R.C.), Drumlochy Road, Ruchazie. 1954–8, by *Charles Gray* of Edinburgh. Early Christian in red and beige brick with pantiles, a short campanile and an arcaded loggia linking sacristies and presbytery. Inside, simple concrete arches and exposed brick transformed by an overwhelming display of popular taste, the hectic STAINED GLASS and MURALS of 1968 by *Thomas Walsh*.

ST PHILOMENA (R.C.), 1255 Royston Road, Provanmill. 1939–40, by *Maxwell, Stewart & Maxwell*. Traditional design, with a Gothic window in the main gable.

ST THOMAS THE APOSTLE (R.C.), Smithycroft Road. 1954–7, by *T. S. Cordiner*. Brick, with a relief of Doubting Thomas on the gable wall looking down Cumbernauld Road. Sub-Gothic window surrounds and very 1950s marble panelling in the sanctuary. The baptistery curves out from the vestibule.

SOUTH CARNTYNE CHURCH, 538 Carntyne Road. 1935–6, by *Miller & Black*. Still in the Free-Style Gothic popular about 1900, but much pared down. Brick with red sandstone dressings. Aisleless, but with pointed shallow arches to broad transepts and chancel. Nice Arts and Crafts-style open timber roof. Wing of halls behind.

PUBLIC BUILDINGS

RIDDRIE LIBRARY, 1026 Cumbernauld Road. 1935–8, by *Thomas Somers* (City Engineer). The first permanent library to be built in a council housing scheme and intended as a model for later ones. Stripped Georgian two-storey centre-piece; splayed back from it, wings (reading room and junior library) with long narrow windows. All of brick, with a hipped slate roof. Between the wings, the flat-roofed lending library. Glass screens originally divided the departments; they were removed in the 1970s.

VOGUE BINGO, 654 Cumbernauld Road. The former Riddrie Picture House, by *J. McKissack & Son*, opened 1936–8 as one of George Singleton's Vogue chain. A cream tiled front with the familiar 1930s cinema curves.

BARMULLOCH COLLEGE OF FURTHER EDUCATION, 168 Rye Road. 1960–4, by *D. Harvey, A. Scott & Associates*. Cleanly detailed blocks of various heights, with a partly exposed concrete frame, glass curtain walling and decorative tiled panels.

CRANHILL SECONDARY SCHOOL, 40 Startpoint Street. 1966, by *Keppie, Henderson & Partners*. A large comprehensive school tightly organized by a formal composition. Tall blocks march down the central axis, with lower ones ranged each side. The buildings themselves have strong vertical mullions and horizontal brick bands. An assertive group when seen from Edinburgh Road below.

EASTMUIR SCHOOL FOR MENTALLY HANDICAPPED CHILDREN, 211 Hallhill Road. By *Boswell, Mitchell & Johnston*, completed in 1963. Against a background of trees, low brick and glass-walled blocks, including the hall with a pleated roof.

GARTHAMLOCK SECONDARY SCHOOL, 43 Craigievar Street. By *Ninian Johnston* of *Boswell, Mitchell & Johnston*, c.1955. An extensive group of flat-roofed blocks of different heights and with a variety of claddings (predominantly blue), strung together by covered walkways. On the same site and by the same architect, the similar WOODCROFT PRIMARY, 5 Findochty Street, of 1958.

QUEENSLIE PRIMARY SCHOOL, 5 Horndean Crescent. By *A. Buchanan Campbell*, 1957–9. Low red brick blocks with weatherboarding and an expressive boilerhouse chimney.

ST ANDREW'S SECONDARY SCHOOL, 47 Torphin Crescent. 1954–7, by *Keppie, Henderson & Gleave*. The usual rendered and curtain-walled blocks, here on a very large scale.

ST MARTHA'S PRIMARY SCHOOL, 85 Menzies Road. By *Gratton & McLean*, 1950–3. Long, low and still with pre-war styling.

ST MODAN'S PRIMARY SCHOOL. *See* Descriptions, below: Garthamlock.

ST THOMAS'S PRIMARY SCHOOL, Smithycroft Road. 1930–1, by the *City Education Office*. The usual stripped classical style in brick and stone. One-storey administration building linked by the hall to two storeys of classrooms with open corridors.

SMITHYCROFT SECONDARY SCHOOL, Smithycroft Road. By *A. G. Jury* (City Architect), 1967–75. A curious, eclectic design. The expensive finishes and enterprising details have a strong period flavour. Three main blocks, clad in dark and light blue vitreous panels, plus a brick gym and swimming pool. Circular classroom block and, within its circular central courtyard, the circular assembly hall, lit from the base of a pleated tent-like roof and, artificially, from behind slatted wall screens. The main staircase, with elegant handrail, flies in two unsupported curves.

WOODCROFT PRIMARY SCHOOL. *See* Garthamlock Secondary School, above.

BARLINNIE PRISON, Lee Avenue, Smithycroft Road. 1880–6. Built for 1,000 prisoners, to relieve the two existing Glasgow prisons and those of local towns. Declared a general prison for Scotland in 1882. The four-storey stone blocks, each for 200 inmates, were linked by corridors in 1890. A chapel was finished in 1893, a cell block for short-term prisoners in 1894.

LIGHTBURN HOSPITAL, 932 Carntyne Road. Only the lodge remains of the Infectious Diseases Hospital of 1893–6 by *James Thomson*. The rest was rebuilt as a geriatric hospital in 1964–8, with low grey brick wards round a garden, designed by the Western Regional Health Board's architect, *R. T. Cunningham*.

WALLACE MONUMENT, by Robroyston Mains Farm Cottages, Robroyston Road. Granite Celtic cross of 1900 raised, according to the inscription, 'to mark the site of the house in which the hero of Scotland was basely betrayed and captured' in 1305. To the NE, at the junction of Robroyston Road and Langmuirhead Road, WALLACE'S WELL, a simple stone well, traditionally associated with Wallace.

DESCRIPTIONS

Barlanark

The first of a series of post-war housing schemes spread along the E boundary which also included Barmulloch, Garthamlock, Cranhill, Ruchazie and Queenslie Industrial Estate (*see* below). Plans were passed in 1946 for 2,311 large four- or five-apartment houses, mostly in four-storey tenements, centred on the wooded grounds that surrounded *David Hamilton*'s Scottish vernacular-style Barlanark House (1822) until it was demolished in the 1970s. The tenements, like those on the neighbouring estates, are rendered with long projecting brick balconies. Those around CALVAY ROAD have been refurbished and restyled as a co-operative venture, with balconies converted to bay windows and folksy lean-to porches added by *McGurn, Logan, Duncan & Opfer*, 1983–6.

Barmulloch

The largest of the post-1945 housing schemes in this part of Glasgow, and interesting because it incorporates a large number of houses of experimental construction, built by a variety of contractors. The plans for a scheme of over 2,000 houses for more than 7,000 people on 372 acres (150·6 ha) were submitted to the Corporation by the Scottish Housing Group (an organization of large contractors) in 1948. Whatever the form of construction (steel panel or pre-cast concrete panel, steel frame or concrete frame, no-fines concrete etc.), the overall impression is of flat-fronted semi-detached or terraced cottages of very simplified design, with rendered walls and (mostly) shallow-pitched roofs, in an almost treeless layout. The timber houses, prefabricated of Swedish timber and built by the S.S.H.A. in terraces and pairs round WALLACEWELL CRESCENT, break the monotony with their more picturesque layout and planting. Before they were modernized, the Corporation's foamed-slag houses in RYEHILL ROAD, with their International Modern styling and flat roofs, also struck a different note.

Blackhill and Provanmill

The BLACKHILL slum clearance scheme, built on the Blackhill Golf Course (by *Wm. McNab*, Director of Housing, 1935–6), did little to ameliorate the lot of the tenants, most of whom were moved from the notorious Old Garngad slums (*see* Royston), just to the W. In 1977 half of its flat-fronted, unadorned concrete-block tenements were demolished because unfit. Some of the rest were rehabilitated, 1978–9, and more went in the path of the M8 in 1983.

Contemporary with the Blackhill tenements, the small group of about 300 cottage flats of various designs built by the Corporation at PROVANMILL. The scheme was extended N of Royston Road in 1947 by a number of prefabricated steel houses in ROBROYSTON AVENUE. There is nothing to be seen now of the small C19 settlement.

Carntyne

An inter-war housing scheme of cottages and cottage flats that stretches from Riddrie in the N to the railway line to Lanark

in the s. The first phase opened in 1933: the second, E of
Gartcraig Road, followed it. The most interesting houses are
the approximately 500 'Sunlit Homes' centred on WAR-
RISTON CRESCENT which were built for the Corporation
c. 1929–33 by *John McDonald (Contractors) Ltd, Sunlit Building Company, Glasgow.* They follow the usual elevations of
two-storey flatted cottages with rendered walls. Some have
traditional bay windows, some do not, but all originally had flat
roofs, for which Mr McDonald's 1931 propaganda publication
Modern Housing claimed extravagant advantages (greater sunlight penetration, economy, bolder lines etc.). The flat roofs,
however, proved less wonderful than promised: hipped roofs
have since been added, most on top of the original roof slabs.
The scheme incorporated a hostel at the s edge, in MYRESIDE
STREET. From the front it looks like a terrazzo-faced
tenement, but at the back it has access balconies serving bed-
sitting rooms, and originally there were bathrooms and washhouses in the wings. Another block of flats, for single women,
was built further N at the E end of WARRISTON STREET in
1944–5, by *R. Bradbury,* Director of Housing. This follows a
similar U-shaped plan, but has an International Modern
veneer (cf. the flats at Crathie Drive, Partick), with a roughcast
finish and angle staircase towers with long metal windows
leading to the continuous access balconies.

Cranhill, Ruchazie, Garthamlock

Three large, adjacent post-1945 housing schemes, predominantly
of dismally arranged three-storey roughcast tenements with
projecting brick balconies shared between two flats (a 1950s
development from the type with long shared access
balconies at Pollok etc.). Some round BELLROCK STREET
have been given a Post-Modern veneer (in 1988). In
BELLROCK CRESCENT and FASTNET STREET, Cranhill,
there are a few of the Corporation's experimental foamed-slag
houses, which had International Modern styling until they
were refurbished with pitched roofs and timber windows; and
a school (St Modan's) of 1957 by *W. N. W. Ramsay.* They lie
just N of a mixed development of 1963–6, designed by *G. Bowie*
for *Crudens Ltd:* three eighteen-storey tower blocks, with
brown and grey rendered infill panels, and some five-storey
blocks with some tile hanging. But making a much more
powerful impression than the high-rise blocks are the great
circular concrete water towers on the brow of the hill at Garthamlock. Below them, at CRAIGEND, an informally laid-out
extension to Garthamlock of houses round pedestrian courts,
begun in 1968.

LETHAMHILL HOUSE stands on the golf course just to the W
of Ruchazie, in GARTLOCH ROAD (No. 121). It is an early
C19 three-bay villa with panelled angle pilasters and a shallow
porch of coupled, fluted Greek Doric columns.

Millerston

Millerston lies mostly beyond the city boundary but, just within it, in CUMBERNAULD ROAD, is THE TOWER, a superficially convincing late C19 reproduction of a C17 tower house with crowstepped gables, gablets with ball finials, rounded angles corbelled out square towards the top, and slit windows to light the stair.

Queenslie

QUEENSLIE INDUSTRIAL ESTATE. A brave post-1945 attempt by Scottish Industrial Estates Ltd to bring new industries to the E end. Most of its factories, built to a uniform design by *George Boswell & Partners* in red or yellow brick and render, with flat roofs and taller staircase towers, are now outmoded and sadly abandoned. The estate's rigid grid-plan has been broken by larger factories and their spreading car parks.

Off Blairtummock Road, at the NE corner of the estate, a small pocket of houses built as one of the last phases of Easterhouse in the early 1960s.

Riddrie

The first large post-1919 municipal housing estate, the Kennyhill and Riddrie Housing Scheme, now mature and pleasantly leafy. Designs by *R. W. Horn* (then Chief Architect of the Corporation's Department of Housing), were approved in 1919, and the last house (of 1,074) was built in 1927.

Fanning out from two crescents on the W side of CUMBERNAULD ROAD (itself constructed on a new straight course in 1920), roads lined with semi-detached and terraced cottages (some, like the earliest cottages at Knightswood, gabled and roughcast, others roughcast with brick below, like the cottage flats at Royston) and with well-spaced three-storey brick tenement blocks with bay-windowed red sandstone façades. As an experiment, all the houses had cavity walling and electric servicing. At the end of Leader Street was the scheme's school (derelict in 1989); opposite, on Cumbernauld Road, its churches and the library (*see* Churches and Public Buildings, above).

In LETHAMHILL ROAD, S of Barlinnie Prison, a few stone-built detached and semi-detached villas already there in 1912.

Springboig

An area of Corporation housing, except for the small group of late C19 terraced and semi-detached villas round BUDHILL PARK near Shettleston Station. N of these, a scheme of Corporation tenements (1938–46) centred on a group in LARCHGROVE ROAD and LARCHGROVE AVENUE, quite

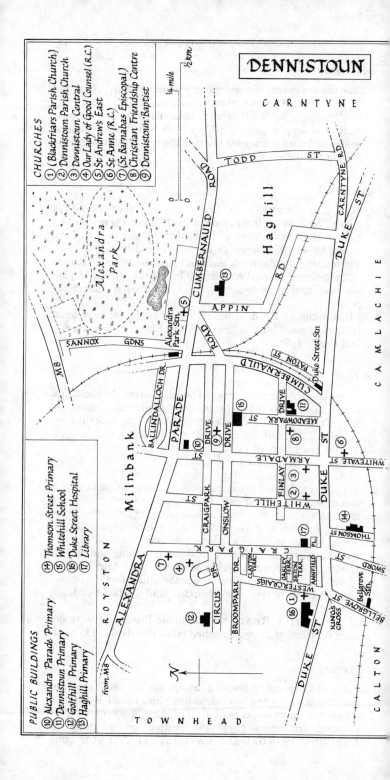

DENNISTOUN

CARNTYNE

Haghill

Alexandra Park

Milnbank

ROYSTON

TOWNHEAD

CALTON

CAMLACHIE

CHURCHES

1. (Blackfriars Parish Church)
2. Dennistoun Parish Church
3. Dennistoun Central
4. Our Lady of Good Counsel (R.C.)
5. St Andrews East
6. St Anne (R.C.)
7. (St Barnabas Episcopal)
8. Christian Friendship Centre
9. Dennistoun Baptist

PUBLIC BUILDINGS

10. Alexandra Parade Primary
11. Dennistoun Primary
12. Golfhill Primary
13. Haghill Primary
14. Thomson Street Primary
15. Whitehill School
16. Duke Street Hospital
17. Library

CUMBERNAULD ROAD
TODD ST
APPIN RD
CARNTYNE RD
DUKE ST
SANNOX GDNS
Alexandra Park Stn.
PATON ST
Duke Street Stn.
BALLINDALLOCH DR.
PARADE
MEADOWPARK ST
DRIVE
ARMADALE ST
WHITEVALE ST
FINLAY ST
WHITEHILL ST
CRAIGPARK
ONSLOW ST
CRAIGPARK DR.
BROOMPARK DR.
CIRCUS DR.
CLAYTON TERR.
OAKLEY TERR.
SETON TERR.
ANNFIELD
WESTERCRAIGS
ALEXANDRA PARADE
SWORD ST
THOMSON ST
Bellgrove Stn.
BELLGROVE ST
KINGS CROSS
DUKE ST
from M8

½ km
¼ mile

N

evidently inspired by Viennese and German examples. An outward-looking square of three-storey tenements, with semi-circular flat-roofed angle towers at the four corners and groups of lower shops, each side marked by slimmer staircase towers. All rendered and painted, and with metal windows.

DENNISTOUN

Dennistoun, planned in the mid-c19 as a moderately priced competitor with the growing western suburbs, rose chiefly on the lands known as The Craigs (from their rocky E–W ridge). Bounded on the E by the Cumbernauld Road, on the S by the Carntyne Loan (later Duke Street), and on the N and W by the Molendinar Burn, they were divided into Easter and Wester Craigs along the line of the present Craigpark. The Merchants' House acquired them in 1650, and by 1700 had divided Wester Craigs into several fields or 'parks' (Craigs Park, Golfhill, Broom Park etc.), which it began to sell off after 1750 to aspiring Glasgow merchants as country estates. Easter Craigs, disposed of in 1700, had by 1738 already been split into three such estates (Whitehill, Craig Park and Meadow Park). The locations of all these are reflected in the street names. Craigs Park, kept by the Merchants' House, became in 1717 a plantation called Fir Park and finally, in 1831, the city's first commercial cemetery, the Necropolis (*see* Townhead, above).

A few streets in the SE corner of the present suburb of Dennistoun, between Duke Street and Gallowgate, had been laid out before 1828 (Whitevale Street, Bluevale Street, Miller (now Millerston) Street) and Whitevale Street had been built up with detached villas. In 1838 John Reid, merchant, bought the lands and villa of Annfield to the W and immediately began to improve the area by paving the Witch Lone (Bellgrove Street), which formed the W boundary of his grounds, and to increase his holdings. Between 1839 and 1844 he bought much of The Craigs and the lands of Bellfield, E of Annfield. In 1851 Reid died, with parts of only one or two streets S of Duke Street feued, and two terraces just N of Duke Street (now Annfield Place) built by a feuar. Alexander Dennistoun quickly assumed Reid's entre-preneurial role and gave his name to the venture. Already the owner of Golfhill and Craigpark, he soon acquired Reid's holding on The Craigs (1853–5), plus, in 1855, Broom Park. *James Salmon*'s ambitious plan of 1854 shows 'an entirely new suburb ... of ornamental villas and self-contained houses', with a generous number of gardens and shrubberies. It bears almost no relation to what was done. The S half of the area was to have been covered by a grid of streets lined with detached villas, interrupted only by a circus and crescent of terraced houses. Terraces were also to form the S boundary. Whitehill Street was intended to be the grand avenue, leading to two stadium-shaped layouts of terraced houses across the whole N half of The Craigs. Circus Drive and Broompark Circus are nominal reminders of these.

Work began in 1857 in Westercraigs (Street) but was not 'proceeded vigorously with' until 1860. The first house there was completed in 1861. At about the same time, Craigpark Street and the terraces linking it with Westercraigs were laid out. Already Salmon's plan had been dispensed with. By 1866 there were seventy houses and more in progress. Only the streets w of Whitehill Street have villas: the rest was developed, starting with Whitehill Street in 1869, more lucratively, with an almost leafless grid of good-quality tenements for the middle classes. (The E end of the city had not proved very attractive to potential villa dwellers.) By the 1890s the entire grid had been established and had been built up as far N as Onslow Drive.

The unfeued parts of Annfield and Bellfield were bought by Dennistoun in 1864 'to secure the amenity ... to the s' and were built up with 'less ornamental houses for artisans', Bellgrove Street, by 1866. On the N edge of the suburb, the City Improvement Trust provided Alexandra Parade, linking it to Townhead. Buildings were slow to appear on the Parade and in the streets off it: the w end, the former Golfhill estate, was not completely developed until after the Second World War.

CHURCHES

Former BLACKFRIARS PARISH CHURCH, 9 Westercraigs. Closed 1983. The successor to the College Church in Blackfriars Street, which in turn was founded in the church of Blackfriars Monastery. By *Campbell Douglas & Sellars*, 1876–7. German Romanesque. E façade of snecked rubble with twin towers, the N one never completed, the s one now lacking its pyramidal stone spire. Centre doorway of three orders with a group of three windows over it. This door and those in the towers have scrolled Romanesque-style ironwork. Plain interior with round-headed windows, a panelled wooden ceiling and an E gallery. – CORONA modelled on the candelabra in Hildesheim Cathedral. – Contemporary ORGAN by *Connacher and Co.*, Huddersfield, its Renaissance-style screen designed by the architects.

MANSE, next door (No. 7), built soon after the church but echoing it only in the round-headed doorway and window, the latter with a very secular relief in the tympanum.

CHRISTIAN FRIENDSHIP CENTRE (former Evangelical Union Church), Meadowpark Street. By *Malcolm Stark Jun.*, 1888–9, in orange Ballochmyle sandstone. Contemporaries described the style as Scottish, shown in the broad diamond-decorated window mullions and in the pedimented doorway enclosed by the large arched window on the gabled entrance façade.

DENNISTOUN BAPTIST CHURCH, Craigpark Drive. 1907–9, by *John M. Crawford*. Free-Style Perp. One huge window flanked by curtailed gallery stairtowers with blind arcading round the tops.

DENNISTOUN CENTRAL CHURCH, Armadale Street. Built as Dennistoun Free Church, 1874, by *James Salmon & Son*. E.E. style. Ugly corner tower (NE), with stone spire and four ungainly pinnacles. Set-back buttresses. Central group of three shafted lancets over a doorway with several orders of shafts. Gallery on cast-iron columns round three sides. Pulpit and communion table later. – ORGAN by *Willis*, brought from Trinity Duke Street Church. Original HALL replaced after 1899 by one of very reduced Gothic style.

DENNISTOUN PARISH CHURCH, Whitehill Street. Built as the Dennistoun United Presbyterian Church in 1869–70, one of the first buildings in Whitehill Street. It looks much earlier. Of smooth cream ashlar, in a very thin lancet style with an over-tall, thin, engaged w tower with tall heavy pinnacles. One simple tall lancet over the w door, plain lancets and no buttresses down the sides. Hall and church officer's house, 1900, by *Miller and Black*.

OUR LADY OF GOOD COUNSEL (R.C.), Craigpark. 1964–6, by *Gillespie, Kidd & Coia*. A quiet neighbour in this suburban street, despite its bold roof rising from low down in one great copper-clad slope, higher towards the altar end. It covers the interior like an awning of timber resting on sturdy concrete columns. Dimly lit interior, with coloured glass windows, randomly set in the vertical surface of the roof, glowing high up. Natural light from a narrow band of windows along the side, from over the gallery, and from the altar end falls obliquely on the fretted timber and patterned brick. Granite altar, font etc. The plan is wedge-shaped, with flights of steps inside, the s one approaching the baptistery, the N one the altar. Along the w side, under the lower roof pitch, a choir gallery above sacristy and confessionals.

ST ANDREW'S EAST, 681–5 Alexandra Parade. 1903–4, by *James Miller*, in an Arts and Crafts interpretation of the late Perp style with a prominent *Westwerk* facing Alexandra Parade. Two sturdy towers, slightly battered and developing at the top into battlemented octagonal bell-chambers clasped by severe octagonal turrets. Between them bridges an arch, making a deep recess in contrast to the subtle modelling of the towers. The arch frames a big window and twin doorways. Perched incongruously above the façade, a square bell turret with wide-eaved roof. The whole composition speaks as much of late medieval castle gateways as of church architecture, though the dramatic central arch may recall Henry Wilson's St Andrew, Boscombe. Simple side elevation of two storeys of windows between buttresses with set-backs. Disappointing interior with no trace of Arts and Crafts-style. Shallow barrel-vault and gallery on three sides. – To the E, the HALL, built before the church (1899) by *James Salmon Jun. and J.G. Gillespie*. Small and low, but with idiosyncratic Art Nouveau Dec details in the end bays.

ST ANNE (R.C.), Whitevale Street. An inventive design of 104 1931–3 by *Jack Coia* of *Gillespie, Kidd & Coia*, the interior especially successful. The w façade, raised above the street and screened by elaborate wrought-iron gates, looks distinctly Italian – a thorough hybrid of Early Christian and early Renaissance styles: pedimented, with volutes screening the aisle roofs, an oculus and three round-arched portals. Concrete frame with walls of red Accrington brick, also used decoratively to complete the volutes begun in stone, round the doorways, and, like Roman tile, in arches rising above the tall round-headed side windows. Stone is restricted to the pediment coping, broken by an Eric Gill-like crucifix, and the heavy arches of the portals, encrusted with interlace ornament and a Madonna and Child keystone, carved by *Archibald Dawson*. Red tile roofs, even on the portals.

The plan is also of Byzantine type: square (allowing an unimpeded view of the altar) with short brick piers at the angles forming the nave into a Greek cross, and screening the Lady Chapel (NE), sacristies (SE) and confessionals (NW, SW). The nave extends w by three more bays, with piers separating it from narrow passage aisles. W choir gallery over the narthex. Shallow three-sided apse, with a classical baldacchino. The brick piers and pulpit are subtly polychrome. Stone capitals with emblems such as the Agnus Dei and Tree of Life, inset stone Stations of the Cross, shaded and gilded; all carved by *Archibald Dawson*. Wide, white groin-vaults. – STAINED GLASS in the circular and two adjacent windows designed by *Charles Baillie* and made by *Guthrie & Wells*.

PRESBYTERY linked to the church and with a view of its interior from an upstairs room. In the same red brick and with an arch of Roman tile over the entrance bay. In the tympanum, a stone relief of vines and a cross as the keystone.

ST BARNABAS (Episcopal), Craigpark (now Potters' Trust Christian Centre). By *Whyte & Galloway*, 1935–6. Tiny and brick-faced.

PUBLIC BUILDINGS

DENNISTOUN PUBLIC LIBRARY, 2a Craigpark. By *J. R. Rhind*, 1903–5. Nicely scaled Baroque façade in cream sandstone, the end bays emphasized with the main entrance (N) and a small dome at the s corner. Interior (originally with a top-lit reading room) completely remodelled in 1967–8 by *Robert Rogerson & Philip Spence*.

ALEXANDRA PARADE PRIMARY SCHOOL, 540 Alexandra Parade. Opened in 1897. Gabled and domestic red sandstone three-storey Board school by *McWhannell & Rogerson*. A hint of the Arts and Crafts style in the asymmetry of the entrance bay, and of Art Nouveau in the relief decoration.

DENNISTOUN PRIMARY SCHOOL, 36 Meadowpark Street. Opened as Dennistoun Public School in 1883. By *James Salmon & Son*. Of grey sandstone, C17 in style. Large mullioned and transomed windows, those in the gable end bays with swan-necked pediments. The three-bay entrance arcade leads into a central hall (here, unusually, filled by staircases), an early variation on the standard plan devised for the Glasgow School Board. Classrooms down the sides.

GOLFHILL PRIMARY SCHOOL, 1–11 Circus Drive. 1902–3, by *A. N. Paterson*. Another three-storey red sandstone Board school (*see* the usual well-carved lettering), this one slightly Baroque, with a concentration of motifs in the centre (blocked rustication, wavy cornices, giant keystones). The janitor's house has a circular projection with tiny cupola.

HAGHILL PRIMARY SCHOOL, Marwick Street. 1902–4, by *A. Lindsay Walker*. Plain three-storey red sandstone Board school with gables and pilasters.

THOMSON STREET PRIMARY SCHOOL, Thomson Street. The original block, at the corner of Reidvale Street, by *James Thomson* of *Baird & Thomson*, opened in 1875. Plain Italianate, with slightly projecting end bays and entrance bay, the latter intended to terminate in a tower. Matching N extension by *Frank Burnet*, 1884.

WHITEHILL SCHOOL, Onslow Drive. 1973–9, by *Baron Bercott & Associates*, in conjunction with the Director of Architecture, Strathclyde Regional Council. Bulky brick envelopes to classrooms and sports hall.

DUKE STREET (formerly Eastern District) HOSPITAL, 253 Duke Street. By *A. Hessell Tiltman*, 1901–4. Facing the street, the red sandstone façade of the administration block, French Renaissance in style. Behind, the wards arranged in three long wings radiating from a round central tower with conical roof, and a single, separate psychiatric wing. All of red brick.

ALEXANDRA PARK, Alexandra Parade. Laid out on the bleak Wester Kennyhill by the City Improvement Trust, 1866–70. Extended in 1874–5, 1891 (when Easter Kennyhill was added) and 1903. At the w entrance in Sannox Gardens, an octagonal stone LODGE by *James Miller*. At the main entrance, a cast-iron DRINKING FOUNTAIN, a good example of a mass-produced C19 type; and N of it the MACFARLANE FOUN- 87 TAIN, designed as a centrepiece for the Glasgow International Exhibition of 1901 by *D. W. Stevenson* and made of cast-iron by *Walter Macfarlane & Co.'s Saracen Foundry*. The top is an open version of the Choragic monument of Lysicrates, crowned with entwined dolphins; the base has four seated classical female figures (Art, Literature, Science, Commerce), all exceedingly sculptural. Finely detailed bronzed reliefs of flora and fauna on each side. Of the 1884 plan by *John Carrick* (City Architect) for feuing the edges of the park, only a small section E of the main entrance still bears any resemblance.

PERAMBULATION

DUKE STREET links Dennistoun with the city centre. Originally called the Carntyne Loan, it stretched no further w than

Drygate until, in 1793, it was connected with George Street. Our perambulation begins towards the E end of the junction known as King's Cross, on the W boundary of the planned suburb. Here, separated by a strip of gardens from the N side of Duke Street, is ANNFIELD PLACE, the only part of Reid's proposed development to have been built before his death in 1851. Two modest terraces of two-storey stone houses, restrainedly Italianate. Four were slightly altered for shops, c. 1931.

S of Duke Street lie the tenements of Dennistoun's artisan development, many (in red sandstone) not built until the 1890s. All those between Bellgrove Street and Sword Street have gone. Amid those that remain, worth visiting are St Anne's Church and Thomson Street Primary School (*see* Churches and Public Buildings, above) and, in WHITEVALE STREET, what may be the only surviving villa of this neighbourhood's early development (i.e. of before 1828). This and the adjoining building (probably built c. 1880 as a school) is now a community centre. In front, a bronze figure group by *Stan Bowner*, 1980, symbolizing the community.

Leading N from King's Cross, WESTERCRAIGS is the earliest street of the planned middle-class suburb. At the S end, the former Blackfriars Church and Manse (*see* Churches, above). Then, on the W side, a number of middle-sized coarsely Italianate villas, the first of them dating from 1861. Some are semi-detached, one has a tower. Off the E side open four contemporary terraces facing each other across strips of garden. Those looking N, SETON TERRACE and CLAYTON TERRACE, are small with tripartite windows; those facing S, OAKLEY TERRACE and the one in BROOMPARK DRIVE, have bay windows. The latter has Romanesque touches of gabled porches and zigzag. More villas in CRAIGPARK and just off it in CIRCUS DRIVE and ONSLOW DRIVE. None is exceptional, though all contribute to the area's character. Largest is HIGHFIELD of c. 1869, on the corner of Broompark Drive (No. 7), its tall entrance tower of a Franco-Flemish cast. Two notable insertions have been made into Craigpark itself: at the S end the Public Library, at the N end the R.C. church, Our Lady of Good Counsel (*see* Churches and Public Buildings, above). Opposite the church, the French Renaissance façade of the originally private DENNISTOUN BATHS, 1883.

Further E, the tight grid of plain but substantial middle-class tenements, and their associated churches and schools, starts with Whitehill Street, the first street of this phase to be begun (1869). The earliest tenements are of cream sandstone; the later ones, mostly towards the N, are of red, that is post-1890. Maintaining the tradition in CRAIGPARK DRIVE, long uniform rows of red sandstone rubble Corporation tenements by *William McNab* (Director of Housing), 1938–43. Just off Alexandra Parade, in MEADOWPARK STREET, is the PARADE CINEMA, of 1920–1 by *McKay Stoddart*, with honed classical detail on the façade (the main feature is the projection box) and within. Much later, and breaking significantly into the grid, is the bulk of Whitehill School (*see* Public Buildings).

The E end of ALEXANDRA PARADE is the earliest part and is still residential. C19 tenements here and in the streets to the N (MILNBANK) are intermixed with C20 public housing: concrete-block tenements of 1936–9 by *William McNab* (Director of Housing), arranged in an unusually picturesque oval in BALLINDALLOCH DRIVE; and later ones (1946–51) with red sandstone facing by *Ronald Bradbury*, McNab's successor, to the NE in SANNOX GARDENS, overlooking Alexandra Park (*see* above). Bradbury acknowledges the International Modern style in flat roofs and cantilevered balconies. The related PRINCESS COURT to the S was built as a single women's hostel.

The W end of Alexandra Parade is known as Tobacco Land from its dominating tobacco factories and warehouses. Most impressive, the huge W. D. & W. O. WILLS factory, designed in 1946–53 by *Imperial Tobacco Company's Engineers' Office*. A hollow brick block (its courtyard filled in up to first-floor level), with a central service tower, corner towers and a grand entrance tower. It looks as if it could have been designed a decade earlier. On the opposite side, GALLAHERS' big blue and silver distribution shed of 1980–3 by *Building Design Partnership*.

HAGHILL, E of the Cumbernauld Road, has the greatest concentration of public housing, bleak slum clearance tenements that replaced a mixture of industry and tenements in the mid-1930s.

CALTON AND CAMLACHIE

Among the pre-war council schemes and the spreading suburban houses with impromptu green spaces established under the Glasgow Eastern Area Renewal (G.E.A.R.) project, can be found a few relics of Glasgow's first C18 suburb and of the intense industry that invaded it in the C19; but there is nothing of the centre of the village of Calton that gave the larger area its name. On weekdays the streets just E of Glasgow Cross are unnaturally silent; at weekends the Barras (Barrows) market (which occupies some of the remaining industrial buildings) erupts.

The present Calton developed during the C18 in three distinct parts: the cotton-manufacturing village itself, where feuing began falteringly in 1706 and more vigorously after 1731; the eastward spread of the ancient Gallowgate, which had reached what is now Barrack Street *c.* 1770; and a new suburb between the village (centred just E of Bain Street) and the burgh boundary. By 1788 Old and New Calton reached as far as the hamlet of Mile-End (just N of Bridgeton Cross). In 1817 Calton with Bridgeton (*q.v.*)

became a Burgh of Barony (population about 15,000). It was annexed to Glasgow in 1846.

Glasgow's first move beyond the burgh boundary was the planting of St Andrew's Church in 1739 just E of the Saltmarket. The first proposals for a suburb here (St James's Square, 1771–3) foundered. Instead, in 1780, Archibald Paterson established Charlotte Street, with strict feuing conditions to ensure uniform design and to keep out the industry that had polluted the burgh. About the same time, Graham Square was laid out much further E, but it failed because of its isolation; by 1817 the council had bought the spare lots for the cattle market. St Andrew's Square, planned in 1786, had also been infiltrated by industry, pressing from both sides, by the 1820s. Great Hamilton Street (now London Road) and Monteith Row, feued from 1812, and London Street, begun in 1823–4, had relatively short lives as fashionable streets, despite their proximity to Glasgow Green, which was made into a positive attraction after 1826, though they remained respectable until the late C19.

From c. 1800, textile mills, chemical works, and breweries, served by the Molendinar and Camlachie Burns, intensified the industrial activity in Calton and to its NE in Camlachie (the site in the C18 both of coal extraction and of several gentlemen's seats). After 1840 carpet weaving began to thrive around Mile-End, and iron and steel works, foundries and engineering shops introduced a new degree of squalor. By 1866 the City Improvement Trust felt bound to drive Bain Street and Claythorn Street through Calton's closes. More slum clearance was done in the early 1930s. For at least a decade the area round the Green has been blighted by proposals for the eastern part of Glasgow's ring road, and at the time of writing demolition of significant buildings has still not been halted. Elsewhere much of the decaying industry has been swept away under G.E.A.R. (1976–87), leaving only fragments of the C19 behind.

CHURCHES

BRIDGETON BAPTIST CHURCH (now a warehouse), 82 Orr Street. By *Miller & Black*, 1905–6. A freely Perp-style church typical of that date.

CALTON NEW PARISH CHURCH, Bain Square, Bain Street. Built as St Luke's Established Church, the parish church of West Calton. 1836–7, by *James Wylson*. Gutted by fire in 1924; the upper walls and interior reconstructed by *J. M. Munro & Son*, 1925–6. Painted ashlar façade with pilastered centrepiece, neo-Greek but of oddly attenuated proportions. Two-storey rubble side elevations. Box-like galleried interior enlivened by two glowing STAINED-GLASS windows flanking the organ case at the E end, 1920s replicas of windows made by *C. & W. Summers* in 1890. Realistic portrayals in classical borders of The Woman of Samaria and The Good Samaritan.

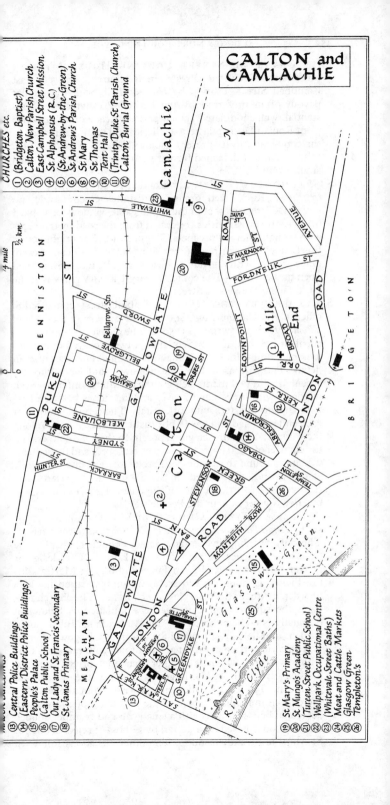

CALTON and CAMLACHIE

CHURCHES etc.
① (Bridgeton Baptist)
② Calton New Parish Church
③ East Campbell Street Mission
④ St Alphonsus (R.C.)
⑤ (St Andrew-by-the-Green)
⑥ St Andrew's Parish Church
⑧ St Mary
⑨ St Thomas
⑩ Tent Hall
⑪ (Trinity Duke St Parish Church)
⑫ Calton Burial Ground

⑬ Central Police Buildings
⑭ (Eastern District Police Buildings)
⑮ People's Palace
⑯ (Calton Public School)
⑰ Our Lady and St Francis Secondary
⑱ St James Primary

⑲ St Mary's Primary
⑳ St Mungo's Academy
㉑ (Tureen Street Public School)
㉒ Wellpark Occupational Centre
㉓ (Whitevale Street Baths)
㉔ Meat and Cattle Markets
㉕ Glasgow Green
㉘ Templeton's

DENNISTOUN

Camlachie

Calton

MERCHANT CITY

BRIDGETON

Mile End

Glasgow Green

River Clyde

N

0   ½ km
0   ¼ mile

EAST CAMPBELL STREET LODGING HOUSE MISSION (originally a United Presbyterian church), 29–35 East Campbell Street. 1863–4, by *Haig & Low*, with the secular flavour often preferred by the United Presbyterians. Substantial, well-modulated Italian palazzo façade of ashlar, with giant Roman Doric pilasters. Galleries and seating removed in the conversion to its present use by *Wylie, Wright & Wylie*, 1932–3. Almost detached former vestries and schoolroom in a similar vein.

ST ALPHONSUS (R.C.), 217 London Road. 1905, by *Pugin & Pugin*. Rock-faced orange sandstone screen façade: no tower. Dec tracery, that in the round gable window formalized into a saltire cross. Aisles concealed from the road by transepts with straight pierced parapets. Stepped buttresses right across the façade, the centre two enclosing an insignificant porch. Nave arcades with fat round polished granite piers. Simplified open timber roof. – The contemporary PRESBYTERY is at the back, facing Stevenson Street.

ST ANDREW-BY-THE-GREEN, Turnbull Street (converted to offices). By *William Paull* and *Andrew Hunter* (masons) and *Thomas Thomson* (wright), 1750–2. The oldest surviving Episcopal church building in Scotland. A two-storeyed domestic-looking composition, Palladian in outline but Baroque in detail. The side as well as the narrower end elevations are accented with pediments belying the orientated interior. Sash windows with lugged architraves and keystones between rusticated giant pilasters without capitals. The central window at each end is arched and has Gibbs rustication. Urn finials along the parapet. C19 half-octagonal porch. In the 1988 conversion, the chancel of 1900 by *J. Stevens* was removed, and the gallery, which ran round three sides and broke forward in a semicircle at the W end, dismantled (in store). – FURNISHINGS also removed. PULPIT and part of the chancel STAINED GLASS by *Alex Walker* now in the People's Palace.

ST ANDREW'S PARISH CHURCH, St Andrew's Square. 1739–56, by *Allan Dreghorn*, with *Mungo Naismith* as master mason. The only building in Glasgow intact enough to display the taste and affluence of her 'Tobacco Lords'. The design is metropolitan, borrowed from James Gibbs's St Martin's-in-the-Fields, London, and in scale and sophistication marks a new departure for Scottish classical churches. The church predates the square around it (*see* Perambulation 1, below); it originally stood, moated by the Molendinar Burn, amid gardens and fields just beyond the burgh of Glasgow.

Hexastyle portico of unfluted Corinthian columns across the whole W front, which is simpler than that of St Martin's. Rococo cartouche with Glasgow's motto in the steep-sided pediment. The tall, slender steeple rises from the body of the church immediately behind the portico, topped by a tall, octagonal bell-chamber with a small cap and trumpet-shaped finial. It too is based on a design by Gibbs – a rejected one for St Mary-le-Strand, London. The other elevations follow St

Martin's very closely, with segmental-headed windows above rectangular ones, all with Gibbs rustication between giant pilasters. E window Venetian.

Sumptuous interior, also based on St Martin's, and finished with lavish rococo plasterwork by *Thomas Clayton*. The dirtiness of the C19 stained glass makes it inappropriately gloomy. Fluted Corinthian columns with tall pedestals and individual entablature blocks, carrying arches cut into the semicircular (rather than elliptical, as at St Martin's) vault, which is panelled in plaster. Gallery round three sides, the mahogany fronts riding between the columns. On the W wall, a magnificent display of plasterwork round the clock.

FURNISHINGS contemporary with the church and also of fine mahogany. – PULPIT of elegant wine-glass type, enriched with carving and reached by a sinuous stair. Its original position is unknown, but there was a matching precentor's desk. – Matching FONT pedestal. – Repewed in 1874 by *Salmon & Son*. – ORGAN. By *Mirrlees* of Glasgow, 1874, divided and enlarged by *Lewis & Co.*, part of the refurbishment of the chancel by *Dr P. Macgregor Chalmers*, 1906. – STAINED GLASS. Mostly by *Adam & Small*, 1874, each window with a plant motif. – Chancel to Dr Runciman † 1872. – By *Stephen Adam*, N side E upper to the Anderson family, 1892; and N side central upper to the Revd E. L. Robertson, 1893.

ST MARY (R.C.), 89 Abercromby Street. By *Goldie & Child*, 1841–2. Classical for the sake of economy, and crudely and unorthodoxly so. No orders except on the projecting porch of 1883–4; just channelled rustication all over the façade, with its two storeys of bleak rectangular windows. Heavy pediment, carved with two angels supporting a cross, and an oblong bell tower above. Tall round-headed windows down each side. Exceptionally broad interior, much altered from the original. Galleries with arcades above them to support a new ceiling inserted in 1865 (the first one collapsed). Pews and cast-iron window frames of *c.* 1896. Sanctuary remodelled *c.* 1870, and refitted with a new altar twenty years later. Walls repainted in a naively illusionistic manner by a Mr *Duffie* in 1926–7, when minor renovations were done by *R. M. Butler*. – ORGAN brought in 1865 from St Mary's Episcopal, which stood in Renfield Street.

PRESBYTERY. Tudorish hoodmoulds and glazing, and the parapet applied by *Cowan & Watson* in 1904 to the once conventional three-storey bay-windowed façade.

ST THOMAS, 790 Gallowgate. 1850. A simple Gothic box with a gabled ashlar façade. Perpish gable window, the rest lancets.

TENT HALL (now Y.M.C.A.), 21 Steel Street. Built in 1876 for the United Evangelical Association, which first met in a mission tent on Glasgow Green in 1874. Cream snecked rubble in an unhistorical Scottish vernacular style.

TRINITY DUKE STREET PARISH CHURCH, 176 Duke Street. Now Kirkhaven Day Centre; built as Sydney Place United Presbyterian Church. 1857–8, by *Peddie & Kinnear*.

Serious Greek façade with two fluted Corinthian columns *in antis*. Large and elaborate rinceau and palmette ornament in the pediment and, on a smaller scale, in the frieze. Prominent antefixae. Interior converted 1975.

CALTON BURIAL GROUND, Abercromby Street. Established by the Calton Incorporation of Weavers in 1786. Extended s in 1822. – MEMORIAL to commemorate the stand made against a reduction in wages in 1787.

PUBLIC BUILDINGS

Former CENTRAL POLICE BUILDINGS, St Andrew's Street. *See* Perambulation 1, below.

Former EASTERN DISTRICT POLICE BUILDINGS, Tobago Street. *See* Perambulation 1, below.

PEOPLE'S PALACE, Glasgow Green. 1893–8, by *A. B. McDonald*, City Engineer, for the recreation and improvement of the inhabitants of Glasgow's East End. Facing N, a palatial range of orange Dumfries-shire sandstone in a pedestrian French Renaissance manner, with mansarded end pavilions and low central dome. The figures are by *Kellock Brown* (Progress with (seated) Science and Art; Shipbuilding; Mathematics, Science, Painting; Sculpture; Engineering; Textiles). Plain interior, formerly with lots of hygienic tiles; now devoted to Glasgow's social history, but originally with reading and recreation rooms on the ground floor, a museum on the first floor, and picture galleries, partly under the dome, along the top. Midway up the staircase, a glazed loggia overlooking the great U-shaped winter garden-cum-concert hall that encloses the back of the building (with its stairtowers by Glasgow's *Department of Architecture*, 1988–90). Four times larger than the museum, the winter garden has a curved roof of steel and glass supported on cast-iron columns close to the perimeter and two shallow transepts forming the side entrances. Set in the glass, four windows from St Ninian's Wynd Church, part of the museum's important collection of STAINED GLASS (and shop and house interiors) preserved from demolished and threatened buildings.

CALTON PUBLIC SCHOOL (now Glasgow College of Printing Annexe), 65 Kerr Street. 1890, by *John Gordon*. Salmon-pink and rock-faced with prominent pavilions (their steep roofs removed). The *Builder* calls it Romanesque, no doubt because of the preponderance of arches.

OUR LADY AND ST FRANCIS SECONDARY SCHOOL, 58–60 Charlotte Street. Closed 1989. The main plain classical block is of 1921–3 by *Thomas Baird*. Behind it, the original school building (pre-1913), stone with a hipped roof. To the N, a simple red brick wing by *Gillespie, Kidd & Coia*, 1950–4. By the same architects, on the site of David Dale's mansion (*see* Perambulation 1, below), a more imaginative addition of 1958–64, its heavily modelled façade in reinforced concrete and blue engineering brick overlooking Glasgow Green. Strong horizontals, the upper two storeys of classrooms boldly cantilevered. The only strong vertical, the recessed stairwell, is accented by the rooftop water tank, angled upward like the cantilevers.

Opposite and until 1989 part of the school, the former ST ANDREW'S R.C. PRIMARY SCHOOL by *J. L. Cowan*, 1896–8. Facing Greendyke Street, the original school of 1855 by *Charles O'Neill* (the City's Assistant Superintendent of Streets and Buildings). An unsophisticated Jacobethan façade with one shaped and one crowstepped gable. Above the single oriel, a relief of a ship, book and globe. Cast-iron Gothic gateway in the railings.

ST ANDREW'S R.C. PRIMARY SCHOOL, Greendyke Street. *See* Our Lady and St Francis Secondary School, above.

ST JAMES PRIMARY SCHOOL, 88 Green Street. 1895, by *Thomson & Sandilands*. The usual red sandstone Board school, the plainness relieved by Gibbs rustication round the first-floor windows.

ST MARY'S PRIMARY SCHOOL, Forbes Street. A large group behind St Mary's R.C. Church (*see* Churches, above), including the main school building (1911–13) and a tall red rock-faced block of former church recreation rooms with ogee-headed windows, by *J. L. Cowan*, 1892–5, facing Orr Street (Nos. 213–229).

ST MUNGO'S ACADEMY, Crownpoint Road. 1972–7, by Glasgow Corporation's *Department of Civic Architecture and Design*. Two big curtain-walled blocks (one single-, one two-storey) strikingly transformed by heavy roof-slabs of polished metal. To the S, the brick and harled gymnasium (1974–5) and, linked to it to the W, the CROWNPOINT SPORTS CENTRE (opened in 1985), including a big shed of profiled metal sheeting and a prominent blue roof.

TUREEN STREET PUBLIC SCHOOL (now Community Industry workshops), Tureen Street. 1875–6, by *John Honeyman*. A restrained Italianate design with pedimented first-floor windows. Second phase (1886) plainer but with a more complicated attic storey. The third phase (1902, by *J. L. Cowan*) has Gibbs rustication round the windows. All in well-matched cream sandstone.

WELLPARK OCCUPATIONAL CENTRE, 120 Sydney Street. Opened in 1867 as Wellpark Institute (the Free Church school). The square corner tower with a domed octagonal belfry is the least successful part of this handsome Italianate design.

WHITEVALE STREET BATHS, Whitevale Street (awaiting conversion in 1989). By *A. B. McDonald* and *W. Sharp* of Glasgow's *Office of Public Works*, 1899–1903. Its long red brick and stone front, more flamboyant than most baths, has an elaborate shaped gable and some nice Baroque details, such as the colonnaded windows. Cast-iron trusses and columns inside.

MEAT AND CATTLE MARKETS, Graham Square, Gallowgate.
The cattle market moved here in 1817 after the failure of
Graham Square as a residential speculation, and the meat
market followed in 1875. On the w side of the square, the
covered MEAT MARKET of c. 1875 by *John Carrick*, City
Architect, constructed of cast-iron and glass; two handsome
Roman Doric entrances with giant coupled columns and pedi-
ments in a stuccoed screen wall. They open into two internal
streets which lead through to two simpler gateways in the
stuccoed wall all along Melbourne Street. At the N end of that
street, the red brick former abattoir. On the N side of Graham
Square, the triumphal arch gateway into the former CATTLE
MARKET and the plain stuccoed Market Hotel, also by
Carrick, who covered over the $3\frac{1}{2}$ acres (1·4 ha) of the market in
1866. The Meat Market is still used; to the NE, a replacement
ABATTOIR (1972) and COLD STORE (1978). Similar gateways set back from Gallowgate in Moore Street, and one in
Bellgrove Street.

GLASGOW GREEN. The medieval Green lay by the Clyde, w
of the present one. By the C17, the expanding city had almost
obliterated it. All the common lands E of the Molendinar Burn
had been sold during the C16, except for the Laigh (Low)
Green. To extend this, the city fathers bought back the
common land parcel by parcel (High Green, Calton or Gallowgate Green, Fleshers' Haugh, King's Park) and laid them
down to grass. By 1730 the 'New Green' extended to 59 acres
(23·8 ha), by 1810 to double that, and, after 1894, to 136 acres
(55 ha). Although serpentine walks and shrubberies were laid
out in 1756, the green was used mainly for grazing, bleaching,
dyeing and washing. By the late C18, it was threatened with
encroachment. In 1793, strips to the w and N were annexed
for roads to the new bridge and a route to the collieries. In
1809 more of it went as a site for the gaol, and in 1812 the city
magistrates cashed in on the East End's growing popularity
by proposing a row of superior houses (Monteith Row).

Protection and improvement of the Green began in 1815,
when, exactly according to the programme devised by *James
Cleland* in 1813, work started on levelling, draining and
turfing; culverting the Molendinar and Camlachie Burns; and
laying gravel paths round the perimeter. Lastly, a carriage
circuit was created in 1827–8, and a road toll and entrance
charge were imposed to ensure the Green's exclusivity. Only
the Low Green remained public, a sheep park ringed with
'pleasant galleries of elms'.

In 1857, to serve the changed population of the by then
industrial East End, the Green became a public park, with an
enclosing belt of trees, flowerbeds, shrubberies and public
amenities, the most ambitious being the People's Palace (*see*
above). In 1899 the last area, Fleshers' Haugh, was drained
for playing fields. The King's Drive, built in 1900 to link
Bridgeton to Hutchesontown via the King's Bridge, divides
these from the rest.

BRIDGES. *See* Crossings of the Clyde and Kelvin, below.

DOULTON FOUNTAIN. A showpiece of yellow terracotta 86 in François I style, designed by *A. E. Pearce* of *Doulton & Co.* (modelling supervised by *W. Silver Frith*) for the Glasgow Exhibition of 1888. Moved here in 1890. Sadly, water no longer spouts from lion masks into the two basins, the upper one sheltering the peoples of the Empire (Australia, South Africa, India, Canada). Above, Scottish, Welsh and English soldiers and a sailor. Reigning over all, Queen Victoria.

DRINKING FOUNTAINS. At the Saltmarket entrance, a sentimental girl with a pitcher by *J. Mossman*, 1881, in memory of Sir William Collins' work for the temperance movement. – At the s end of the People's Palace, a fountain to Hugh McDonald, moved from Paisley in 1880. – N of the People's Palace, a cast-iron Moorish canopy of 1893 to Bailie James Martin.

GLASGOW HUMANE SOCIETY HOUSE, opposite the suspension bridge. 1935–7, in simplified Scottish vernacular style by *J. Thomson King*, successor to the officer's house of 1790, built to succour or shelter victims of drowning.

McLENNAN ARCH. The centrepiece of the façade of *Robert & James Adam*'s Assembly Rooms of 1792, reconstructed by *John Carrick* at the NE end of Greendyke Street when the building made way for the extension of the General Post Office to Ingram Street in 1892; moved here in 1922. The triumphal arch motif, originally with columns rising from a rusticated ground floor and with a tall window in the central arch, is naturally suited for a gateway.

NELSON MONUMENT. 1806, by *David Hamilton* and *A. Brockett* (mason). An obelisk 44 m (144 ft) high on a simple plinth. The first monument in Britain to Nelson's victories. Paid for by public subscription. – To one side, a monument to James Watt, a large boulder erected two centuries after he conceived the idea of steam power while walking on the Green in 1765.

STATUE of James Watt, from the Atlantic Mills, Bridgeton (built 1864, demolished 1966–7), in McPhun's Park, s of King's Drive.

GLASGOW GREEN RAILWAY STATION, Monteith Row. Closed in 1953. Of the station built *c.* 1896 for the Glasgow Central Railway, only the red sandstone surface building with blind arches survives.

WEIR AND PIPE BRIDGE, ST ANDREW'S FOOTBRIDGE. *See* Crossings of the Clyde and Kelvin, below.

PERAMBULATIONS

1. Glasgow Green to Gallowgate

The briefly salubrious suburb round Glasgow Green has left a few significant traces. The most eloquent approach to it is from Saltmarket, where St Andrew's Street frames the façade of St Andrew's Parish Church (*see* Churches, above), a potent symbol of the city's C18 wealth and sophistication.

ST ANDREW'S STREET itself, opened up fifteen years after the church was finished, is now lined with late Victorian buildings. On the S, red sandstone tenements, later variations of those in Saltmarket. On the N, a row of C17-style gables tops the former FAMILY HOME of 1894–6 by *A. B. McDonald* (City Engineer), later converted to police offices and now District Courts. The former CENTRAL POLICE BUILDINGS, also by *McDonald* (1904–8), turn the S corner into St Andrew's Square. Franco-Flemish, in red brick and red sandstone, with big semi-reclining figures of Law and Justice, and a Venetian window lighting the courtroom towards the square.

ST ANDREW'S SQUARE was, until cavalier demolitions in 1988, the ghost of the elegant square planned round the church in 1786 by *William Hamilton* and finished in the early 1790s. Commercial premises had infiltrated as early as 1801, and they came to dominate it. At the SW corner, a coarsely Italianate leather warehouse of 1876–7 (No. 48). On the NW corner, the austere former CITY ORPHAN HOME of 1876 by *Robert Bryden*. Nothing now remains of the simple but palace-fronted C18 terraces that originally lined the rest of the square. Only one early five-bay ashlar fronted house still stands on the E side.

James Morrison Street leads N to LONDON ROAD. This stretch, from Glasgow Cross to Monteith Row, was laid out by *John Weir* in 1824, originally with a grand scheme of tenements. A pedimented fragment is tucked under the railway bridge at the W end. On the corners of James Morrison Street, the cream fluted faience and black tile of the 1930s LAWSON FISHER store, and the pretty timber shopfronts of a cream sandstone tenement (dated 1856). Tall mansard and giant pilasters, linked on the main elevation by a rich foliage frieze. Restored by *Fred Whalley* for *Nicholas Groves-Raines*, 1986–7. A little further E, the long stone C19 warehouse front, more window than wall, of ST ANDREW'S HOUSE (No. 102).

S from the square, past the Tent Hall and the C18 St Andrew-by-the-Green (*see* Churches), the grass and trees of Glasgow Green (*see* Public Buildings). Along its edge, GREENDYKE STREET, an old lane improved in 1824–6. Next to the church, the former HIDE, WOOL AND TALLOW AUCTION MARKET (Nos. 33–9) by *John Keppie*, 1890. Four severe storeys, with a row of giant arches embracing the lowest two. Extended 1891. On the corner of Lanark Street, the Territorial Army's DRILL HALL (built before 1884), like a toy fort in red and white brick.

CHARLOTTE STREET, the next turning, was the first and once the smartest residential street in this quarter. The feuing conditions of 1780 dictated a uniform design for the houses and gave them individual gardens. There were four houses on each side, linked by outbuildings and gates. David Dale's larger and more elaborate house (where the Our Lady and St Francis

School now stands; *see* Public Buildings) stretched the feuing conditions to the utmost. Only one house survives (No. 52), a simple classical villa, ashlar-fronted, of two storeys and five bays, the central three broken forward under a pediment with a small oculus. The only decoration is the Neo-classical reeded frieze with paterae over the door, and urns over pediment and end pilasters (missing in 1989). To be converted to six flats for the National Trust for Scotland by *John Forbes* for *Nicholas Groves-Raines* (1988). The s half of the street was railed off at London Road. The n half was laid out contemporaneously with tenements for artisans: one (No. 24) survives. Brick, with a stone façade, quoins, a dentil cornice and two-light windows in the outer bays. Circular staircase tower.

In MONTEITH ROW, to the e, just one lonely representative (No. 14) of a row of superior tenements overlooking the Green (the rest were demolished by 1980). Plans for them were drawn up in 1812 at the request of the city magistrates. In 1818, the first two westernmost tenements of three simple palace-fronted terraces were built by the contractor *Thomas Binnie*. He completed the rest to a revised design, but not until 1845. Now an estate of dwarfish brick Home Counties-style houses of the early 1980s by *Barratt*'s own architects makes an indecisive edging to the Green.

The glittering colours of TEMPLETON'S CARPET FACTORY 68 (converted to the Templeton Business Centre by *Charles Robertson & Partners*, 1980–5), which vividly advertised the 'orient-dyed' wares produced within, can be glimpsed between the trees. *William Leiper*'s Ruskinian front of 1888, its centrepiece quoted from the Venetian Doges' Palace, is only a curtain concealing a functional mill designed by the mill engineers *Messrs J. B. Harvey*. (In fact the façade, insufficiently tied back, collapsed in 1889. Rebuilding was completed in 1892.) The exotic weave is created with crimson Ruabon brick, red terracotta (for the twisted mullions) and red sandstone; by vitreous enamel mosaic in deep blue, gold, and white within the tympana; and, in the topmost storey, by red and green glazed bricks zigzagged against a bright yellow ground – an ideal High Victorian marriage of medieval forms and modern materials. Later wings surround a courtyard filled, until 1981, with low weaving sheds. Clockwise from the l. of Leiper's façade: facing London Road, an L-shaped wing by *George Boswell* (all the 1920s and 1930s ranges are by him); a plain 1897 wing corner block, banded with windows and concrete and with an eye-catching brick corner tower, 1934; facing Templeton Street, a quieter range of 1927; then a gap before a maverick wing, an automated warehouse by *Munro & Partners*, 1963, facing the Green, and Boswell's last wing, 1936, with its coloured diapering and curved corner windows, taking up the themes of Leiper's façade. On the s side of Templeton Street, the factory's former Social Club (No. 35), late 1920s and probably also by Boswell. Classical in shiny red brick.

N of Templeton Street, in TOBAGO STREET, the former

EASTERN DISTRICT POLICE BUILDINGS (No. 92), 1868–9, by *John Carrick* (City Architect), the third of the nine police stations designed by him, and the only one to survive. A grave sandstone palazzo, with flanking wings for the lighting and cleansing and fire departments. To the S, red and white brick former TRAMWAY STABLES (Nos. 52–74), built in 1883 with 436 stalls, converted to a tobacco factory in 1901 by *G. S. Hill* and altered again in 1914 by *Burnet & Boston*. Opposite, at No. 75, the much more modest stable and store of a rag merchant (1905).

Further N still, the concrete-block Corporation tenements of 1929–33 that replaced much of Old Calton, and just to the E, in Abercromby Street (the E boundary of this perambulation), St Mary's R.C. Church (*see* Churches, above). Back along Millroad Street to more C20 housing linked to the older scheme, this time two groups by the S.S.H.A. The first, most easterly group is of brown brick, two-storey, slightly rustic houses round courtyards (1981–3). It incorporates Tureen Street School (*see* Public Buildings, above) and one of the C18 tenements on Gallowgate (*see* Perambulation 2, below). Big cast-iron arches and brick gatepiers introduce the second scheme (1983–6), with its elaborate paving and planting, and a route through to the Barras with matching arches.

The scheme's yellow and red brick, stepped out to big oriels on the SE corner block, refers to the exuberant former CLAY PIPE FACTORY opposite in BAIN STREET. Three blocks, originally linked, the oldest one on the corner of Gibson Street and Moncur Street. The other two were built to match by *M. Forsyth* of Airdrie, 1876–7, with smart façades to face the City Improvement Trust's Bain Square. Red and yellow brick with rows of arched windows and tall Franco-Flemish centrepieces with oriels. Inside, cast-iron columns and wooden beams. In what remains of Bain Square, Calton New Church (*see* Churches, above).

Bain Street takes us back S to the stretch of LONDON ROAD that was improved from a lane in 1793 as a route from the eastern collieries. The first buildings started to appear along what was then called Great Hamilton Street *c*. 1815. Now there are chiefly later C19 and early C20 tenements, mostly cut down to their ground-floor shops, and, amongst them, St Alphonsus' R.C. Church (*see* Churches) and its neighbour No. 233, the 1903–7 red sandstone front (with later dormers) of the former RUMFORD IRONMONGERY WORKS by *George S. Hill*, now flats. On then to the W where London Road meets Gallowgate and the start of Perambulation 2.

2. Gallowgate to Duke Street

GALLOWGATE is one of the four streets of the medieval burgh, so historically it might seem the obvious place to begin this tour. However, nothing medieval is left; all was swept away by the railway and the City Improvement Trust. Even the later, C19 tenements have in many cases been cut down to ground-floor level. Our perambulation starts past the railway viaduct at the corner of Little Dovehill, with the decorative J. & G. MELIOR BUILDING of 1873, its first-floor windows with shell tympana, its upper ones with segmental pediments and incised anthemion. On the S side the cast-iron entrance arches to the BARRAS market (established here in the 1920s) and its more permanent building, BARROWLAND (1960), the ballroom over the market stalls spangled with neon shooting stars.

Further E, two late C18 tenements. They mark the extent of the building that had spread along Gallowgate by 1780. Both have harled stone façades with band surrounds to the sashes and rusticated quoins, and backs of brick (an unusually early use), with circular stairtowers. Nos. 374–8, *c.* 1780, has a small pediment at the base of the central chimneystack, No. 394 of 1771 (restored by the S.S.H.A. in 1981–3) a two-windowed wallhead gable.

Further E still, GRAHAM SQUARE, the failed speculation of *c.* 1783, and the Meat and Cattle Markets (*see* Public Buildings, above). On the E side (No. 38), the last of the weaving factories that took over the square. The former weaving sheds of 1873–4 are hidden behind the tall red and white brick engineering workshop of 1897 by *Bruce & Hay*. On the E corner, the severe ROYAL BANK OF SCOTLAND by *Clarke & Bell*, 1934. On the opposite side of Gallowgate, the jollier former BRITISH LINEN BANK by *John Fairweather & Son*, 1936, with an Art Deco clock tower of polished granite and an apt bucranium.

A brief excursion for the enthusiast into a concentration of industrial buildings N of Gallowgate. In SYDNEY STREET, No. 118 (Strathclyde Water Department) is a former WATER DEPOT on the site of Glasgow Waterworks Company's basin. Two red and white striped brick blocks flanking a gateway: 1896, by *J. M. Gale* (City Water Engineer). Opposite, an engineering workshop, 1912, by *Miller & Black*, with windows in simple blind arcades. At the N end of Sydney Street, Trinity Duke Street Church (*see* Churches, above). Further W, just into HUNTER STREET, a fine red sandstone ashlar tenement (Nos. 202–4) by *Monro & Son*, 1903. The fine trophy of agricultural implements refers to the potato and seed merchants' warehouse to which it was originally attached. For Duke Street W of Hunter Street, *see* Townhead, above: Perambulation 1. Alternatively, return to Gallowgate to begin Perambulation 3.

3. *Gallowgate S to Bridgeton*

Back now to Gallowgate as far E as Sword Street. Only a few oddments of interest just W of the sweepingly cleared Camlachie. On the corner of Sword Street, the former ORIENT CINEMA, 1931–2, *A. V. Gardner*'s first project without his partner *W. R. Glen*. Mutilated corner entrance in front of a huge auditorium, originally with an oriental theme. Just to the E, another distinctly 1930s building, banded in brick and glass, the BELLGROVE HOTEL, 1935–6, by *McNair & Elder*. Next, a strip of low-rise houses and taller forbidding tenements. At the E end, in WHITEVALE STREET, two exceptionally tall blocks of flats (thirty-one storeys, concrete-clad), part of this mixed development of 1963–9 by *Harvey & Scott*. Also in Whitevale Street, the former Whitevale Street Baths (*see* Public Buildings, above).

S of Gallowgate, St Mungo's Academy with the Crownpoint Road Sports Complex (*see* Public Buildings), and, just off the N side of Crownpoint Road, in Cubie Street, the very handsome Vanbrughian former TELEPHONE EXCHANGE, 1910, by *H.M. Office of Works*, in a mix, unusual in Glasgow, of red brick and brilliant white stone.

S of these, in what was the hamlet of Mile-End, a few C19 industrial buildings among many later ones; but very little evidence of the textile industry and none of the famous carpet weaving, except some very late harsh red brick factories, for example at the S end of Abercromby Street (1927–8, for Templetons, by *G. A. Boswell*); in Crownpoint Road (1929); and in St Marnock Street (1923). BROAD STREET is the main thoroughfare. Here, near the E end, a squarish front (No. 47), patterned in red and white brick, and with a big arched window in place of the original entrance, screens the galleried cast-iron and rolled-steel structure of the first electrical engineering works in the city, designed for Mavor & Coulson by *A. Myles*, 1896–7. To the S of this, in FORDNEUK STREET, MILE END MILLS (Nos. 91–7), the earliest surviving cotton-spinning and power-loom mills, built *c.* 1835 for Fergusson & Co. and much rebuilt in 1914. A three-storey-and-attic red brick building with corner towers. Along the street, a two-storey block with well-detailed blind arcading, all in brick but painted. Off Fordneuk Street, in AVENUE STREET, the red and white brick fragments of Howe's once vast sewing machine factory (No. 48), designed in 1872–3 by *A. Kennedy, Son & Myles*, represent one more strand in the complex textile trade. Back N to Broad Street, which at the E end turns into DAVID STREET. Here (at No. 96) is the battery of abandoned red brick weaving sheds of *c.* 1862 that once formed part of the extensive FORDNEUK FACTORY, founded in the 1840s.

SE of Mile-End, just N of London Road round BARROWFIELD STREET, lies BARROWFIELD, a late scheme of 1930s Corporation tenements (begun in 1938) with some experimental features (flat roofs, cantilevered balconies and metal windows).

BRIDGETON AND DALMARNOCK

Bridgeton, like Calton (*q.v.*) a weaving village, was planted on the Barrowfield lands in 1705, and successfully developed after 1731, when John Orr bought the lands from the original

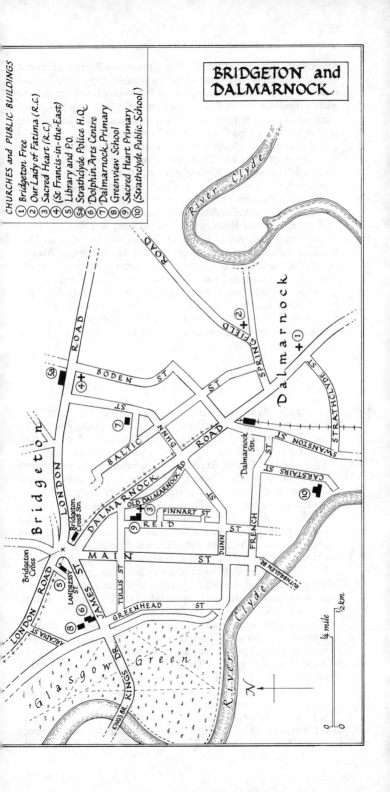

BRIDGETON and DALMARNOCK

CHURCHES and PUBLIC BUILDINGS

① Bridgeton Free
② Our Lady of Fatima (R.C.)
③ Sacred Heart (R.C.)
④ (St Francis-in-the-East)
⑤ Library and P.O.
⑤ₐ Strathclyde Police H.Q.
⑥ Dolphin Arts Centre
⑦ Dalmarnock Primary
⑧ Greenview School
⑨ Sacred Heart Primary
⑩ Sacred Heart Primary (Strathclyde Public School)

River Clyde

SPRINGFIELD ROAD

Dalmarnock

STRATHCLYDE ST

SWANSTON ST

CARSTAIRS ST

Dalmarnock Stn.

BODEN ST

ST

DUNN ST

BALTIC

DALMARNOCK ROAD

Bridgeton

LONDON ROAD

Bridgeton Cross Stn.

Bridgeton Cross

ARCADIA ST

JAMES ST

LANDRESSY ST

MAIN ST

TULLIS ST

GREENHEAD ST

OLD DALMARNOCK RD

FINNART ST

REID ST

DUNN ST

FRENCH ST

RUTHERGLEN BR.

River Clyde

Glasgow Green

KING'S DR

KINGS BR

N

¼ mile

½ km

proprietor, John Walkinshaw. It was known as Barrowfield until the Rutherglen Bridge was built at its s end in 1775–6, and a new road was constructed from there to the village's N boundary at what is now known as Bridgeton Cross. By the early C19 there were several cotton mills and a grid of tenements. Later in the century, a wider range of industries was introduced.

Dalmarnock was developed much later. Although a dyehouse for Turkey red dye had been started on the river bank in 1785, followed by another at Springfield *c*. 1826, most of the land was rural (with two mansion houses of ancient origin) until after 1860, when industries (including ironworks) and services (gasworks, sewage works, power station) were established there.

No trace now of Bridgeton's C18 origins, and little evidence of the C19 except round Bridgeton Cross. Bridgeton with Dalmarnock was declared a Comprehensive Development Area in 1962. The once tenement-lined main streets are now just traffic routes, with attention focused off them into introverted housing schemes. Mixed housing developments studded with high-rise blocks were followed by villagey schemes under the auspices of G.E.A.R. (1976–87). Dalmarnock, only partially rebuilt, is divided between the remnants of industry w of the main road and housing E of it.

CHURCHES

BRIDGETON BAPTIST CHURCH. *See* Calton: Churches.

BRIDGETON FREE CHURCH, 531 Dalmarnock Road. The former Dalmarnock Congregational Church by *J. C. McKellar*, 1901–2. Hall by *McKellar, Davis & Gunn*, 1911–12. Entrance façade with Art Nouveau detailing in the bell turret, tracery, doorway and battered side porches. Disappointingly ordinary galleried interior, with open timber roof.

OUR LADY OF FATIMA (R.C.), Springfield Road. By *Thomas Cordiner*, 1950–3. Little red brick church with a steep-pitched roof, a gable rising into a bellcote and a relief of Our Lady on the gable wall. Concrete portal frames exposed inside.

SACRED HEART (R.C.), 52 Old Dalmarnock Road. 1900–10, by *C. J. Menart*. A basilica of rock-faced red sandstone, with Diocletian windows boldly used on the façade between twin stairtowers with Baroque caps, and in the clearstorey. Inside, passage aisles screened by short sections of wall flanked by fluted pilasters and pairs of marbled Ionic columns *in antis*. Lavish use of marble in the chancel. The curious part-flat, part-segmental ceiling was a structural alteration by *Gillespie, Kidd & Coia*, 1953–4. – Over the Sacred Heart altar, a figure of Christ by *Jack Mortimer*, 1954. – STATIONS OF THE CROSS, 1954, painted on copper by *William Crosbie*, who also restored the original fresco by *Charles Baillie*.

PRESBYTERY. Grey and gabled, 1890, by *Pugin & Pugin*.

ST FRANCIS-IN-THE-EAST, 10–12 Boden Street. A former Free Church of 1878 by *J. McKissack & W. G. Rowan*, converted to a church house in 1947 and thence to a youth centre. Almost unrecognizable except for fragments of E.E. detail and a truncated spire.

PUBLIC BUILDINGS

BRIDGETON LIBRARY AND POST OFFICE, 23 Landressy Street. 1903–6, by *J. R. Rhind*. Edwardian Baroque façade in cream ashlar, with much figurative sculpture. It curves out slightly with the bend in the street between two pedimented end pavilions. These have fluted Ionic columns above each entrance. Top-lit lending section behind. Much of the original woodwork survives inside, though rearranged. The tall reading room to the N, with open timber roof, now the Post Office.

STRATHCLYDE POLICE HEADQUARTERS (Eastern Division), London Road. By *J. C. McDougall* (Strathclyde Regional Council Department of Architecture), opened in 1981. Unexceptional large office block in brown brick, the bays recessed in a repetitive manner.

DOLPHIN ARTS CENTRE, 7 James Street, overlooking Glasgow Green. Built in 1890–3 (architect *James Thomson* of *Baird & Thomson*) as the Logan School of Domestic Economy. Appropriately domestic in style, in snecked red Ballochmyle stone with tiled roofs.

DALMARNOCK PRIMARY SCHOOL, Albany Street. A simple red sandstone Board school by *Robert A. Bryden*, 1892–3.

GREENVIEW SCHOOL, 47 Greenhead Street. A six-bay Italian palazzo designed in 1846 for Duncan McPhail by *Charles Wilson* as Greenhead House. In 1859 it became the Buchanan Institute for destitute children. The first floor of three is emphasized by round-headed windows and balconies with a familiar motif of linked circles, echoed in the frieze below the dentil cornice. The dining hall, with one large window, some heavy Mannerist detailing and the figure of a studious boy, was added in 1873. Workshops, drill hall and janitor's house by *McWhannell & Rogerson*, 1904–5. Interior of house remodelled by *Ninian McWhannell*, 1913–14.

SACRED HEART PRIMARY SCHOOL, 31 Reid Street. 1963–6, by *Lothian Barclay, Jarvis & Boys* in consultation with *A. G. Jury* (City Architect). More imaginative than many contemporary Glasgow schools. Conventional three-storey curtain-walled junior school linked to a group of hexagonal brick infants' classrooms by an administration block arranged round a courtyard.

STRATHCLYDE PUBLIC SCHOOL (now Dalmarnock Adult Training Centre), Carstairs Street. Dated 1903. By *John McKissack*, with Baroque flourishes on its handsome s façade.

BRIDGETON CENTRAL STATION. *See* Perambulation 1, below.

KING'S BRIDGE, RUTHERGLEN BRIDGE, DALMARNOCK RAILWAY BRIDGES, POLMADIE BRIDGE, DALMAR-

NOCK BRIDGE, VIADUCT NEAR CLYDE IRONWORKS. *See* Crossings of the Clyde and Kelvin, below.

PERAMBULATIONS

1. *Bridgeton*

From BRIDGETON CROSS on London Road, the roads through Bridgeton to Gorbals, Rutherglen and Dalmarnock fan out symmetrically across the flat alluvium of the Clyde. At the hub of the junction, a jolly piece of Victorian street furniture, an octagonal cast-iron SHELTER with bright red shingle roof topped by a square clock tower and fancy weathervane; 1874, built by *George Smith & Co.* Forming the two s sides of the triangular-shaped cross, plain cream sandstone tenements by *James Thomson.* They were being built in 1871. Riding above the SE gushet to mark the important meeting of Main Street and Dalmarnock Road, the cone roof and onion finial of the more palatial late C19 BRIDGETON MANSIONS. The visual significance of this meeting of the ways fades sadly away with the low villagey (nay, suburban) shopping centre to the SW (architects *Scott, Brownrigg & Turner*; completed 1987).

Commercial buildings round the corner in London Road. At No. 34 an unconventional French Renaissance façade with a domed bow window within a tall arch, and a tall mansard above an oversized coved cornice to the former GLASGOW SAVINGS BANK, by *John Burnet*, 1876. On the corner of LANDRESSY STREET but making little of its corner site, its successor, now the TRUSTEE SAVINGS BANK (No. 42), by *D. B. Dobson* for *John Gordon*, 1894. A tall Free Style façade disciplined by channelled rustication, and with a neat and respectable temple front of polished granite applied to the banking hall. Big chimneys screen the flat concrete roof, which served the flats above the bank as a drying green. In Landressy Street, the public library (*see* Public Buildings, above).

On the N side of the Cross, at the corner of ORR STREET, the former OLYMPIA THEATRE, a music hall of 1910–12 by *George Arthur & Son* in association with *Frank Matcham*, converted to an ABC cinema by *W. R. Glen* in 1937, and thence to a bingo hall. The red sandstone corner treatment is the usual thing for 1910; semicircular with giant Ionic columns attached and a dome on top. Along London Road from the w corner of Orr Street, a row of red sandstone tenements with the entrance to the disused BRIDGETON CENTRAL STATION (opened in 1872) in the centre and steeply roofed pavilions at each end. Designed as a group for the North British Railway by *Thomson & Turnbull*, 1897–8. (For the streets to the N, *see* Calton: Perambulation 3.)

JAMES STREET runs SW from Bridgeton Cross to Glasgow Green. On the W side, the red and white brick former GREENHEAD WEAVING FACTORY (Nos. 89–91), designed for a power-loom cloth manufacturer by *Ninian McWhannell*, 1888. Further down, a snazzy black and cream tile front, part of the 1938 transformation of a drill hall into the KING'S CINEMA (now industrial premises). At the bottom of James Street, the Dolphin Arts Centre and, next to it, Greenview School (*see* Public Buildings).

More industrial buildings just W of these in GREENHEAD STREET, though not immediately obvious. The frontage of the former GREENHEAD WORKS (for the manufacture of gutta-percha) consists of two classical blocks, built in 1872–3 and 1886 to match the tenements further E along the street, linked by a single-storey brick block of 1886 (architect *G. Boyd*). Behind, a long brick building built *c.* 1840, and a red and white brick block of 1886–9 facing McPhail Street. Just round the corner in ARCADIA STREET, the cement-rendered gable end of the former GREENHEAD ENGINE WORKS (No. 133), built in 1859–63, rebuilt in 1877. Also facing the Green from Greenhead Street (Nos. 97–127), tall cream ashlar Italianate tenements of superior finish, with top balustrades (1865–9). They turn the corner into TULLIS STREET (Nos. 91–101), which leads E to Main Street.

The MAIN STREET of the old village runs S to Rutherglen Bridge. Only the very top has the enclosed C19 character of Bridgeton Cross. The lower end (S of Tullis Street) is an unfocused mix of low brick-built private and S.S.H.A. housing schemes of the 1980s, built through the agency of G.E.A.R.

A little way down Dalmarnock Road, the OLD DALMARNOCK ROAD becomes a backwater, separated from the main traffic route by a strip of green. Here are the Sacred Heart Church and Primary School (*see* above) and, just to the W in FINNART STREET, two courtyards of quietly detailed terraced housing of 1986–8 by *Vernon Monaghan* and *David McMillan* for *Simister, Monaghan, McKinney, MacDonald*. To the E of the newer DALMARNOCK ROAD, a big mixed development (1967–8) of five-storey harled tenements with pitched roofs and minimal styling scattered over a pedestrian network. S of these, three fifteen-storey tower blocks of the familiar *George Wimpey* type, and just one or two unexceptional C19 buildings close by them.

The area SE of this, bordering on DUNN STREET, was once dominated by Sir William Arrol's DALMARNOCK IRON-WORKS, founded *c.* 1868 and built between 1889 and 1911, but only a few fragments have found new uses. Beyond, nearer London Road in BODEN STREET, a former workshop (No. 60) of Grosvenor's EAGLE POTTERY, which flourished here from 1869 until the 1920s. Red and white brick building, with two terracotta roundels, by *John Honeyman*, 1869. Further down there stood (until 1989) the strictly functional complex of the BODEN STREET FACTORY, 1881–1907, the last of Glasgow's weaving factories to close (in 1987).

2. *Dalmarnock*

DALMARNOCK ROAD divides industry from housing. Nothing much along it except the little early C 19 TOLLHOUSE at No. 556, with its half-octagonal bay and pediment doorcase; the Bridgeton Free Church (*see* Churches, above) on the opposite side; and the cast-iron skeleton of a gas-holder (1872), once part of the City and Suburban Gas Company, established here in 1843.

Just a scatter of C 19 industrial buildings to the w. In FRENCH STREET (Nos. 103–5), the former BARROWFIELD WEAVING FACTORY by *M. S. Gibson*, 1889–99. To the street, a long low red and blue brick range. At the corner of REID STREET, the CROWN CHEMICAL WORKS, with a flat-roofed block of 1906 by *W. H. Howie*, and, further up at No. 177, the tall red brick former BARROWFIELD SPIN-NING FACTORY of *c.* 1846, one of the smaller of Glasgow's spinning mills, with an ugly water tower of 1884. S of this, in CARSTAIRS STREET (No. 121), very large former cotton spinning mills of 1884–91 by *Joseph Stott* of Oldham for Glasgow Cotton Spinners Ltd. Prominent stairtowers and a big circular chimney. Opposite, the former Strathclyde Public School (*see* Public Buildings, above). The most interesting building of all in this area, the CALEDONIAN BOILER WORKS, which stood a little further E in STRATHCLYDE STREET (No. 64), has gone, removed to the Railway Pres-ervation Society at Bo'ness in 1989. It was constructed as the Heavy Machinery Hall of the Glasgow International Exhi-bition of 1888 and was re-erected here in 1889. Its cast-iron columns have broad bases for bolting to temporary foundation pads.

SPRINGFIELD ROAD forms the spine through a mix of red sandstone tenements and public housing to the E. On the corner with Dalmarnock Road, attractive courtyards of striped brick houses and flats by the S.S.H.A. (*c.* 1985), just like those near the Barras (*see* Calton, above: Perambulation 2), and, further E, similar terraces round the duller open-ended streets requested by the tenants. As a backdrop, four tall blocks of a mixed development by *Parry & Hughes*, 1962–6.

PARKHEAD

Parkhead, in the 1840s, was a small weaving village that had grown up in the middle of the C 18 at the junction of two main routes, the Great Eastern Road (now Gallowgate and Tollcross Road) and Westmuir Street. In the surrounding countryside were one coal pit, one quarry, and, to the N by the Camlachie Burn, the Parkhead Forge, which had been started *c.* 1837. By 1889 John Carrick could report that 'all along the main thorough-fares the modern tenement has replaced the one-storey thatched

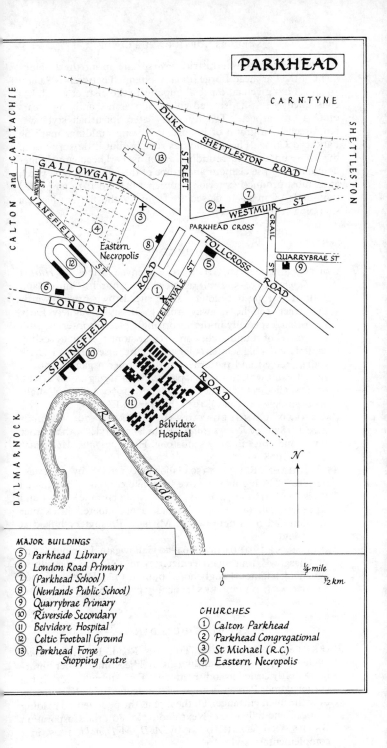

PARKHEAD

CARNTYNE

CALTON and CAMLACHIE

DUKE STREET

SHETTLESTON ROAD

SHETTLESTON

⑬

GALLOWGATE

HOLYWELL ST

JANEFIELD ST

③

④

Eastern Necropolis

⑫

⑧

WESTMUIR ST

② ⑦

PARKHEAD CROSS

CRAIL ST

⑥

LONDON

ROAD

HELENVALE ST

①

TOLLCROSS

⑤

QUARRYBRAE ST

⑨

ROAD

SPRINGFIELD

⑩

Belvidere Hospital

⑪

ROAD

River Clyde

DALMARNOCK

N

MAJOR BUILDINGS
⑤ Parkhead Library
⑥ London Road Primary
⑦ (Parkhead School)
⑧ (Newlands Public School)
⑨ Quarrybrae Primary
⑩ Riverside Secondary
⑪ Belvidere Hospital
⑫ Celtic Football Ground
⑬ Parkhead Forge
       Shopping Centre

0   ¼ mile
0   ½ km

CHURCHES
① Calton Parkhead
② Parkhead Congregational
③ St Michael (R.C.)
④ Eastern Necropolis

cottage ... Numerous industries have sprung up and the development of the Parkhead Forge [greatly extended between 1884 and 1914] ... has given an especial impetus to the district which has consequently lost its isolated village appearance and now wears quite a city aspect.' Twenty years later, its urban style was reinforced by a group of important-looking buildings marking Parkhead Cross. These buildings remain, but little survives of the contemporary surroundings. Nor is Parkhead any longer dominated by the clamour and grime of the famous forge, which at its most productive period between 1884 and 1914 employed thousands of men. It closed in 1976; on the flattened site a shopping centre has risen.

CHURCHES

CALTON PARKHEAD CHURCH, Helenvale Street. By *Hutton & Taylor*, 1934–5. Built as Newbank Church. Church and halls are strung out along a steep site. Brown brick towards the street, roughcast away from it. In style, vaguely Early Christian, especially in the surprisingly pleasant interior, with its arcades of round arches on circular stone piers with scallop capitals and a big semicircular arch to the raised chancel. Brick walls, pierced and patterned to the former organ chambers. Barrel-vault with tie-beams, painted with zigzags. – STAINED GLASS. Chancel window (Crucifixion), 1970, and single-light aisle window (St Luke), 1971, by *Gordon Webster*.

PARKHEAD CONGREGATIONAL CHURCH, 79 Westmuir Street. 1879, by *Robert Baldie*. Plain lancet style, with a corner tower and spire in grey sandstone. Halls by *John McKissack & Son*, 1908–11.

ST MICHAEL (R.C.), 1350 Gallowgate. 1965–8, by *Alexander McAnally*. A big unattractive barn-like church of brown-red brick, with triangular heads to the triple entrance doors and windows. No tower but, instead, a tall tapered brick pier surmounted by a figure of St Michael. Presbytery linked at the w end.

EASTERN NECROPOLIS, 1264–70 Gallowgate. Laid out as one of Glasgow's four main cemeteries in 1847, on the site of Janefield, a famously ugly house built in 1764. Pretty stuccoed LODGE AND GATEPIERS, probably post-1865.

PUBLIC BUILDINGS

PARKHEAD LIBRARY, 64 Tollcross Road. By *J. R. Rhind*, 1904–6. A quite small building given (like Rhind's other libraries) a deftly scaled grand treatment. Two-storey façade with a corner dome. Personification of 'Glasgow' by *Kellock Brown* over the main entrance. To the l. of it, the pedimented reading room of one tall storey. Next door (No. 80), the Corporation BATHS AND WASHHOUSE by *A. B. McDonald*, 1905, in a complementary style.

LONDON ROAD PRIMARY SCHOOL, 1139 London Road. 1907, by *Thomson & Turnbull*. A typical turn-of-the-century Board school (classrooms round a central hall) with a superior English Baroque exterior. Nicely carved ornament. Venetian and circular windows in the pedimented end bays.

NEWLANDS PUBLIC SCHOOL (now Day Centre), 871 Springfield Road. 1895, by *Andrew Balfour*. The plainest kind of red sandstone Board school, pilastered between the upper windows, otherwise rock-faced.

PARKHEAD SCHOOL (now Careers Office), Westmuir Street. The earliest part (1878–9, by *Hugh Maclure*) has French Renaissance details and a roguish bell turret. The later block (1887, by the same architect) has a gambrel roof.

QUARRYBRAE PRIMARY SCHOOL, 153 Crail Street. A Board school of 1902–4 by *McWhannell & Rogerson*. Gabled and exceptionally plain.

RIVERSIDE SECONDARY SCHOOL, 452 Springfield Road. 1935–6, by *William McCaig*. Of between-the-wars type with a three-bay central block and long (here excessively long) wings.

BELVIDERE HOSPITAL, 1400 London Road. The lands of Belvidere were acquired for a hospital in 1870. The original temporary wooden huts were replaced in 1874–7 by five small-pox pavilions designed by *John Carrick* (City Engineer). By 1887 there were the nineteen pavilions of red and white striped brick (some later harled), with arched windows, that flank the drive, together with kitchen, washhouse, mortuary and stores. Facing the river, on the site of the Belvidere Mansion, the gaunt grey stone ADMINISTRATION BUILDING. To the NW, the long striped brick NURSES' HOME of 1892 by *A. B. McDonald* (City Surveyor). Many unremarkable additions of 1960–72.

PERAMBULATION

PARKHEAD CROSS is a grand Edwardian meeting of five main routes (Gallowgate, Duke Street, Tollcross Road, Westmuir Street, Springfield Road). Bold corner towers, typical of their date, to all the buildings. Large and vulgar towers to the NW and N, one Baronial (1902, by *Burnet, Boston & Carruthers*), the other French Renaissance (1905, by *Crawford & Veitch*). More subdued, the pointed caps over the oriel windows of the tenements (1905, by *J. C. McKellar*) between Tollcross Road and Westmuir Street.

On the corner of Burgher Street, at Nos. 1448–56 GALLOWGATE, the tall, attenuated tower of the TRUSTEE SAVINGS BANK, opened in 1908 as a branch of the Glasgow Savings Bank. Designed by *Honeyman, Keppie & Mackintosh*, it is more flamboyant but more conventional than Salmon & Gillespie's Anderston Cross branch (*see* Woodlands and Finnieston, above: Perambulation 4). The sculptural aedicules are

Baroque, the thickly encrusted reliefs over the windows and doors Scottish Renaissance. Above the main door, 'Prudence strangling Want' by *A. Macfarlane Shannon*. Beneath the tower, an octagonal foyer; then a marble-lined passage to the one-storey banking hall in Burgher Street, top-lit from a dome. Facing Gallowgate, two shops and the close to four storeys of tenements entered from galleries at the back.

In GALLOWGATE, past St Michael's Church and opposite the gates to the Eastern Necropolis (*see* Churches, above), is the entrance to the PARKHEAD FORGE shopping centre, a vast utilitarian structure by *Scott, Brownrigg & Turner*, 1986–8, its size partially disguised by an edging of repetitive glass pyramids, which also roof the network of malls. There are no remains of the forge, but further w, among acres of derelict industrial land dotted with small groups of 1930s tenements (in 1989), are two other industrial relics. At No. 1141, the mutilated single-storey office block by *Neil C. Duff* of the HARTSHEAD CURLED HAIR AND BEDDING FACTORY, 1914. Off Gallowgate, in HOLYWELL STREET (No. 49), the big, plain brick PARKHEAD FACTORY, built in 1865–6 for the gingham and pullicate manufacturers, Clark & Struthers.

N of the Cross, in DUKE STREET, the former GRANADA CINEMA (No. 1315, now Mecca Social Club), designed for Alex Fruitin by *Lennox & Macmath*, 1934–5. A deceptively small foyer to a huge auditorium with its original red decoration. Further N still, in SHETTLESTON ROAD, the former EMPLOYMENT EXCHANGE (No. 179) by *H.M. Office of Works*, 1930. Stripped classicism in hard red brick with a giant Ionic order. WESTMUIR STREET, NE from the Cross, deserves a detour for its C19 church and Board school (*see* above).

SE from the Cross runs TOLLCROSS ROAD. The first turning s, with the public library (*see* above) on the corner, is into HELENVALE STREET. Before the Calton Parkhead Church (*see* above), a row of red sandstone tenements (Nos. 52–62) of 1902 by *John Hamilton*, with a distinctly Art Nouveau feeling in the curvy parapets over the bay windows and in the big corbelled-out chimneystacks shooting up between them.

At the s end, on LONDON ROAD, Parkhead's only high-rise flats, 1967–9, by *George Wimpey*'s own architects. Three blocks of the type used by Wimpey at Bridgeton, Scotstoun etc. To the E, the Belvidere Hospital (*see* above). To the w, the famous CELTIC FOOTBALL GROUND, with a prominent red brick s stand of 1929 by *Archibald Leitch*. It was almost identical to his contemporary stand for Rangers at Ibrox Park (*see* Govan: Public Buildings) until it was given its bold roof in 1971 and was extended by *Lang, Willis & Galloway* one hundred years after the club's opening match in 1888. Close to it, London Road Primary School; and more schools (*see* above) in Springfield Road, which leads back to the Cross.

SHETTLESTON AND TOLLCROSS

Shettleston and Tollcross (the latter an estate within the medieval lands of Shettleston) were not absorbed by Glasgow until 1912. By then, they were industrial suburbs. The area had remained rural until the development after 1762 of coal-mining and the opening in 1786 of the Clyde Ironworks. The population of this scatter of hamlets was soon large enough to warrant a chapel-of-ease at Shettleston (1788) and later (1805) a church at Tollcross. Almost nothing survives of these old settlements, though Tollcross still has its original church. In 1848 a Victorian mansion, Tollcross House, was built for a proprietor of the Clyde Ironworks: it replaced the seat of the Corbets, who had held the Tollcross estate since the C13. Later in the century, Shettleston, in particular, was engulfed by tenements spreading E from Parkhead. Within ten years (1891–1901) the population more than doubled from 1,120 to 2,471. Churches and schools were built c. 1900 to serve it. In the 1930s the Corporation linked the two villages with a large housing scheme.

CHURCHES

CARNTYNE OLD CHURCH, 862 Shettleston Road. By *Robert Bryden*, 1892–3. Built as Shettleston Carntyne Free Church. Cream sandstone, Geometrical-style, the main gable between two octagonal buttresses with short spires. Aisleless interior, with W gallery and a pointed barrel-vault with ribs resting on a variety of unarchaeological corbels. Platform modernized in 1948 and the organ in its Gothic case imported from a church in Hawick. Hall and vestry behind the church also of 1892–3, the larger hall facing Shettleston Road of 1914.

EASTBANK PARISH CHURCH, 29 Annick Street and 679 Old Shettleston Road. By *W. G. Rowan*, 1901–4. (The adjoining hall dates from 1897–9.) An important Glasgow-Style church, in red Locharbriggs sandstone with Corncockle stone dressings. Corner tower with a slightly battered profile given by diagonal buttresses stepped up to a narrow horizontal bell-stage and a short recessed tiled spire. Main door and window embraced in a single arch. The Perp tracery in the window and the Perp motifs carved over the door have an Art Nouveau freedom of movement. The interior is exceptional – not for the architecture of plain tall stone arcades with galleries fitted beneath, but for the WOODWORK, from the panelled ceiling painted with the *Te Deum*, to the open timber aisle roofs, to the gallery fronts and platform furnishings with tall slim splayed shafts and a great variety of inventive tracery panels (some designs very reminiscent of Mackintosh). The organ case, canted out like a canopy over the broad pulpit and elders' seats, is of stained pine. The sturdy communion table, with pegged joints in true Arts and Crafts fashion, and the matching lectern and offertory table are of oak. – STAINED GLASS. 1914–18 War Memorial window by *Abbey Studio*.

SHETTLESTON and TOLLCROSS

0 ¼ mile
0 ½ km

Carntyne Stn

Shettleston Stn

OLD SHETTLESTON ROAD

ANNICK ST

DALZIEL DR

ELVAN ST

SHETTLESTON

DRIVE

MURYFAULD

DRUMOVER DR.

TENNYSON DR.

Tollcross Park

PARKHEAD

TOLLCROSS

Shettleston

ARDGAY

ACADEMY ST

KILLIN ST

ST

ROAD

Egypt

WELLSHOT

ALTYRE ST

Braidfauld

BRAIDFAULD ST

BRAIDFAULD GDNS

Tollcross

AMULREE

TOLLCROSS ROAD

Fullarton

FULLARTON AVE

CAUSEWAYSIDE ST

LONDON

Dalbeth ROAD

R. Clyde

SANDYHILLS

N

CHURCHES
① Carntyne Old Church
② Eastbank Parish Church
③ Shettleston Old Parish Church
④ St Barnabas (R.C.)
⑤ St Joseph (R.C.)
⑥ St Margaret Tollcross
⑦ St Mark (R.C.)
⑧ St Serf
⑨ (Tollcross Central)
⑩ Tollcross Park
⑪ Victoria Tollcross

PUBLIC BUILDINGS
⑫ Shettleston Hall and Library
⑬ Sports Centre
⑭ Tollcross House
⑮ Eastbank Academy
⑯ (Tollcross Public School)
⑰ St Vincent's School
⑱ Wellshot Road Primary

ST BARNABAS (R.C.), Darleith Street. 1960–2, by *T. S. Cordiner*. Unambitious. Flimsy bracing of metal and timber between the confessionals, and roof-slab projecting on the N side. Timber-lined boxy interior.

ST JOSEPH (R.C.), 14 Fullarton Avenue. 1978–80, by *Nicholson & Jacobsen*. Bold and complicated copper roof hooded over the raised clearstorey, which lights a fan-shaped auditorium. Projecting top-lit vestibule, the entrance framed by polygonal bays. Corresponding presbytery.

ST MARGARET TOLLCROSS, 179 Braidfauld Street. 1900–1, by *W. G. Rowan*. An Arts and Crafts-style church which looks as if it belongs in an English village. Characteristic of the style, the stubby, slightly battered tower with wide-spreading slated cap, the big black and white half-timbered porch, and the low aisle gathered in under one sweeping roof. The once-charming interior, equally redolent of English villages, despite its Glasgow-Style chancel furnishings, has been distressingly mutilated in the conversion into a multi-use church centre (1987–8). Few churches could be less appropriate, in style or quality, for that purpose. What remains in 1989 (though for how long is uncertain) is the nave and low S aisle and transept, with nice open timber roofs; the chancel, with no chancel arch but an elegant timber screen of slender splayed shafts and panelling incorporating arcaded elders' seats along the back wall (a simpler version of Rowan's furnishings at Eastbank Church; *see* above); the pulpit; and the red sandstone font with its niche for an ewer. N transept and tower divided off as a hall and meeting rooms; pews removed. Characteristic timber fireplace in the polygonal vestry.

ST MARK (R.C.), Edenwood Street. 1980. Small and harled with a split-pitched roof.

ST PAUL (R.C.). *See* Sandyhills and Mount Vernon.

ST SERF, 1464 Shettleston Road. 1934–6, by *Whyte & Galloway*. Brick and Early Christian. Entrance through a square tower.

SHETTLESTON OLD PARISH CHURCH, 99 Killin Street. A large former Free Church of 1895–1903 by *W. F. McGibbon*. French C13 style, the exterior in red snecked rubble (with no accent except a bellcote), the very serious interior in grey sandstone. High nave with a massive hammerbeam roof and circular clearstorey windows. In the nave, the aisle arcades have round piers with plain moulded capitals; the deep chancel has square piers with shafts attached each side and foliage capitals. Furnishings in the same style and traceried screens dividing chancel and aisles. Lancet windows, mostly with STAINED GLASS. Chancel, 1913, by *Alfred Webster*. – Three windows by *Gordon Webster* (N aisle, 1962, 1972; S aisle, 1967).

To the S, the large group of HALLS, one contemporary, with an octagonal NW entrance porch with conical cap.

TOLLCROSS CENTRAL CHURCH, 1089 Tollcross Road, set back from the street. Closed. By *John Brash*, 1805–6. Square plan, with the end bays at the front broken forward under hipped roofs and a vestry projecting behind. Two storeys of sash windows. Harled. Attached in the centre of the façade, a tower of 1834–5 in droved ashlar, pedimented at eaves level and with a square clock-stage, octagonal bell-stage and short stone spire above. The whole exterior very unsophisticated in design. Reroofed in 1884. Interior reseated in 1858, pulpit rearranged in 1904–5, when an organ chamber was constructed between it and the vestry. – ORGAN. By *Brindley & Foster* of Sheffield, 1904.

CHURCH HALLS with two curved gables by *Robert Gifford*, 1891. – CHURCHYARD. Contemporary with the church, with old stone walls, a watchhouse of 1828–30 and a number of early C19 tombstones.

TOLLCROSS PARK CHURCH, 16 Drumover Drive. A former United Free Church of 1904–5 by *Duncan & Alan G. McNaughtan*. Sheer cream sandstone façade with a low pent-roofed narthex between big buttresses. SE porch with Perpish detail, given a severe Glasgow-Style cast and buttresses invitingly splayed. Barn-like interior, with a massive timber roof on arched braces. – HALL. 1901–2, by *Watson & Salmond* with Art Nouveau curves to the mouldings and a hipped roof to the N porch. All enclosed in Mackintoshy railings.

VICTORIA TOLLCROSS CHURCH, 1154 Tollcross Road. A former United Free Church of 1900–2 by *R. A. Bryden*. Quite large, of red sandstone with Perp windows. Entrance façade prolonged into two octagonal-ended gallery stairtowers. Plain galleried interior, with central Gothic pulpit. – ORGAN. 1912, by *Norman, Beard & Co.* – STAINED GLASS. One contemporary window of Belgian manufacture, one of 1968 by *T. B. Milligan*.

The original small grey church of 1869 (now the hall and minus its bellcote and plate tracery) stands behind, facing Causewayside Street.

PUBLIC BUILDINGS

SHETTLESTON HALL AND PUBLIC LIBRARY, 150–4 Wellshot Road. Handsome buildings of 1922–5 by Glasgow's *Office of Public Works*. In the tradition of Wren at Hampton Court, but fiercely stripped down to essentials. Hard red brick with grey ashlar dressings. Low, more domestic former clinic behind.

SHETTLESTON SPORTS CENTRE, 86 Elvan Street. The former baths and washhouse, in the same style as the Hall and Library (*see* above): by the *Office of Public Works*, 1924.

TOLLCROSS HOUSE AND PARK, 591 Tollcross Road. 1848, by *David Bryce* (then in partnership with *William Burn*) for James Dunlop, one of the proprietors of the Clyde Ironworks, replacing a 'substantious house' built by the Corbets, the original owners of the estate. A loose Baronial composition (of the type Burn invented in the late 1820s; cf. Milton Lockhart of 1829), with crowstepped gables, square bartizans, circular towers with conical caps, massed chimneys, and some of the windows mullioned, some sashed. The grey stugged ashlar is relieved by buckle quoins and carved dormer gables. The method of planning, too, is derived from Burn and had been developed by Bryce at, e.g., Balfour Castle (1847): N of the compact main block the service wing comes forward picturesquely in an L-shape on the entrance front (W) to protect the privacy of the reception and family rooms on the S and E fronts. The latter overlook a secluded wooded valley. Some of the Baronial detail survived the conversion to a children's museum in 1897 and is being restored in the conversion to flats by *Nicholas Groves-Raines* (job architect *Fred Whalley*) in 1989. The grounds became a public park in 1897.

WEST LODGE, Tollcross Road, and STABLES, Wellshot Road, by *Bryce*. – CONSERVATORY, N of the house. Mid-C19. Latin-cross plan with a dome at the crossing and semicircular ends to the cross wings. Mostly cast-iron (see especially the scrolled buttresses) and glass.

EASTBANK ACADEMY, 1346–64 Shettleston Road. By *John McKissack*, opened 1894. Of the two-storey type with projecting wings. Similar in style to Wellshot Road Primary (*see* below) but more fully Flemish, with big shaped gables and rusticated giant pilasters. On the far side of Academy Street, an additional Free Style block of 1911 by *J. McKissack Junior*. Behind it, big late C20 extensions.

Former TOLLCROSS PUBLIC SCHOOL, 1196 Tollcross Road. Late C19. Two-storey in grey snecked rubble, its central gable with plate tracery.

ST VINCENT'S SCHOOL FOR THE BLIND AND DEAF, Fullarton Avenue. Blocks of red brick with flat, slightly projecting roof slabs; a late (1966) and particularly well-built version of Glasgow's post-World War II schools.

WELLSHOT ROAD PRIMARY SCHOOL, 249 Wellshot Road. A three-storey red sandstone school erected by Shettleston School Board in 1902–4 to designs by *James Lindsay*. Some Dutch or Flemish detail: two bays emphasized by curly pediment and the luxury of a timber cupola. Facing Altyre Street, an additional block of classrooms by *John McKissack*.

CAMBUSLANG FOOTBRIDGE, CLYDESFORD ROAD BRIDGE, BOGLESHOLE ROAD BRIDGE, CARMYLE RAILWAY VIADUCT. *See* Crossings of the Clyde and Kelvin, below.

DESCRIPTION

On SHETTLESTON ROAD (cut through in the early C19), one or two pre-Victorian survivals at the centre of the old village, one with a wallhead chimney and cherry-cocked stonework, and the stylish PORTLAND ARMS (1937, by *Thomson, Sandilands & McLeod*). Off the S side, the Egyptian foyer of the former BROADWAY CINEMA in AMULREE STREET (1929–

30, by *John McKissack*) catches the eye. Round Tollcross
Park, pockets of villas, very modest NE of it around ELVAN
STREET, smarter W of it at the bottom of MUIRYFAULD
DRIVE (where the terraced red sandstone houses of *c*. 1900
have nice cast-iron gates and fences), in TENNYSON DRIVE,
and in DRUMOVER DRIVE, where the villas are slightly
earlier and more picturesque, especially Nos. 90 and 102 with
little cast-iron crested towers and wide timber eaves. All along
the S and E sides of the park in TOLLCROSS ROAD and
WELLSHOT ROAD, the stately regularly repeated bows and
bays of tall red and cream sandstone turn-of-the-c 19 tenements.

Municipal housing predominates, though: N of Shettleston Road,
minimal 1930s Corporation tenements (Nos. 1485–1505
SHETTLESTON ROAD distinguished by their more pretentious cantilevered and curved concrete balconies); S of it,
between Shettleston and Tollcross, a large cottage estate of
1936–7 (EGYPT).

No memorable buildings in the centre of Tollcross, although
most of those round the old Tollcross Central Church (*see*
Churches, above) on TOLLCROSS ROAD are still the C 19
miners' cottages, some tenemented and still with outside staircases.

SANDYHILLS AND MOUNT VERNON

Sandyhills was one of Shettleston's outlying mining settlements,
no more than a group of cottages along the main road. The
first church was built here in 1854. Sandyhills and Shettleston
gradually grew towards each other, but significant expansion did
not occur until the 1920s, when Glasgow Corporation built a big
cottage scheme S of the main road.

Mount Vernon had a different character. The ancient name of
this high and commanding ridge was Windy Edge. In 1755
George Buchanan, a Glasgow merchant, built his house, Mount
Vernon, here; it was followed a century later by a number of
smaller villas, the first built in 1860, the rest mostly after 1878,
when the branch railway line opened. This isolated group was
engulfed by suburban housing in the 1930s and afterwards.
Mount Vernon itself was demolished in 1932.

CHURCHES AND PUBLIC BUILDINGS

KENMUIR MOUNT VERNON CHURCH, London Road. 1883.
Severe lancet style in blackened snecked rubble with a spirelet.
Halls to match.

ST PAUL (R.C.), 1697 Shettleston Road. 1957–9; one of *Gillespie, Kidd & Coia*'s last basilican churches. Brick with a
portal frame. In front a big tower, the lower part inter-
penetrated by the entrance porch, the upper part an open

frame for the large copper silhouette of the Crucifixion by *Jack Mortimer*. A spacious interior, with much marble and slate and a plethora of symbols, carved on the furnishings and etched on the windows.

EASTBANK PRIMARY SCHOOL, Gartocher Road. By *A. G. Jury* (City Architect), 1964–9. A neat and substantial brick-clad three-storey block with one longer, lower wing.

NORTH MOUNT VERNON PRIMARY SCHOOL, Penryn Gardens. Completed in 1974; by *Fraser Cook* (Lanarkshire County Architect's Department). Circular and open-plan, with brick walls and a perspex dome over the assembly hall.

DESCRIPTIONS

Sandyhills

Along BAILLIESTON ROAD, only a fragment of the original mining village: a few stone single-storey cottages and a couple of tenement blocks. To its s, a large mid-1920s cottage estate stretches down to SANDYHILLS PARK, an informally land-scaped band of green laid out about 1980 (to replace a scheme of prefabs) along the N side of SANDYHILLS ROAD. One or two late C19 villas survive here. On the N side, a pair of C19 gatepiers now serves four tall and sheer slab blocks of 1964–70 by *Baron Bercott & Associates*. Opposite is the Victorian ELIZABETH LODGE (hotel), a rather English-style neo-C17 villa, facing Sandyhills Golf Course and the countryside beyond. Further E, one short stretch of smaller detached and semi-detached villas before the mass of inter- and post-war speculatively built housing begins.

Mount Vernon

At Mount Vernon's heart is still the secluded group of villas built on the steep hillside by Glasgow businessmen after 1860. Most modest are Nos. 1–10 GRANTLEA TERRACE, a neat terrace of debased Italianate two-storey two-bay stone houses. On BOWLING GREEN ROAD, grander double-fronted villas look s over the bowling green. At the w end they are debased classical in style, at the E end *cottage-orné* with gabled dormers. No. 17 at the E end is dated 1880. There are more such villas, many still with gardens of shrubs and evergreens in mid-C19 taste, along the commanding ridge in CARRICK DRIVE. Nos. 26 and 30 are of identical cottagey design: No. 24 is similar. On the corner, No. 2 MANSIONHOUSE ROAD has two handsome bows. Most of the other villas in this road are cottage-style, No. 7 especially pretty with fretted bargeboards and arched windows. In HAMILTON ROAD, s of the large estate of inter-war private houses that skirts the golf course, are a few more villas in well-wooded gardens, varied only by the terrace of late C19 three-storey red sandstone houses set back in BUCH-ANAN GARDENS.

EASTERHOUSE

Of Glasgow's four major peripheral housing schemes, Easterhouse is probably the best-known, because of its notorious decay and deprivation. It is the least favoured topographically, spread out over an exposed and lumpy landscape. The land belonged to Lanarkshire until 1938 and was originally part of Monklands (a former possession of the monks of Newbattle Abbey), which extended to the E and S. Coal had first been exploited by the monks; in the early C 19, most of the settlements in this area (including Baillieston (*q.v.*) and Swinton) were mining hamlets. In the late C 19, Easterhouse had two miners' rows facing each other across the main road, which were served by Bargeddie Church, now just E of the city boundary.

The land was annexed by Glasgow in 1938, but it was not until 1953 that plans were approved for a self-sufficient satellite township with 7,200 houses for 25,000 people. The first houses were built in 1954–6 at Wellhouse Farm, adjacent to Barlanark (*see* Carntyne and Robroyston). By 1958, four areas S W of Westerhouse Road–Easterhouse Road were complete, the last being Blairtummock, where houses went up around the C 18 mansion. A little pocket of houses, isolated to the W at Provanhall, was built in 1958–9, followed by Bishoploch, Lochend and Rogerfield (the N E sector) in 1959. A few houses were built at Queenslie (*see* Carntyne and Robroyston) last of all. The first church (St John Ogilvie) appeared in 1958, the first primary school in 1959, the first secondary one in 1962, but it was not until 1969–71 that the Township Centre, the hub of the whole satellite idea, was constructed. By then, the desperate tenants had begun to move away. In the 1980s private developers have been brought in and housing co-operatives formed to try to rescue the many empty tenements.

CHURCHES

LOCHWOOD CHURCH, Lochend Road. A hall church by *Walter Ramsay*, 1963–4.

ST BENEDICT (R.C.), 755 Westerhouse Road. 1962–5, by *Gillespie, Kidd & Coia*; one of their most straightforward designs of this period, but still the most distinctive building in Easterhouse. Church and presbytery are linked in a long low composition parallel with the road. Over the church, a big split-pitched copper roof with the clearstorey facing the road and the roof diving very low at the back. The harled walls (originally painted white) are unpierced except for the entrance doors. Against the side walls several narrow, randomly spaced buttresses. The plan is a simple rectangle, with seating all round the altar platform.

ST GEORGE AND ST PETER, Boyndie Street. 1959–60, by *A. Buchanan Campbell*. Wedge-shaped, with open framing at the lower end forming the entrance porch, which forms a link to the church hall and a support for the cross. – Some FURNISHINGS from the church of the same name which stood in Elderslie Street, Anderston.

ST JOHN OGILVIE (R.C.), Newhills Road. 1957–60, by *Alexander McAnally*. Simplified Gothic with a corner tower and spire.

PUBLIC BUILDINGS

ST BENEDICT'S PRIMARY SCHOOL, 754 Westerhouse Road. 1959–60, by *Keppie, Henderson & Partners*. Brick gable ends, a curtain-walled façade and, unusual for its date, a steeply pitched roof swept down low at each end.

PROVANHALL PRIMARY SCHOOL, Balcurvie Road. 1957–9, by *Keppie, Henderson & Gleave*. Like St Benedict's Primary School (*see* above), it has an unusual pitched roof.

GARTLOCH HOSPITAL, Gartloch Road. A gigantic institution built for 500 patients in 1890–7 to Scottish Baronial designs by *Thomson & Sandilands*. At the centre, the original first-class asylum for paying inmates, its narrow front range (administration) with two top-heavy towers. Flanking it the equally Baronial boilerhouse and laundry, and workshops: behind it, the separate dining hall and ward blocks. To the NE, the equally large but slightly more utilitarian former pauper asylum is linked in an H-plan to the hospital. Further N still, the sanatorium, the farmstead (built on the site of the home farm of the mansion that the asylum replaced) and rows of employees' cottages facing the road. Many later additions within the wooded grounds, including the NURSES' HOME, 1937–9, by *Thomas Somers* (City Engineer), with Dutch-influenced stripes of brick and render and big bowed lounges at each end.

PROVAN HALL, Auchinlea Road. Picturesquely set in the marshy 4 ha (10 acres) of the District Council's Auchinlea Park, a fragment of the 800 ha (2,000 acres) that, in the Middle Ages, belonged to the prebendary of Barlanark and spread out to the W. The hall was probably begun in the late C15. It passed, with the whole estate, out of ecclesiastical hands into those of the son of Canon William Baillie by means of a feu charter confirmed in 1565, and thence to Sir Robert Hamilton of Goslington in 1593. Glasgow Burgh bought it in 1667 and repaired it the following year. The estate was divided in 1729 between five merchants (the names of most of these lands are enshrined in the names of the C20 housing schemes that cover this area), and in 1767 the council sold Provan Hall, which stood on the lands they had kept to ensure the water supply to the town mills. It was bought by Dr John Buchanan in 1778 and stayed in that family until 1938, when it was sold to the National Trust for Scotland (from which the District Council now leases it).

The Hall was the prebendary's country seat. It comprises

two blocks of similar size which face each other across a courtyard, closed on the E and W with rubbly whinstone walls. The
enclosure is entered from the E by an archway pierced through
the medieval wall, which must have been defensive (*see* the
shot-holes and look-out platform, reached by a flight of steps).
Over the archway, a pedimented plaque with Hamilton arms,
R.H., and the date 1647. The lower, W wall is more recent,
though probably on the line of the original.

The N BLOCK is evidently late medieval, probably late C15
(it has features in common with Provand's Lordship; *see*
Townhead, Public Buildings, above). At the NE corner, a
stubby defensible stairtower with a conical cap, and shot-holes
and slit windows. The gables are crowstepped; all the rear
windows have chamfered jambs, and the chimney cope and
eaves course are moulded. On the ground floor, three barrel-
vaulted rooms, two interconnecting and vaulted N to S, the
separate kitchen vaulted E to W. It has a fireplace the full width
of the gable wall, an oven in the S wall and a drain in the N
one. A door in the fireplace gable has been blocked. Upstairs,
two rooms, each with a fireplace similar to those in Provand's
Lordship, and a mural chamber off the W room. Blocked
doorway in the W gable.

The S BLOCK was latterly the dwelling house, and may be
either C15 fabric much altered or a new C18 house. The
external rendering, sash windows and pedimented stone doorcase with pulvinated frieze, and the plastered lining conceal
the truth. A formal garden to the S probably belongs to the
C18.

DESCRIPTION

WESTERHOUSE ROAD and EASTERHOUSE ROAD form the
sharply curved main route through the scheme, dividing the
earlier houses at Blairtummock, Easthall, Kildermorie and
Wellhouse to its SW from the slightly later ones at Provanhall,
Bishoploch, Lochend and Rogerfield to its NE. Most of the
houses are tenements with particularly uneventful flat façades
of the late 1950s type, with individual recessed balconies to
each flat and a dreary coat of grey harl. The patches of contemporary and later two-storey houses do little to relieve the
monotony: neither does the TOWNSHIP CENTRE of 1968–
71 on WESTERHOUSE ROAD, with its one-storey shopping
mall and separate mediocre swimming pool, library and police
station along SHANDWICK STREET. St Benedict's Church
and School (*see* above) opposite make a much happier picture.
SE of the centre, in WARDIE ROAD, the plain C18 BLAIR-
TUMMOCK HOUSE (stone, two storeys and seven irregular
bays of sash windows) lies on the edge of the local park, closely
clipped by the M8 to the S. S of LOCHDOCHART ROAD, in
SOUTH ROGERFIELD, derelict tenements have been refurbished (*c.* 1987) and made more fashionably 'Olde English',

with timbered gables, timber oriels in place of balconies, and pantiled lean-to porches (cf. Barlanark; *see* Carntyne and Robroyston). There is a different and earlier expression of confidence along a wall curving round from LOCHEND ROAD into AUCHENGILL ROAD, where a mosaic mural evolves from simple landscape themes into seascape and more complex social themes. Designed and partly made by *Hamilton, Lydon, Massey, Kane* and *Kelly*, 1984.

BAILLIESTON

In 1833, when the chapel-of-ease (within Old Monkland Parish) was built at Crosshill, there was no settlement called Baillieston, only Baillieston House. Baillieston village seems to have grown as an extension of Crosshill, which it then absorbed. The area's main industry was mining, which began with the opening of the Monkland Canal in 1790 and superseded weaving, but declined decisively in the 1920s. Thereafter the area became a dormitory (annexed to Glasgow in 1975), with an increase in population from about 5,000 in 1911 to over 15,000 in 1983. Council housing engulfed the mining village of Swinton in the 1920s; private housing did the same for the Garrowhill estate in the 1930s, the area s of Main Street in the 1950s and the grounds of Baillieston House in the 1960s. It continues to spread.

Of the once idyllically situated riverside villas, the estate of Calderpark (now Glasgow Zoo) by the Calder and the dovecot of the former Daldowie mansion by the Clyde are the only evidence. Two motorway interchanges, amongst other developments, have completed the despoliation begun by mining and ironworking in the C19.

CHURCHES

BAILLIESTON OLD CHURCH (disused in 1989), Church Street. 1833. Built as a chapel within Old Monkland Parish; it became Crosshill Parish Church in 1872. Simple stuccoed, pedimented façade, with segment-headed windows. Pilastered bell turret with domical cap.

MURE MEMORIAL PARISH CHURCH, Maxwell Drive, Garrowhill. 1936–40, by *George Arthur & Son*. Cheaply built in brick, with no historicist references. Nave, aisles, saddleback-roofed tower over the pulpit end; large halls behind. Similar flavour to the simple interior with its brick chancel arch.

ST ANDREW (Baillieston Parish Church), Muirhead Road. 1973–6, by *Jas. Houston & Son*. Of blue engineering brick and stained timber with a tiled roof. Hexagonal, with a projecting N porch and, flanking it, mullioned windows filling two sides of the hexagon.

ST BRIDGET (R.C.), Swinton Road. 1891–3, by *Pugin &*

Pugin. Rock-faced red sandstone. Dec, with nave and aisles. An elaborate NE tower with spire was never built. A corridor (with confessionals) links the W end to the PRESBYTERY, a simple gabled house in pinkish ashlar by *William Ingram*, 1880–2. Inside the church, arcades of octagonal piers with moulded caps. Open timber roof on ugly wall-shafts. E window a rose within a spherical triangle. – STAINED GLASS. Nine windows by *John Hardman Studios*: Lady Chapel E (1945), E window (1947), and seven others (1948–9).

ST JOHN (Episcopal), Swinton Road. 1850–1. Very small, E.E. with nave and chancel of pinkish droved ashlar. Unpleasant flat-roofed vestry (1963).

DALDOWIE CREMATORIUM, Hamilton Road. Built as the Lanarkshire Crematorium in 1950 (County Architect *William Watt*) on the estate of the ancient manor house of Daldowie, owned by the Stewarts of Minto from the C16. A later house, built *c.* 1731–45 by the Bogles, was extended by John Dixon of Calder Ironworks in 1830 and 1837. All that remains from the time of the C18 mansion is the DOVECOT, some way to the W, within the curtilage of the sewage works. An immense sandstone cylinder with a tiled ogee roof. Below the eaves, a ring of nesting holes within a band of ashlar, and a wide ledge. Inside, the original wooden potence pole and nesting boxes.

4 M8 BAILLIESTON INTERCHANGE. A spectacular gateway to Glasgow with its series of carriageways looping overhead as one crosses the city boundary. Engineers: *Babtie, Shaw & Morton, c.* 1977.

The path of the M8 here follows the course of the part of the Monkland Canal which was infilled in 1972.

PUBLIC BUILDINGS

GARROWHILL INSTITUTE, Maxwell Drive. The C18 Garrowhill House (five-bay, with hipped roof, Venetian ground-floor windows, harling), extended by *George Arthur & Son*, 1935–8, as a community institute for the Garrowhill housing scheme. It lies in what remains of its grounds, now a small public park.

CALDERPARK ZOO, Baillieston Road. A handsome early C19 villa, Calderpark House, was demolished when the zoo was established here during World War II.

BANNERMAN HIGH SCHOOL, Glasgow Road. On the site of the early C19 Baillieston House (demolished in 1964). One- and two-storey ranges, system-built of grey aggregate panels and cheered up by sculpture in the courtyard and mosaics at the entrance.

GARROWHILL PRIMARY SCHOOL, Springhill Road. 1935–8, by *John Stewart* (Lanarkshire County Architect). Streamlined brick central block and rendered wings bent back round a garden, originally intended to be completely enclosed but never completed.

ST BRIDGET'S PRIMARY SCHOOL, Camp Road. 1931–7, by *John Stewart* (Lanarkshire County Architect), an extension to the original chapel-cum-school of 1880 (replaced by a parish centre, 1974–6). Two-storey wings form a hexagon enclosing an internal courtyard (cf. Garrowhill Primary, above). Slight classical reminiscences in the corner entrance block. All rendered.

CALDERBANK HOUSE, Muirhead Road. A late C 19 Baronial house on the site of an older house (recorded in 1796), reconstructed as a maternity hospital in 1931 by *J. Stewart* (Lanarkshire County Architect) and now a rehabilitation centre. Symmetrical front, with crowstepped gables and blocked columns to the porch. Fine staircase window with brilliantly coloured depictions of Morning, Hospitality and Evening: unsigned.

ST CATHERINE'S HOUSE (home for the elderly), Swinton Road. The former Mure Memorial Miners' Church of 1882 by *McKissack & Rowan*, simply and successfully converted to its present use by *Thomas Cordiner*, 1949–53. The main façade, with lancet windows between a pair of buttresses, is intact. Along the sides, two storeys of windows in the original long window opening: dormers above.

DALDOWIE DOVECOT. *See* Daldowie Crematorium, above.

CUILHILL BASIN of the Forth and Clyde Canal on the city boundary s of the Edinburgh Road. Built *c.* 1843. The central 'island', with masonry quay walls, has curved recesses for turning barges. The basin was originally linked with pits s of it by the Drumpeller railway.

DESCRIPTIONS

Baillieston

MAIN STREET still has the character of a mining village, with only a few simple buildings that look earlier than the mid-c 19. To the SE, the older settlement of CROSSHILL retains a slightly rural feeling in CHURCH STREET, despite the infiltration of industry. To the N of Main Street, SWINTON ROAD, with some villas of 1908 and St Bridget's Church (*see* above), is in its width the country road into which it peters out N of Edinburgh Road (constructed in 1924–8). The only evidence of the formerly independent village of SWINTON is the former church, one or two large houses of *c.* 1900, and, N of RHINDMUIR ROAD, in the midst of C20 housing, RHINDMUIR HOUSE, a late C18 five-bay house of painted stone, with semicircular Tuscan-columned porch, rusticated quoins and scrolled skewputts. One ugly C19 bay window.

Garrowhill

The Garrowhill Garden Estate was founded as a co-operative venture in 1923 by J. M. Scott Maxwell on orthodox, socially enlightened garden-suburb principles. His pamphlet *The housing scheme as a social training centre* (1935) set out his ideals of social education, community involvement and creative leisure. The estate was to be provided with a church, primary school, institute and playing fields to form 'that most essential feature of the scheme ... the community centre'.

The 180 acres (72·8 ha) of the Garrowhill estate were surveyed by *Maurice Arthur* in 1923 and plans were prepared; but ten years of effort produced no result until private enterprise from s of the border saw the possibilities. In 1934 building of 1,850 houses began (architects *George Arthur & Son*, contractor *H. Boot*). By 1939, 1,376 houses, the church and the school were complete. The N part was finished after the war. Unfortunately, the estate has none of the leafy cottagey attractiveness of Hampstead or Letchworth, though roads were laid along the contours in approved fashion and many old beech trees were kept. The houses (mostly four-in-a-terrace, with some detached, semi-detached and bungalows) are of the most ordinary speculative type, pebbledashed, tile-hung. At the centre, a small park, the remnant of the old country estate, with church, school and the Garrowhill Institute (*see* Public Buildings). To the E, a circus of simple single-storey shops in the same style.

CARMYLE

'Village' is a rather optimistic name for this collection of Lanarkshire County Council houses ringed by despoiled countryside. The riverside is promising, and it was here that the settlement had its origins, in the meal mills established by the bishops of Glasgow in the c 13. The village itself started as a muslin weaving settlement c. 1741, and grew after ironstone was discovered c. 1790. By 1882 it had a station and a 'straggling rural appearance'. The old centre of the village is round the church.

CARMYLE CHURCH, South Carmyle Avenue. A former United Free Church of 1906–7 by *Alexander Petrie*. Late c 16 Gothic in red sandstone, with a sturdy battlemented tower, topped by an octagonal Perp belfry and ogee dome. Inside, a hammerbeam roof, s gallery and chancel or, rather, organ recess.

ST JOACHIM, Inzievar Terrace. 1954–5, by *Gillespie, Kidd & Coia*. A nicely unassuming grey brick box with a shallow copper roof, and a concrete bell-frame creating the entrance. Diamond-shaped aisle windows below tall clearstorey ones. Shallow barrel-vault over the nave. – BALDACCHINO inlaid in silver with symbols of the Trinity and Evangelists. – STAINED GLASS. Two windows (St Joachim and St Anne) by *Nina Miller Davidson*.

CARMYLE HOUSE (originally Carmyle Cottage), 138 Carmyle Avenue. The gatepiers and an avenue of trees are the introduction to one of *William Burn*'s characteristic 'cottage houses' of the 1830s, designed in 1836 for John Sligo. Asymmetrical Jacobean of stugged ashlar. w entrance in a narrow gabled bay with shaped pediment over the door and a tall chimneystack flanking. The windows have flat lugged margins and mullions. Lower service wing to the l. in a favourite Burn composition (cf. Bryce's Tollcross House: *see* Shettleston and Tollcross: Public Buildings). The other façades have canted bay windows and dormers. Modest internal details.

CARMYLE RAILWAY VIADUCT. *See* Crossings of the Clyde and Kelvin, below.

PUBLIC BUILDINGS
⑦ Town Hall
⑧ (Parochial Offices)
⑨ Library and Post Office
⑨a Burgh Primary
⑨b Macdonald Centre and Nursery
⑩ Stonelaw High School
⑪ Stonelaw High School—
    Gallowflat Annexe
⑫ Maternity Hospital
⑬ Overtoun Park

RUTHERGLEN
TOWN CENTRE

FARME CROSS

DALMARNOCK RD

CAMBUSLANG RD

GLASGOW ROAD

Rutherglen Stn.

HIGH ST
GREENBANK ST
Queen ST
King ST
Victoria ST
FARMELOAN
Eastfield

MAIN   STREET

MILL ST
KIRKWOOD ST
STONELAW
HAMILTON ROAD

Gallowflat

BANKHEAD RD

GREENHILL   ROAD

Clincarthill

MELROSE AVE

Wardlawhill

MILL STREET

JOHNSTONE   DRIVE

DRYBURGH AVE

ROAD

STONELAW DR.

OVERTOUN

DRIVE

N

Overtoun
Park

RODGER   DRIVE

Burnside

0   ¼ mile
0   ½ km

CHURCHES
① Rutherglen Old Parish Church
② Rutherglen Baptist
②a St Columbkille (R.C.)
③ (Rutherglen East)
④ (Rutherglen Evangelistic Institut
⑤ Rutherglen Wardlawhill
⑤a Stonelaw Parish Church
⑥ Rutherglen West Parish Church

SUBURBS SOUTH OF THE CLYDE

RUTHERGLEN

Rutherglen stands upon a ridge above the point where the Clyde becomes tidal. Until its annexation by Glasgow in 1975 it was a proudly independent town. It was erected into a royal burgh, with a wide taxable area that included Glasgow, in the reign of David I. A charter of 1179–89 confirms this, although there is no evidence for the traditional date of 1126. As a trading centre it was superior to Glasgow until, in the late C12, Glasgow was also erected into a burgh of barony for its bishop and began the expansion that curtailed Rutherglen's prosperity and completely eclipsed her importance as a sea port. Despite this, the burgh remained important in national affairs and was represented regularly after 1478 in the Scottish Parliament.

The medieval town can still be recognized from its wide main street and back raw (King Street), linked by several wynds, and by fragments from its medieval parish church. No trace remains of the pre-1221 castle, which was sited near the present junction of King Street and Castle Street, and was almost completely destroyed at the battle of Langside in 1568. One tower, refurbished by the Hamiltons of Eliston, was ruinous by c. 1710.

By then, even Rutherglen's inland trade had dwindled. It was reduced to 'a quiet country village' (though still with eight fairs a year), trading mainly in coal, extracted from more than twenty neighbouring pits. On the riverside plains and s of the main street, Glasgow merchants acquired and remodelled or built country seats, such as Shawfield (1788), the c15 Farme Castle, Cathkin House (1799) and Gallowflat (1769). Most of these were obliterated by the industrial and suburban expansion that began in the last decade of the c18, after river trade in coal ceased in 1775 with the construction of a new bridge from Rutherglen to Bridgeton, and of an obstructive weir up-river at Glasgow Bridge in 1786. The new enterprises included printfields, a bleachfield at Shawfield (which became a soap and soda works in 1807 and gradually obliterated with its waste the ancient Town Green), a small cotton mill and a dyeworks at Farme. The population rose from 988 in 1755 to 5,502 in 1831, about 500 of whom were handloom weavers for Glasgow manufacturers.

Later in the c19 the soda manufactory developed into a chemical works which overran the old quayside at the bend of the river. Other heavy industry, including steamer building, steel production and ropeworks, spread along the Clyde. In Main Street and King Street, tenements replaced village buildings and sprang up N and s of them. The tolbooth, rebuilt in 1766 at the low point in the town's fortunes, was superseded in 1862 by an imposing Town Hall. After 1890, suburbs spread s towards Cathkin Braes over the wooded farmland dotted with pits and quarries, and became the home of Glasgow commuters as well as the local middle class. The population more than doubled between 1871 (10,766) and 1911 (24,319) and rose particularly fast between 1905 and 1908. At Stonelaw a pit was still in operation in 1900, yet by 1920 twenty-five drives and avenues had been built there. After 1918, Rutherglen spread its boundaries still further with low-density housing schemes provided all round the centre for those displaced from decaying c19 tenements. Redevelopment after 1945 swept away dying heavy industry and has left (in 1989) large areas of dereliction.

CHURCHES

BLAIRBETH RODGER MEMORIAL CHURCH, Kirkriggs Gardens. A hall church of 1954–6 by *Watson, Salmond & Gray*.

BURNSIDE PARISH CHURCH, Church Avenue. 1909–11, by *Stewart & Paterson*. Built as St Gilbert's, Pollokshields, and re-erected here in 1950–4. Prominently sited, large and of insistent E.E. design with rows of lancets, but without tower or *flèche*. Cruciform, with one aisle between the transept and big porch. A polygonal end to the E transept. The tall unmoulded aisle arcade passes without break in front of the transept. Deep panelled chancel, with tall chancel arch. Open timber roof. All the furnishings were imported with the church, including the STAINED GLASS (undated and unsigned). – S window, scenes of charity, for some reason enacted in C18 dress. – N window, a First World War War Memorial with a collage of boldly drawn scenes. – Only the ORGAN came from elsewhere – from Belmont Church.

Polygonal session house and large E.E. hall, designed as a hall church in 1926–8 by *J. J. Craig & Son*.

FERNHILL AND CATHKIN CHURCH, Neilvaig Drive. Opened 1962. A harled box with steep green slate roof and 'fire-station' tower by *Rogerson & Spence*.

RUTHERGLEN BAPTIST CHURCH, Stonelaw Road. 1903–4, by *William Ferguson*. Lancet-style, in red sandstone.

RUTHERGLEN EAST CHURCH, Farmeloan Road. Opened as a Reformed Presbyterian Church; closed 1981. By *G. P. Kennedy & R. Dalglish*, 1871–2: repaired 1895–8, re-roofed 1910. Geometrical, of grey snecked rubble. The tower with its short stone spire marks the street corner. Galleries reached via a tower and by the low polygonal projection. – ORGAN. 1904, by *Norman & Beard* of Norwich.

Former RUTHERGLEN EVANGELISTIC INSTITUTE (now flats), Greenbank Street. In an unsophisticated, even roguish, classical style, embellished with fancy cast-ironwork but spoilt with cement-render of 1988. Plans for the large hall, behind the committee and class rooms facing Greenbank Street, were drawn up in 1884 by the Revd Armstrong and improved by *J. J. Craig* (Burgh Surveyor). Completed 1887. A gymnasium and, above, a reading room lit by the narrow oriel were added in 1894–5 to Craig's design. On the other side of the little garden, the bathhouse, with hallkeeper's house above: 1901, by *George Sinclair*.

RUTHERGLEN OLD PARISH CHURCH (ST MARY THE VIRGIN), Main Street. In an ancient and still countrified churchyard, the tower of the medieval church stands dwarfed by *J. J. Burnet*'s large, towerless E.E.-style church of 1900–2.

The medieval church was assigned to Paisley Abbey before 1189. According to Ure (1793), the nave was 62 by 25 ft (19 by 7·6 m), plus two aisles. Each arcade had five pillars, 'smooth and round, except the middle ones which are octagonal', and slightly pointed arches. The fragments of capitals (scallop and waterleaf) that survive in the Rutherglen Museum fit the description of a Transitional building. The chancel was demolished before 1793; its E gable, with characteristic masonry, stands on the E side of the tower. The nave was replaced in 1794 by *James Jeffrey* and again by Burnet.

The tower was built much later than the C12, probably in the late C15 or early C16, completely independently against the E wall of the chancel. In 1710 it was given its timber and slated broach spire with four lucarnes. – BELL. 1635, cast by *Michael Burgerhuys* of Middleburgh, Holland (cf. Carmunnock).

The present church lies over the site of the medieval nave but lies N-to-S, not E-to-W. Of cream snecked rubble of the most mechanically finished kind, with lancets cut crisply out of large expanses of plain wall. No decoration except for the tabernacle and shafted doorway with carved tympanum on the broad W porch, and the narrow turret with a curious crown on the S façade alongside the gallery stair projection. The interior is grim in its plainness. Just a flat E wall pierced by lancets and unrelated to the broad arches carrying a gallery over the very broad W aisle, divided off as church halls, 1989. Vestibule screened off at its S end. Chancel marked only by steps, panelling and by flanking pulpit and reading desk. Arched-braced timber roof over the nave. – STAINED GLASS. All quite horrible. – Three-light window, 1911, by *James M. Benson* of Glasgow (the Ascension, with Christ on clouds like rocks above a stolid crowd). – Three-light (S) War Memorial (Sacrifice, Triumph, Peace), 1922, a confused collage by *W. Meikle & Sons*. – Single light by *Abbot & Co. (Lancaster) Ltd*.

GATEWAY to churchyard from Main Street. 1662–3, by *John Scott*. Classical but uncomfortably squat. Aonghus MacKechnie justly compares this gateway, with its unusual detail of a pair of consoles accompanied by another pair drawn in relief, with the doorway at the contemporary Kinneil House (Lothian), built for the Duke of Hamilton, who was chief heritor of Rutherglen Church. WARDENS' BOXES of stone (one dated 1761) flank the church path. For the churchwardens making collections. – STATUE. Built into the wall at the corner of the churchyard, a bronze seated but vigorous figure of Dr James Gorman † 1899 by *Johan Keller*, 1901. – Some C18 and early C19 GRAVESTONES.

RUTHERGLEN WARDLAWHILL CHURCH, Hamilton Road. A Congregational chapel of 1881–2, by *Robert Dalglish*; acquired by the Church of Scotland in 1884. Dull throughout. Plate tracery in the large gable window, the rest lancets. Extended by the rebuilding of the S gable and E addition of session house and vestry in 1936. Galleried interior with a flat ceiling. – STAINED GLASS. Two three-light windows (a War Memorial) by *R. Douglas McLundie*, unveiled 1949. – Two to commemorate the centenary by *Smith*, 1984. – HALLS, 1909.

RUTHERGLEN WEST PARISH CHURCH, Glasgow Road. A former Free Church of 1848–50 by *Charles Wilson*. A simple ashlar preaching box with lancets, distinguished by a supertall, super-slim partly engaged tower with a forest of tall, oversized pinnacles. The interior is charming, remarkably complete and perfectly adapted for preaching: the minister from his high pulpit commands the low curved gallery with its steeply raked gated pews. There are two tiers of cast-iron columns, the upper ones with leafy capitals carrying the plaster rib-vault with foliate bosses. Gabled Gothic organ case and pulpit and original pews, grained a light ochre. E window with the original patterned stained glass. – Large halls and church house by *Miller & Black*, 1929–30.

ST ANTHONY, Mar Gardens, High Burnside. By *Peter Whiston & Partners*, 1967–70. Harled, with a shaped slated roof.

ST COLUMBKILLE (R.C.), Main Street. 1934–40, by *Gillespie, Kidd & Coia*. The brick façade, with the severity of an Egyptian pylon, masks a basilican church, its Early Christian style modified by the late C17 domestic profile of the hipped roofs over the projecting confessionals. Tall, excessively narrow transepts and, at the SE angle, the presbytery, built first in 1935.

Round the entrances to both church and presbytery, the same enjoyable textures of patterned bricks and carved stone as at Coia's St Anne's, Whitevale Street (*see* Dennistoun); the triple narthex doors and the windows between them are outlined in five arches of brick and stone. – SCULPTURE by *Archibald Dawson*, completed by *Mortimer, Willison & Graham*. Over the doors, bas-reliefs of St Columba and his tutors. Along the blank wall above, figures of Christ and the Evangelists. – Set in a border round the presbytery door, ribbed with Roman tiles, blocks of stone carved with touchingly portrayed Biblical scenes and with the names of the incumbents of Rutherglen parish. Above the door, the Good Shepherd.

Inside, a wide flat-ceilinged nave and chancel and low passage aisles. The arcades have smooth, inflated curves, unbroken by capitals, in brownish Blaxter stone. Apsidal chancel, the arches to the side chapels and presbytery corridor suggesting an ambulatory, with an original classical baldacchino. Lavish but subtly coloured decoration at the E end, with much green marble and silvered wrought-iron. – PAINTING. The side chapels' barrel-vaults are decorated in contrasting styles. – Sacred Heart Chapel by *Walter Pritchard*. Baroque Crucifixion and Resurrection in transparent colours on an aluminium leaf ground. – Lady Chapel by *William Crosbie*. The Life of the Virgin, also on metal foil, but with the tight drawing and solid colour typical of the Early Renaissance. – STATUES in the chapels designed by *Coia* himself. – SANCTUARY LAMP AND ORGAN from the previous church (1853, by *R. Baird* of Airdrie). – STATIONS OF THE CROSS. Figurative, in glass mosaic by *Jessie McGeehan*.

ST MARK (R.C.), Fernhill Road, Burnside. 1957–61, and typical of the work of *Alexander McAnally & Partners*. An informal variation on the round-arched style, in brick and stone. Cruciform, with a gabled W tower. Plastered interior with wide unmoulded stone arches to the crossing and passage aisles. Panelled sanctuary. Wrought-iron screens to baptistery and mortuary chapel. – ORGAN by *Andrew Watt & Son*.

STONELAW PARISH CHURCH, Stonelaw Road. 1910–12, by *J. B. Wilson*. Originally United Presbyterian. A big but squat and towerless church on a site that slopes steeply S, allowing another storey beneath the nave, its red sandstone tooled in an unattractive chequer pattern. A polygonal vestibule with pinnacles, panelled at the tops, faces the road. Free Perp tracery in all the windows. Inside, cream snecked rubble with red sandstone dressings. Galleries on three sides, canted out between the tall arches of the two arcades. Tie-beam roof with traceried trusses. Only the 'ship's bridge' pulpit original. – STAINED GLASS. Contemporary three-light window by *William Meikle & Sons*, a confusing representation of the Raising of Souls.

PUBLIC BUILDINGS

TOWN HALL (now Glasgow District Council Offices), Main Street. 1861–2, by *Charles Wilson*, in Baronial style; extended
43 E in 1876 by *Robert Dalglish & John Thomson*. The most imposing building in Main Street, with a tall clock tower, 33·5 m (110 ft) high, of dramatic profile. All the details (battlements, machicolations and so on) are cut like pastry out of the cream sandstone ashlar. Decoration is restricted to armorial panels, a little strapwork, and big cast-iron lion's-mask waterspouts. In the tower (with clock by *Muirhead*), the main staircase to the grand meeting hall, which is lit by the large oriel. Below the oriel, arched windows, originally to shops (a courtroom lay behind them). Cast-iron entrance canopy of 1902. The 1876 extension r. of the tower, though, intended to be in harmony with the rest, is smaller in scale and more Jacobethan than Baronial. On the ground floor was the police office, on the first the council chamber, and, above that, constables' houses. Nothing inside survived the drastic conversion to offices by *Rogerson & Spence*, 1967.

Former PAROCHIAL OFFICES, Main Street. By *J.J. Craig* (Burgh Surveyor). Dated 1893. The shaped and pedimented gable, which marked the first-floor boardroom, is the only distinctive feature of this two-storey red sandstone façade.

LIBRARY AND POST OFFICE, Main Street. The library with two gables was built in 1905–7 by *Sinclair & Ballantine*; the post office was added in 1910–11 by *J.J. Craig* (Burgh Surveyor). All of white Bannockburn ashlar in a hybrid but predominantly late C17 style. Despite modernization by *Rogerson & Spence* in 1967, some nice interior features survive: plasterwork; stained glass in the former reading room dome by *John C. Hall*, with C17 motifs in an Art Nouveau manner; and a fireplace in the former committee room upstairs.

BURGH PRIMARY SCHOOL, King Street. A three-storey red sandstone Board school by *William Ferguson*, opened 1902. The best façade is to High Street, with tall roofs on the end pavilions and big arched upper windows.

Former EASTFIELD PUBLIC SCHOOL, Cambuslang Road. An earlier Board school by *William Ferguson*, 1898. Carved segmental pediment and other Wrenaissance detail.

GALLOWFLAT PUBLIC SCHOOL. *See* Stonelaw High School,
below.

MACDONALD CENTRE AND NURSERY, King Street. The
Macdonald School of 1865 has been demolished. What survives is the 1891 extension by *William Ferguson*. Three storeys
under a hipped roof with a central cupola.

STONELAW HIGH SCHOOL, Melrose Avenue. A Board school
of 1885–6 by *J.J. Craig* (Burgh Surveyor); extended in 1905
(date on tower). Of two storeys except for the tall Italianate
central tower, with banded rustication on the columns and
pilasters to emphasize the entrance. – GALLOWFLAT
ANNEXE, McCallum Avenue. Much more inventive than
Craig's school, an unusually asymmetrical and domestic block,
with beehive caps over the entrance towers, by *D. McNaughtan
& Son*, 1907, the only block of Gallowflat Public School's
original three to survive a fire of 1941.

RUTHERGLEN MATERNITY HOSPITAL AND HEALTH
CENTRE, Stonelaw Road. 1972, by *Frank Campbell*. A neat
five-storey system-built cube, wrapped round with glass
balconies.

OVERTOUN PARK, Mill Street. Opened in 1908 on land
donated by Lord Overtoun. By *Watson & Salmond* (1906),
the Free-Style GATEPIERS and charming LODGE, its red-
tiled roof swept out from a central chimneystalk over a broad
bay window facing the park. A shelter and ladies' waiting room
project to the E. – BAND STAND in cast- and wrought-iron by
J. & A. McFarlane, 1914, temporarily removed in 1988. –
DRINKING FOUNTAIN of cast-iron by the *Saracen Foundry*,
erected at the w end of Main Street in 1897 to celebrate Queen
Victoria's Diamond Jubilee (it has a bust of the monarch under
a domed canopy); moved here in 1911.

RUTHERGLEN BRIDGE. *See* Crossings of the Clyde and
Kelvin, below.

GALLOWFLAT. A mound, measuring about 31 m in diameter
and over 2 m high. Like the former cairn on Cathkin Braes, it
was surrounded by a ditch (which was widened in 1773 to
form a fishpond for Gallowflat House, but has been filled in
during recent landscaping). Gallowflat House was demolished
in 1914. A 'passage' leading to the summit was found during
the C18 work, as well as objects of C1 or C2 A.D. date, including
two Roman bronze *paterae*, three melon-shaped beads and
part of a rotary quern. These items were subsequently lost,
except for one of the melon beads, which is in Rutherglen
Museum. A stone cup-shaped lamp was also found in the
tumulus at some date and is now in the Royal Museum, Edinburgh.

DESCRIPTION

MAIN STREET is wide and tree-lined, recalling Rutherglen's
history as a market town. The broad loanings (now pavements)

were the site of horse and cattle fairs until 1900. Scenically, the street is rewarding: architecturally, there is little to recommend it except the churches and public buildings (*see* above).

On the N SIDE, the irregular curve of the building line recalls the site of the old Tolbooth (demolished in 1900). Here, near the site of the original (removed in 1777), stands a reconstruction of the MERCAT CROSS (made in 1926 from written descriptions). On a flight of twelve circular steps, a column carrying a lion holding the burgh arms. Most of the low thatched houses were replaced by tenements after 1873. A few, disguised by modern fronts, survive.

On the S SIDE, dominated by the powerful W front of St Columbkille's (*see* Churches, above), nondescript commercial buildings. Largest in scale is the MITCHELL ARCADE, a commonplace shopping mall of 1976 by *Keppie, Henderson & Partners*. Most diverting is the former VOGUE CINEMA (MECCA BINGO) by *John McKissack & Son*, 1935–6, reviled in 1946 (*Clyde Valley Plan*) for its 'disastrous effect' on the street. Egyptian overtones inside.

At each end of Main Street, the sense of enclosure was lost when roads were rebuilt and widened. At the W end, mid-C20 medium-rise blocks, rising out of waves of interwar cottages, make a bathetic distant prospect. Isolated by the carriageways of GLASGOW ROAD, opposite Rutherglen West Church, is the WAR MEMORIAL (unveiled in 1924), a granite cenotaph by *Robert Gray* with a bronze figure of Courage by *G. H. Paulin*.

N of Main Street and linked to it by one or two wynds, KING STREET is the medieval Back Raw. No buildings to suggest that now, only a school (*see* Public Buildings, above) that belonged to the tenements that used to stand here. E of Farmeloan Road, the former BURGH HALLS, built to a depressingly sober design of 1906 by *George Boyd* of Shettleston, originally for a temperance society.

FARMELOAN ROAD leads N to FARME CROSS, where until the 1960s a busy junction was enclosed by red sandstone tenements built soon after a destructive flood in 1903. These survive only at the NE corners. On the W side of the Cross, the Glasgow Style offices of BRITISH ROPES LTD, by *E. A. Sutherland*, 1912, its round red sandstone corner capped by a characteristic flattened ogee dome with long spindle finial. Further N, along DALMARNOCK ROAD (No. 26), STEWARTS & LLOYDS' PHOENIX TUBE WORKS, with an Italianate brick office block of *c.* 1905, pilastered in stone, and huge workshops in similar style but all of brick.

On the SE corner of the Cross, a pocket park opens up a view of the isolated enclave of artisans' cottages off CAMBUSLANG ROAD, four parallel terraces built by the Glasgow Working Men's Investment Trust & Building Society for local coal and steel workers. SMITH and MILLAR TERRACES were built first in 1875–7 and are of a type found more frequently, and earlier, in Edinburgh (but cf. Scotstoun and Springburn). Flatted stone cottages of two storeys plus attics, the ground-floor cottages entered from one side of the row, the upper ones by outside staircases from the other. CARLYLE TERRACE (1881–2) and RUSKIN TERRACE (1888–9) are single-storey with some bay windows: alternate cottages are entered from opposing sides.

Back to Main Street. S of it, streets of tenements have been replaced by the Mitchell Arcade (*see* above) and contemporary deck-access housing of the most austere kind. Further S rise the leafy suburbs of Clincarthill, Wardlawhill, High Crosshill and Burnside, which grew up rapidly between 1880 and 1914 with a mixture of unexceptional but well-preserved villas and terraces round a string of public parks. The largest houses are off STONELAW ROAD, which still preserves some of its wooded charm. For example, to the W in BROOMIEKNOWE ROAD, Nos. 32 (WESTKNOWE, 1901, by *Thomas Baird*) and 34 (dated 1878), both Scottish Baronial. In Wardlawhill, tenements and more modest villas, originally rented by the lower middle class.

Around BURNSIDE station a particular cohesive group of *c.* 1900–10, with red sandstone tenements on the main BURNSIDE ROAD, and terraced villas off it in Douglas and Peveril Avenues and at the start of BLAIRBETH ROAD. The last (Nos. 76–90) have many Glasgow Style touches, including the stained glass in windows of the detached corner house, dated 1907. Opposite, four large cream sandstone villas behind long gardens (Nos. 71–7), all earlier and very plain, except perhaps DUNCRAGGAN (No. 73) with its more generous bay. Further W, on the S side, BLAIRBETH TERRACE, a handsome tenement block in French Empire style, with tall mansards and gently bowed end bays. It began with the big L-shaped block at the E end, originally a villa converted to flats in 1896. W of that and S in STIRLING DRIVE, more modest houses of 1898–9 by *James Cunningham*.

At HIGH BURNSIDE, on the ridges to the S, several houses built in the late 1870s which stood in rural isolation for over twenty years. For example, in LOWER BOURTREE DRIVE, a plain double villa by *Francis Armstrong* of Dalbeattie, 1877, and in LOCHBRAE DRIVE, several more, including a sequence with Gothic gables and porches by *Harry Blair* of Glasgow, 1878–81. Of the larger houses, No. 14 Burnside Road (THE INGLE), with its corner tower and big bargeboards, is most appealing.

Fringing Cathkin Braes (now the very S edge of Glasgow) were a number of country retreats. Most important is CATHKIN HOUSE, designed for Walter Ewing Macrae in 1799 by the Edinburgh architect and landscape gardener *James Ramsay*. The S front has slightly projecting end bays marked by giant angle pilasters. The porch, shown in a view of *c.* 1878, was extended later by two bays and the Roman Doric doorcase removed. The same giant pilasters and bold coved cornice continue on the N front with its broad central bow and large

Adamesque Venetian windows. Later E addition. Converted into flats, 1989. Right at the S end of Burnside Road is MID-CATHKIN FARM, one of the Cathkin estate farms. A much altered rubble-built house, dated 1799 over the door.

Public housing schemes completely surround the town centre and the inner suburbs. Despite variations in style, from 1919 to 1960 their composition was consistent: mostly rendered cottages and cottage flats laid out along the contours. Earliest are the semi-detached cottages (1919–22) and slightly later tenements in GALLOWFLAT, at the E end of Main Street. Next came the monotonous area of 1,500 interwar flatted cottages of minimal design W of Main Street, begun in the early 1930s by *Hugh Inglis* (Burgh Surveyor). On MILL STREET, one or two more stylish tenements, pebbledashed with brick trim. Those at the corner of GREENHILL STREET are marked by almost circular bays.

EASTFIELD, E of Gallowflat, is also a scheme of the 1930s but is by Lanarkshire housing architects, *Peter Smith* succeeded by *William Brown*. Along CAMBUSLANG ROAD, their tenements have an Art Deco flavour, with brick trim, stepped parapets, flat roofs, rounded corners and metal windows.

SPITTAL (W) and FERNHILL AND CATHKIN (S) were built after 1945, with only slight variations on earlier themes.

CAMBUSLANG

Cambuslang comprises numerous small settlements. Some of them, like Flemington and Hallside, originated in the C17 and C18 as miners' and weavers' hamlets. Others were country estates, either ancient like Newton and Morriston, or more modern, like Wellshot and Rosebank, favoured in the late C18 and C19 as country seats conveniently near Glasgow. All were developed after industry began to expand rapidly *c.* 1860, either with suburban housing (e.g. Wellshot, the Coats) or with mines, manufactures and their associated dwellings (e.g. Rosebank, Morriston, Hallside, Westburn, Newton).

The name Cambuslang is relatively modern and was not applied to the barony of Drumsagard until the C17. The barony can be traced back to the reign of Alexander II (1214–49), when it belonged to Walter Olifard, justiciary of Lothian. In 1455 it passed, indirectly, to the Hamiltons, who remained feu superiors until 1922. The site of Drumsagard Castle lies SE of Hallside (*see* Descriptions, below). The position of the medieval church is unknown. Traditionally the founder was the C6 St Cadoc, but the first ecclesiastic was mentioned in connexion with barony *c.* 1180. In 1429 the church became a prebend of Glasgow Cathedral, and by the mid-C15 there was a village, probably round this church.

Post-Reformation history is more certain. A church (probably

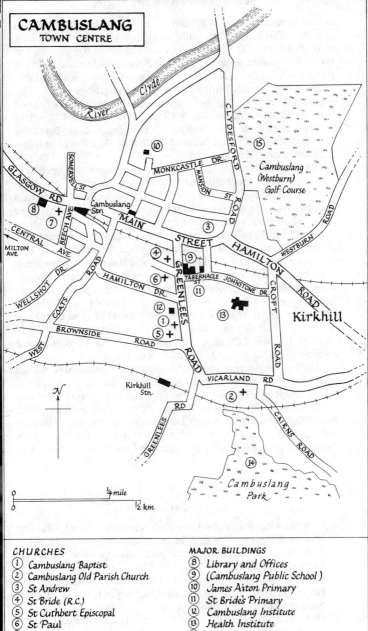

CAMBUSLANG
TOWN CENTRE

River Clyde

Cambuslang (Westburn) Golf Course

GLASGOW RD
SOMERVELL ST
MONKCASTLE DR.
CLYDESFORD ROAD
MANSION ST

Cambuslang Stn

CENTRAL AVE
MILTON AVE.
BEECH AVE
Cambuslang Stn
MAIN STREET
HAMILTON ROAD
WESTBURN ROAD

WELLSHOT DR
COATS ROAD
HAMILTON DR.
GREENLEES ST.
TABERNACLE ST.
JOHNSTONE DR.
CROFT ROAD

Kirkhill

WEST
BROWNSIDE ROAD

Kirkhill Stn
GREENLEES ROAD
VICARLAND RD.
CAIRNS ROAD

N

Cambuslang Park

0		¼ mile
0		½ km

CHURCHES
1. Cambuslang Baptist
2. Cambuslang Old Parish Church
3. St Andrew
4. St Bride (R.C.)
5. St Cuthbert Episcopal
6. St Paul
7. Trinity Parish Church

MAJOR BUILDINGS
8. Library and Offices
9. (Cambuslang Public School)
10. James Aiton Primary
11. St Bride's Primary
12. Cambuslang Institute
13. Health Institute
14. Cambuslang Park
15. Cambuslang Golf Course

not the first since 1560) was built on the site of the present parish
church at Kirkhill in 1626, and a village grew up around it. There
were coal-heughs at Morriston and Greenlees in the C17; and in
the C18, domestic weaving and spinning spread throughout the
parish, after 1780 mainly for Glasgow muslin manufacturers.
A short-lived cotton mill opened at Flemington in 1787. The
population in 1755 was less than 1,000. Heavy industry arrived
with the opening of Dunlop's Clyde Ironworks N of the river
in 1786. The iron and steel trade encouraged more extensive
exploitation of coal, and between 1801 and 1851 the population
doubled, from 1,616 to 3,306.

Cambuslang Station on the Carlisle to Glasgow line opened in
1849, but it was not until the 1870s that what is now the main
part of the village, Cambuslang Town, began to grow from a
collection of farm buildings. N of the main street, tenements were
built to house the workers in the riverside industries. S of it, near
the stations (Kirkhill opened in 1904), Glasgow commuters,
attracted by the still beautiful countryside, began to move into
the new suburb on the ridge overlooking the river. Commuters,
both middle- and working-class, and employees of the new steelworks at Hallside (opened in 1873), of new mines in the outlying
hamlets, and of new industries by the Clyde (e.g. Rosebank
Dyeworks, 1881; Mitchell Engineering, 1891) swelled the population (1851: 3,306; 1881: 9,447; 1891: 15,364; 1901: 20,211; 1911:
24,864). It levelled off after 1921 (26,130) and has been dropping
steadily up to the present day (21,886 in 1981).

Much of the decayed industrial housing and many rural village
buildings were replaced by large housing schemes in the 1930s,
1950s and 1960s. Industrial decline and the closure of many
mines during the 1940s and, since 1970, of all the steelworks
have blighted the area, which has increasingly become a dormitory. 270 acres (109 ha) of derelict land N and S of the Clyde were
declared a recovery area by the Scottish Development Agency in
1975.

CHURCHES

CAMBUSLANG BAPTIST CHURCH, Greenlees Road. 1895, by
William Ferguson. Classical, in cream sandstone with red ashlar
dressings. Hall beneath. At the back, the ingeniously planned
MEMORIAL HALL by *Miller & Black*, 1932.
CAMBUSLANG FLEMINGTON HALLSIDE CHURCH, 228
Hamilton Road, Flemington. Built in 1885 as Hallside Church.
Simplest lancet style. Halls of 1929.
CAMBUSLANG OLD PARISH CHURCH, Cairns Road. 1839–
41, by *David Cousin*. The third church known to have occupied
this site; its Transitional style may consciously recall a medieval predecessor. Its distant silhouette, with tall tower and
recessed spire rising above the trees of a large churchyard,
looks medieval and English; but, close to, the box-like nave
and unarchaeological detail reveal the church as distinctly early

C19. The nave and chancel in grey ashlar have flat buttresses, a simplified corbel table, angle pinnacles, and tall round-headed windows, moulded and with nook-shafts. The upper stage of the tower also has exceptionally tall and slim triplets of these windows. The spire has lucarnes (and, inside, a stone inscribed A M T 1626, which may survive from the first pre-Reformation church). The main door leads through the tower (which houses twin gallery staircases) to a classically groin-vaulted vestibule. In contrast, the body of the church is dominated by a splendid plaster vault of Tudor rather than Gothic inspiration. Moulded diaphragm arches meet in pendant finials and corbels shaped like crowns. More crowns act as stops to the hood-moulds over the gallery windows. All round the walls at this level, shields display the arms of the heritors. The arms of the Duke of Hamilton (as chief heritor) occur a dozen times. The curved gallery rests on simple cast-iron columns. The chancel was rebuilt in 1919–22 to plans prepared by *Macgregor Chalmers* in 1913. He moved the organ from within the chancel arch to its own chamber.

The pleasingly bold and coherent decorative scheme dates from 1957–8 and should be preserved. The ceiling was painted dark blue, the woodwork stripped and stained glass put in all the windows. – The STAINED GLASS was designed by *Sadie McLellan* with a light but decisive touch. E window (The Life and Words of St Cadoc; Christ as Head of the Church), nave windows (symbols of the Passion within broad wavy borders, set in clear glass), tower windows (Angels). – TAPESTRIES also by *McLellan*. Altar frontal (Agnus Dei); pulpit frontal (Burning Bush); hanging in vestibule (Te Deum Laudamus). – ALTAR CROSS, with trails of silver and copper leaves, to a design by *McLellan*. – ORGAN. 1896, by *Abbot & Smith* of Leeds; rebuilt by *Peter Conacher* of Huddersfield, 1968. – BELL, E end of nave. Inscribed M I H 1612 (for John Houston) and CH (possibly for *Charles Hogg*, an Edinburgh bell-founder). – WAR MEMORIAL, 1921, designed by *MacGregor Chalmers*. – GATEPIERS. Decorated with intersecting arcading, zigzag and dogtooth.

HALLS. 1895–7, by *A. Lindsay Miller*. Gothic, with some trefoil-headed windows. Extended in 1968.

ST ANDREW, Main Street. 1961–6, by *Beveridge & Dallachy*, with many popular mannerisms: a shallow-pitched roof, patterns of snapped headers on the blank chancel and transept walls, random stone facing, green slate window surrounds, coloured spandrels in the large W window. To the N, a courtyard enclosed by vestries (E), the hall (N), and an open walkway (W). On one courtyard wall, a relief of Christ and St Andrew by *Thomas Whalen*. Inside, a single passage aisle (N) with simple cylindrical piers. Contemporary furnishings: FONT and CHANCEL PAVEMENT (with Evangelist symbols) by *Whalen*; COMMUNION TABLE by *Thomas Beveridge*; wrought-iron RAIL with abstract crosses designed by *Colin M. Middleton*, made by *John Allan*. – C19 furnishings and STAINED GLASS

SE window from Rosebank Church and West Parish Church. –
ORGAN by *Compton*.

ST BRIDE (R.C.), Greenlees Road. Behind the squat church
of 1902 by *Joseph Cowan & Sons*, the tall presbytery of 1896–
8, with fancy ironwork cresting.

ST CADOC (R.C.), Wellside Drive, Halfway. 1955–60, by
Thomas Cordiner & Partners.

ST CHARLES (R.C.), Newton Brae, Westburn Road. Reconstructed by *L. A. M. Fraser*, after a fire in 1981, to the original
plain design of 1927. To the W, the original red sandstone
church of 1894 by *Joseph Cowan*, now in industrial use.

ST CUTHBERT (Episcopal), Brownside Road. The hall of a
church planned in 1909 by *H. D. Walton* but never built. Rock-
faced, lancet-style façade. Open timber roof inside.

ST PAUL, Bushyhill Street and Hamilton Drive. Designed as a
United Free Church in 1904–5 by *Alexander Petrie*. Rock-
faced Locharbriggs sandstone. Tall (with halls beneath the
church), and ecclesiastical-looking only from Hamilton Drive.
Horseshoe gallery. Panelled ceiling carried on columns and
pointed arches. – PULPIT and choir redesigned in 1938.

TRINITY PARISH CHURCH, Glasgow Road at Beech Avenue.
1897–9, by *William Ferguson*. A very large, originally United
Presbyterian church of red Corncockle sandstone, in a freely
interpreted Perp style. Flat-roofed staircase projections and,
above them, square pinnacles clasped by buttresses built up
into a substantial entrance front. Rooftop bell turret, with tall
spiky finial. At the N end of the gabled side elevation, two more
tower-like bays flank the manager's room. Behind this, the
hall. Inside, tall quatrefoil piers support a dark-stained open
timber roof. Between the piers the gallery projects in canted
bays. – ORGAN, 1900, with an elaborate display of pipes within
a tall arch. – STAINED GLASS. Gallery W by *Stephen Adam*
(Resurrection), post-1914. – Aisle E by *Gordon Webster* in dull
blues (Christ's Entry into Jerusalem), 1947. – Several pictorial
windows of the 1930s.

PUBLIC BUILDINGS

CAMBUSLANG PUBLIC LIBRARY AND OFFICES, Glasgow
Road. By *John Stewart* (Lanarkshire County Architect), 1936–
8. One long range with stripped classical detail.

VOGUE BINGO, Main Street. The Savoy Theatre of 1929 by
John Fairweather became a Vogue cinema in the 1930s. The
façade is still stuccoed and classical, with a modified order of
Doric pilasters, in the C19 theatre tradition. Unspoilt (though
shrouded) classical interior, and engraved glass shopfronts.

CAMBUSLANG BOWLING CLUB, Westcoats Road. The club
was founded in 1874; the classical gateway and pavilion, with
miniature Baronial tower, look a little later.

CAMBUSLANG PUBLIC SCHOOL (Cambuslang College
Annexe), Greenlees Road. By *A. Lindsay Miller*, 1882–3.
Tudor-Gothic. The most decorative façade, with some nice

carving, faces Greenlees Road. Plainer extensions of pre-1910 to Tabernacle Street.

DALTON SPECIAL SCHOOL, Stoneymeadow Road, Dalton. 1931, by *John Stewart* (Lanarkshire County Architect) with the county's familiar style and layout for schools at this date.

JAMES AITON PRIMARY SCHOOL, Morriston Street. 1974, by *Edward Allan* for Lanarkshire County Council. Circular, single-storey, and prefabricated.

ST BRIDE'S PRIMARY SCHOOL, Tabernacle Street. Designed as an R.C. Advanced Division school in 1936 by *John Stewart* (Lanarkshire County Architect) in a particularly severe stripped classical manner.

CAMBUSLANG INSTITUTE, Greenlees Road. 1892–8, by *A. Lindsay Miller*; extended in 1906 and 1910. L-shaped, with a large hall behind in the angle. Plain wings of grey snecked rubble contain the library and recreation rooms. At the corner, a tower with strange spear-like shafts engaged by roll mouldings round the drum of the dome. Interior modernized 1978–83.

HEALTH INSTITUTE, Johnstone Drive. 1926, by *John Stewart* (Lanarkshire County Architect). Its plan, with splayed wings, recalls contemporary schools, but the style is more domestic, with pitched tiled roofs and brick and harled walls. Modernized inside by *Strathclyde Architects' Department*, 1982–3.

Former POLICE BARRACKS, Mansion Street. Built *c.* 1911 and converted into sheltered accommodation by the Scottish Housing Association in 1982. Institutional-looking, with two gabled and bay-windowed wings following the curve of the street. At the corner, a handsome late C17-style doorcase, its scrolled pediment enclosing a shield of arms.

CAMBUSLANG PARK. Opened in 1913 as a ribbon of open land following the natural declivity of Borgie Glen. Just S of the Parish Church, the PREACHING BRAES, a natural amphitheatre made famous by the revivalist meetings (the Cambuslang Wark) held there in 1742 by William McCulloch, a local clergyman, and the evangelist George Whitefield. 50,000 attended the second communion of the meeting.

CAMBUSLANG FOOTBRIDGE, CLYDEFORD ROAD BRIDGE, BOGLESHOLE ROAD BRIDGE. *See* Crossings of the Clyde and Kelvin, below.

DESCRIPTIONS

Cambuslang

MAIN STREET completely lost its village character in the 1960s, when it was transformed into a dual carriageway and the area of C19 tenements that had shut it off from the river and riverside industry was comprehensively redeveloped. Before then it was lined with tenements and punctuated with churches, just like many similar village main streets (*see*, e.g., Shettleston).

The late C19 and early C20 tenements that survive are on the S side. Simple though they are, they form an almost unbroken line. On the N side, the ground level, with shopping parades and a public square, is sunk below street level and linked only tenuously to it by ramps and steps. The public square is enclosed by two storeys of shops and defined on the E side by a slab block on tall *pilotis* (KYLE COURT, completed in 1965). Further W, three more cross-shaped tower blocks amongst an estate of medium-rise system-built slabs, some on *pilotis* where the ground slopes away. Linking staircase towers are patterned in brick or concrete. Beyond, in MONKCASTLE DRIVE, a few modest C19 villas.

Of the few riverside industrial buildings that survive, the former ROSEBANK DYEWORKS in SOMERVELL STREET is most important. The production of Turkey red yarn began here soon after 1881 and stopped *c.* 1945. The building, banded with Greek key pattern in white brick on red and with a double-pitched roof with bell turret, is prominent in the view S from Main Street. Also in Somervell Street, the HOOVER FACTORY, 1946, large but not visually striking.

Trinity Church, at this (W) end of the village's main street, hints at the prosperity of the suburbs to its S. The first were laid out on the Wellshot estate *c.* 1869. (WELLSHOT HOUSE itself, of 1806, survives, much altered, in MILTON AVENUE off Buchanan Drive.) A few houses are large and detached, but many, e.g. those in HAMILTON DRIVE, are semi-detached and less pretentious, often with only one-and-a-half storeys.

Of the old village to the SE at KIRKHILL, there is now only the parish church (*see* above). The last low thatched cottages were replaced with tenements by Lanarkshire County Council in the 1930s. Further E still, off Hamilton Road, in WESTBURN ROAD and CALEDONIAN CIRCUIT, some County Council tenements in a more distinctive 1930s style, with Art Deco-ish brick trim on whitened render.

N of these, on the Cambuslang Golf Course, Clydeford Road, the C18 DOVECOT of Westburn House; octagonal, single-chambered with an ogee slate roof, two circular windows and a low door. Round the top, four dove-holes and below them a continuous stringcourse-cum-perch. Harled in 1974. Inside, 488 nest-holes with slate perches. Westburn House itself was built in 1685 and added to in 1703; it was ruinous by 1895 and demolished shortly afterwards.

Halfway, Hallside, Newton, Westburn

These villages and hamlets are scattered over rolling countryside, scarred by derelict industrial sites and bings.

HALFWAY is the dominant settlement, a C19 mining village with only a few of its stone cottages left on the shopping street along HAMILTON ROAD and the redundant C19 Gilbertfield Church at the junction with Lightburn Road. 1930s and 1950s public housing built by Lanarkshire County Council predominates. To the N, off MILL ROAD, a large, nicely land-scaped S.S.H.A. scheme of the 1970s. Just beyond the city boundary to the S are the ruins of GILBERTFIELD CASTLE, an L-shaped tower house of 1607.

HALLSIDE, to the NE, was built to house workers from the adjacent steel works (which opened in 1873 and were demolished exactly 100 years later). Some of the cottages remain, more or less in their original state, from the once much larger settlement. The terraces, built in the 1870s of stone with brick dressings, lie at r. angles to the road. At the end of a slight ridge to the SE is the site of DRUMSAGARD CASTLE, represented by a circular mound, level on top and about 6 m high and 43 m in diameter. No trace now of the castle: its stones were used c. 1775 to build Hallside Farm. The barony originated in the early C13 (see above).

WESTBURN was also designed to serve steelworks. Mostly tenements here, built by Lanarkshire County Council in the 1930s. More interesting are the 1930s timber-clad Corporation cottages in NORTHBANK AVENUE, and some post-war steel-clad houses near the former steelworks in NEWTON AVENUE. (For Westburn House dovecot, see Cambuslang, Description, above.)

At NEWTON, the salubrious Newton House of 1825 acquired a mining settlement as a neighbour in the C19 and was later demolished. The miners' cottages have been almost completely replaced in the 1980s by speculative housing.

Beyond these villages, rising to a ridge in the S, pastoral landscape, dotted with farms and their associated terraced cottages. Of the many villas built in this area, the only one that remains is CALDERGROVE HOUSE (Hamilton Road) in the wooded valley of the Rotten Calder. It is now just the shell of a plain villa of c. 1830, spoilt in 1875 by a mansard roof and Ionic porch. The interior, lavishly decorated in 1875 and 1919, was remarkably well preserved until 1983, when it was burnt out.

GORBALS

The name of Gorbals evokes the memory of notorious slums, of decaying tenements with a warren of bed-and-kitchen houses and single-ends; but its history is longer and far more complicated than that outdated and always inaccurate image suggests, and makes an interesting study in the sometimes unfortunate fate of planned development. The first attempt to impose a plan on the ancient lands of Gorbals (and the medieval Gorbals village) was made in the late C18, when the Glasgow Town Council, which had annexed them to Glasgow in 1661, split them between three beneficiaries. The city of Glasgow took Gorbals village and lands to the S, and part of Kingston; the Trades' House, the area between what is now West Street and Bridge Street; and

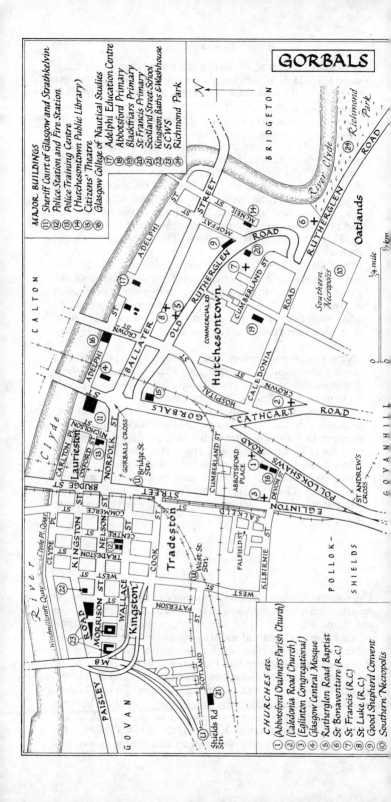

GORBALS

MAJOR BUILDINGS

⑪ Sheriff Court of Glasgow and Strathkelvin
⑫ Police Station and Fire Station
⑬ Police Training Centre
⑭ (Hutchesontown Public Library)
⑮ Citizens' Theatre
⑯ Glasgow College of Nautical Studies
⑰ Adelphi Education Centre
⑱ Abbotsford Primary
⑲ Blackfriars Primary
⑳ St Francis Primary
㉑ Scotland Street School
㉒ Kingston Baths & Washhouse
㉓ SCWS
㉔ Richmond Park

CHURCHES etc.

① Abbotsford Chalmers Parish Church
② (Caledonia Road Church)
③ (Eglinton Congregational)
④ Glasgow Central Mosque
⑤ Rutherglen Road Baptist
⑥ St Francis (R.C.)
⑦ St Bonaventure (R.C.)
⑧ St Luke (R.C.)
⑨ Good Shepherd Convent
⑩ Southern Necropolis

Hutchesons' Hospital the land E of Main (now Gorbals) Street, plus a separate slice between the present Nicholson Street and Bridge Street which they feued to James Laurie in 1801. Tradeston was laid off first between 1790 and 1798, to a grid plan devised by *John Gardiner*, surveyor. Hutchesontown, laid out between 1790 and 1813, was linked to Glasgow in 1794–5 by the short-lived Hutchesons' Bridge (replaced in 1829–34 and again in 1868–71 by Albert Bridge), which turned Crown Street into its main thoroughfare. The feuing conditions demanded uniformly four-storey houses along streets of generous and equal width. In 1802 James Laurie began his even grander plans for a suburb of streets named after the English nobility with Carlton Place; the neighbourhood's amenity was soon destroyed by the tramway that the ironmaster William Dixon built to link his colliery and the Clyde, but Laurie persevered and some of the whole district's smartest tenements were built along the Portland Street–Abbotsford Place axis as late as the 1830s. Gorbals retained its village character, with thatched cottages and early C18 tenements alongside a chapel of 1727 and the mansion built in the C16 by the Elphinstons, then rentallers of Gorbals.

These plans had to compete with the growth of transport and industry. The Glasgow, Paisley and Ardrossan Canal and its terminus, Port Eglinton, opened in 1814, and were superseded in 1840 by the railway and Bridge Street Station. Weaving factories and engineering works were started in Tradeston and Kingston, cotton mills in Hutchesontown. The Clyde Navigation Trust developed the riverside with Clyde Place Quay (1832–4) and Windmillcroft Quay (1840). The medieval bridge was replaced by Victoria Bridge in 1851–4. By then Tradeston was irredeemably industrial and artisans' tenements had spread W into Laurieston. Although some middle-class tenements were being built in Hutchesontown in the 1850s, S of them lay a mix of mills, workshops and workers' houses. Gorbals' overcrowded and elderly property was replaced by the City Improvement Trust between 1871 and 1891. Then the whole district was about as large as C19 Cardiff and crammed with twice as many people (1851: 36,147; 1871: 44,042; 1891: 39,806).

Despite overcrowding, the purpose-built tenements of Gorbals and Hutchesontown remained structurally sound until they were demolished in the 1950s. Pockets of the earlier, smarter houses of Laurieston and Hutchesontown remained in middle-class ownership until after 1945, but most had become teeming slums. The great development schemes of the 1950s and 1960s were aimed as much at rehabilitating Gorbals' reputation as at physically improving it. Decayed and sound houses, with industry intermingled, were indiscriminately swept away, leaving a few scattered public buildings and churches; some commercial premises in Bridge Street and industrial ones in Tradeston; a fringe of houses in Carlton Place; and a patch of C19 tenements at Oatlands.

Hutchesontown-Gorbals (E of Gorbals Street) was one of the first three Comprehensive Development Areas to be designated

in Glasgow; at the time it was the biggest in the United Kingdom.
The plan was approved in 1957. *Robert Matthew* and *Basil Spence*
were appointed design consultants to *A. G. Jury* (City Architect
and Planner). The first three schemes were completed by 1965,
two others by 1970. By the time the much smaller Laurieston-
Gorbals C.D.A. was designated in 1965, cost had curtailed any
visionary planning. Its four slabs were set down in a windswept
open space between roads and railway lines. The tide had turned
in favour of rehabilitation before the third C.D.A. (Hut-
chesontown-Polmadie) could be started. There the worst housing
has been cleared, but many tenements have been retained and
improved.

CHURCHES

Former ABBOTSFORD CHALMERS PARISH CHURCH, 100
Pollokshaws Road. Built as a Free Church in 1897–8. An
ungainly, unclassifiable, but more or less Italianate design by
H. & D. Barclay, with a tall semicircular portico, a wheel
window in the gable and a stumpy *tempietto* above. (STAINED
GLASS by the *Blythswood Stained Glass Co.*)

CALEDONIA ROAD CHURCH, 1 Caledonia Road. The burnt-
out shell of *Alexander Thomson*'s first church (1856–7) is a
memorable landmark on the route N through Gorbals. A fragment of Greek Ionic temple and an extremely tall tower of
Lombardic origin, recalling Thomson's earliest Italianate
essays, are tied together in a Romantic composition by a tall
plinth, banded in Schinkel's manner, and by the weighty backdrop of the body of the church, banded below but opened into
a continuous glazed colonnade above. The forms are more
solid and have less spatial trickery than the later St Vincent
Street Church (*see* Commercial Centre, above: Churches). The
plinth is pierced only by twin Vitruvian openings, which gave
access into the vestibule. The interior was tall like a classical
cella, with a boldly constructed timber roof and an architecturally treated platform, similar to those of St Vincent
Street. Light came from high up, from the clearstorey and
from within the portico. The plan was well adjusted to the
gushet site, with the additional wedge of space to the W taken
by the church hall, and the elevations were originally subtly
echoed in tenements to the N.

EGLINTON CONGREGATIONAL CHURCH (closed), 341
Eglinton Street. 1866, by *John Burnet*. French Gothic exterior
with an engaged corner tower and short spire. (Remarkable
interior decoration of 1895 designed by *W. J. Anderson*, including the MURAL on the E wall, painted by *J. Moodie* to represent
a Byzantine iconostasis, and the copper and wrought-iron
CORONAS, made by *J. Milne & Sons*. – STAINED GLASS.
Circular windows: C13 style, by *W. & J. J. Kier*, 1866.)

GLASGOW CENTRAL MOSQUE, Gorbals Street. Completed in
1984 by the *Coleman Ballantine Partnership*. It unfortunately
takes no advantage of its commanding site on the banks of the

Clyde. Round three sides of an irregular paved courtyard, the mosque (E) linked to a community hall (W) by a low range of ancillary rooms (S). The otherwise simple roofline is punctuated by a multi-faceted golden dome and a tall slender concrete minaret, which seem as insubstantial as a child's spinning top and stick. The mosque's brick walls are pierced by diagonally cantilevered bay windows of brick and glass and by a large concrete portal. The other buildings, also of brick, have shallow-arched concrete surrounds to windows and doors. Interior decoration is limited to geometric patterns contrasted with fields of strong colour.

RUTHERGLEN ROAD BAPTIST CHURCH, Old Rutherglen Road. The former Augustine Free Church of 1872. E.E. with a spheric-triangle window in the gable and a jazzy metal finial of modern origin on the stunted SE tower.

ST BONAVENTURE (R.C.), 473 Caledonia Road. Designed by *J. Honeyman* and built in 1877–8 as the Buchanan Memorial Church; converted in 1953 from use as a factory to an R.C. church by *Gillespie, Kidd & Coia*. The style is French Gothic, reminiscent of E. W. Pugin's, with its row of sharp gables and traceried windows along the side and its picturesque composition of gabled halls, nave façade with a rose window and SE tower with an apse. A copper cap has been plonked on the tower in place of a spire. Simple interior. – REREDOS and Passion series round the gallery painted by *William Crosbie*.

ST FRANCIS (R.C.), 405–7 Cumberland Street. 1868, by *Gilbert Blount*; rebuilt, including the Tudor Gothic Friary, by *Pugin & Pugin* (nave 1878–81, chancel and chapels completed 1895). Lumpish rock-faced Dec, characteristic of Pugin & Pugin. No tower, just a polygonal stair-turret on the façade topped by a statue of St Francis. Private SE chapel off the corridor that leads to the Friary. Octagonal piers, moulded arches, wall-shafts carrying a wagon roof, clearstorey lancets screened by continuous arcading. In each aisle bay a mosaic within a niche is flanked by lancets with deep, arched recesses below. At the NE end, the usual elaborate stone altars. – PULPIT. 1887, executed by *Boulton* of Cheltenham in alabaster and marble, with Caen stone reliefs.

ST LUKE (including St John) (R.C.), Ballater Street. Completed 1975. By *William J. Gilmour* in conventional but unattractive materials. A steep monopitch copper roof sweeps up to a prow-like NW tower.

GOOD SHEPHERD CONVENT, Old Rutherglen Road. Part of the former Hayfield Public School (1903, by *John Hamilton*). A long, loosely composed front, with a few Glasgow Style touches. Handsome timber roof over the galleried hall projecting at the back.

SOUTHERN NECROPOLIS, Caledonia Road. 11 acres (4·5 ha) were opened in 1840. It was extended E in 1846 and W in 1850. The massive castellated gateway, with vaguely Norman arch and arcading round the windows above, is by *Charles Wilson*, 1848.

PUBLIC BUILDINGS

Sheriff Court of Glasgow and Strathkelvin,
116 Gorbals Street. By *Keppie, Henderson & Partners*, 1980–6.
Dumb monumentalism in the form of a very late descendant
of Kallman McKinnell & Knowles's Boston City Hall (U.S.A.)
of 1962–7, with its lower storeys graduated behind a sub-
classical framework of heavy lintel and narrow piers. Here the
weight of this darker framework seems to press the building
(which is sunk to accord with the neighbouring Carlton
Terrace) into the ground. Though aligned with Carlton
Terrace, the building stands as aloof as a fortress from the
river and its neighbours, separated from them by a broad
terrace. The materials and finishes inside and out speak of vast
cost. Outside, the coffee-coloured Danish marble of the outer
framework contrasts with honey-coloured sandstone cladding,
channelled on the lowest storey. The interior, its narrow top-
lit spine overlooked by access balconies and crossed by glass
and metal bridges, continues the 1960s manner in pale Hoptonwood limestone, terrazzo, cream plaster and dark hard-
woods, but is given a 1980s gloss with Mackintosh-inspired
chequered screens and a few Post-Modern flourishes. Above
the central desk, a RELIEF of St Mungo by *Jake Kempsell*. N
of the spine overlooking the river lie the offices and sheriffs'
suite; s of it, the twenty-one courtrooms, with six double-
height criminal jury courts on the ground floor, and smaller
courts above and below them.

Police Station and Fire Station, Wallace Street and
Centre Street. The former Southside Fire Station of 1914–16,
by Glasgow's *Office of Public Works*. Two Wrenaissance-style
blocks striped in brick and stone and joined by an archway.
The present Police Station (Wallace Street) was built as
accommodation for the firemen; the Centre Street block incorporated an engine room and firemen's houses.

Police Training Centre, 71 Oxford Street. A police office
and barracks of 1892–5 by *A. B. McDonald* (City Engineer).
Red-painted palazzo façades to Oxford Street and Nicholson
Street; the rest of pressed red brick, with mid-c20 additions
towards Norfolk Street.

Hutchesontown Public Library (now day nursery),
McNeil Street. 1904–6, by *J. R. Rhind*. A very handsome
and subtly asymmetrical Loire-style design, with beautifully
carved architectural and sculptural detail in red sandstone
ashlar. The three bartizans have domed lead caps with complicated modelling, the slightly off-centre square tower a stone
top with the same detail, supported by gryphons and with a
slender female figure holding a book as a finial. Over the broad
entrance, a low-relief frieze of half-figures: St Mungo blessing,
flanked by Della Robbia-style maidens carrying the emblems
of Glasgow (ship, tree etc.). More such emblems in plaques
on the bartizans.

Citizens' Theatre, Gorbals Street. The untheatrical yellow

brick façade and foyer of 1989 by *Building Design Partnership* screens a C19 theatre, built in 1878 as Her Majesty's (later Royal Princess) Theatre by *Campbell Douglas*, originally with Doric columns from David Hamilton's Union Bank in Ingram Street (1841). The parapet statues of Burns, Shakespeare and the muses by *Mossman* are now ranged behind the generous band of glazing above the canopied entrance. The interior, with two horseshoe tiers on cast-iron columns, is more or less intact. It was altered in 1887 by *A. Skirving* with elaborate decoration by *Joseph Sharp*, including the stage boxes, with muses of a fairground quality copied from Mossman's sculptures. Proscenium decorated by *Thos. Lawrie*, 1895. It became the Citizens' Theatre in 1945.

COLISEUM, 79–85 Eglinton Street. A music hall of 1903–5 by *Frank Matcham*, built for Moss Empires. First converted to a cinema in 1925. The Franco-Flemish-style façade has an elaborate corner pavilion, originally topped by a revolving electric advertisement within the cupola. Behind is a red brick box with COLISEUM in raised letters. The interior, with cantilevered galleries based on the Ardwick Empire, Manchester, was destroyed in 1962.

NEW BEDFORD PICTURE HOUSE (Mecca Bingo), 121 Eglinton Street. 1932, by *Lennox & Macmath*, with an angular Art Deco façade of painted reconstituted stone, and until 1988 a night-sky mosaic and coloured zigzags round the central arch.

COLLEGE OF BUILDING AND PRINTING (Annexe), 7 Florence Street. A large classical Board school (the former Adelphi Terrace Public School), by *T. L. Watson*, 1894.

GLASGOW COLLEGE OF NAUTICAL STUDIES, Ballater Street. By *Robert Matthew, Johnson-Marshall & Partners*, 1962–70. A clean-cut white-tiled cube with a forest of rooftop radar masts, giving a truly nautical look. Facing the main gate, the domed planetarium. Towards the river a deck-like podium with brown-clad assembly hall and dining room, a ship's mast and an overhead link to a riverside block and jetty. To the W, a simple marine engineering workshop (1971, by Glasgow's *Department of Architecture and Civic Design*) and toffee-brown residential blocks.

ADELPHI EDUCATION CENTRE, Commercial Road. Designed as a junior secondary school by *Boissevain & Osmond*, 1963–6. Of one and two storeys round a central courtyard; neat and impersonal, with its neutral colours and precise detailing.

ABBOTSFORD PRIMARY SCHOOL, 129–31 Abbotsford Place. A Board school by *H. & D. Barclay*, opened in 1879. It is a cream ashlar Roman palazzo with a deep timber cornice, pedimented entrance bay and stress on the more highly modelled first floor, with its subtly grouped windows. Central hall. To the N, a simplified version by the same architects, 1893.

BLACKFRIARS PRIMARY SCHOOL, Cumberland Street, and ST FRANCIS PRIMARY SCHOOL, Old Rutherglen Road. Two well-detailed and compactly planned schools, with curtain-walled classroom blocks, for Hutchesontown-Gorbals C.D.A. by *J. L. Gleave & Partners*, 1961–4.

SCOTLAND STREET PUBLIC SCHOOL, 225 Scotland Street. 1904–6, by *Charles Rennie Mackintosh* (by then a partner in *Honeyman, Keppie & Mackintosh*) for Govan School Board. Its N front and its glittering stairtowers can be clearly seen from the motorway now that the surrounding tenements and most of the industry have gone. Closer to, the building can be read as a conventional Board school, but one which, like the Martyrs' School, has been infused by a singular architectural imagination. The plan is one of the two types favoured by local School Boards, with a drill hall on the ground floor (which doubled as an infants' classroom), classrooms above, a practical room above that and staircases and cloakrooms for boys and girls at each end. The rear elevation is, apart from the extraordinary decoration, conventionally flat, with three storeys of windows, but the front is wonderfully expressive, with staircases pulled out (as Honeyman had done at Rockvilla School (*see* Possilpark and High Possil) thirty years earlier) into bold glazed semicircular towers, given a hint of Scottishness by the pointed bell-cast caps. The cloakrooms too are clearly expressed by the bands of windows stepped back from the towers. Otherwise, the façade is severe, with plain sash windows and the suggestion of an eaves gallery *à la* Alexander Thomson or J. J. Burnet. No hint of the fluid Art Nouveau style of the 1890s here, except in the charming infants' porch and the swooping entrance arches: the decoration is, like the glazing, severely geometric on the front and back elevations, with their crisp flutes and zigzags, in the railings, and in the hall, with its almost Egyptian green tile capitals.

The staircases are the most dramatic feature inside as well as out, flooded with light (Mackintosh would have liked black tiling to set this off) and with the same boldness in the steel structure supporting roofs and balconies that appears later at the School of Art. Mackintosh also wanted full-height vertical railings, like those of the Willow Tearooms, rather than the standard-issue balustrades he was forced to have. The hall was, unusually, originally open between the piers to the corridors and stairwells (and may be restored like this). Otherwise, the interior (opened to the public by Strathclyde Regional Council) is interesting mainly as an example of early C 20 Board school architecture. Upstairs, one classroom is restored to its original appearance with the usual tiered seats and a fitment designed by Mackintosh but distinguished only by its curved hand-holds. In the barrel-vaulted cookery room, a dresser by Mackintosh.

KINGSTON BATHS AND WASHHOUSE, Paterson Street. 1954–6, by *A. G. Jury* (City Architect). Two crisp cubes of red pressed brick and a big octagonal chimney.

CLYDE PLACE QUAY. At Bridge Wharf, the STEAMER TERMINAL AND TRANSIT SHED, a long red brick shed dated 1929, with an Italianate timber clock tower that looks older.

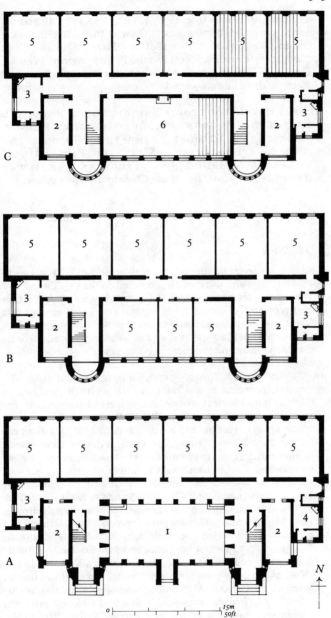

Scotland Street School: plans
A ground floor, B first floor, C second floor
1 hall, 2 cloaks, 3 staff, 4 head,
5 classroom, 6 cookery room
(Redrawn from a survey plan of 1947)

The quay itself dates from 1832–4. The TRANSIT SHED adjacent to the w on Windmillcroft Quay is the oldest surviving one in Glasgow: w half of 1861 by *Andrew Duncan* (Clyde Navigation Trust Engineer) and the Paisley engineers *Hanna, Donald & Wilson*; E half of 1866. Of one storey, in brick and stone, with sliding wooden doors, continuous on the N and W elevations.

ALBERT BRIDGE, VICTORIA BRIDGE, SOUTH PORTLAND STREET SUSPENSION BRIDGE, GLASGOW BRIDGE, GEORGE V BRIDGE, KINGSTON BRIDGE, ST ANDREW'S FOOTBRIDGE, WEIR AND PIPE BRIDGE, POLMADIE BRIDGE, CALEDONIAN RAILWAY BRIDGES. *See* Crossings of the Clyde and Kelvin below.

PERAMBULATIONS

1. Tradeston

The homogeneous texture of this regular grid of C19 and early C20 factories and warehouses, bounded on the E by the railway viaduct and on the w by the M8, has been broken by demolition and rebuilding, leaving large expanses of waste ground and late C20 industrial sheds and their car parks. A few remarkable industrial buildings survive, as well as a scatter of more ordinary red sandstone commercial buildings of *c.* 1900, e.g. Nos. 28–30 Clyde Place.

In CLYDE PLACE, Nos. 35–7, with a trabeated and classically decorated structure, was built as early as 1878 for Duncan MacGregor, nautical instrument makers. Further E is the former Steamer Terminal (*see* Public Buildings, above: Clyde Place Quay). Just to the S, at the corner of KINGSTON STREET and Centre Street, Nos. 56–64, a draper's warehouse, is also dated 1878. It is impressively large and regular (five storeys and sixteen bays) with a variety of basket, ogee and shouldered arches, all outlined in half-round mouldings. Round the corner, facing CENTRE STREET, No. 100, the D & D WAREHOUSE by *Elder & Cannon*, 1981–2, in a polychrome Post-Modern manner, is the only late C20 industrial shed and car park to be styled with any panache. Further S still, in WALLACE STREET, is the Police and Fire Station (*see* Public Buildings), and, w of it, at the corner of WEST STREET (Nos. 155–9), the prominent brick water tower of the former VICTORIA GRAIN MILLS (now wholesale warehouse) by *Wm. F. McGibbon*, 1886–96, his first and simplest medieval Italian-style building in this area. Facing Wallace Street (No. 133), an earlier part of the same mills (1894, by *McGibbon*) in Flemish style. Further E, at the corner of Wallace Street and Tradeston Street (No. 86), Glasgow's only surviving coppersmith's works, low brick buildings of 1876 disguised by harling.

At the corner of TRADESTON STREET (No. 118) and Cook

Street, *McGibbon*'s larger and more decorative example of his Ruskinian style, with a crenellated tower, machicolations, tall lancets and patterns of brick and terracotta. Built in 1900, it is the last and most prominent part of the former CLYDESDALE PAINT COLOUR AND OIL WORKS, which lie between Tradeston, Cook and West Streets. They were begun in 1876 for Blacklock & MacArthur (whose stag's head trademark is prominently displayed) and still have a remarkably full complement of structurally complete buildings. Earliest are the ashlar offices (1876) at Nos. 161–77 WEST STREET, given a mansard in 1896 by *McGibbon*. (The similar building next door was a formerly independent dyeworks.) Next to be built, in 1888, was the four-storey paint warehouse by *H. & D. Barclay* at Nos. 104–6 Tradeston Street, and behind it the contemporary paint-grinding and mixing rooms, with glazed roofs, ventilators and brick chimneys. Facing the yard is the varnish factory, with an iron colonnade on the ground floor (1896, by *McGibbon*). The later buildings have iron columns and steel beams, with floors of timber (1888 warehouse), sheet iron (grinding and mixing rooms) and corrugated iron and steel (1900 warehouse).

COOK STREET at the junction with West Street is lined with plain stone buildings. On the N side, Nos. 54–6 is a former engineering shop of 1854, rebuilt as Tradeston Paint Mill in 1866 and lengthened by a two-storey block in 1907 by *R. Thomson*. Opposite is the extensive and well-preserved EGLINTON ENGINE WORKS, built from *c.* 1855 for A. W. Smith (later SMITH-MIRRLEES), sugar machinery manufacturers, the last to operate in the United Kingdom (closed 1989). The seventeen-bay block along Cook Street (No. 57) was originally the fitting shop (later offices). The W part still has cast-iron columns with fittings for the shaftings and wrought-iron (probably replacing timber) beams. Along WEST STREET (Nos. 181–3), one-to-four-storey blocks. Of *c.* 1855, the original, one-bay engine shop (which powered the whole works), the four-storey former smithy and pattern-makers' shop (with iron columns and wooden beams), and the ground-floor façade of the two adjacent two-storey buildings which once fronted the original boiler shop. It was altered to machine shops in 1866–8. The later boiler shop (with large arched doorway) was added in 1874–5. All these buildings have king-post trussed roofs on brick arcades. Much further N up West Street, at No. 38, the nicely modelled brick façade of the big courtyard carting stables built for the haulage contractors Wordie & Co. in 1895 (architect *W. Tennant*).

Centred on MORRISON STREET to the NW and powerful in size and scale, whether seen from the street or from the flyover above, are the warehouses of the CO-OPERATIVE WHOLE-SALE SOCIETY LTD, until 1973 the Scottish Co-Operative Wholesale Society, founded in 1868 and established on this site soon after. The ordinary Victorian warehouse on the gushet site between Clyde Place and Morrison Street is the earliest. It was begun at the E end in Laidlaw Street by *J. Spence*, 1872–3, continued W with four storeys in 1873–6 (doorways enlarged by *Bruce & Hay*, 1907) and was completed with the clock-crowned triangle facing down Paisley Road in 1876. Eclipsing this is *Bruce & Hay*'s huge warehouse of 1886–95, almost tucked under the flyover. The N parts are earliest, done in association with *James Davidson* (Clerk of Works to the SCWS's own building and surveying department). The first part (1886–7), facing Dalintober Street, is Franco-Flemish, with a big shaped gable and bartizan. On the top floor, above the warehouse, is the panelled Dalintober or Co-Operative Hall, with hammerbeam roof and cast-iron Corinthian columns, and, behind it, the committee room. A crowstepped block of 1888 joins this to the Jacobean-style former stables, ham-curing department and grocery store (1891–3) facing Carnoustie Street. The massive front block (1892–7) was the Society's showpiece. Its design, in French Second Empire-style, inspired by the New Louvre, was recycled (though the architects denied it) from their City Chambers competition design of 1880. All the parts and the details are crisply articulated, but less skilfully assembled. The corner pavilions, with their clustered giant Composite columns and square domes, make a stronger accent than the pedimented centre topped by a dome on a tall colonnaded drum. On the top, the personification of Light and Liberty brandishes an electric light. Crowded into the central pediment, the figures of Justice, Commerce and the Four Continents, with Cybele and two lions as finials. Handsome lamp-standards flank the entrance to a marble-lined vestibule and staircase with wrought-iron balustrade, a grand prelude to a simple warehouse with cast-iron columns and wooden beams, carved and plastered in the clerks' room. The neighbouring warehouse of 1919 by *James Ferrigan* (SCWS's Chief Architect) is just as grandiose. Here the detail, still French and rather flabbily carved, is subservient to what appears from Morrison Street to be one massive block. It is in fact hollow, round three sides of a brick-lined light-well. Behind it, in Wallace Street, were other SCWS buildings (including another huge warehouse by *Bruce & Hay*, 1882 and 1892).

CENTENARY HOUSE, on the wedge-shaped site between Morrison Street and Paisley Road, continued to advertise the SCWS boldly, even brashly, with an extremely mannered design of 1962–9 by the SCWS's Chief Architect, *Kenneth F. Masson*. The simple curtain-walled office block revealed in the central courtyard is screened from the outside by walls clad in white and grey mosaic, curved and angled towards Paisley Road, decorated with *brises-soleil*, sunken panels and relief motifs, and pierced round the top where the frame is left open. Opposite, by the Clyde, an opportunity missed. Laing's tall beige blocks of flats (*c.* 1986–8) show none of the verve displayed in some of London's contemporary Dockland housing.

Finally, an excursion s w into what was once part of Kinning Park (*see* Govan: Perambulation 3) but has now been cut off from it by the M8, and back s e again to Eglinton Road. SCOTLAND STREET leads w from further down West Street to the famous Scotland Street School at No. 225 (*see* Public Buildings, above). At its E end, the street is still lined with C 19 industrial premises. On the N side is another large portion of the Smith-Mirrlees Works, i.e. the former SCOTLAND STREET ENGINE WORKS begun for P. & W. McOnie in 1850 and continued after 1862 for the marine engineer James Howden. It comprises: in West Street, the office block dated 1850, and an adjacent building of *c.* 1870 (Nos. 220–8); in Scotland Street, a long building of the 1870s, with four smaller bays surviving from the 1850s (Nos. 2–4); in Paterson Street, a formerly polychrome brick block of 1878 (Nos. 64–75); and in the centre of the works, an unpainted polychrome building. Nos. 8 and 14 Scotland Street were used between 1891 and 1903 by Blair, Campbell & McLean as part of Scotland's largest copper works. The eleven-bay block dates from 1864–5, the office block from 1870–1.

JAMES HOWDEN & CO. LTD's present works lie further w. Part of them (since 1940) is the red brick former GLASGOW AND DISTRICT SUBWAY POWER STATION (No. 175), with red brick engine hall, boilerhouse, superintendent's house and workshops designed in 1895 in a rather English Arts and Crafts manner by *John Gordon*, architect, and *Simpson & Wilson*, engineers, with *D. Home Morton* as consultant. The world's only cable-hauled underground passenger system was powered from here between 1896 and 1935 (when it was converted to electric traction). Howden's main works, built in 1897 (engineer *James Nisbet*) and 1907–8 (architects *Bryden & Robertson*), are at Nos. 191–7. Ashlar lodge and gatepiers, 1897; office block, 1897 (with 1907 mansard for drawing offices); altered lodge, 1902; two-storey workmen's messroom and pressed brick machine shop with two gables to the street, 1908. Behind the offices, machine shops of all the above dates.

KILBIRNIE STREET turns E from the S end of West Street. At the E end, No. 44 (ARNOLD CLARK LTD) was a coach-building premises (William Park's) built in 1913–14 to a design supplied by Kahn's *Trussed Concrete Steel Co. Ltd* of Westminster (executive architect *Richard Henderson* of Glasgow). It incorporates beams drilled to take drive shaftings and changes in machinery layout. The boldly exposed frame has suggestions of pilasters and stepped, almost Art Deco, angle parapets screening storage tanks for paint and oil. Round the corner, at the junction of SALKELD STREET (No. 140) with Mauchline Street, a bold circular tower marks the former depot of the LEYLAND MOTOR CO. (probably 1937 by *James Miller*). The familiar ribbed faience panels, strip windows and columned vestibule look the worse for wear. Just behind, in FALFIELD STREET, a relic of Tradeston's weaving industry, the FALFIELD MILLS (Nos. 8–38), a partly cut-down eigh-

teen-bay red brick power-loom cotton mill of *c.* 1840, with a
lower stone wing, probably of 1861.

2. Hutchesontown

BALLATER STREET divides the two initial phases of Hutchesontown-Gorbals C.D.A. Almost nothing but a few churches, schools, a library (*see* Churches and Public Buildings,
above) and a couple of industrial buildings has survived the
comprehensive redevelopment of the area between 1957 and
1974. The first phase to have been completed is N of Ballater
Street by the river. It is an undemonstrative, friendly-looking
mixed development by *Robert Matthew, Johnson-Marshall &
Partners*, 1958–65. The design is consistently rectilinear, from
the patterning of the eighteen-storey slab blocks, with their
glass balconies slotted into the exposed frame, to the tight
organization round hard-landscaped courts. Warmth is added
to both slabs and flat-roofed maisonettes by the yellow and
brown brick cladding and load-bearing walls.

112   In contrast, *Sir Basil Spence*'s wall of flats, 1960–6, silhouetted
in the view S from here, is highly expressionist and sculptural –
though topped now by absurd pitched roofs. It lies S of OLD
RUTHERGLEN ROAD, which still winds along most of its old
course and has been retained as an access road to the housing
S of Ballater Street. Near its W end (a cul-de-sac where it
used to meet Crown Street) is the only COTTON MILL to be
preserved in an area once dominated by them. It is the oldest
fireproof mill surviving in Glasgow and possibly in Scotland.
The main six-storey mill (No. 189) was built in 1816–21: it
probably ceased spinning in the 1860s. On each floor, two rows
of cast-iron columns and beams support low brick-arched
ceilings and fittings for line shaftings. C 20 attic, except in the
S bay. The S wing (No. 203) was built in 1817–21. On the S
side of the road is a relic of old Gorbals village, the BURIAL
GROUND purchased by the Gorbals feuars in 1715. The
remaining slabs are propped against the old walls.

QUEEN ELIZABETH SQUARE, beyond, is the centre of Hutchesontown, newly created by *Sir Basil Spence, Glover &
Ferguson*, 1960–6. The shopping area, between Old Rutherglen
Road and Cumberland Street, is dull: just a single shopping
mall (with a deck above giving access to three stubby four-
storey office blocks) and a flat-roofed block of shops N of the
great wall of flats. The Franciscan church and Blackfriars
Primary School on the remains of Cumberland Street, and a
former Free church, a former Board school and St Francis
Primary School on Old Rutherglen Road (*see* Churches and
Public Buildings) complete the centre.

A single and two linked slabs of flats form one overwhelming
side of the square. They are the most complex of all the
city's multi-storey blocks, powerful in silhouette (before their
maltreatment in 1987), elevation and detail but brutal as an
environment, with dark and dramatic spaces between the

strongly curving concrete pylons at the level of the square, and long spinal corridors, reached from one bold concrete service tower per block, which lead to the deep garden-cum-drying decks cantilevered at each end, and to the 400 scissor-plan maisonettes. The harsh surfaces are of board-marked concrete and pebble aggregate.

CUMBERLAND STREET ends to the W at the third phase (1968–74) of the Corporation's part of the plan. As with Laurieston C.D.A., at this late date the Corporation accepted a package-deal for system-built flats. 756 deck-access flats (demolished in 1987) originally accompanied the more conventional tower blocks by the same contractors (*Gilbert Ash*) which still stand. To the S, the gaunt shell of the Caledonia Road Church (*see* Churches, above) forms the only C19 landmark in this inhospitable area.

The SE part of Hutchesontown-Gorbals, S and E of Cumberland Street, was developed by the S.S.H.A. The first scheme, of 1961–5, opposite Queen Elizabeth Square, is predominantly of three- and four-storey maisonettes for families. Of a traditional kind, with coloured harling and pitched roofs, they are ranged round hard-surfaced pedestrian courts and play areas 'on a Georgian pattern', according to the S.S.H.A.'s Chief Technical Officer, *Harold Buteux*. Along Old Rutherglen Road, hoisted up on decks sheltering cars and shops, are the four twenty-four-storey slabs intended for the childless. By the river, eight stubby mosaic-clad towers of familiar S.S.H.A. type (1963–8). A brief detour N up McNEIL STREET to the distinguished former district library (*see* Public Buildings), then on to Oatlands.

OATLANDS, S of Rutherglen Road, opposite Richmond Park (which opened in 1899), belongs to the last Gorbals C.D.A., Hutchesontown–Polmadie, never begun (instead it was designated in 1970 one of Glasgow's first housing treatment areas). Slum clearance tenements (W) have been demolished for low-rise spec. housing, and rows of standard red sandstone tenements (E) have been improved by housing associations, or selectively demolished to provide a wide-open square. To the SW, beyond the Southern Necropolis (*see* above), the DIXON'S BLAZES INDUSTRIAL ESTATE occupies the site of the famous ironworks.

3. Laurieston

BRIDGE STREET and the railway viaduct that runs down its W side divide Tradeston from Laurieston. First of interest on the W side, nearest the bridge, is the former COMMERCIAL BANK OF SCOTLAND, 1884. It has bold shell tympana and other coarse Early Renaissance detail in cream ashlar. Nos. 36–54 was the fore-building of BRIDGE STREET STATION, built in 1889–90 (architect *James Miller*, engineer *George Graham*) and closed in 1906 when Central Station had been extended. Eighteen bays of grey stone in late C17 domestic style, with

touches of François Premier-style decoration. The arched
entrance to the booking hall, always sandwiched between
ground-floor shops, is concealed by a shop fascia. At each end
are the former entrances to the high-level platform.

The other buildings worth noting start on the E side, at the
corner of Norfolk Street, with a particularly elaborate cream
sandstone tenement of 1898, with (modernized) pub beneath,
by *James Miller*, who has synthesized the free, asymmetrical
Glasgow Style, represented by oriels, saucer dome and bold
chimney stacks, with richly carved Edwardian Baroque detail.
Further N, at Nos. 63–7, is an odd juxtaposition of the two
upper floors of a mid-C19 grey stone tenement and two red
sandstone lower ones inserted in 1888 by *John Gordon* for
the southern branch of the GLASGOW SAVINGS BANK.
Handsome polished granite columns and wrought-iron gate
on the ground floor; relief plaques of appropriate subjects such
as scales, globe and anchor etc. between the windows above.
The surprise is the large banking hall, lit from the glazed
coffers of its dome, added to the back of the tenement. The
Egyptian decoration of No. 61 is of a different era: 1935, by
Cornelius Armour (SCWS architect), built as an extension to
the KINNING PARK CO-OPERATIVE SOCIETY BUILD-
ING, 1902, by *Bruce & Hay* (Nos. 47–61), which has another
façade to Coburg Street.

CARLTON PLACE, the most prestigious street of Laurie's
suburb, named in honour of the Prince Regent, turns the
corner into Bridge Street with a commercial building, the
BANK OF SCOTLAND. *J. Burnet* replaced the w pavilion of
the w terrace in more ponderous style in 1857. Two classical
figures holding the bank's arms stand above the bowed and
colonnaded corner. Both terraces – the E, Nos. 40–61, of 1802–
4, and the w, Nos. 62–84, of 1813–18 – have lost their w
pavilions, destroying the simple symmetry of their façades, the
first palace-fronted ones, it seems, to be built on a grand
scale in Glasgow, seventy years after the formula appeared in
London. The architect was *Peter Nicholson*, who left Glasgow
while the w terrace was being built; *John Baird I* finished it.
This dignified river frontage was completed on the E (until
1973) by *David Hamilton*'s Gorbals Parish Church, 1806–10,
with its tall spire.

The overall design of the terraces, with their channelled ashlar
ground floors, long first-floor windows (with cornices only in
the end and centre bays), and pedimented centre with Doric
pilasters and frieze, is not particularly sophisticated. Most
curious is the use of three-bay houses throughout, resulting in
an uncomfortable central pilaster and divided porch in the
middle of the projecting centre bays. Even the three classical
porches are of rather ungainly proportions, though, if original,
the segmental one at Nos. 51–2 is an especially early example
in Glasgow of Greek Doric. Much of the other detail dates
from *Philip Cocker & Partners*' restoration, 1989–90.

Along the w terrace, No. 78, the CLYDE SHIPPING CO. LTD

was altered in the late C19 and still has the staircase and other fittings of that date. Only the domed top-light of the original stair survives in an upper room. No. 76 still has the upper flights of its stair, its arcaded landing and reeded doorcases and plasterwork in its first-floor rooms. Nos. 71–3 has been thoroughly remodelled, most recently (1986–8) by *Ian Bridges* as the PRINCE AND PRINCESS OF WALES HOSPICE. The end pavilion, No. 65, was converted to a bank, with big Baroque doorway, in 1893 by *Baird & Thomson*. The earlier E terrace was brutally treated. A stumpy red sandstone block of 1908 (fronting a taller range to South Portland Street) has replaced the W pavilion. Only the centre houses (Nos. 51–2) are at all intact internally. No. 52 (LAURIESTON HOUSE) was Laurie's own house. Inside, the most handsome domestic interior of its date in Glasgow, including a staircase crowned by a colonnaded rotunda with fine Neo-classical plasterwork. No. 40 at the E end shows the original pattern of the pavilions. The rubble backs of both terraces, with a few bows at the E end, and one taller, later tower, are easily seen from Oxford Street. Behind the houses in CARLTON COURT, a handsome range of former carting stables built for the Clyde Shipping Co. *c.* 1895.

Between Carlton Place and Norfolk Street the old street pattern is preserved, though no original buildings survive. Beyond the wide traffic route of Norfolk Street, four massive package-deal slabs (by *Crudens*, 1970–3) rise out of partly contoured but still barren surroundings, edged on the W by dismal grey harled tenements of the 1970s and on the S, where some of the old streets can again be traced, by red brick low-rise of the 1980s.

Only a very few older buildings lie on these fringes (*see* Public Buildings, above). Just one C19 tenement survives in GORBALS STREET (Nos. 162–70); it is by *Salmon, Son & Gillespie*, 1900, and has a few of their idiosyncrasies. Good wrought-iron gate to the former BRITISH LINEN CO. BANK on the ground floor. Indistinguishable from a tenement is what remains of CUMBERLAND STREET STATION of 1900 at the W end of Cumberland Street (mostly demolished *c.* 1969).

Gorbals Street continues S as the more built-up POLLOKSHAWS ROAD to St Andrew's Cross and the massive ST ANDREW'S WORKS, the first of two large electricity generating stations built *c.* 1900 for Glasgow Corporation Electricity Department. It was designed by *A. Myles*, 1899–1900. Part was converted to a printworks in 1937. Along the street, a fifteen-bay, steel-framed block with walls of red pressed brick, a pediment and vast windows within a blind arcade. The only decoration is terracotta roundels. At the S end the sandstone-faced entrance bay to the S wing (the Battery House), its two storeys of arched windows outlined in white brick facing the railway line.

Pollokshaws Road meets Eglinton Street at EGLINTON TOLL, alternatively called St Andrew's Cross, the name inscribed on the plain pub-and-tenement block that faces S. Behind its simple corner dome is a railed flat roof, probably a rooftop drying area. Just N of it, the tenements (Nos. 345–63 Pollokshaws Road), dated 1888, are lifted slightly out of the ordinary by the row of gables corbelled out between the chimneystacks. More noticeable are the red sandstone and green slate of the late Tudor-style former YMCA hall and classrooms (by *Robert Miller*, 1896–7) at the corner of Maxwell Road, which leads w into Pollokshields (*q.v.*). Other routes s from the crossroads lead sw into Queen's Park or se into Govanhill (*qq.v.*).

GOVANHILL

Govanhill is still a relatively undisturbed example of late Victorian tenement development, apart from demolitions on the NE edge. William Smith Dixon, proprietor of the Govan Iron Works, which lay to the N, started selling feus here *c*. 1869. By 1877 it was a police burgh of 7,212 inhabitants; by 1891 the population had risen to 10,000. Much of the tenement development of this twenty-year period survives in a band to the w of Cathcart Road, laid out in a compact grid. The only open space was Govanhill Park, a recreation ground laid out in 1894 and surrounded by plain red sandstone tenements.

Cathcart Road and Calder Street were the principal Victorian thoroughfares, with the Candlish Polmadie Church (*see* Churches, below) acting as a landmark at their intersection. Sadly, various demolitions and the building of the suburban-style GOVANHILL HEALTH CENTRE, 1983, have eroded the late Victorian character of CALDER STREET. ALLISON STREET, another thoroughfare with tenements over shops, remains largely intact. Nos. 265–9 is an intriguing block for which *Alexander Thomson* prepared a design *c*. 1875. It was completed to a simpler design by *R. Turnbull*, *c*. 1878.

The s side of DIXON AVENUE (Nos. 42–106) has terraces of two-storey houses with front gardens. The designs are all variations on a theme, with good cast-iron finials (Nos. 42–4), curious narrow trilobe-headed doorways (Nos. 54–74), and a variety of bow and bay windows throughout. Nos. 92–106 are by *Robert Duncan*, 1900. Nos. 112–14, of 1898, have bays of a curious flat-fronted profile and balustraded sills between storeys.

More recent housing in the w part of Govanhill beyond Hickman Street is of little interest, although at Nos. 85–93 GOVANHILL STREET, *Simister, Monaghan, McKinney, MacDonald* have skilfully reinterpreted the character of neighbouring tenements in a Post-Modern work (completed 1983), using concrete blocks, overhanging tiled roofs and timber lattice balcony fronts. Ironically the neighbouring tenements were refurbished soon afterwards using superficial Post-Modern elements. At Nos. 364–72, another Post-Modern design by the *Holmes Partnership*, *c*. 1987.

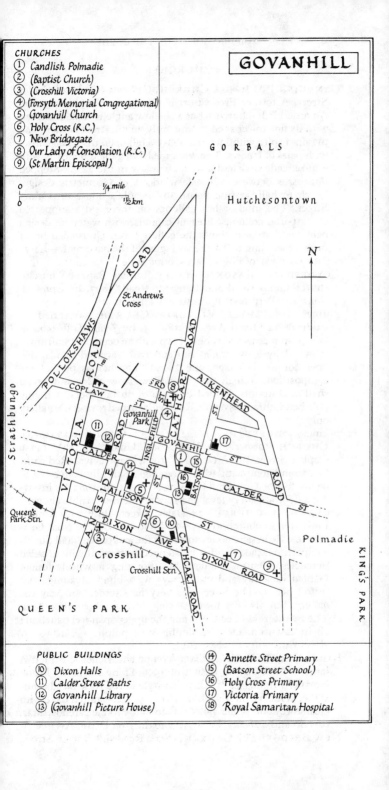

CHURCHES

1. Candlish Polmadie
2. (Baptist Church)
3. (Crosshill Victoria)
4. (Forsyth Memorial Congregational)
5. Govanhill Church
6. Holy Cross (R.C.)
7. New Bridgegate
8. Our Lady of Consolation (R.C.)
9. (St Martin Episcopal)

GOVANHILL

0   ¼ mile
0   1½ km

GORBALS

Hutchesontown

N

St Andrew's
Cross

POLLOKSHAWS ROAD

ROAD

Strathbungo

COPLAW

Govanhill
Park

3RD ST

CATHCART ROAD

AIKENHEAD ROAD

INGLEFIELD ST

GOVANHILL ST

VICTORIA

CALDER

ROAD

LANGSIDE

ALLISON

DAISY ST

DIXON

AVE

ST

CATHCART ROAD

CALDER ST

Queen's
Park Stn

Polmadie

KING'S PARK

Crosshill

Crosshill Stn

DIXON ROAD

QUEEN'S PARK

PUBLIC BUILDINGS

10. Dixon Halls
11. Calder Street Baths
12. Govanhill Library
13. (Govanhill Picture House)
14. Annette Street Primary
15. (Batson Street School)
16. Holy Cross Primary
17. Victoria Primary
18. Royal Samaritan Hospital

CHURCHES

CANDLISH POLMADIE CHURCH, Cathcart Road and Calder Street. A former Free Church. 1874–7, by *John Honeyman*. An aisled E.E. church set at a shallow angle to Calder Street, with its fine tower sited prominently on the street corner. Tall pyramid spire with lucarnes above a tall open third stage inset with pairs of lancets. The w façade has a gabled doorway with blind arcade over and a wheel window in the gable. Stepped buttresses between tall aisle windows of Geometric design. Porch to hall, session house and beadle's house on Calder Street. The interior has galleries on three sides supported on cast-iron columns. Elegant capitals, with waterleaf design below and stiffleaf above the gallery level. Unusual band of timber panelling below the springing of the nave roof. – Large ORGAN CASE of filigree late Gothic style.

CLYDESDALE MASONIC HALLS (former Baptist Church), Butterbiggins Road and Langside Road. 1897, by *Stark & Rowntree*. Perp revival; drastically altered.

Former CROSSHILL VICTORIA CHURCH (converted to studios), 32 Dixon Avenue. 1891–3, by *John H. Wilson*, in salmon-pink snecked rubble. Perp with an octagonal stairtower crowned by a pyramidal cap and two traceried bands, one open for the bellstage, one glazed. The hall is part of the composition. A high interior with narrow aisles and broad shallow transepts divided by arcades on tall piers of highly polished Labrador syenite. Roof with cusped timbers. N gallery only.

Former FORSYTH MEMORIAL CONGREGATIONAL CHURCH (formerly an Evangelical Union church), 147–9 Coplaw Street. By *H. Campbell*, 1903. Perp revival. Red rock-faced sandstone with ashlar dressings. Skilfully converted to offices for the Govanhill Housing Association, 1983, by inserting a floor at gallery level and leaving the roof visible above.

GOVANHILL CHURCH, 24 Daisy Street. Built as a United Presbyterian church in 1878–80 by *Robert Baldie*. Neat Geometric style in sandstone ashlar. On the axis of Bankhall Street, a tripartite façade divided by stepped buttresses with arcaded pinnacles. Central window incorporating a wheel design. Gabled doorway and outer bays with blind arcading with trefoil heads. The interior is very handsome; not only the gallery, but also the lower seating, follow a horseshoe plan. The two storeys of columns and the upper spandrel panels are all in cast-iron. Original double-stair pulpit. – ORGAN by *Abbot & Smith* of Leeds, 1912.

HOLY CROSS (R.C.), Dixon Avenue and Belleisle Street. A large and impressive design of 1909–11 by *Pugin & Pugin*. Northern Italian Early Christian style in red rock-faced sandstone. Wide narthex, shallow-arched barrel-vaulted nave with clearstorey and organ gallery. Elaborate marble reredos, altar, *cancelli* and *ambones*. Presbytery to the E on Dixon Avenue.

NEW BRIDGEGATE CHURCH, Dixon Road and Warren Street.

Built in 1923 as a United Free Church by *Thomson, Sandilands & McLeod*. Late Gothic in red sandstone. Prominent tower, with short recessed spire built as a war memorial. Expectations raised by the vestibule, with its elaborate marble and stained timber panelling and decorative glass, are dashed on entering the plain aisled interior. – STAINED GLASS. On the N side of the nave, 1927: Christ bearing the Cross and Christ and Mary Magdalene in the Garden of Gethsemane.

OUR LADY OF CONSOLATION (R.C.), 130 Inglefield Street. By *Scott, Fraser & Browning*, 1967–71. Unattractive exposed reinforced concrete and brick façades. The church is at first-floor level, reached by a partly enclosed flight of steps. Staircase and lift from the car park on the ground floor are carried up as the main tower, which is surmounted by a wooden cross. Squarish plan with choir gallery and clearstorey lighting.

ST MARTIN'S EPISCOPAL CHURCH, 139 Dixon Road. Now converted to housing. By *McKissack & Rowan*, 1887. Simplified E.E., with S aisle and transept of 1903 in neo-Norman by *H.D. Walton*.

PUBLIC BUILDINGS

DIXON HALLS (in use as a day centre since 1978), Dixon Avenue and Cathcart Road. A gift of William Smith Dixon of the Govan Iron Works to the burghs of Govanhill and Crosshill, the boundary of which bisected the building E to W. 1878–9, by *Frank Stirrat*, who won the commission in competition. Ebullient Scottish Baronial style. Tall and narrow, with clock tower at the E corner and a busy skyline of angle turrets and crowstepped gables. Its commanding appearance is enhanced by its siting at 45° to Dixon Avenue and Cathcart Road. Two staircases (one now blocked) at the front of the building led up to the grand hall at first-floor level. The hall has a balcony and an open timber roof, but it is now subdivided and masked with false ceilings. Courtrooms and ancillary accommodation for the two burghs on the ground floor, with separate entrances on appropriate sides of the original boundary.

CALDER STREET PUBLIC BATHS AND WASHHOUSE, 99 Calder Street. 1912–17, by *A.B. McDonald* (Office of Public Works). Long low façade of red sandstone ashlar, with twin Roman Doric pedimented doorways. Lavish interior, substantially unaltered. Two top-lit swimming ponds with ferroconcrete arched ribs. Hot baths at attic level. Washhouse (since 1971 a launderette) at rear, entered from Kingarth Street.

GOVANHILL LIBRARY (formerly Govanhill and Crosshill District Library), 170 Langside Road and Calder Street. By *James R. Rhind*, 1902–6. Edwardian Baroque, with coupled unfluted Ionic columns. Sculptured figures on balustrade; dome over the Langside Road entrance with a winged figure in copper. Interior modernized, with ugly false ceilings throughout, by *Robert Rogerson & Philip Spence*, 1969–71.

GOVANHILL PICTURE HOUSE (in use as a warehouse, 1989),

49 Bankhall Street. By *Eric A. Sutherland*, 1925–6. Egyptian-style frontage with Hindu-inspired domes. Striking grey and white tile centrepiece with lotus-bud columns. Original interior destroyed.

ANNETTE STREET PRIMARY SCHOOL (formerly Govanhill Public School). 1886, by *H. & D. Barclay*. In an imposing palazzo style. Three storeys (originally one each for infants, juniors and seniors); boys' and girls' playgrounds to either side with separate entrances and separate staircases within the building. Axial entrance on Annette Street, with elegant square fluted pilasters. The first floor has pedimented windows and end bays with semicircular niches. Top floor of panelled piers alternating with dwarf columns under a bracketed cornice. Altogether a very accomplished design.

BATSON STREET SCHOOL (used by a social work department, 1989), 291–311 Calder Street. Datestone 1874; opened 1875. In revived Scottish Jacobean style; central bay with a crow-stepped gable and a pair of spiral chimneys.

HOLY CROSS PRIMARY SCHOOL (formerly Calder Street Public School), 316 Calder Street. Datestone 1914. By *Andrew Balfour*. Large and stylish stripped Baroque in red sandstone. Rock-faced base with smooth horizontally channelled ashlar above. Quarter Ionic columns in the end bays.

VICTORIA PRIMARY SCHOOL (formerly Victoria Public School), Govanhill Street and Batson Street. Datestone 1903; opened 1905. A three-storey plain Italianate design by *Andrew Balfour*, in red sandstone.

ROYAL SAMARITAN HOSPITAL FOR WOMEN, Coplaw Street. Originally established in Cumberland Street, Hutchesontown, in 1886, it moved to St James Street, Kingston, in 1889. All the major buildings on the present site were designed by *McWhannell & Rogerson*. The sketch design was prepared in 1893. The first section of the hospital (1894–6) consists of the administration block and a ward block (datestone 1896) linked to the W, all built in cream rock-faced stone with red sandstone dressings. The administration block has a two-storey asymmetrical bay window, stylish Art Nouveau details and the building's name in handsomely carved letters. A typical Arts and Crafts angled entrance porch at the side. E ward block added in the same style, 1899–1907. On the corner of Victoria Road, the ALICE MARY CORBETT MEMORIAL NURSES' HOME, 1904–5, in free Baronial style: extended N in 1923–6 (datestone 1925) and E by *R. Walker* in 1931. The same architect imaginatively reinterpreted the earlier style for the ward block at the E edge of the site in 1923–7 (datestone 1924). Behind the hospital on Butterbiggins Road, the AGNES BARR DISPENSARY, opened in 1898. Later additions by *Walker, Hardy & Smith*: Radiology Department, 1934, Paying Patients' Wing, 1936.

KING'S PARK

The development of the new suburb of MOUNT FLORIDA started in the 1870s and was boosted when the Cathcart District Railway was extended there in 1886. Its main street is CATHCART ROAD, lined with late C19 and early C20 tenements. The finest of them is at the junction with Carmunnock Road, a red sandstone Glasgow Style composition with lead-covered bell-shaped corner towers and carved panels of gorgons' heads at second-floor level. At the corner of Battlefield Road are BATTLEFIELD and LANGSIDE COURTS, two twenty-storey L-shaped tower blocks of 1964–7 built by *George Wimpey*.

Rising E from the junction of Cathcart Road and Carmunnock Road is MOUNT ANNAN DRIVE, which climbs the hill and offers a varied sequence of picturesque views. On either side, a variety of late C19 and early C20 villas, the most interesting of which is No. 70 by *Richard Henderson* (1906), a Free-Style design of great originality. Opposite a terrace of two-storey houses (Nos. 63–79) set back behind front gardens: again, a Free-Style composition with canted bay windows and, on panels beneath the upper windows, a series of cartouches.

Near the S end of Cathcart Road is KING'S PARK ROAD, which leads E with a broad sweep of red sandstone two-storey villas, with three pairs of cream and stone double villas interspersed. Nos. 12 and 14 have castellated bay windows.

At the eastern edge of Mount Florida is HANGINGSHAW, formerly the site of the Aikenhead Colliery. It is now characterless apart from the extraordinarily well-preserved scheme of prefabs s at the junction of PROSPECTHILL ROAD and AIKENHEAD ROAD. This scheme of fifty-two E.F.M.s (emergency factory-made dwellings) was probably one of the last to be laid out in Glasgow. The layout was prepared in November 1948 and the houses, transported in four sections from the Blackburn Aircraft factory at Dumbarton, were erected on site soon after. This type of prefab, known as the A.I.R.O.H. (Aircraft Industry's Research Organization on Housing) house, has aluminium sandwich panel walls and corrugated aluminium roof panels. Even the garden sheds, also prefabricated, survive in large numbers.

To the N, the now desolate wastes of POLMADIE, where the Dubs' QUEEN'S PARK LOCOMOTIVE WORKS thrived from 1896 until 1963. Only a few of its steel-framed corrugated-iron-clad sheds, designed by *Sir William Arrol & Co.* (1904–14), still stand. Opposite in JESSIE STREET, the pattern-making shop and offices of Alley & McLellan's SENTINEL WORKS, a four-storey structure of reinforced concrete designed by *Archibald Leitch* with *Brand & Lithgow* and built in 1903–5, using the *Mouchel-Hennebique* system – the earliest known use of reinforced concrete in Glasgow.

To the E is TORYGLEN, an extensive post-war housing scheme. PROSPECTHILL CIRCUS gives access to a mixed development by *Laing* (1963–9), including three slab blocks of twenty-one storeys. Nos. 3, 7 and 11 PROSPECTHILL CRESCENT and No. 999 PROSPECTHILL ROAD, 1954–6, by the S.S.H.A., are blocks of ten storeys (insisted on by the City Engineer, who was experimenting with multi-storey housing at this time) on Y- and (slightly later) T-plans. An early example of no-fines concrete with an oversailing concrete flat roof. Professor *Deininger* and *Ludwig Kresse* of Stuttgart acted as consultants for this part of the scheme. S of Prospecthill Road much of the housing is unremarkable.

KING'S PARK and CROFTFOOT developed between the wars as commuter suburbs. Much of the two-storey housing is by *Mactaggart & Mickel*.

CHURCHES

BATTLEFIELD EAST CHURCH (former Cathcart Free Church), 1216 Cathcart Road and Battlefield Road. The first church on this site, flanking Battlefield Road, is by *John Honeyman*, 1864–5. E.E.-style, with a cruciform plan and an apsidal E end. It became the hall in 1912, when the adjacent large rock-faced red sandstone church by *John Galt* was opened. This has a spacious interior with galleries supported on cast-iron columns. – STAINED GLASS. One window by *Sadie McLellan*, 1972 (Agony in the Garden).

CHRIST THE KING (R.C.), 220 Carmunnock Road. By *Thomas S. Cordiner*, 1957–60. A simple orange brick clear-storey-lit box with an eye-catching front facing King's Park. In the centre a tall, thin, helm-roofed tower; below, a cantilevered canopy sheltering a relief of Christ the King on a random rubble wall. – ORGAN CASE by *Hill, Norman & Beard*, 1960.

CROFTFOOT PARISH CHURCH, Croftpark Avenue and Crofthill Road. By *John Keppie & Henderson*, 1934–6. A neat Byzantine design in plum-coloured brick, with strongly contrasting white pointing. The main entrance, adjacent to the bell tower, has an elaborate semicircular stone hood, its tympanum carved with a tree and, above it, a text (*nec tamen consumebatur*). Brightly lit interior with short aisles and gallery, all in fair-faced brick. Sanctuary framed by pair of large stone columns.

CROFTFOOT UNITED FREE CHURCH, Croftpark Avenue and Carmunnock Road. By *Noad & Wallace*, c. 1949. Harled, pitched-roofed and box-like, with apsidal projections.

KING'S PARK PARISH CHURCH, 242 Castlemilk Road. 1931–2, by *Hutton & Taylor*. Byzantine-style, in rustic red brick with stone dressings. Cruciform plan: the lower transepts have hipped roofs, and the crossing has a bell housing. Fine triple-arched entrance façade with patterned brick spandrels and stone columns carved simply. The interior is aisled, with exposed brick arcades supporting a sweeping white plastered barrel-vault over the nave. – STAINED GLASS. At the crossing, clearstorey windows by *Sadie McLellan* and *Gordon Webster*, *c.* 1980. – Commemorative glass to Sir John Auld Mactaggart † 1956 (nave over entrance) and to Lady Lena Mactaggart † 1958 (chancel).

MOUNT FLORIDA PARISH CHURCH (former United Presbyterian Church), 1123 Cathcart Road. A temporary wooden church was opened here in 1877. The present building, in snecked sandstone, is by *J. Hamilton*, 1884–8. Spire never built. A large barn-like church without aisles, but with a gallery at the w end. The elaborate painted decoration of 1892 by *McCulloch & Gow* has been entirely obliterated. Adjoining the church, in the cul-de-sac, is the WAR MEMORIAL HALL by *George Boswell*, 1924.

ST BRIGID (R.C.), Prospecthill Road and Prospecthill Crescent. 1955–7, by *Thomas S. Cordiner*. Steel portal frames, clad in brick and with a tiled roof. The entrance has sliding doors leading to a narthex with flanking baptistery. Long aisleless nave; short narrow chancel. Light and refreshing interior, with the walls and ceiling gaudily painted yellow, tangerine, violet and turquoise. Painted figures on the sloping ceiling. Nave windows of frosted glass with leading like crazy-paving and brightly coloured figures and symbols. Five-light window of vivid stained glass over the choir gallery. Zigzag altar rails. One of the best 1950s interiors left in Glasgow.

ST OSWALD'S EPISCOPAL CHURCH, 260 Castlemilk Road. The original red sandstone, lancet-style church (1930–1, by *Whyte & Galloway*) is now used as a hall. The new church of 1966 by *Jeremy Wells-Thorpe* is an original design using bold brick panels in an elaborate relief pattern. Plain interior with steel trusses.

SOVEREIGN GRACE BAPTIST ZION CHURCH (former Polmadie United Presbyterian Church), Calder Street and Polmadie Road. 1895–7, by *D. McNaughtan*. Free-Style Gothic with lancet windows. Grey snecked rubble with red sandstone dressings. Two floors of halls at the E end, church at the w end. Galleried interior with mock hammerbeams and arched braces with wrought-iron tie-rods.

TORYGLEN PARISH CHURCH, Glenmore Avenue. 1953, by *Gratton & McLean*. A busy design with echoes of Arts and Crafts motifs. Brick walls, gambrel roof covered in pantiles, dormer windows with copper dressings. A hall church, with a platform at one end and a sanctuary and choir at the other.

PUBLIC BUILDINGS

Former CATHCART PARISH COUNCIL CHAMBERS (Mount Florida Health Clinic), 183 Prospecthill Road and Cathcart Road. By *A. R. Crawford & Veitch*, 1907. The grand English Baroque front elevation masks a modest building with a triangular plan. The lead-covered dome over the entrance hall has a miniature temple as a cupola. Interior mutilated, but some carved panelling survives in the former Council Room.

Former STATE CINEMA, 271 Castlemilk Road and King's Park

Avenue. 1937, by *Charles J. McNair & Elder*. The entrance block has a curved corner and a streamlined horizontal-banded window. The foyer (with island paybox) and auditorium survive. There are striking metal grilles adjacent to the former cinema screen. (Closed as a cinema in 1971; used since then as a bingo hall.)

HAMPDEN PARK FOOTBALL GROUND, Mount Annan Drive. It is 'a huge elongated bowl on the slopes of Mount Florida ... like the mouth of a volcano' (Simon Inglis): the shape no doubt helps to create the famous Hampden Park roar. This ground, the third home of Queen's Park Football Club, was established in 1903, with *Archibald Leitch* advising on the layout. *J. Miller* prepared the design for the S stand; it was in three sections, with a lofty centrepiece. The outer two sections of this survive, but after a fire in 1905 the centre pavilion was rebuilt in 1914 by *Babtie, Shaw & Morton*, civil engineers, as a grand red brick composition in Scottish Castle style. This façade was later flanked by semicircular twin towers in an Art Deco manner.

KING'S PARK PRIMARY SCHOOL, Kingsbridge Drive. Early 1930s, by *Ninian McWhannell*. A long angled block in three sections fitting the curve of the road. Red brick, with stone dressings emphasizing the horizontal lines. Art Deco details: especially good is the ironwork over the central entrance.

KING'S PARK SECONDARY SCHOOL, Fetlar Drive. 1956–63, by *Gillespie, Kidd & Coia*. A group of buildings in blue brick and strongly expressed reinforced concrete set round a courtyard on a steeply sloping site. The four-storey classroom block, with each floor cantilevered out on a chamfered concrete slab, dominates from the hilltop. Parallel with it, the administration block, one-storey towards the courtyard, three-storey to the N and with zigzag roofs over the assembly and dining halls.

MOUNT FLORIDA PUBLIC SCHOOL, 1133 Cathcart Road. Built for the Cathcart School Board in 1895–7 by *H. & D. Barclay*. A neat Greek cross plan fitting the triangular site between Carmunnock Road and Cathcart Road. In rock-faced red sandstone with ashlar dressings.

ST MIRIN'S PRIMARY SCHOOL, 260 Carmunnock Road. 1954, by *T. S. Cordiner*. A compact group of single-storey blocks in brick with, unpredictably, monopitch roofs.

KING'S PARK. A public park formed from part of the policies of Aikenhead House in 1930. AIKENHEAD HOUSE, at the centre of the park, was built in 1806 for the tobacco merchant John Gordon, probably from a design by *David Hamilton*, who added the wings in 1823. The present mansion, built on the site of a C17 house, was divided into fourteen flats in 1986. It has a two-storey central block with flanking one-and-a-half-storey wings in a subtle design. Chaste decoration, including panelled pilasters (cf. Camphill House; *see* Queen's Park, Public Buildings, below, under Queen's Park), shows off the fine quality of the pink ashlar. Strongly contrasting portico of yellow sandstone using a finely carved fluted Corinthian order.

To the S, at the entrance to the walled garden, an elaborate SUNDIAL, with a datestone of 1885: a copy of one of a pair erected in 1635 at Newbattle Abbey, Midlothian. This one was made for Douglas Castle, Lanarkshire, and moved here soon after 1930.

Further S, and reached from Croftpark Avenue, the former STABLES, a simple courtyard layout with a Palladian ashlar façade to the road. Opposite, two stone estate cottages.

CASTLEMILK

One of the peripheral housing schemes of the 1950s and 1960s, built by the Corporation on the Castlemilk estate, which had belonged to the Stuarts since the C13. The Corporation bought the estate in 1938 for a peripheral scheme to house over 30,000 people; detailed plans for the layout had been drawn up by 1941, but building did not begin until 1954. Some of the grounds of Castlemilk House (then a children's home, since demolished) were retained as a public park (see below), and the five neighbourhoods of houses and one small industrial area were laid out round the estate's existing plantations.

The dramatic landscape of wooded hills relieves a little the monotony of the three- and four-storey tenement blocks interspersed with a few terraces of three-storey houses and pairs of two-storey cottages, grouped in indistinguishable neighbourhoods. Even the shopping centre and minimal facilities grouped at the centre off CASTLEMILK DRIVE are totally lacking in visual impact.

Most prominent are the twenty-storey tower blocks of the scheme's post-1959 extension. The three in DOUGRIE ROAD (by *A. G. Jury*, the City Architect, 1960–6) have been reclad in ochre and brown profiled metal. The five point blocks off ARDENCRAIG ROAD, which look to the S over Cathkin Braes Park, still have *George Wimpey*'s livery of 1963–5.

CHURCHES

CASTLEMILK EAST CHURCH, Barlia Terrace. 1956–9, by *W. N. W. Ramsay*. A grey harled box with, on the shallow pitched roof, a shallow drum carrying a spike.

CASTLEMILK WEST CHURCH, Carmunnock Road and Glenacre Terrace. 1957–9, by *Gratton & McLean*. An extravagantly shaped and detailed exterior in an overabundance of materials leads to disappointment inside: just a plain box-like church above the ground-floor hall.

ST BARTHOLOMEW (R.C.), 32 Croftfoot Drive. 1955–8. Unmemorable.

St Margaret Mary (R.C.), 99 Dougrie Road. By *T. S. Cordiner*, 1956–7. Buff brick with a great high barn-like slated roof and an integral tower thrusting towards the street. Church under the roof; hall beneath.

St Martin (R.C.), 201 Ardencraig Road. 1959–61, by *Gillespie, Kidd & Coia*. Its present dismal condition gives no idea of its original appearance or of the size and simple grandeur of the interior. Outside, the dapple-grey brick walls and shuttered concrete details have been obliterated by a coat of harling, and the rocky slope, the skeleton of the design, is denuded of its trees. There is no prominent roof shape in this design (as there is at, e.g., St Benedict, Drumchapel). The presbytery, built into the slope of the cliff, dominates the approach: from the road, the church looks like a blank low box. Inside, the wide, slightly splayed auditorium of pearly grey brick culminates in a broad apse, with the altar majestically raised on a flight of steps. Light floods down on to it from the complex timber roof (supported on a series of vertically glazed bow-string trusses) which seems suspended above the auditorium. The small square side windows, with harshly tinted glass, illuminate only the Stations of the Cross carved on to the wide-splayed stone jambs. The w window is a similarly decorative panel of coloured glass. Simple FURNISHINGS: timber pews and w gallery (with confessionals beneath); brick pulpit, reading desk and font (moved from the former baptistery behind the narthex); stone altar on a simple cylindrical pedestal.

PUBLIC BUILDINGS

Glenwood Secondary School, 17 Ardencraig Road. The most distinctive school in the area, still with the bold stylistic traits of Glasgow's 1930s schools, though of 1954–8, by *Burnet, Boston & Partners*. Flat-roofed and symmetrical blocks, with angular brick trim and window strips that wrap around the corners.

The other 1950s SCHOOLS, although by various architects, all of similar standard type, with linked, mainly brick-built blocks: e.g. St Dominic's Primary, Ardencraig Drive, and Windlaw Primary, Dunagoil Road, both by *Glasgow Corporation Architects' Dept*, 1957–9; Tormusk Primary, 128 Tormusk Road, by *Sam Bunton & Associates*, 1957–8; and Braeside Primary, Machrie Drive, by *Baron Bercott*, 1955–7.

Castlemilk House was demolished in 1972, leaving only its stables at the E end of Barlia Terrace, a bridge SE of the stables, and a pair of modest gatepiers to the NE, at the sharp NE corner of Croftfoot Road. The house stood a little to the NE of the stables. The earliest parts were late medieval and formed the centrepiece of the larger C18 and C19 castellated mansion of the Stuarts.

The STABLE BLOCK (used by the Parks Department) was

built *c*. 1800. Four ranges round a courtyard with N and S carriage arches. The N range is formal with a central octagonal tower. This has Gothick glazing in round-headed windows.

The BRIDGE was remodelled in 1833. Castellated parapet and a single wide arch.

CARMUNNOCK

In the welcome breathing-space between Glasgow and East Kilbride, a village with a good deal of rural charm, the only such within Glasgow's boundaries. It once belonged to the Castlemilk estate.

CARMUNNOCK PARISH CHURCH, Kirk Road. 1762–7, repaired in 1838–40. A T-plan church (made cruciform by a lower vestry of *c*. 1819) set in a big, much older churchyard. It was rebuilt on the site of an earlier church of unknown date: the unusual orientation may suggest an early origin. Some of the fabric is of rubble, some, like the N end of the W gable, of big squared stones. The site is said to have been established by St Cadoc in 528, but the first record of an incumbent was made in 1177. About three years later, the church of 'Cormonnoc' was given to Paisley Abbey. A bell inscribed *1618. Michael Bergerhuys me fecit* was replaced in 1893–4 by the present one (by *Warner & Co*).

At the N and S ends, stone fore-staircases, with iron railings of *c*. 1819, mount to stone porches. Blind arches are inscribed on the flanking walls. The W burial aisle of the Stuarts of Castlemilk has a broader scale-and-platt stair on the S side to what was the laird's loft and retiring room. All three gables have scrolled skewputts. Some of the square-headed windows have been given round heads later. Naively classical bell-housing on the S arm, like a squat baldacchino. On the W side of the N projection, a blank tablet with an hourglass, skull and crossbones on the classical surround.

The interior has, unhappily, been recast. In 1871 the side lofts were enlarged and the body of the church was repewed. In 1948 the C19 ORGAN (by *Wadsworth* of Manchester, from St Michael's, Edrom Street, Glasgow) was installed in the laird's loft. – Four STAINED-GLASS windows behind the octagonal pulpit on the W wall: they are a War Memorial by *Norman Macdougall*, 1922; only two of them figurative. – The VAULT (entered from the S) is jack-arched and marble-lined with late C19 and C20 memorial tablets.

Several C18 tombstones in the CHURCHYARD: the oldest is of 1744. WATCHHOUSE, by the gate. The painted regulation boards for the watch are dated 1828.

At the N entrance to the village, the just Italianate former CASTLEMILK HALL AND READING ROOM, 1893. Just beyond, KIRK ROAD, the old main street through the village, begins with the first of the modest whitewashed houses. On the W side, an C18 pair: No. 2, with carved plaques in traditional style recording the restoration of 1972–4; No. 8, with a wallhead gable and scrolled skewputts, said to be of medieval origin and with an ancient well behind it. On the opposite corner, the CLASON HALL, the former Free Church of 1865 (E.E., with bellcote and apse), spoilt by its 1950 entrance. Facing it from Waterside Road, the former SCHOOL of c. 1870, its long windows an alteration from two storeys of 1904. Just beyond the church gate, a row of single-storey cottages, the last one (No. 24) C17, with a crowstepped gable and external shutter hinges. Further on, another row, the middle one Victorianized (like many in the village), the W one with a scrolled skewputt.

To the E, overlooking the triangular village green, Nos. 1–3 GREENSIDE, though dated 1825 and with a smarter symmetrical front, still has a wallhead gable. More low C17 but Victorianized cottages W of the green in MANSE ROAD. No. 7, the schoolhouse between 1700 and 1870, has a crowstepped gable, a 1776 datestone (S gable), and a 1601 date over the fireplace.

Among the fringe of C20 suburban houses, CARMUNNOCK PRIMARY SCHOOL, a circular timber-clad building of 1973 by *Lanarkshire's County Architect* (cf. James Aiton Primary, Cambuslang).

CATHCART

Cathcart was one of the three ancient parishes that ringed Glasgow to the S, the others being Govan and Eastwood. It stretched from Pollokshaws to Muirend, an area gradually covered, since the turn of the century, by speculative housing, which ranges from the cottage villas of Cathcart village to the tenements of Clarkston Road, the palatial houses of Newlands, the bungalows of Muirend and the public housing of Merrylee.

The parish church was donated to Paisley Abbey c. 1179 and was not disjoined until 1596. Its site is unknown. There are, however, very meagre remains of Cathcart Castle, built in the C15 by the Cathcarts, who had held the lands of Cathcart since the C12. The castle was abandoned c. 1750, and fell into ruin. In 1791 the population of the whole, almost entirely agricultural, parish was only 697. The only well-established industry was paper-making at Millholm, begun c. 1729 and developed by the Coupers in the mid-C19. Another paper mill by the Old Bridge opened in 1812. At about the same time a new village (New Cathcart) grew up along the line of the road to Ayrshire (the present Clarkston Road), constructed c. 1810. In the old village, a new church was built in 1831 to replace an C18 one. Ten years later the total population of Old and New Cathcarts was still only 745, but by 1891 it had swelled to 16,589, owing to the influx of commuters attracted by the opening of the Cathcart District

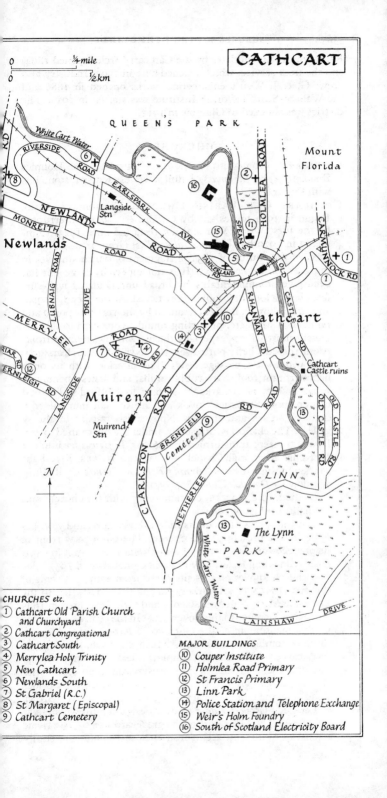

CATHCART

0 ¼ mile
0 ½ km

QUEEN'S PARK

Mount Florida

White Cart Water

RIVERSIDE ROAD

⑥ ✕

✕ ⑧

EARLSPARK AVE

Langside Stn

LANGSIDE ROAD

NEWLANDS

MONREITH ROAD

Newlands

NEWLANDS ROAD

LUBNAIG ROAD

DRIVE

MERRYLEE

MERRYLEE ROAD

ROAD

✕ ⑦

COYLTON RD

✕ ④

⑯ ⌐

HOLMLEA ROAD

② ✕

SPEAN ST

⑪ ✕

⑮ ✕

⑤ ✕

TANKERLAND RD

① ✕

CARMUNNOCK RD

① ✕

①

Cathcart

RHANNAN RD

⑩

③ ✕

⑭ ■■

OLD CASTLE RD

Cathcart Castle ruins

Muirend

Muirend Stn

CLARKSTON ROAD

BRENFIELD RD

Cemetery

⑨

NETHERLEE RD

OLD CASTLE RD

OLD CASTLE RD

⑬

LINN

PARK

⑬ ■ The Lynn

White Cart Water

LAINSHAW DRIVE

N

FRIAR...

FERNLEIGH RD

⑫ ■

LANGSIDE

CHURCHES etc.
① Cathcart Old Parish Church and Churchyard
② Cathcart Congregational
③ Cathcart South
④ Merrylea Holy Trinity
⑤ New Cathcart
⑥ Newlands South
⑦ St Gabriel (R.C.)
⑧ St Margaret (Episcopal)
⑨ Cathcart Cemetery

MAJOR BUILDINGS
⑩ Couper Institute
⑪ Holmlea Road Primary
⑫ St Francis Primary
⑬ Linn Park
⑭ Police Station and Telephone Exchange
⑮ Weir's Holm Foundry
⑯ South of Scotland Electricity Board

Railway in 1884, and later by the Cathcart Circle (opened 1894) and the tram service, which reached here in 1902. Industry also grew: G. & J. Weir's engineering works opened in 1886 and the Wallace-Scott Tailoring Institute was started in 1913. The district was annexed to Glasgow in 1912.

CHURCHES

CATHCART CONGREGATIONAL CHURCH, 56 Holmlea Road. 1934, by *Stellmacs*. A dull towerless red sandstone box with Dec tracery.

CATHCART OLD PARISH CHURCH, Carmunnock Road. Begun in 1914 to designs by *Clifford & Lunan*; interrupted by the First World War and not restarted until 1923. Completed in 1929 by *Watson, Salmond & Gray*. It was built to succeed the church of 1831, a fragment of which survives in the graveyard (*see* below). It is not especially large but has been given monumentality by broad unarticulated wall-surfaces with a look of knobbly grey tweed. At the N end, a squat and square tower, its size enhanced by the very low porch and range of vestries etc. projecting round a courtyard to the NE. Details mostly Perp, especially the big windows of the E front. Along the side, hefty buttresses step down from the clearstorey over windowless passage aisles. The interior, with its open hammerbeam roof, bare rubble walls, and aisles opening in squat arches, is remarkably similar to Clifford's Titwood church (now St James Pollok), as are the tall unmoulded s transept arches and the Art Nouveauish tracery of the w gallery. The chancel is, unusually, under the rib-vaulted tower. Low N transept transformed in 1962 by *T. Beveridge* into the McKellar Memorial Chapel. – STAINED GLASS. Five-light window designed by *R. Anning Bell* for *Guthrie & Wells*. – Window by *Douglas Hamilton*, 1950.

To the N, the MANSE, contemporary with the church, and the halls, the last of 1964.

The GRAVEYARD, with its funereal ivy, laurel and yew, lies opposite the present parish church. The Gothick w front of its predecessor, designed by *James Dempster* and built in 1831, faces Kilmailing Road. The rest was demolished in 1931. The first church known on this site dated from 1707, but some of the MONUMENTS are earlier. Among the oldest, that to the Polmadie Martyrs (Thom, Cooke and Urie), executed in 1685 for their adherence to the Covenant. – In the centre, the gabled Gothic mausoleum of the Gordons of Aikenhead. – Near it, the C18 tombstone of Francis Murdoch, Dean of Guild of Ayr, carved with Christ trampling Death accompanied by Father Time. – To the s, a circular Byzantine mausoleum with stone dome and grotesque corbels. – Close to the Carmunnock Road gate, the C18 classical burial chamber of Thomas Brown of Langside (*Robert Adam* made a design for Brown's house at Langside). – The s part of the graveyard was a C19 private extension. Within it, a cast-iron enclosure round the family burial place of Neale Thomson of Camphill † 1867. – Against the wall, a neo-Greek sarcophagus designed by *Alexander Thomson* and erected in 1867 to commemorate the son of his collaborator, 'John McIntyre, Builder in Glasgow'. – Built into the angle of the wall s of the ruined church, an early C19 WATCHHOUSE.

CATHCART SOUTH CHURCH, 40–2 Clarkston Road. 1893–4, by *W. G. Rowan* for the United Presbyterians. Dec, with much crocketed finials on the main gable and flanking pinnacles. Disappointing interior, with NW organ recess and galleries at the SE end and in the two transepts. – STAINED GLASS. Above the organ, a five-light First World War memorial window by *R. Anning Bell*, 1920 (the Virgin, Abraham and Isaac, Christ, David and Goliath, Dorcas). – Two nave windows by *James Wright*, 1937: NE (Conversion of Paul) and SW (Glory of Jesus). – Transepts: NE by *Douglas Hamilton*, 1939; SW by *Gordon Webster*, 1938.

A low session house links the church to its Dec predecessor of 1889 (now the HALL, modernized in 1975). Behind it, the BUCHANAN HALL of 1912, unexpectedly elaborate, with Art Nouveau stained glass filling the dome and in the doors and exuberant plasterwork. More STAINED GLASS in the SW window by *Alfred Webster*, 1912. - KENT HALL to the NE, by *Honeyman, Jack & Robertson*, 1959, with a STAINED-GLASS window by *Gordon Webster*, 1960.

CHRIST THE KING (R.C.), 220 Carmunnock Road. *See* King's Park: Churches.

MERRYLEA HOLY TRINITY PARISH CHURCH, 80 Merrylee Road. 1912–15, by *P. Macgregor Chalmers*. S aisle and transept 1921–5. Chalmers' favourite Scottish Romanesque style in cream Auchenheath stone, with a green slate roof that cat-slides over the porch where the tower was originally designed to rise. Simple but majestic unplastered and clearstoried interior enlivened by the wooden barrel-vault. E apse lined with the blind arcading of the stone elders' stalls and an apsidal baptistery.

Original FURNISHINGS in the Romanesque vein reflect the blind arcading of the apse. – ORGAN, 1948. The War Memorial case by *Leslie Grahame Thomson* classical rather than Roman-esque. – STAINED GLASS. Three apse windows, 1916 (Baptism, Crucifixion, Resurrection), by *Guthrie & Wells*. – Baptistery window, 1918 (Virgin and Child), probably by the same artists. – S aisle. Five windows by the *St Enoch Studio*, 1947–8 (Scenes from the Early Life of Christ). – W window. Three-light outer ones a War Memorial, the centre one to the Rev. Hugh Sutherland, 1922, by *Stephen Adam* (The Last Supper). – N aisle window signed with a bishop's mitre, 1961. – N aisle E window, 1922, by *C. Paine* (Virgin and Child).

The church was linked *c*. 1925 to a large HALL (N) and offices (W), including a bay-windowed church officer's house more redolent of Gloucestershire than Glasgow.

NEW CATHCART CHURCH, 218 Newlands Road. Built as

Cathcart Free Church. By *J. B. Wilson*. A long red rock-faced composition of hall (1898) and church (1907–8), linked by a slim octagonal tower which bristles at the top with rainwater spouts and crockets. The church is Perp, with a big two-storey NW porch.

NEWLANDS SOUTH CHURCH, 83 Langside Drive. 1901–3, by *H. E. Clifford*. Dull, Perp and towerless, of snecked Giffnock rubble outside and with Auchenheath stone dressings within. Broad arches with low octagonal piers divide off the passage aisles, a favourite Clifford formula. Open hammerbeam roof. Most of the original woodwork and Art Nouveau light fittings survive.

The Dec HALL facing Riverside Road was the original church of 1898–9 by *Stark & Rowntree*. Undistinguished extension of 1965.

ST GABRIEL (R.C.), 83 Merrylee Road. 1955, by *Thomas Cordiner*. Simple rectangle of concrete block and facing brick with a shallow pitched roof, the minimal ornament concentrated on the shallow recessed entrance and on the Festival of Britain-style star over the high altar.

ST MARGARET (Episcopal), 351–5 Kilmarnock Road. *P. Macgregor Chalmers'* most ambitious and most impressive Glasgow church, and one of the few of his churches to receive its tower. His favourite Romanesque style here has a Germanic cast, with apses flanked by pyramid-capped towers at each end. It was designed in 1895 but built in four stages: hall and vestries, 1908; nave and lower part of the tower, 1910–12; chancel, 1922–3; tower top, 1934–5. *Gordon Galloway* of *Whyte & Galloway* (executives after Chalmers' death in 1922) modified the tower design to omit the spire. Beautifully built throughout of very local pale buff Auchenheath stone.

Externally, all the emphasis is on the bold E and blind-arcaded W apses, and on the almost free-standing NW tower, with its vaulted porch, open bell-stage and bold pinnacles: the sides are quite plain. Halls and vestries lie round a courtyard to the N and screen a charming polygonal sacristy, like a chapter house, linked at the NE corner of the church.

65   The interior, a model of Ecclesiological correctness, is a rather dry and perhaps over-studied essay. The arcades have plain round arches of two orders and capitals of two main forms (scallop in the nave, cushion, with a complicated outline and carved volutes, in the chancel): no two capitals are exactly the same. Over the nave, a simple timber barrel-vault, with stone wall-shafts only in the more elaborate chancel. The apses differ: the E one (sanctuary) has a ribbed half-dome, the W (baptistery) a plain one. Both have MOSAICS: E, Christ in Glory; W, the Descent of the Holy Spirit. – The chancel FURNISHINGS are all of a piece, from the blind-arcaded stone altar to the Bishop's throne, pews, kneeling desks and the case of the *Willis* organ (1924), which repeat the same Romanesque motifs in oak. – FONT. An oddly incongruous choice, a marble angel holding a shell copied by *Galbraith & Winton* from a

Thorwaldsen sculpture. – SCULPTURE. Plaster relief roundels of St Martin and St Margaret by *A. & W. Young*, 1916 and 1918. – STAINED GLASS. In the w apse, late glass by *Morris & Co.*, 1923. That in the chancel matches in style and date but is unattributed. – Two choir windows of the 1940s and two Lady Chapel windows by *St Enoch Studio*. – Also in a choir window, a solitary hooded figure, a modest memorial to the stained-glass artist Hugh McCulloch † 1925. – Lady Chapel E window: St Margaret's Last Communion in a setting that recalls this church (dedicated to George Herriot † 1920). – Aisles: three windows by *Gordon Webster*, 1950, 1954, 1971; two by *St Enoch Studio*, 1949.

CATHCART CEMETERY, Brenfield Road. Laid out from plans of *W. R. McKelvie* of Dundee and opened in 1878. At the entrance, a picturesquely asymmetrical lodge with a small round tower.

LINN CREMATORIUM, Lainshaw Drive. By *T. S. Cordiner*; opened in 1962. Long and low but with a strongly mannered silhouette. Expressionist canopies on tapering *pilotis* stretch out either side of the central block.

PUBLIC BUILDINGS

COUPER INSTITUTE, 84–6 Clarkston Road. 1887–8, by *James Sellars* of *Campbell Douglas & Sellars*, funded by a bequest from Robert Couper of the local Millholm Paper Mills. The remaining part of the original building, the hall, is like an early Georgian Town House with a Venetian window and a stairtower with arcaded bell-stage and short spire. Originally a library and reading room in the same style continued the composition informally to the S. They were replaced by an additional hall in 1923 and the books were moved to the new PUBLIC LIBRARY (1923–4, by *J. A. T. Houston*). Hall and library follow their own familiar Glasgow precedents. The interior of the halls was modernized in 1971–3: the library is well-preserved.

POLICE STATION AND TELEPHONE EXCHANGE, 141–3 Merrylee Road. The former (1892 and 1911, by *C. Davidson* of Paisley) of ashlar in Scottish c 17 style; the latter very plain, in rubble, more Cotswolds than Scottish (1928, by *H.M. Office of Works, Edinburgh*).

CANNON (former Toledo) CINEMA, Clarkston Road, Muirend. 1933, by *William Beresford Inglis*. In *hacienda* style inside and out.

VOGUE BINGO (former Kingsway Cinema), Cathcart Road. 1929, by *J. McKissack* for the Vogue chain, with a fantastically Hispanic-style foyer curved along the street.

HOLMLEA PRIMARY SCHOOL, Holmlea Road. By *A. Balfour*, 1907–8. Inscribed *Cathcart Parish School Board: Holmlea Public School*. c 17 domestic style in pink ashlar with two identical two-storey ranges linked by a slightly more elaborate entrance bay. Glasgow-Style railings, with the typical inverted heart motif.

ST FRANCIS PRIMARY SCHOOL, 33 Briar Road, in the grounds of the Franciscan Convent (a mid-C19 villa with ecclesiastical-looking additions). By *Gillespie, Kidd & Coia*; completed 1968. Only two storeys, but with the cantilevered, chamfered floor slabs familiar from the much larger King's Park and Our Lady and St Francis (Calton) secondary schools.

LINN PARK was acquired by the Corporation in 1919 and opened to the public in 1921 and (lower part) 1927. At its heart the small, undistinguished and much abused summer retreat (THE LYNN) built for Colin Campbell *c.* 1828 and enlarged in 1852 by John Gordon of Aikenhead to designs by *Charles Wilson*. – To the W, an iron BRIDGE of *c.* 1835 spans the Cart in one elegant arch. It is apparently a one-piece casting and is the oldest complete iron bridge in the city. – At the N end of the park, off Old Castle Road, lie the meagre ruins of CATHCART CASTLE, atop a cliff overhanging the Cart. Only the lowest courses survive of the C15 keep built by the Cathcarts. It was abandoned as a dwelling *c.* 1740 and sold for building materials. In 1866 it still had five storeys and was surrounded by smaller buildings. It was a simple oblong structure within a barmkin and had a first-floor hall over a crudely vaulted ground floor.

CATHCART STATION, Clarkston Road. The remains of a pretty wooden station building like those at Maxwell Park and Pollokshields West, and also built *c.* 1894 for the Cathcart and District Railway.

NEW BRIDGE. *See* Descriptions, below: Cathcart.

CATHCART OLD BRIDGE across the White Cart Water. Datestone 1624 (*ex situ*). The bridge is probably late C18; one arch (S) narrow and semicircular, the other (N) wide and segmental.

DESCRIPTIONS

Cathcart

HOLMLEA ROAD and CLARKSTON ROAD form the main artery through the area. They were constructed, together with the NEW BRIDGE across the White Cart, in 1900–2 to carry trams into Cathcart. W of Holmlea Road, streets of mid-1930s Corporation tenements, sandstone-faced, lead to SPEAN STREET which follows the White Cart in a loop round the former Wallace-Scott Tailoring Institute of 1913–22 by *Sir J. J. Burnet*, converted in the late 1950s to the headquarters of the SOUTH OF SCOTLAND ELECTRICITY BOARD. The Institute was notable in 1922 both for its advanced, functional design and for the facilities provided for its staff. It originally faced towards a continuation of Inverlair (then Minto) Avenue. Almost all its formally laid surroundings of garden, tennis courts, bowling green and sports ground, ringed with clipped bushes and pollarded trees, have disappeared under later buildings and a sea of tarmac and cars: two tower-like gate lodges remain. The main entrance now is via the E footbridge, replaced and augmented with a road bridge. This approach is dominated by a curtain-walled office slab of 1969. A glass-fronted foyer links it to the former factory and to the computer suite (1976–80) with its ungainly roofline. The former Tailoring Institute itself has been butchered twice and now presents a bland late C20 face. The glazed polychrome brickwork facing the floor slabs was removed in the 1950s; in 1976–80, 1950s windows were replaced by *Harvey, Scott & Partners* with bronze glazing and spandrels. The big concrete parapets that turned the angles into towers, and the handsome glass entrance canopy have also gone. The U-shaped plan, originally closed on the E side by a corridor and cloakroom block, and with open-plan workrooms and a social and educational institute in the wings, has been destroyed. Three storeys of offices have been inserted into the courtyard.

In NEWLANDS ROAD, just to the S, are other important industrial buildings at G. & J. Weir's HOLM FOUNDRY (No. 149). The W block was built in 1912 to a design bought in the U.S.A. by William Weir from Kahn's *Trussed Concrete Steel Co.*: *Albert Kahn* had already used the design for the No. 10 factory of the Packard Automobile Company in Detroit. Here concrete infill panels were used instead of brick. The frame, although clearly expressed, is still moulded at each storey with vestiges of classical cornices. Weir fitted out the interior in traditional style with wood panelling and stained glass: the entrance gates are Art Nouveau. Top storey by *James Miller*, 1928. The E block looks the same but is steel-framed with brick infill and was not built until 1949–51. Round the corner in Inverlair Avenue is the MINTO BUILDING, designed in 1913 by *Moritz Kahn* in the London office of the T.S.C. Company. E of the gateway on Newlands Road, the former Social Welfare building with the curved and streamlined details of 1930s modernism: 1937, by *Wylie, Wright & Wylie*.

CLARKSTON ROAD, S of the New Bridge, divides Cathcart village and Linn Park from Newlands (*see* below) and Muirend. Along most of its length, from the New Bridge across the White Cart to Muirend Station, it is lined with a haphazard mixture of late C19 tenements-with-shops, terraced houses, maltreated rural cottages and mid-C20 houses, garages and supermarkets. The few churches and public buildings along or close to this main road are of interest (*see* above), but otherwise the only diversion is one small classical bank of 1925–7 by *Paterson Stoddart* (once a branch of the Glasgow Savings Bank) and the fantastic Cannon Cinema (*see* Public Buildings, above), both close to the city boundary.

CATHCART VILLAGE to the E lacked cohesion in the mid-C19 and still does. It stretches from the ruined parish church and graveyard to the White Cart near the ruins of Cathcart Castle. The area round the present parish church is dominated by ugly arterial roads and mid-C20 suburbia, but KILMAILING

ROAD, to the S, has a more villagey character, with tenements opposite the ruined church and *cottage-orné*-style double villas of the late C19 further down. Plenty of rural charm is still to be found in the wooded glen of the White Cart where the pedestrian Cathcart Old Bridge (*see* Public Buildings) crosses the river. By the bridge on the E bank towers the tall, narrow and crowstepped LINDSAY HOUSE (No. 38 SNUFF MILL ROAD) by *John Baird II*, a tenement built in 1863–4 by David Lindsay (*see* his monogram above a side door). The much-restored so-called SNUFF MILL lies on the S side of the bridge. Built as a meal mill in the C18, it was converted to a cardboard mill in 1812 for Solomon Lindsay of Penicuik. The small W section became a snuff mill in 1814. Adjacent to it, the MILL HOUSE of *c.* 1902. The group of late C19 *cottages ornés* behind in Snuff Mill Road completes the picture. Upstream, past the cliff-top ruins of Cathcart Castle, the river opens out into the rolling expanse of Linn Park (*see* Public Buildings).

In NETHERLEE ROAD, on the W bank, the early C19 classical villa CARTBANK faces the castle. One storey and with bowed ends towards the drive; two storeys towards the river. The famous HOLMWOOD, further down Netherlee Road, designed by *A. Thomson* for James Couper of Millholm Mills, is (in 1989) in Eastwood District outwith the city boundary.

Newlands

Newlands presents a remarkably unspoilt picture of a turn-of-the-century suburb with its double villas of consistent size and type, plots of equal size and roads of uniform width, lined with low walls and privet hedges and made green by the trees of mature gardens. None of the plots is as large as most of those in Pollokshields, none of the houses is as opulent, and none of the streets so leafy; but what it lacks in scale and grandeur and semi-rural atmosphere, it compensates for with a kind of stolid consistency. Newlands Road was constructed in 1895, and by 1905 the heart of the area had been built up from Earlspark Avenue in the N to Monreith Road in the S with a spine of houses extending down Langside Drive. The area W of Langside Drive, still occupied by Merrylee Farm in 1900, followed. The *Glasgow Herald* noted that the building boom in this suburb had tailed off noticeably by 1907.

NEWLANDS ROAD is one of the smartest roads, with proportionately more detached houses. Few, however, depart from the standard double-fronted design with bay windows and a hipped roof. Those that do are therefore more conspicuous: from the W, No. 9 (GARTHLAND) is red, rock-faced and Baronial; No. 11 (DUNSTAFFNAGE) has an elaborate conservatory on the side and belvedere platform on the roof; No. 21, like many houses in the area, still has a lot of leaded and stained glass. On the S side, flanking Lubnaig Road, two large Free-Style houses: No. 40 (THE OAKS) faced with harl and cream polished ashlar; No. 42 (BRACKLEY) with Dutch details in red sandstone on harling and a cartouche dated 1905. At the far end of Langside Drive, the villas are more modest and probably later. They peter out into the Corporation scheme off Clarkston Road. In the parallel but less interesting MONREITH ROAD, only the half-timbered Nos. 19–21 and 25–7, probably as late as the 1920s, and No. 17, which duplicates No. 9 Newlands Road, stand out.

LUBNAIG ROAD leads S and has, at its S end, where it joins Merrylee Road, a group of red sandstone villas with variously castellated, half-timbered and conical trimmings to otherwise identical bay-windowed fronts. The housing in MERRYLEE ROAD is more varied, with prominent blocks of late C20 flats. Best are the houses at the W end: No. 23 with a corner bay and much stained glass; Nos. 10–12 with fancy half-timbering in the gables; and Nos. 3 and 5 (KINHOLM and DRUMGARTH), a Free-Style variation on the double villa, with copper saucer domes over the bay windows and corner porches. LANGSIDE DRIVE crosses Merrylee Road further E.

In Langside Drive, N of Merrylee Road, two interesting late C19 houses linked to form SCOTT HOUSE, an old people's home. At the Baronial No. 56, built by Scott the shipbuilder, a huge conservatory wrapped round the side and a main reception room in the spirit of a medieval hall, with open timber roof, inglenook fireplace and a chimneypiece of glazed tiles embossed with marine monsters. Nos. 52–4, a red sandstone house trimmed with cream sandstone and with ironwork cresting over the two bows, was apparently designed as a double villa but was certainly occupied from 1897 as a single house (HUGHENDEN) by Hugh McCulloch of the firm of interior decorators and stained-glass makers. Much of the decoration that he commissioned survives. In the music room windows (S bow), late C19 stained glass with charming Pre-Raphaelite maidens playing musical instruments, adaptations of designs made for *McCulloch & Co.*, by *David Gauld*. The Glasgow-Style fireplace and glass-fronted cabinets over recessed seats are later, by *E. A. Taylor*, c. 1902–4. Here and in the drawing room, friezes painted with maidens in stylized bowers by Taylor in the weakly romantic manner of Jessie M. King, his future wife. On the N staircase, a glorious golden harvest scene of classical maidens by *Harrington Mann*; on the S staircase, a jewel-coloured galleon, attributed by Donnelly to *E. A. Taylor*. S of Merrylee Road, two exceptionally handsome and distinctive houses with recessed first-floor loggias: No. 81 (STONELEIGH) with Domestic Revival overtones in the knubbly wall surface and steep-pitched red-tiled roofs; and No. 83 (THE BEECHES), more formal and of ashlar, with C17 details, such as the mullioned and transomed windows, the cartouche supported by cherubs above the broad porch and the hefty balustrade enclosing the loggia.

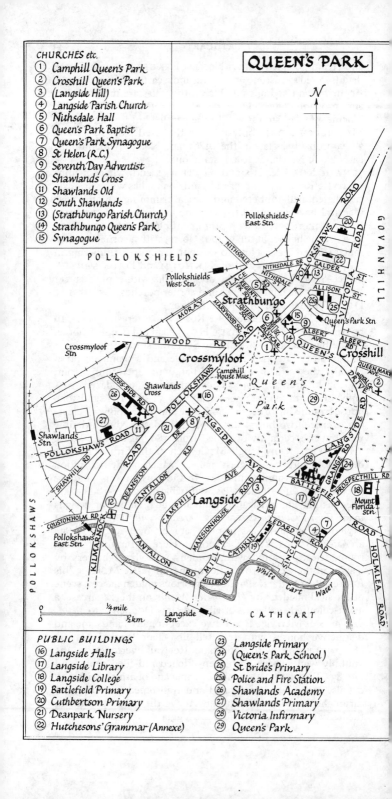

QUEEN'S PARK

CHURCHES etc.
1. Camphill Queen's Park
2. Crosshill Queen's Park
3. (Langside Hill)
4. Langside Parish Church
5. Nithsdale Hall
6. Queen's Park Baptist
7. Queen's Park Synagogue
8. St Helen (R.C.)
9. Seventh Day Adventist
10. Shawlands Cross
11. Shawlands Old
12. South Shawlands
13. (Strathbungo Parish Church)
14. Strathbungo Queen's Park
15. Synagogue

PUBLIC BUILDINGS
16. Langside Halls
17. Langside Library
18. Langside College
19. Battlefield Primary
20. Cuthbertson Primary
21. Deanpark Nursery
22. Hutchesons' Grammar (Annexe)
23. Langside Primary
24. (Queen's Park School)
25. St Bride's Primary
25a. Police and Fire Station
26. Shawlands Academy
27. Shawlands Primary
28. Victoria Infirmary
29. Queen's Park

QUEEN'S PARK

Round Queen's Park lie salubrious suburbs linked by more work-aday tenements and shops. In their midst the steep Camp Hill rises out of Queen's Park and descends gradually towards the White Cart, with the avenues of Langside tracing its southern contours. Round the northern fringe of the park lie the wooded villadom of Crosshill and the broad sweep of Queen's Drive, and to the w and s e the flatter grids of villas, terraces and tenements in Strathbungo, Crossmyloof, Shawlands and Battlefield.

CHURCHES

CAMPHILL QUEEN'S PARK CHURCH, Balvicar Drive. Gothic hall next to the park, 1873: architect unknown. The church (originally Camphill United Presbyterian) by *William Leiper* followed in 1875–8. The spire was finished in 1883. For the Normandy-Gothic steeple soaring above the nave, Leiper was indebted to J. L. Pearson's St Augustine, Kilburn (London), which was being planned when Leiper was in Pearson's office in 1870. The façade is also French Gothic. In the main gable, two large traceried windows within an enclosing arch: in the spandrel, an angel with outspread wings by *Mossman*. The rest of the carving is by *McCulloch & Co.*, mostly concentrated on the gabled porch (musician angels in the tympanum, rich foliage on the shafted doorway). The graceless curtain-walled health centre slapped up at the w end spoils the setting. The interior has a few Pearson motifs too, especially the group of tall w lancets, but in plan it conforms to Church of Scotland prescriptions, with a short wide nave and galleries behind the tall arcades. These have twin-shafted stone columns with foliage capitals. Though plain, all this originally glowed with colour (as Leiper's Dowanhill Church did too). Apart from the tie-beams, the roof is ceiled and still stencilled with golden flowers, but the coloured wall-stencilling designed by Leiper has been whitewashed over. Ill-chosen central PULPIT and reredos (Italian Gothic) of 1947. – STAINED GLASS. Fine original three-light w window by *Cottier* (Faith, Hope, Charity).

CROSSHILL QUEEN'S PARK CHURCH, 40 Queen's Drive. 1872–3, by *Campbell Douglas & Sellars*. Like Leiper's later Camphill Church (*see* above), the former Queen's Park High Church has a handsome tall s e steeple, but with a heavier silhouette and roguish details. A stairtower emerges from the angle buttresses against the nave and disappears again near the top. The layered arrangement of broaches, tabernacles, and linking arcading defies description. All this is reminiscent of Townhead Church (*see* Royston, above) and may have been designed by *J. J. Stevenson*, the former partner of Campbell Douglas, before he left for London in 1873. The squarish body of the church is conventionally French, with big traceried windows and a gabled porch. Inside, galleries on three sides, with two tiers of heavy Gothic columns and clearstorey windows very high up above the Gothic arches of the upper tier – a variation on the arrangement at Townhead. Open timber roof with arched braces. – LECTERN. Elaborate symbolism on this Second World War Memorial. – STAINED GLASS. Big S window (Adoration of the Magi) by *C. Paine* for *Guthrie & Wells*, 1957. – Two sets of 1914–18 War Memorial glass either side of the platform. Brought from Crosshill Victoria Church.

LANGSIDE HILL CHURCH, 22 Langside Road. Ruinous (in 1989) but still impressive. A Free Church of 1894–6 by *Alexander Skirving*. Graeco-Roman. The façade is as Greek as one could expect from a former assistant of Alexander Thomson, with an Ionic hexastyle portico raised above a triple entrance porch. The podium's channelled rustication wraps right round the two staircase projections, formed like the *cellae* of circular temples. The pediment sculpture was never done: it was to have shown John Knox remonstrating with Mary, Queen of Scots. The side elevations could be called Roman, with arched windows over the square ones. So was the interior, which had arcades of Corinthian columns supporting a deep coved ceiling and a horseshoe layout of galleries and pews.

LANGSIDE PARISH CHURCH, 167 Ledard Road. The former Battlefield West Church of 1908–9 by *H.E. Clifford*. In orangy-pink Corsehill sandstone with green slate roofs. Simple façade modelled on Dunblane Cathedral. Galleried interior with tall slender arcades and a central (N) organ recess. – STAINED GLASS. Jubilee windows (W side of nave, commemorating the building of the church) and windows flanking the entrance by *Gordon Webster*, 1952.

Prettily composed Arts and Crafts-inspired Allan Halls to the E. World War II Memorial Hall to the W, its S window etched with Christ, St Andrew and a commemorative inscription.

NITHSDALE HALL (The Brethren), 41–3 Nithsdale Road. Built in 1888 as Nithsdale United Presbyterian Church. A simple red and white brick box screened by a small but substantial Greek façade in Alexander Thomson's manner. Temple front with four pilasters between the two pylon-like projections. Elaborate approach with anthemion railings and (decapitated) lamp-standards. The snecked rubble has the obvious white pointing often specified by Thomson.

QUEEN'S PARK BAPTIST CHURCH, 178 Queen's Drive. By *McKissack & Rowan* and begun the same year (1886) as Strathbungo Parish Church (*see* below), but squat and more thoroughly Romanesque in style. *Westwerk* with stumpy towers and chevron-decorated doorway. Chunky stepped buttresses and biforated windows down the sides. Uncarved (or unfinished?) capitals to the main doorway and windows. The nave arcades are equally chunky, with wide cruciform scalloped capitals on painted granite columns. Whole church extensively modernized by *Davis Duncan Partnership*, 1983–4.

QUEEN'S PARK SYNAGOGUE, Falloch Road. 1924–6 (and dated 5886) by *Ninian McWhannell*, in red-painted artificial stone. The façade is in a curious combination of styles: Italian Romanesque for the outer bays, C 15 Venetian for the entrance. The apse, with its half-glazed dome, can be seen from Lochleven Road.

ST HELEN (R.C.), 30 Langside Avenue. Built as a United Presbyterian Church in 1896–7: architect *John B. Wilson*. Yellow snecked rubble, red ashlar dressings. Uninspired Perp. Entrance through the base of what was to have been the NE tower; the top and spire were never built. Over the door, a weathered stone figure clasping a fish, evidently *ex situ*. Octagonal cast-iron columns carry an open timber roof, with giant cusping, over nave and galleries.

ST NINIAN (Episcopal). *See* Pollokshields.

SEVENTH DAY ADVENTIST CHURCH, 174 Queen's Drive. Built in 1895–7 as the Swedenborgian New Jerusalem Church. A horribly crude E.E. design by *J. B. Wilson* in a deep but vivid red rock-faced sandstone. Conventional plan, with double transepts and apse.

SHAWLANDS CROSS CHURCH, 1114 Pollokshaws Road. A former United Free church of 1900–3 by *Miller & Black*. An elaborate version of their favourite late Perp style in silvery-grey sandstone. The octagonal buttresses, with lantern-tops and spiky pinnacles flanking the main gable, lift the design out of the ordinary. No tower, but a pretty octagonal timber bell turret perches on the roof ridge. A broad, airy interior; tall Perp arcades and galleries with Perp details carried between them on three sides. Simple roof with arched braces. Usual platform arrangement.

To the SE, the Arts and Crafts-style HALL of 1898–9 by *John Hamilton*, which seems to have set the style.

SHAWLANDS OLD PARISH CHURCH, 1120 Pollokshaws Road. 1885–9, by *J. A. Campbell* of *John Burnet, Son & Campbell*, in white Giffnock stone and without a tower for economy's sake. Advantage has been taken of the necessary simplicity. The church is severely E.E. with large expanses of mechanically cut snecked rubble walling. Along the defensive street elevation, with its deep gloomy porch, tiny unmoulded lancets which light the aisles, clearstorey, and the hall and session house at the S end (1893). Drama is reserved for the N end facing the Shawlands Cross; the three boldly recessed lancets and vesica between two buttresses of massive and primitive outline are quoted from Dunblane Cathedral. Equally severe, the high nave with aisle arcades of alternately round and octagonal piers on high bases and with a little nailhead in the capitals. Simple open timber roof with tie-beams. Unusual repoussé metal linings to the doors. – Stone PULPIT also in a hefty E.E. style. – STAINED GLASS. Three-light E window (War Memorial on the subject of Redemption) by *Douglas Hamilton*, 1950. – In the modern hall extension, six panels from the former Park Church, Lynedoch Place (*see* Woodlands and Finnieston: Perambulation 1); the four in the chapel in the vigorous style of *J. T. & C.E. Stewart*.

SOUTH SHAWLANDS CHURCH, Regwood Street and Deanston Drive. The hall (1909) preceded the church (1912–13), which is towerless and Perp in *Miller & Black*'s familiar manner. Unencumbered interior with cantilevered galleries. Halls beneath. – STAINED GLASS. Chancel, 1954, by *Douglas Hamilton*.

STRATHBUNGO PARISH CHURCH, 601–5 Pollokshaws Road. Derelict in 1989. 1886–7, by *McKissack* (who as a member of the congregation did most of the design) *& Rowan*. Of blackened cream sandstone. A bold but awkwardly scaled composition building up from a low half-octagonal stairchamber via a narrow, heavily buttressed Romanesque nave façade to the big tower in Scottish late Gothic style, which climbs higher than the neighbouring tenements. The tower is almost sheer to the bell-stage: then a crown of four ribs flying from the domed finials of the buttresses clasps a little octagonal lantern, itself with a dome of open ribs.

Incorporated in the gables of the church hall, three windows from the previous modest Transitional-style church of 1839–41 by *Charles Wilson*.

STRATHBUNGO QUEEN'S PARK CHURCH, Queen's Drive and Albert Avenue. 1873–5, by *James Thomson*. The least innovative of the three spired churches on the N side of Queen's Park. Straightforward Dec with the prescribed spire, recessed behind a quatrefoil parapet, and a variety of tracery patterns. Galleried interior with cast-iron columns carrying a painted barrel-vault. – ORGAN, 1902, providing the only decorative element since the stencilling on the NE wall was painted over. – STAINED GLASS. Flanking the entrance, two windows by *Douglas Hamilton* in memory of Miss Jane Haining, who died in a German concentration camp (Greater Love Hath No Man). – HALL to the NW with a pretty bay-windowed session room.

SYNAGOGUE, 125 Niddrie Road. 1926–7, by *Jeffrey Waddell & Young*. Much less ambitious than the almost contemporary Queen's Park Synagogue (*see* above) but also with Romanesque overtones.

PUBLIC BUILDINGS

LANGSIDE HALLS, 1 Langside Avenue. A rebuilding, almost stone-for-stone, of *John Gibson*'s National Bank of Scotland of 1847. The Corporation moved it from No. 57 Queen Street when it was replaced by a warehouse in 1901, and the City Engineer, *A. B. McDonald*, converted it into public halls in 1902–3. The façade is an early and intensely rich Palladian version of Gibson's palazzo style, with two orders of pilasters (and, in the centre, attached columns) against a rusticated background. The frieze of fruity swags, the bearded faces on the keystones (representing the Clyde, Thames, Severn, Tweed and Humber), the vase finials, and the royal arms flanked by Peace and Plenty, and every other detail exquisitely done by *John Thomas* of London, who had worked on the Houses of Parliament. The interior had already been remodelled by *James Sellars* in 1856. McDonald made the front of the building a green-tiled entrance hall with double staircase leading up to the small hall, and transformed Sellars' single-storey banking hall into the large hall, removing the celebrated stained-glass-filled dome and substituting the present elaborate plasterwork.

POLICE STATION (and former Fire Station), Craigie Street. 1892–8, by *A. B. McDonald* (City Engineer). Unimaginative Scottish C17 style.

LANGSIDE LIBRARY, Sinclair Drive. 1912–13, by *George Simpson*. A simple single-storey C17-classical block in red sandstone, raised above the road. Extended and made open-plan inside, but the main reading room still has a mural painting (oil on canvas) of *The Battle of Langside* by *Maurice Greiffenhagan*, A.R.A., 1919, given by the governors of Glasgow School of Art.

CAMPHILL HOUSE (Museum of Costume). *See* under Queen's Park, below.

LANGSIDE COLLEGE OF FURTHER EDUCATION, 50 Prospecthill Road, incorporates the former Deaf and Dumb Institution of 1876–8 by *Salmon, Son & Ritchie*, an early example in Glasgow of polychromatic Ruskinian Gothic. A long façade, banded in pink and cream stone, with the characteristic naturalistic foliage decoration carried even to the cast-iron cresting of the complicated French pavilion roofs.

The purpose-built part, dominated by the four-storey slab on the summit of the hill, is by *Boissevain & Osmond*, 1958–65. A neat steel frame and neutral curtain walling, with stove-enamelled steel panels, originally enlivened by some areas of glazed brick in primary colours.

BATTLEFIELD PRIMARY SCHOOL, Carmichael Place. Two former Board schools on one site: that of 1904–6 by *A. Balfour* cut down to its plinth, now used as a base for prefabricated classrooms; the other of 1912 by *McWhannell, Rogerson & Reid* of pink Corsehill sandstone, with no superfluous ornament, only crisply cut C17-style architectural detail.

CUTHBERTSON PRIMARY SCHOOL, Cuthbertson Street. 1906, by *James Miller*, the main block plain in an English C17 domestic manner with slightly advancing end bays and a hipped roof. The flat-roofed wings each side have handsome Venetian windows.

DEANPARK NURSERY SCHOOL, 10 Deanston Drive. The former Crossmyloof Public School of 1877–9 by *James Thomson*. Two-storey and absolutely plain except for two shallow gables with fancy bargeboards and brackets.

HUTCHESONS' GRAMMAR SCHOOL (Annexe), Kingarth Street. The main school is in Beaton Road (*see* Pollokshields: Public Buildings); this was the Girls' Grammar School of 1910–12 by *Thomson & Sandilands*. In general outline like a High Renaissance palazzo, flanked by two staircase towers with Baroque detail, including Vanbrughian arcaded tops. Glazed loggia to the central hall. Above it the large art room windows; below, the insignificant entrance to the one-storey offices. Contemporary former domestic economy and gymnasium block (facing Calder Street) and janitor's house.

LANGSIDE PRIMARY SCHOOL, 203–33 Tantallon Road. 1904–6, by *Andrew Balfour*. A rich Renaissance design in pink sandstone with giant Ionic pilasters, handsome lettering between the two storeys, and other well-carved details. The projecting end bays are more Vanbrughian.

Former QUEEN'S PARK SCHOOL (Teachers' Resource Centre), 75 Grange Road. Four school buildings on the site. The earliest, second from the s, is dated 1874. The next, in similar Gothic style, faces the road junction. The three-storey red sandstone block with Vanbrughian details (1912, by *Thomson & Sandilands*) was designed to replace the first two buildings but was never completed because of the First World War (*see* the rendered end wall). N of it, the two-storey Higher Grade School of 1900–2 by *H. & D. Barclay*.

ST BRIDE'S R.C. PRIMARY SCHOOL, 83 Craigie Street. The former Strathbungo Public School, dated 1894, with two Ionic temple fronts applied flatly towards each end of the big plain red rubble façade.

SHAWLANDS ACADEMY, 31 Moss-side Road. 1930–3, by *Thomas Baird*. A very large example of the type of school building that became standard between 1920 and 1939, with an assembly hall and offices at the centre of wings of classrooms. The style here is stripped classical, the material brick with stone dressings. Many later additions.

SHAWLANDS PRIMARY SCHOOL, 1284 Pollokshaws Road. By *James Hamilton*, 1893; the first building for Shawlands Academy (*see* above). Italianate with a renewed third storey. On the side, the original arrangement with pedimented end bay and pedimented dormers.

Former DRILL HALL (Third Lanarkshire Rifle Volunteers), 35 Coplaw Street. 1884–5, by *John Bennie Wilson*, in a cheerful domestic Gothic style, the battlemented tower suggesting its military use.

VICTORIA INFIRMARY, Langside Road. The competition for this southern counterpart to the Royal and Western Infirmaries was won by *Campbell Douglas & Sellars* in 1882, but building of the administration block and the first of three pavilions did not start until 1888, the year of Sellars' death. Subsequent architects to the hospital were *Campbell Douglas & Morrison* (1888–1903); *H.E. Clifford* (1903–25); and *Watson, Salmond & Gray* (from 1925).

The ADMINISTRATION BLOCK (and former Nurses'

Home) faces Queen's Park. In the central pedimented gable, the arms of Queen Victoria, and a puma (symbolic of medical care). Flanking it, open arcaded cupolas, repeated on the towers at the ends of all the ward pavilions. The first two PAVILIONS (S) were built between 1888 and 1902 to Sellars' design; the third is by *H. E. Clifford* (1902–6). Their end elevations were crudely boxed in in yellow brick in the 1960s. The fourth (1923–7) was built to a modified design: its big bowed end has five storeys of cantilevered metal balconies. W of the pavilions, facing Langside Road, a lower domestic-looking block built as the Nurses' Home in 1892. Attached to it, a taller extension of 1903–6.

E of the pavilions, dominating the Grange Road junction, the former PRIVATE PATIENTS' WING of 1931 (extended 1935), designed by *John Watson* in an extremely simple classical style, with just a hint of the Baroque over the entrance. The attic and the canted ends to the splayed wings are almost fully glazed. The contemporary JOHN INNES MEMORIAL CHAPEL has a Neo-Norman interior. The OUTPATIENTS' DEPARTMENT of 1966–7 on Grange Road screens large additions of the late 1960s, including the small PATHOLOGY DEPARTMENT of 1965, worth examining for the touching Eric Gill-ish relief of The Reaper over the mortuary door (W).

The NURSES' HOME (1928–30; extended 1937) lies N of the main entrance on a narrow dark site, overlooking the park. Simply classical in style but rock-faced and with Art Deco touches round the doorways. It incorporates, at the N end, a dull late C19 villa (QUEEN'S PARK HOUSE).

QUEEN'S PARK, Queen's Drive. Opened in 1862. The name commemorates, not Victoria, but Mary, Queen of Scots, and the site of the battle of Langside (1568) on the S edge of the park. The land, 143 acres (57·8 ha) of Pathhead Farm, was bought by the Corporation from Neale Thomson of Camphill in 1857. *Paxton*'s plans of 1860, which included a lavish winter garden and a lake, were modified by *John Carrick*, the Corporation's Master of Works. He also produced feuing plans for the margins of the park. The high terraced site of the winter garden, aligned on the main gate, was prepared, but a flower garden, originally 'in the old Dutch style', took the place of this expensive building. The lake was omitted altogether.

CAMPHILL HOUSE (Museum of Costume) and its grounds were added to the park in 1894; the house was converted to a museum in 1895–6. It had been built some time between 1800 and 1818 by Robert Thomson, cotton manufacturer. This compact, four-square classical house has affinities with the central block of Aikenhead House, 1806 (*see* King's Park, above: Public Buildings), attributed to *David Hamilton*: prominent, panelled angle pilasters over which the cornice is broken out, sashes with plain classical surrounds but a distinctive glazing pattern with margin lights. On the N FRONT a portico with coupled, fluted Ionic columns, leads via a coffered passage to the central hall, which has a Soanian plaster-vaulted ceiling. Rooms open off all round it, the s ones with simple original plasterwork. To the N W, the enclosed oval staircase. Fireplaces removed, probably during the conversion of 1895–6.

PROPAGATING HOUSES for all the Corporation parks overlook Battle Place. 1905, by Glasgow's *Office of Public Works*. A domed glasshouse with slated cupola fronts the long range of low glasshouses.

An EARTHWORK measuring about 120 m by 100 m lies just off the summit of Camp Hill, a spot which offers exceptional views over the city; the bank is still clear in places, but an encircling path has now obliterated the outer ditch. Entrance in the S E, where excavation revealed part of an inner stockade. Medieval pottery from the excavation of the ditch; Roman sherds recently found in the bank. Presumably the earthwork has its origin in the Iron Age.

ELECTRICITY SUBSTATION, 18 Battlefield Road. 1923–4, by *R. B. Mitchell*, in the Wrenaissance style then favoured by Glasgow Corporation. Just in Millbrae Road (No. 15), the later LIGHTING DEPARTMENT (1937–9, by *Sam Bunton*), with all the attributes of the Modern Movement expressed in silver-grey brick, with blue tile trim and glass bricks.

ELECTRICITY SUBSTATION, Ellangowan Road and Haggs Road. 1908, and almost perfectly disguised, in this residential neighbourhood, as a little villa.

BATTLEFIELD REST, on an island between Battlefield Road and Grange Road. Unique in Glasgow – a tramcar shelter of 1914–15, by *Burnet & Boston*, striped in green and cream tiles. In one of the half-octagon ends, the public conveniences; in the other, under a spreading tiled roof and domed clock tower, a kiosk.

PERAMBULATIONS

1. Strathbungo and Crosshill

Strathbungo has a longer history than Crosshill. It grew up in the C 17 as a group of weavers' and miners' cottages at the junction of the road from Glasgow with that from Hamilton and Paisley (now Nithsdale Road). Until the mid-C 19, it was the only village between Gorbals and Pollokshaws. Suburban development, encouraged by the creation of Queen's Park, began with the private Regent's Park promoted by *Alexander Thomson* and his colleagues, the builder John McIntyre and Alexander Stevenson, the lessee of Giffnock quarry.

Queen's Park and (as a part of the same plan) the continuation S of Eglinton Street as Victoria Road, also attracted more residents to Crosshill, until then just a scatter of early Victorian villas on the hilltop. By 1871 the district was populous enough to be declared a police burgh. In 1872 Tweed complained of 'the mixture of dwelling houses and shops . . .', particularly in Victoria

Road, ' ... which forbids it ever becoming an aristocratic or select retreat'. He did, however, approve of the 'best portions', especially the handsome Queen's Drive. By 1900 Strathbungo and Crosshill had almost grown together, and by 1914 the last of old Strathbungo, between Pollokshaws Road and Victoria Road, was replaced by red sandstone tenements.

REGENT'S PARK. It was in MORAY PLACE that the suburban 41 development of Strathbungo began in 1859 with *Alexander Thomson*'s terrace (Nos. 1–10) at the N end. The choice of this peculiar site seems to have been more expedient than wilful: in 1859 the surroundings were still industrial, except to the N W, where Darnley Gardens lay beyond the railway line. The restricted position, however, worked to Thomson's advantage by forcing the dramatic perspective view, which increased what he called 'the mysterious power of the horizontal element in carrying the mind away into space and into speculation upon infinity'. The stress of the design is indeed on the unbroken horizontal of the first floor, with its regular parade of square stone mullions. The windows, their frames hidden behind slivers of pilasters, are set well back between them, and only blank panels, invisible in an oblique view, mark the division between the houses. Even the decoration is unobtrusively incised. In the pedimented end pavilions, there is subtle play between the horizontal element and the illusion of an open temple portico. No. 1 was Thomson's own house (1859–61), extended in the same style *c*. 1930. The surprisingly plain rubble back elevations have brick and stone outshots and a regular row of lotus-topped chimneypots. The interiors are also quite modest: No. 2, for instance, has joinery treated in simple planes as if it were stone and plasterwork with the familiar disk, lotus and anthemion bands.

The rest of Moray Place was built by speculative builders to more conventional designs. In Nos. 11–36 (*c*. 1864–5) Thomson is recalled but not understood. Though the windows have pilasters between them and the doorways splayed surrounds, the openings are all conventional holes-in-the wall. On Nos. 19–25 (*c*. 1874) only the bands of Greek key and anthemion hark back to Thomson. Here, the end pavilions project as broad bows. By the time Nos. 26–32 were built (after 1878), the design was eclectically Victorian, with gabled L-shaped terminations. The other terraces of this once private estate are more modest and conventional. The flat-fronted two-storey terraces with tall basements in REGENT PARK SQUARE (still with its gatepiers at the E end) and the N side of QUEEN SQUARE were built before 1878. The similar but bay-windowed ones (Queen Square S side and MARYWOOD SQUARE) followed in the 1880s. The suburb is bounded on the E by the classically detailed cream stone tenements of the 1860s and 1870s which line Pollokshaws Road. Nos. 706–22, with semi-circular brick staircase towers, look the earliest.

Just N W of them, N of Regent's Park, is another group of buildings with immediately recognizable Thomson characteristics. It dates from after 1878 and may have been designed by *Turnbull*, Thomson's partner, after the latter's death in 1875. Along the N side of NITHSDALE ROAD (Nos. 18–76), and turning the corner into NITHSDALE STREET, a row of exceptionally plain tenements with small, deeply set windows, and only a flat band rising and falling over the upper windows as a recognizable Thomson hallmark. Rounding the corner between Nithsdale Street and NITHSDALE DRIVE, the SALISBURY QUADRANT bursts with Thomson's mannerisms combined without discipline in an evidently late Victorian fashion. Simpler but similar tenements adjoin each side (Nos. 40–6 Nithsdale Road, Nos. 65–73 Nithsdale Drive). There is more of the Thomson flavour further E along Nithsdale Drive in the Nithsdale Hall (*see* Churches, above) and due W in Pollokshields (*q.v.*).

Nithsdale Drive continues E to POLLOKSHAWS ROAD. There is now no immediately visible trace here of the old village of Strathbungo. It was all rebuilt, including Strathbungo Parish Church (*see* Churches), between 1880 and 1914. The unexceptional tall cream and red stone tenements round the ancient junction of what is now Nithsdale Road and Pollokshaws Road close all views S in a way now quite rare on the main roads out of Glasgow. Especially bold is the one with a Franco-Flemish gable on the corner of Allison Street.

QUEEN'S DRIVE. From Allison Street, Victoria Road, of generous width but with a mundane mixture of tenements and shops, leads S to the main gates of Queen's Park (*see* Public Buildings, above) and to the grand drive round its N edge. Feuing plans were made for Queen's Drive by *John Carrick* (the Corporation's Master of Works) when the park was laid out in 1860. He gave the churches a picturesque role in the overall design by prescribing spires and, in contrast, established a plain standard design for the tenements, with bay windows at the ends of each three-storey-plus-basement block. Most elevations conform to the standard, but plans and details vary according to each building phase. At the W end, the last of the tenements to be built (in 1895), round NIDDRIE SQUARE and in BALVICAR STREET. These, by *Alexander Petrie*, are quite grand, with two-flat houses only. Next to the E, Nos. 120–50 Queen's Drive, feued in 1871, maintain Carrick's elevational standard, with the addition of railings in a tough design of interlaced circles at Nos. 152–64. Each central close has a dog-leg stair: the oval top-lit stair at No. 150 is exceptional.

BALMORAL CRESCENT (Nos. 78–118), just E of the park gates, looks far more impressive. It is one of Glasgow's most extravagant and eccentric tenement blocks (by *W. M. Whyte*, 1884–6), aggrandized by very tall basements, steep pavilion roofs with some curly-pedimented dormers, and a variety of curved bay windows. Along most of the ground floor, carrying the balustraded sills above, are brackets supported by grotesque squatting figures, some monstrous, some medieval and some classical, but all obviously Victorian folk, with, it has been said, identifiable faces. The large, many-windowed flats contrasted with meanly narrow closes and dog-leg stairs, but all has been rebuilt behind the façade by *McGurn, Duncan, Logan & Opfer*, 1988–9. After this come the earlier, more restrained tenements of ROYAL CRESCENT, the first stretch of Queen's Drive (Nos. 44–76) to be laid out (in 1869). They have faceted bays with prominent roofs, and small square stairwells at the front instead of conventional closes. Large villas of the mid-1870s start beyond Crosshill Queen's Park Church (*see* Churches, above). Three pairs (Nos. 26–38) with big bow windows have (or have had) much fretted timber for bargeboards and porches. Slotted amongst the villas, a close of simple brick cottages for the elderly (QUEEN'S PARK DRIVE), designed in 1949–50 by the *City Architect* 'in a more traditional and sentimental style ... than normally used on our housing schemes'.

It leads through to the once rural villadom that grew up on CROSSHILL after *c.*1840. In the private CROSSHILL AVENUE, several bow- and bay-windowed villas, built before 1878, lie behind long gardens. Their backs, with long staircase windows, give on to the s side of QUEEN MARY AVENUE at Nos. 50, 52, 54, and 62–4. Only No. 58, a flat-fronted three-bay villa, and No. 56 (FERNBANK), with anthemion pattern fretted on the bargeboards and incised round the Thomsonish window, face the E end of the street. Opposite, a small Baronial red sandstone villa of 1895 by *J. W. Stafford* (No. 55) and then five pairs of cream stone double villas (1893, by *George Boyd*), built after the railway arrived in 1886. Further W, several earlier villas: Nos. 29 and 25, with some Greek detail, and Nos. 27 and 23, smaller and more Picturesque. All have the same blank fleshy shields. Towards the bottom of the hill at the W end of the street are terraced houses (N) and tenements (S) with façades of untutored faintly Greek design. The houses (Nos. 3–11) have classical leaf friezes below the eaves and windows with lugged surrounds; the tenements (Nos. 10–32), pilasters applied without structural logic. More villas to the N in the parallel ALBERT ROAD. The only ones of particular interest are early ones at the E end: No. 102 with double gables and nice fretted bargeboards; LORETTO, jettied under two steeply peaked gables and with arched windows; and Nos. 80–6, a series with intricate classical decoration in bas-relief.

2. Crossmyloof and Shawlands

In 1850 Crossmyloof consisted of only the huge bakery opened by Neale Thomson of Camphill in 1847 to supply the whole of Glasgow, in London fashion, with quartern loaves, and an associated group of operatives' houses. They lay just W of Pollokshaws Road, near Camphill House. Tenements spread s from there down the roads to Pollokshaws and Kilmarnock after 1860, and N towards Strathbungo after 1890. Villas were built quite early in a pocket between the main roads at Shawlands, and after 1894, when Shawlands Station opened, on the hill around it.

Among the red sandstone tenements of POLLOKSHAWS ROAD, near the entrance to Camphill House, are two striking developments, both designed by *John Nisbet*. SPRINGHILL GARDENS (1904) opens off the main road round three sides of a square with especially tall tenements. Vestigial pediments like eyebrows are the only ornament on the narrow projecting bays. CAMPHILL GATE (Nos. 988–1004 Pollokshaws Road), 1905–6, is more obviously Glasgow Style, with well-carved lettering, corner bays with saucer domes and spindle finials, and a flat roof fenced with an iron balustrade instead of a drying green. Opposite Langside Halls (*see* Public Buildings, above) at the corner of Langside Avenue, the tiny CORONA BAR of 1912–13 by *Clarke & Bell*, held in the angle of a tall, angular red sandstone building. The bar has an openwork parapet, diminutive corner dome and top-lit interior, still with etched and stained glass.

At SHAWLANDS CROSS, where Pollokshaws Road and Kilmarnock Road meet, two handsome churches in contrasting styles (*see* Churches, above) and the domed TRUSTEE (formerly Glasgow) SAVINGS BANK by *Neil C. Duff*, 1905–6, decorated in C17 style with lots of fleshy strapwork. Just around the corner in MOSS-SIDE ROAD (not developed until the 1920s) are Shawlands Academy (*see* Public Buildings) and the former WAVERLEY CINEMA, 1923, by *Watson, Salmond & Gray*, its eye-catching corner dome ringed by Egyptianizing columns. Further into SHAWLANDS down Pollokshaws Road, the C19 predecessor to Shawlands Academy (*see* Public Buildings) and the banal back of the 1960s SHAWLANDS SHOPPING ARCADE, which leads through to a more stylish front on KILMARNOCK ROAD, the district's main shopping street. Several stretches of cream sandstone tenements survive along here, those between CARMENT DRIVE and COUSTONHOLM ROAD with unusual pediments linked over the windows.

w of Kilmarnock Road, a tenement neighbourhood of the 1890s centred on Tassie Street gives way further w to a variety of earlier small cream sandstone villas around SHAWHILL ROAD and along POLLOKSHAWS ROAD, where Nos. 1365 and 1381 have a more substantial Baronial presence, with crowstepped gables and rope moulding. N of Pollokshaws Road, on the hill round Shawlands Station (opened *c.* 1894), streets of substantial terraced and double villas, remarkable for their uniformity and no doubt part of a single development.

3. Langside

Langside began as a planned development. In 1852 Neale Thomson added the Langside estate of the Browns to his Camphill lands with the intention of developing it. *A. & G. Thomson* prepared a feuing plan for the edge of the estate in 1853, con-

sisting of inner and outer crescents of villas (reflected in the
present layout) and terraces along the Kilmarnock Road. Only
one double villa (now No. 25 Mansionhouse Road) was designed
by *Alexander Thomson* and built in 1856–7. Apart from one close
neighbour (Rawcliffe Lodge, 1861, now a monastery), it stood
alone until the 1870s, when other villas were built. Villas gave
way to tenements in the 1880s and 1890s, and the very last houses
did not appear until the 1920s. There was a Langside village, a
weavers' hamlet just s of Battle Place, but this was obliterated in
the 1890s by respectable middle-class tenements which spread s
between 1898 and 1903 right to the banks of the White Cart. In
this neighbourhood, the washed-out pinky-orange of Dumfries-
shire stone is as common as the red of Locharbriggs and the
cream of Giffnock.

This longer perambulation starts back at the w end of LANG-
SIDE AVENUE, where flats, designed for Strathclyde Housing
Association by *Derek Stephenson & Partners* and completed in
1976, have replaced three parallel avenues (Langside, Dirleton,
Lethington) of 1870s villas. It is an imaginative substitution
in the spirit of the original houses but with no trace of dull
cribbing. The layout round formal squares respects the old
grid of streets, and the squarish buff brick blocks of three and
four storeys, with tall hipped slate roofs and canted bays,
standing alone or linked in terraces, recall the former large
detached or double villas. Marking the NW and SE limits of
the scheme, much taller (eight-storey) pavilion-roofed blocks,
heavily modelled with concrete lintels and chamfered sills *à la*
Maisons Jaoul. To the w in TANTALLON ROAD, the old
public school (*see* Public Buildings: Deanpark Nursery School)
belongs to the 1870s phase of development. Most of the rest
of this street dates from after 1880. The villas (Nos. 163–277)
that flank Langside School (*see* Public Buildings) were built
in the 1880s. No. 277 (HOLYROOD HOUSE) has a rooftop
viewing platform railed in elaborate cast-iron.

Tantallon Road leads round to MILLBRAE CRESCENT. On the
s side, a long, smooth, shallow curve of low two-storey terraced
houses, Thomsonesque in detail, and possibly by *Turnbull*
after his partner's death in 1875. Double entrances divided by
lotus-headed columns, recessed panels with anthemion under
the eaves, groups of lotus-topped chimneys; the shallow gables
of the end houses have bargeboards with anthemion fretwork.

Camphill Avenue turns off Millbrae Road a little further N.
Rounding the corner of MANSIONHOUSE ROAD, the first
turning, are the high stone walls of the CARMELITE MON-
ASTERY (No. 29), converted in 1919 from Rawcliffe Lodge,
an extensive mansion of 1861. Its François Premier-style tourelles, shell-carved tympana and higher s block with iron-
crested mansard, can just be glimpsed. Nos. 25 and 25a,
designed by *Alexander Thomson* and built in 1856–7, at first
appears to be an unexceptional Victorian villa like its neighbours of the 1870s (the Italianate No. 23 and the Tudor Gothic
No. 27), and the later Nos. 30 (by *H. E. Clifford*, 1899, now

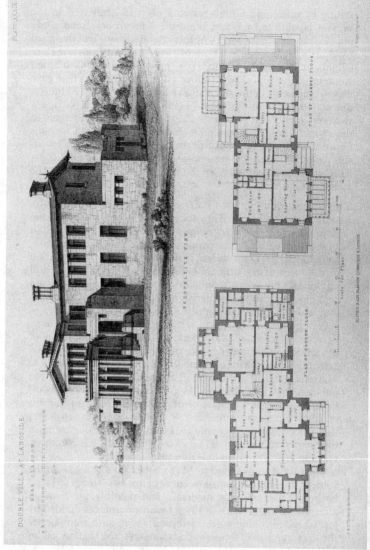

Double villa,
Mansionhouse Road
(Reproduced from
Blackie's *Villa and
Cottage Architecture*,
1868)

part of the prominent Bon Secours Hospital) and 32 (1896) opposite. It is, however, not a single but a double villa, one part of which faces E towards the pre-existing Millbrae Road, the other W towards the new road laid out to this point according to *Thomson*'s feuing plan of 1853 (*see* above). Others were intended but not built. The main advantage of the design, whatever the theory, was to combine two quite small houses in one larger, asymmetrical and therefore more romantic composition, with the heavily modelled and ornamented façade of No. 25 contrasted against the flat and austere back of No. 25a and vice versa. But the design gives neither the improved privacy nor the equality of aspect claimed for it. The kitchens (although provided with frosted glass) overlook the main entrances and, because of the steep site, one house is close to the road and the driveways to both houses, while the other enjoys a long terraced garden. The composition is of a picturesque Loudonesque type, with overhanging eaves, made more Greek by the temple-like form of the clearly expressed blocks, by the classical mullions that screen the windows (set well back behind them) and by the exotic decoration, including incised friezes and lotus chimneypots. The plan (despite inventive features, e.g. the wine-bins beneath the hinged floor of the dining room) is straightforward, but the decoration is idiosyncratic. The walls are panelled in varnished natural yellow pine boarding (some now painted). On the dining room ceiling, a symbolic sun (day); on the drawing room ceiling, within a rich border of disks, daisies etc., tiny stars (night). The joinery of the doors, in flat unmoulded planes, has the character of stone.

Tenements at the N end of Mansionhouse Road turn the corner into Langside Avenue (where their craggy plinths appear to have been hewn out of the cliff) and again into CAMPHILL AVENUE. Here, more interesting than this first stretch (with the exception of the Free-Style Nos. 3–11), is the pompous crescent of 1903 by *John C. McKellar* (Nos. 23–53), raised high above the road on a steep embankment fringed by trees. It has the grand air of mansion flats but the arrangement of conventional tenements, with double flights of steps up to each main door and close (with fine swing doors and tiling). Beyond them the hillside, with its mixture of modest housing, retains some of the character of the Langside estate's pleasure-grounds. The road winds round the long empty site of LANGSIDE HOUSE, probably designed in 1777 by *Robert Adam* for Thomas Brown. To the S the wooded slope drops away suddenly to reveal a panorama over the flat expanse of Newlands.

MILLBRAE ROAD is the way to return N, catching a glimpse of the E sides of the Carmelite Monastery and, still just possible, of Thomson's double villa *en route*. At the top, No. 22 (MISTLEBANK), a very plain stone villa of rural character, looks like an early survivor of the area. Opposite it, part of the Electricity Substation (*see* Public Buildings). BATTLE

PLACE, a high artificial plateau, is the end of the perambulation, apart from a few excursions E and S to take in public
buildings (*see* above) and the two rows of semi-rural cottages
lying parallel in PROSPECTHILL ROAD and VALEVIEW
TERRACE. The BATTLE MONUMENT (1887–8, by *Alexander Skirving*) makes a suitable climax, commemorating the
battle of Langside (1568) between the forces of the Regent
Moray and Mary, Queen of Scots. The column is spiralled,
not with battle scenes like Trajan's, but with thistles and fleur-
de-lis. From the top, a lion with his paw on a cannon ball looks
E over the battlefield. Two contrasting churches, both designed
by *Skirving*, originally formed backdrops: one, the Gothic
Langside Old Parish Church of 1882–5, has been demolished;
the other, the classical Langside Hill Church (*see* Churches,
above), lies derelict. The gap-toothed surroundings, especially
on the S side, seem sadly inadequate.

POLLOKSHAWS AND EASTWOOD

Pollokshaws retained the flavour of a crowded independent
manufacturing town until the late 1950s, despite its annexation
to Glasgow in 1912 and the stranglehold of suburban sprawl.
Then, in the 1960s, it was entirely redeveloped, and now slabs
of flats tower dramatically over the main street and the White
Cart river.

The town originated as an early C18 weaving settlement in the
parish of Eastwood, which then stretched from Crookston Castle
(W) to Cathcart (E), and from Strathbungo (N) to just beyond
Thornliebank (just S of the present city boundary). In the late C18
industry expanded, with bleachfields at Auldhouse and calico-
printing and cotton-spinning factories. Eastwood Parish Church
was rebuilt in 1781 nearer the village. By 1793 the population
was 2,642, and in 1812 Pollokshaws was made a Burgh of Barony,
stretching N to Shawlands and S to the present city boundary.
Although more diverse industries were introduced after 1850,
textile manufacture predominated. In the late C19, the old village
was concentrated round the old Burgh Buildings, with a ribbon
of newer, more urban tenements running down Shawbridge
Street and into Harriet Street. Beyond, at Mansewood, were
businessmen's villas. Industry (more diverse than in the late C18,
but still predominantly textiles) was most concentrated E of the
old centre along the banks of the White Cart, where some still
remains.

By the mid-C20, the mixture of C18 and C19 houses and
industry was considered overcrowded and insanitary. In 1958 a
tract from Shawhill Road to Nether Auldhouse Road was
declared a Comprehensive Development Area and was obliterated in a two-part development, leaving just a few public
buildings, churches, and isolated rows of tenements.

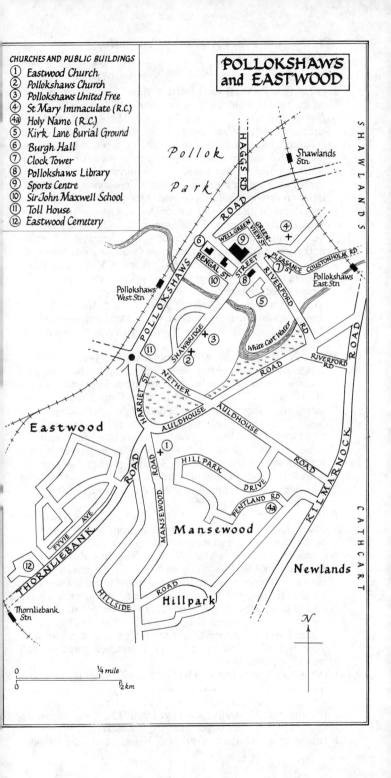

CHURCHES AND PUBLIC BUILDINGS
1. Eastwood Church
2. Pollokshaws Church
3. Pollokshaws United Free
4. St Mary Immaculate (R.C.)
4a. Holy Name (R.C.)
5. Kirk Lane Burial Ground
6. Burgh Hall
7. Clock Tower
8. Pollokshaws Library
9. Sports Centre
10. Sir John Maxwell School
11. Toll House
12. Eastwood Cemetery

POLLOKSHAWS and EASTWOOD

Pollok Park

SHAWLANDS

Shawlands Stn

Pollokshaws West Stn

Pollokshaws East Stn

HAGGS RD

POLLOKSHAWS ROAD

WELLGREEN

GREENVIEW ST.

BENGAL ST.

STREET

PLEASANCE ST.

COUSTONHOLM RD.

RIVERFORD RD.

SHAWBRIDGE

White Cart Water

RIVERFORD RD.

Eastwood

HARRIET ST.

NETHER

AULDHOUSE ROAD

AULDHOUSE

ROAD

KILMARNOCK ROAD

CATHCART

MANSEWOOD ROAD

HILLPARK DRIVE

PENTLAND RD.

Mansewood

Newlands

FYVIE AVE

THORNLIEBANK ROAD

HILLSIDE ROAD

Hillpark

Thornliebank Stn

N

0   ¼ mile
0   ½ km

CHURCHES

EASTWOOD PARISH CHURCH, 5 Mansewood Road, perched on the side of a hill. 1862–3, by *Charles Wilson*, succeeded by *David Thomson*. Given by Sir John Maxwell to replace a church of 1781. Mixed Gothic style, with little archaeological accuracy, and cruciform, fronted by a s tower and broach spire flanked by clumsy staircase projections with rows of lancet windows. Inside, four equal arms dominated by a part-ceiled timber roof which meets in a cross of free-flying beams. Galleries on cast-iron columns round three sides, coming forward in a curve at the SE and SW angles. Conventional platform with organ case arranged to suggest a chancel. – The STAINED GLASS, filling almost every window, is inescapable but mostly unfashionable. Two of the windows (N to Sir John Maxwell † 1865 and W to Lady Harriet † 1857) are of Munich glass, the third (E to Walter McCrum † 1867) a superior design. – Of the others, most interesting is Melchizedeck by *J. T. & C. E. Stewart* for *William Meikle & Sons*, 1904–7; and the Song of Songs and the Madonna, *c.* 1894, by the same unknown artist. – Three windows by *Gordon Webster*, and one by *Guthrie & Wells*, 1932.

HOLY NAME (R.C.), 4 Pentland Road. 1983–4, by *Elder & Cannon*. None of the free oblique planning of the 1960s: the sources appear to have been the basilican form and the style of Alexander Thomson. Steep-pitched nave roof and tall clearstorey above the blank outer walls, rusticated at the base. The ceiling is stepped down to suggest aisles. – LECTERN. Post-Modern, nicely made in brass and bronze.

POLLOKSHAWS CHURCH, 215–29 Shawbridge Street. Built as Pollokshaws Original Secession Church in 1843, but from the outside it is indistinguishable from a boxy late Georgian villa. The centre of the three-bay snecked rubble façade is slightly broken out under a pediment.

POLLOKSHAWS UNITED FREE CHURCH, 169 Shawbridge Street, has a flat mid-C19 cream ashlar front, with plate tracery outlined in half-round mouldings.

ST MARY IMMACULATE (R.C.), Shawhill Road. By *W. Nicholson* of Manchester, opened in 1865. Of cream snecked rubble with conventional Dec tracery in undersized windows. SE tower; spire not built. Open timber roof over the nave, and aisle arcades of wide, pointed arches on polished granite columns. N aisle extended by one bay by *Pugin & Pugin*, 1900. Insignificant clearstorey. – STAINED GLASS. W window by *John Hardman Studios*, 1938. – The attached PRESBYTERY was added after 1879.

EASTWOOD CEMETERY. The Old Cemetery, on the w side of Thornliebank Road, was the site of the parish church until 1781, and is said to include early Christian burials. It contains the Stirling Maxwells' MAUSOLEUM. The New Cemetery, opened in 1900, lies beyond the city boundary.

KIRK LANE BURIAL GROUND belonged to the village's

earliest church, built for the Associate Session of Pollokshaws in 1764; it was Glasgow's first Secessionist church, and was in use until 1871. Fragments of two walls survive. Robert Burns's daughter Betty (Mrs John Johnstone) is buried here.

PUBLIC BUILDINGS

BURGH HALL, Pollokshaws Road. 1895–8, by *Robert Rowand Anderson*, who, according to Sir John Stirling Maxwell, 'deliberately set out to save from oblivion some of the fine features of the old Glasgow College', which was demolished in the 1880s. The tower with its timber bell-stage and cap, although squatter, is the most prominent borrowing. Its main entrance, with Gibbs rustication and arms within an aedicule flanked by two vases above, is a politer, more C18-style rendering of the robust mid-C17 main entrance to the College. Both the informal composition of the halls and the details (crowstep gables, 'pediments' of strapwork) recall the overall grouping of the College buildings and their C17 style.

The entrance through the tower leads into a range of office buildings that link the large hall on its E–W axis and smaller hall facing Bengal Street. The interior was modernized in 1968–9 and 1973–4, but the large hall was always simple, with a partly open timber roof and a minimum of classical decoration.

CLOCK TOWER, Pleasance Street. A fragment of the old Burgh Buildings of 1803 (*see* datestone) topped by a squat tower and spire. The entrance bay is classical, the outer bays halfheartedly Gothic with battlements, machicolations and cusped upper windows.

POLLOKSHAWS LIBRARY, Shawbridge Street. 1960s, by *A. G. Jury* (City Architect). Mostly glazed and with a zigzag roof. At the NW corner, the exposed frame forms a tall entrance porch.

POLLOKSHAWS SPORTS CENTRE, Ashtree Street. The former public baths and washhouse of *c.* 1920 by the Corporation's *Office of Public Works*, of shiny red brick and stone dressings in their usual style at this period. On the adjoining playground, the swings have elaborate cast-iron frames.

SIR JOHN MAXWELL SCHOOL, 28 Bengal Street. By *John Hamilton* for Eastwood School Board; completed 1907. A severe classical design in red sandstone ashlar, disregarding Anderson's wish that the school should be in keeping with his Burgh Hall.

TOLLHOUSE, preserved on a roundabout at the junction of Pollokshaws, Barrhead and Nether Auldhouse Roads. Circular, with a conical roof and central chimneystack; *c.* 1820.

POLLOKSHAWS WEST STATION, Pollokshaws Road. Raised on an embankment, the long up-platform building, built to serve the Glasgow, Barrhead and Neilston Railway *c.* 1847.

The associated POLLOKSHAWS VIADUCT, skirting the E side of Pollok Park, was completed in 1847; engineer, *Neil Robson*.

PERAMBULATIONS

1. Pollokshaws

Our perambulation starts at the junction of Pleasance Street and Greenview Street with the CLOCK TOWER (*see* Public Buildings, above), the most venerable amongst the fragments of the village's nucleus that have been preserved within the N part of the redevelopment scheme (1960–71, by *Dorward, Matheson, Gleave & Partners*). The four featureless 18–22-storey Bison-system blocks on the hill above in SHAWHILL ROAD belong to this. From the hilltop a view SE over the remnants of Pollokshaws' industry, with, in the foreground, its last remaining textile factory (D. & H. COHEN LTD) in COUSTONHOLM ROAD. The buildings are post-war but succeed the village's first large weaving factory (opened in 1854).

W of the Clock Tower, more of the N part of the 1960s scheme in WELL GREEN, where three-to-four-storey flats, cleverly designed to the traditional tenement pattern of main-door flats and closes, look on to a courtyard of tortuous hard landscaping and scratchy shrubs. The concrete-framed fronts have timber cladding with spandrels vibrantly coloured in lilac, turquoise and blue. The backs are of orange brick, with pebble-panels randomly set. All very stylish. To the N and E, more of the same and, in contrast, at the W end of GREENVIEW STREET, a tall Edwardian survivor (Nos. 64–8), its ground floor recessed behind three broad arches with Gibbs rustication.

Further W still, at the junction of POLLOKSHAWS ROAD and HAGGS ROAD, OLD SWAN CORNER, two runs of plain red sandstone tenements meeting at the acutely angled OLD SWAN INN (dated 1901), marks a turn in the history of Pollokshaws, and indeed of Glasgow. This formed the first major 'treatment area' of structurally sound but overcrowded tenements to be improved by the Corporation. The decision to rehabilitate them was made in March 1971, three years before the last of Pollokshaw's multi-storey blocks was completed, and three years before rehabilitation became the Corporation's established policy.

Back to the Clock Tower, the only remnant of the island of encroachment that divided the original town square. This has been recast as a dismal paved space, enclosed only by a row of pre-war single-storey shops (E) and by the SHAWBRIDGE ARCADE (W), the redevelopment's inadequate sunken shopping precinct.

SHAWBRIDGE STREET is the axis through the S half of the scheme, designed by *Boswell, Mitchell & Johnston*, 1961–74.

The view down it presents the most classically Utopian vision of any of Glasgow's redevelopments. Looking s from the Shaw Bridge, slab blocks set at right angles to the gently curved street shut out the distant prospect. Between them, medium-rise (five-storey) blocks enclose grassed courts. The artificial landscaping is minimal but the river passes through as a quiet, wooded, almost rural band. w of the bridge, the welcome disorder of the remaining industrial premises and the weir that used to serve an early C19 grain mill. Otherwise the magnificent homogeneous modernity of the scene is broken only by the retention of two churches, one dwarfed and unhappy behind a dull paved square, and by the unfortunate intrusion (c. 1984) of folksy red brick sheltered housing. The slabs (of 16–20 storeys) vary slightly. Those further N have continuous balconies left raw grey concrete or clad in white mosaic. Those further s have no balconies. All the end elevations have been reclad in a distinctly Post-Modern pattern of pink and cream slabs with stripes of red and green or red and blue linking the windows. The lower blocks are of brick, linked by recessed decks and more highly modelled with projecting and recessed balconies.

The scheme ends at the Toll House roundabout: beyond, HARRIET STREET, still lined with tenements, leads to Eastwood Parish Church (*see* Churches, above) on its wooded hillside and to Auldhouse, where Perambulation 2 starts.

2. Eastwood

AULDHOUSE lies just s of Eastwood Church at No. 140 THORNLIEBANK ROAD. The oldest part, the crowstepped L-shaped SE block, was probably built by George Maxwell, Minister of Mearns, or by his son John, Minister of the High Kirk. The lintel over the kitchen fireplace has the date 1631. This house was an L-shaped tower with two rooms on each of the three floors and an entrance in the re-entrant angle. Three first-floor rooms were panelled in the C18. About 1800, four rooms were added to the W, doubling the house in size and making the W front symmetrical. It was given a classical entrance door and sash windows with red sandstone surrounds. Substantial C19 additions have been replaced by ungracious concrete-block flats. The surviving strip of the lands stretches N as Auldhouse Park. Just by the park, at No. 230 AULDHOUSE ROAD, an eye-catching early C20 DRILL HALL, whitewashed and Free-Style, with twin saucer-domed towers and C17-style dormers.

At MANSEWOOD to the E, the villas built by Pollokshaws businessmen, which date from the 1870s onward. Their setting is semi-rural. Above them to the N, silhouetted along the ridge, two stumpy eight-storey blocks and the embracing deck-access blocks of HILLPARK DRIVE (1966–73, by the *City Architect*). The earlier Corporation EASTWOOD SCHEME was built W of Thornliebank Road in the first years of the 1950s. The three- and four-storey tenements in FYVIE AVENUE, devised in 1949 by *A. G. Jury* (then Director of Housing) to more lavish standards than pre-war housing, won a Saltaire Society Award in 1951 and became the model so monotonously repeated in all the peripheral estates of the 1950s. They are built of pebble-faced concrete blocks and have shallow pitched brown tiled roofs. In the centre of each block, recessed access balconies, each one shared between two houses. Porthole windows light the balconies and the stairs. 'Light cheerful colours' on metal-mesh balcony fronts, on windows and doors were used to enliven the whole scheme.

POLLOKSHIELDS

West Pollokshields, a large and leafy Victorian and Edwardian suburb, demonstrates vividly the prosperity and taste of Glasgow's citizens during those eras. Sir John Maxwell of Pollok contemplated developing a residential suburb on his lands as early as 1834, when he commissioned plans for Kinning Park (*see* Govan: Introduction). These unrealized plans were succeeded more than a decade later by others for the countryside s of the Paisley, Johnstone and Glasgow Canal. Maxwell's first step, in 1849, was to bridge the canal and railways and to begin a road (the present St Andrews Drive) leading s w from Kinning Park to Pollok. The proposals for the lands w of this road, drawn up by *David Rhind*, took picturesque advantage of the hills, with broad winding drives following the contours instead of a Neo-classical layout like that which had been planned for Kinning Park. Strict feuing conditions permitted only villas in their own grounds and forbade shops and trade. Feuing started in the N in 1851 with sites along St Andrews Drive. It was lined with villas by the mid-1860s. By 1875 all the roads N of Nithsdale Road and E of the southern part of Albert Drive had been built up, and the population was large enough (1,518) to justify the creation of the police burgh of West Pollokshields.

The flatter land E of what is now Shields Road was not feued until the 1860s, and then it was developed with the tenements and shops, churches and schools barred from West Pollokshields. There was a small group of tenements at the w end of Princes Street (now Maxwell Road), by 1865, and another pocket close to Strathbungo by 1875. The continuation of Shields Road s of the junction with Albert Drive after 1870 encouraged more building. When the independent police burgh of East Pollokshields was formed in 1880 there were 4,000 residents. Within the next ten years tenements of a substantial middle-class kind had spread all over this area, and West Pollokshields, which by then stretched down to the N edge of Maxwell Park (opened in 1890) had over 400 villas. Both burghs were annexed to Glasgow in 1891. The last sections of Maxwell's land to be feued were those s of Maxwell Park and in the far w, where avenues, with

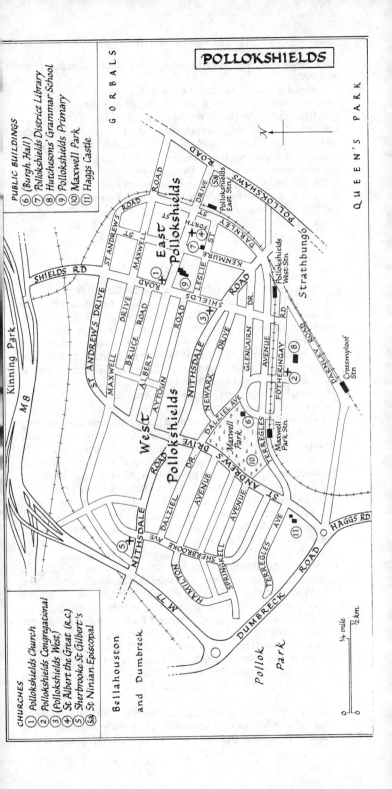

POLLOKSHIELDS

CHURCHES
① Pollokshields Church
② Pollokshields Congregational
③ (Pollokshields West)
④ St Albert the Great (R.C.)
⑤ Sherbrooke St Gilbert's
⑤ₐ St Ninian Episcopal

PUBLIC BUILDINGS
⑥ (Burgh Hall)
⑦ Pollokshields District Library
⑧ Hutchesons' Grammar School
⑨ Pollokshields Primary
⑩ Maxwell Park
⑪ Haggs Castle

GORBALS

QUEEN'S PARK

Kinning Park

M8

SHIELDS RD

ST ANDREWS ROAD

MAXWELL ROAD

ST ANDREWS DRIVE

MAXWELL DRIVE

BRUCE ROAD

ALBERT ROAD

AYTOUN ROAD

NITHSDALE ROAD

NITHSDALE ROAD

SHIELDS ROAD

NEWARK DRIVE

DALZIEL AVE

DALZIEL DR

SHERBROOKE AVE

SPRINGKELL AVE

TERREGLES AVE

HAMILTON DR

ST ANDREW'S DRIVE

GLENCAIRN DR

FOTHERINGAY RD

DARNLEY ST

KENMURE ST

LESLIE ST

FORTH ST

East Pollokshields

West Pollokshields

Maxwell Park

Pollokshields East Stn.

Pollokshields West Stn.

Strathbungo

DARNLEY ROAD

POLLOKSHAWS ROAD

Crossmyloof Stn.

Maxwell Park Stn.

HAGGS RD

DUMBRECK ROAD

Pollok Park

Bellahouston and Dumbreck

¼ mile
½ km

the biggest and most opulent houses, were laid out in the 1890s and 1900s.

Pollokshields has remained remarkably intact, disturbed only by subdivision of the largest gardens for smaller suburban houses and flats, the decay of the northern fringe of East Pollokshields because of industrial encroachment, and the demolition of the earliest part of West Pollokshields for council flats. It is disappointing that, with the exception of *Alexander Thomson*, who was responsible for several villas, few of Glasgow's most talented architects make an appearance here; commissions for individual villas and speculative developments seem often to have gone to the conservative and even dull, such as *Thomson & Sandilands* and *Fryers & Penman*.

CHURCHES

POLLOKSHIELDS CHURCH, 274 Albert Drive. Built as Pollokshields Established Church. The hall opened in 1875: the church, also by *Robert Baldie*, followed in 1877–8. Mixed Gothic: an E.E. corner tower with tabernacles above the broaches of the spire; a w front with a big Geometrical window and rows of trefoil-headed windows with stiffleaf capitals; and aisles and clearstorey with pairs and triplets of lancets. This is all quite grand, and so is Baldie's interior, with aisle arcades on polished granite piers, with high octagonal bases and French Gothic leaf capitals, and its high scissor-braced roof; but it is the lavish furnishings and stained glass that speak most volubly of Pollokshields' C19 and C20 wealth. – With the magnificent Perp case of the divided *Harrison & Harrison* ORGAN, *H. E. Clifford* created, in his 1913 reordering of the platform, what amounts to a chancel. The pews, arranged in collegiate fashion, match the organ case, but the COMMUNION TABLE (by *W. G. Rowan*) is even more intricately Perp. Inserted in the reredos in 1928, three pieces of C14 textile. – PULPIT. 1914, by *P. Macgregor Chalmers*, an elaborate Perp confection of white marble and alabaster on an arcaded base. – Black and white marble PAVEMENT, now sadly covered by a carpet.

Every window has STAINED GLASS, mostly by *Stephen Adam* at various phases of his career. – w aisle: all of 1878, the first four from the s all by Adam. The first three of them have simply drawn and subtly coloured figures in clearly depicted settings, with rich foliage, fruit and flowers in the heads; the fourth design still employs a Gothic canopy. – E aisle (from the N): first and third windows by *W. & J. J. Kier* (Beatitudes), in jewel-like colours, 1882. – The others are all by Stephen Adam. The second (by *Stephen Adam & Son*, 1900) with a rendition of the Sistine Madonna in the deep colours he then favoured; the fourth (to James Morland † 1893), with deep colours, but still with strong leadlines; the fifth (1899) completely different in character, with fearsomely animated plant forms, etiolated angels and some curious results from the decay of Adam's experimental colours. – s wall (under the gallery) all of 1878 and all probably by Adam, with luscious fruit and flowers. – Clearstorey windows: all early C 20, including the sentimental NE triplet to Agnes Eadie † 1908 by *Robert Anning Bell* (Suffer the Little Children). – N window: to the brother of William McOnie † 1850 (The Law and the Prophets). – s window: 1878, with heads of the Apostles, illustrations of Scriptural quotations and much light-coloured patterned glass. – Vestibule: Ecclesia, designed by *Clifford*, 1914. – Church hall: w window of 1875.

CHURCHYARD. War Memorial modelled on the Ruthwell and Bewcastle crosses, 1921.

POLLOKSHIELDS CONGREGATIONAL CHURCH, 63 Fother-ingay Road. 1902–3, by *Steele & Balfour*. Mixed Gothic tracery in a simple towerless red sandstone building, con-temporary with the adjoining tenements.

POLLOKSHIELDS GLENCAIRN CHURCH, 67 Glencairn Drive. This large and important church of 1890–1, by *W. G. Rowan* (which opened as Trinity United Presbyterian Church), was destroyed by fire in 1988. The FURNISHINGS, designed by Rowan, and the STAINED GLASS were especially rich: fortunately much has been removed to the People's Palace.

Former POLLOKSHIELDS WEST CHURCH, 614 Shields Road. Built as a Free Church in 1875–9 to debased Greek designs by *McKissack & Rowan*. The corner tower is modelled on Stark's St George's Tron (*see* Commercial Centre: Churches) but given Greek bulk and entasis (inspired, no doubt, by Alexander Thomson). The Ionic porticoes, raised above a podium, also speak of Thomson. They occur on three sides of this very square plan. On the fourth is a later square-ended chancel: the interior was remodelled in 1923. The entrance, through the podium, is flanked by Greek Doric columns *in antis*. – STAINED GLASS of *c.* 1950 by *Alfred Webster* and *Nina Miller Davidson*.

ST ALBERT THE GREAT (R.C.), 153 Albert Drive. Designed as Albert Road United Presbyterian Church in a free Italian Renaissance style by *J. B. Wilson*, 1886–7. Bold exterior with a half-octagonal vestibule facing Albert Drive, a dramatically tall tower with arcaded bell-stages and a dome, and liberal carved ornament with a suggestion of false perspective in the arches over the vestibule windows. Disappointing galleried interior; the part-coved, part-open timber roof is the only curiosity.

ST NINIAN (Episcopal), 1 Albert Drive. 1872–7, by *David Thomson*; extended w in 1887. The first Episcopal church to be built on Glasgow's south side. Towerless early French Gothic, in grey snecked rubble, with aisles and two N porches, the most westerly one part of the 1887 extension. All the architectural attention is concentrated on the polygonal apse facing the main Pollokshaws Road. It has crocketed hood-moulds and saints and prophets as gargoyles. Tiny hexagonal s link to the hall, which is dated 1893. The interior is High Victorian and quite impressive. Disproportionately long and narrow nave and chancel continuous under a timber barrel-vault. Circular arcade piers with stiff leaf capitals and twin arches screening the Lady Chapel (N) and organ chamber (S). – REREDOS. Gothic, by *H. D. Walton*, 1899. Sculpted in stone, marble and alabaster by *William Vickers*. – MURAL PAINT-ING round the chancel. The *Benedicite* by *William Hole*, 1901. Charming Pre-Raphaelite-style angels in subdued colours within a pilastered framework. – PULPIT by *Howie & Walton*, 1889. Oak with traceried panels on a circular stone base. – Eagle LECTERN, 1895. – STAINED GLASS. Several windows by *Heaton, Butler & Bayne*, including a five-light one (1888) and four two-light ones (two of 1891, one of 1902, one of 1903) in the chancel, and one in the S aisle (to the wife of Robert Alexander Ogg † 1911). – Several windows by *William Meikle & Sons* dated between 1893 and *c*. 1922. – Baptism of Christ (1889) and the Good Samaritan (1890, S chancel aisle) by *Stephen Adam*.

SHERBROOKE ST GILBERT'S, 240 Nithsdale Road. The hall of the former Sherbrooke United Free Church opened in 1894, the church in 1900. It makes a large but bland group. The details are French C13, orthodox, as might be expected, even at this late date, from its architect, *W. F. McGibbon*; the composition, with porch, stair-turret and hall vestibule forming a link between church and hall, is less conventional. The porch's column figures are Knox and Calvin. The interior is aisleless but has double transepts and a simple hammerbeam roof. The majority of the original FURNISHINGS survive. – ORGAN. 1910, by *Norman & Beard*. – STAINED GLASS. Two windows of 1910. Two-light window on the E side of the nave by *Gordon Webster*, 1964.

PUBLIC BUILDINGS

Former BURGH HALL, 72 Glencairn Drive. 1888–90, by *H. E. Clifford*, within the curtailage of Maxwell Park (*see* below) and incorporating in the design the Jacobethan park GATES and park-keeper's LODGE. A small but ungainly building, of un-attractively finished crimson Ballochmyle stone. The bulky Baronial tower (no distinctive part of the plan) dominates the low façade with its three windows (one an oriel) lighting the committee room. The hall itself is later in style, with William-Adamish Venetian windows. Below the N one a panel of masonic emblems recording No. 772 Lodge, which was held in the room designed for it beneath the hall. It was entered via the arcade across the back. The hall's C17-style STAINED GLASS is well sprinkled with masonic emblems, along with the Maxwell arms in a frame of false perspective (E), female personifications of Art, Music and Literature (S) and figures of SS John and Andrew.

POLLOKSHIELDS DISTRICT LIBRARY, 30 Leslie Street. 1904–7. *Thomas Gilmour* of the City Engineer's Department won the competition: his designs were revised by his superior, *A. B. McDonald*. Nicely carved cartouches and panels (inscribed *Literature*; *History*; *The Arts*) enliven a rather dull and stiff Edwardian Baroque design. The interior, slightly rearranged in 1926, has STAINED GLASS designed and made by *John C. Hall*.

HUTCHESONS' GRAMMAR SCHOOL, 21 Beaton Road. By *Boswell, Mitchell & Johnston*, 1957–60. The school, founded in 1795, moved from Ingram Street to Crown Street in 1840, and from there to this site 120 years later. There is nothing in its grouping of one- to three-storey blocks or in its materials (buff brick and curtain walling) to distinguish it from contemporary state schools. (For the annexe, the former Girls' Grammar School, *see* Queen's Park: Public Buildings.)

POLLOKSHIELDS PRIMARY SCHOOL, 241 Albert Drive and 11 Melville Street. Two of *H. & D. Barclay*'s palazzo-style schools for Govan School Board: the one in Melville Street (now an annexe) is of 1878–9, the other (with some Quattrocento-style carving) of 1882. The later part on Herriet Street (the former Albert Road Academy of 1901) is a less orthodox classical composition by the same architects, with big windows to light the art rooms.

MAXWELL PARK, Glencairn Road. Twenty acres (8 ha) of marshy land were presented by Sir John Stirling Maxwell in 1878. The Burgh Hall (*see* above) was built on the NE corner; Hall and park were opened in 1890. After Glasgow annexed the burgh in 1891, the belt of trees was rearranged to allow visitors 'a view of the villas in the vicinity, with their ornamental pleasure grounds' (McLellan). – The FOUNTAIN, surrounded by clipped hedges and carpet bedding, was designed in 1907 by *Burnet, Boston & Carruthers*, in memory of Thomas and John Hamilton, and made in Carrara Stoneware (since painted) by *Doulton & Co*. French Renaissance in style, with a figure in hunting dress atop the three basins of diminishing size.

STATIONS. MAXWELL PARK and POLLOKSHIELDS WEST, Fotheringay Road and Terregles Avenue. Both were built *c.* 1894 for the Cathcart District Railway. Wooden island platform buildings in a cutting, with footbridges to the ticket offices above waiting rooms with pretty scalloped canopies sheltering the platforms.

HAGGS CASTLE (Children's Museum), 100 St Andrews Drive. The small castle gives a distinctly Victorian impression which belies its real age. It was begun in 1585 by John Maxwell (the 12th of Pollok) on the edge of the moss, which stretched far to the N, and by the side of the old Pollokshaws-to-Govan Road (the lane to the W). It replaced the Low Castle of Pollok, by then in disrepair (*see* Pollok Park: Pollok House), and was almost finished in 1587, when Maxwell borrowed money to complete the interior. Until 1595 it was the Maxwells' main seat: thereafter it became a dower house. Abandoned in 1753, by the 1840s it was a ruin, with a smithy on the lower floor. Work was begun in the 1850s to consolidate the building, already engulfed in the suburbs; by 1860 *John Baird II* had restored it as a house for the Maxwells' factor. The N wing and staircase projection were added in 1899–1900 for Sir John Stirling Maxwell (*MacGibbon & Ross* were consulted, as unexecuted schemes attest, but the additions carried out betray no distinct hand). The house was then let. It was divided into flats in the late 1940s and converted by Glasgow District Council into a children's museum in 1972–6.

Haggs is of the compact L-plan type, originally with the main staircase in the projecting s wing. Mostly built of coursed rubble, but with lower courses of random rubble in the E and w elevations, the exterior is distinguished by the amount of rich proto-Renaissance decoration. The cable motif is particularly in evidence, as stringcourses (knotted at the ends) round dormers, and looped round the decorative panels above the door. On the lowest panel the (recut) inscription reads 1585 / NI DOMIN 9 / AEDES STRUXE / RIT FRUSTRA STRUIS / SR JHON MAXWELL OF POLLOK KNY / GHT AND D MARGARET CONYNGHN / HIS WYF BIGGET THIS HOWS. In the upper panels two shields and two embracing figures, possibly moved from the dormer kneelers. In the dormers, rows of curious reel ornaments linked by an entwined thread.

The mid-C19 work is quite easily catalogued. The s end of the s wing was built up anew, minus a storey and with fabricated decoration. Most of the other openings, despite the enlargement of some of them, are in their original positions. One or two have been added to the s front, particularly the l. one on the first floor and the centre one below it. The wallhead chimney replaced a dormer, which was added to the small eaves-level window to its l. Most obviously C19 is the octagonal bay built in 1899–1900 to enlarge the staircase tower. This, formerly corbelled out from first-floor level, was also raised and given its exaggeratedly tall cap. At the back (N), the original garderobe shaft and the two-storey wing of 1899–1900 with its coarsely crowstepped gables over each bay. Fire-escape (w) 1972–6. On the w side another circular stairtower, corbelled out square at the top but lacking a cap. Slit windows and horizontal gunloops (originally also on the main front) are still in evidence here. Cloakroom projection 1972–6.

INTERIOR. The main stair to the hall was removed from the s wing when the other staircase was extended to the ground floor and enlarged. The ground floor looks most authentic, with its three tunnel-vaulted rooms linked by a vaulted passage (no longer with a dividing wall). The KITCHEN has a deep chimney recess, lit from each end. On the breast a deer (Maxwell) and a heart (Cunningham). Upstairs, the HALL has been divided into one large room and a wide passage to the drawing room. The hall fireplace (with a C19 Baronial sur-

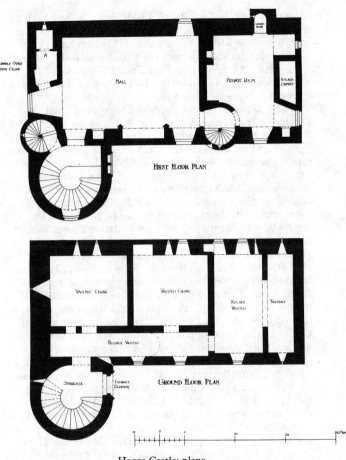

Haggs Castle: plans
(Reproduced from MacGibbon and Ross, *Castellated and
Domestic Architecture of Scotland*, 1887–92)

round) was moved from the S to the N wall in the 1850s. The
curved wall of the staircase projects into the SOLAR and is
divided into panels by giant chevron and roll mouldings, also
carried round the cornice. The Baronial fireplace has an C18-
style festoon. The clash of styles is continued into the
DRAWING ROOM, where the barrel-vaulted ceiling in C17
style has plasterwork with Rococo motifs, including musical
instruments.

COTTAGE. An earlier building much enlarged in the C19.
The decoration of the castle's dormers is repeated round the
gable window.

PERAMBULATIONS

1. East Pollokshields

ALBERT DRIVE is East Pollokshields' main street, with two churches and a primary school (*see* Churches and Public Buildings, above) in addition to the shops that were unwelcome in West Pollokshields. Towards the E end, within the industrial fringe along the railway line, the French Renaissance No. 100 was once the GLASGOW LAUNDRY AND CARPET BEATING WORKS of *c.* 1895.

DARNLEY STREET crosses Albert Drive here. Just into its S half are the premises built for MILLER & LANG ART PUBLISHERS (since divided between the printers G. & G. Ponton and an evangelical church), one of the most characteristic buildings of the Glasgow Style, designed in 1901–3 by *D. B. Dobson* of *Gordon & Dobson*. The façade is full of unclassifiable Mackintosh-inspired detail: a sinuous moulding embracing the entrances, including the big door into the printing works, and, above, two oriels, one large and shallow with a stepped parapet topped by a gesticulating figure, the other bowed and decorated more conventionally with *grotteschi*. Two very utilitarian clearstorey lights across the roof create the kind of contrast familiar, say, from the School of Art. (The plainer but visually related warehouse next door was designed by *Gordon, Son, Dobson & Sturrock*, 1903–4.) But the exterior is only a foretaste of the richness of the first-floor office. Its stained glass, designed by *W. G. Morton* for *John C. Hall & Co.*, is exotic and original in both imagery and design, with the leadlines describing flowing Art Nouveau forms round rippled, figured and opalescent glass. The staircase from the street is equally decorative, with a mosaic floor and an enamelled panel of an ethereal girl in the vestibule, flowery tiles, and two stained-glass roundels (The Birth of Venus; a mermaid entwined in seaweed). In the upper hallway, another naked nymph, this time in mosaic. The office is divided into passage and office by a screen glazed with monstrous whales. The glass in the top of the passage doors symbolizes the seasons and the passage of time (Father Time; Father Christmas; Neptune; Mother and Child; Death) and may relate to the greetings cards that the firm produced. The fingerplates are hammered with plant forms and, above the doors, a writhing dragon is transfixed in marble. The boardroom is plain, but has specially designed furniture (cupboard moved to the entrance hall).

Just E of the railway bridge, the former COPLAWHILL TRAMWAY WORKS AND TRAM DEPOT at No. 25 Albert Drive. The depot is a two-storey, nine-by-four-bay ashlar-fronted building, originally with stables on the first floor, designed for the Corporation Tramways Department by their engineer, *W. Clark*, 1894. The main single-storey workshops (of nine bays, with steel roof trusses on cast-iron columns and brick walls) followed in 1899–1912. In the main frontage, eleven round-headed doorways, all but two of them blocked.

Further E still, on the corner of Pollokshaws Road, St Ninian's Episcopal Church (*see* Churches).

Back in ALBERT DRIVE, beyond Forth Street, the grid of cream sandstone tenements, the heart of the C19 burgh, begins. The earliest ones, of the 1860s, are to the N at the W end of Maxwell Road. Those SE of Albert Drive, adjacent to Strathbungo, in Melville Street, Leven Street etc., are slightly later, e.g. those at Nos. 84–112 NITHSDALE ROAD, attributed to *Thomson & Turnbull*, 1873–8. The tenements in Albert Drive itself followed after *c.* 1875. Most have rusticated ground floors and, frequently, Italianate detail: some have conical or bell-shaped caps to corner bays, especially those that mark ALBERT CROSS at the junction with Kenmure Road. Along this stretch, the tenements incorporate shops.

The latest tenements, built *c.* 1885–1900 SW of Nithsdale Road, are on a much larger scale, with four- to six-room houses in blocks edged with small front gardens and interspersed with wedges of green where the street pattern fitted awkwardly between the railway lines. Most interesting are those by *H. E. Clifford* in TERREGLES AVENUE (Nos. 44–84, of 1895–6) and FOTHERINGAY ROAD (*c.* 1902), which face each other across the cutting of the Cathcart Circle. The Terregles Avenue blocks, of cream sandstone, have the severest elevations, with the unmoulded canted bay windows, overhanging eaves and prominent downpipes and chimneystacks of the Glasgow Style. The deep red Fotheringay Road houses are slightly more elaborate, with a variety of tops to the bays (caps, saucer domes, wavy parapets etc.) and hints of late C17 detail, carried into the large drawing rooms. Round the corner in DARNLEY ROAD, a long row of more conventionally detailed tenements looks SE across the Glasgow–Barrhead line towards Regent's Park (*see* Queen's Park: Perambulation 1).

2. West Pollokshields N of Nithsdale Road

Development in this part of Pollokshields, bounded on the W by Albert Drive, began in 1851 and was complete by the mid-1870s. ST ANDREWS DRIVE is where the earliest villas were built in the 1850s. The very first ones at the E end (including four by Alexander Thomson) have all gone: the trees of their mature gardens form a setting for the 530 flats of a 1966–72 Corporation scheme (designed by *A. G. Jury*, City Architect). Five-storey brown brick and exposed concrete deck-access blocks, uneasily topped by later profiled steel mansards, are linked by stairtowers round a large landscaped square. To the W of the square and on the N side of St Andrews Drive, the seven simple square blocks of eight storeys belong to the same scheme.

MAXWELL DRIVE now has the earliest surviving houses (apart from The Knowe in Albert Drive: *see* below). This broad, leafy, almost rural road is lined with stone walls, overgrown gardens and, on the S side, a variety of mid-C19 villas, e.g.

No. 23, a *cottage orné* with steep pitched gables and fancy bargeboards; No. 25, with twin bows and a Corinthian porch; Nos. 27–9, a double villa with cast-iron crestings to the bows just beneath the deep eaves; No. 31, simple and classical; and No. 33, cottagey, with a Tudor-Gothic doorway. W of St Andrews Drive is a much more handsome and refined Italianate villa (No. 43) with an arcaded corner porch and tower, triplets of arched windows and a bargeboard pierced with anthemion and rinceau. The ground-floor bows and bays have parapets of linked circles (cf. Breadalbane Terrace, Garnethill, of the 1840s).

In Bruce Road, Albert Drive and Aytoun Road to the S, the villas date mainly from the mid-1860s and 1870s. In BRUCE ROAD, they are mostly very restrained, but the plain exterior of No. 23 at the W end conceals good interior decoration of *c.* 1898, especially in the former dining room, which has rich relief designs round the walls and elaborate metal door furniture, bell pulls etc. Most of the houses at this end of ALBERT DRIVE (starting at St Andrews Drive) are plain classical (some with big bracketed eaves and columned porches, e.g. No. 357); but a few, e.g. No. 354, with crude bargeboards, are gabled and Gothic. No. 336 is an inelegant Greek villa completed by *Thomson & Turnbull* in 1877. Its asymmetrical composition of three disparately sized blocks echoes the E section of Thomson's Castlehill (*see* Nithsdale Road, below). No. 328 (part of Craigholme School) also has Thomson-inspired mannerisms, such as the banded rustication of the porch, the window lights divided by pilasters and bizarre inverted capitals, but in general is more decorative. The bay turns from polygonal on the ground floor to semicircular, with a squat colonnade, above.

THE KNOWE (originally Knowe Cottage) by *Alexander Thomson*, at the corner of Albert Drive and Shields Road, is the most famous of Pollokshields' early villas. It was begun for John Blair, a hatmaker, in 1852–3 and continued in several stages over the next twenty years. The LODGE on Albert Drive, altered from the coachhouse *c.* 1873, is almost a miniature of the house. The embanked drive sweeps in a broad curve through the grounds (built up with flats as KNOWEHEAD GARDENS and TERRACE) which drop away steeply from it 33 to the NE. The S entrance façade is consequently cottagey in scale, and designed in the rather tough rendering of the Picturesque Italian style that Thomson favoured for some of his early villas. The only extraordinary feature of the original cottage (which must be imagined as very compact, without the NE wing which was built in 1855–8 on the site of an earlier, smaller addition) is the curious reversed entasis of the porch columns. The original phase is unexceptional in its interior decoration, except for the elongated Corinthian column balusters of the staircase and the timber pilasters lining the S bow. (In the staircase window, STAINED GLASS depicting Egyptian scenes and motifs: it may date from when the house was renamed Nile Park in 1899.) The second phase is more obviously Greek inside, with doorcases derived from the Erechtheion, and Greek and slightly Egyptian motifs on ceilings and fireplaces. *J. McKellar* added the big S E billiard room in 1899, in Thomson's style externally, but with many Art Nouveau flourishes inside. The grounds are bordered to Aytoun Road with a wall with fireclay balusters designed by *Thomson* in c. 1873. The dreary late C 20 flats within the grounds make only a token gesture to the villa in the triplets of windows with arches impressed into the crude concrete lintels.

In SHIELDS ROAD, just round the corner from The Knowe, a terrace (Nos. 553–609) of modest three-bay houses built in 1874–6 marks the transition from the tenement area of East Pollokshields to the villadom to the w, and, at attic level, lightheartedly acknowledges Thomson's inspiration with chimneypots derived from the gatepiers of The Knowe, acroteria and arched windows.

NITHSDALE ROAD, w of Shields Road, has more Thomsonesque villas and two by *Thomson* himself. No. 161 (converted to a synagogue in 1928) combines in an uncomfortable way twin temple fronts (expressed in the topmost storey) with large and severe bows on battered basements and, squeezed between them, a narrow Ionic porch. The usual plain bay-windowed villas continue until No. 200, one of the large and very secluded houses on the N side. This is *Thomson*'s Egyptian-style ELLISLAND, designed in 1871 for William Johnson, a gas-fitting manufacturer, and a curiosity amongst Thomson's villa designs because of its square, single-storey, block-like form. The façade is flat and unexpressive except for two painted lotus-headed columns solemnly sunk into it either side of the door. The mysterious quality of this entrance is heightened by the massive unmoulded plinths of the lamp-standards guarding it. The other elevations are equally plain, the roof shallow and wide-eaved with lotus-topped chimney-stalks and a cast-iron cresting, which originally surrounded a large flat rooflight and is repeated along the tops of the screen walls that extend E and W from the façade. The interior, probably richly coloured originally with stencilled decoration, has been altered beyond recall, but the effect of the wide central top-lit entrance hall must have been dramatic. CASTLEHILL (No. 202, part of St Ronan's Preparatory School) was designed by *Thomson* in 1870, slightly earlier than Ellisland. It takes more advantage of its site, spreading along the ridge with the main rooms looking s, but from the outside it looks uninteresting. The interior, however, is completely idiosyncratic, with no trace of conventional High Victorian taste. The spine corridor is panelled in pitch pine, the glass doors etched with neo-Greek motifs, the cornices starred with the familiar flat daisies, and the stair is squeezed into an extremely narrow top-lit well.

After this, there is nothing of especial note until Albert Drive is reached; but Albert Drive marks the beginning of a later phase in West Pollokshields development, which is described below.

3. West Pollokshields s of Nithsdale Road

The houses along the w part of Nithsdale Road and in Dalziel
Drive date from after 1880 and display a greater variety of
styles and more architectural pretensions. Round the junction
with Albert Drive, No. 231 NITHSDALE ROAD, the Italianate
OAKLEIGH (now Xaverian House), and the Baronial
ALLERLY (No. 229), a disappointing design of *c.* 1887 by
W. F. McGibbon for himself, are particularly large, with the
conventional bay windows carried upwards into towers. The
gabled ARDENWOHR (No. 233), 1893, by *James Lindsay* for
Alex. Massey, looks remotely Jacobean, with a repulsive red
rock-faced finish. Its rather average neighbours further w (and
the modern infill flats) sit high up on embankments screened
by trees. A brief detour down GOWER STREET for a spectacular view over to Gilmorehill demonstrates all the advantages of their siting. The astonishing SHERBROOKE CASTLE
HOTEL (No. 11 Sherbrooke Avenue) is further w, looking
down on Sherbrooke St Gilbert's Church (*see* Churches,
above) from high above the road. It is the apotheosis of the
Baronial style in Glasgow, utterly uninspired in detail and
with an over-tall tower that makes a coarse and obvious impact.
It was designed for the contractor John Morrison in 1896 by
Thomson & Sandilands. The interior has been battered by its
use as a hotel: there is nothing exceptional except the grand
central staircase, top-lit from panels of stained-glass foliage
and fruit. A little further on, at the bottom of MAXWELL
DRIVE, there is a number of identical, gawky red sandstone
double villas (Nos. 89–105) by *A. J. Fryers*, just like those in
Hamilton Avenue (*see* below).

DALZIEL DRIVE returns e a few yards down Sherbrooke
Avenue. At its w end, No. 58, by *J. B. Wilson* for Dr Forrest
(1907), has French Renaissance ornament in red terracotta on
red sandstone. There are two big houses at the corner of Albert
Drive: SURBITON (No. 52, originally Clifton Hall), a long
red sandstone house of 1891 by *John Gordon* with many squarish bays; and No. 31, by *H. E. Clifford* for William Geddes, a
Free-Style composition of 1902 in cream snecked rubble with
a red tiled roof and abstracted strapwork decoration.

Along the next stretch, the most remarkable houses are on the n
side (those on the s are mostly smaller red and cream rock-
faced double and detached villas, with a few minor variations
on this well-tried theme). No. 48 (n side) was designed by
W. F. McGibbon for John Barr in 1892, and, with its château-
style tower rising above the entrance, is not dissimilar to his
own house in Nithsdale Road. After two identical villas with
columned porches (Nos. 44 and 46), the next three houses
strike a surprising note. All have unmoulded, unornamented
and unorthodox Baronial features cut out of the cheese-like
cream sandstone. HAZLIEBRAE (No. 38) and DYKENEUK
(No. 40), both with large conservatories, are dated 1886.
Dykeneuk is most wilfully odd, with chamfered corners and a

diagonal arch linking chimneystalk (W) and crowstepped gable
(S). Its interior, with Art Nouveau chimneypieces, bookcases,
etc., may be slightly later. Patriotic stained glass in the stair
window (Mary, Queen of Scots; Bruce; Wallace); in the hall
window, a galleon. THE MOSS (No. 30) of c. 1892, at the
corner of St Andrews Drive, is far more elegant, with its
columned porch and balcony linking shallow bays and a single-
storey billiard room and service court lifting it above the
average.

The E part of Dalziel Drive dates from the early 1880s, but the
other roads E of Maxwell Park were created after the park
opened in 1890. The group of houses in GLENCAIRN DRIVE,
GLENCAIRN GARDENS and TERREGLES AVENUE,
designed for James Marr by *Alexander Petrie*, 1897, all have
symmetrical façades with bay windows linked by arcaded or
columned porches; some have a small tower on the side.
LOUDON HOUSE, on the corner of Terregles Avenue and
Glencairn Gardens, has, unlike the others, a big bowed staircase window full of stained glass. NEWARK DRIVE has a
greater variety of designs (from W to E): Nos. 39–41 has Italian
details; No. 35, crowstepped gables and a long balcony on
oversized brackets; No. 33 and No. 27, a French Neo-classical
look with channelled rustication all over and (No. 33) a big
iron-crested belvedere; No. 32, more conventional French
features. Several of the other, mostly bow-windowed villas
have a judicious application of carved decoration. In ST
ANDREWS DRIVE, overlooking the W side of Maxwell Park,
the sedate and uniform row of red sandstone villas forms part
of *Fryers & Penman*'s development for George Hamilton (1902
and 1905) which extends into the SE part of Sherbrooke
Avenue. Further S at No. 100 is the Victorianized Haggs Castle
(*see* Public Buildings, above).

The most individual and the grandest villas, almost on the scale
of country houses, are hidden amongst the overhanging trees
that cover the hill SW of DALZIEL DRIVE and ST ANDREWS
DRIVE. This was the last area of West Pollokshields to be
developed in the late 1890s and early 1900s, with uniform
avenues mostly transformed by the contours of the land and
by the variety of architectural design. The latest houses are
furthest S and W. This almost rural enclave is most easily
penetrated from Maxwell Park via HAMILTON AVENUE,
broad and flat at its E end and lined with quite ordinary villas,
except for HOLMWOOD (now Craigholme School) on the
corner of St Andrews Drive (No. 72), built in 1891–2 and
bought by James Weir of the Cathcart Foundry; and Nos. 9–
11 Hamilton Avenue, a red brick 'Old English' pair by *John
Gordon* for Colin Young, 1895, which would look more at home
in London's Bedford Park. After the junction with Sherbrooke
Avenue, a steep winding stretch with a row of six coarse red
villas, with crowstepped gables and angled porch projections,
by *A. J. Fryers* for George Hamilton, 1896 (cf. Maxwell Drive;
see above). Right at the S end is DUNHOLME (No. 76), like a

Cotswold manor house, designed by *James Miller*, 1909, for Duncan McCorkindale.

BENEFFRY is secluded round the corner at the W end of SPRING-KELL AVENUE (No. 124). Built for John Anderson in 1910 and now a Strathclyde University hall of residence, it is in a coarsened version of William Leiper's villa style by his partner and successor *William Hunter McNab*. The interior looks more Tudorbethan, with much oak panelling, low beamed ceilings and carved stone overmantels. The ornamental plasterwork on friezes, corbels etc. is of excellent quality, as might be expected from the specialist *G. Bankart* of *G. Jackson & Sons Ltd*. At KELMSCOTT, by *John Nisbet*, c. 1903, Scottish Baronial is admixed with Queen Anne, especially evident in the red tile roof with its timber cornice and dormers. Next we reach two big houses at the corner of Sherbrooke Avenue (*see* below) and, beyond them, No. 99 Springkell Avenue, a Free-Style design by *H. E. Clifford*, 1903–4, with boldly half-timbered wing and haphazard fenestration, much more striking than Clifford's more sober Free-Style house at No. 96, built in 1903 for A. N. Hunter. All the other houses (Nos. 82–94) on this flatter, more open stretch were designed by *Alexander Petrie* for James Marr between 1899 and 1902. Nos. 89–94 have conical-capped bows on the side, with big mullion-and-transom windows lighting the staircases and little timbered attics in the centres of the hipped roofs. Nos. 85–90 are red rock-faced, with crenellated and conical-capped bows.

Returning to SHERBROOKE AVENUE, the houses on the SW and NW corners are both of 1902 by *J. McKellar*; OAKLANDS (No. 31) for James Donald and REDHILLS (No. 42) for J. Duncanson. Oaklands looks disorganized, its oddest features the big square tower, with a timber-framed cap-house flanked by cylindrical chimneys. There is Art Nouveau glass in the big staircase window. Redhills, in red ashlar, has more conventional, Baroque details. The SE corner is filled by MATHERAN (No. 29, Glasgow School of Occupational Therapy), notable for its size rather than its beauty. It is a large variation of 1902–3 by *Burnet, Boston & Carruthers* for Hugh Dunsmuir on the theme of the bay-windowed villa with a corner tower. Its Baronial interior is arranged round the barrel-vaulted double-height hall: the staircase goes up behind the curved chimneybreast with its plaster strapwork and sentimental motto, and the panelled reception rooms are entered from the timber arcaded passage round two sides.

N of Springkell Avenue are slightly earlier houses: No. 25 (DUN-CAIRN) on the corner of Sutherland Avenue dates from 1892 and is similar to No. 19 (CRUACHAN) and No. 17 (SHER-BROOKE HOUSE), further N, both Baronial monsters in red sandstone. No. 23 (CORRIESTON) on the opposite (NE) corner has an Italianate tower and gatepiers, and No. 34 (CAIRN O'MOUNT) is another reticent house of c. 1900 by *H. E. Clifford*. The smaller BALMORY (No. 21), c. 1893, by *W. J. Anderson* looks much more original in black snecked rubble with polished red sandstone dressings, including an unexpected metope frieze below the Arts-and-Craftsy saucer dome of the round corner tower.

s of Springkell Avenue lie two more houses of 1902–3, both part of PATRICK HOUSE, an old people's home. No. 35, by *Gavin Paterson* for William Wallace, has a c 17-Scottish-style façade in silver-grey snecked rubble. No. 39 (WOODMAILING) is a more interesting Baronial exercise, by *Burnet, Boston & Carruthers* for Andrew Biggart, with Glasgow-Style touches, especially at the entrance, which has nice Celtic carving on the porch imposts and mauvish stained glass in the grid-pattern front door, and in the white-painted double-height entrance hall. Opposite, the symmetrical, classical WAVERLEY (No. 52), by *John Reid* for Colin Young, looks late Georgian rather than of 1904. Further round the corner, on the flatter ground, more of the simpler, more closely packed houses by *Fryers & Penman* (1902 and 1905) also found in St Andrews Drive (*see* above) bring us back to Maxwell Park.

BELLAHOUSTON AND DUMBRECK

The affluent villa suburb of Bellahouston and Dumbreck, split apart by the M8, was originally part of Govan rather than of Pollokshields, with which it is now more closely associated. The former parish church is in Clifford Street and the private academy that served the area is in Paisley Road West, both north of the motorway. The estate of Dumbreck was added to the adjacent one of Bellahouston by Mr Steven, owner of Bellahouston, in the early c 19. He changed the name of Dumbreck House, which had been built late in the previous century by William Wardrop, to that of the larger estate. After *c.* 1860, Glasgow businessmen began to build villas on these estates; by 1865 there was a small group of them and a church in the NE corner near Paisley Road, and a cluster further s, including the predecessor of the present Hazlewood House. There was even greater activity in the last three decades of the c 19, when new streets were formed, and villas and, in the N, tenements erected. The first houses were in Urrdale (then Manor) Road. By 1887, long before the rest of the Bellahouston estate was turned into a park by the Corporation in 1896, all the roads between it and Dargavel Avenue were laid out and partly built up. By 1915 the whole suburb, very similar in character to Pollokshields, was complete.

BELLAHOUSTON PARK, made famous by the Empire Exhibition of 1938, opened as a public park in 1896 and was extended in 1901. From that layout, all that is left is the Jacobethan GATE LODGE on Paisley Road West (1907, by *A. B. McDonald* of Glasgow's Office of Public Works).

The PALACE OF ART by *Launcelot Ross* lies further s. It 106 is the only survivor from the Empire Exhibition and was the only building designed to be permanent – for the display of the civic art collection. It looks dingy and sad. The portico of six tall blue-tiled pillars was glazed in when the Exhibition ended, and a flimsy timber porch has since been added. The characteristic lettering has gone from the granite-clad façade (though some still remains on the side); stuccoed additions and courtyard corridors of the 1951 conversion to community use have spoilt the clarity of the original design (just four simple galleries round a courtyard).

Only the most vivid imagination could conjure all the other, temporary structures, pastel-coloured and transformed at night by coloured floodlighting. The Exhibition was conceived in 1936 to attract new industry to depressed Glasgow. *T. S. Tait* was elected architect-in-chief, and his plan was unveiled in 1937. The (in Tait's words) 'essentially modern' buildings were mainly inspired by Asplund's Stockholm Exhibition of 1930 and were designed by a team of ten architects including *Coia*, *J. T. Thomson*, *Basil Spence* and *Launcelot Ross*. Others, e.g. *Emberton* and *Misha Black*, took independent commissions. Standardization of materials and components and the use of a module ensured continuity of design. Above all, on top of the hill, stood Tait's tall silver observation tower. Up there now, just the MEMORIAL of the start of the Exhibition, unveiled by the King and Queen in 1937.

In 1989 plans are afoot to execute here *C. R. Mackintosh*'s idealistic and fragmentary drawings for a 'House for an Art Lover' (1901).

PERAMBULATION

To make sense of this suburb, first visit Ibrox Parish Church in Clifford Street, the C19 Bellahouston Academy, and the tenements around them (*see* Govan: Churches; Public Buildings; Perambulation 3). Then, at the W end of Clifford Street, cross the footbridge over the M8 to URRDALE ROAD, where the earliest houses, large but undistinguished (dating from *c.* 1870–80), stand in huge sloping gardens.

CRAIGIE HALL, 1872, by *John Honeyman*, round the corner in ROWAN ROAD, is much more interesting. Its exterior is deceptively plain and mildly Italianate, with an Ionic doorcase on the entrance front, and to the E a lower link to a large service wing. On the W front an elaborate columned bay window overlooks the lush grounds. S of it, the billiard room screens a glass-roofed, stone-walled winter garden, part of the 1890s work. The interior is exceptionally sumptuous, both the original work and the additions made to it by *John Keppie* and *Charles Rennie Mackintosh* for *Honeyman & Keppie* in the mid-1890s. The HALL shows the contrast, with Art Nouveau overdoors added in 1892 to the original classical decoration of marbled walls and Corinthian angle columns. Corinthian colonnettes divide the stained-glass panels of courtly lovers above the staircase. Stained glass also in the front door and in the service passage. In the two RECEPTION ROOMS, deep plaster friezes, delicately modelled with swags, garlands, grotesques and birds, inlaid parquet floors, and hints of the Jacobean style in the ceilings and joinery. The LIBRARY and MUSIC ROOM, designed for Thomas Mason, have Keppie's and Mackintosh's hallmarks. In the library, the Edwardian classical shelving is made sinuous and the glass doors given Art Nouveau leading: in the music room the large organ case and panelling (1897) have the forms of Mackintosh's early style. There is a similar but less extravagant fireplace here, and another one in the BILLIARD ROOM.

Rowan Road is a steep narrow lane lined with stone walls which conceal a few similar large houses and many more modern houses and flats. It leads up to BEECH AVENUE and, at No. 5, the R.C. Church of ST LEO THE GREAT by *Alexander McAnally*, which opened in 1976. To the s are the same sort of thickly treed suburban roads as in the western part of West Pollokshields, but here the lime trees almost overwhelm the narrower roads and smaller houses on smaller plots, fenced with low walls and privet hedges. The houses are particularly closely packed in the side roads, but almost all are of the same bay-windowed double type. A few (e.g. in DARGNAVEL AVENUE) are more cottagey. The red sandstone houses of uniform design in TORRIDON AVENUE are just like those of the 1890s by *A. J. Fryers* across the railway line in Pollokshields (*see* Hamilton Avenue, Maxwell Drive).

DUMBRECK AVENUE turns w off Dumbreck Road. s of it, a solitary pocket of public housing by *A. G. Jury* (City Architect), 1968–72. Tenements round green courts and two L-shaped twenty-two-storey tower blocks with a spectacular view over Bellahouston Park. N of Dumbreck Avenue, amid small bungalows built over its grounds in 1915, is the Jacobean HAZLEWOOD HOUSE, designed in 1882 by *J. M. Munro* as a successor to the original mid-C19 Hazlewood, whose stables survive at the back. Bay windows look down gardens to the s; the E entrance leads into an inner hall lit by a large cupola with painted glass, on a massive enriched coving.

GOVAN

Govan was once a thriving independent town famous for shipbuilding, but, since it was annexed by its greater neighbour in 1912, it has gradually been transformed into just an outlying district of Glasgow. The Victorian and Edwardian buildings that survive chart the growing prosperity of the town and its entrepreneurs: the vitality and clamour once prevalent all along this stretch of the river is now only recalled by the Fairfield Yard close to Govan Road.

The district now known as Govan is only a fragment of the original parish, which, as late as 1770, stretched to Gorbals and Govanhill in the E, and, until the mid-C19, to Strathbungo and

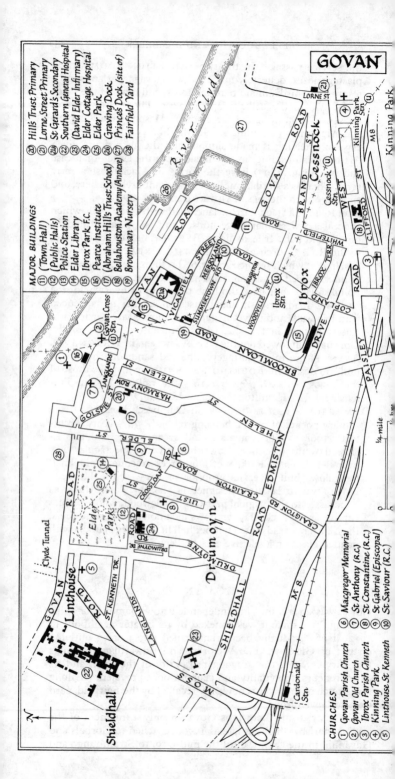

GOVAN

MAJOR BUILDINGS
⑪ (Town Hall)
⑫ (Public Halls)
⑬ Police Station
⑭ Elder Library
⑮ Ibrox Park F.C.
⑯ Pearce Institute
⑰ (Abraham Hill's Trust School)
⑱ Bellahouston Academy (Annexe)
⑲ Broomloan Nursery

⑳ Hills Trust Primary
㉑ Lorne Street Primary
㉑ᵃ St Gerard's Secondary
㉒ Southern General Hospital
㉓ (David Elder Infirmary)
㉔ Elder Cottage Hospital
㉕ Elder Park
㉖ Graving Dock
㉗ Prince's Dock (site of)
㉘ Fairfield Yard

CHURCHES
① Govan Parish Church
② Govan Old Church
③ Ibrox Parish Church
④ Kinning Park
⑤ Linthouse St Kenneth

⑥ Macgregor Memorial
⑦ St Anthony (R.C.)
⑧ St Constantine (R.C.)
⑨ St Gabriel (Episcopal)
⑩ St Saviour (R.C.)

Dumbreck in the s and Kelvinside in the N. The ecclesiastical importance of Govan dates back at least to the c 10. The name Govan appears for the first time in a charter granting the lands and church of Govan to the see of Glasgow in 1147. Soon after 1153 they became a prebend. By the c 16 Govan was, according to Bishop Leslie, 'a gret and ane large village', surrounded by coal pits. During the c 18 the villagers lived by salmon fishing and weaving, but early in the next century fishing was succeeded by silk manufacture and dyeing. In 1836 the population was 2,122. Thatched cottages lined the main street (the Greenock turnpike), which ran in a shallow crescent N of the present Govan Cross.

Shipbuilding transformed Govan. It began with the founding of Mackie & Thomson's yard just N of Govan Cross in 1840. Within twenty years the whole waterfront between there and Highland Lane had been developed by Robert Napier and by Smith & Rodgers, who launched the first ship in 1844. About 1860 middle-class suburbs (fragments of which remain) began to develop to the s and E, with tenements in and around Orkney (then Albert) Street and villas and terraces as far s as Ibrox. The burgh was established in 1864 with a population of 9,058. It soon became one of the largest and most populous in Scotland, for that year saw the introduction of shipyards on a much larger scale, and of the associated metal-working and engineering industries. Randolph, Elder & Co.'s Fairfield Yard opened in 1864, Stephen & Sons' Linthouse Yard in 1868. Tenements began to spread in earnest. The population rose to 33,126 in 1874, 58,569 in 1884, and 90,908 in 1904. Nothing illustrates the burgh's aggrandizement so well as the two municipal buildings: the modest former Burgh Chambers of 1866–7 (now a police station) in Orkney Street and the grandiose Town Hall of 1897–1901 further E. The influence of the shipyard owners can be seen in their philanthropic gestures – in the park, library, cottage hospital and infirmary provided by the Elders and in the workingmen's institute paid for by Lady Pearce. Their patronage was architecturally enlightened: Mrs Elder employed *J. J. Burnet*, Lady Pearce *Robert Rowand Anderson*.

By 1904 outlying settlements had engulfed or obliterated the c 18 and early c 19 mansions from Linthouse (w) to Plantation (E). The first estate to be exploited was that of Kinning House, where in 1834 Sir John Maxwell planned a 'Model New Town' to the designs of *Peter Macquisten*. The plan, which centred on a huge circus, did not materialize and, although some tenements for the middle classes were built in 1842, it was not until Kingston Dock opened in 1867 that Kinning Park and its neighbour Plantation grew into an industrial suburb. Cessnock House disappeared when the Prince's Dock was constructed in 1893–7. By the 1880s Govan and Glasgow were physically joined.

After Govan had surrendered her independence in 1912, Glasgow Corporation began to replace and supplement the housing with her standard tenement and, at Drumoyne, cottage schemes. The decline of shipbuilding since 1960, together with the transfer of shipping upstream to Shieldhall and beyond, the decay of C19 housing and a fall in population, prompted radical changes. In 1969 Govan was designated a Comprehensive Development Area. The results show the Corporation's change of heart from post-war utopianism. Dreary medium- and low-rise schemes, some with a stylistic nod to the rural Scottish vernacular, have replaced large areas of tenements, although many have been saved and improved, initially by the pioneering efforts of a team of community architects called *Assist*. Elder Park and Kinning Park (the latter split in two by the M8; *see* also Gorbals) were designated C.D.A.s in 1975, late enough to show the effects of the District Council's policy for a mixture of public and private development. In 1989 the riverside is again being transformed, this time from a hive of industry to a chain of dormitory suburbs with leisure facilities, like that to be built on the infilled Prince's Dock, the site of Glasgow's 1988 Garden Festival.

CHURCHES

GOVAN PARISH CHURCH, 866 Govan Road, set well back in a churchyard of great antiquity (as the collection of monuments in the church clearly shows). The present church of 1883–8, by *Robert Rowand Anderson*, is the last in a long series of churches on this site. The exterior of grey snecked rubble with green slate roofs seems dull without the intended lavish tower and spire (*see* the foundations on the W side) and the unexecuted band of relief sculpture across the façade, though the plans are ambitious and the interior is splendid. The minister who promoted rebuilding, John Macleod, was a pioneer of Scoto-Catholicism and a believer in the beauty of worship as inspiration for the working classes. The style is E.E. in the Scottish manner, with details (especially the chancel gable) based on Pluscardine Priory near Elgin. Ashlar chancel, higher than the nave, extended in 1911–12, with octagonal stairtowers at the angles. The walls are striped in red brick and stone, a vibrant effect dimmed with age. The size of the interior, with broad high nave and narrow passage aisles, owes much to the preaching churches Macleod had visited in Italy. The aisle arcades are of broad moulded piers dying into the arches, but the clearstorey is more decorative, each bay with one tall window flanked by two nook-shafted lancets. Between the bays, wall-shafts carrying the arched braces of the roof, which cross the boarded cove before spanning the roof high above the nave. Only one galleried (W) transept, opening with two clustered piers. The rhythm of one large and two small arches is repeated with the openings to the deep chancel and the choir aisles, one with the choir gallery, the other (originally the baptistery) with the ORGAN (by *Brindley & Foster*) over. The chancel ends in an elegant blind arcade and band of foliage. Each side, top-lit passages in the depth of the walls; they lie over those that lead to the stairs in the angles. Fine wrought-iron screens divide the chancel aisles, the w one continuous with the large square Steven Chapel, ringed with lancets. The furnishings are simple and unobtrusive.

STAINED GLASS. Twelve windows are by *C. E. Kempe*, part of a unified but uncompleted scheme commissioned soon after the church was finished. – Chancel: first completed and dedicated to John Macleod † 1898; Christ enthroned (oculus), above scenes of the main events in His life. – Choir and transept galleries (Angels of Faith and Hope). – Transept lancets (figures of Faith flanked by Noah and Abraham, and Hope flanked by Moses and Jacob). – Clearstorey (E): Witnesses of the Resurrection. (The w clearstorey windows were designed but not inserted.) – s window over the gallery, particularly beautiful: Our Lord the King of Angels, with the three arch-angels and thirteen angel musicians. – E chancel aisle, windows by *Shrigley & Hunt*. – In the Steven Chapel, a good undated display by *Clayton & Bell* (The Power of Our Lord; and eight Old Testament prophets, with finely illustrated scenes from their lives), and the Supper at Emmaus by *Heaton, Butler & Bayne*. – Above the font, a window by *Kempe* from St Margaret Polmadie dedicated to Dr Macleod who also founded that church.

MONUMENTS. The W transept and chancel contain one of the most remarkable assemblages of Early Christian sculpture in Scotland, most of which were moved inside the church from the graveyard in 1926. Five main types of sculpture are represented: a richly ornamented sarcophagus; hogbacked tombstones; cross-shafts; upright crosses; and recumbent slabs. – The sarcophagus in the chancel, one of three that survived until 1762, is a single block of sandstone hollowed out internally to receive the burial; the top part of each side is carefully shaped to allow the cover slab (perhaps a gabled block) to fit tightly. The sides and ends of the sarcophagus are decorated with panels of interlace and figural ornament. On one side, a panel including two pairs of beasts, the lower pair having tails and ears which interknot, and a panel with a pair whose necks are intertwined. The other side has a hunting scene in Pictish style. The sarcophagus is of the C 10–11 A.D. – The five hogbacked stones are bowed and gabled blocks, with decoration representing the square shingles of a wooden roof. Several of the stones have roughly carved animal heads with the forepaws continuing along the sides. Of Scandinavian inspiration, such slabs can be paralleled in the Anglian areas of Northern England and are probably of the mid- to late C 10 A.D. – The better-preserved of the two cross-shafts, which formerly stood at Jordanhill (whither it had been moved from Govan after the demolition of the medieval church), bears elaborated panels of interlace ornament and a panel with a man on horseback. Another fragment bears on one side what has been described as 'a blundered representation' of an interesting scene in the iconography of the early church – S S Paul and

Govan Sarcophagus
(Reproduced by permission of RCAHMS)

Anthony breaking bread in the desert. – The better-preserved of the two upright crosses, of the C 10 A.D., bears a cross filled with interlace above a panel depicting a horseman with a spear; on the reverse, there is a boss from which emerge four serpents above a panel of interlace. The other upright cross is now broken, but a fragment with a man on horseback remains. – Finally, there is a large group of recumbent cross-slabs or grave-markers, all bearing a central cross surrounded by interlace ornament.

GOVAN OLD CHURCH, Govan Cross. Built as St Mary Govan Free Church. 1873, by *Robert Baldie*. A flat three-gabled façade with Geometrical tracery, lancets and shafted portals. No tower. The halls shield the church from Govan Road. Simple interior, broader than long with raked pews and gallery curving round the platform and organ. Beamed ceiling on pendentives and patterned glass in the windows.

IBROX METHODIST CHURCH, 534 Paisley Road West. Built as Ibrox United Presbyterian Church. By *Angus Kennedy*, 1867–8. Originally a two-storey box (aisleless church above halls) with a corner tower. Chancel and transepts added 1896–7 by *Bruce & Hay*. Grand façade with a shafted E.E. main doorway and reticulated window, and s w tower, its spire with stunted pinnacles and lucarnes. The nave is long and plain, with Y-tracery in the lancets, but the transepts have big Geometrical windows and the chancel, linked to the transepts by little gabled bays set diagonally, is quite pretty. Inside, an elaborate open roof. Chancel panelled and given its stained-glass window (Virgin and St John) in 1958.

IBROX PARISH CHURCH, Clifford Street. Opened in 1863 as Bellahouston Church, but cut off from the suburb it served by the M8. A brutish design in cream ashlar by *James Smith* of Glasgow. The bell tower (NE) is especially hamfisted, not unlike a contemporary drinking fountain with its stubby spire resting on a bell-stage of squat E.E. columns. Breaking into the large blank expanse of the main gable, a window with lots of prickly cusping and a six-pointed star. Lower down, two rows of shafted lancets lighting the vestibule. Double transepts and polygonal chancel with conventional Geometrical detail, and a little Perp session house, all added by *W. F. McGibbon*, 1897–8. Inside, the ugly panelled ceiling (with stone piers along the walls) replaces an open timber roof burnt down in 1968. Aisleless nave with W gallery into the vestibule, two arches into each transept, and a ribbed vault over the apse. This plainness is relieved by vivid STAINED GLASS in every window. – Nave. Most interesting are the fine examples with brightly enamelled pictorial medallions against a background of Gothic grisaille. They are by *Ballantine & Son* and were given by the Stephen family, the benefactors of the church. The earliest (W), now lost, was of 1863. Earliest now, two small Evangelist windows in the gallery (1868). The nave windows (from W to E) are pairs: Jesus and the Woman of Samaria and Jesus and Nicodemus, given by Moses Stephen, 1869; Jacob and the Angel and Jacob's Ladder, undated; Jesus with Martha and Mary, 1873, and Jesus with Nathaniel, 1874, given by Elizabeth and Grace Stephen. – Apse. Three single-light windows in the style of late medieval engravings, by *Clayton & Bell*, post-1899. – Also by *Clayton & Bell*, The Rest on the Flight into Egypt, dedicated to George Boyd † 1899 (S transept). – Three clumsy crowded compositions by *David Gauld* for *Guthrie & Wells*, after 1897: Annunciation and Nativity and the Evangelists (transepts), and St Paul Preaching in Athens (nave). – Nave S wall. The Good Samaritan, *c.* 1918, by *R. Anning Bell* for *Abbey Studio*. Moved from Springburn Parish Church. – Gallery window. First World War Memorial. A strong Arts and Crafts composition updated post-1945 and marred by the fire.

KINNING PARK CHURCH, 15 Edwin Street. The former Paisley Road United Free Church. 1874–6, by *McKissack & Rowan*. An unhappy design. Weedy pinnacles with over-large spirelets flank the main gable. The Geometrical tracery in the W window is picked out in half-round mouldings. A narrow tower, with pyramidal copper cap, rises up at the E end.

LINTHOUSE ST KENNETH, 7–9 Skipness Drive. Originally Govan Linthouse United Free Church. 1899–1900, by *James Miller*. A curious marriage of styles, particularly jarring where the distinctly Arts and Crafts battered towers, topped by miniature Ionic *tempietti* with saucer domes, meet the four-square classical nave front with its applied Ionic colonnade and peculiarly austere windows. Baroque appears as well, used for the entrance and for the tower windows, with organic-looking consoles.

MACGREGOR MEMORIAL CHURCH, 137 Crossloan Road. 1902–4, by *James Miller*. The only interesting feature is the inventive Art Nouveau tracery of the main window and tower bell-openings. Otherwise a straightforward design, with NW corner tower and NE porch of neo-Perp outline. A row of buttresses with set-offs along the aisleless nave. Galleried interior.

OUR LADY AND ST MARGARET (R.C.), 110–18 Stanley Street. Only the gatepiers, a few loose fragments and the presbytery survive from *Pugin & Pugin*'s church of 1882. The presbytery's tall rock-faced façade culminates in an ecclesiastical gable with cross finial, round-traceried window and crocketed tabernacle (marking an oratory?).

PLANTATION ST ANDREW, 115 Plantation Street. 1874. A prominent landmark amongst the late C20 low-rise housing that replaces the suburb of Plantation. The hefty tower, its stone spire ringed with gables at the base, is sandwiched between two gabled bays with rows of lancets. Entrance through the tower.

ST ANTHONY (R.C.), 839 Govan Road. 1877–9, by *John Honeyman*. Italian Romanesque (an uncommon style for Glasgow churches at that date), of cream snecked rubble banded and striped in pink stone. Blind arcading in the broad gable and round the attached campanile, fronted by a big square porch. Classical interior with a N gallery and a gallery over the broad E aisle, which opens into the nave with giant Corinthian columns. Marble-lined apse; the classical altar canopy looks later. – PRESBYTERY, to the S facing Langlands Road. 1892. Asymmetrical, with Gothic windows over the door and a timbered gable poking up from the roof.

ST CONSTANTINE (R.C.), Uist Street. Dated 1921. Gabled red sandstone façade with one big mullioned-and-transomed window. The tall narrow PRESBYTERY of pressed red brick looks more interesting.

ST GABRIEL (Episcopal), 40 Greenfield Street. By *James Chalmers*, 1901–2. In pressed red brick, with white stone dressings. Round-headed windows and simplified chevron.

ST SAVIOUR (R.C.), Merryland Street. 1899, by *Joseph Cowan*. The simplest kind of rendered box, with Perpish glazing bars. Associated schools facing Summertown Road, 1896, also by Cowan.

SALVATION ARMY CITADEL, Golspie Street. 1904. Free Style, with C17 overtones. Short battered tower.

SHIELDHALL AND DRUMOYNE CHURCH, 9 Langcroft Road. 1934–5. One of *Stellmacs*' brick and rendered designs (cf. United Free Church, Knightswood).

WESLEYAN CHURCH, 147 Elder Street (now Harmony Row Youth Club). 1883, by *W. F. McGibbon*. Cream snecked rubble, with elaborate plate tracery. Gabled s porch. Gabled halls with trefoil windows.

PUBLIC BUILDINGS

GOVAN TOWN HALL, 401 Govan Road. 1897–1901, by *Thomson & Sandilands*. A large and magnificent building, demonstrating volubly Govan's status at the turn of the century, but not a confident design. French Second Empire and Neo-classical elements of disparate and uncertain scale are combined into an elaborate Beaux Arts composition in red sandstone ashlar. The council chamber and office suites face E and s. Flanking the main entrance, medallion busts of Provost James Kirkwood and Bailie John Marr. Over the N one, the bust of Councillor Richard Russell. Facing Summertown Road, the more attractive Italianate façade of the concert hall, carved with *grotteschi*, cartouches of music and drama, and a delightful frieze (by *Macfarlane Shannon*) of garlanded *putti* pulling a chariot. The small hall, with its lower, more domestic façade, was inserted into the open N courtyard in 1902. Council chamber roof reconstructed 1973–6.

Former KINGSTON HALLS AND PUBLIC LIBRARY, 330 Paisley Road. 1904–5, by *R. W. Horn* of the City Engineer's Department. Burnt down in 1948; reopened in 1957. Used (in 1989) as a night shelter. Horn modelled his less bravura performance on J. J. Burnet's narrow-fronted Athenaeum, giving the halls a three-bay Edwardian Baroque front (pretty but conventional) and the library a one-bay, slightly deferential façade. Figure in the aedicule over the library door. The carved gilt lettering is tinged with Art Nouveau.

PUBLIC HALLS, Langlands Road. 1923–6, by Glasgow's *Office of Public Works*. A large but (in 1989) derelict example of this handsome classical type.

POLICE STATION, 18–20 Orkney Street. Designed by *J. Burnet*, 1866–7, as the Burgh Chambers, and extended s in the same style, as the police and fire station in 1899. Channelled rustication over the whole of the long blockish façade. The first-floor windows are set, in Thomson's manner (though less daringly), within a range of pilasters.

ROYAL MAIL SORTING OFFICE, 400 Paisley Road. By *Cunningham Glass Partnership*, 1983–4. A transparent tunnel leads from Paisley Road to a silver and red high-tech shed set below street level, on the site of the railway lines (for coal transport) at General Terminus Quay. By the same architects, the transport workshop, 1985–6.

ELDER LIBRARY, 228a Langlands Road. 1901–3, by *J. J.* [89] *Burnet*. A park pavilion with continental Baroque grace. Along the front a colonnade swells out, following more curvaceously the domed bow in the façade. Despite this dramatic centrepiece there is neither a grand entrance (it is tucked inconspicuously round the side of the bow) nor axis inside. On the balustrade, the figures of a shipwright and a draughtsman flank the Govan arms. The back, rebuilt a few feet further out in 1921–5 (by the *City Engineer*), is a severer composition with two canted bay windows. The interior was repanelled and opened up in 1959–62 by *A. McGuire*. The hall, with tessellated floor, stained wood and glass screens and BUSTS of Mr & Mrs John Elder by *Macfarlane Shannon*, retains the original character.

IBROX LIBRARY, Midlock Street. By *Rogerson & Spence*, c. 1980. A simple concrete-framed envelope with slim panels of blue brick and glass and a deep concrete fascia. The centre of the library is double-height and galleried (cf. Cardonald Library; *see* Craigton etc.).

IBROX PARK (Rangers Football Club), Edmiston Drive. Towards the road, the vast S stand of 1927–9 in pressed red brick, with RANGERS F.C. lettered proudly in a central tiled panel. It marked the pinnacle of *Archibald Leitch*'s career as leading designer of football grounds and at the time was the largest (with 10,000 seats) and most lavish stand ever built. The rest of the ground was rebuilt in an innovative oval form in 1978–81 with three stands by *T. M. Miller & Partners*.

88 PEARCE INSTITUTE, 840 Govan Road. An institute of 1902–6 for workingmen and women, convincingly disguised by the scholarly *Sir R. Rowand Anderson* as a large C17 Scottish town house. The larger hall wing is a rich composition, with octagonal staircase tower, balconied cupola and much strapwork. It ends in a shaped gable with exquisite ship finial. The rest, with a balancing crowstepped gable, is intentionally less sophisticated, despite the oriel and the handsome clock. Nothing at all elaborate about the interior. – STATUE, opposite. Sir William Pearce, by *Onslow Ford*, 1894. Bronze figure standing woodenly on a tall granite base.

Former ABRAHAM HILL'S TRUST SCHOOL, 65–9 Golspie Street. 1874, by *James Thomson* of *Baird & Thomson*. An endowed school. Plain and two-storey with a hipped roof and central entrance bay extended into an Italianate tower with triplets of arched windows.

BELLAHOUSTON ACADEMY (Annexe), 425 Paisley Road West. 1874–6, by *Robert Baldie* in a distinctly Scottish version of what the *British Architect* called 'Early Domestic Gothic'. One long range with crowstepped gables, oriels in the end bays, spired ventilators and a central tower with bartizans and tall mansard roof crested with ironwork. The academy began as a private, part-boarding school; the dormitories were in the attics and an assembly hall took up most of the first floor. Altered in 1903–5 (after Govan School Board took over in 1885) to a standard Board school arrangement. The severer block to the W was designed as the pupil-teacher institute by *Bruce & Hay*, 1899–1901. To the S, its shed-like gymnasium and swimming pool by *Samuel Preston* (Govan School Board Master of Works), 1903–5. (The rest of the school is in Pollokshields.)

BROOMLOAN NURSERY (former Broomloan Road Public School), 71 Broomloan Road. The earliest Italianate part, by *Alexander Watt*, is dated 1875. Second red sandstone building in similar style by *D. Barclay*, 1894.

HILL'S TRUST PRIMARY SCHOOL, 29 Nethan Street. By *Thomson, Taylor, Craig & Donald*, 1974–5. In contrast to its predecessor (*see* above), a low, single-storey school, the main block, with brown brick and harled walls, modelled into chamfered and big drum-like bays beneath a bold, unifying roof slab.

IBROX PRIMARY, 46 Hinshelwood Drive. Dated 1906. A plain red sandstone Board school on an enormous scale, vying with the Ibrox Park football stand opposite.

KINNING PARK NURSERY SCHOOL, 540 Scotland Street. An early Govan Board school in cream snecked rubble with tall mansards over the end bays and a central bell turret. Big plain block by *S. Preston* (the Board's Master of Works), 1912.

LAMBHILL PUBLIC SCHOOL, 36 Lambhill Street. 1875–6, by *James Salmon & Son*. Elizabethan with mullioned and transomed windows, and a pyramidal slated roof behind the curved central gable. To the N, a red ashlar block of *c.* 1931 by *Glasgow Corporation Education Department* in a reduced Baroque style much grander than the original school. Part disused; part health centre (1989).

LORNE STREET PRIMARY SCHOOL, 58 Lorne Street. 1892. A handsome Italian palazzo façade with a subtly modulated rhythm of bays in the manner of *H. & D. Barclay*. Bold Ionic aedicule surrounds to the first-floor windows. Fluted pilasters and diamond panels in the storey above.

ST GERARD'S SECONDARY SCHOOL. *See* Perambulation 2, below.

OUR LADY AND ST MARGARET'S PRIMARY, Stanley Street. 1910, by *Bruce & Hay*, on a huge scale; it could be mistaken for a warehouse or mill. Gothic overtones in the gabled buttresses dividing the end bays and the castellated parapet.

DRILL HALL (Royal Naval Reserve), 130 Whitefield Street. The three-storey office building has angle bartizans. Adjoining it, the drill hall and sturdy N tower. All in red brick. 1905–6, by *Burnet, Boston & Carruthers*.

DAVID ELDER INFIRMARY, Langlands Road. 1924–7, by *Keppie & Henderson*. A variation on the C17 domestic theme of the Elder Cottage Hospital (*see* below) but pared down to a plain harled box without quoins. C17-style doorcase and three of seven dormers with vestigial alternating pediments in a steep green-slated mansard. Plain, deep frieze inscribed 'David Elder Infirmary 1925' in bold Roman letters. In the entrance hall, a bronze dedication TABLET by *Benno Schotz*, 1927: Pity succouring suffering humanity (the hospital was founded for charity cases, especially sick and injured workers); bas-relief of classical figures in Ghiberti's late style.

ELDER COTTAGE HOSPITAL, 1a Drumoyne Road. 1910–12, by *J. J. Burnet*. An essay in the late C17 English domestic style, modified by its squat proportions, cottagey lower windows and very Scottish snecked rubble. Opulent semicircular doorhood, with carved consoles and fruity swags. Above it, a nice relief of a mother nursing her baby (the hospital was initially intended to be a maternity home).

The cottage theme is taken up more strongly opposite in the contemporary NURSES' HOME, with its half-timbered gables.

ST FRANCIS MATERNITY AND NURSING HOME. *See* Perambulation 2, below.

SOUTHERN GENERAL HOSPITAL, Govan Road. Opened as Govan Combination Poorhouse in 1872. The original building (1867–72, by *James Thomson*) lies towards the S end of the E drive: French Renaissance, with a clumsy central bell tower and steeply mansarded, iron-crested pavilions. In the centre, the former poorhouse, flanked by the almost detached hospital wings. N of it, and in similar style, a hospital block of 1883 by *H. McLachan*, extended at the back in 1897–9 by *H. & D. Barclay*. Prominent sanitary towers at the angles. Flanking this, but facing the W drive, the NURSES' HOME, 1905, by *Thomson & Sandilands*, extended to the E in a more convincing Scottish domestic style by H. & D. Barclay in 1926; and the MORTUARY (attached to a later Pathology Department), KITCHEN, LAUNDRY and BOILERHOUSE, all of the 1930s by *Thomas Somers* (City Engineer). SE of these, alongside the former poorhouse, the original ASYLUM (psychiatric wards), also extended by H. & D. Barclay, 1926.

W of the W drive, the former CHILDREN'S HOME of 1901 by the *Barclays*, in late C17 style with a hipped roof and cupola, curiously rusticated quoins and two lower pavilions; the severe WARD BLOCKS, 1906–9, by Thomson & Sandilands; and, set back beyond them, the former FEMALE DEFECTIVES' HOME (1926, by H. & D. Barclay) in Scottish Domestic style with angle bartizans.

At the S end of the site, extensive additions, mostly planned in 1961 by *T. D. W. Astorga* (Western Regional Health Board architect) and *Keppie Henderson & Partners*. The INSTITUTE OF NEUROLOGICAL SCIENCES (1967–72, by Astorga) is linked across Langlands Road to the earlier ACCIDENT AND ORTHOPAEDIC BLOCK (by Keppie Henderson & Partners, 1957–64), its concrete frame projecting like fins. It is on the site of Shieldhall Hospital: some pavilions of this survive further S. To the W, low harled teaching blocks, including the WALTON CONFERENCE CENTRE, 1971, and the MATERNITY HOSPITAL, 1964–7, another long slab bridging the road.

BATHS AND WASHHOUSE, Harhill Street. Built *c.* 1922. The usual handsome classical composition in shiny red brick and stone, done by Glasgow's *Office of Public Works* in the early 1920s.

SHIELDHALL SEWAGE WORKS, Renfrew Road. By *Rogerson & Spence*, *c.* 1980. Buildings of concrete and blue engineering brick, with effectively repeated concrete barrel-vaults.

GOVAN GRAVING DOCKS, Stag Street. Built for the Clyde Navigation Trust, 1869–98; closed 1988. The first, nearest the river, was constructed 1869–75 (engineers *Bell & Miller*); the second was opened in 1886 (engineer *Archibald Hamilton*) and the third and largest (constructed in mass-concrete) in 1898.

KING GEORGE V DOCK, Renfrew Road. Opened for the Clyde Navigation Trust in 1931. A large single basin with unrestricted access from the river. W side developed after 1945.

PRINCE'S DOCK, Govan Road. Infilled and landscaped for Glasgow's Garden Festival of 1988, and thereafter to be used for houses. The dock was built in 1893–7 for the Clyde Navigation Trust and until its opening in 1897 was known as Cessnock Dock. The three basins, two-storied warehouses (unique in Glasgow) and hydraulically powered cranes and capstans have gone, but the HYDRAULIC PUMPING STATION still stands at the NW corner: 1894, by *Burnet, Son & Campbell*. The N end is a splendid accumulator tower with machicolations in medieval Italian style. At the S end the stump of an octagonal chimney in the form of the 'Tower of the Winds', with relief panels set in the frieze. Another accumulator tower was built at the SW corner in 1911–12.

GOVAN STATION, Govan Cross. One of the series of underground stations on the Argyle Line designed by *Holford Associates*. A free-standing block of blue engineering brick, 1980.

ELDER PARK. A park of 37 acres (15 ha) laid out on flat farmland in 1883–4 to plans by *John Honeyman*. – BANDSTAND. Octagonal, cast-iron. On the base, reliefs of shipbuilding, music and art. – STATUES. John Elder, by *Sir J. E. Boehm*, 1887–8. A bronze standing figure with his hand resting on a compound engine. – Mrs John Elder, a bronze seated figure by *A. Macfarlane Shannon*, 1905–6. – PORTICO of the demolished Linthouse mansion, designed for Mr Spreull by *Robert Adam* in 1791. Erected here 1921.

CLYDE TUNNEL AND EXPRESSWAY, BELL'S BRIDGE, HARBOUR TUNNELS. *See* Crossings of the Clyde and Kelvin, below.

PERAMBULATIONS

1. Govan Cross, Elder Park, Drumoyne

GOVAN CROSS. This irregular open space is still the visual hub of the much rebuilt town centre. Govan Old Church (*see* Churches, above) and tall red sandstone façades shelter its E and W sides. In the centre, the domed cast-iron canopy of the AITKEN MEMORIAL FOUNTAIN, 1884.

On the SW corner, the BANK OF SCOTLAND, designed as the British Linen Bank (No. 816 GOVAN ROAD) and Post Office (No. 818), by *Salmon, Son & Gillespie*, 1897–1900. Free-Style, with a tall narrow corner bay topped by an open crown of wavy ribs. In contrast to the austere elevations, the inventive

82   and expressive sculpture. Over the entrance, a ship (complete
with tiny figurehead) blown forth by winged wind gods,
who sit on the columns flanking the door and appear bowed
beneath the weight of the upper storeys: carved by *Derwent
Wood*. In a completely different, more meticulous style are
the tiny workmen (bee-keeper, navigator, fisherman etc.,
by *Johan Keller*) ensconced in the Byzantine capitals between the bank windows. Other Art Nouveau touches (the
window of No. 818 and the ironwork over the side door to the
warehouses above the bank) were replaced, along with the
interior, in 1970–3 by *Watson, Salmond & Gray*. Next door,
the Y.M.C.A. of 1898 (Nos. 5–9 WATER ROW) has an unexceptional symmetrical façade. The open space continues on
the s side of Govan Road and spreads amorphously round the
Underground Station (*see* Public Buildings, above) to form a
bus station and car park behind the unambitious GOVAN
CENTRE (1981–3, by *Cunningham Glass Partnership*) with its
few touches of polychrome brickwork. Inside, a single shopping mall.

To the w stand the most substantial remains of old Govan, the
Parish Church, St Anthony's and the Pearce Institute (*see*
above). Prominent on the gushet site opposite the Pearce Institute, BRECHIN'S BAR (dated 1894), with its squat Baronial
tower. NW of it, the former LYCEUM CINEMA (County
Bingo), 1937–8, by *McNair & Elder*, follows the corner in one
sweeping curve. Of the few remaining stretches of tenements,
most eye-catching, in an angular Baroque way, are those on
the corner of SHAW STREET.

The FAIRFIELD YARD of Govan Shipbuilders Ltd (Nos. 1030–
48 Govan Road) faces Elder Park (*see* Public Buildings, above).
A long red sandstone ashlar office block by *John Keppie* of
Honeyman & Keppie, 1889–91, screens the shipyard. The style
is Italian Renaissance. On the first floor, two continuous strips
of window light the two drawing offices: between them, a
staircase window within the central temple front. Statues of a
shipwright and an engineer stand on stylized ships' prows
flanking the doorway. Three-storey offices in Elder Street,
1903. Art Deco w block, 1940, by *G. Bestwick*. NW of this, the
fine engine works of 1874 with pilastered brick walls which
conceal a magnificent interior of massive cast-iron stanchions
and raking stays, deep wrought-iron crane girders and substantial pine roof trusses.

The w and s edges of Elder Park are fringed with late C19 houses.
The tenements of LINTHOUSE, the grid of streets on the w
edge, originally housed workers from the Stephen & Sons'
shipyard, which opened in 1868 in the grounds of the Linthouse mansion (*see* Elder Park, above) and is now cut off from
the rest of the area by the Clydeside Expressway. Its elegant
engine shed of 1873 has been moved to the Scottish Maritime
Museum at Irvine. In ST KENNETH DRIVE are terraced
and semi-detached villas in yellow and red sandstone, and an
associated Board school of 1898. Flats by *Building Design*

Partnership with sub-Mackintosh detail took the place of *Mac-gregor Chalmers'* St Kenneth's Church (1897–8) in 1982–5.

LANGLANDS ROAD winds back towards Govan Cross; from the SE gates of Elder Park, it is a pedestrian route between red brick housing. On the N side, attractive courtyard blocks of terraced houses and flats by *Simister, Monaghan, McKinney,* 122 *MacDonald,* 1984–6, which avoid the cloying folksiness of their speculative neighbours. Their wide-eaved roofs have frilly red terracotta ridge tiles, their smooth brick walls some black and red tile patterns. The former Abraham Hill's Trust School (*see* Public Buildings) closes the view E. Beyond, to the SE, lie informal housing schemes of the 1970s, side by side with 1930s tenements and the remains of C19 industry.

DRUMOYNE, which lies well to the S of Elder Park, is a 1920s Corporation scheme of cottage housing; it is contemporary with Mosspark and the earliest phases of Knightswood and has the same house types, though it is less picturesque in its layout. In the 1930s an extension with straight wads of tenements was built S of Shieldhall Road. NW of these, much later S.S.H.A. terraces, tenements and two fifteen-storey tower blocks, 1960–3.

Further W at SHIELDHALL are the Southern General Hospital and the Shieldhall Sewage Works (*see* Public Buildings), both along Govan Road. Further W still is the SHIELDHALL INDUSTRIAL ESTATE, off Renfrew Road, where in 1978 large steel sheds replaced the unique industrial estate built in 1887–1929 by the Scottish Co-Operative Wholesale Society on the site of the mid-C18 Shieldhall mansion. Thirty-eight manufacturing departments supplied all SCWS outlets from here with a complete range of goods. Of all the red brick buildings (laid out by *James Davidson,* SCWS Clerk of Works), the only ones to survive are the former Chemical and Sundries Factory (1910) in Bogmoor Road and the former Cabinet Works (1929) in Hardgate Road. On RENFREW ROAD itself, the SCWS's most stylish industrial building, the former LUMA LIGHTBULB FACTORY (1936–8) by *Cornelius Armour,* the SCWS's architect. Very Scandinavian and like something from an aerodrome, with a glazed conning tower.

2. Govan Cross to Ibrox

E of GOVAN CROSS the tenements have almost all gone, marooning one or two interesting C19 and early C20 buildings. Just E of the Cross, between Govan Road and the river, a 1970s Corporation housing scheme on the site of Harland & Wolff's Shipyard. From the well-planted riverside walk, with its captivating view of Gilmorehill, it has a promising villagey grouping but, closer to, the grey harled tenements and bare courtyards prove disappointingly bleak.

On the opposite side of GOVAN ROAD (S), the solitary TRUSTEE SAVINGS BANK (No. 705) was once an important corner building for the Glasgow Savings Bank by *E. A. Suth-*

erland, 1906. Conventional except for its elongated stone dome and drum encircled with fins. Carving by *Richard Ferris*. Further E (N side), the eccentric NAPIER HOUSE (Nos. 638–46), a model lodging house by *Wm. J. Anderson*, 1898–9. Its then-experimental structure (partly steel-framed, with concrete floors) is most obvious at the sides and back, although the deeply recessed triplets of windows on the stone-clad elevations hint at it. Large sheer areas of wall, wilful asymmetry and unmoulded openings, all traits of the Glasgow Style.

Further E again (s side), the former GOVAN PRESS BUILDING (No. 577) by *Frank Stirrat*, 1889–90, with busts of Gutenberg, Scott, Burns and Caxton.

Govan Road then passes the Graving Docks (*see* Public Buildings, above), which, until they closed in 1988, gave an impression of the vitality and noise once prevalent along Govan's waterfront. The road (diverted in 1892) then turns to skirt Prince's Dock, deserted by shipping and being redeveloped. Opposite, the latest phase (1970s) of a mass of Corporation housing fringes the road and stretches right up to the Town Hall (*see* Public Buildings).

W and sw of the Town Hall, the remains of a middle-class residential suburb, already established *c*. 1865. In MERRY-LAND STREET, Loudonesque villas with *cottage-orné* or Italianate details. Four of those on the N side now form the ST FRANCIS MATERNITY AND NURSING HOME. Conversion into a cottage hospital was begun by *D. Andrew* in 1909 and 1912, but much was done (quite obviously) in the mid-1930s. Just round the corner in COPLAND ROAD, slightly later and fairly smart tenements with neo-Greek details (Nos. 74–84). Along the next stretch (Nos. 86–120), two-storey terraced houses of *c*. 1860 in plain cream ashlar with rusticated basements and balustraded parapets. These return into BRIGHTON PLACE, where there are also shorter terraces of three houses each, the outer ones with bay windows and rusticated quoins.

Surrounding this older group, 1930s tenements and a big associated school (ST GERARD'S, 1935–7, by *Walker, Hardy & Smith*). Amongst them in BROOMLOAN ROAD, three unadorned towers faced in grey and yellow brick (*Crudens Ltd*, 1967–71). Just to their s, in BROOMLOAN PLACE, a charmingly incongruous survival: a short row of mid-C19 rural stone cottages. Three more tall blocks rise up at the far s end of Broomloan Road, grey *Reema* slabs of twenty-one storeys with louvred attics and recessed balconies, by *Miller & Black* in association with the City Architect, 1963–7.

Next a brief detour W along Edmiston Road to see the big former marine engineering works of BRITISH POLAR ENGINES in HELEN STREET (No. 161), with six large bays of engineering shops (1884–1905) and a later Art Deco office block (on the site of the Govan Electricity Generating Station of 1899–*c*. 1911 by *W. Arnott*, engineer). The route back E again along Edmiston Road, past Ibrox Park (the Rangers' football

ground) and Ibrox Primary School (for both, *see* Public Buildings), reaches COPLAND ROAD, where the housing changes
to four-storey red sandstone tenements, fairly uniform in style.
Off the W side, amongst the industry in WOODVILLE
STREET, is the Flemish-gabled COPPER WORKS (No. 143)
of Blair, Campbell & McLean (1903), by *A. Hamilton*). Back
in Copland Road, near the S end, the long, Italianate IBROX
TERRACE of two-storey houses opens off the E side. It is a
fragment of the mid-C19 suburb of IBROXHOLM, which gives
its name to the Corporation scheme built on the site of several
large villas and softened by the trees that originally surrounded
them. Three L-shaped blocks with long glazed balconies and
brown brick and aggregate cladding, accompanied by pitched-
roofed walk-up blocks, all thoughtfully designed and laid out
by *A. G. Jury* (City Architect), 1962–6.

3. Cessnock, Plantation, Kinning Park

On PAISLEY ROAD WEST, the middle-class suburb that began
with villas at Ibroxholm (*see* above) was continued by cream
sandstone tenements. They stretch from Copland Road to
Harvie Street and date mainly from after 1865. Most are plain
and three-storey, with simple classical detail. Nos. 520–32,
just beyond Ibrox Methodist Church (*see* Churches, above),
are exceptional. They have many of the distinctive details
seen in Alexander Thomson's Walmer Crescent further E (*see*
below), e.g., flat bandcourses ornamented with disks, recessed
panels between the upper windows, and incised anthemion
decoration. Just after Whitefield Street, also on the fringes of
the former villa development at Ibroxholm, Nos. 498–90 are
also above average in detail, but still in the Georgian tradition.
Nos. 492–90 seem to have been truncated above ground-floor
level. This row faces the C19 Bellahouston Academy (*see*
Public Buildings). Behind it, in CARILLON ROAD, CLIF-
FORD STREET etc., a homogeneous development of tenements in rough yellow and cross-hatched pink sandstone
followed the building of the Academy in the late 1870s and
1880s. It is now, with its church (*see* Churches: Ibrox Parish
Church), cut off from the rest of Bellahouston (*q.v.*) by the
M8.

WALMER CRESCENT, on the opposite side, is screened from
Paisley Road West by the commercial property that has
invaded its gardens. Designed by *Alexander Thomson* and built
in 1857–62, it stood for some years almost alone, 'occupied
exclusively by rich merchants' (Brotchie). It is a gentle curve of
tenements (two main-door houses with bay windows flanking a
simple close door) tied together, despite the ungracious blocks
of its bay windows, by strong horizontals: channelled rustication, an unbroken strip of top-floor windows divided regularly by thick mullions, a disk-ornamented bandcourse rising
and falling over the first-floor windows. There is the usual
play with the depth of the wall surface and many other subtle-

ties, e.g., chimneys used like attics to stress the main-door bays. The tenements return into Cessnock Street with a bowed corner.

The next stretch of tenements is contemporary with Walmer Crescent. Beyond that, at the corner of HARVIE STREET, a Chambord-style roofline on Nos. 252–6 by *James Sellars*, 1882. Then a detour down LORNE STREET (with its early former CINEMA by *John Fairweather*, 1925–7) to a handsome Board school and the pumping station at Prince's Dock (*see* Public Buildings); and the long brick GOVAN TRAM DEPOT, 1913–14, designed for electric trams by the engineer, *J. Ferguson*, just in BRAND STREET (Nos. 29–35).

The route back to Paisley Road West is through PLANTATION, once 'an intensely modern and workaday district' (T. C. F. Brotchie, *History of Govan*, 1905) of grey tenements laid out after 1867 on the grounds of the C18 Plantation House (demolished *c.* 1900). Except for Plantation St Andrew (*see* Churches), it has been entirely rebuilt with grey harled terraces and tenements and speculative red brick houses of the 1970s and 1980s.

The suburb of KINNING PARK has likewise been almost entirely obliterated, the E part by the M8. Formally planned on a grand scale in 1834 (*see* Govan: Introduction), it began slowly but smartly *c.* 1842 with Pollok Street, but spread s to Scotland Street (*see* Gorbals: Tradeston) and w with intermingled tenements and factories in the late 1860s and 1870s. A few of these remain: e.g., at the corner of MILNPARK STREET and Middlesex Street, the KINNING PARK COLOUR WORKS of *c.* 1895, with quite a showy polychromatic office block, probably by *Bruce & Hay*; and, at the s end of STANLEY STREET, opposite the R.C. school and presbytery (*see* Churches and Public Buildings), the biscuit factory of GRAY DUNN & CO. LTD (Nos. 75–115), a row of red and white brick buildings, homogenized by paint and render. N block by *John Baird II*, 1875 (top storey C20); two blocks with arched openings by *Stark & Rowntree*, 1893–7; s block by *Watson, Salmond & Gray*, *c.* 1940.

Back in PAISLEY ROAD WEST, plain classical three-storey tenements of *c.* 1870, and, further on, near the junction of the roads to Paisley and Govan, a few slightly earlier ones. On the gushet, commanding what until 1912 was the main E entrance into Govan from Glasgow, an extravagantly opulent late C19 building, with a *tempietto* and winged figure perched on the taller and most complicated of its steep pavilion roofs. NW of it, just in GOVAN ROAD, flats and workshops, designed by *Graham Wylie & Isabel Court*, 1987–8, open round a cloister with a faint ring of C19 philanthropic ventures. s of the junction, on the w corner of Admiral Street, the modern exterior of the OLD TOLL BAR hides a saloon of 1892–3, lavishly decorated with painted and engraved glass and mirrors, and with an elaborate bottle display behind a single long counter.

In ADMIRAL STREET itself, at No. 31, a former RIVET WORKS
of *c.* 1888 with a long red and white brick front. At the s end
of it, the two wide bays of the ADMIRAL STREET SUB-
STATION, added in 1901. E in SEAWARD STREET, the tall
red brick KINNING PARK SEWAGE PUMPING STATION
of 1909–10, designed in connection with the Shieldhall Outfall
Works by the engineers *D. & A. Home Morton.* Originally
with steam pumps.

CRAIGTON, MOSSPARK, CARDONALD, PENILEE, CROOKSTON

Paisley Road West is the corridor through this sea of mostly
interwar housing. The only older buildings belong to the small
suburbs that grew up between the stations at Cardonald (opened
in 1879) and Crookston (1885). They housed commuters who
travelled by train and, after 1903, by tram to both Paisley and
Glasgow. The first wave of building activity reached its peak in
1905.

In the early C19 there was only the hamlet of Halfway on the
Paisley turnpike (opened in 1753) and a scattering of farms
and country houses (Craigton House and Ralston House, both
demolished, and Maryland House, which survives). Their estates
were C18 subdivisions of the Cardonald estate, which had been
carved out of the lands of Crookston in the C15 for the illegitimate
son of the first Earl of Lennox.

The first municipal housing to invade the farmland in 1921–3
was the garden suburb of Mosspark, wound round the drumlin
s of Bellahouston Park, and the severer tenements of Craigton to
the N. Next, in the 1930s, Corporation and S.S.H.A. flatted
cottages spread across the steep ridge at Cardonald and over
South Cardonald below it. During the Second World War the
experimental houses at Penilee were constructed on the flattest
land to the W, to serve the adjacent Hillington Industrial Estate
(over the city boundary). Amongst this low-rise housing, a few
taller blocks sprang up, led by the innovatory flats at Moss
Heights (1950–4).

CHURCHES

CARDONALD PARISH CHURCH, 2141 Paisley Road West.
1888–9. *P. Macgregor Chalmers'* first, exceedingly modest
church, towerless in red sandstone with only lancet windows.
The aisles (w one of 1899) are almost as broad as the nave. A
surprising variety of STAINED GLASS enriches this otherwise
plain interior, including six lancets in the E aisle by *Sadie
McLellan, c.* 1960 (Scenes from the Last Days of Christ's
Life); two lancets on both aisle s walls, one of them a centenary
window, 1988; w aisle N wall, lancet by *Gordon Webster,* 1933.

CHURCH OF THE ASCENSION (Episcopal), Mosspark Drive. 1925–6, by *H.O. Tarbolton*, linked in one composition to the later hall by *Spiers Ltd*, 1937–8.

GOOD SHEPHERD (Episcopal), Hillington Road. By *Noad & Wallace*, 1939–40. – STAINED GLASS. Four windows by *Margaret Chilton* (Celtic Saints), 1940.

HILLINGTON PARK CHURCH, Berryknowes Road. The hall opened as a United Free Church in 1908. The harled church with red sandstone Dec façade was added in 1924–5.

MOSSPARK CONGREGATIONAL CHURCH, Ladybank Drive and Mosspark Boulevard. 1937–8, by *Balfour & Stewart*. Harled. Intersected tracery in red sandstone is the only embellishment.

MOSSPARK PARISH CHURCH, Ashkirk Drive. By *Thomson, Sandilands & Macleod*, 1925–9. A red sandstone church, substantial but without the short SW tower originally projected. There are still Art Nouveau touches, e.g., in the chancel tracery and exterior ironwork, despite the late date. Projecting organ chamber, polygonal apse and, linked to the W end, large halls, stone-faced towards the road. The interior has much in common with Clifford's Cathcart Old Parish Church (being completed about this time). Open timber roof with decorative bracing, low passage aisles with broad arches to the nave. – ORGAN (from Kingston Halls; *see* Govan) donated in 1933 by John Auld Mactaggart (Mactaggart & Mickel built the Mosspark scheme).

OUR LADY AND ST GEORGE (R.C.), Sandwood Road. 1957–9, by *T.S. Cordiner*. Brick, with a shallow pitched roof. Instead of a tower, a tapering concrete pier, carrying a cross, rises through the central glazed recess in the gable end.

OUR LADY OF LOURDES (R.C.), Lourdes Avenue. 1937–9, by *Stellmacs Ltd, Designers and Builders*. A quite ambitious though traditional design exploiting the decorative potential of the rustic brown brick pointed in white, both outside and within. NW tower, with an angular outline of sharply stepped buttresses. Inside, passage aisles, an apsidal baptistery (NW) and mortuary chapel (SW). Partly ceiled timber roof. – STAINED GLASS. Three vivid E lancets (Crucifixion; Virgin; St John) contemporary with the church. – Chancel (saints) and Lady Chapel (two windows), 1952, by *Guthrie & Wells*; nave (Five Joyful Mysteries and St Anne); W (Assumption, 1952), all pictorial glass of the 1950s.

PENILEE ST ANDREW, Bowfield Crescent. Facing down Bowfield Drive, the main E approach to Penilee, the hexagonal church of 1963–5 by *James Houston & Son*, its façade projecting like a prow. Linked behind, the extensive halls of 1949–50 by *Abercrombie & Maitland*.

ST NICHOLAS, Hartlaw Crescent, Cardonald. By *James Miller*, 1935–6. Long and low on the S slope of the hill. Church and hall of brown brick with no historicist details.

NAZARETH HOUSE, Paisley Road West. Built in 1906 as a home for the aged poor and destitute children in the grounds of MARYLAND HOUSE, a three-bay two-storey Greek villa with panelled angle pilasters in the style of David Hamilton and a Greek Doric portico. Ugly pebbledashing etc. but inside a cantilevered stone staircase with cast-iron balustrade. Nazareth House itself has a long red sandstone front with gables and dormers in a steep slate roof and castellated staircase towers each end. The repetitive buttresses are the only overtly ecclesiastical feature, apart from the CHAPEL of 1922 at the W end with a wheel window in its gable end.

CARDONALD CEMETERY, Corkerhill Road. 1922. Gates etc. by *Burnet & Boston, c.* 1936.

CRAIGTON CEMETERY, 1578 Paisley Road West. Opened as Govan Burgh Cemetery, 1873. – LODGE, gabled with a Gothic porch. – MONUMENT to Sir William Pearce † 1888, who is buried at Gillingham, Kent; by *Honeyman & Keppie,* 1891. Bronzes by *Alfred Toft.* A domed cenotaph ringed by Corinthian columns and pilasters in Creetown granite with bronze capitals. Above them, four bronze boys (Labour, Design, Engineering, Navigation). In a niche facing the entrance a bust of Pearce and, below, plaques depicting shipbuilding and engineering. The finial is a ship in full sail.

PUBLIC BUILDINGS

CARDONALD LIBRARY, Mosspark Drive. By *Rogerson & Spence,* 1968–70. An exposed concrete frame clad with alternate panels of grey granite and glass. Brick interior, with a wooden gallery in a more rustic idiom. Almost identical to Ibrox Library, Govan (*q.v.*).

CARDONALD COLLEGE OF FURTHER EDUCATION, Mosspark Drive. 1968–72, by *Alison & Hutchison.* Predominant is the curtain-walled slab with a glass entrance hall tucked between the stilt-like *pilotis.*

CRAIGTON PRIMARY SCHOOL, Morven Street. A Board school of 1901 by *Watson & Salmond.*

HOWFORD SCHOOL FOR THE HANDICAPPED, 487 Crookston Road. 1961–3, by *Gillespie Kidd & Coia,* whose characteristics of that time can easily be spotted. Flat-roofed blocks lit from clearstories and from windows punched randomly low down. Split-pitched roofs over the circulation areas and bold entrance canopies flying above roof level.

LOURDES SECONDARY SCHOOL, Kirriemuir Avenue. 1951–7, by *T. S. Cordiner.* Linked brick blocks with shallow pitched roofs and a number of porthole windows.

SANDWOOD PRIMARY SCHOOL, 120 Sandwood Road. 1955–9, by *T. S. Cordiner.* A friendly-looking assemblage in brown brick, with a shallow curved roof over the main block, snapped headers, a pattern of glazing bars and other popular mannerisms of the time.

ROSS HALL HOSPITAL, 197 Crookston Road, occupies a large Baronial mansion of red sandstone built for the Cowans of

Hawkhead in 1877. Partly obscured from the road by a sleek aluminium-clad ward block of 1983–4 by *Spence & Webster*, linked by a neat space-frame canopy. The gabled main front overlooks a well-preserved Victorian garden and small lake laid out *c.* 1900 by *Pullman & Son*, extended and altered in 1908. The main rooms are in a subdued Jacobethan style. In the centre of the house, a full-height heavily panelled hall lit from a glass barrel-vault and with arches opening to the first-floor galleried landing. On the staircase, two STAINED-GLASS windows, the lower one with three seated maidens representing the Arts by *W. & J.J. Kier*, 1886, the upper one in different style and unsigned. Floral motifs and three medallions of historical figures. – To the N, the matching LODGE at the entrance to the rest of the grounds, now a public park.

CROOKSTON STATION. 1885. One of the original stations on the line built by the Glasgow and South Western Railway on the course of the derelict Glasgow to Johnstone Canal. Stone, single-storey, with an arcaded and timber screen to the offices. Lattice girder footbridge by *Arrol Bros.*, Germiston Iron-works.

DESCRIPTIONS

Craigton and Mosspark

Bordering the W edge of Bellahouston Park (*q.v.*), two of the Corporation's first housing schemes.

CRAIGTON (1921–3), like Riddrie (*see* Carntyne and Robroyston: Descriptions), is a mixed scheme of tenements in short detached blocks, mainly along PAISLEY ROAD WEST and N of it, and of flatted cottages in BELLAHOUSTON DRIVE and the streets behind it. Tenements and cottages are of red brick with plain rock-faced red sandstone fronts.

MOSSPARK lies S of Craigton and is completely different in character. It was the Corporation's first scheme laid out on garden-suburb principles entirely with cottages and flatted cottages intended for slightly more affluent tenants. The layout of narrow tree-lined roads encircling the steep hill was approved in 1922. The first houses, designed in 1920 by *Robert Horn* (Chief Architect to *Peter Fyfe*, Director of Housing), were let in 1923. There are nine different house types, mainly three-apartment flats (four in each block) and four- to five-apartment cottages, semi-detached and in terraces of four or six. Some of the houses, e.g. in Ashkirk Drive and Mosspark Boulevard, have terrazzo fronts (since painted): most are rendered with brick quoins, doorways and patterns of headers. The variety of Arts and Crafts details (small paned windows, bracketed doorhoods and so on) is familiar from the earliest English garden suburbs and cities. Most appear identically at Knightswood, the second such estate (*q.v.*). Here they are now endangered by the insidious insertion of lattice windows and pseudo-Georgian doors. Ten additional types, predominantly five-apartment and constructed more economically of concrete blocks, were added to the repertoire in 1923. Altogether 1,510 houses were built, 1,000 of them cottages. All have, in different combinations, at least a living room and interconnected scullery, a bathroom and independent bedrooms.

On the E edge, in ARRAN DRIVE, the sweet, slightly *chinois* pavilion was built in 1926 as the Union Bank by *Geo. Arthur*. Next to it, the simple LIBRARY of 1949 and, set back further s, the single-storey TENNIS CLUB PAVILION, converted into a house. Round the corner, in TANNA DRIVE, a row of pebbledashed, tile-hung and pantiled Royal Artillery War Memorial cottages, strung together artfully in a picturesque composition of 1948–51 by *C. C. Powell* for the British Legion Haig Homes. Near the top of the hill, in ASHKIRK DRIVE, is Mosspark Parish Church (*see* Churches, above).

Cardonald, South Cardonald, Penilee, Crookston

Along PAISLEY ROAD WEST, w of the Craigton scheme, is the entrance to Craigton Cemetery (*see* above). Along the E edge, a few terraces of one-and-a-half-storey C19 stone cottages. The gable end of one of them, No. 10 CROSSLEE STREET, abutting the monumental mason's yard by the cemetery gate, is decorated with classical and Gothic patterns of seashells. Further w, along the main road, C19 fragments of the old hamlet of HALFWAY, including the POLICE STATION of *c.* 1900 by *C. Davidson* of Paisley. Opposite, a serious-looking former cinema (now the FLAMINGO) of 1933–4 by *Bryden, Robertson and Boyd*.

High up along the ridge crowned by the cemetery, MOSS HEIGHTS, 1950–4, commands a panoramic view over Pollok Park. It is one of the two prototype high-rise projects developed by *Ronald Bradbury* (Director of Housing) in 1946 (cf. Crathie Drive, Partick). Three long ten-storey concrete-framed slabs follow the contours of the slope, reflecting the post-war interest in the Picturesque. The cream panel cladding of 1987–8 has destroyed the cheerful character of the façades, which were enlivened in 1950s taste with concave-curved balcony fronts and clad in pre-cast concrete panels with red whinstone (plinth) and ochre pebble finish. Round the sliding main doors was blue tiling. The backs are sheer and rendered and have towers with staircases and emergency access balconies, linked at the fourth and eighth floors by decks. Below, to the w, two four-storey blocks with flat roofs and individual metal-railed balconies, similar to those built at Pollok.

Opposite, on the s side of Paisley Road West, the large grounds of Nazareth House, and, E and w of it, the associated church and school (Our Lady of Lourdes and Lourdes Secondary: *see* above). Beyond them, along the main road and just N and s of it, the sprinkling of early C20 villas that form the core of Cardonald, and its parish church (*see* above). In LAMINGTON ROAD, TRAQUAIR DRIVE and TWEEDSMUIR ROAD, N of the main road, a concentration of red sandstone villas of *c*. 1905–6 and, near the top of the ridge, a slightly earlier terrace of Italianate houses in HILLINGTON PARK CIRCUS. It is terminated by tenements in similar style (N) and by a pair of villas in WEDDERLEA DRIVE (Nos. 106–8). On the s side of Paisley Road West, starting with No. 1979, a small development (originally known as THISTLE PARK) by the *Scotstoun Estate Building Co.* (1906) of their distinctive one-and-a-half-to two-storey cottage terraces (cf. Scotstoun). Here the w terraces (also in SELKIRK AVENUE) are of red sandstone: the E ones (also in FIFE AVENUE and WALKERBURN ROAD) are cream with half-timbered gables.

But it is the pebbledashed fringes of the two large public housing schemes that predominate along this route. On the s side, the big 1930s *Mactaggart & Mickel* scheme of SOUTH CAR-DONALD, acres of four-in-a-block cottage flats with a southern English flavour in the tile-hung bays and slated gambrel roofs. On the E edge of the scheme, in TARFSIDE OVAL, a group of four twenty-four-storey L-shaped slabs with glass balconies (cf. Ibroxholm; *see* Govan: Perambulation 2), surrounded by the usual walk-up tenements: 1966–9, by *A. G. Jury* (City Architect).

On the N side, spread across from Berryknowes Road to Hillington Road South, is a corresponding 1930s Corporation scheme (CARDONALD), with the types of flatted cottages familiar from the later phases of Knightswood. It is punctuated only by the tower blocks in QUEENSLAND DRIVE (1966–9, by *Geo. Wimpey*) and in SWINTON DRIVE (1968–72, by *A. G. Jury*). Stepping down the steep slope far to the NW, between HARTLAW CRESCENT and Chirnside Road, a row of six deck-access blocks divided by wedges of landscaping (1966–9, by *A. G. Jury*).

PENILEE lies w of Sandwood Road. This wartime scheme (1939–47) of about 2,000 homes was designed by the Corporation's Chief Housing Architect, *J. H. Ferrie*, to accommodate war workers from the adjacent and contemporary Hillington Industrial Estate (over the city boundary in Renfrewshire). Here is some of the most advanced wartime housing in Britain. Because of the restriction on timber, the houses were experimentally constructed. External walls were at first built of brick, then, like the internal walls, of foamed-slag blocks. Eight different types of concrete roof and floor slab were supplied by specialist firms. Details were cast *in situ* (e.g. the tenements' lattice balconies) or pre-cast at the Corporation's own works (stairs, lintels etc.). In contrast to the cosy naturalness of Mosspark, the layout here is strongly geometrical, on a completely flat barren 85·4 ha (211 acres). It centres on a stadium-shaped park edged by school and church (Penilee St Andrew: *see* Churches, above). The terraced cottages, cottage flats and tenements also have a strong International Modern flavour, with flat roofs, horizontal, porthole and glass brick windows; *pilotis* in the recessed porches and some ship-deck balcony

A

B

Penilee
A perspective of three-storey tenement block
B perspective of two-storey cottage block
(Reproduced from S. Gale, *Modern Housing Estates*, 1949)

rails. The colours were far removed from the white mistakenly
ascribed to the modern movement: white, light and dark brown
for walls, cream for window surrounds and balconies, pale
blue and white for windows and primary colours for doors.
Even internal doors were in pastel colours. Many blocks have,
alas, been made stylistically, and literally, cosier with pitched
roofs, timber windows and pastel colours. A row of stubby
towers off SANDWOOD ROAD (1967–70, by *A. G. Jury*, the
City Architect) marks the southern perimeter of the site.

CROOKSTON has little to offer apart from its station, Ross Hall
(*see* above) and the semi-rural setting of its mostly post-war
spec. housing. The remains of the medieval Castle lie further
s in Pollok (*q.v.*).

POLLOK

The first of Glasgow's four huge peripheral estates, Pollok set the low-density pattern for all the others (Castlemilk, Drumchapel, Easterhouse). The model was the garden suburb, as stipulated by Sir John Stirling Maxwell, who sold this part of his Pollok estates to the Council in 1935. Advised by *Patrick Abercrombie*, he imposed a scheme of cottage houses and flats at twelve houses per acre, with unfenced gardens and open spaces, and dual-carriageway main roads defining neighbourhoods.

In the first parts of the scheme (1937–9 and 1942–5), round the old mining villages of Nitshill and Househillmuir and on the E edge of Pollok (*see*, e.g., the s end of BRAIDCRAFT ROAD), cottages of the latest, most simplified Knightswood type were built. Some of the cottages were of the experimental foamed-slag type used at Penilee (e.g. along PEAT ROAD at Old Nitshill); like the Penilee cottages, they have been given pitched roofs. By 1945, 744 houses of the 5,200 originally envisaged had been built.

These designs were replaced after 1945 by new schemes for flat-fronted rendered and brick cottages with metal windows and doorhoods on twin metal poles. These are ubiquitous in the areas built up before 1951, when cottages were almost completely phased out. New varieties of two-, three- and four-storey tenement blocks were also invented. The style, with rendered brick or concrete block walls, flat roofs and shared-access balconies with brick or sheet steel or mesh fronts and porthole windows, quite obviously reflects International Modern taste; so did the colours (light brown for the render, turquoise for the balconies, and signal red for all metal posts).

POLLOK, N of Barrhead Road, except for Househillwood, has a garden-suburb air despite neglect and decay. The Levern Water winds through the scheme, flanked by wide grassy banks. The cottages, with their mature gardens, cover the knolls, four-storey flats line the dual carriageways and other main roads, e.g. along BROCKBURN ROAD and NETHERPLACE ROAD (1947–9). Two-storey ones in LEVERNSIDE CRESCENT. In CALFHILL ROAD, CALFHILL COURT, by *A. G. Jury* (City Architect), 1952, the later of Pollok's two single women's hostels, in a softer style with pitched roofs, coloured roughcast and wrought-iron balconies. There is a focal point at the central roundabout below the harsh ruins of Crookston Castle, where the flat-roofed blocks of the earlier hostel for single women (1947) step down the hill, and the similar CROOKSTON CASTLE SCHOOL steps up toward the castle.

CROOKSTON CASTLE can be reached from the w through its ringwork defence, which dates from the late C12, when Sir Robert Croc of Neilston held the manorial lands. The enclosure is roughly oval, within a broad ditch accompanied by a counterscarp bank. There was most likely a timber palisade rather than a stone wall, and the original buildings were also probably of timber. The stone remains are of an early C15 tower house, partially taken down in the late C15 and deserted by the late C16. It had a particularly unusual plan; a central rectangular block, with barrel-vaulted cellar, hall and solar one above the other, and four angle towers with smaller rooms, of which only the NE and SE towers survive.

S of Barrhead Road, the scheme (here generally known as NITS-HILL) lacks coherence and is considerably bleaker. The spine of 1930s and 1940s cottage flats through Househillwood and Old Nitshill spreads out E and W into Muirshiel and Craigbank with post-war versions. Along the S edge, a chaos of tenement blocks, both the standard 1940s type (e.g. round Newfield Square) and later ones with pitched roofs; tenements made unsightly by added roofs; and insignificant houses dumped down to replace demolished flats.

Off BARRHEAD ROAD, E of Peat Road, the TOWNSHIP CENTRE. As in all the other peripheral schemes, it arrived almost too late and under private initiative. It took the place of pre-war cottages in Househillwood. The blank red brick SHOPPING CENTRE (1977–9, by *Ian Burke & Associates*), in its dreary setting, does nothing to give visual heart to the scheme. Alongside, the slightly more cheerful LEISURE POOL (1984–6, by the *City Architect's Department*), with its pyramidal glass roof and colourful cross-braced walls. E of it, at the corner of Boydestone Road, the huge NATIONAL SAVINGS BANK HEADQUARTERS completed in 1970 by the *Ministry of Building and Public Works*. All of concrete, including a mural by *K. Dobson* on the theme of banking. Off Barrhead Road, at the W edge of the scheme, EAST HURLET HOUSE, said to be of 1763. Very plain. Two storeys and three bays, with one-and-a-half-storey wings. Harled, with stone margins round the windows.

CHURCHES

PRIESTHILL PARISH CHURCH, Freeland Drive. An octagonal brick pill-box of 1971–3 by *A. Buchanan Campbell*, now half-smothered in roofing felt. Attached to the former hall church of 1952.

ST BERNARD (R.C.), Wiltonburn Road. By *T. S. Cordiner*, 1961–4.

ST CHRISTOPHER, Meikle Road. By *A. Buchanan Campbell*, 1961–2. The open concrete frame of the bell tower draws attention to this simple brick church with a subdued butterfly roof and a pattern of mullions and transoms in the glazed side walls of the sanctuary. It is attached to the former hall church of 1940 by *Abercrombie & Maitland*.

ST CONVAL (R.C.), 21 Hapland Road. By *Alexander McAnally*, 1953–6. Simple and of red brick, with an Italianate triple entrance, a thin bell tower and a lower balancing buttress rising above the gable.

ST JAMES CROOKSTON (R.C.), Crosstobs Road. By *Alex-*

ander McAnally, 1965–8. A tentative move towards centralized planning in this odd-shaped church, with its conventional nave and chancel and big semicircular side chapels. Outside of pink Accrington brick, except for the gabled stone façade; inside of cream brick with a cedar ceiling and a lavish use of coloured marbles and wrought-iron, the latter by *Thomas Bogie & Sons* of Edinburgh.

St James Pollok, 165 Meiklerig Crescent, looks particularly large and solid compared with its flimsy domestic neighbours. It was built in 1893–5 as Pollokshields Titwood Church (*H. E. Clifford*'s first church), and was moved here from the corner of Glencairn Drive and Leslie Road by *James Taylor Thomson, McCrea & Sanders* in 1951–3. Perp and cruciform. The nave lies parallel with the road. No tower (the SE porch was to have been the base of tower and spire in the original design). Big Perp clearstorey windows over windowless passage aisles opening into the nave with low broad arches. Galleries at the end of the nave and set behind the two tall arches into the W transept.

St Robert Bellarmine (R.C.), 310 Peat Road. By *Pugin & Pugin*, 1955–9. Fairly large, with low aisles but towerless; in pink brick with stone Dec tracery. – STAINED GLASS. E and W windows by *John Hardman Studios*, 1958. Contemporary PRESBYTERY.

PUBLIC BUILDINGS

Police Station, Brockburn Road. The flat-roofed red brick original was built in the 1950s. By *J. C. McDougall* (Strathclyde Regional Architect), friendly extension of the late 1980s: a neat plum brick pavilion with a mirror-glass clearstorey and recessed entrance bay, the latter spanned by a clever eye of wrought-iron. Opposite, the more conventional FIRE STATION (1959–62, by Glasgow Corporation's *Department of Architecture and Planning*).

Pollok Library, 100 Peat Road. Probably of the early 1960s. Low and brick-built, with a paraboloid roof.

Leverndale Hospital, 510 Crookston Road. The Hawkhead Asylum of 1890–5 by *Malcolm Stark Junior*, with extensive additions of 1903–5 by *H. & D. Barclay*. At the top of the hill, the main building, with its ogee- and pyramid-capped towers, massive bay windows, and tall pencil-slim water tower which can be seen for miles around. Spreading like fingers from this, lower S pavilions in the same style and much later N ones in brick and render. Lower down the slope towards the gates, another large group with a long Elizabethan-style façade screening lower pavilions. Just to the E, what is now the PSYCHO-GERIATRIC DEPARTMENT, its rendered wings of 1965 and CLASP wards of the 1970s very unrewarding. By the gate, the NURSES' HOME, inter-war neo-Georgian of the meanest kind, and incongruously cosy staff accommodation, *c.* 1970.

CROOKSTON HOME, 837 Crookston Road. A former Renfrewshire Combination Hospital converted to a Home for the Aged
Poor in 1934–6 by *W. Barrie* of the Glasgow Public Assistance
Department. Enclosed verandas and open concrete balconies
give the old hospital blocks a Modern Movement veneer. At
the back, streets and grassed courts of individual houses, two-
storey with open-access balconies and a variety of details,
like Art Deco brickwork on the little angular corner cottages,
semicircular brick entrance porches, and covered walkways.

DARNLEY, ARDEN AND CARNWADRIC

CARNWADRIC CHURCH, 556 Boydestone Road. By *William
Nimmo & Partners*; dedicated 1952.
DARNLEY UNITED REFORM CHURCH, Glen Moriston
Road. By *Hamilton Associates*; opened 1981. Small, neat and
white-rendered, with a series of monopitches.
ST LOUISE (R.C.), Nitshill Road, Arden. 1983, by *Nicholson
& Jacobsen*.
DARNLEY HOSPITAL, Nitshill Road. Late C19. Central block
of yellow sandstone, with a shaped central gable and Flemish
Baroque details, in front of simple pavilions.
KENNISHEAD STATION, Kennishead Avenue. Built *c.*1848
for the Glasgow, Barrhead & Neilston Railway. Stone building
with a house on the up-platform.
DESCRIPTIONS. DARNLEY is grimly impressive. It was
designed by Glasgow Corporation's *Department of Architecture and Planning*, begun *c.*1970 and completed *c.*1975.
Six- to eight-storey linked deck-access blocks snake along the
contours of the wide open site dictated by the Brock Burn.
They have castellated silhouettes, much exposed concrete and
bands of coloured render. To the S of Nitshill Road in CORSE-
LET ROAD, DARNLEY MILL FARM incorporates one C18
cottage with crowstep gables and a fat round tower with tall
conical cap.
ARDEN, an earlier S.S.H.A. scheme, looks quite friendly. The
pitched-roofed tenement blocks are similar to the Corporation
type of the 1950s, but the S.S.H.A.'s careful landscaping and
maintenance make all the difference.
CARNWADRIC. Amongst the 1920s Corporation cottage flats
(accompanied by a typical red brick school of the mid-1930s
in Capelrig Street), one attractive Arts and Crafts-style terrace
in CARNWADRIC ROAD (Nos. 18–32) which really belongs
to Thornliebank just over the city boundary. To the NW, a
row of five high-rise blocks (in KENNISHEAD AVENUE)
punctuates the skyline: part of a mixed development of 1965–
70 by *Parry & Hughes*.

POLLOK PARK

Pollok House and Park were given by the Maxwell family to the City of Glasgow in 1966. The house (with its famous collection of paintings) and the 146 ha (361 acres) of parkland (in which a new home for the Burrell Collection was completed in 1983) are open to the public.

POLLOK HOUSE

Although the present house dates only from the late 1740s, the Maxwell family, who built it, was established at Pollok by the mid-C13. Their first fortified dwelling is said to have been sited by the White Cart river. The second stood higher up and was inhabited until the mid-C16; a large beech, E of the house, marks its site. The Maxwells' next seat, the Laigh or Low Castle, was built in the late C14 where the stable court now stands: the wall of the adjacent garden incorporates remains of one of its towers (*see* below). On the W bank of the river, connected to the castle by a ford, lay the dependent settlement of Pollock Town, which was obliterated when the grounds were improved in the late C18.

The idea of a new house on a new site took shape in 1737, when Sir John Maxwell (second Baronet) apparently consulted *William Adam*. However, building did not start until 1747, a few months before Adam died, and was not finished until 1752, probably by the cultivated third Baronet. There is no evidence that the house was built to the 1737 designs, although Sir John Stirling Maxwell (tenth Baronet), who enlarged the house between 1890 and c. 1908, gradually convinced himself that William Adam had been the designer. His own architects, *Sir Robert Rowand Anderson* and (for at least the later work) his partner *A. F. Balfour Paul*, evolved their designs in increasing sympathy with Adam's style.

Sizeable extensions were needed not only for domestic convenience but also to house the library and large collection of paintings acquired by Sir John's father in the 1840s and 1850s (half of which are still on display at Pollok). The C18 core is a puzzle, and the lack of documents hampers its solution. Some alterations were made c. 1778 and more in the mid-C19. It is also unclear exactly what may have been done when the new entrance hall was added in the 1890s. Certainly the plan with its two axial corridors and evenly sized rooms is strangely symmetrical for such a modest house. It must be remembered that Sir John became an architectural connoisseur (in 1937 he published *The Shrines and Homes of Scotland*) and that his architects were, as the S front shows, masters of historical pastiche, often based directly on existing examples.

EXTERIOR. The C18 house is of the tall, compact and austere type evolved during the late C17 and early C18 by Sir William Bruce and James Smith. It is of seven by three bays and has three storeys above a tall basement, the top storey tucked under the elegantly upswept eaves of the shallow hipped roof. The walls are of ashlar, with prominent rusticated quoins and a plain bandcourse which emphasizes the first floor. On the ENTRANCE FRONT (N) the three centre bays are slightly broken forward under a pediment (the shield is C 19). More restrained outside than within, the single-storey porch projection, added by *Robert Rowand Anderson* in 1890, with the C 18 pedimented doorcase re-used for the new entrance. Sir John's extensions to E and W are displayed more prominently on the garden front.

The GARDEN FRONT (S) is more distinctive. It is flat and unemphatic except for the slightly uneven window rhythm, which allows space for pairs of carved festoons to flank the first- and second-floor windows. On the ground floor, a 'Venetian' garden door, enriched with Gibbs rustication, and a handsome sweep of steps with wrought-iron balustrades. The wings were conceived in their final restrained form *c.* 1904. Hipped-roofed pavilions, with Venetian windows imitating the garden door and carved festoons, are held slightly away from the main house by narrow balustraded links in a classical composition that would have met with William Adam's approval.

INTERIOR. From the restrained N front, we step into an ENTRANCE HALL of such size and opulence that it raises expectations of grandeur in the rest of the house. Begun in 1890, before Sir John's architectural taste was fully formed, it smacks more of the contemporary preference for the Baroque rather than of the C 18. Steps lead down in the centre to three arches screening the basement and up either side to the HALL of the original house. This is restrained by comparison, although it has, at the junction with the E–W spine corridor, a fine quartet of Ionic columns with loosely rolled, fleshy volutes. To the r., the staircase, on an oval plan, has a handsome swept handrail and balusters that seem somewhat slender and refined for *c.* 1750. One fireplace looks C 18 (*in situ?*), the other, of reeded marble, early C 19. The S part of the hall may have been partitioned off originally to form a garden hall.

The two E rooms have almost no decoration. The MORNING ROOM (NE), with a plain C 19 fireplace, was first a parlour and then, from *c.* 1830 to 1908, the library. The DRAWING ROOM in 1902 had, according to drawings made by the National Art Survey of Scotland, an overmantel with a surround almost identical to that in the dining room. The ceiling plasterwork was created from squeezes of the dining-room ceiling after a fire in the drawing room *c.* 1910. (An earlier ceiling, painted pale green and with a coved edge and gilt fillet, has been discovered above it.) The crimson of the walls (like the deep green in the dining room) was chosen by Sir John Stirling Maxwell to set off his paintings. In the LIBRARY, the screens of Ionic columns originally had basket arches, more in William Adam's manner (cf. e.g. The Drum, Gilmerton, Edinburgh). The plasterwork and fireplaces (with overmantels designed to

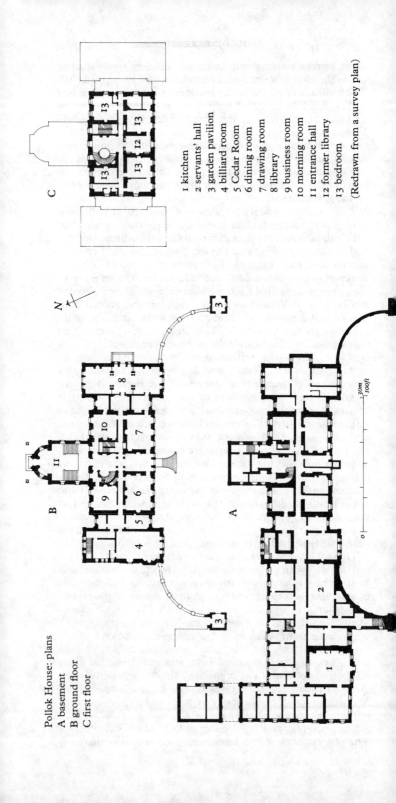

Pollok House: plans
A basement
B ground floor
C first floor

1 kitchen
2 servants' hall
3 garden pavilion
4 billiard room
5 Cedar Room
6 dining room
7 drawing room
8 library
9 business room
10 morning room
11 entrance hall
12 former library
13 bedroom

(Redrawn from a survey plan)

accommodate El Greco's *Lady in a Fur Wrap*), although less robust, harmonize with those in the rest of the house.

The DINING ROOM, with its handsome plasterwork, is the most elaborate of the C18 rooms. The rococo motifs are boldly and somewhat flatly handled, the pendant bouquets round the alcove rather stiff; but the shell swags flanking the buffet and the hunting equipment trophy in the overmantel are exquis- 16 itely detailed. Very similar plasterwork in the BUSINESS ROOM. Especially pretty is the basket of flowers raised on trelliswork over the pier glass. The CEDAR ROOM, in the link, was converted from a servery to a panelled smoking room in 1929. It adjoins the BILLIARD ROOM, smaller and plainer than the library and with a coved ceiling.

On the FIRST FLOOR, the small room in the centre of the S front was the LIBRARY in the C18 (upstairs libraries were common in Scottish houses of the period). The original bookcases are now display cabinets. The SE BEDROOM had a very rococo gilt overmantel mirror (removed). In the NW BEDROOM, the arch of a bed alcove (partitioned off in the C19) can still be seen.

The layout of the BASEMENT service rooms, with the huge W extension, was finalized as early as 1900. Their brown and cream paint, tessellated floors and fittings in the kitchen (now tearoom) are typical of the date.

The GARDENS and GROUNDS are largely the creation of Sir John Stirling Maxwell, who began his improvements by planting the lime avenue leading to the N front to commemorate his twenty-first birthday (1888). From then, he steadily transformed the park with tree and rhododendron planting. Immediately E and S of the house are the parterres he designed in the C17 manner; the lower lawn was originally laid out similarly. Setting off the S front, formal terracing and twin pavilions designed in 1901. The LIONS here are by *Hew Lorimer*, 1940s. – BRIDGE across the Cart, 1757–8. One single shallow span, stone balustrades. – STABLES, to the SE. An C18 quadrangle incorporating earlier fragments, including a C17 surround to the main arch and, as part of the adjacent garden wall, a fragment of a tower added to the C14 Laigh Castle in *c.* 1536. Stable roof raised and fenestration altered *c.* 1867. – SAWMILL, SW of the stables. Brick, single-storey, probably mid-C19. The mill is driven by a Holyoake turbine (1888) in place of the original low-breast waterwheel. Adjacent, the disused POWER STATION with Waverley turbine (Ritchie's patent) made by *Carrick & Ritchie* of Edinburgh. – DOVECOT on the W bank of the Cart river. C17, square, roofless. – NE LODGE, 97 Haggs Road. 1892, by *R. R. Anderson*. Scottish C18 style, with broad semi-circular bay. Inscribed 'I am ready: gang forward'. Gatepiers with rampant lions. – LODGE, 300 Barrhead Road. Simple C18-style lodge. Late C18 rusticated gatepiers.

BURRELL COLLECTION

Won in competition by *Barry Gasson & John Meunier* with *Brit Andreson*, 1972; realized by *Barry Gasson Architects* and opened in 1983. The celebrated collection of works of art was bequeathed to Glasgow Corporation by Sir William Burrell in 1944. Fearing the damaging effects of Glasgow's air, he specified that it was to be housed at least sixteen miles from the centre of the city. Cleaner air meant that a parkland setting within the city boundary could finally be chosen: a gently sloping field with a mature wood to the N. The architects have placed their building right up against the wood and left most of the field untouched. It is a low and rather wandering building, largely of glass, stainless steel and smooth pink stone from Dumfries-shire.

A plain stone gable, into which has been set the remains of a C14 arch from Hornby Castle, Yorkshire, clearly marks the entrance. Once inside, the long axis of the entrance hall is centred upon another and grander gateway from Hornby, in three stages, with a lavish heraldic display above the arch. Burrell acquired these, and the other examples of architectural stonework built into the galleries at various points, from the legendary Randolph Hearst. At the far end of the entrance hall
118   to the r. is a brightly lit covered courtyard, with the Warwick Vase given pride of place in its centre. Arranged on three sides of this courtyard are the re-created rooms using the architectural features and fittings that had been introduced by Burrell into Hutton Castle (C15 and C16), his home near Berwick-on-Tweed. They are (from l. to r.) the drawing room, hall and dining room, all looking rather lifeless.

Beyond the Hornby Castle gateway, the gallery proper starts. It is light and airy, with a long glass wall right up against the trees on the l. The columns are of smooth grey concrete, the roof of knotty timber, the glass cases butt-jointed. All sufficiently restrained to avoid overwhelming the works of art. Under the mezzanine to the r., dimly lit enclosed spaces for the display of textiles and drawings. Beyond these, a long glass wall, facing S, with display panels and roundels of stained glass. To the SE, reached by a flight of stone stairs, is the restaurant, double-height and with the atmosphere of a conservatory.

BRONZE AGE MOUND. In trees to the left of the eighth fairway of Pollok Golf Course; one of the few surviving prehistoric monuments in Glasgow. The mound is about 15 m in diameter and 2.5 m high; when it was dug into in 1863 an inverted cinerary urn, covering a cremation, was discovered. An amber bead was found nearby; these finds are now lost.

EARTHWORK to the NE of the pond in the North Wood. Possibly of early medieval date, 30 m in diameter, entrance causeway on E; excavations in 1959–60 revealed a circular house, shale discs and part of a rotary quern.

CROSSINGS OF THE CLYDE
AND KELVIN

BY TED RUDDOCK

Crossing the Clyde has been important throughout the history of Glasgow. In Roman times there was a regular ford near the site of the present Victoria Bridge, and the ford was probably responsible for the early growth of the town in the area round Trongate and Glasgow Cross. A wooden bridge was erected before A.D. 1285 and a stone bridge probably *c.* 1400. In the C 18 this bridge proved quite inadequate for the traffic; by the middle of the century heavy horse-drawn vehicles had to cross by fords which were maintained beside the bridge on both the upstream and downstream sides.

Glasgow's subsequent development, like that of most large seaports, has required continual deepening and extension of the river and docks at the same time as industry required more and better vehicular crossings – two types of development which are always in conflict. The geology of the area is a critical factor in the design of both river crossings and port facilities, and knowledge of the geology of Glasgow and the Clyde channel has grown step by step with the construction of bridges, quays and docks.

Upstream from Cambuslang the bed of the Clyde is generally formed at the level of the rock. From Cambuslang to the western limits of the city, its channel is cut in beds of alluvium; most of them were formed before the Ice Age but in some places they are covered or interspersed with boulder clay of glacial origin. The rounded hills on which much of the middle of the city is built are 'drumlins' formed of boulder clay but mostly with a core of rock, and the course of the River Kelvin has been cut through Carboniferous rocks right down to Yorkhill, a very short distance from the Clyde. Here for a considerable distance the Clyde flows in alluvium which is 18–30 m (60–100 ft) deep but very near the buried rock scarp which forms the northern boundary of the alluvium. Bridge-builders have therefore had great difficulty in making foundations sufficient to support their structures on the Clyde, while there was no such problem in bridging the Kelvin. Moreover, several of the bridge-builders' best efforts were rendered ineffective after a few decades by the harbour authority's success in deepening the Clyde and so undermining the bridge foundations.

In 1755 the city fathers commissioned their first report on the condition of the harbour and the need for better river crossings. In 1760 the material of the river-bed was described by *John Smeaton*, after making borings at seven different possible bridge sites between Glasgow Green and the Broomielaw, as everywhere 'mud or sleech' (the latter is a term still used in Belfast to describe exceptionally unstable foundation strata). The first new bridge, built at the Broomielaw in 1768–72, was founded on wooden piles but needed the protection of a weir until it was replaced in the 1830s by a bridge with deeper foundations. Victoria Bridge (1851–4) was possibly the last, and is now the only remaining, bridge founded on wooden piles and platforms. By the advent of the first railway crossings, techniques for sinking foundations to much greater depths were available. The large-diameter cast iron cylinders of 1859–61 which are still to be seen at Dalmarnock were presumably sunk by excavating the material from inside them. This method was certainly used for the cast iron cylinders of Albert Bridge (1870–1) and of the Caledonian Railway's approach to Central Station (1876–8), where the cylinders reached rock at 26 m (85 ft) below high-water level. Most of the later Clyde bridges, possibly beginning with Glasgow Bridge (1895–9), have been founded by sinking 'pneumatic' caissons of steel either to rock or to firm layers within the alluvium, the caissons being filled with compressed air to allow manual excavation of the ground within, a technique used for similar depths in construction of the St Louis Bridge in the United States (1869–70) and previously used only at modest depths in Britain.

In 1768, at the same time as the construction started of the first Broomielaw Bridge, the process of deepening the river, essentially by narrowing the channel, was begun. The technique was surprisingly successful, as was the use of a fleet of dredgers to continue the process in the c 19. Agreement about the target depths of dredging had to be negotiated on various occasions between the Clyde Navigation Trust and the Glasgow Bridge Trustees, together with the various railway companies; several bridges were threatened and Hutcheson Bridge lost in 1868 as inevitable results of the harbour development. Between 1755 and 1925 the depth of water in the channel between Glasgow Bridge and Dumbuck Ford, a mile or so E of Dumbarton, was everywhere increased by a minimum of 6 m (20 ft).

Both the Bridge Trustees and the railway companies were sometimes forced to adapt the form and dimensions of their bridges to the wishes of the Navigation Trust. This is evident especially in the matching alignment of piers and heights of navigation clearance of four bridges built within a short distance downstream from Glasgow Bridge. The Trust's interests were still a critical factor in the design of Kingston Bridge in the 1960s.

The art of construction has been well represented in the super-structures of Glasgow bridges. The c 15 Stockwell Bridge was of the type built near the mouths of Scottish rivers, mostly under the patronage of bishops, and of which the Brig' of Ayr, Aberdeen's Bridge of Dee and Guard Bridge in Fife are surviving examples. The new generation of stone-arch bridges which began with Westminster Bridge in London in 1736–50 was represented by the first Broomielaw (now called Glasgow) Bridge (1768–72) by *William Mylne* and Rutherglen Bridge (1775–6), probably by

James Watt, both since replaced. The oldest stone bridge now standing on the Clyde is Victoria Bridge, which replaced Stockwell Bridge in 1851–4; the first two wrought iron bridges, South Portland Street and St Andrew's suspension footbridges were contemporary with it. Cast iron arches were considered by John Rennie in 1815 and the old Stockwell Bridge was widened with them in 1820, but there have not been any other cast iron arches over the Clyde. Albert Bridge (1870–1) has wrought iron arches covered on the elevations by massive cast iron decorative spandrel panels, and this type of façade was favoured again for three bridges over the Kelvin. In two of these three, Partick Bridge (1876–8) and Great Western Bridge (1891), the arch ribs are of cast iron, but the third and smallest, the Gibson Street to Eldon Street Bridge (1895), has steel spandrel-arch ribs behind its cast iron façades. The decorated façades show Glasgow's pretensions to civic dignity, and perhaps its wealth, in the late Victorian years; so does the general use of granite (and for balustrades and similar features polished granite), the most expensive as well as most enduring of the common building stones. With similar pride the city demanded of the railway companies that they use good materials and aesthetic enrichments in their viaducts built across the Clyde. Masonry piers and towers were emphasized because steel girders, such as those used in the Central Station bridges, were considered ugly, and steel arches, as used in City Union Railway Bridge and the second Dalmarnock railway bridge, little better.

The latest of the structural materials is concrete. Many tons of it were used as filling in the cylinder and caisson foundations of c 19 and early c 20 bridges, but reinforced concrete was not used for superstructures until the 1920s. Even then it was usually faced with stone, as in King George V Bridge and Queen Margaret Bridge. Concrete, like steel, was, until the late 1950s, allowed to appear only in structures conceived as entirely utilitarian.

After concrete became respectable, there were at least two worthy designs: the simple five-span concrete girder footbridge over the Clyde at Polmadie (1955) and another footbridge of 1964 in Kelvingrove Park with a profile derived from the bridges of Robert Maillart. Only a few years in time but an enormous difference in function separate these from the motorway Kingston Bridge by *W. A. Fairhurst & Partners* (1967–70), a concrete structure clad with specially textured pre-cast panels.

The few bridges built to cross rivers in the 1960s, 70s and 80s expose their structural concrete or steel quite freely, as do the much greater number of bridges and viaducts of the main roads and motorways which now weave through the city. Civic dignity is no longer demanded of these structures, and excessive traffic noise makes many of them offensive to any but the car-borne observer. But those who walk on riverside paths can enjoy the comfortable proportions and simple use of materials and texture in some of the recent engineers' designs, and occasionally, as under Kingston Bridge, some exciting vistas.

CLYDE CROSSINGS

Described from downstream to upstream

CLYDE TUNNEL. From Whiteinch on the N bank to Linthouse
on the S. Built 1957–64, but first planned just after the Second
World War, when bridges over the navigable approach to the
city could not be contemplated. Engineer *Sir Wm. Halcrow &
Partners* of London, whose associate architect *E. J. D. Mans-
field* designed the ventilation buildings and the landscaping of
the approaches; contractor *Charles Brand & Son Ltd*. The
planning consultant for the Tunnel and Clydeside Expressway
junction was *William Holford & Associates*. A short tunnel of
two separate tubes, each containing two lanes of road traffic
and, under the road, a cycle track and pedestrian passage; one
tube for northbound travel, one for southbound.

The tunnel is approached down ramps through cuttings and
underpasses, all of grey concrete which is generally dirty, and
entered under the ventilation buildings, fronted by the wide
glazing of the tunnel control rooms. A steep descent (1 in 16)
and immediate change to ascent reflect the narrowness of the
river. Despite the tunnel's shortness, widely varying geological
strata made the construction difficult.

At each end a swirl of approach roads. The best hard landscaping is under the flyover of the Clydeside Expressway
(A814) at Broomhill Drive a little to the E, where pleasant
pedestrian routes run through the junction in several directions.

BELL'S BRIDGE. From the Scottish Exhibition Centre to the
Glasgow Garden Festival site. A footbridge completed in April
1988 for the Scottish Development Agency; engineer *Crouch
& Hogg*; builder *Lilley Construction*; mechanical design and
construction *Barback & Primrose*; consultant architect *Boswell
Mitchell & Johnston*. The deck and steel plate girders which
form both sides of the bridge are gently arched from quay to
quay in a symmetrical curve, supported by a structure which
is original in form and detail. Three spans, the N one supported
simply by the quay wall and a pier in the river, the remaining
two spans balanced about a second pier as a pair of cable-
stayed cantilevers, this whole unit being designed to pivot on
the pier, opening the river for passage of tall vessels. As all the
cables radiate from a point high on a tapered pylon which rises
from the pier at the middle of the bridge's width, they slope
laterally and the plate girders of the whole bridge have a
corresponding inward tilt – a purposeful and interesting form,
to which gaiety is added by the upward extension of the pylon
to a needle point and by a translucent canopy cantilevered out
like many butterfly wings from a line of steel columns and
beams along the middle of the deck. Unfortunately, some
engineering detail is hidden by enclosing the cables in plastic
sheathing and their connexions to the girders in black steel
boxes.

HARBOUR TUNNELS. From Tunnel Street, Finnieston, to Mavisbank Quay. 1890–6, for Glasgow Harbour Tunnel Co.; engineer *Wilson & Simpson*; contractor *Hugh Kennedy & Sons* of Partick. The ends of the tunnels, just W of the line of Finnieston Street, are marked by domed rotundas on both banks of the Clyde, covering the vertical shafts of 24-m (80-ft) diameter which gave access to three parallel 5-m (16-ft) diameter tunnels, two for horse-drawn vehicles (one travelling northwards and one south), the third for pedestrians going both ways. Each rotunda and shaft contained stairs for the pedestrians and six hydraulic vehicle lifts by *Otis Elevator Co.*, with supporting steelwork by *Findlays* of Motherwell. The tunnels were never financially successful and in 1943 the lift machinery was removed as scrap metal for the war effort; but the pedestrian tunnel reopened in 1947 and was used until 1980. It contains a 900-mm (3-ft) diameter water main, installed in 1938, for which access is maintained at the S end. The tunnels were lined with cast iron segments under the river and with brickwork under the quays, the shafts with double-skin cast iron segments filled with concrete.

In 1986–7 the vehicle tunnels were sealed off at each end, the shafts filled with granular material and concrete floors laid at ground level to convert the rotundas to new uses. The steel ribs, timber, slates and glass of the roofs were repaired. Of the circular wall of each rotunda, originally built in twelve equal bays, six bays were vehicle entries framed by cast iron Corinthian columns and a continuous steel lintel; the openings are now glazed but the structure is unchanged. The red and white brick towers adjacent to the rotundas, which housed the hydraulic accumulators for the lifts, and the company's boilerhouse and power station at the S end have all been demolished.

KINGSTON BRIDGE. The urban motorway's great leap over the Clyde, completed in 1970. Engineer *W. A. Fairhurst & Partners*; consulting architect for landscape works *Wm. Holford & Associates*; contractor *Logan-Marples Ridgeway Joint Venture*. The river crossing consists of two parallel structures, each 21 m (68 ft) wide and carrying five lanes of traffic, supported by a pier on each quay. They are triple-cell pre-stressed concrete box girders with arched soffit profiles, cast *in situ* as free cantilevers to keep the river and the quayside streets open during construction, and joined for continuity when they met at midspan. The clear height of 18 m (60 ft) was required for dredgers to go upstream as far as George V Bridge. The main river span is 143 m (470 ft), with balancing spans of 62·5 m (205 ft) reaching from the quayside piers to the approach viaducts; the viaducts are supported by tall columns twice-tapered to match the structural forces acting in them, following precedents in the work of the Italian engineer P. L. Nervi. These colonnades, together with the quayside piers, both splashed with shafts of light from the gap between the two bridge decks overhead, create some dramatic views through the vast spaces underneath, especially along the axis northward from the river. Many more vistas, good and bad, under the three miles of elevated approach roads, ramps and intersections. To give, in the engineer's words, 'a standard of finish comparable with that of a modern building', the outer spandrels of the bridge are clad with exposed-aggregate panels showing vertical joints. Bands of similar texture but visually jointless outline the curves of the soffit edges and the cantilevered edges of the road slabs.

KING GEORGE V BRIDGE. The most recent of the bridges near the old city centre, crossing the river askew from Commerce Street to Oswald Street, and built 1924–7, though first proposed in 1914. It pretends to be, in the tradition of Glasgow civic bridges, a three-arch bridge of granite, but it is not. After a proposed granite duplicate of Glasgow Bridge had been vetoed by the Navigation Trust, *Thomas P. M. Somers* (City Engineer) decided on a reinforced concrete bridge, invited competitive designs and chose that of *Considère Constructions Ltd*; contractor *Melville, Dundas & Whitson*. There are three 'arches'; the two piers aligned in relation to those of the adjacent railway bridges and giving a middle span of 44·5 m (146 ft), with a height of 5·5 m (18½ ft) above high water to accommodate coasting vessels, including the famous Clyde 'puffers' which used the Broomielaw quays under and upstream of the railway bridges. The resulting profile of road and parapet is unusual and rather inelegant, rising from the river banks by straight lines which are joined by a short curve over the crown of the middle arch. The 'arches' are actually reinforced concrete box girders with curved soffits, the façades clad with grey Dalbeattie granite modelled to represent arches, spandrels, and cornice. The balustrade is also granite, solid and polished. The concrete soffit of the box girders has been covered with a roughcast rendering, probably in response to weathering.

CALEDONIAN RAILWAY BRIDGES. Of the first bridge, built in 1876–8 (engineer *B. H. Blyth*, of *Blyth & Cunningham* of Edinburgh; contractor *William Arrol & Co.*), contemporary with the first part of Central Station, only the piers remain just upstream of the second (and current) bridge, the tracks and girders having been removed in 1966–7. For each pier two cast iron cylinders, 4·5 m (15 ft) diameter in the river and 4 m (13 ft) on the banks, were sunk to bedrock, filled with concrete and extended above the river-bed with masonry, the outside stones being of Dalbeattie granite. The two granite shafts of each pier rise high out of the water and are still linked by arched cast iron frames placed there, by the engineer's admission, purely for ornament.

The second bridge, built in 1899–1905, when the station was enlarged (engineer *Donald A. Matheson* of the Caledonian Railway Co.; contractors *Sir Wm. Arrol & Co.* and *Morrison & Mason*), carries up to ten tracks, its width varying from 35 to 62·5 m (114 to 205 ft), with a minimum of eight parallel main girders in the width. The façades are enlivened by the cantilevering of latticework parapets from the main girders on large curved brackets, throwing the heavier steelwork into shadow. The main structure spreads low over the Broomielaw quay below, a dark and complex monster of steel. Each of the two supports in the river is a line of five granite-faced cylinders linked by arches just above low-water level. Deep underneath are rectangular steel caissons covering the whole area of the piers and filled up with concrete and brickwork. They were sunk by the compressed-air process to a firm sand and gravel stratum at depths 12 to 21 m (40 to 70 ft) below high water.

GLASGOW (or JAMAICA STREET) BRIDGE. Built in 1895–9. Engineer *Blyth & Westland* of Edinburgh; contractor *Morrison & Mason* of Glasgow; steel cylinders for foundations by *Sir Wm. Arrol & Co*. It replaced a handsome seven-arched bridge in classical style by *Thomas Telford*, which was too narrow, its foundations too shallow and the size of its arches inconvenient for shipping. *Blyth & Westland* therefore made a design of four larger arches with roadway 100 ft (30 m) wide, but had to alter it to a virtual replica of the former bridge, with 80 ft (24 m) roadway, after 'an outcry in Glasgow against not retaining the beautiful lines of Telford's bridge' and objections from the Corporation to the estimated cost. The engineers, and doubtless the shipowners, thought it a very retrograde change. The piers stand on concrete-filled steel cylinders sunk by the compressed-air method to minimum depth of 23 m (75 ft) below the arch springings. Semicircular arches above low-water level link the heads of four cylinders to make up each pier. The piers, arches and façades of the bridge are of grey granite, much of it taken from the old bridge and redressed, and the old balustrades and copestones were also redressed and polished. Only the pedestals over the piers depart from Telford's architectural treatment. Like the pilasters they replace, they are semi-octagonal in plan, but more bulky and with S-curved vertical profiles.

The first bridge on the site was Glasgow's second bridge over the Clyde, called Broomielaw Bridge and built 1768–72 to the design of *William Mylne* of Edinburgh, contractor *John Adam* of Glasgow. Telford's bridge replaced it in 1833–5 for reasons similar to those which caused his to be replaced in the 1890s.

SOUTH PORTLAND STREET FOOTBRIDGE. 1851–3. A 30 wrought iron suspension bridge, the ironwork designed by *George Martin*, engineer, and the supporting stone pylons by *Alexander Kirkland*, architect. It was erected at the expense of the heritors of Gorbals to replace a wooden bridge near the same spot which had been built for temporary use while Broomielaw Bridge was rebuilding in 1833–5 but was much used until it became unsafe in 1846. In 1870–1 *Bell & Miller*, engineers, altered the ironwork, lowering the main chains and deck at midspan and adding lattice girders to the side-rails. There were further repairs to the deck and side-rails in 1926. The fine profile should be seen against the sky, not, as it appears from most viewpoints, with a background of buildings. The pylons, of yellow-brown sandstone, are triumphal arches of Grecian composition, with square pilasters at the outer corners, pairs of fluted Ionic columns flanking the entries, and over the entablatures massive ashlar plinths through which the chains pass to rest on their saddle supports. There are two chains on each side of the bridge, each chain link being five flat wrought iron bars; wrought iron suspenders at about $1 \cdot 5$ m (5 ft) spacing; and a deck of wrought iron or steel cross beams and wooden floor.

VICTORIA BRIDGE. 1851–4. Engineer *James Walker* of London; contractor *Wm. York* of Glasgow. Of sandstone faced with granite from Kingstown (now Dun Laoghaire) near Dublin, which is darker than the Dalbeattie granite used for other bridges down river. It is a generation older than those bridges – and now the oldest Clyde bridge in the city – and more restrained in its design of five segmental arches (span of the largest: 80 ft – 24 m) under a parapet which makes a continuous low curve in elevation. The tails of the voussoirs are cut to form steps matching the courses in the spandrels, the cutwaters curved from the sides of the piers to a sharp point and topped by a domical shape of solid granite. There are simple rectangular pilasters up the spandrels over the piers. The parapet balusters are carved to a square shape in plan, an elegant touch.

This replaced the medieval bridge of Glasgow (otherwise Stockwell Bridge), partly rebuilt in 1671, nearly ruinous by 1758, strengthened and widened in 1774–8, and widened again in 1821 by *Thomas Telford* by the novel device of cast iron footway arches spanning between the protruding cutwaters.

CITY UNION RAILWAY BRIDGE. 1897–9. Engineer *William Melville*; contractors *Morrison and Mason* for foundations and masonry and *Sir William Arrol & Co.* for steelwork. It carries four lines of track, replacing the two-track bridge of 1870. Five spandrel-braced arches of riveted steelwork over the river, each of two ribs, and a lattice girder span over the street on each bank. Steel caissons sunk to almost 18 m (60 ft) below the river-bed support cylindrical piers of rock-faced Shap granite, from which the arch ribs spring at a height of $7 \cdot 5$ m (25 ft) above low-water. A complex system of cross girders between the arches carries the 14-m (45-ft) wide track bed, the form of the structure having been largely dictated by the need to construct it under the old bridge, which was still in use. There is a decorative cast iron cornice and parapet on all the river spans, punctuated by crenellated half-turrets of Dumfries-shire red sandstone at the piers and bigger towers in the same style at the abutments. It served the main routes from the s to the now demolished St Enoch Station.

ALBERT BRIDGE. 1868–71. Engineers *R. Bell & D. Miller* of Glasgow; contractor *Hanna, Donald & Wilson* of Paisley. One *Adamson* of Edinburgh has been mentioned as architect, prob-ably for the ornamental masonry and ironwork. There are three arches, the largest of 35 m (114 ft) span, and each with eight ribs of riveted wrought iron construction. Abutments and piers of grey granite founded on concrete-filled cast iron cylinders. The arch ribs are hidden by cast iron spandrel fascias bearing the royal arms and the arms of Prince Albert and of various corporate bodies. Cast iron parapets with the ancient arms of Glasgow facing the road at midspan, and imposing granite pedestals terminating the parapets and bearing roundels with sculpted heads of Victoria and Albert facing the river. Over the semi-octagonal cutwaters, stocky half-columns of polished pink granite with Corinthian capitals.

This is the fifth bridge to be built at or near the end of Saltmarket. The first, partly funded by the patrons of Hutchesons' Hospital and called Hutchesontown Bridge, was begun in 1794–5 by *John Roberton* or *Robertson*, a mason of Pollokshaws, but destroyed by a flood in November 1795 and found impossible to rebuild. In 1803 a fine timber footbridge designed by *Peter Nicholson* was erected on a site just upstream. It stood until another stone bridge called Hutcheson Bridge was built in 1829–34, the engineer being *Robert Stevenson* (grandfather of Robert Louis Stevenson). By 1868 it had become unsafe owing to the deepening of the river and had to be demolished. A temporary timber bridge carried the traffic until Albert Bridge opened (1871).

WEIR AND PIPE BRIDGE ABOVE ALBERT BRIDGE. The present steel structures, completed in 1949, were supplied by *Ransome & Rapier* of Ipswich; engineer *Robert Bruce* (City Engineer). Two parallel bridges each carrying a large pipe by spandrel-braced arches over three openings. Sluice-gates in the river across the openings control the flow to maintain a fairly constant depth of water upstream; they are raised and rotated by chains to allow boats to pass under them at full tide. The red sandstone piers and abutments with neat classical details survive from similar sluices also supplied and erected by *Ransome & Rapier* in 1896–1901, engineer *A. B. McDonald* (City Engineer), with *Sir Benjamin Baker* as consultant; the gates themselves were designed by *F. G. M. Stoney*. They were built to stop the extensive erosion of the river banks and the siltation in the harbour reaches downstream which resulted from the removal in 1879 of the first river control works on this site, a fixed weir and navigation lock constructed in 1852.

ST ANDREW'S FOOTBRIDGE. A wrought iron suspension [31] bridge built in 1854–5 to replace a busy ferry, and not much altered since. Engineer *Neil Robson* of Glasgow; architect for the supporting pylons *Charles O'Neill*; contractor *P. & W. McLellan*. The spanning structure, 67 m (220 ft) over the river, is all of wrought iron, comprising chains of multiple flat links, suspender bars and riveted deck structure. The pylons are portals of fine cast iron work, each with four fluted Corinthian columns almost 6 m (20 ft) high and correct entablature with the chains going through the frieze to their saddle supports. Cast iron lamp-standards also serve as posts for iron gates by which the portals can be closed. An excellent example of 1850s iron bridge construction.

KING'S BRIDGE. From King's Drive to Ballater Street. 1930–3. Engineer probably *T. P. M. Somers* (City Engineer); contractor *Sir Wm Arrol & Co*. A bridge so flat and wide – 21 m (70 ft) between parapets – that one can easily cross without noticing its existence; it has four equal spans, each of eleven parallel steel plate girders of riveted construction carrying a reinforced concrete road slab. The abutments and piers are of concrete, faced with smooth, fine-jointed granite, the parapet granite in simple rectilinear shapes. There are arches through the piers, showing that they are built on deep cylinders or caissons. The outsides of the external girders are encased in concrete made with fine granite aggregate, brushed or blasted to match the sawn granite of the parapets, and, to be fashionable in the 1930s, moulded to a pattern of longitudinal grooves interrupted at intervals by protruding square blocks. Unfortunately, corrosion of the reinforcement in these facings is causing spalling and staining.

The first bridge here was a wooden bridge 15 m (50 ft) wide built in 1901 with timbers from the dismantled service bridge used during the reconstruction of Glasgow Bridge in 1895–9.

POLMADIE BRIDGE. 1954–5. Engineer *Robert Bruce*; contractor *Melville, Dundas & Whitson*. A prestressed concrete footbridge of plain elevation, sitting happily in its parkland setting. 3·6 m (12 ft) wide, its tall slim piers supporting five spans of white concrete beams and simple balustrade, set in a slightly rising curve and all with exposed-aggregate texture. It occupies the site of a wooden footbridge 4·9 m (16 ft) wide, built in 1901 (like the predecessor of King's Bridge) with timber salvaged from Glasgow Bridge's service bridge. It was burnt and rebuilt at least once before being replaced by the concrete bridge.

RUTHERGLEN BRIDGE. From Main Street to Shawfield Drive. 1893–6. Engineer *Crouch & Hogg* of Glasgow; contractor *Morrison & Mason*. With the dignified and rather solemn aesthetic of a Glasgow civic bridge in the expected material, grey granite. 18 m (60 ft) wide, three arches of low segmental form, supported on V-jointed piers and abutments, solid pilasters over both. A rounded solidity characterizes the details at arch springings, caps of cutwaters and the copings of the solid parapets. It replaced the first Rutherglen Bridge, of five masonry arches, built 1774–5, its engineer said to be *James Watt* during his early practice as a civil engineer.

RAILWAY BRIDGES, DALMARNOCK. Only relics survive of the first bridge at the site, a two-track iron girder bridge built in 1859–61. Engineer *George Graham* of the Caledonian Railway Co., possibly with *Blyth & Cunningham*. Some fine chunky castings; large-diameter vertical cylinders, three in line for each support, X-framed bracing panels between them and thick I-beams spanning across their tops. The girders, deck and track have gone.

The second bridge, also for the Caledonian Railway, and on a pronounced skew, has three steel arches over the river and three brick arches in the approaches; piers and abutments of sandstone. A construction joint through the middle of all the piers shows that there were two periods of building, probably 1893–7 and *c.* 1923. Each arch is of ten ribs, five in each construction period. The spandrel members are vertical and carry the track bed on steel cross beams with brick jack-arches.

DALMARNOCK BRIDGE. 1889–91. Engineer *Crouch & Hogg*; contractor *A. H. Boyle* of Bonnybridge; iron and steel fabricators *Jardine & Co.* of Motherwell. A perfectly horizontal five-span bridge of riveted steel plate girders hidden behind cast iron fascia panels with repeating quatrefoil motif. The piers, founded on iron caissons, are of sandstone with a granite impost, the sandstone then extended up in moulded panels to the top of the parapet, which is formed of cast iron Gothic arcading. On the sides of the abutments, pairs of polished pink granite columns. Wooden bridges had been built here in 1821 and 1848.

VIADUCT NEAR CLYDE IRONWORKS. A low four-arched sandstone viaduct opened by the Caledonian Railway Co. in 1865 and still carrying two tracks. The arch spans are about 18 m (60 ft). Arch, spandrel and parapet surfaces are of rock-faced ashlar; cutwaters semicircular in plan.

BOGLESHOLE ROAD BRIDGE. Only a few yards upstream from the last viaduct. 1986. Engineer *Strathclyde Regional Council*; builder *Raynesway Construction Services Ltd.* A steel plate girder bridge of moderate span, the girders tapering in depth to show a gently arched soffit line in the main span and matching curves in the two half-spans reaching from thin concrete supporting piers on the banks of the river to the ends of the approach embankments. Concrete deck and simple tubular steel railings.

CAMBUSLANG BRIDGE. From Cambuslang Road to Bridge Street. 1892. Engineer *Crouch & Hogg*. The flimsiest bridge in the city to carry road traffic over the Clyde and subject to a vehicle weight restriction. Three spans of steel lattice girders, only two girders in the width and about 30 m (100 ft) span, supported by cylindrical masonry piers which rise almost 6 m (20 ft) above water level.

CAMBUSLANG FOOTBRIDGE. A simple but distinguished bridge parallel to the road bridge and not many yards upstream. 1977. Engineer *Strathclyde Regional Council*; builder *Fairclough Ltd.* 3·3 m (11 ft) wide and perfectly level across four spans. Solid concrete piers support plate girders of rust-coloured weathering steel, over which is a wide band of well-finished concrete forming the deck kerb and white-painted steel railings of closely spaced verticals with top and bottom runners. Under the deck it carries two substantial pipes. There are neat lamp-standards of green-painted tubular steel.

CLYDEFORD ROAD BRIDGE. Opened in 1976. Engineer

Strathclyde Regional Council; builder *Murdoch & McKenzie*. Two parallel steel box girders of constant trapezium cross-section, continuous over two spans on concrete columns rising from a single pier in the river-bed. A cast-*in-situ* concrete deck cantilevers out both sides of the girders and carries side-rails of grey steel tubes and wire mesh.

CARMYLE RAILWAY VIADUCT. 1897. At the river end of Carmyle village, upstream from a fine horseshoe weir, is this striking disused viaduct of three long lattice-girder spans, with an extra short span at each end. The girders, all below the track, are of riveted and presumably steel construction. Side railings of the typical Victorian railway close-lattice form. The tall piers are of stone for most of their height, the upper part slightly tapered, but change to blue engineering brick a few feet below the girder bearings.

KELVIN CROSSINGS

Only a selection of the most interesting bridges across the Kelvin is described (from downstream to upstream). For the Kelvin Aqueduct of the Forth and Clyde Canal, *see* Maryhill, above.

PARTICK BRIDGE. Built in 1876–8 for the Trustees of Glasgow and Yoker Turnpike Roads. Engineers *R. Bell & D. Miller*; contractor *Hugh Kennedy*. A pretentious bridge of one large cast iron arch and a masonry flood-discharge tunnel at the eastern end; the arch four-centred with an obtuse angle at the crown, and formed of nine ribs resting on abutments which are very skew to the direction of span. There are green-painted cast iron parapets and fascias with white shields in the spandrels; wingwalls of red sandstone ashlar with large semi-octagonal towers rising to the parapet at the abutments.

Very close beside it on the downstream side is a curious bridge which carries a very large pipe across the river. Two routine steel lattice girders painted white form the spanning structure, which is covered by a pitched roof and adorned at each end of the span with a substantial sandstone 'building', featuring four corner towers with dome-shaped sheet metal hats.

A short distance away on the upstream side, an earlier freestone bridge of three arches shows through a thick mantle of ivy. It was built in 1800 and presumably closed to traffic since 1878.

KELVIN WAY BRIDGE. A red sandstone bridge of 1913–14 in Kelvingrove Park. Engineer *Alex B. McDonald* (City Engineer); contractor *John Emery & Sons*. A single arch with generous roadway, 18 m (60 ft) wide between the parapets. On high pedestals at the four corners of the span, bronze sculptures by

Paul Raphael Montford, commissioned in 1914 but not erected until *c*. 1920, each of two figures representing Peace and War, Progress and Prosperity, Navigation and Shipbuilding, and Commerce and Industry. Each pair is grouped about a sandstone pillar carved with strapwork and topped by four dolphin heads and a lamp-standard.

FOOTBRIDGE IN KELVINGROVE PARK. 1964. Engineer *W. T. Docherty* of *Ronald Walker & Co*. A single span of white reinforced concrete, the form derived from Robert Maillart's three-hinged arch designs in Switzerland in the interwar years, but the profile exceptionally low. The deck is 3·6 m (12 ft) wide, with neat side rails of closely spaced steel uprights with a timber handrail.

PRINCE OF WALES BRIDGE, KELVINGROVE PARK. 1894–5. Engineer *Alex B. McDonald* (City Engineer); contractor *P. McKissock & Son*. A single elliptical arch of red sandstone with no stinting of materials or classical details; 12 m (40 ft) wide, with quadrant wingwalls, carved decoration over the whole of the spandrels, and Peterhead granite balustrades. It replaced a timber bridge painted to look like masonry, built in 1868 to the design of *John Carrick*, City Architect.

GIBSON STREET-ELDON STREET BRIDGE. A road bridge opened in 1895 at the joint expense of Glasgow and Partick. Engineer *Formans & McCall*. The main arch is segmental, about 21 m (70 ft) span; width between parapets is 20 m (65 ft). Parapets and fascias are of cast iron decorated in the style of the earlier Partick and Great Western Bridges and painted bottle-green, but the seven arch ribs behind the fascias are of riveted steelwork.

GREAT WESTERN BRIDGE. 1889–91. Engineer *Bell & Miller*; contractor *Morrison & Mason*; iron and steel by *Wm. Arrol & Co*. A classic of late Victorian engineering, it can be crossed almost unnoticed because its road is level with the streets at both ends; but it is very impressive from the riverside. It is a scaled-up version of the earlier Partick Bridge by the same engineers, comprising two large cast iron arches of four-centred profile, each 27·7 m (91 ft) span and of nine parallel ribs, a 9·4-m (31-ft) cast iron arch at each end and short approaches faced with sandstone. The smoothly moulded arch segments, spandrel members and bracing units, with three-dimensional bolted connexions, are vintage structural cast iron. Like Partick Bridge, the spandrels are clad with fascias of decorative cast iron bearing the arms of Glasgow. Parapet mainly of cast iron, but granite to crown the big semi-octagonal turrets of polished red granite on the faces of the bridge over the piers. The road is laid on riveted steel girders (from the firm which had just finished building the world's greatest steel bridge across the Forth) and brick jack-arches.

QUEEN MARGARET BRIDGE. 1926–9. Designed by *T. P. M. Somers* (City Engineer), with *Considère Constructions Ltd*; contractor *Wm. Taylor & Son*. A large reinforced concrete arch over the river with pedestrian arches through both abutments, and carrying Queen Margaret Drive high across the valley. The arch is a little askew and spans 41 m (135 ft). The façades are clad with very smooth and finely jointed red Corncockle sandstone, mimicking voussoir arches with keystones, and topped by cornice and parapet of polished red Peterhead granite, including short lengths of open balustrade. The width between parapets is a generous 24 m (80 ft).

KIRKLEE BRIDGE. From Kirklee Road to Clouston Street. 1899–1901. Engineer *Charles Formans* of *Formans & McCall*; contractor *William & Charles Wilson*. Probably the best stone bridge in Glasgow, certainly the most exuberant. In its high semi-elliptical arch and pairs of Ionic columns at the abutments, it adheres precisely to the architecture of Robert Mylne's Blackfriars Bridge in London (1760–9; demolished 1864) and the Piranesi engraving from which Mylne drew his inspiration, spurning later adaptations by Rennie (at Kelso and at Waterloo Bridge, London) and others. It is of red sandstone, except the Ionic columns and the balustrades, which are of polished pink granite. The entablature over the columns lines up with a fine cornice over the large arch. Projecting mouldings outline the border of each spandrel and the circumference of a circle inscribed in it; and filling the circle, also in relief, are the arms of the city – all this carved *in situ* on the coursed sandstone of the façades. Tall tunnels through both abutments are of V-jointed ashlar and entered through semicircular arches with carved keystones. The soffit of the large arch is also V-jointed. Public parkland on the w bank allows good access and views of the bridge.

GLOSSARY

Particular types of an architectural element are often defined under the name of the element itself; e.g. for 'dog-leg stair' see STAIR. Literal meanings, where specially relevant, are indicated by the abbreviation *lit*.

ABACUS (*lit*. tablet): flat slab forming the top of a capital; *see* Orders (fig. 16).

ABUTMENT: the meeting of an arch or vault with its solid lateral support, or the support itself.

ACANTHUS: formalized leaf ornament with thick veins and frilled edge, e.g. on a Corinthian capital.

ACHIEVEMENT OF ARMS: in heraldry, a complete display of armorial bearings.

ACROTERION (*lit*. peak): pointed ornament projecting above the apex or ends of a pediment.

ADDORSED: description of two figures placed symmetrically back to back.

AEDICULE (*lit*. litle building): term used in classical architecture to describe the unit formed by a pair of orders, an entablature, and usually a pediment, placed against a wall to frame an opening.

AFFRONTED: description of two figures placed symmetrically face to face.

AGGER (*lit*. rampart): Latin term for the built-up foundations of Roman roads.

AGGREGATE: small stones added to a binding material, e.g. in harling or concrete.

AISLE (*lit*. wing): (1) passage alongside the nave, choir or transept of a church, or the main body of some other building, separated from it by columns or piers; (2) (Scots) projecting wing of a church for special use, e.g. by a guild or by a landed family whose burial place it may contain.

AMBULATORY (*lit*. walkway): aisle at the E end of a chancel, usually surrounding an apse and therefore semicircular or polygonal in plan.

ANNULET (*lit*. ring): shaft-ring (*q.v.*).

ANSE DE PANIER (*lit*. basket handle): basket arch (*see* Arch).

ANTA: classical order of oblong section employed at the ends of a colonnade which is then called *in antis*. See Orders (fig. 16).

ANTEFIXAE: ornaments projecting at regular intervals above a classical cornice. *See* Orders (fig. 16).

ANTHEMION (*lit*. honeysuckle; plural: *anthemia*): classical ornament like a honeysuckle flower (*see* fig. 1).

Fig. 1.   Anthemion and palmette frieze

APSE semicircular (i.e. apsidal) extension of an apartment. A term first used of the magistrate's end of a Roman basilica, and thence especially of the vaulted semicircular or polygonal end of a chancel or a chapel.

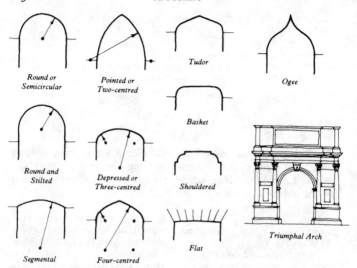

Round or Semicircular

Pointed or Two-centred

Tudor

Ogee

Round and Stilted

Depressed or Three-centred

Basket

Shouldered

Segmental

Four-centred

Flat

Triumphal Arch

Fig. 2.   Arch

ARABESQUE: light and fanciful surface decoration. *See* Grotteschi.

ARCADE: series of arches supported by piers or columns. *Blind arcade*: the same applied to the surface of a wall. *Wall arcade*: in medieval churches, a blind arcade forming a dado below windows.

ARCH: for the various forms *see* fig. 2. The term *basket arch* refers to a basket handle and is sometimes applied to a three-centred or depressed arch as well as the type with a flat middle. *Transverse arch*: across the main axis of an interior space. A term used especially for the arches between the compartments of tunnel- or groin-vaulting. *Diaphragm arch*: transverse arch with solid spandrels spanning an otherwise wooden-roofed interior. *Chancel arch*: across the W end of a chancel. *Relieving arch*: incorporated in a wall, to carry some of its weight, some way above an opening. *Strainer arch*: inserted across an opening to resist any inward pressure of the side members. *Triumphal arch*: Imperial Roman monument whose elevation supplied a motif for many later

classical compositions. *Blind arch*: framing a wall which has no opening. *Overarch*: framing a wall which has an opening, e.g. a window or door.

ARCHITRAVE: (1) formalized lintel, the lowest member of the classical entablature (*see* Orders, fig. 16); (2) moulded frame of a door or window. Also *lugged* or *shouldered architrave*, whose top is prolonged into lugs (*lit*. ears).

ARCHIVOLT: continuous mouldings of an arch.

ARRIS (*lit*. stop): sharp edge at the meeting of two surfaces.

ASHLAR: masonry of large blocks wrought to even faces and square edges. *Droved ashlar* (Scots) is finished with sharp horizontal tool-marks.

ASTRAGAL (*lit*. knuckle): moulding of round section, and hence (Scots) wooden glazing-bar between window-panes.

ASTYLAR: term used to describe an elevation that has no columns or similar vertical features.

ATLANTES: male counterparts of caryatids, often in a more demonstrative attitude of support. In sculpture, a single figure of the god Atlas may be seen supporting a globe.

ATTACHED: description of a shaft or column that is partly merged into a wall or pier.

ATTIC: (1) small top storey, especially behind a sloping roof; (2) in classical architecture, a storey above the main cornice, as in a triumphal arch.

AUMBRY: recess or cupboard to hold sacred vessels for Mass.

BAILEY: open space or court of a stone-built castle; *see also* Motte-and-bailey.

BALDACCHINO: tent-like roof supported by columns, e.g. over some monuments of the C 17–18.

BALLFLOWER: globular flower of three petals enclosing a small ball. A decoration used in the first quarter of the C 14.

BALUSTER (*lit.* pomegranate): hence a pillar or pedestal of bellied form. *Balusters*: vertical supports of this or any other form, for a handrail or coping, the whole being called a *balustrade*. *Blind balustrade*: the same with a wall behind.

BARBICAN: outwork defending the entrance to a castle.

BARGEBOARDS: boards, often carved or fretted, hanging clear of the wall under sloping eaves.

BARMKIN (Scots): enclosing wall.

BARONY: *see* Burgh.

BARROW: burial mound.

BARTIZAN (*lit.* battlement): corbelled turret, square or round, at the top angle of a building.

BASE: moulded foot of a column or other order. For its use in classical architecture *see* Orders (fig. 16). *Elided bases*: bases of a compound pier whose lower parts are run together, ignoring the arrangement of the shafts above. Capitals may be treated in the same way.

BASEMENT: lowest, subordinate storey of a building, and hence the lowest part of an elevation, below the piano nobile.

BASILICA (*lit.* royal building): a Roman public hall; hence an aisled church with a clearstorey.

BASTION: projection at the angle of a fortification.

BATTER: inward inclination of a wall.

BATTLEMENT: fortified parapet with upstanding pieces called merlons along the top. Also called Crenellation.

BAYS: divisions of an elevation or interior space as defined by any regular vertical features.

BAY WINDOW: window in a recess, with a consequent projection on the outside, named according to the form of the latter. A *canted bay window* has a straight front and bevelled sides. A *bow window* is curved. An *oriel window* does not start from the ground.

BEAKER: type of pottery vessel used in the late third and early second millennia B.C.

BEAKHEAD: Norman ornamental motif consisting of a row of bird or beast heads with beaks biting usually into a roll moulding.

BEE-BOLL: wall recess designed to contain a beehive.

BELFRY (*lit.* tower): (1) bell turret set on a roof or gable (*see also* Bellcote); (2) room or stage in a tower where bells are hung; (3) bell tower in a general sense.

BELL-CAST: *see* Roof.

BELLCOTE: belfry as (1) above, with the character of a small house for the bell(s), e.g. *birdcage bellcote*: framed structure, usually of stone.

BERM: level area separating ditch from bank on a hillfort or barrow.

BILLET (*lit.* log or block) FRIEZE: Norman ornament consisting of small blocks placed at regular intervals (*see* fig. 3).

Fig. 3. Billet frieze

BIVALLATE: of a hillfort: defended by two concentric banks and ditches.

BLIND: *see* Arcade; Arch; Balustrade; Portico.

BLOCKED: term applied to columns

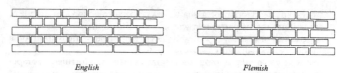

English   Flemish

Fig. 4. Bond

etc. that are interrupted by regular projecting blocks, e.g. to the sides of a Gibbs surround (*see* fig. 10).

BLOCKING COURSE: plain course of stones, or equivalent, on top of a cornice and crowning the wall.

BOLECTION MOULDING: moulding covering the joint between two different planes and overlapping the higher as well as the lower one, especially on panelling and fireplace surrounds of the late C 17 and early C 18.

BOND: in brickwork, the pattern of long sides (stretchers) and short ends (headers) produced on the face of a wall by laying bricks in a particular way (*see* fig. 4).

BOSS: knob or projection usually placed to cover the intersection of ribs in a vault.

BOW WINDOW: *see* Bay window.

BOX PEW: pew enclosed by a high wooden back and ends, the latter having doors.

BRACE: *see* Roof (fig. 22).

BRACKET: small supporting piece of stone, etc., to carry a projecting horizontal member.

BRESSUMER: (*lit.* breast-beam): big horizontal beam, usually set forward from the lower part of a building, supporting the timber superstructure.

BRETASCHE (*lit.* battlement): defensive wooden gallery on a wall.

BROCH (Scots): circular tower-like structure, open in the middle, the double wall of dry-stone masonry linked by slabs forming internal galleries at varying levels; found in W and N Scotland and probably dating from the earliest centuries of the Christian era.

BRONZE AGE: in Britain, the period from *c.* 2000 to 600 B.C.

BUCRANIUM: ox skull.

BULLSEYE WINDOW: small circular window, e.g. in the tympanum of a pediment.

BURGH: formally constituted town with trading privileges. *Royal Burghs*, which still hold this courtesy title, monopolized imports and exports till the C 17 and paid duty to the Crown. *Burghs of Barony* were founded by secular or ecclesiastical barons to whom they paid duty on their local trade. *Police burghs* were instituted after 1850 for the administration of new centres of population and abolished at local government reorganization in 1975. They controlled planning, building, sewerage, lighting and cleansing.

BUT-AND-BEN (Scots, *lit.* outer and inner rooms): two-room cottage.

BUTTRESS: vertical member projecting from a wall to stabilize it or to resist the lateral thrust of an arch, roof or vault. For different types used at the corners of a building, especially a tower, *see* fig. 5. A *flying buttress* transmits the thrust to a heavy abutment by means of an arch or half-arch.

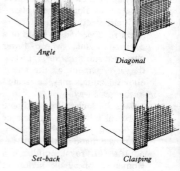

Angle   Diagonal

Set-back   Clasping

Fig. 5. Buttresses at a corner

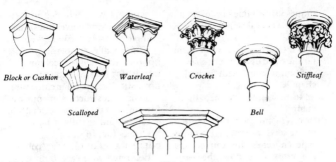

Fig. 6. Capitals

Block or Cushion   *Waterleaf*   *Crocket*   *Stiffleaf*

Scalloped   *Bell*

Elided

CABLE MOULDING or ROPE MOULDING: originally a Norman moulding, imitating the twisted strands of a rope.

CALEFACTORY: room in a monastery where a fire burned for the comfort of the monks.

CAMBER: slight rise or upward curve in place of a horizontal line or plane.

CAMES: *see* Quarries.

CAMPANILE: free-standing bell tower.

CANDLE-SNUFFER ROOF: conical roof of a turret.

CANOPY: projection or hood over an altar, pulpit, niche, statue, etc.

CANTED: tilted, generally on a vertical axis to produce an obtuse angle on plan, e.g. of a canted bay window.

CAP-HOUSE (Scots): (1) small chamber at the head of a turnpike stair, opening onto the parapet walk; (2) chamber rising from within the parapet walk.

CAPITAL: head or top part of a column or other order; for classical types *see* Orders (fig. 16); for medieval types *see* fig. 6. *Elided capitals*: capitals of a compound pier whose upper parts are run together, ignoring the arrangement of the shafts below.

CARTOUCHE: tablet with ornate frame, usually of elliptical shape and bearing a coat of arms or inscription.

CARYATIDS (*lit.* daughters of the village of Caryae): female figures supporting an entablature, counterparts of Atlantes.

CASEMENT: (1) window hinged at the side; (2) in Gothic architecture, a concave moulding framing a window.

CASTELLATED: battlemented.

CAVETTO: concave moulding of quarter-round section.

CELURE or CEILURE: panelled and adorned part of a wagon roof above the rood or the altar.

CENOTAPH (*lit.* empty tomb): funerary monument which is not a burying place.

CENSER: vessel for the burning of incense, frequently of architectural form.

CENTERING: wooden support for the building of an arch or vault, removed after completion.

CHAMBERED TOMB: burial mound of the Neolithic Age having a stone-built chamber and entrance passage covered by an earthen barrow or stone cairn.

CHAMFER (*lit.* corner-break): surface formed by cutting off a square edge, usually at an angle of forty-five degrees.

CHANCEL (*lit.* enclosure): that part of the E end of a church in which the altar is placed, usually applied to the whole continuation of the nave E of the crossing.

CHANTRY CHAPEL: chapel attached to, or inside, a church, endowed for the celebration of masses for the soul of the founder or some other individual.

CHECK (Scots): rebate.

CHERRY-CAULKING or CHERRY-COCKING (Scots): masonry techniques using a line of pin-stones in the vertical joints between blocks.

CHEVET (*lit.* head): French term for the E end of a church (chancel and ambulatory with radiating chapels).

CHEVRON: zigzag Norman ornament.

CHOIR: (1) the part of a church where services are sung; in monastic churches this can occupy the crossing and/or the easternmost bays of the nave, but in cathedral churches it is usually in the E arm: (2) the E arm of a cruciform church (a usage of long standing though liturgically anomalous).

CIBORIUM: canopied shrine for the reserved sacrament.

CINQUEFOIL: *see* Foil.

CIST: stone-lined or slab-built grave. First appears in Late Neolithic times. It continued to be used in the Early Christian period.

CLAPPER BRIDGE: bridge made of large slabs of stone, some built up to make rough piers and other longer ones laid on top to make the roadway.

CLASSIC: term for the moment of highest achievement of a style.

CLASSICAL: term for Greek and Roman architecture and any subsequent styles inspired by it.

CLEARSTOREY: upper storey of the walls of a church, pierced by windows.

CLOSE (Scots): courtyard or passage giving access to a number of buildings or dwellings.

COADE STONE: artificial (cast) stone made in the late C18 and the early C19 by Coade and Sealy in London.

COB: walling material made of mixed clay and straw.

COFFERING: sunken panels, square or polygonal, decorating a ceiling, vault or arch.

COLLAR: *see* Roof (fig. 22).

COLLEGIATE CHURCH: a church endowed for the support of a college of priests, especially for the singing of masses for the soul of the founder. Some collegiate churches were founded in connexion with universities, e.g. three at St Andrews and one at King's College, Aberdeen.

COLONNADE: range of columns.

COLONNETTE: small column.

COLUMN: in classical architecture, an upright structural member of round section with a shaft, a capital and usually a base. *See* Orders (fig. 16).

COLUMNA ROSTRATA: column decorated with carved prows of ships to celebrate a naval victory.

COMMENDATOR: one who holds the revenues of an abbey *in commendam* (medieval Latin for 'in trust' or 'in custody') for a period in which no regular abbot is appointed. During the Middle Ages most Commendators were bishops, but in Scotland during and after the Reformation they were laymen who performed no religious duties.

COMPOSITE: *see* Orders.

CONDUCTOR (Scots): down-pipe for rainwater; *see also* Rhone.

CONSERVATION: a modern term employed in two, sometimes conflicting, senses: (1) work to prolong the life of the historic fabric of a building or other work of art, without alteration; (2) work to make a building or a place more viable. Good conservation is a combination of the two.

CONSOLE: ornamental bracket of compound curved outline (*see* fig. 7). Its height is usually greater than its projection, as in (*a*).

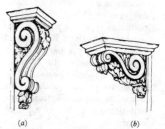

(*a*) (*b*)

Fig. 7. Console

COOMB CEILING or COMB CEILING (Scots): ceiling whose

slope corresponds to that of the roof.

COPING (*lit.* capping): course of stones, or equivalent, on top of a wall.

CORBEL: block of stone projecting from a wall, supporting some feature on its horizontal top surface. *Corbel-course*: continuous projecting course of stones fulfilling the same function. *Corbel table*: series of corbels to carry a parapet or a wall-plate; for the latter *see* Roof (fig. 22).

CORBIE-STEPS (Scots, *lit.* crow-steps): *see* Gable (fig. 9).

CORINTHIAN: *see* Orders (fig. 16).

CORNICE: (1) moulded ledge, decorative and/or practical, projecting along the top of a building or feature, especially as the highest member of the classical entablature (*see* Orders, fig. 16); (2) decorative moulding in the angle between wall and ceiling.

CORPS-DE-LOGIS: French term for the main building(s) as distinct from the wings or pavilions.

COUNTERSCARP BANK: small bank on the down-hill or outer side of a hillfort ditch.

COURSE: continuous layer of stones etc. in a wall.

COVE: concave soffit like a hollow moulding but on a larger scale. A *cove ceiling* has a pronounced cove joining the walls to a flat surface in the middle.

CREDENCE: in a church or chapel, a side table, often a niche, for the sacramental elements before consecration.

CRENELLATION: *see* Battlement.

CREST, CRESTING: ornamental finish along the top of a screen, etc.

CROCKETS (*lit.* hooks), CROCK-ETING: in Gothic architecture, leafy knobs on the edges of any sloping feature. *Crocket capital*: *see* Capital (fig. 6).

CROSSING: in a church, central space opening into the nave, chancel and transepts. *Crossing tower*: central tower supported by the piers at its corners.

CROWNPOST: a vertical timber standing vertically on a tie-beam and supporting a central horizontal longitudinal timber.

CROWSTEPS (Scots): squared stones set like steps to form a skew; *see* Gable (fig. 9).

CRUCK (*lit.* crooked): piece of naturally curved timber combining the structural roles of an upright post and a sloping rafter, e.g. in the building of a cottage, where each pair of crucks is joined at the ridge.

CRYPT: underground room usually below the E end of a church.

CUPOLA (*lit.* dome): (1) small polygonal or circular domed turret crowning a roof; (2) (Scots) small dome or skylight as an internal feature, especially over a stairwell.

CURTAIN WALL: (1) connecting wall between the towers of a castle; (2) in modern building, thin wall attached to the main structure, usually outside it.

CURVILINEAR: *see* Tracery.

CUSP: projecting point formed by the foils within the divisions of Gothic tracery, also used to decorate the soffits of the Gothic arches of tomb recesses, sedilias, etc.

CYCLOPEAN MASONRY: built with large irregular polygonal stones, but smooth and finely jointed.

DADO: lower part of a wall or its decorative treatment; *see also* Pedestal (fig. 17).

DAGGER: *see* Tracery.

DAIS or DEIS (Scots): raised platform at one end of a room.

DAL-DE-VERRE: a French term for stained glass set directly into a slab (*dal*) of concrete.

DEC (DECORATED): historical division of English Gothic architecture covering the period from *c.* 1290 to *c.* 1350.

DEMI-COLUMNS: engaged columns, only half of whose circumference projects from the wall.

DIAPER (*lit.* figured cloth): repetitive surface decoration.

DIOCLETIAN WINDOW: semi-circular window with two mullions, so called because of its use in the Baths of Diocletian in Rome.

DISTYLE: having two columns; cf. Portico.

DOGTOOTH: typical E.E. decoration applied to a moulding. It consists of a series of squares, their centres raised like pyramids and their edges indented (*see* fig. 8).

Fig. 8. Dogtooth

DONJON: *see* Keep.

DOOCOT (Scots): dovecot. Free-standing doocots are usually of *lectern* type, rectangular in plan with single-pitch roof, or *beehive* type, circular in plan and growing small towards the top.

DORIC: *see* Orders (fig. 16).

DORMER WINDOW: window standing up vertically from the slope of a roof and lighting a room within it. *Dormer head*: gable above this window, often formed as a pediment.

DORTER: dormitory, sleeping quarters of a monastery.

DOUBLE-PILE: *see* Pile.

DRESSINGS: features made of smoothly worked stones, e.g. quoins or stringcourses, projecting from the wall which may be of different material, colour or texture.

DRIPSTONE: moulded stone projecting from a wall to protect the lower parts from water; *see also* Hoodmould.

DROVED ASHLAR: *see* Ashlar.

DRUM: (1) circular or polygonal vertical wall of a dome or cupola; (2) one of the stones forming the shaft of a column.

DRUMLIN: long oval mound of Glacial formation.

DRY-STONE: stone construction without mortar.

DUN (Scots): a small stone-walled fort.

E.E. (EARLY ENGLISH): historical division of English Gothic architecture covering the period 1200–1250.

EASTER SEPULCHRE: recess with tomb-chest, usually in the wall of a chancel, the tomb-chest to receive the Sacrament after the Mass of Maundy Thursday.

EAVES: overhanging edge of a roof; hence *eaves cornice* in this position, and *eaves gallery*, the storey below the eaves with large openings or a continuous gallery.

ECHINUS (*lit.* sea-urchin): lower part of a Greek Doric capital; *see* Orders (fig. 16).

EDGE-ROLL: moulding of semi-circular or more than semi-circular section at the edge of an opening.

ELEVATION: (1) any side of a building; (2) in a drawing, the same or any part of it, accurately represented in two dimensions.

ELIDED: term used to describe (1) a compound architectural feature, e.g. an entablature, in which some parts have been omitted; (2) a number of similar parts which have been combined to form a single larger one (*see* Capital, fig. 6).

EMBATTLED: furnished with battlements.

EMBRASURE (*lit.* splay): small splayed opening in the wall or battlement of a fortified building.

ENCAUSTIC TILES: glazed and decorated earthenware tiles used for paving.

EN DÉLIT: term used in Gothic architecture to describe attached stone shafts whose grain runs vertically instead of horizontally, against normal building practice.

ENGAGED: description of a column that is partly merged into a wall or pier.

ENTABLATURE: in classical architecture, collective name for the three horizontal members (architrave, frieze and cornice) above a column; *see* Orders (fig. 16).

ENTASIS: very slight convex deviation from a straight line; used on classical columns and sometimes on spires to prevent an optical illusion of concavity.

ENTRESOL: mezzanine storey within or above the ground storey.

EPITAPH (*lit*. on a tomb): inscription in that position.

ESCUTCHEON: shield for armorial bearings.

EXEDRA: apsidal end of an apartment; *see* Apse.

FERETORY: (1) place behind the high altar where the chief shrine of a church is kept; (2) wooden or metal container for relics.

FESTOON: ornament, usually in high or low relief, in the form of a garland of flowers and/or fruit, hung up at both ends; *see also* Swag.

FEU (Scots): land granted, e.g. by sale, by the *feudal superior* to the *vassal* or *feuar*, on conditions that include the annual payment of a fixed sum of *feu-duty*. The paramount superior of all land is the Crown. Any subsequent proprietor of the land becomes the feuar and is subject to the same obligations. Although many superiors have disposed of their feudal rights, others, both private and corporate, still make good use of the power of feudal control which has produced many well-disciplined developments in Scotland.

FIBREGLASS: *see* GRP.

FILLET: narrow flat band running down a shaft or along a roll moulding.

FINIAL: topmost feature, e.g. above a gable, spire or cupola.

FLAMBOYANT: properly the latest phase of French Gothic architecture, where the window tracery takes on undulating lines, based on the use of flowing curves.

FLATTED: divided into apartments.

But flat (Scots) is also used with a special colloquial meaning. 'He stays on the first flat' means that he lives on the first floor.

FLÈCHE (*lit*. arrow): slender spire on the centre of a roof.

FLEUR-DE-LIS: in heraldry, a formalized lily as in the royal arms of France.

FLEURON: decorative carved flower or leaf.

FLOWING: *see* Tracery (Curvilinear).

FLUTING: series of concave grooves, their common edges sharp (arris) or blunt (fillet).

FOAMED SLAG: blast-furnace slag which has been treated during cooling to give it a foamy texture. It is used as a lightweight insulating material in concrete.

FOIL (*lit*. leaf): lobe formed by the cusping of a circular or other shape in tracery. *Trefoil* (three), *quatrefoil* (four), *cinquefoil* (five) and *multifoil* express the number of lobes in a shape; *see* Tracery (fig. 25).

FOLIATED: decorated, especially carved, with leaves.

FORE- (*lit*. in front): *Fore-building*: structure protecting an entrance. *Forestair*: external stair, usually unenclosed.

FORM-PIECE: tracery bar.

FOSSE: ditch.

FRATER: refectory or dining hall of a monastery.

FREE STYLE: characteristic of British architecture 1880–1914, in which historical styles are composed in an eclectic and free manner.

FREESTONE: stone that is cut, or can be cut, in all directions, usually fine-grained sandstone or limestone.

FRESCO: painting executed on wet plaster.

FRIEZE: horizontal band of ornament, especially the middle member of the classical entablature; *see* Orders (fig. 16). *Pulvinated frieze (lit*. cushioned): frieze of bold convex profile.

FRONTAL: covering for the front of an altar.

GABLE: (1) peaked wall or other vertical surface, often triangular, at the end of a double-pitch roof; (2) (Scots) the same, very often with a chimney at the apex, but also in a wider sense: end wall, of whatever shape. *See* fig. 9. *Gablet*: small gable. *See also* Roof, Skew.

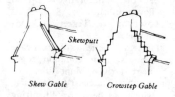

Skewputt

Skew Gable   Crowstep Gable

Dutch Gable

Curvilinear or Shaped Gable at wallhead

Fig. 9. Gables

GADROONING: ribbed ornament, e.g. on the lid or base of an urn, flowing into a lobed edge.

GAIT (Scots) or GATE: street, usually with a prefix indicating its use, direction or destination.

GALILEE: chapel or vestibule usually at the W end of a church enclosing the porch; *see also* Narthex.

GALLERY: balcony or passage, but with certain special meanings, e.g. (1) upper storey above the aisle of a church, looking through arches to the nave; also called tribune and often erroneously triforium. (2) balcony or mezzanine, often with seats, overlooking the main interior space of a building. (3) external walkway projecting from a wall.

GARDEROBE (*lit.* wardrobe): medieval privy.

GARGOYLE: water spout projecting from the parapet of a wall or tower, often carved into human or animal shape.

GAZEBO (jocular Latin, 'I shall gaze'): lookout tower or raised summer house overlooking a garden.

GEOMETRIC: historical division of English Gothic architecture covering the period *c.* 1250–90. *See also* Tracery. For another meaning, *see* Staircase.

GIBBS SURROUND: C18 treatment of door or window surround, seen particularly in the work of James Gibbs (1682–1754) (*see* fig. 10).

GLASGOW STYLE: the idiosyncratic variations of Art Nouveau peculiar to certain Glasgow architects and designers of the late C19 and early C20.

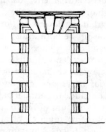

Fig. 10. Gibbs surround

GNOMON: vane or indicator casting a shadow on to a sundial.

GRC (glass-reinforced concrete): concrete reinforced with glass fibre, formed in moulds, often used for the multiple repetition of architectural elements.

GROIN: sharp edge at the meeting of two cells of a cross-vault; *see* Vault (fig. 26a).

GROTTESCHI or GROTESQUE (*lit.* grotto-esque): classical wall decoration of spindly, whimsical character adopted from Roman examples, particularly by Raphael, and further developed in the C18. Its foliage scrolls incorporate ornaments and human figures.

GRP (glass-reinforced polyester): synthetic resin reinforced with glass fibre, formed in moulds, sometimes simulating the outward appearance of traditional materials.

GUILLOCHE: running classical ornament formed by a series of circles with linked and interlaced borders (see fig. 11).

Fig. 11. Guilloche

GUNLOOP: opening for a firearm.

GUTTAE: see Orders (fig. 16).

HAGIOSCOPE: see Squint.

HALF-TIMBERING: timber framing with the spaces filled in by plaster, stones or brickwork.

HALL CHURCH: (1) church whose nave and aisles are of equal height or approximately so. (2) (Scots C20): church convertible into a hall.

HAMMERBEAM: see Roof.

HARLING (Scots, lit. hurling): wet dash, i.e. a form of roughcasting in which the mixture of aggregate and binding material (e.g. lime) is dashed onto a rubble wall as protection against weather.

HEADER: see Bond.

HENGE: ritual earthwork with a surrounding bank and ditch, the bank being on the outer side.

HERITORS (Scots): proprietors of a heritable subject, especially church heritors who till 1925 were responsible for each parish church and its manse.

HERM (lit. the god Hermes): male head or bust on a pedestal.

HERRINGBONE WORK: masonry or brickwork in zigzag courses.

HEXASTYLE: term used to describe a portico with six columns.

HILLFORT: Iron Age earthwork enclosed by a ditch and bank system; in the later part of the period the defences multiplied in size and complexity. Hillforts vary in area and are usually built with careful regard to natural elevations or promontories.

HOODMOULD or label: projecting moulding above an arch or lintel to throw off water.

HORSEMILL: circular or polygonal farm building in which a central shaft is turned by a horse to drive agricultural machinery.

HUNGRY JOINTS: see Pointing.

HUSK GARLAND: festoon of nut-shells diminishing towards the ends (see fig. 12).

Fig. 12. Husk garland

HYPOCAUST (lit. under-burning): Roman underfloor heating system. The floor is supported on pillars and the space thus formed is connected to a flue.

ICONOGRAPHY: description of the subject matter of works of the visual arts.

IMPOST (lit. imposition): horizontal moulding at the spring of an arch.

IN ANTIS: see Anta.

INDENT: (1) shape chiselled out of a stone to match and receive a brass; (2) in restoration, a secretion of new stone inserted as a patch into older work.

INGLENOOK (lit. fire-corner): recess for a hearth with provision for seating.

INTERCOLUMNIATION: interval between columns.

IONIC: see Orders (fig. 16).

JAMB (lit. leg): (1) one of the straight sides of an opening; (2) (Scots) wing or extension adjoining one side of a rectangular plan, making it into an L or T plan.

KEEL MOULDING: see fig. 13.

Fig. 13. Keel moulding

KEEP: principal tower of a castle. Also called Donjon.

KEY PATTERN: *see* fig. 14.

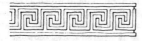

Fig. 14. Key pattern

KEYSTONE: middle and topmost stone in an arch or vault.

KINGPOST: *see* Roof (fig. 22).

LABEL: *see* Hoodmould. *Label stop*: ornamental boss at the end of a hoodmould.

LADY CHAPEL: chapel dedicated to the Virgin Mary (Our Lady).

LAIGH or LAICH (Scots): low.

LAIRD (Scots): landowner.

LANCET WINDOW: slender pointed-arched window.

LANTERN: a small circular or polygonal turret with windows all round crowning a roof (*see* Cupola) or a dome.

LAVATORIUM: in a monastery, a washing place adjacent to the refectory.

LEAN-TO: term commonly applied not only to a single-pitch roof but to the building it covers.

LESENE (*lit*. a mean thing): pilaster without base or capital. Also called pilaster strip.

LIERNE: *see* Vault (fig. 26b).

LIGHT: compartment of a window.

LINENFOLD: Tudor panelling ornamented with a conventional representation of a piece of linen laid in vertical folds. The piece is repeated in each panel.

LINTEL: horizontal beam or stone bridging an opening.

LOFT: three special senses: (1) *organ loft* in which the organ, or sometimes only the console (keyboard), is placed; (2) *rood loft*: narrow gallery over rood screen, q.v.; (3) (Scots) reserved gallery in a church, e.g. a *laird's loft*, or a *trades loft* for members of one of the incorporated trades of a burgh.

LOGGIA: sheltered space behind a colonnade.

LONG-AND-SHORT WORK: quoins consisting of stones placed with the long sides alternately upright and horizontal, especially in Saxon building.

LOUIS: convenient term used in the antique trade to describe a curvaceous chimneypiece of Louis XV character.

LOUVRE: (1) opening, often with lantern over, in the roof of a room to let the smoke from a central hearth escape; (2) one of a series of overlapping boards to allow ventilation but keep the rain out.

LOZENGE: diamond shape.

LUCARNE (*lit*. dormer): small window in a roof or spire.

LUCKENBOOTH (Scots): lock-up booth or shop.

LUGGED: *see* Architrave.

LUNETTE (*lit*. half or crescent moon): (1) semicircular window; (2) semicircular or crescent shaped surface.

LYCHGATE (*lit*. corpse-gate): wooden gate structure with a roof and open sides placed at the entrance to a churchyard to provide space for the reception of a coffin.

LYNCHET: long terraced strip of soil accumulating on the downward side of prehistoric and medieval fields owing to soil creep from continuous ploughing along the contours.

MACHICOLATIONS (*lit*. mashing devices): on a castle, downward openings through which missiles can be dropped, under a parapet or battlement supported by deep corbels.

MAINS (Scots): home farm on an estate.

MAJOLICA: ornamented glazed earthenware.

MANSARD: *see* Roof (fig. 21).

MANSE: house of a minister of religion, especially in Scotland.

MARGINS (Scots): dressed stones at the edges of an opening. 'Back-set margins' (RCAHMS) is a misleading term because they are actually set forward from a rubble-built wall to act as a stop for the harling. Also called Rybats.

MARRIAGE LINTEL (Scots): on a house, a door or window lintel carved with the initials of the owner and his wife and the date of the work – only coincidentally of their marriage.

MAUSOLEUM: monumental tomb, so named after that of Mausolus, king of Caria, at Halicarnassus.

MEGALITHIC (*lit.* of large stones): archaeological term referring to the use of such stones, singly or together.

MERCAT (Scots): market. The *mercat cross* was erected in a Scottish burgh, generally in a wide street, as the focus of market activity and local ceremonial. Most examples are of post-Reformation date and have heraldic or other finials (not crosses), but the name persisted.

MERLON: *see* Battlement.

MESOLITHIC: term applied to the Middle Stone Age, dating in Britain from *c.* 5000 to *c.* 3500 B.C., and to the hunting and gathering activities of the earliest communities. *See also* Neolithic.

METOPES: spaces between the triglyphs in a Doric frieze; *see* Orders (fig. 16).

MEZZANINE: (1) low storey between two higher ones; (2) low upper storey within the height of a high one, not extending over its whole area.

MISERERE: *see* Misericord.

MISERICORD (*lit.* mercy): ledge placed on the underside of a hinged choir stall seat which, when turned up, provided the occupant with support during long periods of standing. Also called Miserere.

MODILLIONS: small consoles at regular intervals along the underside of some types of classical cornice.

MORT-SAFE (Scots): device to assure the security of a corpse or corpses: (1) iron frame over a grave; (2) building or room where bodies were kept during decomposition.

MOTTE: steep mound forming the main feature of C 11 and C 12 castles.

MOTTE-AND-BAILEY: post-Roman and Norman defence system consisting of an earthen mound (motte) topped with a wooden tower within a bailey, with enclosure ditch and palisade, and with the rare addition of an internal bank.

MOUCHETTE: motif in curvilinear tracery, a curved version of the dagger form, specially popular in the early C 14 in England but in the early C 15 in Scotland; *see* Tracery (fig. 25).

MOULDING: ornament of continuous section; *see* the various types.

MULLION: vertical member between the lights in a window opening.

MULTI-STOREY: modern term denoting five or more storeys.

MULTIVALLATE: of a hillfort: defended by three or more concentric banks and ditches.

MUNTIN: post forming part of a screen.

MUTULE: square block under the corona of a Doric cornice.

NAILHEAD MOULDING: E.E. ornamental motif, consisting of small pyramids regularly repeated (*see* fig. 15).

Fig. 15. Nailhead moulding

NARTHEX: enclosed vestibule or covered porch at the main entrance to a church; *see also* Galilee.

NECESSARIUM: medieval euphemism for latrines in a monastery.

NEOLITHIC: term applied to the New Stone Age, dating in Britain from the appearance of the first settled farming communities from the continent *c.* 3500 B.C. until the beginning of the Bronze Age. *See also* Mesolithic.

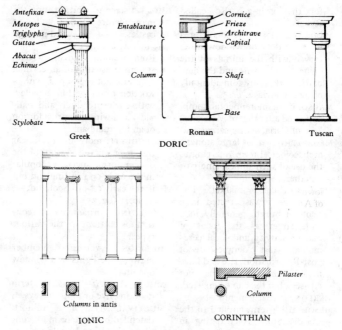

Fig. 16. Orders

NEWEL: central post in a circular or winding staircase, also the principal post when a flight of stairs meets a landing.

NICHE (*lit.* shell): vertical recess in a wall, sometimes for a statue.

NIGHT STAIR: stair by which monks entered the transepts of their church from their dormitory to celebrate night services.

NO-FINES CONCRETE: concrete without a fine aggregate (i.e. sand).

NOOK-SHAFT: shaft set in an angle formed by other members.

NORMAN: *see* Romanesque.

NOSING: projection of the tread of a step. A *bottle nosing* is half round in section.

OBELISK: lofty pillar of square section tapering at the top and ending pyramidally.

OGEE: double curve, bending first one way and then the other. *Ogee* or *ogival arch*: *see* Arch.

ORATORY: small private chapel in a house.

ORDER: (1) upright structural member formally related to others, e.g. in classical architecture a column, pilaster, or anta; (2) one of a series of recessed arches and jambs forming a splayed opening. *Giant* or *colossal order*: classical order whose height is that of two or more storeys of a building.

ORDERS: in classical architecture, the differently formalized versions of the basic post-and-lintel structure, each having its own rules of design and proportion. For examples of the main types *see* fig. 16. Others include the primitive Tuscan, which has a plain frieze and simple torus-moulded base, and the Composite, whose capital combines Ionic volutes with Corinthian foliage. *Superimposed orders*: term for the use of Orders on successive levels, usually in the upward sequence of Doric, Ionic, Corinthian.

ORIEL: *see* Bay window.

OVERARCH: *see* Arch.

OVERHANG: projection of the upper storey(s) of a building.

OVERSAILING COURSES: series of stone or brick courses, each one projecting beyond the one below it; *see also* Corbel-course.

PALIMPSEST (*lit.* erased work): re-use of a surface, e.g. a wall for another painting; also used to describe a brass plate which has been re-used by engraving on the back.

PALLADIAN: architecture following the ideas and principles of Andrea Palladio (1508–80).

PALMETTE: classical ornament like a symmetrical palm shoot; for illustration *see* Anthemion, fig. 1.

PANTILE: roof tile of curved S-shaped section.

PARAPET: wall for protection at any sudden drop, e.g. on a bridge or at the wallhead of a castle; in the latter case it protects the *parapet walk* or wall walk.

PARCLOSE: *see* Screen.

PARGETING (*lit.* plastering): usually of moulded plaster panels in half-timbering.

PATERA (*lit.* plate): round or oval ornament in shallow relief, especially in classical architecture.

PEDESTAL: in classical architecture, a stand sometimes used to support the base of an order (*see* fig. 17).

Fig. 17. Pedestal

PEDIMENT: in classical architecture, a formalized gable derived from that of a temple, also used over doors, windows, etc. For the generally accepted meanings of *broken pediment* and *open pediment see* fig. 18.

PEEL (*lit.* palisade): stone tower,

e.g. near the Scottish-English border.

PEND (Scots): open-ended passage through a building on ground level.

PENDANT: hanging-down feature of a vault or ceiling, usually ending in a boss.

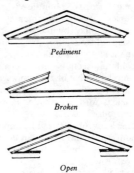

Pediment

Broken

Open

Fig. 18. Pediments

PENDENTIVE: spandrel between adjacent arches supporting a drum or dome, formed as part of a hemisphere (*see* fig. 19).

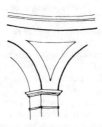

Fig. 19. Pendentive

PEPPERPOT TURRET: bartizan with conical or pyramidal roof.

PERISTYLE: in classical architecture, a range of columns all round a building, e.g. a temple, or an interior space, e.g. a courtyard.

PERP (PERPENDICULAR): historical division of English Gothic architecture covering the period from *c.* 1335–50 to *c.* 1530.

PERRON: *see* Stair.

PIANO NOBILE: principal floor, usually with a ground floor or basement underneath and a lesser storey overhead.

PIAZZA: open space surrounded by buildings; in the C17 and C18 sometimes employed to mean a long colonnade or loggia.

PIEND: see Roof.

PIER: strong, solid support, frequently square in section. *Compound pier*: of composite section, e.g. formed of a bundle of shafts.

PIETRA DURA: ornamental or scenic inlay by means of thin slabs of stone.

PILASTER: classical order of oblong section, its elevation similar to that of a column. *Pilastrade*: series of pilasters, equivalent to a colonnade. *Pilaster strip*: see Lesene.

PILE: a row of rooms. The important use of the term is in *double-pile*, describing a house that is two rows thick.

PILLAR PISCINA: free-standing piscina on a pillar.

PILOTIS: French term used in modern architecture for pillars or stilts that carry a building to first-floor level, leaving the ground floor all or partly open.

PINNACLE: tapering finial, e.g. on a buttress or the corner of a tower, sometimes decorated with crockets.

PINS (Scots): small stones pushed into the joints between large ones, a technique called cherry-caulking.

PISCINA: basin for washing the communion or mass vessels, provided with a drain; generally set in or against the wall to the S of an altar.

PIT-PRISON: sunk chamber with access above through a hatch.

PLAISANCE: summerhouse, pleasure house near a mansion.

PLATT (Scots): platform, doorstep or landing. *Scale-and-platt stair*: see Stair.

PLEASANCE (Scots): close or walled garden.

PLINTH: projecting base beneath a wall or column, generally chamfered or moulded at the top.

POINTING: exposed mortar joints of masonry or brickwork. The finished form is of various types, e.g. *flush pointing, recessed pointing*. *Bag-rubbed pointing* is flush at the edges and gently recessed in the middle of the joint. *Hungry joints* are either without any pointing at all, or deeply recessed to show the outline of each stone. *Ribbon pointing* is a nasty practice in the modern vernacular, the joints being formed with a trowel so that they stand out.

POPPYHEAD: carved ornament of leaves and flowers as a finial for the end of a bench or stall.

PORCH: covered projecting entrance to a building.

PORTCULLIS: gate constructed to rise and fall in vertical grooves at the entry to a castle.

PORTE COCHÈRE: porch large enough to admit wheeled vehicles.

PORTICO: in classical architecture, a porch with detached columns or other orders. *Blind portico*: the front features of a portico attached to a wall so that it is no longer a proper porch.

POSTERN: small gateway at the back of a building.

POTENCE (Scots): rotating ladder for access to the nesting boxes of a round doocot.

PREDELLA: in an altarpiece the horizontal strip below the main representation, often used for a number of subsidiary representations in a row.

PRESBYTERY: the part of the church lying E of the choir stalls.

PRESS (Scots): cupboard.

PRINCIPAL: see Roof (fig. 22).

PRIORY: monastic house whose head is a prior or prioress, not an abbot or abbess.

PROSTYLE: with a row of columns in front.

PULPITUM: stone screen in a major church provided to shut off the choir from the nave and also as a backing for the return choir stalls.

PULVINATED: see Frieze.

PURLIN: see Roof (fig. 22).

PUTHOLE or PUTLOCK HOLE: putlocks are the short horizontal timbers on which during construction the boards of scaffold-

ing rest. Putholes or putlock
holes are the holes in the wall for
putlocks, and often are not filled
in after construction is complete.
PUTTO: small naked boy (plural:
putti).

QUADRANGLE: inner courtyard in
a large building.
QUARRIES (*lit*. squares): (1) square
(or sometimes diamond-shaped)
panes of glass supported by lead
strips which are called *cames*; (2)
square floor-slabs or tiles.
QUATREFOIL: *see* Foil.
QUEENPOSTS: *see* Roof (fig. 22).
QUIRK: sharp groove to one side of
a convex moulding, e.g. beside a
roll moulding, which is then said
to be quirked.
QUOINS: dressed stones at the
angles of a building. When rusticated they may be alternately
long and short.

RADIATING CHAPELS: chapels
projecting radially from an
ambulatory or an apse; *see*
Chevet.
RAFTER: *see* Roof (fig. 22).
RAGGLE: groove cut in masonry,
especially to receive the edge of
glass or roof-covering.
RAKE: slope or pitch.
RAMPART: stone wall or wall of
earth surrounding a castle, fortress, or fortified city. *Rampart
walk*: path along the inner face
of a rampart.
RANDOM: *see* Rubble.
REBATE: rectangular section cut
out of a masonry edge.
REBUS: a heraldic pun, e.g. a fiery
cock as a badge for Cockburn.
REEDING: series of convex mouldings; the reverse of fluting.
REFECTORY: dining hall (or frater)
of a monastery or similar establishment.
REREDORTER (*lit*. behind the
dormitory): medieval euphemism for latrines in a monastery.
REREDOS: painted and/or sculptured screen behind and above
an altar.
RESPOND: half-pier bonded into a

wall and carrying one end of an
arch.
RETABLE: altarpiece; a picture or
piece of carving standing behind
and attached to an altar.
RETROCHOIR: in a major church,
an aisle between the high altar
and an E chapel, like a square
ambulatory.
REVEAL: the inward plane of a
jamb, between the edge of an
external wall and the frame of a
door or window that is set in it.
RHONE (Scots): gutter along the
eaves for rainwater; *see also* Conductor.
RIB-VAULT: *see* Vault.
RIGG: a strip of land leased for
building, usually with a narrow
street frontage and extending to
a considerable length.
RINCEAU (*lit*. little branch) or
antique foliage: classical ornament, usually on a frieze, of leafy
scrolls branching alternately to
left and right (*see* fig. 20).

Fig. 20. Rinceau

RISER: vertical face of a step.
ROCK-FACED: term used to
describe masonry which is cleft
to produce a natural, rugged
appearance.
ROCOCO (*lit*. rocky): latest phase
of the baroque style, current in
most Continental countries
between *c*. 1720 and *c*. 1760, and
showing itself in Britain mainly
in playful, scrolled decoration,
especially plasterwork.
ROLL MOULDING: moulding of
semicircular or more than semicircular section.
ROMANESQUE: style in architecture
current in the C11 and C12 and
preceding the Gothic style (in
England often called Norman).
(Some scholars extend the use of
the term Romanesque back to
the C10 or C9.)
ROOD: cross or crucifix, usually
over the entry into the chancel.
The *rood screen* beneath it may
have a *rood loft* along the top,
reached by a *rood stair*.

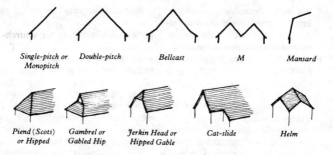

Single-pitch or Monopitch   Double-pitch   Bellcast   M   Mansard

Piend (Scots) or Hipped   Gambrel or Gabled Hip   Jerkin Head or Hipped Gable   Cat-slide   Helm

Fig. 21.   Roof forms

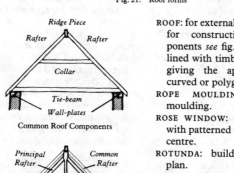

Common Roof Components

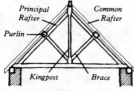

Roof with Kingpost Truss

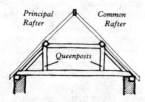

Roof with Queenpost Truss

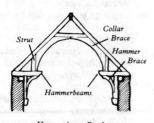

Hammerbeam Roof

Fig. 22.   Roof construction

ROOF: for external forms *see* fig. 21; for construction and components *see* fig. 22. *Wagon roof*: lined with timber on the inside, giving the appearance of a curved or polygonal vault.

ROPE MOULDING: *see* Cable moulding.

ROSE WINDOW: circular window with patterned tracery about the centre.

ROTUNDA: building circular in plan.

ROUND (Scots): useful term employed by the RCAHMS for a bartizan, usually roofless.

RUBBLE: masonry whose stones are wholly or partly in a rough state. *Coursed rubble*: of coursed stones with rough faces. *Random rubble*: of uncoursed stones in a random pattern. *Snecked rubble* has courses frequently broken by smaller stones (snecks).

RUSTICATION: treatment of joints and/or faces of masonry to give an effect of strength. In the most usual kind the joints are recessed by V-section chamfering or square section channelling. *Banded rustication* has only the horizontal joints emphasized in this way. The faces may be flat but there are many other forms, e.g. *diamond-faced*, like a shallow pyramid, *vermiculated*, with a stylized texture like worms or worm-holes, or *glacial*, like icicles or stalactites. *Rusticated columns* may have their joints and drums treated in any of these ways.

RYBATS (Scots): *see* Margins.

SACRAMENT HOUSE: safe cupboard for the reserved sacrament.

SACRISTY: room in a church for sacred vessels and vestments.

SALTIRE or ST ANDREW'S CROSS: with diagonal limbs. As the flag of Scotland it is coloured white on a blue ground.

SANCTUARY: (1) area around the main altar of a church (*see* Presbytery); (2) sacred site consisting of wood or stone uprights enclosed by a circular bank and ditch. Beginning in the Neolithic, they were elaborated in the succeeding Bronze Age. The best-known examples are Stonehenge and Avebury.

SARCOPHAGUS (*lit.* flesh-consuming): coffin of stone or other durable material.

SARKING (Scots): boards laid on the rafters (*see* Roof, fig. 22) to support the covering, e.g. metal or slates.

SCAGLIOLA: composition imitating marble.

SCALE-AND-PLATT (*lit.* stair and landing): *see* Stair (fig. 24).

SCARCEMENT: extra thickness of the lower part of a wall, e.g. to carry a floor.

SCARP: artificial cutting away of the ground to form a steep slope.

SCREEN: in a church, usually at the entry to the chancel; *see* Rood screen and Pulpitum. *Parclose screen*: separating a chapel from the rest of the church.

SCREENS or SCREENS PASSAGE: screened-off entrance passage between the hall and the kitchen in a medieval house, adjoining the kitchen, buttery, etc.; *see also* Transe.

SCUNTION (Scots): equivalent of a reveal on the indoor side of a door or window opening.

SECTION: view of a building, moulding, etc. revealed by cutting across it.

SEDILIA: seats for the priests (usually three) on the S side of the chancel of a church; a plural word that has become a singular, collective one.

SESSION HOUSE (Scots): (1) room or separate building for meetings of the elders who form a kirk session; (2) shelter by entrance to church or churchyard for an elder receiving the collection for relief of the poor, built at expense of kirk session.

SET-OFF: *see* Weathering.

SGRAFFITO: scratched pattern, often in plaster.

SHAFT: upright member of round section, especially the main part of a classical column. *Shaft-ring*: motif of the C12 and C13 consisting of a ring like a belt round a circular pier or a circular shaft attached to a pier.

SHEILA-NA-GIG: female fertility figure, usually with legs wide open.

SHOULDERED: *see* Arch (fig. 2), Architrave.

SILL: horizontal projection at the bottom of a window.

SKEW (Scots): sloping or shaped stones finishing a gable which is upstanding above the roof. *Skewputt*: bracket at the bottom end of a skew.

SLATE-HANGING: covering of overlapping slates on a wall, which is then said to be *slate-hung*.

SNECKED: *see* Rubble.

SOFFIT (*lit.* ceiling): underside of an arch, lintel, etc.

SOLAR (*lit.* sun-room): upper living room or withdrawing room of a medieval house, accessible from the high table end of the hall.

SOUNDING-BOARD: horizontal board or canopy over a pulpit; also called Tester.

SOUTERRAIN: underground stone-lined passage and chamber.

SPANDRELS: surfaces left over between an arch and its containing rectangle, or between adjacent arches.

SPIRE: tall pyramidal or conical feature built on a tower or turret. *Broach spire*: starting from a square base, then carried into an octagonal section by means of triangular faces. *Needle spire*: thin spire rising from the centre of a tower roof, well inside the parapet. *Helm spire*: *see* Roof (fig. 21).

SPIRELET: *see* Flèche.

SPLAY: chamfer, usually of a reveal or scuntion.

SPRING: level at which an arch or vault rises from its supports. *Springers*: the first stones of an arch or vaulting-rib above the spring.

SQUINCH: arch thrown across an angle between two walls to support a superstructure, e.g. a dome (*see* fig. 23).

Fig. 23.   Squinch

SQUINT: hole cut in a wall or through a pier to allow a view of the main altar of a church from places whence it could not otherwise be seen. Also called Hagioscope.

STAIR: *see* fig. 24. The term *perron* (*lit.* of stone) applies to the external stair leading to a doorway, usually of double-curved plan as shown. *Spiral*, *turnpike* (Scots) or *newel stair*: ascending round a central supporting newel, usually in a circular shaft. *Flying stair*: cantilevered from the wall of a stairwell, without newels. *Geometric stair*: flying stair whose inner edge describes a curve. *Well stair*: term applied to any stair contained in an open well, but generally to one that climbs up three sides of a well, with corner landings. *Winder stair*: a stair constructed in a circular shaft round a central newel with steps (*winders*) that narrow at one end.

STALL: seat for clergy, choir, etc., distinctively treated in its own right or as one of a row.

STANCHION: upright structural member, of iron or steel or reinforced concrete.

STEADING (Scots): farm building or buildings. A term most often used to describe the principal group of agricultural buildings on a farm.

STEEPLE: a tower together with a spire or other tall feature on top of it.

STIFFLEAF: *see* fig. 6.

STOUP: vessel for the reception of holy water, usually placed near a door.

STRAINER: *see* Arch.

STRAPWORK: C16 and C17 decoration used also in the C19 Jacobean revival, resembling interlaced bands of cut leather.

STRINGCOURSE: intermediate stone course or moulding projecting from the surface of a wall.

STUCCO (*lit.* plaster): (1) smooth external rendering of a wall etc.; (2) decorative plaster-work.

STUDS: intermediate vertical members of a timber-framed wall or partition.

STUGGED (Scots): of masonry that is hacked or picked as a key for rendering; used as a type of surface finish in the C19.

STYLOBATE: solid structure on which a colonnade stands.

SWAG (*lit.* bundle): like a festoon, but also a cloth bundle in relief, hung up at both ends.

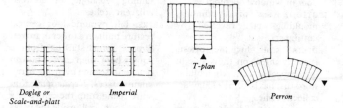

Dogleg or   *Imperial*   *T-plan*   *Perron*
Scale-and-platt

Fig. 24.   Stair

TABERNACLE (*lit.* tent) (1) canopied structure, especially on a small scale, to contain the reserved sacrament or a relic; (2) architectural frame, e.g. of a monument on a wall or free-standing, with flanking orders. Also called an Aedicule.

TAS-DE-CHARGE: coursed stone(s) forming the springers of more than one vaulting-rib.

TENEMENT: this term for a holding of land is also applied to the building upon it, which usually contains several dwellings.

TERMINAL FIGURE or TERM: upper part of a human figure growing out of a pier, pilaster, etc. which tapers towards the bottom.

TERRACOTTA: moulded and fired clay ornament or cladding, usually unglazed.

TESSELLATED PAVEMENT: mosaic flooring, particularly Roman, consisting of small *Tesserae* or cubes of glass, stone, or brick.

TESTER (*lit.* head): bracketed canopy, especially over a pulpit, where it is also called a sounding-board.

TETRASTYLE: term used to describe a portico with four columns.

THERMAL WINDOW (*lit.* of a Roman bath): *see* Diocletian window.

THREE-DECKER PULPIT: pulpit with clerk's stall below and reading desk below the clerk's stall.

TIE-BEAM: *see* Roof (fig. 22).

TIERCERON: *see* Vault (fig. 26b).

TILE-HANGING: *see* Slate-hanging.

TIMBER FRAMING: method of construction where walls are built of timber framework with the spaces filled in by plaster or brickwork. Sometimes the timber is covered over with plaster or boarding laid horizontally.

TOLBOOTH (Scots): tax office containing a burgh council chamber and a prison.

TOMB-CHEST: chest-shaped stone coffin, the most usual medieval form of funerary monument.

TOUCH: soft black marble quarried near Tournai.

TOURELLE: turret corbelled out from the wall.

TOWER HOUSE (Scots): compact fortified house with the main hall raised above the ground and at least one more storey above it. A medieval Scots type continuing well into the C17 in its modified forms, the L plan and so-called Z plan, the former having a jamb at one corner, the latter at each diagonally opposite corner.

TRACERY: pattern of arches and geometrical figures supporting the glass in the upper part of a window, or applied decoratively to wall surfaces or vaults. *Plate tracery* is the most primitive form of tracery, being formed of openings cut through stone slabs or plates. In *bar tracery* the openings are separated not by flat areas of stonework but by relatively slender divisions or bars which are constructed of voussoirs like arches. Later developments of bar tracery are classified according to the

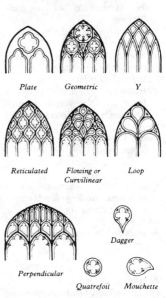

Plate   Geometric   Y

Reticulated   Flowing or   Loop
               Curvilinear

Perpendicular   Dagger

Quatrefoil   Mouchette

Fig. 25. Tracery

GLOSSARY

character of the decorative pattern used. For generalized illustrations of the main types *see* fig. 25.

TRANSE (Scots): passage, especially screens passage.

TRANSEPTS (*lit.* cross-enclosures): transverse portions of a cross-shaped church.

TRANSOM: horizontal member between the lights in a window opening.

TREFOIL: *see* Foil.

TRIBUNE: *see* Gallery (1).

TRICIPUT, SIGNUM TRICIPUT: sign of the Trinity expressed by three faces belonging to one head.

TRIFORIUM: middle storey of a church treated as an arcaded wall passage or blind arcade, its height corresponding to that of the aisle roof.

TRIGLYPHS (*lit.* three-grooved tablets): stylized beam-ends in the Doric frieze, with metopes between; *see* Orders (fig. 16).

TRIUMPHAL ARCH: *see* Arch.

TROPHY: sculptured group of arms or armour as a memorial of victory.

TRUMEAU: stone pillar supporting the tympanum of a wide doorway.

TUMULUS (*lit.* mound): barrow.

TURNPIKE: *see* Stair.

TURRET: small tower, often attached to a building.

TUSCAN: *see* Orders (fig. 16).

TYMPANUM (*lit.* drum): as of a drum-skin, the surface framed by an arch or pediment.

TYNECASTLE TAPESTRY: a patented wallpaper resembling woven fabric.

UNDERCROFT: vaulted room, sometimes underground, below the main upper room.

UNIVALLATE: of a hillfort: defended by a single bank and ditch.

VASSAL: *see* Feu.

VAULT: ceiling of stone formed like arches (sometimes imitated in

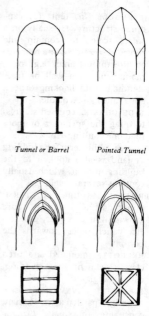

Tunnel or Barrel   *Pointed Tunnel*

Pointed Tunnels with Surface Ribs

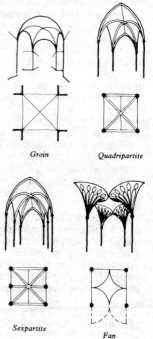

Groin   *Quadripartite*

Sexpartite   *Fan*

Fig. 26. (a) Vaults

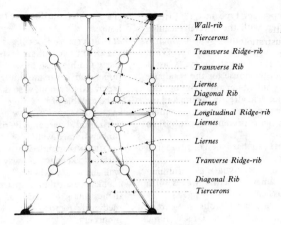

Wall-rib
Tiercerons
Transverse Ridge-rib
Transverse Rib
Liernes
Diagonal Rib
Liernes
Longitudinal Ridge-rib
Liernes
Liernes
Tranverse Ridge-rib
Diagonal Rib
Tiercerons

Fig. 26.   (b) Ribs of a late Gothic vault

timber or plaster); *see* fig. 26a. *Tunnel-* or *barrel-vault*: the simplest kind of vault, in effect a continuous semicircular arch. *Pointed tunnel-vaults* are frequent in Scottish late medieval architecture but otherwise rare. A Scottish peculiarity is the *pointed tunnel-vault with surface ribs* which are purely decorative in intention. *Groin-vaults* (usually called *cross-vaults* in classical architecture) have four curving triangular surfaces produced by the intersection of two tunnel-vaults at right angles. The curved lines at the intersections are called groins. In *quadripartite rib-vaults* the four sections are divided by their arches or ribs springing from the corners of the bay. *Sexpartite rib-vaults* are most often used over paired bays. The main types of rib are shown in fig. 26b; *transverse ribs, wall-ribs, diagonal ribs*, and *ridge-ribs*. *Tiercerons* are extra, decorative ribs springing from the corners of a bay. *Liernes* are decorative ribs in the crown of a vault which are not linked to any of the springing points. In a *stellar vault* the liernes are arranged in a star formation as in fig. 26b. *Fan-vaults* are peculiar to English Perpendicular architecture and differ from rib-vaults in con-

sisting not of ribs and infilling but of halved concave cones with decorative blind tracery carved on their surfaces.

VAULTING-SHAFT: shaft leading up to the springer of a vault.

VENETIAN WINDOW: *see* fig. 27.

Fig. 27.   Venetian window

VERANDA(H): shelter or gallery against a building, its roof supported by thin vertical members.

VERMICULATION: *see* Rustication.

VESICA (*lit.* bladder): usually of a window, with curved sides and pointed at top and bottom like a rugger-ball.

VESTIBULE: ante-room or entrance hall.

VILLA: originally (1) Roman country-house-cum-farmhouse, developed into (2) the similar C 16 Venetian type with office wings, made grander by Palladio's varied application of a central portico. This became an important type in c18 Britain, often with the special meaning of (3) a country house which is not a principal residence. Gwilt (1842) defined the villa as 'a country house for the residence of opulent persons'. But devaluation had already begun, and the term implied, as now, (4) a more or less pretentious suburban house.

VITRIFIED: hardened or fused into a glass-like state.

VITRUVIAN SCROLL: running ornament of curly waves on a classical frieze. (*See* fig. 28.)

VOLUTES: spiral scrolls on the front and back of a Greek Ionic capital, also on the sides of a Roman one. *Angle volute*: pair of volutes turned outwards to meet at the corner of a capital.

VOUSSOIRS: wedge-shaped stones forming an arch.

WAINSCOT: timber lining on an internal wall.

WALLED GARDEN: c17 type whose formal layout is still seen in the combined vegetable and flower gardens of c18 and c19 Scotland. They are usually sited at a considerable distance from a house.

WALL-PLATE: *see* Roof (fig. 22).

WATERHOLDING BASE: type of Early Gothic base in which the upper and lower mouldings are separated by a hollow so deep as to be capable of retaining water.

WEATHERBOARDING: overlapping horizontal boards, covering a timber-framed wall.

WEATHERING: inclined, projecting surface to keep water away from wall and joints below.

WEEPERS: small figures placed in niches along the sides of some medieval tombs; also called mourners.

WHEEL WINDOW: circular window with tracery of radiating shafts like the spokes of a wheel; *see also* Rose window.

WINDER STAIR: *see* Stair.

WYND (Scots): subsidiary street or lane, often running into a main street or gait.

YETT (Scots, *lit.* gate): hinged openwork gate at a main doorway, made of wrought-iron bars alternately penetrating and penetrated.

Fig. 28.   Vitruvian scroll

INDEX OF ARTISTS

Thorburn, Twigg, Brown & Partners, 208

Thornycroft, (Sir) William Hamo (sculptor, 1850–1925), 55, 178, 305, Pl. 94

Thorwaldsen, Bertel (sculptor, 1768–1844), 61, 539

Tiltman, Alfred Hessell (1854–1910), 447

Timpson, F., 290

Tinworth, George (sculptor, 1843–1913), 284

Toft, Alfred (sculptor, 1862–1949), 603

Traquair, Phoebe (painter, 1852–1936), 79, 303, 391

Truscon, 403, 434

Trussed Concrete Steel Co., 71, 387, 517, 541; see also Kahn, Albert; Kahn, Moritz

Tudsbery, M. T., 346

Turnbull, Robert (?1839–1905), 313, 320, 368, 522, 554, 557; see also Thomson & Turnbull

Underwood (Walter) & Partners, 76, 150, 151, 167, 198, 248, 263, 284, 343, 415

Vaughan, Dai (artist), 221

Verity & Beverly, 82, 231

Vickers, William (sculptor), 136, 171, 247, 265, 570

Victoria Park Feuing Co. (builders), 380

Waddell, John Jeffrey (1876–1941), 304, 398, 406; see also Waddell (Jeffrey) & Young

Waddell (Jeffrey) & Young (John Jeffrey Waddell, q.v.), 548

Wadsworth, Ernest (organ builder), 533

Wagner Associates, 193

Wailes, William (glass-stainer, 1808–81), 295

Walker, A. Lindsay, 447

Walker, Alex (glass-stainer, fl. 1896–1920), 452

Walker, Alexander, 162

Walker, Hardy & Smith, 526, 598

Walker, James (engineer), 624

Walker, R., 526

Walker (Ronald) & Co., 629

Wallace (sculptor) of London, 139

Walsh, Thomas (painter), 436

Walton, Edward Arthur (painter and designer, 1860–1922), 162

Walton (G.) & Co., 314

Walton, George (1867/8–1933), 67, 171, 215, 313

Walton, Henry Davison (fl. 1887–1919), 160, 389, 502, 525, 570

Ward & Hughes (glass-stainers: Thomas Ward, 1808–70; Henry Hughes, q.v.), 62, 157, 302, 303

Warner & Co. (bell founders), 533

Warren, William (sculptor, fl. 1790–1828), 55, 140

Waterhouse (Alfred) & Son (Alfred Waterhouse, 1830–1905; Paul Waterhouse, q.v.), 231

Waterhouse, Paul (1861–1924), 68, 231

Watson, John (b. 1901), 551; see also Watson & Salmond; Watson, Salmond & Gray

Watson & Salmond (John Watson, q.v.), 207, 370, 476, 495, 603

Watson, Salmond & Gray (John Watson, q.v.), 82, 159, 200, 207, 234, 490, 536, 550, 556, 596, 600

Watson (T. L., q.v.) & Henry Mitchell, 243

Watson (T. L., q.v.) & W. J. Millar, 214

Watson, Thomas Lennox (c. 1850–1920), 60, 61, 72, 94, 134, 149, 203, 232, 269, 334, 511; see also Watson (T. L.) & Henry Mitchell; Watson (T. L.) & W. J. Millar

Watson, Walter R. (c. 1873–1932), 269, 373, 381, 423; see also Cowan & Watson

Watt, Alexander, 275, 593

Watt (Andrew) & Son (organ builders), 493

Watt, James (engineer, 1736–1819), 619, 626

Watt, William, 484

Waugh, D. S. R., 342; see also Hughes (T. Harold) & D. S. R. Waugh

Webb, Christopher Rahere (glass-stainer, 1886–1966), 132

Webster, Alfred A. (glass-stainer, d. 1914), 157, 302, 475, 537, 569; see also Adam (Stephen) Studio

Webster, Gordon (glass-stainer, b. 1908), 80, 131, 132, 133, 302, 317, 326, 327, 339, 357, 371, 378, 379, 392, 415, 470, 475, 502, 528, 537, 539, 546, 562, 570, 601

Webster, Thomas (1773–1844), 270

Weddell & Inglis, 83, 221, 243, 329, Pl. 107

Weddell, Inglis & Taylor, 416

Weddell & Thomson (J. W. D. Thomson), 221, 288

Weir, Robertson (painter), 415

Weir, W. J., 424

Wells, Andrew (glass-stainer), 356, 421; see also Guthrie & Wells

Wells-Thorpe, Jeremy, 529

Westwood & Emberton (Percy Westwood, 1878–1958; Joseph Emberton, 1889–1956), 226

INDEX OF STREETS AND BUILDINGS

This index includes streets and major buildings. Principal references are in **bold** type; demolished buildings are shown in *italic*.